EARLY PRAISE FOR *UNCREDITED*

"Uncredited by Allison Tyra is an amazing compendium of stories about hundreds of women – left out, ignored, misnamed, erased, mansplained, reframed and uncredited (to name just a few). As a historian of women for over a half century, I was blown away and somewhat ashamed that I had never heard of or read about at least 2/3 of these remarkable actors. Tyra, the creator and manager of Infinite Women, an ever-expanding encyclopedia of women, has given us an extraordinarily documented, theorized, and passionate account of the hows, whens and whys women have been hidden from history...film, medicine, science...you name it. A must!"
—Barbara Winslow, Professor Emerita, Women and Gender Studies Brooklyn College US

"For centuries, women's contributions to every field of human discovery have been downplayed, underappreciated, erased, or outright stolen. Allison Tyra's encyclopedic compendium of groundbreaking accomplishments by women who have been unfairly omitted from our shared history fundamentally shifts the balance when it comes to accurately attributing credit where credit is due. Thoroughly researched and written in accessible, engaging prose, *Uncredited* is an invaluable resource for historians, educators, and anyone seeking a more accurate understanding of the past."
—Lorissa Rinehart, Author of *First to the Front, The Untold Story of Dickey Chapelle, Trailblazing Female War Correspondent*

"Uncredited illustrates the breadth and depth of women's accomplishments throughout history, but then clearly answers the question 'Why haven't I heard of these women before?' It is essential reference material for anyone who might have doubted women's accomplishments or assumed that these were only unacknowledged a few times."
—Kimberly Hess, author of *A Lesser Mortal: The Unexpected Life of Sarah B. Cochran*

"Uncredited sets the record straight by celebrating the all-too-little known and unheralded accomplishments of women, and makes painfully clear the cost we all pay for having learned a woefully lopsided version of history."
—Dana Rubin, author of *Speaking While Female: 75 Extraordinary Speeches by American Women*

"Giving credit where it is long overdue, Allison Tyra puts stories of hundreds of women in their proper place, while pointing out the structural blocks that have kept their accomplishments — around the world and through the centuries — from being rightly celebrated."
—Carrie Gibson, author of *El Norte: The Epic and Forgotten Story of Hispanic North America*

"Can a book be depressing and uplifting at the same time? As hunters and warriors, as writers, artists, rocket scientists, spies, pirates, sports heroes, explorers, physicians, inventors, monarchs--you name it--women have always been the equals of men, argues Allison Tyra. And they have almost always been overlooked. In Uncredited, Tyra returns hundreds of such women to the records of history and proves how bias and misogyny have long striven to erase their accomplishments.

Eye-opening and provocative, Uncredited belongs in every library. Every girl should have the chance to read it, to see what her future could bring if she follows her heart, instead of doing what she's told."
—Nancy Marie Brown, author of *The Far Traveler: Voyages of a Viking Woman*

"Allison Tyra's Uncredited is a fascinating examination of how women have long been denied credit for their own work. This book is stunning in its scope, with stories from ancient Greece to the present, and tales of women's struggles all over the world to get what they deserve. By looking at everything from whose records are seen as worth preserving to double standards to assumptions that wives are just extensions of husbands, Tyra reveals all the ways women have been made invisible, whether by being seen as not believable, unintelligent, untalented, or just too weak to hack it. But you'll also get a chance to hear the incredible stories of female pirates, empresses, athletes, warriors, scientists, revolutionaries, and entertainers while you're at it. This book will inspire you – and make you mad enough – to make sure that the women of the past, present, and future get the recognition they deserve for their achievements!"
—Sarah Horowitz, author of *The Red Widow*

"Allison Trya's vital volume marks impactful strides in shifting centuries-old unconscious bias that permeates our daily lives. This volume stands as a necessary starting-place to begin balancing centuries of uneven understanding on the roles, contributions and advances emanating from generations of remarkable women. Brava!"
—Mindy Johnson, Author / Historian of *The Only Woman Animator – Bessie Mae Kelley & Women at the Dawn of an Industry* and *Ink & Paint – The Women of Walt Disney's Animation*

UNCREDITED

Women's Overlooked, Misattributed, and Stolen Work

ALLISON TYRA

Text copyright © 2024 by Allison Tyra

All rights reserved. For information regarding reproduction in total or in part, contact Rising Action Publishing Co. at http://www.risingactionpublishingco.com

Cover Illustration © Nat Mack
Distributed by Simon & Schuster

Line Edit by Tina Beier
Proofread by Sally O'Keef
Formatting by Shannon Sullivan

ISBN: 978-1-998076-63-5
Ebook: 978-1-998076-64-2

HIS058000 HISTORY / Women
SOC010000 SOCIAL SCIENCE / Feminism & Feminist Theory
BIO022000 BIOGRAPHY & AUTOBIOGRAPHY / Women

#UncreditedBook
#InfiniteWomen

Follow Rising Action on our socials!
Twitter: @RAPubCollective
Instagram: @risingactionpublishingco
Tiktok: @risingactionpublishingco

For Gerard. He knows what he did.

UNCREDITED

CONTENTS

INTRODUCTION	1
How to Use this Book	1
GETTING PAST THE GATEKEEPERS	3
WHAT GETS RECORDED IN THE FIRST PLACE	5
Journalism	8
Sports Coverage	17
Documentation	20
Mrs. Nameless	27
PRIORITIES AND PRESERVATION	33
Lost and Rediscovered	38
Editors Deciding What Gets Changed Posthumously	41
Work Destroyed	45
MUSEUMS AND GALLERIES	52
SCHOLARLY ANDROCENTRISM	57
ARCHAEOLOGICAL ANDROCENTRISM	63
TRANSLATION	73
EDUCATION GATEKEEPERS	77
Deciding What is Taught	77
INDUSTRY GATEKEEPERS	89
WIKIPEDIA'S GENDER BIAS	99
VISUAL REMINDERS	103
Censorship	114
MEDIA REPRESENTATION	118
CREDIT STOLEN	134
WHEN OTHERS MISATTRIBUTE	142
PLAGIARISM BEGINS AT HOME	152
The Husbands	153
STOLEN WORK	162
CONTRIBUTIONS IGNORED	179

THE SCIENTISTS	186
THE ARTS	207
THE ACTIVISTS	213
THE ARCHITECTS	218
BEHIND THE WRITER	222
THE INVENTORS	226
THE MILITARY	229
HER CHOICE?	233
Male Pseudonyms	236
THE POWER BEHIND THE THRONE	247
IGNORED FOR AWARDS	251
UNDERMINED	264
NO ASSUMPTION OF CREDIBILITY	271
Mansplaining	276
Assumed Lack of Capability	279
Giving Men the Unearned Benefit of the Doubt	285
No Girls Allowed	289
Schools	290
Jobs	300
Professional Organisations	310
Women Who Changed the Rules	313
Yes, Women *Are* Funny	317
THE PINK GHETTO	323
Refusing to Invest in Women	329
YOU TALK TOO MUCH	334
Beyond Mansplaining	342
BEHAVIOURAL DOUBLE-STANDARD	346
NO BUSINESS LIKE SHOW BUSINESS	353
WHEN WOMEN DO SUCCEED, THEY'RE EXCLUDED	355
THE GLASS CLIFF	363
PERSONALLY AND PROFESSIONALLY UNDERMINED	368

Men in Personal Life Actively Sabotaging	369
MALE ADVISORS/BOSSES TELLING WOMEN	378
NOT TO PURSUE IMPORTANT THINGS	378
ALGORITHMIC BIAS	382
WOMEN BRINGING WOMEN DOWN	387
RESPECTABILITY	394
PSYCHOLOGICAL BARRIERS TO SUCCESS	401
She's a Witch!	405
SLUT SHAMING	410
Overshadowed by Personal Life	420
"Science says..."	427
HOW FEMALE ATHLETES DRESS	432
SACRIFICING FOR FAMILY	438
Anti-Nepotism Policies	447
THE COST OF DISREGARDING WOMEN	452
Medical	453
BAD BUSINESS	458
WARTIME	463
PUBLIC GOOD	466
ONE FINAL NOTE	474
ABOUT THE AUTHOR	475
FURTHER READING	476
GLOSSARY	482
PLAYLIST	486

INTRODUCTION

> *"For most of history, Anonymous was a woman."*
> —Virginia Woolf

Hedy Lamarr was a bombshell. Promoted by the head of Hollywood studio MGM as "the world's most beautiful woman," she starred in more than 30 films in the 1930s, 1940s, and 1950s. It wasn't until the 2010s that she was widely recognized for her work as an inventor, which included technology that would later serve as the basis for Bluetooth, GPS, and Wi-Fi.[1]

She was one of countless women whose work has been overlooked, misattributed or outright stolen. Perhaps the greatest offence of women not being credited for their work is that it is likely impossible to ever truly calculate the scope of their erasure. However, thanks to the work of historians, filmmakers, and women who refused to be silenced and ignored, many of these stories are coming to light. Although it cannot right the wrongs these women experienced, acknowledging the truth of their contributions can at least ensure their legacy and remind future generations that brilliant, passionate, and talented women have always been here—if you know where to look.

HOW TO USE THIS BOOK

This book is a collection of the stories of hundreds of women, combined with statistics, results of research studies, and anecdotal examples of the key factors that

---

[1] Cheslak, Colleen, "Hedy Lamarr," *National Women's History Museum*, 2018, https://www.womenshistory.org/education-resources/biographies/hedy-lamarr

contribute to women not receiving credit for their work and accomplishments. It came out of seeing the same stories told over and over again—but when they're told in isolation, it's easier to dismiss those larger patterns at play.

Because we are looking at the issue broadly, we won't go too deeply into any one woman's story, and it is my fondest wish that you will set this book down periodically because you are intrigued by the brief introduction to various women and just cannot wait to go learn more about them. Go with my blessing, but please come back!

Because our focus is on those larger patterns, the book is divided by the themes involved: documentation and gatekeepers, credit actively being stolen, contributions being overlooked, women being undermined, and the impacts of respectability expectations. If you're interested in a particular woman, topic, or group, please check the index to direct you to the correct part of the book. We also have a recommended reading list at the end with books that delve more deeply into specific areas, because there is always more to tell.

GETTING PAST THE GATEKEEPERS

"You can't be what you can't see."
—Marian Wright Edelman[2]

In a 2013 study, Swiss students delivered persuasive political speeches to a virtual reality audience, with the virtual room's back wall featuring a picture of Hillary Clinton, Angela Merkel, Bill Clinton, or no image. When presented with a female role model, the female speakers were more likely to speak longer, rate their performance more highly, and be rated more highly by others.[3]

Representation matters. Whether in reference to fact or fiction, we are taught expectations from the earliest ages by what we see around us—in media, in school, and in our own lives. The problem has always lain with the gatekeepers at different levels, deciding who and what gets attention in the first place, and what is saved and what is featured. In other words, if a woman accomplishes something and no one acknowledges it, no one else will know about it in the future.

Throughout this section, and indeed the entire book, consider the biases at play, both individual and societal. Every source is shaped by biases—who benefits from framing things in a certain way? What do they actually know, and what are they assuming or guessing? What prejudices might they hold that shape their thinking? And most importantly: who do we trust, especially when different sources

---

2 "Representation Matters: Madam Vice President," January 20, 2021, Children's Defense Fund, https://www.childrensdefense.org/blog/madam-vice-president-representation-matters/
3 Latu, Ioana M., Marianne Schmid Mast, Joris Lammers, and Dario Bombari, "Successful Female Leaders Empower Women's Behavior in Leadership Tasks," *Journal of Experimental Social Psychology* 49, No 3. (2013): 444–48, https://doi.org/10.1016/j.jesp.2013.01.003

tell conflicting stories?

Men have traditionally been the gatekeepers of what information is recorded, what records are saved, and what information is featured when presented to the public. From male reporters and editors who insist their readers aren't interested in "women's" stories to curators and school boards deciding that women's history isn't important to teach young people, men (and some women, to be sure) have decided time and again that women's stories aren't worth telling. Just as the victors write history, so do men.

WHAT GETS RECORDED IN THE FIRST PLACE

> "Florence Nightingale was never called 'the Lady with the Lamp,' but she was called 'the Lady with the Hammer,' an image deftly readjusted by the war reporter of the Times since it was far too coarse for the folks back home. Far from gliding about the hospital with her lamp aloft, Nightingale earned her nickname through a ferocious attack on a locked storeroom when a military commander refused to give her the medical supplies she needed."
> —Rosalind Miles, *Who Cooked the Last Supper: The Women's History of the World*[4]

If a woman accomplishes something, but there is no record of it, did she accomplish anything at all? To paraphrase the internet, "docs or it didn't happen." If we have no way of knowing, much less proving, that someone did something, that achievement essentially disappears. This makes the journalism and documentation gatekeepers incredibly powerful, and their decisions devastatingly important.

Ada Blackjack thought Harold Noice was her saviour. Instead, he did everything he could to destroy her reputation, not out of malice, but out of greed and self-preservation. In 1921, unable to find work that would enable her to care for her son, who was sick with tuberculosis, Blackjack accepted a job that would turn into hell on earth. Vilhjalmur Stefansson, one of many white guys with more money than sense, devised a cockamamie plan to claim Wrangel Island in the Arctic and then try to sell it to the UK, Canada (then part of the UK Commonwealth) or the US. So, he sent four white guys and Blackjack, of the Iñupiat, off

---

4   Miles, Rosalind, *Who Cooked the Last Supper?: The Women's History of the World* (Three Rivers Press, 2001).

with only six months of supplies for a one-year expedition that ended up lasting two. Their rations, of course, ran out and the group were unable to hunt enough food to survive. Stefansson's foolishness had also created an international incident, which impeded much-needed supplies from getting to the group. Three of the men sledded off to get help and were never seen again. The fourth man, Lorne Knight, was sick with scurvy and so was left behind with Blackjack to care for him. Despite her best efforts, he died in June 1923, just under a month before the rescue team, led by Harold Noice, showed up.[5]

Even before Noice had set out, he was anticipating making money off the disaster, as his lawyer had sold exclusive newspaper rights for $3,000 for the story of the relief expedition. This included telling the members of the party—which turned out to only be Blackjack – not to speak with the press themselves. But, of course, Blackjack didn't know that as she collapsed with relief at being rescued, having spent almost a month with no company except a dead body and a cat named Victoria. Meanwhile, Noice immediately began looting the camp, taking both Knight's and Blackjack's diaries, without her consent, as well as photos she had taken on the island, the other men's papers, and items like a typewriter. He would later ignore her requests for the return of her belongings.

Reading Knight's diary, Noice was struck by both the incompetence and the mistreatment of Blackjack—struck by "Arctic hysteria," she had experienced a mental health crisis early on, including propositioning one of the men—which combined with a rumor he'd heard in Nome, Alaska, that she was a sex worker, painted a particular kind of picture in his head. The rumor may have come from the facts that she was poverty-stricken, Indigenous, and a single mother, having divorced the abusive husband she married at sixteen and left at twenty-two, as well as someone who may have drowned her sorrows in alcohol and taken up with unsuitable men (though these rumours, too, may have been unfounded). But it was that desperation and need to care for her son that led her to take a job no one else wanted.

During her "hysteria," the men responded by withholding food, forcing her

---

5 Niven, Jennifer, *Ada Blackjack: A True Story of Survival in the Arctic* (Hachette Books, 2003).

to sleep in the cold and tying her to a flagpole. It is incredibly impressive that she managed to recover—and this was at the start of the two years.

Noice took it upon himself to censor the diaries, removing whole blocks of pages (including the final ten) and erasing then blacking out sections, ostensibly to protect the men's reputations. He also knew that missing information would heighten the scandal he already knew would come from the situation and enable him to spin falsehoods and innuendo that complete copies of the diaries would belie. Despite having told multiple people he was going to censor the diaries, he would later try to blame Blackjack for the mutilations, trying to undermine the lone survivor's ability to counter his lies.

Any claims of protecting the men's reputations were soon proved false as he, the man in charge on-site, openly criticized Stefansson and Knight. For her part, Blackjack spent months adamantly avoiding the press that hounded her. While Noice's criticisms of the men were arguably well-founded—the expedition was a mess from start to finish – that wasn't enough. Spurred by his new, rich, and incredibly jealous wife, he began spreading lies about Blackjack as well. Unstable and obsessed with "correcting" the heroic depictions of Blackjack that were appearing in the press, Fanny Noice badgered her husband into publicising the lies he had told to appease her. One of these was the promiscuity, which only convinced Fanny that Noice himself must have slept with Blackjack as well. In addition to the claims that Blackjack was a sex worker who had been taken along to service the men in that capacity rather than cooking, sewing, and hunting, he claimed she was lazy, that she refused to work because none of the men would agree to marry her, and rather than caring for Knight, had let him die. He claimed she refused to check the traps for animals that could be killed for food, and implied she feigned her inability to shoot (having lived her whole life in missionary or city environments, Blackjack had no skill with a gun prior to the expedition, but out of necessity, did learn how to shoot while on Wrangel Island). Though he had previously published an article describing her as frail and small, weighing less than one hundred pounds, his new story was that Knight's body was emaciated while Blackjack was found "well and fat," claiming that she had saved her own life eating the food that would have saved Knight. Blackjack herself stated that she weighed only ninety pounds, a 25% weight loss from her typical one hundred and twenty. To support his other lies, Noice also made-up things that he claimed she had said, but she maintained she never had.

Blackjack was hesitant to speak out against him for several reasons–a naturally private person, she had no desire to engage the reporters who were constantly following her. She had also promised both her employer and her rescuer that she would not speak with reporters, a vow she took seriously. She also felt indebted to Noice as the man who saved her. But with his baseless attacks on her, she finally overcame these barriers, breaking her silence on February 26, 1924. She spoke with the *Los Angeles Times*, which printed three extensive articles over five days.

Blackjack also had one advantage many women of color don't have in cases of "he said, she said"—a rich white guy in her corner. As the instigator and funder of the expedition, Stefansson had a vested interest in combatting Noice's work, both the truths and the lies, as they reflected badly on his expedition and therefore his own reputation. Neither man seems to have cared about Blackjack as a person, but for Stefansson, defending her and undermining Noice was also defending himself. Stefansson was able to force Noice to write an extensive retraction, which Stefansson published in his own book in 1925, destroying Noice's reputation and ensuring that his version of events would not go down in history as the main narrative of Blackjack's story.

JOURNALISM

In 1963, when Maria Goeppert Mayer won the Nobel Prize in Physics, the newspaper in her hometown of San Diego ran the headline, "S.D. Mother Wins Nobel Prize."[6] When Dorothy Crowfoot Hodgkin won the Nobel Prize in Chemistry the following year, her headlines read "Nobel prize for British wife," "Oxford housewife wins Nobel prize" and "Nobel prize for a wife from Oxford."[7] After

---

6   "Maria Goeppert-Mayer – in Honor of Women's History Month," Www.ans.org., Accessed July 15, 2023, https://www.ans.org/news/article-1929/maria-goeppert-mayer-in-honor-of-womens-history-month/
7   "Jan Royall: Why We Must Champion Dorothy Hodgkin for the £50 Note," Somerville College Oxford, November 30, 2018, https://www.some.ox.ac.uk/news/jan-royall-why-we-must-champion-dorothy-hodgkin-for-the-50-note/

Australian painter Nora Heysen won the Archibald Prize—arguably the country's most prestigious art award—The Australian Women's Weekly ran an article with the headline "Girl Painter Who Won Art Prize is also Good Cook," listing three of the twenty-eight-year-old Heysen's favourite recipes along with her strategies for meeting her domestic duties and leaving time for painting.[8] When Alison Hargreaves, who summited Everest without the assistance of sherpas or oxygen, later died while climbing, *The Guardian* asked, "Alison Hargreaves: Unfit Mother?"[9] *The New York Times* ran the headline, "Sherry Lansing, former model, named head of Fox Productions," when Lansing became the first woman in the modern era to run a major motion picture studio in 1980. Many news outlets credited her as being "the first woman to run a motion picture studio," erasing women like Mary Pickford, Alice Guy-Blaché, and Lois Weber who ran production companies from the earliest days of the film industry.[10]

It is unfortunately not uncommon even in the 2020s to see articles with titles in the vein of "Did a woman ACTUALLY do a thing?" and then proceed to provide the evidence that yes, in fact, a woman did do the thing. Examples include "Did Khutulun and Other Warrior Women Actually Fight in the Mongol Army?," which had the sub-headline "From wielding lethal bows to commanding troops, the female soldiers of the Central Asian steppe were formidable foes." (*Atlas Obscura*, July 12, 2022[11]). Another from *Smithsonian Magazine* on March 3, 2021 read, "Did a Viking Woman Named Gudrid Really Travel to North America in 1000 A.D.?," followed immediately by, "The sagas suggest she settled in Newfoundland and eventually made eight crossings of the North Atlantic Sea."[12]

---

8   "Girl Painter Who Won Art Prize Is Also Good Cook," *Australian Women's Weekly*, February 4, 1939, https://trove.nla.gov.au/newspaper/article/55464841
9   Barnard, Josie. "Parents: Alison Hargreaves, Unfit Mother?" *The Guardian*, August 28, 2002, https://www.theguardian.com/world/2002/aug/28/gender.familyandrelationships
10 Higgins, Bill. "Backlot: 80 Years of The Hollywood Reporter." *The Hollywood Reporter*, December 7, 2010, https://www.hollywoodreporter.com/movies/movie-news/backlot-80-years-hollywood-reporter-2-56669/.
11 Durn, Sarah. "Did Khutulun and Other Warrior Women Actually Fight in the Mongol Army?" *Atlas Obscura*, July 12, 2022, https://www.atlasobscura.com/articles/mongol-female-warrior-women-china
12 Durn, Sarah. "Did a Viking Woman Named Gudrid Really Travel to North America in 1000 A.D.?" *Smithsonian Magazine*, March 3, 2021, https://www.smithsonianmag.com/history/did-viking-woman-named-gudrid-really-travel-north-america-1000-years-ago-180977126/

This is part of the practice referred to as framing, when journalists and editors choose how to present the content of a story. This includes phrasing, what quotes to include and exclude, what sources to cite, what facts to leave in or out, and so on.

In November, 2021, *The New York Times* claimed "With Jules Verne and the publisher Hugo Gernsback, H.G. Wells invented the genre of science fiction," ignoring Mary Shelley's *Frankenstein* which was published before either man was even born. While framing is more subtle and subjective, claims like this are just inaccurate—and thus easily disproved. That's what makes framing much more dangerous.[13]

Depending on the biases of journalists, editors, publishers, and sources, an article may be 100 percent accurate but still entirely misleading. Some outlets lean so heavily into this that they have mastered techniques to skirt the edges of defamation and other legal consequences. Such tactics include:

- presenting a commentary program as entertainment rather than news.
- framing assertions as questions rather than statements.
- allowing sources to make questionable claims and hiding behind simply repeating what the source said.
- selecting sources who will match the narrative they are trying to build, regardless of validity.
- repeating disproven claims, including invalidated "studies."
- not offering corrections or updates when it is shown they've presented inaccurate information, or burying these where they're unlikely to be noticed.

Even today, journalists' personal biases shape stories. In her memoir *Making a Scene*, actress Constance Wu recounts an interview where the journalist, a fellow Asian woman, insisted that Wu's mother must be a stereotypical "tiger mom" like the character Wu played on the television show *Fresh Off the Boat*. She disregarded Wu's assertions that this was completely untrue, and instead quoted the show's creator (the son of the woman Wu's character was based on) claiming that Wu's

---

13 Shotwell, Alyssa, "Twitter Reminds NYT Women Exist after H.G. Wells Credited with Creating Sci-Fi." *The Mary Sue*, November 22, 2021, https://www.themarysue.com/new-york-times-mary-shelley-scifi-hg-wells/

mother must be like his own.¹⁴ It's unclear what he was basing that claim on, or if he'd even met Wu's mother. Here we see multiple framing elements: the journalist choosing to present someone else's less-informed opinion over Wu's, which quotes to use, and how to phrase the surrounding text, all to shape a narrative that fits the journalist's view of the world, rather than the truth.

And sometimes women are cut out entirely. In 2014, the *BBC* aired "The Brits Who Built the Modern World," about five male architects including Michael Hopkins. His wife, Patty Hopkins, was co-founder and equal partner of Hopkins Architects, known for designs including the Glyndebourne Opera House in Sussex and the Frick Chemistry Lab at Princeton University. She was deliberately edited out of a photo used for promotional materials, leaving only the men.¹⁵

Decades earlier, journalist Dickey Chapelle was in Cuba in 1958, covering the work of revolutionary forces. As noted in a biography of Chapelle, "she tried in vain to publish a piece about these two women warriors (Celia Sanchez and Vilma Espín) and those like them who fought with equal ferocity and valor as their male counterparts. But no matter how heroically she wrote them in her pitches, Dickey's editors didn't think their stories were worth printing."¹⁶

Ann Lowe was the first African American to become a major fashion designer in the modern era, from the 1920s through the 1960s. She was best known for designing Jacqueline Bouvier's wedding dress when she married John F. Kennedy in 1953—or rather, she should have been. Although her work is recognized now, Jackie never publicly credited Lowe for the most talked-about dress of the year. Even though Lowe had been working with the Bouvier family for years, when asked who designed the dress, Jackie reportedly replied "I wanted to go to France, but a coloured dressmaker did it." The dress, which cost $500 (approximately $5,000 today), was described in detail in *The New York Times*'s coverage of the

---

14 Wu, Constance, *Making a Scene* (Simon and Schuster, 2022).
15 Waite, Richard. "BBC Slammed for 'Bias' after Patty Hopkins Is Sidelined in TV Show," *The Architects' Journal*, March 5, 2014, https://www.architectsjournal.co.uk/news/bbc-slammed-for-bias-after-patty-hopkins-is-sidelined-in-tv-show
16 Rhinehart, Lorissa, *First to the Front: The Untold Story of Dickey Chapelle, Trailblazing Female War Correspondent* (MacMillan, 2023).

wedding, but Lowe's name was never mentioned. Even worse, she lost money on the project—ten days before the wedding, a pipe burst in her studio, ruining the dress as well as nine others for members of the wedding party. Lowe and her team worked day and night to re-create the masterpieces in a week and a half. She ended up losing $2,200—about $21,000 in today's currency. Then, when she hand-delivered the gowns in Newport, R.I., she was told to enter through a service entrance in the back.[17] Lowe replied that either the dresses went with her through the front door or they went back with her to New York. Lowe also designed the dress Olivia de Havilland wore to the 1947 Oscars, when she won for Best Actress. The name on the label, however, was Sonia Rosenberg, the store for which Lowe worked at the time.[18]

Historically, many media outlets have not been overly concerned with accuracy in the first place, as exemplified by the phrase "if it bleeds, it leads." Sensationalism sells, and often there were (and are) scant repercussions when the targets were not wealthy or powerful. Perhaps the most legendary example of this type of "yellow journalism" is an exchange between famed publishing magnate William Randolph Hearst and illustrator Frederick Remington. Remington, who had been sent to Cuba to cover a brewing conflict, cabled to Hearst that there was no war—to which Hearst allegedly replied, "You furnish the pictures. I'll furnish the war."[19]

In the 1960s, Boston journalists Loretta McLaughlin and Jean Cole worked to publicize what would become known as the Boston Strangler murders. "An editor disputed the worth of a series on the four dead women, noting that they were 'nobodies,'" McLaughlin later recalled. The reporters' first major story ran with the headline "Two Girl Reporters Analyze Strangler"—never mind that both were experienced investigative journalists in their thirties. "Being a female reporter was often semi-apologetically noted for the readers," McLaughlin observed. "Among

---

17 "How black designer of Jackie Kennedy's wedding dress was snubbed by bride and press," *The Washington Post*, September 1, 2019, https://www.scmp.com/lifestyle/fashion-beauty/article/3025023/how-black-designer-jackie-kennedys-wedding-dress-was
18 Hess, Liam. "Pioneering Designer Ann Lowe Gets Her Due in This Year's Met Exhibition," *Vogue*, April 27, 2022, https://www.vogue.com/article/ann-lowe-met-exhibition-2022
19 "Crucible of Empire – PBS Online," PBS, 2019, https://www.pbs.org/crucible/bio_hearst.html

my newsclips are several with a headline stating, 'Girl reporter covers' whatever it was, from murder to presidential elections." [20]

China's last and most famous empress, Cixi (1861 – 1908), also became its most infamous in part due to slanderous rumours by her political opponents, but also thanks to the concerted efforts of Oxford-trained linguist Edmund Backhouse, who, among other things, claimed to have been her lover for years, including coercive and sadistic practices, and that she disguised herself to sneak into a brothel and watch the patrons have sex. Backhouse's lies repeatedly made it into the *Times of London* via the dispatches of a Peking correspondent who made the mistake of trusting Backhouse's "reporting." When the correspondent discovered that much of what Backhouse had told him was completely fabricated, it was too late—it would have damaged his own reputation to reveal the falsehoods.[21] Among other things, Backhouse claimed to have overheard or been told any number of fabricated statements by Cixi and others, and purported both that Cixi died of illness and to have witnessed her murder by stabbing.[22]

Two years after the empress's death, Backhouse doubled down with *China Under the Empress Dowager*. Published in 1910 and written by Backhouse and British journalist J. O. P. Bland, the book was hailed as a thoroughly researched biography, but scholars later discovered that Backhouse had forged many of the documents he and Bland claimed to cite. Presenting Cixi as a cruel and greedy tyrant, it was considered the authority on her for decades, until Hugh Trevor-Roper's 1976 biography *A Hidden Life: The Enigma of Sir Edmund Backhouse*, published in the United States under the title *Hermit of Peking*, exposed the lies. As *Smithsonian Magazine* writes, "It's hard to know what Backhouse's motivations may have been for this historical hoax, but perhaps sensational lies simply paved

---

20   Smith, Nathan, "The Tenacious Women Reporters Who Helped Expose the Boston Strangler," Smithsonian.com, March 16, 2023, https://www.smithsonianmag.com/history/the-tenacious-women-reporters-who-helped-expose-the-boston-strangler-180981786/
21   Fiegl, Amanda, "Cixi: The Woman behind the Throne," Smithsonian.com, March 1, 2008, https://www.smithsonianmag.com/history/cixi-the-woman-behind-the-throne-22312071/
22   Heineken, Brian, "A Hermitage Revisited: The Literary Afterlife of Sir Edmund Trelawny Backhouse," University of Minnesota–Twin Cities, May 6, 2016, https://conservancy.umn.edu/bitstream/handle/11299/181378/Brian%20Reinken%20summa%20CLA%20sp2016.pdf?sequence=1

an easier path to fame than nuanced truth."

It is within this mindset that women's stories have often been ignored or misrepresented. Even if a journalist wanted to cover serious women's stories, if the male editors and publishers didn't think it would sell, the stories were often scrapped. So-called girl stunt reporters were sometimes able to bridge this gap, as with Nellie Bly's famous exposé of horrific conditions at the Women's Lunatic Asylum on New York's Blackwell's Island. Yet even the term used to describe them diminished the women as "girls" and their investigative work as "stunts," and they were often only able to carry out assignments, like visiting an illegal abortion clinic, that a male reporter could not.[23]

When Mary Sherman Morgan died in 2004, her son George submitted an obituary for her to the *Los Angeles Times*, which they "refused to print [...] on the grounds they could not verify any of its information," he later recalled. Mary, the only female engineer among 900 rocket scientists at North American Aviation in the early 1950s, invented hydyne, the rocket fuel that successfully boosted America's first satellite into orbit in 1958. This spurred George to write a stage play and popular non-fiction biography, *Rocket Girl: The Story of Mary Sherman Morgan*, to ensure her legacy would not be lost.[24]

In 1855, Mary Seacole travelled 3,000 miles from England to the Black Sea on a mission to set up a canteen for soldiers at war. *London Times* special correspondent William Howard Russell reported the news in his dispatch. Russell was embedded with British troops outside Sevastopol, and informed his editor that "Inter alia, we are to have an hotel at Balaclava. It is to be conducted by 'Mrs. Seacole, late of Jamaica.'" When his dispatch was reprinted across the British newspapers, almost every one changed her gender, assuming that "Mrs." must have been an error—surely he meant "Mr." As *Smithsonian Magazine* notes, "By the time British troops left in July 1856, everybody in Crimea knew Mrs. Seacole, or, as she was better known, "Mother Seacole."" Her fame spread to the U.K. as

---

23 Todd, Kim, *Sensational* (HarperCollins, 2021).
24 "Mary Sherman Morgan – Rocket Girl," *Cosmos Magazine*, June 20, 2021, https://cosmosmagazine.com/science/mary-sherman-morgan-rocket-girl/

well, once the newspapers figured out their mistake, and she was as well-known as Florence Nightingale, becoming arguably the most famous Black woman in the British empire.

Even today, there are blatant disparities. Women are much more likely to be asked about their physical appearance—diet and exercise regimen, clothing designers, intimate bodily questions—and personal lives, like dating, whether they're pregnant, how they balance work and home, and questions about their children. During a press tour for 2012 Marvel movie *The Avengers*, a male reporter asked Scarlett Johansson—who at the time played the only female Avenger—if she wore underwear under her very tight costume. And he wasn't the only one. "You're like the fifth person that's asked me that today," she responded. "What is going on? Since when do people start asking each other in interviews about their underwear?" The SAME male reporter, who worked for *Extra*, also notoriously asked Anne Hathaway about her diet and exercise regimen when she played Catwoman in *The Dark Knight Rises*. After multiple asinine questions, Hathaway also wasn't having it, asking "Are you trying to lose weight? What's the deal, man? You look great. No, no seriously. We have to talk about this. What do you want? Are you trying to fit into a catsuit?" [25]

In a 2015 radio interview, two male hosts asked Ariana Grande if she could get through a day without either make-up or her phone. She laughed and responded, "Is this what you think girls have trouble choosing between? Is this men assuming that that's what girls would have to choose between?" Sienna Miller also shut down a reporter asking about her romantic life, saying "I can guarantee you, having read enough interviews about this, that these questions aren't mentioned with men." When asked what her favourite position was (the implication being sexual) on SiriusXM in 2012, reality star Lauren Conrad snapped back, "CEO."[26]

And, of course, it's not just women in entertainment who are the target of sexist questions. In a 2011 interview, Hillary Clinton was asked, "Which designers

---

25 Phan, Delenne, "Interviewing Female Superheroes," Department of Linguistics, April 24, 2022, https://www.colorado.edu/linguistics/2022/04/24/interviewing-female-superheroes
26 "21 Times Women Had the Perfect Response to Being Underestimated," *Elle*, March 7, 2021, https://www.elle.com.au/culture/women-responses-to-sexist-questions-12528

do you prefer?" Her answer: "Would you ever ask a man that question?"[27] Elena Soreva, the first Russian woman to go to the International Space Station, was asked at a 2014 press conference how she was planning to do her hair in space. She replied, "Aren't you interested in the hair styles of my colleagues?"[28]

The trend is also exacerbated for any women with other marginalizations. Carly Findlay is an Australian disability advocate who regularly faces invasive questions and insulting comments about her skin condition, ichthyosis. Perhaps the most offensive setting was in a radio interview for the Australian Broadcasting Corporation in 2018, where she was there to discuss that exact topic, yet comments from host Jon Faine included asking her to justify calling herself disabled because she was not in a wheelchair, saying she looked like a burn victim and suggesting her face would be good at Halloween. When she mentioned that people have the gall to ask whether she can have sex, he asked, "What's the answer?" When she said that she doesn't like when people say they'll pray for her, he jumped in to defend the behaviour she just said was offensive. [29]

It's also a question of who's doing the reporting. The UK's National Union of Journalists says only seventeen percent of their photographer and videographer members are women; the British Press Photographers Association reports 12.5 percent, and the Association of Photographers puts their female Accredited and Assisting Photographers at only eighteen percent—yet seventy-five percent of their student members are female. Even in fields like fashion, where the primary audience is female, only 13.7 percent of 2017 magazine covers from the ten leading US publications were shot by female photographers. *Women Photograph* routinely analyses ratios of men's and women's photographs that lead on the first pages of major publications (non-binary folks are grouped with women). In the fourth quarter of 2021 (October to December), they analysed *The Wall Street Journal*

---

27 Amira, Dan, "Hillary Clinton Is Asked What Designers She Wears Moments after Making Point about Sexism," *Intelligencer*, Dec 2, 2022, https://nymag.com/intelligencer/2010/12/hillary_clinton_asked_what_des.html
28 *Ibid.*
29 Findlay, Carly, "Talking Microaggressions with Jon Faine on ABC Radio," Carly Findlay, March 28, 2018, https://carlyfindlay.com.au/2018/03/28/talking-microaggressions-with-jon-faine-on-abc-radio

(12.5 percent of lead photos had a woman's byline), *The Guardian* (14.3 percent), the *Los Angeles Times* (20.8 percent), *The Globe and Mail* (22.5 percent), *Le Monde* (24.4 percent), *The New York Times* (25.3 percent), *The Washington Post* (28.6 percent) and the *San Francisco Chronicle* (53.1 percent).[30]

In Somalia, the first all-women media outlet, *Bilan*, was launched in 2022 with funding support from the United Nations. "It is sad that our country needs a women-only media house but that is the reality here. Women are expected to babble all they like in the kitchen but to keep their mouths firmly shut in public," says editor-in-chief Nasrin Mohamed Ibrahim. "'Men think you should come in, read the news and go home." *Bilan* also gives Ibrahim the chance to tell important stories that would otherwise be censored: "I have been a journalist since I was a teenager in secondary school. In the 12 years I have been working, there have been stories I have never been able to tell ... One reason why women's stories are rarely told in the Somali media is that most reporters are men." Her deputy editor, Fathi Mohamed Ahmed, spoke of the rampant sexual harassment women journalists face: "The biggest challenge facing female journalists in Somalia is abuse, especially from male journalists," she said. "They offer to help you but only if you give them something in return."[31] [32]

SPORTS COVERAGE

Sport coverage is a massive part of the media industry and, like most sectors, there is a clear gender gap. As of 2019, women made up 40 percent of all participants in sports in the US, yet received only four percent of sports media coverage.[33] It

---

30 Fielder, Jez, "Women Photographers in Focus as Industry Still Needs to Sharpen Up," *Euronews*, March 7, 2022, https://www.euronews.com/culture/2022/03/07/women-photographers-in-focus-as-industry-still-needs-to-sharpen-up
31 Choat, Isabel, "All-Female Newsroom Launched in Somalia to Widen Media's Scope," *The Guardian*, April 11, 2022, https://www.theguardian.com/world/2022/apr/11/all-female-newsroom-launched-in-somalia-to-widen-medias-scope.
32 Ibrahim, Nasrin Mohamed, "Women Are Expected to Keep Their Mouths Shut Here in Somalia. But Not Any More," *The Guardian*, April 11, 2022, https://www.theguardian.com/global-development/2022/apr/11/women-are-expected-to-keep-their-mouths-shut-here-in-somalia-but-not-any-more/
33 MacKenzie, Macaela, "Female Athletes Receive Only 4% of Sports Media Coverage—Adidas Wants to Change That," *Glamour*, July 15, 2019, https://www.glamour.com/story/female-athletes-receive-only-4-of-sports-media-coverage-adidas-wants-to-change-that/.

creates a catch-22 cycle, in which executives refuse to invest in women's sports because they don't get enough attention (and therefore the organisations can't make as much money off them), so there is less of a push for women's sports to succeed. This was the reasoning for the Tour de France organizers to end the women's race after only a few years in the 1980s—televised airings of the race were bringing in big money in advertising and sponsorships, focusing, of course, on the male riders, so they dropped the women's race to capitalize on the men's larger audience.[34] Yet even when women do get more screen time, the pay doesn't match—in 2021, it was reported that athletes in women's sports received more than 59 percent of screen time in primetime Olympic coverage, but were still generally paid less than their male counterparts.[35] More recently, the 2024 US college basketball National Collegiate Athletic Association (NCAA) women's championship game attracted 18.9 million viewers – around 28 percent more than the men's game, which had 14.8 million. However, the television rights for the women's game only cost $6.5 million, while the men received $873 million.[36] The Respect Her Game report from 2021 also showed that:

- 82 percent of Olympic commentators are men.
- More than two-thirds of women athletes (69.6 percent) wear revealing outfits compared to half of men athletes (53.5 percent).
- Women athletes are about ten times more likely to be visually objectified with a camera angle than men athletes (5.7 percent compared with 0.6 percent).
- Men athletes are referred to as "male [athlete/sport]" just 2.0 percent of the time compared with 13.6 percent for women athletes. This reinforces the idea that men are "real" athletes while women are secondary, that men are the default while women are an anomaly.

---

34 Cross, Kim, "The Real Reason There's No Tour de France for Women," *Outside Online*, July 23, 2018, https://www.outsideonline.com/outdoor-adventure/biking/why-there-no-womens-tour-de-france/
35 "Respect Her Game," The Representation Project, https://therepproject.org/wp-content/uploads/2021/08/Respect-Her-Game-Report.pdf
36 Bachman, Rachel and Simonetti, Isabella, 2024, "NCAA Women Beat Men in Finals' Ratings for First Time—but Got 99% Less TV Money," *Wall Street Journal*, April 9, 2024, https://www.wsj.com/business/media/the-womens-ncaa-tournament-outshone-the-mens-but-it-got-99-less-tv-money-74806707/

- Women athletes are seven times more likely to be referred to using a gender diminutive (such as "girl") than men athletes.[37]

And then there are instances like what happened right after Hungarian swimmer Katinka Hosszú broke a world record at the Rio Olympics in 2016. NBC cut away from Hosszú to her volatile coach/husband in the stands, with a commentator declaring him "the guy responsible for turning [her] into a whole different swimmer." Never mind that she's been an Olympian since she was 15—years before she met him—and had been winning gold medals at the European Championships before he started coaching her, and that he was himself a failed wannabe professional swimmer who, at only a year older than her, had little experience.[38] This is also a guy who, at an event for 10 - and 11-year-olds, of whom he was the coach, exploded into a profanity-laced rant, yelling "fuck you" and flipping his middle fingers at an official.[39] Hosszú filed for divorce a year and a half later. He retaliated by trying to delete her public Facebook page. He subsequently coached Italian swimmer Ilaria Cusinato, but they "parted ways" within nine months. Meanwhile, without his coaching, Hosszú became the most decorated female swimmer at the European Championships in 2020, when her total medal count reached 24—with her 25th (won at the 2022 European Championships), she was just one shy of tying Alexander Popov, who holds the overall record with 26.

During a live broadcast of the FIDE Women's Grand Prix chess tournament in 2022, grandmaster and commentator Ilya Smirin admitted to saying chess is "maybe not for women." He defended himself to his fellow commentator, Women's International Master Fiona Steil-Antoni, that it had been in a private conversation. She pointed out that he had recently complimented a woman competitor by saying that she was "playing like a man." He had also asked why a player would want to

---

37 *Ibid.*
38 Stubbs, Roman, "'The Man Responsible': NBC Broadcaster Draws Ire after Crediting World Record to Swimmer's Husband," *The Washington Post*, November 27, 2021, https://www.washingtonpost.com/news/early-lead/wp/2016/08/07/the-man-responsible-nbc-broadcaster-draws-ire-after-crediting-world-record-to-swimmers-husband/
39 Anderson, Jared, "Tusup Talks about Regrets, Burying the Hatchet in Eurosport Interview," *SwimSwam*, August 12, 2020, https://swimswam.com/tusup-talks-about-regrets-burying-the-hatchet-in-eurosport-interview/

be like a male grandmaster. He was immediately fired from the role, but such swift and significant consequences are often few and far between.[40]

Former tennis star, frequent high-profile commentator, and noted jackass John McEnroe claimed in 2017 that although Serena Williams was without a doubt the best female tennis player of all time, she would rank 700th if she were competing with men. It's one of countless, nonsensical sexist remarks made about Serena and other female athletes. In contrast, Andy Murray, who has paired with Williams in mixed doubles, notoriously corrected a BBC host who congratulated Murray on becoming "the first person ever to win two Olympic tennis gold medals." Without missing a beat, Murray pointed out, "I think Venus and Serena have won about four each." It wasn't a one-off either—Murray was also quick to correct another reporter at Wimbledon in 2017 who called his opponent "the first US player to reach a major semi-final since 2009"—at the time, Williams had already won 23 (not just made it to the semi-final). Murray interrupted the reporter mid-question with, "Male player, right?"[41] If only there were more men willing to fact-check such comments in real time.

DOCUMENTATION

Cinema pioneer Alice Guy-Blaché was the first female film director, but that didn't keep a man from trying to write her out of history. Starting in 1896, she created more than 1,000 films for studio founder Léon Gaumont's Gaumont Film Company and is considered the first director to systematically develop narrative filmmaking, as well as pioneering various filmmaking techniques. She was the company's head of production for 10 years, yet she later discovered Gaumont had erased her from the company's history —her name had been removed from most, if not all of her films, and she was not mentioned in the 1930 publication of the company's history. She spent years communicating with colleagues and film

---

40 Coventry, James, "Chess Grandmaster Sacked for Saying Chess 'Maybe Not for Women,'" *ABC News*, September 28, 2022, https://www.abc.net.au/news/2022-09-29/chess-commentator-sacked-for-saying-chess-not-for-women/101484600
41 Proudfoot, Jenny. "Throwback To: Serena Williams Praising Andy Murray for Calling out Sexism," *Marie Claire UK*, July 3, 2019, https://www.marieclaire.co.uk/entertainment/people/serena-williams-andy-murray-522993

historians to correct the record and compiled long lists of her films, to the best of her recollection, to repair the damage to her reputation. Meanwhile, having been forced out of Gaumont's employment after her marriage, she and her husband started their own studio, making her the first woman studio owner. Yet she was not welcome at distributor meetings because, as her husband alleged, her presence would "embarrass the men."[42]

Beyond journalism, it's important to keep in mind who is responsible for and capable of producing records. In Guy-Blaché's case, her former boss was able to erase a decade of her work. In ancient Egypt, cultural norms prevented women from holding bureaucratic or administrative positions in government. As such, although there is significant documentation of male medical practitioners, we have none of that type for the women who practised medicine.[43] This has enabled historians to disregard the evidence that does exist, including mentions of such women in non-government documents—for more on this, see the "Scholarly Androcentrism" section.

In ancient Greece, Greek geographer and travel writer Pausanias wrote that it was decreed that, while unmarried women were allowed to participate, if a married woman was caught at the Olympic Games, she would be cast down from Mount Typaeum and into the river flowing below. Given that physical fitness was valued by many ancient Greeks for women as well as men, the ladies decided to have their own competition and the Herean Games were born. Unfortunately, unlike the Olympic Games, few records remain (if they ever existed). While some use the lack of formal records to claim that the games didn't happen, others point to the likelihood that the women's games were simply considered insignificant by the record-keepers of the time, such as the poets who wrote odes to Olympic athletes.[44]

Beyond this, women have often been kept illiterate throughout the centuries,

---

42 Wills, Matthew. "Hollywood Froze out the Founding Mother of Cinema." *JSTOR Daily*, March 13, 2019, https://daily.jstor.org/hollywood-froze-out-the-founding-mother-of-cinema
43 Reser, Anna, and Leila Mcneill, *Forces of Nature: The Women Who Changed Science* (Frances Lincoln, 2021).
44 Young, Lauren, "When Ancient Greece Banned Women from Olympics, They Started Their Own," *Atlas Obscura*, August 10, 2016, https://www.atlasobscura.com/articles/when-ancient-greece-barred-women-from-even-watching-the-games-they-started-their-own-olympics

particularly if those women were poor or otherwise marginalized. As such, we often must rely on the narratives of men to tell the stories of women's lives—and those men are often unreliable narrators, when they bother at all. Just as the victors write history, so do those in power.

One major example this is James Marion Sims, who has been held up as the "father of modern gynaecology" despite the well-documented fact that his "discoveries" were based on his horrific torture of a dozen enslaved women. He meticulously detailed the appalling experiments he conducted on these women but did not even write down the names of most of his victims. Because they were enslaved, we have no record of Anarcha, Betsey, Lucy, and nine other nameless women's experiences beyond what Sims wrote. There is no documentation from their perspectives, of how it felt to be strapped down naked in front of curious strangers and operated on without anaesthesia, or when they were forced to participate in his surgeries on each other, and nurse each other back to health, knowing it would only mean more pain and trauma.[45] (See "Statues" section for more on Sims)

Sims is only one of countless "doctors" to torment, maim and kill people who had no ability to say no to their "treatments," alongside the likes of Nazi concentration camp officials Josef Mengele and Carl Clauberg, or 19th century English surgeon Isaac Baker Brown, who sliced off women's clitorises without the consent or knowledge of his patients or their families because he thought masturbation caused epilepsy and the ever-popular "hysteria."[46] Depending on the circumstances, victims of such men are often incapable of telling their own stories.

In scholarship, there are primary sources—original documents, eyewitness accounts, photos, video footage, etcetera—and secondary sources, like journal and newspaper articles, critics' reviews, and so on. Primary sources are highly valued, but like anything created by humans, they are not infallible or free from bias.

Anna Reser and Leila McNeill write in their book, *Forces of Nature: The Women who Changed Science,* about the scant documentation from Imperial China and the Imperial Court, and the fact that the writings that do exist were generally

---

45 Cleghorn, Elinor. *Unwell Women: Misdiagnosis and Myth in a Man-Made World,* (Dutton, 2021).
46 Ibid.

produced by men. " In China, these writings were often very dismissive of women practitioners, whom male doctors described as unlearned, crude, and wiley ... As with ancient Egyptian medicine, records by or about women medical practitioners are very scarce. Male doctors described women medical practitioners as three of the six "grannies:" medicine sellers, shaman healers, and midwives. Of the stereotypes of women that a family might encounter, the grannies were among those that male writers warned families against."[47]

Similarly, the major historian of the Crusades was William of Tyre, who largely ignored the influential women from that period, such as Queen of Jerusalem Morphia of Melitene; Queen Melisende of Jerusalem, Princess Alice of Antioch, Countess Hodierna of Tripoli, Abbess Yvette of Bethany, Princess Constance of Antioch, Agnes of Courtenay, Queen Sibylla of Jerusalem and Eleanor of Aquitaine. In her book, *Queens of Jerusalem: The Women Who Dared To Rule*, Katherine Pangonis writes, "He does not give much credit to the notion that the women he writes about were individuals as complex as the men, and he prefers to cast women as literary tropes rather than depict them as living, breathing humans."[48] Indeed, the description for Kate Lombard's *Queens of Outremer* sums up the situation: "William of Tyre, the key historian for this period, gives a sympathetic portrayal of just one queen, and writes off the rest as manipulative harridans, or barely worth the words. He devotes the fewest possible pages in his hefty chronicle to the deeds of women, when indeed women played a key role in both the crusades themselves and the foundation of the Kingdom of Jerusalem. There is a trend for male chroniclers of the crusades to concern themselves with the deeds of men, and this has carried over to much modern scholarship too."[49]

Katharina Kepler became a side character in her own trial for witchcraft in 1615 when her son, the well-known astronomer Johannes Kepler, famously defended her. She was imprisoned for 14 months and threatened with torture before finally

---

47 Ibid.
48 Macquire, Kelly, "Interview: Queens of Jerusalem, the Women Who Dared to Rule by Katherine Pangonis," *World History Encyclopedia*, March 22, 2022, https://www.worldhistory.org/article/1969/interview-queens-of-jerusalem-the-women-who-dared/
49 Lombard, Kate, *Queens of Outremer: The Christian Princesses of Medieval Palestine* (Orion, 2021).

being released and dying six months later, and even her other son, Heinrich, accused that she had "ridden a calf to death and prepared him a roast dish from it, [and] he himself wanted to accuse her before the authorities."[50] Yet when her story is told, it is with titles like "Johannes Kepler Defended His Mother in a Witchcraft Trial" (Smithsonian Magazine, 2015). Indeed, although she testified in her own defence, only her son's arguments are preserved verbatim in the trial documents—and he'd been documented as calling the septuagenarian Katharina "the author of her own lamentable misfortune."[51] A book about the trial, titled *The Astronomer and the Witch: Johannes Kepler's Fight for his Mother*, features neither Katharina's image nor her name on the cover. The official description ends with the line, "even Katharina's children wondered whether their mother really did have nothing to hide…"[52]

Pirate and governor Sayyida al Hurra is arguably one of the most intriguing Muslim women in history—certainly of the 1500s. Yet Islamic records do not mention her exploits as either the ruler of Tetouan in Morocco or the terror of Iberian and North African waters. She is ignored in favour of her ally, the male corsair Hayreddin Barbarossa. After her husband's death in 1515, Sayyida—who had previously ruled in his place when he was away—was accepted by her people as independent governor, believed to be the last woman in Islamic history to do so. When she married no less a man than the sultan of Morocco, she made him come to Tetouan for the wedding, the only time in the country's history a sultan has wed outside the capital.

At the same time, she wreaked havoc on the Spanish in retribution for her family being forced from Granada because of their faith during the Reconquista. She led her own fleet and established herself as the undisputed pirate queen of the western Mediterranean, Iberia, and Morocco's Atlantic coast. Because she was seen

---

50 Rampling, Jennifer, "History of Science: Trial by Gender," *Nature* 527, no. 7577 (2022): 164–64, https://doi.org/10.1038/527164a

51 Maksel, Rebecca, "Johannes Kepler Defended His Mother in a Witchcraft Trial," *Smithsonian Magazine,* December 28, 2014, https://www.smithsonianmag.com/air-space-magazine/johannes-kepler-mother-witch-180957616/

52 Rublack, Ulinka, *The Astronomer and the Witch: Johannes Kepler's Fight for His Mother* (Oxford University Press, 2015).

as the main contact to negotiate the return of Christian captives, it is these records that give the fullest account of Sayyida and her life. Among her own people, whom she dedicated her life to, there is little mention in surviving documents.[53] [54]

Anne Chambers, author of the bestselling 1979 biography *Granuaile*, observes a similar issue with the subject of her book, the Irish tribal leader and warrior known to the English as Grace O'Malley. "It is quite an irony of history that Grace O'Malley's factual records should have been written by her presumed enemies—the English. From all these military men who came to conquer her country, that the story, the factual story of Grace O'Malley is written in the dispatches they sent back to court and back to England during these disturbed times. Imprisoned almost in that was the real story of Grace O'Malley. So really in effect, she—and we—would have to thank her enemies, that they at least wrote something about her. Otherwise she would have been totally lost history."[55]

American abolitionist, women's rights activist, and former slave Sojourner Truth's most famous speech is known as the "Ain't I a Woman?" speech, delivered at the Women's Rights Convention in 1851. However, it is highly unlikely that Truth actually used the phrasing "Ain't I a Woman?" A contemporaneous transcript of the speech was published in the *Anti-Slavery Bugle* on June 21, 1851. However, the 1863 version by white abolitionist Frances Dana Barker Gage changed Truth's speech patterns, giving her the speech characteristics of Southern slaves. Truth was born and raised in New York and spoke only Dutch until she was 9 years old—there is no indication that she would have spoken in this dialect and it appears to be either faulty memory or deliberate changes on Gage's part. Gage also added made-up statements—Truth saying she could bear the lash as well as a man, that no one ever offered her the traditional gentlemanly deference due a woman, and that most of her 13 children were sold away from her into slavery.

---

53   Duncombe, Laura Sook, "Sayyida Al-Hurra, the Beloved, Avenging Islamic Pirate Queen," *Jezebel*, March 3, 2015, https://jezebel.com/sayyida-al-hurra-the-beloved-avenging-islamic-pirate-1685524517
54   Idrissi Azami, R., Touzani, H and Sabil, A. (2023). "Female agency, history, and the current discourses of representation: Sayyida Al-Hurra (ruler of Tétouan) as a case study," *Journal of Applied Language and Culture Studies*, 6 no 3 (2023): 91-106.
55   "Warrior Women." Episode 2: Grace O'Malley: The Pirate Queen, Discovery Channel, 2003, https://www.imdb.com/title/tt0387790/

Truth is widely believed to have had five children, one of whom was sold away, and was never known to claim more children.[56] Gage even contradicted herself, writing in 1851 that the environment was friendly but then writing in 1863 that attendees and organizers were afraid of "mobbish" opponents. Gage also claimed that Truth was not well-received, which directly conflicts with other eyewitness accounts that attendees were "beaming with joyous gladness" and there was not "one discordant note." Unfortunately, Gage's version is the one that gained popularity, reprinted in 1875, 1881, and 1889, and it wasn't until historian Nell Irvin Painter published her 1997 biography *Sojourner Truth: A Life, A Symbol* that Gage's version was discredited. However, the legacy remains, as it is still known as the "Ain't I a Woman?" speech.[57]

In 2023, Lesley Paterson won her first BAFTA for writing her film adaptation of *All Quiet On The Western Front*. For some reason, the BBC chose to leave her acceptance speech out of the official broadcast. Her response? "It is what it is and hopefully I'll get to say a speech at the Oscars" (she was also nominated for Best Adapted Screenplay that year but did not win). The movie won seven of the 14 BAFTAs it was nominated for, including Best Film and Best Director.[58]

In many instances, lack of documentation is due to women actively seeking to conceal their identities due to sexism or other reasons. As *Smithsonian Magazine* noted in an article on female architects, because they were unlikely to get steady work if it was well-known a woman was designing the buildings, "working women architects, in an effort to survive in the business, disguised their efforts so well that no solid record links them to having designed anything at all." The article cites as an example Lady Elizabeth Wilbraham, believed to have designed Wotton House in Surrey, England in 1704. "Wilbraham, an aristocratic Englishwoman who lived from 1632 to 1705 and studied architecture, is rumored to

---

56   "Compare the Speeches — The Sojourner Truth Project. 2014," The Sojourner Truth Project, https://www.thesojournertruthproject.com/compare-the-speeches
57   Mabee, Carleton and Susan Mabee Newhouse, *Sojourner Truth: Slave, Prophet, Legend* (NYU Press, 1995, pp. 67–82).
58   Welsh, Daniel, "All Quiet on the Western Front Writer Vents 'Frustration' as Bafta Speech Is Cut from Broadcast," *HuffPost UK*, February 20, 2023, https://www.huffingtonpost.co.uk/entry/all-quiet-on-the-western-front-speech-cut-baftas_uk_63f359aee4b0a209e828bb45

have designed 400 buildings. Wotton House, a 17th-century Baroque country estate commonly believed to be designed by William Winde, was attributed to Wilbraham by architectural historian John Millar based on designs she made for her family—though no drawings or invoices have her signature."[59]

MRS. NAMELESS

Arguably the world's most successful pirate of all time has largely lost her true name to history. In records, she is referred to as variations on Zheng Shi, Madam Ching, Ching Shih—all meaning simply the wife or widow of Cheng I. In 1801, the woman who would be known as Ching Shih was a young sex worker who married a pirate lord, Cheng I. It's said that she demanded an equal share and command before she would marry him, to which he agreed. Six years later when her husband died, Ching Shih, in her early 30s, took command of the Guangdong Pirate Confederation, putting her in charge of about 400 junk ships and 40,000 to 60,000 pirates. Years earlier, she had helped her husband form the confederation, in which different pirate leaders each sacrificed some autonomy for collective benefit. Her political savvy and knowledge of players, relationships, and dynamics helped her not only gain power but keep the confederation together after Cheng I's death. [60]

She then wrecked havoc on the South China Sea for years—under her command, the confederation was far more active. Ching Shih took on everybody who was anybody, including the East India Company, the Portuguese Empire, and the Qing Chinese navy. One captive estimated that Ching Shih had 80,000 pirates, 1,000 large junks, and 800 smaller junks and rowboats under her command in 1809.

She also ruled with an iron fist—any pirate caught giving his own orders or disobeying those of a superior was to be beheaded on the spot. It was also a capital offence to steal from the common treasury or from villagers who supplied the pirates. Additionally, if a pirate raped a female captive, he would be put to death, but if sex was consensual, both would be put to death, though a captive was allowed

---

[59] Billock, Jennifer, "Six Wonders Built by Pioneering Women Architects," *Smithsonian Magazine*, March 9, 2021, https://www.smithsonianmag.com/travel/six-wonders-built-pioneering-women-architects-180977099/
[60] Banerji, Urvija, "The Chinese Female Pirate Who Commanded 80,000 Outlaws," *Atlas Obscura*, April 6, 2016, https://www.atlasobscura.com/articles/ching-shih-chinese-female-pirate/

to marry a pirate if they wanted to.

Perhaps the most impressive part of her piratical career was its ending. Ching Shih was such a powerful enemy that she was able to arrange a peaceful surrender in 1810. At the time, she was in command of 17,318 pirates, 226 ships, 1,315 cannons, and 2,798 assorted weapons; her personal command encompassed 24 ships and 1,433 pirates. The terms of surrender included pardons, pork, wine and money for her crews, and her lover Zhang Bao was awarded the rank of lieutenant and allowed to keep a private fleet of 20 to 30 ships. She then married him, retired to run a gambling house in Macau, had more children, and lived to be almost 70.

Yet for all her accomplishments, historian Dian Murray's 1987 book *Pirates of the South China Coast, 1790-1810*, is the first modern Western source of Ching Shih's story.

While it is maddening to see this erasure in modern times, it carries on a long habit of burying women's identities in the interest of seeing them as only an extension of their husbands. This can also impact the woman's professional reputation in fields where name recognition is vital to being taken seriously—if all your work has been done under one name, it can be difficult to "re-establish" yourself under a new one that no one knows.

Transgender people often have the same issue with their dead names, which has led to some bizarre expressions of misogyny. The brilliant neurobiologist Ben Barres famously told of a colleague overhearing someone remark, "Ben Barres gave a great seminar today, but then his work is much better than his sister's." The speaker had assumed Barres, a transgender man, was a different person than when he was presenting as female and using his dead name – the non-existent "sister" was Barres himself.[61]

The name of the massive toy corporation Mattel comes from a combination of the two founders' names: Elliot Handler and Harold "Matt" Matson. Just one problem: there were three founders. Ruth Handler, wife of Elliot, creator of the

---

[61] Kaplan, Sarah, "'A Towering Legacy of Goodness': Ben Barres's Fight for Diversity in Science," *The Washington Post*, December 28, 2017, https://www.washingtonpost.com/news/speaking-of-science/wp/2017/12/28/a-towering-legacy-of-goodness-ben-barress-fight-for-diversity-in-science/

iconic and bestselling Barbie doll and the company's first president, was part of the team who built the company over the course of thirty years from 1945 to 1975. Meanwhile, Matson left the company the year after its founding, but his name remained for decades while Ruth's was left out.[62]

To be fair, in some instances it has been a strategic choice on the woman's part. Publishing tycoon Miriam Leslie inherited her husband's business upon his death and legally changed her own name to Frank, so she was Mrs. Frank Leslie in all senses.[63] Until even a few decades ago, it was common for women to be addressed as simply the "Mrs." of their husband, their own name and identity essentially absorbed into his. The business-savvy and perception-conscious Frank knew the power of her husband's brand and recognized that the move would strengthen her position in the male-dominated 1880s American publishing industry.

The erasure of women's names can also make it more difficult for future historians to connect work to the person. For example, if an artist like Jane Frank's early education and work was done under her family name, Jane Schenthal, it may be difficult for scholars without additional context to connect the two. This is especially true for women who married multiple times.

Tennis star Billie Jean King won the Wimbledon tournament six times, yet like other women champions, her identity was erased on the official display of winners' names. Instead of B. J. King (the format for the men), she is listed as "Mrs. L. W. King." L.W. referred to Larry, her husband. British tennis player Roger Cawley never won Wimbledon, but his name is on the list thanks to his marriage to winner Evonne Goolagong Cawley, listed as "Mrs. R. Cawley" for her 1980 win. The single ladies fared little better, getting their own initials for lack of a man to credit, but still having "Miss" tacked on, meaning Cawley's 1971 win is acknowledged to "Miss E. F. Goolagong." Chris Evert was listed as Miss C. M. Evert for her first two wins, then Mrs. J. M. Lloyd after her marriage. It's also notable that the board was never updated after Evert's and King's marriages ended, so their ex-husbands'

---

62   Chang, Andrea, "Elliot Handler dies at 95; co-founder of Mattel, inventor of Hot Wheels," Los Angeles Times, July 23, 2011, https://www.latimes.com/local/obituaries/la-me-elliot-handler-20110723-story.html

63   Prioleau, Betsy, *Diamonds and Deadlines: A Tale of Greed, Deceit, and a Female Tycoon in the Gilded Age* (Abrams Press, 2022).

initials lived on until the tournament finally ended the sexist tradition in 2022.[64]

As noted in the book *Wise Gals: The Spies Who Built the CIA and Changed the Future*, this erasure also happened in the field of espionage. Regarding Mary Hutchison, who had initially been offered only a secretarial position despite her significant qualifications, "She was frequently identified as the wife of Captain Gregory L. Hutchison in her reports, and never as Dr. Hutchison, a distinction markedly different than that of the male officers she worked alongside." She was also working against the perception of being a "contract wife," a woman hired because she was married to another intelligence officer.[65]

During the U.S. Civil War in 1863, runaway slave couple Dabney and Lucy Ann Walker joined Union troops at a camp near Fredericksburg, Virginia. A few weeks later, Lucy returned to Confederate territory to serve as a laundress and personal servant to a Southern woman who lived nearby. Shortly afterward, Dabney, who served as a cook, began reporting Confederate movements to General Joseph Hooker's staff. His information was reliably accurate and timely: he knew which units were moving, where they were going, how long they'd been marching, and how many troops they had. Dabney's information usually reached Hooker just hours after it was discussed by rebel commanders.

When asked where he got his information, Dabney led Union army officers to a hilltop, where they had a clear view of Fredericksburg and much of the surrounding area. He pointed to a house on the outer edge of the town, near the riverbank. In the yard was a clothesline where laundry was hung out to dry.

Dabney explained that he and Lucy Ann had worked out their own signalling system using the laundry line. When she saw troops moving through the area or overheard Confederate soldiers talking about future plans, she rushed to the clothesline and hung items in particular patterns to send her husband a coded message. Until Hooker moved the camp, the couple provided him with some of the best intelligence of the campaign. Yet Lucy Ann is not named in many references,

---

[64] Carayol, Tumaini, "New Boards Please: Wimbledon to Drop Mrs and Miss on Women's Honour Roll," *The Guardian*, May 26, 2022, https://www.theguardian.com/sport/2022/may/26/wimbledon-to-drop-mrs-and-miss-before-names-womens-honour-roll-tennis/

[65] Holt, Nathalia, *Wise Gals: The Spies Who Built the CIA and Changed the Future*, (Icon Books, 2023).

only called "Dabney's wife," though her name is listed on a Freedman's Bank record from March 2, 1871.[66] [67]

In the archives of the Smithsonian Institution, a black and white photograph filed as Image No. SIA2008-0031 features a man and a woman. The woman, Marion Brickwedde, held a B.S. in chemistry (1929) and M.S. in physics (1930), and went on to teach physics at George Washington University and Pennsylvania State University, and served on the research staffs of the U.S. National Bureau of Standards and Los Alamos National Laboratory. The photograph's original caption reads, "Dr. F. G. Brickwedde and his wife with the apparatus for making heavy water."[68]

When the first US Army Signal Corps codebreakers received their training at the privately run codebreaking school at Riverbank, four of their wives completed the course as well. In a letter commending them to the War Department, Riverbank owner George Fabyan listed not their names, but the names of their husbands.[69]

Even today, we see women reduced to the status of "(man)'s wife." When American athlete Corey Cogdell-Unrein won the bronze medal in women's trap shooting at the Rio Olympics in 2016, the *Chicago Tribune* reported it as, "Wife of a Bears' lineman wins a bronze medal today in Rio Olympics," prioritising her husband's status over her sport or her achievements as a multiple medal winner and three-time Olympian, much less her name.[70]

Even if women want to keep their own last name after marriage, it's not always an option—at least, not in Japan. Under Japanese law, married couples are required to have the same surname, and around ninety-six percent choose the man's (as of

---

66   Crotty, Rob, "Confederate Dirty Laundry: Spies and Slaves," *Pieces of History*, February 11, 2011, https://prologue.blogs.archives.gov/2011/02/11/confederate-dirty-laundry-spies-and-slaves/
67   Halfmann, Janet, *The Clothesline Code: The Story of Civil War Spies Lucy Ann and Dabney Walker* (Brandylane, 2021).
68   Smithsonian Institution Archives, Accession 90-105, Science Service Records, Image No. SIA2008-0031. https://siarchives.si.edu/collections/siris_arc_290569
69   Fagone, Jason, *The Woman Who Smashed Codes: A True Story of Love, Spies, and the Unlikely Heroine Who Outwitted America's Enemies* (Dey St, 2018).
70   Tesema, Martha, "Chicago Tribune Scrutinized for Sexist Olympic Medalist Headline," *Mashable*, August 8, 2016, https://mashable.com/article/corey-cogdell-chicago-tribune/

2022, a judge has upheld as constitutional the country's ban on same-sex marriage). The legal ban on different last names was upheld in court as recently as 2021.[71]

Also in 2021, a *Smithsonian Magazine* article title referred to a portrait of Antoine and Marie Anne Lavoisier as being of "French Chemist and His Wife"—Marie Anne was also a chemist, and the article even acknowledges "Though she went unrecognized at the time, Marie also played an instrumental role in (her husband's) achievements."[72]

That same year, at an event honouring BioNTech founders Ugur Sahin and Özlem Türeci, who are married, Turkish president Recep Tayyip Erdoğan referred to Türeci as "Ugur Sahin's wife" rather than by name. In addition to co-founder, Türeci serves as chief medical officer for the company, which produced the first messenger RNA-based vaccine approved for use against COVID-19.[73]

---

71 Inuma, Julia Mio, "Japan Says Married Couples Must Have the Same Name, so I Changed Mine. Now the Rule Is up for Debate," *The Washington Post*, March 11, 2021, https://www.washingtonpost.com/world/asia_pacific/japan-names-marriage-women/2021/03/11/0fd38bca-7c30-11eb-8c5e-32e47b42b51b_story.html
72 McGreevy, Nora, "Iconic Portrait of French Chemist and His Wife Once Looked Entirely Different," *Smithsonian Magazine*, September 3, 2021, https://www.smithsonianmag.com/smart-news/jacques-louis-david-portrait-once-carried-entirely-different-meaning-conservators-find-180978564/
73 "Erdoğan Draws Ire for Omitting Name of Woman behind Coronavirus Vaccine," *Turkish Minute*, July 9, 2021, https://www.turkishminute.com/2021/07/09/erdogandraws-ire-for-omitting-name-of-woman-behind-coronavirus-vaccine/

PRIORITIES AND PRESERVATION

"Without recognition women lose their history. They do these extraordinary things, and then they are forgotten and denied to ever have existed, so women keep reinventing the wheel."
—Dr. Marjorie Snyder, Senior Research Advisor at the Women's Sports Foundation.[74]

Shakespeare's First Folio, compiled after his death by two actors, preserved his works for future generations. Without it, "we wouldn't even be talking about Shakespeare," says Oxford Shakespearean scholar Emma Smith. Instead, because two men cared enough to preserve his work, he became the best-known playwright in the world for centuries to come.[75]

When it comes to maintaining, preserving, and restoring documents, it will always be a question of how best to allocate the available resources. But what is "best" depends on the priorities of the decision-makers—priorities that often leave women out. This leaves historians to piece together stories of women based on passing mentions and scant official records.

Margaret W. Moodey was one of the Smithsonian Institution's first female staff members. By 1924, an annual report states that she "had the entire responsibility and care of the collection of cut gems." Although she worked there for more than forty years, starting as a scientific aide in the geology department around 1900, and despite both the importance of her duties and her role as a rare woman in the

---

74 Ryzik, Melena. "Too Good to Be Ignored: Women Who Reached the Top in Sports," *The New York Times*, 24 Oct. 2016, www.nytimes.com/2016/10/30/books/game-changers-women-who-reached-the-top-in-sports.html
75 Wexler, Ellen, "Without the First Folio, Half of Shakespeare's Plays Would Have Been Lost to History," *Smithsonian Magazine*, April 21, 2023, https://www.smithsonianmag.com/history/without-first-folio-william-shakespeare-plays-lost-history-180982021/.

organisation, her papers were not saved. Those of her male colleagues were, so we are left with only men's records that mention her as documentation of more than four decades of work.[76]

Works by ancient thinkers like Hypatia and writers like Sappho survive only in the merest scraps, though the same could be said of many of their male contemporaries, so it is impossible to say how much of the lack of preservation might be attributable to sexism. In more recent times, the evidence of destruction may itself be destroyed, making it harder to distinguish this very issue. Among her hundreds of letters to her friend Ellen Nussey, Charlotte Brontë wrote plainly of her dissatisfaction with her marriage to Arthur Bell Nicholls, which she agreed to out of duty rather than desire.[77] "Dear Ellen, Arthur complains that you do not distinctly promise to burn my letters as you receive them. He says you must give him a plain pledge to that effect – or he will read every line I write and elect himself censor of our correspondence. He says women are most rash in letter-writing – they think only of the trustworthiness of their immediate friend – and do not look to contingencies," she wrote on October 31, 1854.[78] Nussey agreed to the promise, seemingly with no intent of keeping it, thankfully, for subsequent generations benefited from such candid and extensive insight into Brontë's life and mind. Nicholls' demands and threats of censorship illustrate, however, how the destruction of documents not only hides evidence of women's thoughts and experiences, but also shields the men who clearly intend that exact outcome.

Florence Price, the first African American woman recognized as a symphonic composer and to have her work played by a major orchestra, was prolific. From 1927 until her death in 1953, she composed more than 300 pieces, including symphonies, concertos, choral works, art songs, chamber music, and solo pieces. In 2009, new manuscripts were found in an abandoned summer home of Price's. Dating back decades, the writing included several orchestral pieces that were

---

[76] Cohen, Sara E, "Using Data Science to Uncover the Work of Women in Science," *Smithsonian Magazine*, March 15, 2022, https://www.smithsonianmag.com/blogs/american-womens-history-initiative/2022/03/15/using-data-science-to-uncover-the-work-of-women-in-science/

[77] Traister, Rebecca, *All the Single Ladies* (Simon & Schuster. 2016).

[78] Bronte, Charlotte. *Letter to Ellen Nussey,* October 31, 1854.

subsequently made available for performance, but it is unclear why no one had sought them out for more than fifty years, particularly as her works were performed by major symphony orchestras during her lifetime.[79]

After five years of diligent work, botanist Jane Colden completed her manuscript on the plants of New York in 1758. While there is no documentation on why her manuscript—full of vibrant descriptions of hundreds of native plants, as well as practical uses and beautiful illustrations—was never published, it appears she ceased her botany work after marrying in 1759. While she was leery of her growing fame, the timing may also indicate her husband was not supportive of her pursuits, as it seems unlikely that a woman who had put so much of herself into a project and was in regular correspondence with other botanists of the day would have simply dropped her work without significant reason. Being in her thirties—well into "spinsterhood" by the standard of the day—she may have been forced to choose between the relative security of marriage and a passion she had apparently been pursuing since she was a teen.[80]

After her death in 1766, her manuscript disappeared for more than a decade, but by the 1780s, it came into the possession of a Hessian soldier and botanist. *Flora of New York*, as the manuscript came to be called, was also the uncredited source for several plants in *Materia Medica Americana*, published in 1787 by another German in the United States. After passing to a British botanist and plant collector, the book eventually ended up in the collection of the Natural History Museum, London. While this is the best possible outcome, it begs the question of how the manuscript went missing. If indeed her husband was unsupportive, he may have simply given the manuscript away at some point, or never bothered going through her papers after her death. Such a possibility stands in stark contrast to the countless supportive wives who have dedicated their lives to preserving and promoting their husbands' legacies.

While we are fortunate that Colden's *Flora of New York* survived, many other

---

79 Roberts, Maddy Shaw, "Lost Manuscripts by Composer Florence Price Unearthed and Published," *Classic FM*, March 3, 2020, https://www.classicfm.com/music-news/florence-price-composer-manuscripts-discovered/
80 Imbler, Sabrina, "Centuries Later, America's First Female Botanist Lives on in a Community Garden," *Atlas Obscura*, September 20, 2019, https://www.atlasobscura.com/articles/jane-colden-first-american-female-botanist

works have not been so lucky. In 1842, New Zealand painter Martha King was commissioned by the Wellington Horticultural and Botanical Society to produce "two sets of drawings of the most interesting indigenous botanical specimens, and specimens of native woods." While one set of forty watercolours is in the collection of Wellington's Alexander Turnbull Library, the second set disappeared without a trace.[81] In 1859, Australian painter Adelaide Ironside won renown with "The Pilgrim of Art, crowned by the Genius of Art," but due to improper storage, all that remains of the piece is a photograph from the 1930s, as the work itself had deteriorated beyond repair.[82]

While documents are the most common, it is not only writings that can go missing over time. Etheldred Benett amassed an impressive collection of fossils in the early 1800s, at one point encompassing thousands of specimens. Well-known to European geologists of the time, the core of her collection was purchased by T. B. Wilson and donated to the Academy of Natural Sciences in Philadelphia, which seems to have put everything in storage and promptly forgotten about it. After Benett's death in 1845, the collection was assumed lost, only "relocated" in the 1980s. The rediscovery led to renewed interest in her academic work and the value of the collection itself.[83]

Fanny Mendelssohn Hensel was a brilliant composer—possibly superior to her brother Felix, who passed her work off as his own. (See the "Plagiarism begins at home" section for more about Fanny's life). Due to her controlling father and brother, most of her more than 400 compositions remained unpublished during her life. After her untimely death at age forty-one, her personal documents were left to her family, who did as much to support her career as they had during her life: nothing. In 1965, most of her works became part of the West Berlin State Library's

---

81 Long, Moira M, "King, Martha," *The Dictionary of New Zealand Biography*. https://teara.govt.nz/en/biographies/1k12/king-martha
82 Lindsey, Kiera, *Wild Love: The Ambitions of Adelaide Ironside, the First Australian Artist to Astonish the World* (Allen & Unwin, 2023).
83 Spamer, Earle E., Arthur E. Bogan and Hugh S. Torrens, "Recovery of the Etheldred Benett Collection of Fossils Mostly from Jurassic-Cretaceous Strata of Wiltshire, England, Analysis of the Taxonomic Nomenclature of Benett (1831), and Notes and Figures of Type Specimens Contained in the Collection," *Proceedings of the Academy of Natural Sciences of Philadelphia* Vol 141 (189): 115–80. https://www.jstor.org/stable/4064955

Mendelssohn Archive, under the control of Dr. Rudolf Elvers, who likewise largely kept her works from the public for decades. As reported in 1986:

> But he says the rest of her work must first be carefully transcribed and checked against all available source material, and that qualified musicologists are not interested. "I am waiting for the right man for the job to come along," he adds, after first complaining about "all these piano-playing girls who are just in love with Fanny." Contrasting her life with Felix's, he says, "She was nothing. She was just a wife" with the name Mendelssohn.
>
> He maintains that serious musicologists and publishers have little interest in her work because "it's too much, and it's not so good."
>
> Elvers also told a small gathering of scholars at Brandeis recently, "I don't believe she will play an eminent role in music history."

Because her works were not published, they generally do not meet the criteria for public domain, and groups that wanted to perform her pieces were typically denied by Elvers, as were scholars wanting access for research purposes. This was not the proverbial benign neglect of so many individuals and institutions towards women's work—this was a misogynist deliberately undermining and gatekeeping the work of someone whose legacy he was entrusted with. When he said, "I don't believe she will play an eminent role in music history," this was a prophecy he did his best to see fulfilled—we are only fortunate that her legacy outlived him.[84]

In an article about forgotten women pioneers of electronic music, BBC journalist Allyson McCabe writes, "In some cases, significant works by women weren't preserved. In others, preservation was limited to rare anthologies, compilation albums that have gone out of circulation, or one-off recordings on media formats that are now obsolete. Yet perhaps the biggest limitation of all is the unconscious reproduction of biases that determine whose voices are amplified and whose remain muted."[85] A 2019 report from the University of Portsmouth in the UK

---

84 Swan, Christopher, "The Other Mendelssohn," *Christian Science Monitor*, March 27, 1986, https://www.csmonitor.com/1986/0327/zfanny.html.
85 McCabe, Allyson, "Oksana Linde and the Forgotten Pioneers of Electronic Music," *BBC*, May 18, 2022, https://www.bbc.com/culture/article/20220513-oksana-linde-and-the-forgotten-pioneers-of-electronic-music

estimated that less than ten percent of DJs, and only five percent of recognized electronic music producers are female-identifying.[86]

And of course, it is not always men concealing women's work. Jane Austen was very forthright in her letters, which is why her sister Cassandra and other members of her family destroyed the majority of her personal correspondence after her death, forever limiting subsequent generations' knowledge of her as a person.[87] Ironically, Matilda Gage, the namesake of the Matilda Effect (the bias against acknowledging the contributions of women whose work has been credited to men), had credit stolen from her by two of America's most prominent women's suffragists.[88] Following an ideological split from Gage, Elizabeth Cady Stanton and Susan B. Anthony removed her name as an author from the *History of Woman Suffrage*, which she co-wrote, edited, and extensively researched. The work also largely left out parts of the movement that did not perfectly align with Anthony's and Stanton's views, barely mentioning major figures like Alice Paul and Lucy Stone. Stanton and Anthony also notoriously excluded women of colour from their work, so the exclusion of women like Ida B. Wells comes as little surprise.

LOST AND REDISCOVERED

In the arts and beyond, there are several stories of women whose work was unearthed long after their deaths. A recurring theme both here and throughout the book is the need for advocates who will fight for someone's legacy, whether that person is a family member or a stranger. The oldest extant Korean cookbook, written circa 1670 by Lady Jang Gye-hyang, was passed down through generations of her descendants without it ever occurring to any of them that this held more significance than a family recipe book. It was only in the early 2000s that Jo Gwi-bun, who married into the family, brought *Eumsik-dimibang* to wider attention.

---

86 "The lack of gender diversity in electronic dance music." University of Portsmouth. July 21, 2019. https://www.port.ac.uk/news-events-and-blogs/news/the-lack-of-gender-diversity-in-electronic-dance-music
87 Flood, Alison, "Rare Jane Austen Letter to Sister to Be Sold at Auction," *The Guardian*, October 7, 2019, https://www.theguardian.com/books/2019/oct/07/rare-jane-austen-letter-to-sister-to-be-sold-at-auction,
88 "Gage, Matilda Joslyn – Freethought Trail – New York," Freethought-Trail.org, https://freethought-trail.org/profiles/profile:gage-matilda-joslyn/.

She helped to research *Comments on Eumsik-dimibang*, published in 2006, which provided modern measurements and ingredients to replicate the dishes. "I couldn't turn away from the food of my in-laws, and felt I must promote the book and keep it alive," she says. "Once I married into this family, I had an obligation to shine a light on its legacy."[89]

In 1924, Edith Lake Wilkinson was institutionalized at the age of 56, and all her possessions packed away and sent to her nephew. The trunks remained untouched in an attic for decades until the nephew's sister-in-law rediscovered it; it contained dozens of Wilkinson's paintings. Some of those paintings are now held in collections at The Huntington Museum of Art and The Provincetown Art Association and Museum, while others were sold off by the family at garage sales, quite possibly never to be seen again. Her great-niece, Emmy-winning screenwriter Jane Anderson, is largely responsible for bringing Wilkinson's work to public attention. *Packed in a Trunk: The Lost Art of Edith Lake Wilkinson*, a documentary co-written by Anderson, was released in 2015.[90]

Argentine photographer Josefina Oliver was largely unknown until her great-niece found her archives in 2006, fifty years after she died. In Oliver's diary, Patricia Viaña discovered more than 150 photos between the pages—a collection that grew to more than 2,500 as she dug through twenty volumes of diaries. In 2007, she established the Archivo Josefina Oliver, researching to establish the facts of Oliver's life and working to bring her great-aunt's oeuvre to public and industry attention, including organising the digitisation of her photographs to better share them with the world. Oliver's work was exhibited at Buenos' Aires' Palais de Glace in 2014. Alejandro Castellanos, Director of the Centre of the Image in Mexico City, described the collection as "a very important archive for Latin American photography."[91]

Street photographer Vivian Maier's work was discovered shortly before her

---

89   Yoon, Hahna, "The Oldest Cookbook in Korean Was Written by a Genius Noblewoman," *Atlas Obscura*, September 3, 2020, https://www.atlasobscura.com/articles/first-korean-cookbook
90   Anderson, Jane, "Edith Lake Wilkinson – Chronology," Edith Lake Wilkinson, https://www.edithlakewilkinson.com/about/chronology
91   "Josefina Oliver," https://josefinaoliver.com/

death, but did not achieve recognition until years later. In 2007, the eighty-one-year-old Maier failed to keep up with payments for a storage space she had been renting, and the contents—including well over 100,000 negatives, prints, audio recordings, and 8mm film—were auctioned off. Fortunately, one of the buyers was John Maloof. He knew Vivian's name from the boxes the materials were stored in but could not locate her until he found her obituary in April 2009. Six months later, he posted some of the photos and information about her online, and her work went viral. Maloof also co-directed the popular documentary *Finding Vivian Maier*, released in 2013. Several books about her life and work have since been published by Maloof and others.[92]

Lee Miller started as a fashion and fine art photographer before becoming *Vogue*'s war correspondent in World War II, shooting everything from the London Blitz to the liberation of Paris to the concentration camps at Buchenwald and Dachau. Yet she did little to promote herself as an artist during her lifetime and her own son was largely unaware of her work. Her son, Antony Penrose discovered around 60,000 photographs, negatives, documents, journals, cameras, love letters, and souvenirs in cardboard boxes and trunks in her attic after her death and has since spent decades promoting his mother's legacy. In addition to creating the Lee Miller Archives, Penrose published the first biography of his mother in 1985, *The Lives of Lee Miller*. He collaborated with photojournalist and editor David Scherman on the 1992 book *Lee Miller's War: Photographer and Correspondent With the Allies in Europe 1944–45*, and interviews with Penrose form the foundation of the 1995 documentary *Lee Miller: Through the Mirror*.[93]

Bessie Mae Kelley was a pioneer of early animation, but she was lost to history and would have remained lost were it not for the efforts of animation historian Mindy Johnson. Johnson was deliberately looking for women who had been erased from history when she came across Kelley's image in an illustration depicting pioneers of the industry. One of Johnson's colleagues dismissed her as a cleaning

---

92 "History," Vivian Maier Photographer. https://www.vivianmaier.com/about-vivian-maier/history/
93 Villa, Angelica, "Photographer Lee Miller's Subversive Career Took Her from Vogue to War-Torn Germany," *ARTnews*, March 19, 2021, https://www.artnews.com/feature/lee-miller-photography-vogue-man-ray-1234587240/

lady or secretary—begging the question of why he thought an illustrator would include someone unimportant in their work, but sexism is rarely logical. Johnson was able to locate Kelley's living relatives, who had kept some of Kelley's materials almost 100 years after their creation in the 1920s. From the letters, artwork, and film reels, Johnson was able to piece together Kelley's work and life story. Kelley hand-drew cartoons in collaboration with Paul Terry for his famed animated adaptation of *Aesop's Fables*. "Even Walt Disney is on record as saying that when he began his studio in Kansas City, he wanted to make cartoons as good as *Aesop's Fables*," Johnson told NPR.[94]

The 1932 opera *Tom-Tom: An Epic of Music and the Negro* was groundbreaking. Not only was it written by an African American woman, Shirley Graham Du Bois, it featured an entirely African American cast and orchestra and attracted 25,000 attendees to the Cleveland Stadium over two nights. Incorporating elements of blues, spirituals, and jazz, the score was believed lost until it was rediscovered after Harvard University purchased Du Bois's papers in 2001. Dr. Lucy Caplan, who studied the work as part of her doctoral research, calls it "epic in scale," saying, "It covers centuries of history, goes through zillions of musical styles and attempts to tell a monumental story."[95]

EDITORS DECIDING WHAT GETS CHANGED POSTHUMOUSLY

As a writer, French queen Marguerite de Navarre is best remembered for her short story collection, the *Heptameron*. Originally intended to encompass 100 stories, only seventy-two were completed at the time of her death in 1549. The collection, framed as stories shared between a group of travellers, was not published until almost ten years later, in 1558, and the (male) editor responsible for the first edition cut several of the stories, as well as the prologues and epilogues

---

94 Mehta, Jonaki, Dorning, Courtney and Kelly, Mary Louise, "Bessie Mae Kelley Is One of the Earliest Known Women to Hand-Draw Animated Films," *NPR*, December 19, 2022, https://www.npr.org/2022/12/19/1144237423/bessie-mae-kelley-is-one-of-the-earliest-known-women-to-hand-draw-animated-films

95 Neville, Samantha, "Finding "Tom-Tom," Office for the Arts at Harvard, February 21, 2018, https://ofa.fas.harvard.edu/blog/finding-tom-tom.

that accompanied all the stories, and much of the interstitial content. He also changed the order in which the remaining pieces appeared, ignoring Marguerite's intentions.⁹⁶

Part of the issue with the preservation of documents is who controls them after the creator has died. Perhaps the best-known diary in modern history is that of Anne Frank, a young Jewish girl who kept her journal while in hiding from the Nazis during the occupation of the Netherlands. Sadly, the Frank family were exposed and Anne died in the Bergen-Belsen concentration camp in 1945. Miep Gies, who sheltered the family, gave the diary to Anne's father, Otto, the only surviving family member. First published in 1947, it has since been translated into more than 70 languages around the world. But that first edition was incomplete.

Almost four decades later, in 1986, the Dutch Institute for War Documentation released the "critical edition," which included sections that had previously been edited out to make Anne seem more childlike and innocent.⁹⁷ In the passages, the teenaged Anne talked about her sexuality, touching her friend's breasts, and menstruation. A subsequent 1995 edition included Anne's description of exploring her genitals and her thoughts on sex and childbirth.⁹⁸ In 1998, five additional pages were made public, reputedly removed by Otto Frank and later given to Cornelis Suijk, former director of the Anne Frank Foundation and then-president of the U.S. Center for Holocaust Education Foundation. It is worth noting that Otto Frank died in 1980, meaning Suijk waited an additional 20 years to release the pages, which were critical of her parents' strained marriage and discussed Anne's lack of affection for her mother.⁹⁹

In one instance, Anne herself was the one hiding her words. More than 70 years after the diary was first published, the Anne Frank House museum shared

---

96 "The Heptameron, Volume I," The Gutenberg Project, February 7, 2006, https://www.gutenberg.org/files/17701/17701-h/17701-h.html
97 Hampl, Patricia, "The Whole Anne Frank," *The New York Times*, March 5, 1995, https://archive.nytimes.com/www.nytimes.com/books/97/10/26/reviews/frank-definitive.html
98 Waaldijk, Berteke, "Reading Anne Frank as a Woman," *Women's Studies International Forum* Vol16, No 4 (1993): 327–35. https://doi.org/10.1016/0277-5395(93)90022-2
99 Blumenthal, Ralph, "Five Precious Pages Renew Wrangling over Anne Frank," September 10, 1998, https://www.nytimes.com/1998/09/10/world/five-precious-pages-renew-wrangling-over-anne-frank.html

that staff had uncovered concealed pages that Anne had likely hidden herself, with risqué jokes and notes about sex, menstruation, and sex work. Each revelation has helped form a more complete picture of a real teenaged girl, rather than an idealised, sexless, perfect child. As a result, it has been subject to a different form of censorship as groups in the U.S. have tried to ban it in different settings.[100]

Now regarded as one of America's great poets, none of Emily Dickinson's work was published until years after her death. In her later years, Emily made her sister Lavinia promise to burn all her correspondence, which Lavinia did after Emily passed in 1886. But she had also left behind a chest full of her poetry, including 40 notebooks. A battle for control of the papers ensued between her brother's mistress, Mabel Loomis Todd, and his wife, Susan Huntington Gilbert, who was also Emily's lover. Todd won, and she and Thomas Wentworth Higginson published the first, massively edited, collection of Emily's poetry in 1890. Among other things, Todd repeatedly removed Susan's name, including removing dedications to at least 11 poems. Todd later claimed that only necessary changes were made, but in addition to removing Susan, they changed Emily's punctuation, capitalisation, and even her wording, all of which impacts the tone and meaning of the poetry. It wasn't until 1955 that academic Thomas H. Johnson published the first complete and mostly unaltered collection of Dickinson's poems.[101]

Protestant martyr Anne Askew was one of only two women known to have been both tortured in the Tower of London and burned at the stake. Before she was executed for heresy in 1546, at age 25, so badly injured from being "stretched" on the rack that she couldn't walk, she wrote her own first-person account of her ordeal and beliefs. To add insult to literal injury—her hips, shoulders, elbows, and knees had all been dislocated during the torture—after her death, her words were changed by two different Johns to serve their own purposes.

Her account was first published by John Bale—known as "bilious Bale" by

---

100   Chiu, Allyson, "Anne Frank's Hidden Diary Pages: Risque Jokes and Sex Education," *The Washington Post*, May 16, 2018, https://www.washingtonpost.com/news/morning-mix/wp/2018/05/16/anne-franks-hidden-diary-pages-risque-jokes-and-sex-education/
101   Horan, Elizabeth, "To Market: The Dickinson Copyright Wars." The Emily Dickinson Journal Vol 5. no 1 (1996): 88–120. https://doi.org/10.1353/edj.0.0117

contemporaries for his sour demeanour—as *The Examinations of Anne Askew*. Later analysis indicated that he added parts and removed others to frame Anne as a "weak vessel of the Lord" rather than a strong and independent woman who left a bad marriage and a thoughtful theologian brave enough to share her thoughts. John Foxe also made changes when he published her writing in his *Acts and Monuments* (1563). Although he rescinded Bale's changes, he made his own and added new information without any indication of where it came from.[102] [103]

In her book, *Unsuitable for Publication: Editing Queen Victoria*, Yvonne Ward explores how two men censored the British monarch's own words when preparing her correspondence for publication after her 1901 death. The resulting book shaped how the late queen was perceived, which arguably also impacted how many saw the country itself, with Ward making the case that these changes impact generations of people's perception of the Victorian period. Significant aspects of her life were deemed inappropriate for public consumption, including her experiences as a mother, her struggle to combine the roles of ruler and wife, and her close friendships with other European royal women. Similar to the situation with Anne Frank, men removed the humanising parts of a woman's story to create an idealised version at the expense of the true experiences that make a person relatable to audiences.[104]

It is not only the women's own writing, but documentation about them that may be removed posthumously, as Jack Weatherford notes in his book, *The Secret History of the Mongol Queens: How the Daughters of Genghis Khan Rescued His Empire*. He recounts how *The Secret History of the Mongols*—considered the single most significant account of Genghis Khan's life—censored the Khan's words he had spoken in 1206 at the founding of the Mongol Empire. After text about the rewards the Khan showered upon men for their contributions to his rise to power, this unknown editor removed all mention of women but the tantalising sentence,

---

102   Freeman, Thomas S and Sarah Elizabeth, "Racking the Body, Shaping the Text: The Account of Anne Askew in Foxes "Book of Martyrs,"" *Renaissance Quarterly*, Vol 54, No 4-Part1 (2001): 1165–1196.
103   Hickerson, Megan L, "'Ways of Lying': Anne Askew and the Examinations," *Gender & History*, Vol 18, no 1 (2006): 50–65.
104   Ward, Yvonne M, *Unsuitable for Publication: Editing Queen Victoria* (Black Ink, 2013)

"Let us reward our female offspring," repeated twice. As Weatherford observes, "Perhaps the copyist was careless in repeating it, or perhaps the censor deliberately sought to emphasize what was missing or even to taunt future generations with the mystery of what had been slashed away."[105]

WORK DESTROYED

While some men have been content to undermine their female relatives' pursuits, men like Henry Collier took things one step further. His daughter Edith Marion Collier began a promising painting career in the United Kingdom after moving there in 1912, but things took a bad turn when her family convinced her to move home to New Zealand in 1921. As an unmarried daughter in her thirties, she was immediately thrust into caregiving duties, leaving little time for painting. Although she continued exhibiting for years, the combination of criticism and expectations from her family eventually wore her down and she gave up. A contributing factor was that her disapproving father burned many of her best paintings of female nudes.[106]

A family member's approval or disapproval can hold great power, as seen in the case of lesbian Anne Lister and her coded diaries. More than 50 years after her 1840 death, her family home was occupied by a distant relative, John Lister, who deciphered the diaries with the help of an antiquarian, Arthur Burrell. Burrell later recounted that "The part written in cipher – turned out after examination to be entirely unpublishable. Mr Lister was distressed but he refused to take my advice, which was that he should burn all 26 volumes. He was as you know an antiquarian and my suggestion seemed sacrilege, which perhaps it was." Instead, he placed the diaries back behind the wall panel where Anne herself had hidden them decades earlier. This one seemingly small act preserved for future generations one of the most complete known accounts of a historical queer person's life.[107]

---

105 Weatherford, Jack, *The Secret History of the Mongol Queens: How the Daughters of Genghis Khan Rescued His Empire* (Crown, 2010).
106 Drayton, Joanne, "Collier, Edith Marion." The Dictionary of New Zealand Biography. 1998. https://teara.govt.nz/en/biographies/4c25/collier-edith-marion
107 "Anne Lister–The Journals," The West Yorkshire Archive Service. https://wyascatablogue.wordpress.com/exhibitions/anne-lister/anne-lister-the-journals/

In the 1910s, painter Helen Saunders was one of only two women (the other being Jessica Dismorr) involved in the Vorticists, an artistic movement formed in 1914 by Wyndham Lewis. After Saunders and Lewis became estranged in 1919—and Saunders moved increasingly away from the avant-garde toward realism—Lewis subsequently destroyed one of Saunders' paintings, *Atlantic City*, by painting over it to create his own *Praxitella* in 1921.[108] While some may argue that he just needed a canvas and didn't want to spend his own money, it seems likely that it was more personal. He was a blatant misogynist and womaniser, as well as a raging homophobe and racist who, incidentally, wrote an entire book about how great Hitler was. He was also known to be petty and jealous, and his so-called literary magazine *BLAST* has the same premise as a middle school mean girl clique's burn book—it was a space to "blast" things Lewis didn't like. (It only had two issues, failing as quickly as its successor, *The Tyro*.)[109] So, it's no stretch of the imagination to think Lewis would deliberately destroy a woman's work—especially one who had rejected him and his art form—to create space for his own.

In more than one critic's opinion, painter Jean Cooke was at least as talented as, if not more talented than, her husband John Bratby. He reputedly forced her to stop signing her work with her married name, out of jealousy at her success. Per *The Times*'s obituary on Jean, "[John] feared and resented the competition she offered to his reputation as the one and only painting Bratby." He also limited the amount of time she was "allowed" to work on her art, and would paint over her canvases, ostensibly because he needed one for himself. But the fact that he also slashed her canvases when he was "displeased" suggests he painted over her works out of reasons more personal than practical. As Art UK notes, "Jean Cooke lived and painted in his shadow, and it is a sign of her prodigious output that she

---

108   Katz, Brigit, "Lost Vorticist Masterpiece Found Hidden beneath Another Painting ," August 24, 2022 , *Smithsonian Magazine*, https://www.smithsonianmag.com/smart-news/lost-vorticist-masterpiece-found-hidden-beneath-another-painting-180980630/

109   Carlston, Erin G, "'Acting the Man': Wyndham Lewis and the Future of Masculinity," Modernism/Modernity Print Plus, Johns Hopkins University Press, November 28, 2018, https://modernismmodernity.org/articles/acting-man

is remembered at all, her work surviving against all the odds." [110]

In 2022, Anna Leporskaya's *Three Figures* painting was defaced by, of all people, a museum guard. The painting, which was insured for £740,000, was on display at Ekaterinburg's Boris Yeltsin Presidential Center when the guard drew on it using a ballpoint pen.[111] The 63-year-old man later said he was tricked into the vandalism by teenagers, one of whom claimed it was their work.[112]

In some instances, men destroy women's work after the woman has died. After Australian painter Clarice Beckett died of pneumonia in 1935, her father destroyed many of her paintings. The remainder were carelessly stored in a shed, where the damp and rodents destroyed more of them. It took until the 1960s for Beckett's sister to bring them to a Melbourne curator, and Beckett is now regarded as one of the country's most loved artists.[113]

Although Sylvia Plath had been separated from her husband, Ted Hughes, for months at the time of her suicide in 1963, they were still legally married. As such, he inherited her entire estate, including all of her writings. He deliberately burned her last journal, ostensibly because he "did not want her children to have to read it." While we will never know what was in the journal because of Hughes' actions, it seems likely that she would have written about the impact of finding out Hughes was having an affair with and had impregnated poet Assia Wevill, who also later committed suicide.[114] In 2017, previously unpublished letters to Dr. Ruth Barnhouse, dated between 1960 and 1963, revealed Plath told her former therapist

---

110   Tresadern, Molly, "The Women Artists Obscured by Their Husbands," Artuk, November 14, 2017, https://artuk.org/discover/stories/the-women-artists-obscured-by-their-husbands
111   Cain, Sian, "Russian Painting Vandalised by 'Bored' Gallery Guard Who Drew Eyes on It," *The Guardian*, February 10, 2022, https://www.theguardian.com/artanddesign/2022/feb/10/russian-painting-vandalised-by-bored-gallery-guard-who-drew-eyes-on-it
112   Solomon, Tessa, "Security Guard Who Drew Eyes on Russian Painting Opens Up: 'What Have I Done?'" ARTnews, February 14, 2022, https://www.artnews.com/art-news/news/anna-leporskaya-vandalism-security-guard-explained-1234619113/
113   Crawford, Amy, "The Great Australian Modernist the World Almost Never Knew," *Smithsonian Magazine*, April/May 2023, https://www.smithsonianmag.com/arts-culture/clarice-beckett-great-australian-modernist-world-almost-never-know-180981834/
114   Trinidad, David, "Hidden in Plain Sight: On Sylvia Plath's Missing Journals," *Plath Profiles: An Interdisciplinary Journal for Sylvia Plath Studies* Vol 3 (September): 124–57, https://scholarworks.iu.edu/journals/index.php/plath/article/view/4514/4139

that Hughes had physically abused her two days before she had a miscarriage, and had wished her dead. He also claimed to have "lost" another journal as well as an unfinished novel, and instructed that the collection of her papers and journals not be released until 2013.[115]

While Hughes had personal reasons for his destruction and apparent carelessness, Martin Mobarak destroyed a woman's work for financial gain. In July 2022, he hosted a grand party just so he could burn a Frida Kahlo drawing in front of a huge crowd and post it to YouTube. The stunt was to announce that his company would be selling 10,000 non-fungible tokens (NFTs) of the image, reputedly the original *Fantasmones Siniestros*, a 9—by 6-inch ink and watercolour work that Kahlo drew in her diary in 1944. The Mexican government subsequently initiated an investigation—if the stunt was real, Mobarak committed a federal crime by destroying an important cultural work, whereas if it were a hoax, it would constitute fraud, as Mobarak was using the destruction to sell a product.[116] However, more than two years later, there was no further news of charges being brought. As to whether it was the genuine piece, the person that Mobarak claimed to have bought the work from insisted she had never heard of him prior to his YouTube stunt – though it does seem unlikely that a reputable dealer would want to be publicly associated with the situation, and if the burned copy was a fake, no one else has come forward with the real *Fantasmones Siniestros* as of this writing.[117]

Of course, some destruction is neither gendered nor avoidable. Polish astronomer Maria Cunitz lost much of her work when a massive fire broke out in her town of Byczyna on May 25, 1656. Her home was among the many destroyed, and with it, her large collection of astronomy equipment, academic books and papers, detailed correspondence with other astronomers and of course years' worth of

---

115   Kean, Danuta, "Unseen Sylvia Plath Letters Claim Domestic Abuse by Ted Hughes," *The Guardian*, February 22, 2018, https://www.theguardian.com/books/2017/apr/11/unseen-sylvia-plath-letters-claim-domestic-abuse-by-ted-hughes

116   Feldman, Ella, "Did This Man Destroy a Frida Kahlo Drawing to Make an NFT?" *Smithsonian Magazine*, November 10, 2022, https://www.smithsonianmag.com/smart-news/this-man-set-an-alleged-frida-kahlo-drawing-on-fire-then-he-started-selling-its-nft-180981110/

117   "The burning of a $10 Million Dollar Frida Kahlo Painting," we3magazine, November 22, 2022, https://medium.com/we3-magazine/the-burning-of-a-10-million-dollar-frida-kahlo-painting-61844c2483a5

her own research. One saving grace was that her *Urania propitia*, an influential work in the field, had been privately published in 1650, and so was not a victim to the flames. As of 2016, nine physical copies remain, and it has been digitized and made available online.[118]

Sometimes the destruction happens on a much larger scale, and of course not all is inherently gendered. In the 1930s and '40s, the Nazis censored both men and women's work in their purge of so-called "degenerate" art, including works by Friedl Dicker, Ilse Twardowski-Conrat, Elena Luksch-Makowsky, Teresa Feodorowna Ries, Anita Rée, Elfriede Lohse Wächtler, Emilie Mediz-Pelikan and Broncia Koller-Pinell. At best, the works were confiscated and later recovered, but countless pieces were destroyed and their creators harassed, harmed, and killed, like Wächtler, who stopped painting after being forced to undergo surgical sterilisation; she was later murdered by the Nazis in 1940. Dicker was killed in Auschwitz, while Twardowski-Conrat and Rée committed suicide.[119,120,121,122]

Many of Rée's works survived because a groundskeeper at the Kunsthalle Hamburg hid them in his apartment, at great personal risk. Ries's studio was ransacked in 1938, and after fleeing Austria in 1942, she was forced to leave all her works in Switzerland.[123] Gabriele Münter hid her own artwork and that of other artists in her home, where, despite several searches, they were never found.[124]

While not actively seeking to destroy art, other governments did their own

---

118 O'Connor, J. J. and Robertson, E.F, "Maria Cunitz – Biography," MacTutor, School of Mathematics and Statistics, University of St Andrews, Scotland, https://mathshistory.st-andrews.ac.uk/Biographies/Cunitz/
119 Makarova, Elena, "Friedl Dicker-Brandeis," Jewish Women's Archive. https://jwa.org/encyclopedia/article/dicker-brandeis-friedl
120 "Vienna Rescues Forgotten Women Artists Censored by the Nazis," BBC News, January 26, 2019, https://www.bbc.com/news/world-europe-46992369
121 Ewald, Simone, "The Artist Elena Luksch-Makowsky: Between St. Petersburg, Munich, Vienna, and Hamburg," *In Marianne Werefkin and the Women Artists in Her Circle*, 2017, 175–90, http://www.jstor.org/stable/10.1163/j.ctt1w8h0q1.19
122 Lutz, Petra, "Elfriede Lohse-Wächtler | German Expressionist Painter," Britannica, https://www.britannica.com/biography/Elfriede-Lohse-Wachtler
123 "The Collection of Groundkeeper Wilhelm Werner," Hamburger Kunsthalle. https://www.hamburger-kunsthalle.de/en/exhibitions/collection-groundkeeper-wilhelm-werner
124 Prodger, Michael, "How Gabriele Münter Painted 'the Content of Things,'" *New Statesman*. September 23, 2020, https://www.newstatesman.com/long-reads/2020/09/gabriele-munter-blaue-reiter-kandinsky-expressionism

damage during that time. Hisako Hibi and her husband were two of the more than 125,000 people of Japanese descent imprisoned in internment camps by the United States government during World War II. Because they were severely limited in what they could bring with them, the couple—both painters—had to leave most of their work with friends in San Francisco. When they returned more than three years later, those pieces had been lost.[125]

During the French Revolution, portraitist Adélaïde Labille-Guiard saw the destruction of her most ambitious work to date, as well as other paintings of royals. *Reception of a Chevalier de Saint Lazare by Monsieur Grand Master of the Order* was commissioned to honour the brother of King Louis XVI, who would later rule France from 1814 to 1824 as King Louis XVIII. Two and a half years of her life went into the painting, which was destroyed by Revolutionists in 1793. She was also never paid the 30,000 livres she was owed for the work, as well as other unpaid royal bills, due to her patrons' flights into exile.[126]

There is also the destruction of documentation to consider. One of the greatest crimes against cultural history was the looting of the Benin Bronzes by the British in 1897. The Bronzes consisted of thousands of plaques and sculptures created to recount the history of the Benin people. They not only decorated the royal palace of the Oba, but shared important stories. Many of these were to honour the Iyoba of Benin, or the queen mother. In addition to damage and destruction in individual pieces, by ripping them from their original context, much of the meaning has been irretrievably lost, as there is no record of the order the pieces appeared in. The British did not bother to document that, though they did take photos of the piles of stolen pieces. The photos are labelled "loot." While some museums have repatriated Bronzes back to Nigeria, as of this writing, the British Museum

---

125   Ault, Alicia, "From the Inventor of Mass-Market Paper Bags to a Scientist Who Unraveled the Mysteries of Polio, Meet Five American Women Whose Remarkable Achievements Have Long Been Overlooked," *Smithsonian Magazine*, March 12, 2024, https://www.smithsonianmag.com/smithsonian-institution/from-inventor-mass-market-paper-bags-to-scientist-who-unraveled-mysteries-of-polio-meet-five-american-women-whose-remarkable-achievements-have-long-been-overlooked-180983931/

126   McPhee, Peter, "Hidden Women of History: Adélaïde Labille-Guiard, Prodigiously Talented Painter," *The Conversation*, February 7, 2019, https://theconversation.com/hidden-women-of-history-adela-de-labille-guiard-prodigiously-talented-painter-107801

has steadfastly refused to even consider returning the 200 or so in its collection, as is the case with countless other cultural objects the museum has obtained from Europeans who stole them from around the world. But the British Museum is not alone—approximately 2,400 of the Bronzes are in collections in Europe and the United States, while only a few dozen are in Nigeria.[127]

---

127 Marshall, Alex, "This Art Was Looted 123 Years Ago. Will It Ever Be Returned?" *The New York Times*, January 23, 2020, https://www.nytimes.com/2020/01/23/arts/design/benin-bronzes.html

MUSEUMS AND GALLERIES

"Museums, in general, mirror the power structures in our society, structures that in the arts, for example, privilege the history of white men's accomplishments."
—Susan Fisher Sterling, director of the National Museum of Women in the Arts (US)[128]

For more than 300 years, Flemish painter Michaelina Wautier's portraits were credited to male artists such as Jacob Van Oost or were simply forgotten in the storage rooms of museums. Although she was well established during her lifetime in the 1600s—despite women not being allowed to paint or draw by studying live models—she fell into obscurity after her death. It was only through the efforts of art historian Katlijne Van der Stighelen that she gained modern recognition. "If she was not a woman, her works would have been considered in the same breath as art made by the great male contemporaries of the 17th century," Van der Stighelen says, "such as Peter Paul Rubens and Anthony van Dyck."[129]

While trying to convince galleries to display Wautier's work, Van der Stighelen encountered a catch-22: "Organising an exhibition of an unknown female artist, I was told, would be financially catastrophic for their museums." Yet exhibitions are one of the main avenues for artists to become better-known. Antwerp's Museum aan de Stroom finally exhibited Wautier's works in 2018, followed in 2022 by the Museum of Fine Arts, Boston. The Boston curator and director of the museum's Center for

---

128   Le Brun, Lily, "Women artists get a raw deal in historical collections. Will that ever change?" *Apollo*, March 2, 2015, https://www.apollo-magazine.com/inquiry-wall-flowers-women-historical-art-collections/
129   Esterow, Milton, "For Centuries, Her Art Was Forgotten, or Credited to Men. No More," *The New York Times*, December 2, 2022, https://www.nytimes.com/2022/12/02/arts/design/michaelina-wautier-artist-boston.html

Netherlandish Art, Christopher Atkins, worked with Van der Stighelen on the show, commenting, "I'm a specialist in 17th-century Dutch and Flemish art, and I'd never heard of her until relatively recently." A key patron, Rose-Marie van Otterloo, noted "I'm from Belgium and I read about Wautier about four years ago ... I'd never heard of her. After thirty years of collecting old masters, how could I not have heard of her?"[130]

Historically, men have often been the gatekeepers of museums, deciding what is collected and what is displayed for the public to engage with. Even today, disparities exist when we look at who the decision-makers are, and that in turn impacts what we see in gallery spaces. A 2018 study of 820,000 exhibitions across the public and commercial sectors found that only one third featured women artists.[131] [132] The same year, an analysis of the collections of 18 major U.S. art institutions found that their collections were 87 percent by male artists and 85 percent by white artists.[133] A 2019 study found that over the previous decade, only 11 percent of all acquisitions and 14 percent of exhibitions at 26 major U.S. museums were of work by female artists.[134] As of 2022, less than 1 percent of London's National Gallery collection is by female artists (21 works out of 2,300).[135]

In other words, apart from the historical issue of collecting and featuring works primarily by men, the issue is continuing to be perpetuated in terms of what museums buy and what they show the public. When she was chief curator at the Museum of Contemporary Art, Los Angeles, Helen Molesworth commented,

---

130   Solly, Meilan, "'Baroque's Leading Lady' Artist Michaelina Wautier Finally Gets Retrospective," *Smithsonian Magazine,* August 17, 2018, https://www.smithsonianmag.com/smart-news/antwerp-hosts-first-retrospective-dedicated-baroque-artist-michaelina-wautier-180970055/

131   National Museum of Women in The Arts, "Get the Facts about Women in the Arts," NMWA, 2022, https://nmwa.org/support/advocacy/get-facts/

132   Shaw, Anny, "Gallery Representation Dwindles for 'Established' Female Artists, New Research Finds," The Art Newspaper – International Art News and Events, January 25, 2019, http://www.theartnewspaper.com/news/gallery-representation-dwindles-for-more-established-female-artists-new-research-finds

133   Topaz, Chad M., Bernhard Klingenberg, Daniel Turek, Brianna Heggeseth, Pamela E. Harris, Julie C. Blackwood, C. Ondine Chavoya, Steven Nelson, and Kevin M. Murphy, "Diversity of Artists in Major U.S. Museums," *PLOS ONE,* Vol 14, no 3. https://doi.org/10.1371/journal.pone.0212852.

134   Halperin, Julia, and Burns, Charlotte, "Museums Claim They're Paying More Attention to Female Artists. That's an Illusion," Artnet News, September 19, 2019, https://news.artnet.com/womens-place-in-the-art-world/womens-place-art-world-museums-1654714

135   Preston, Edwina. n.d, "'No Woman Could Paint': The Story of Art without Men Corrects Nearly 600 Years of Male-Focused Art Criticism," *The Conversation,* https://theconversation.com/no-woman-could-paint-the-story-of-art-without-men-corrects-nearly-600-years-of-male-focused-art-criticism-184458.

"Most museums still maintain a commitment to an idea of the best, or quality, or genius. And I'm not saying I don't agree with those as values. But I think those values have been created over hundreds of years to favour white men." Molesworth was fired in 2018, after clashing with the (male) director, who claimed Molesworth was "undermining the museum." Given the acclaim and popularity of shows she had curated, it was not an issue of her work. Rather it seems that Molesworth daring to comment on gender, race and other disparities led to her termination. *The LA Times* noted that the situation recalled the director's "high-profile exhibitions for two white male artists and Molesworth's for an African American male artist and a Latin American female artist." In 2017, she had sarcastically commented, "The patriarchy is over in L.A.!... I am never under pressure to support the work of extremely affluent white male artists who are collected by the affluent white male people who run the museum."[136]

Molesworth's firing gained attention not only in its own right, but as part of a larger pattern. Only the week before, María Inés Rodriguez, who spent four years as the director of Bordeaux's Contemporary Art Museum, had been fired for "managerial difficulties."[137] This prompted almost 80 prominent members of the art world to publish a letter decrying the action, saying "We are stupefied by the announced dismissal of a consummate professional who is internationally renowned for her curiosity, the pertinence of her curatorial programme, and the quality of her exhibitions."[138]

Molesworth's comments, sarcastic though they were, highlight an important point—even if curators and collection managers are women, they are still subject to the influence of directors, board members, and other stakeholders. Three of the world's most prominent museums, the British Museum, the Louvre, and The Metropolitan Museum of Art, have never had female directors, even though MOMA was founded by three women: Abby Aldrich Rockefeller, Lillie P. Bliss, and Mary

---

136 Knight, Christopher, "MOCA Fires Its Chief Curator," *Los Angeles Times*, March 13, 2018, https://www.latimes.com/entertainment/arts/la-et-cm-moca-fires-molesworth-vergne-20180313-story.html

137 Wilson, Michael, "It's 2018. Why Can't Museums Let Female Curators Do Their Jobs?" *Garage*, March 15, 2018, https://garage.vice.com/en_us/article/xw5eb3/female-museum-curators-fired-molesworth

138 "Museum Directors Condemn the Removal of CAPC Bordeaux Director," *Frieze*, March 10, 2018, https://www.frieze.com/article/museum-directors-condemn-removal-capc-bordeaux-director

Quinn Sullivan. The 2018 Art Museum Staff Demographic Survey found that although women make up the majority of professional staff, they remained underrepresented among leadership roles.[139]

Even for directors, there is someone above—the board. Laura Raicovich resigned from her post as Executive Director of the Queens Museum in January 2018 as the result of differences with the board over activism and political engagement, which she felt was important for the museum to encourage. One journalist writing about the situation opined, "This feels like the start of something. As an arts community we can't afford to watch our best talent shoved under the bus for fear that we might lose a limb while digging them out. We're in this together." [140]

Outdoor sculpture exhibition Sonsbeek made headlines in October 2022 when the entire artistic staff quit after years of sexism and institutional racism, citing a culture of neglect behind a "facade" of diversity and inclusion.[141] In June 2021, the board of directors at Brussels's new Kanal-Centre Pompidou overruled the decision of the independent panel of experts selected to choose the museum's inaugural artistic director. The board announced that Bernard Blistène, an older white man, would be joint artistic director alongside Kasia Redzisz, whom the panel had selected as artistic director. Blistène had gotten only four votes on the ten-person panel—the other six voted for Redzisz. There had been no indication that the board was considering two artistic directors until after Blistène lost. Within days, the backlash caused the board to back down, and Redzisz was installed as sole artistic director.[142]

The gender bias in collecting even extends to the animals displayed in natural history museums—a study published in 2019 found that centuries' worth of bias

---

139 Westermann, Mariët; Sweeney, Liam and Schonfeld, Roger C. "Art Museum Staff Demographic Survey 2018," January 28, 2019, Andrew W. Mellon Foundation, Ithaka S+R, the Association of Art Museum Directors, and the American Alliance of Museums, https://sr.ithaka.org/publications/art-museum-staff-demographic-survey-2018/
140 Wilson, Michael, "It's 2018. Why Can't Museums Let Female Curators Do Their Jobs?" *Garage,* March 15, 2018, https://garage.vice.com/en_us/article/xw5eb3/female-museum-curators-fired-molesworth
141 "Sonsbeek Artistic Director, Curators Resign over 'Unbearable' Working Conditions," Art Forum, October 03, 2022, https://www.artforum.com/news/sonsbeek-artistic-director-curators-resign-over-unbearable-working-conditions-89407
142 Rea, Naomi, "A Museum's 'Sexist' Decision to Overrule the Appointment of a Female Director Has Sparked Outcry in the Brussels Art Scene," *Artnet News,* June 23, 2021, https://news.artnet.com/art-world/kanal-centre-pompidou-director-controversy-1982629

toward male specimens over female ones skewed representation in museums around the world. The resulting impact is that any research done using those specimens is potentially incomplete or inaccurate because they are limited to male subjects.[143]

In an unquestionably unethical move, the U.S. National Archives in 2020 altered an image that was presented in relation to an exhibition on women's rights. The photo, from the January 21, 2017, Women's March in Washington D.C., had several protest signs blurred because they featured slogans negative toward then-president Donald Trump. Words relating to women's body parts were also censored from the image. Moreover, the photo was not even their own, but one the Archives had licensed to promote the exhibition. It was only after the actions were exposed by the *Washington Post* that the Archives acknowledged and apologized for trying to erase the words of activist women.[144]

Frederick Ilchman, the chairman of the Art of Europe department at the Museum of Fine Arts, Boston, expressed the hope that as more women artists like Michaelina Wautier are "rediscovered" and given attention, that more women artists would follow—"we will surely learn more about her and her achievement; there must be other women artists from her era who deserve similar attention."[145]

The lack of visibility of women artists and their work also creates a self-reinforcing cycle, as American artist Martha Edelheit noted—"It didn't really occur to me that I could be an artist. All the artists in the museums were men."[146]

---

143 Fleming, Amy, "Why Sexist Bias in Natural History Museums Really Matters," *The Guardian*, October 23, 2019, https://www.theguardian.com/science/shortcuts/2019/oct/23/bad-science-sexist-bias-natural-history-museums-specimens

144 Bekiempis, Victoria, "National Archives Sorry for Blurring Anti-Trump Signs in Women's March Photo," *The Guardian*, January 18, 2020, https://www.theguardian.com/us-news/2020/jan/18/national-archives-sign-womens-march-photo

145 Esterow, Milton, "For Centuries, Her Art Was Forgotten, or Credited to Men. No More," *The New York Times*, December 2, 2022, https://www.nytimes.com/2022/12/02/arts/design/michaelina-wautier-artist-boston.html

146 McEwan, Olivia, "A Women's History of Global Abstraction," Hyperallergic, March 7, 2023, https://hyperallergic.com/805770/a-womens-history-of-global-abstraction-whitechapel-gallery/

SCHOLARLY ANDROCENTRISM

In the Christian New Testament, Junia is a follower of Jesus, mentioned alongside Andronicus in Paul's letter to the Romans as "outstanding among the apostles, and they were in Christ before I was." Yet many centuries later, mediaeval scholars began deliberately changing the feminine Junia to the masculine Junias, literally rewriting history.[147]

Androcentrism is a mindset that assumes male as the default, particularly in powerful roles. Warriors, rulers, scholars—all may be inherently assumed to be male unless proven otherwise. And even when proven otherwise, androcentrism may be so strong that archaeologists, historians, and other academics will argue the point beyond logic or reason. Some people simply cannot fathom or accept that women have held many roles and accomplished countless achievements throughout human history, to the point of rejecting proof of those facts. Their reasoning typically boils down to the deep-seated conviction that "a woman couldn't possibly have done this."

As researcher Leila A. McNeill writes, "With hundreds of books and academic articles attached to its name, The Manhattan Project has generated a publishing industry as wide-reaching in scope as the Project itself, which many consider to be the largest organized scientific endeavor in history." Yet almost none of the scholarship included the women who worked on the project until physicists Ruth

---

[147] Brooten, Bernadette, "Junia: A Woman Apostle Named in Scripture," *Women's Ordination Worldwide*, January 14, 2020, from Women Priests, Arlene Swidler & Leonard Swidler (eds.), *Paulist Press 1977*, pp. 141-144, http://womensordinationcampaign.org/timeline-links/2020/1/14/junia-a-woman-apostle-named-in-scripture

Howes and Caroline Herzenberg published *Their Day in the Sun: Women of the Manhattan Project* in 1999, more than 50 years later. It was then another 14 years before a work was published in the popular history arena, with journalist Denise Kiernan's *The Girls of the Atomic City: The Untold Story of the Women who Helped Win World War II*. Far more common is for media and academia to mention women in the context of being wives of the scientists, rather than the thousands of women employed on the project.[148]

Today, mathematician Ada Lovelace is widely recognized as the world's first computer programmer, writing algorithms a century before computers even existed. She corresponded extensively with her collaborator Charles Babbage on an idea for an "analytical machine" that could think. In 1843, she wrote detailed notes on how such a device could "weave algebraic patterns just as the Jacquard loom weaves flowers and leaves." Even though the letters are in her handwriting, signed and in other ways verifiable as her own work, historians still spent years debating who the "real" author was. Never mind the evidence that she studied mathematics from a young age—her mother, who also had a love of maths, had prioritised it in Ada's education to offset Ada's father, Lord Byron's, literary tendencies. She learned advanced calculus with the mathematician Augustus De Morgan, including the "numbers of Bernoulli" (that formed the algorithms in question).[149]

When Mary Shelley's *Frankenstein* was originally published anonymously, many assumed the author was her husband, poet Percy Shelley, who had written its preface. As recently as 2007, an entire book was published about this fringe theory, claiming that a young woman (she was 20 when it was published in 1818) with no formal education could not have written such a book.[150] Never mind that she was the daughter of two prominent philosophers and writers, and that her father was also a publisher. She would have been an extremely well-read woman by the standards of early 1800s Britain.

---

148 McNeil, Leila, "Manhattan's Missing Women," *Lady Science*, February 20, 2015, https://www.ladyscience.com/manhattans-missing-women/1q7yzyca3by0txurbbdqeu8touq5np

149 Morais, Betsy, "Ada Lovelace, the First Tech Visionary," *The New Yorker*, October 15, 2013, https://www.newyorker.com/tech/annals-of-technology/ada-lovelace-the-first-tech-visionary

150 Lauritsen, John, *The Man Who Wrote Frankenstein* (Pagan Press, 2007).

As to her age, no one has ever claimed that Mozart was too young to have written the entire symphonies he composed as a teenager. S. E. Hinton—whose publisher suggested she use her initials to disguise her gender—wrote her classic coming-of-age novel *The Outsiders* while still in high school herself.[151] Most of poet Arthur Rimbaud's work was done in his mid–to late teens in the 1870s.[152] Christopher Paolini's bestselling YA book *Eragon*, Miles Franklin's Australian classic *My Brilliant Career*, Helen Oyeyemi's acclaimed *The Icarus Girl* and of course *The Diary of Anne Frank*—all written by teenagers.[153][154][155]

Given Shelley's incredible cultural impact and name recognition, it's almost impressive that people can still ignore her contributions. Yet as recently as November 2021, the *New York Times* published a piece claiming "With Jules Verne and the publisher Hugo Gernsback, H.G. Wells invented the genre of science fiction." Academic and artist Mame-Fatou Niang perhaps best captured the feeling of many with her Twitter response: "When Mary Shelley wrote #Frankenstein in 1818 (aged 19), neither Jules Verne, nor Welles were born yet (Allan Poe was 9). A teenage girl wrote what is still considered today the 1st science fiction novel. This article continues the long tradition of erasing her."[156]

Androcentrism also leads to a conviction that legendary men likely did exist while legendary women did not. The same historian convinced that *The Iliad* is a historical account may also bend over backward to deny that the Amazons—who do feature in *The Iliad*—were real. Nancy Marie Brown, author of *The Real Valkyrie: The Hidden History of Viking Warrior Women*, has encountered this mindset in relation to shieldmaidens and women like Gudrid, whom she wrote about in

---

[151] Michaud, Jon, "S. E. Hinton and the Y.A. Debate," *The New Yorker*, 2017, https://www.newyorker.com/culture/cultural-comment/hinton-outsiders-young-adult-literature

[152] "Arthur Rimbaud," Poetry Foundation, April 12, 2020, https://www.poetryfoundation.org/poets/arthur-rimbaud

[153] Strauss, Valerie, "The Education of a Best-Selling Teenage Author," Nov 10, 2014, https://www.washingtonpost.com/news/answer-sheet/wp/2014/11/10/the-education-of-a-best-selling-teenage-author/

[154] Franks, Rachel, "Miles Franklin," State Library of NSW, March 5, 2018, https://www.sl.nsw.gov.au/stories/miles-franklin

[155] Dotinga, Randy, "When the Very Young Write That First Big Book," *Christian Science Monitor*, July 25, 2005, https://www.csmonitor.com/2005/0725/p12s01-bogn.html

[156] Swanner, Rebecca, "Twitter Reminds the NYT That No, H.G. Wells Didn't Invent Science Fiction," *Darcy Magazine*, November 21, 2021, https://darcymagazine.com/nyt-books-mary-shelley-tweets-memes/

The Far Traveler: Voyages of a Viking Woman and Margaret the Adroit, whom she argues made the Lewis Chessmen in *Ivory Vikings: The Mystery of the Most Famous Chessmen in the World and the Woman Who Made Them*. As she puts it, "There's this concept that a woman couldn't have done this, so therefore she must be imaginary. You see this all the time."[157]

It is also not uncommon for scholars to simply ignore women's documents even when they do exist. In 2021, a book was published entitled *The Howe Dynasty: The Untold Story of a Military Family and the Women Behind Britain's Wars for America*. Among these was Englishwoman Jane Strachey, whose husband was across the Atlantic Ocean in the midst of the American Revolution. As author Julia Flavell puts it, "The private correspondence of a middle-class English wife, they have been virtually ignored by historians of the home front in Britain during the American Revolution. Yet they open a unique window into the experience of ordinary British women. And their intimate tone, everyday detail and authentic chronicling of wartime events provide a fascinating parallel to [Abigail] Adams' letters."[158]

As in natural history museums, academic androcentrism applies to other areas as well, as Australian biologist Helene Marsh discovered. In 1981, she and her mentor, Toshio Kasuya, announced a major discovery. The prevailing theory of the time was that wild animals did not typically live past their reproductive years. But after years of studying reproduction in short-finned pilot whales, they had found that female whales stopped reproducing around age 36 but lived to be around 50 years old. It was the first discovery of menopause in a non-human animal. However, the reaction of the crowd at her presentation of the breakthrough was less than receptive.

"The mainly male audience was quite scathing," Marsh later recalled. "They couldn't believe that there would be females in a population that had stopped breeding, because the reason they were there was to breed."

Calling the response "incredibly sexist," Marsh recalled comments like "This

---

[157] Durn, Sarah, "The Patriarchal History of Viking Warrior Women's Mythic Status," *Lady Science,* April 22, 2021, https://www.ladyscience.com/features/the-patriarchal-history-of-viking-warrior-womens-mythic-status-2021

[158] Flavell, Julie, "What an Englishwoman's Letters Reveal about Life in Britain during the American Revolution," *Smithsonian Magazine,* August 16, 2021, https://www.smithsonianmag.com/history/what-english-abigail-adams-letters-reveal-about-life-britains-home-front-during-american-revolution-180978427/

cannot be true. There would be no point in the females remaining alive if they weren't reproducing."

Although their research failed to gain traction, more than 30 years later, a University of Exeter paper showing that orcas also experience menopause was picked up by media including *The New York Times* and the BBC. Subsequent research documented menopause in false killer whales, narwhals, and beluga whales. The Exeter study's senior scientist credited Kasuya and Marsh's paper as the foundation for all later research on the topic. [159]

In the 1880s, activist Charlotte Smith convinced the U.S. Patent Office to compile an official, comprehensive list of women who had been granted patents. The list, collected by four Patent Office clerks and published in 1888, was deeply flawed—the clerks had spent 10 days compiling data from patentees whose names sounded female, which likely left many out and resulted in under-counting the total number, in addition to simply missing unmistakably feminine names and not listing all patents for women who had more than one. It's also worth noting that the ones that did make the list were often for domestic use, while women's inventions for military and industrial use were more likely to be overlooked. As recounted by the Smithsonian Institution, scholar Autumn Stanley "suspects that the clerk-compilers, upon finding a woman's name associated with an industrial invention, simply assumed that it could not be true, and omitted these patents from the list. Through their incomplete compilation, the clerk-compilers of the LWP both reflected and reinforced the stereotype that women only invented in so-called domestic areas." Almost 100 years later, Stanley did her own audit for the year 1876, finding 33 patents awarded to people with female names who were not included in the 1888 list. Because the list only included 124 women's patents for that year, the ratio came out to at least one in five women being overlooked. If that ratio is consistent across the entire date range of 1790 to 1888, this means that the list of 5,535 women should actually exceed 7,000. [160]

This is, of course, not a new phenomenon—Confucian historians were

---

[159] Bodin, Madeline, "A Whale of a Tale about a Science Breakthrough Ignored for Decades," *Atlas Obscura*, March 17, 2022, https://www.atlasobscura.com/articles/animal-menopause

[160] "Counting Women Inventors." Lemelson Center for the Study of Invention and Innovation, March 21, 2017, https://invention.si.edu/counting-women-inventors

rewriting Chinese history centuries ago to fit their narrative of women as subservient and inferior to men. Such "scholars" would routinely downplay women's stories or exclude them entirely, attributing their achievements to their close male relatives, or—if ignoring them wasn't an option—framing powerful women like A Nong as witches who committed ritual human sacrifice.[161]

Screenwriter Gennifer Hutchison perfectly summed up the mindset in a Twitter thread on July 26, 2022:

> My favorite historical "discoveries" are ones male anthropologists/historians just *can't* figure out for YEARS that are swiftly answered by a woman when one is finally given access.
> "But what could this ancient tablet of instructions even MEAN!"
> Woman: "it's a recipe."
> They're almost always things traditionally associated with women or the domestic sphere.
> "Why did they keep knives up on the ceiling beams?! Must be about being closer to their gods."
> Woman: "To keep the kids from getting them."
> And a lot of times, it's like these men forget women existed.
> "The hands in these ancient cave paintings are so small! Must have been the young men painting them!"
> Woman: "Women painted them." [162]

---

161 Barlow, Jeffrey G. 1987. "The Zhuang Minority Peoples of the Sino-Vietnamese Frontier in the Song Period", *Journal of Southeast Asian Studies*, Vol 18, no 2 (250–269),
162 Hutichson, Gennifer, Twitter, July 26, 2022< https://twitter.com/GennHutchison/status/1551677318912847872

ARCHAEOLOGICAL ANDROCENTRISM

"When I was a student at Cambridge I remember an anthropology professor holding up a picture of a bone with 28 incisions carved in it. 'This is often considered to be man's first attempt at a calendar,' she explained. She paused as we dutifully wrote this down. 'My question to you is this—what man needs to mark 28 days? I would suggest to you that this is woman's first attempt at a calendar.' It was a moment that changed my life. In that second I stopped to question almost everything I had been taught about the past. How often had I overlooked women's contributions?"

—Sandi Toksvig[163]

Cavemen were not the first artists—cavewomen were, at least the majority. That was the conclusion of a 2013 analysis of ancient handprints found in eight cave sites in France and Spain. Pennsylvania State University archaeologist Dean Snow estimated that three-quarters of the handprints were female, based on the relative lengths of certain fingers.

"There has been a male bias in the literature for a long time," said Snow, whose research was supported by the National Geographic Society's Committee for Research and Exploration. "People have made a lot of unwarranted assumptions about who made these things, and why."[164]

---

[163] Toksvig, Sandi, "Sandi Toksvig's top 10 unsung heroines," *The Guardian*, October 28, 2009, https://www.theguardian.com/books/2009/oct/28/sandi-toksvig-unsung-heroines

[164] Hughes, Virginia, "Were the First Artists Mostly Women?" *National Geographic*, October 10, 2013, https://www.nationalgeographic.com/adventure/article/131008-women-handprints-oldest-neolithic-cave-art

Nuwer, Rachel, "Ancient Women Artists May Be Responsible for Most Cave Art," *Smithsonian Magazine*, October 9, 2013, https://www.smithsonianmag.com/smart-news/ancient-women-artists-may-be-responsible-for-most-cave-art-1094929/

Those assumptions include attributing cave paintings to men because many of them show hunting scenes—which researchers also assumed was a primarily male pastime, known as the "Man the Hunter" model. However, a 2020 study challenged this assumption as well, based on the discovery of a woman's body, buried with hunting tools around 9,000 years ago in the Andean highlands. Intrigued, researchers reviewed evidence of other skeletons from the Americas in the same time period, focusing on graves that also held tools associated with big-game hunting. Of the 27 skeletons whose sex could be determined, 11 were likely female. [165] [166] While at least one male anthropologist tried to challenge the assumption, claiming that male hunters could have buried their tools with deceased loved ones as a sign of grief, anthropologist Kathleen Sterling (who was not involved in the study) pointed out that such challenges are never raised when such tools are found buried with men. "We typically don't ask this question when we find these toolkits with men," she noted. "It's only when it challenges our ideas about gender that we ask these questions." [167]

Noting that many cultures do not even have strict gender binaries, anthropologist Marin Pilloud (who was also not involved in the study) observed that scholars often interpret information through their own cultural lenses, creating a subjective rather than objective analysis. [168] "The past can serve to legitimise the present," she observed. "I know in my own research it's been hard to challenge that paradigm ... When we step back from our own gendered biases we can explore the data in nuanced ways that are likely more culturally accurate." [169] Even then,

---

165 Wei-Haas, Maya, "Prehistoric Female Hunter Discovery Upends Gender Role Assumptions," *National Geographic*, November 4, 2020, https://www.nationalgeographic.com/science/article/prehistoric-female-hunter-discovery-upends-gender-role-assumptions

166 Milks, Annemieke, "Did Prehistoric Women Hunt? New Research Suggests So," *The Conversation*, November 5, 2020, https://theconversation.com/did-prehistoric-women-hunt-new-research-suggests-so-149477

167 Gershon, Livia, "This Prehistoric Peruvian Woman Was a Big-Game Hunter," *Smithsonian Magazine*, November 5, 2020, https://www.smithsonianmag.com/smart-news/9000-year-old-big-game-hunter-peru-prompts-questions-about-hunter-gatherer-gender-roles-180976218/

168 Saplakoglu, Yasemin, "9,000-Year-Old Grave of a Female Hunter in Peru Shows Women Tackled Big Game, Too," *ScienceAlert*, November 4, 2020, https://www.sciencealert.com/9-000-year-old-grave-a-powerful-huntress-and-her-weapons-found-in-peru

169 Fater, Luke, "Reintroducing the Big-Game Huntresses of the Ancient World," *Atlas Obscura*, November 30, 2020, https://www.atlasobscura.com/articles/ancient-female-huntress

that modern lens may be filtered through personal biases: a study published in 2023 found that women hunted in almost 80 percent of foraging societies from the 1800s to present day.[170]

Archaeologist Margaret Conkey encourages others in her field to reconsider the meanings ascribed to Palaeolithic art, saying "we can't explain 25,000 years of material by saying it was all related to hunting."

There have also been many examples in recent years of individual warriors that were, by default, assumed to be male, but upon closer examination were revealed to be women. These include:

- A Scythian warrior girl, around 13 years old, buried in Tuva (Siberia), was discovered in 1988 and for more than three decades was assumed to be male until DNA sequencing was done in 2020. She was buried with an axe, a one-metre birch bow, and a quiver with ten arrows about 70 centimetres long. [171]
- A Viking woman discovered in Solør, Norway was identified as female but discounted as a warrior because of her gender, even though she was buried with weapons and a horse. A 2019 CT scan showed she died of a blow to the head, presumably a battle injury. [172]
- A 2,000-year-old body found entombed with a sword was discovered in Tabriz, Iran—initially assumed to be male because of the sword, tests in 2004 confirmed it was a woman. [173]
- The Viking warrior interred in Birka, Sweden combined both examples of misogyny—first, it was assumed that she was a man for almost 130

---

170 Osborne, Margaret, "Early Women Were Hunters, Not Just Gatherers, Study Suggests," *Smithsonian Magazine*, June 30, 2023, https://www.smithsonianmag.com/smart-news/early-women-were-hunters-not-just-gatherers-study-suggests-180982459/
171 Liesowska, Anna, "Ancient Girl Amazon Warrior No Older than 13 Is Confirmed by Modern Scientific Techniques," *Siberian Times*, June 16, 2020, https://siberiantimes.com/science/casestudy/news/ancient-girl-amazon-warrior-no-older-than-13-is-confirmed-by-modern-scientific-techniques/
172 Alberge, Dalya, "Meet Erika the Red: Viking Women Were Warriors Too, Say Scientists," *The Guardian*, November 2, 2019, https://www.theguardian.com/uk-news/2019/nov/02/viking-woman-warrior-face-reconstruction-national-geographic-documentary.
173 "Woman Warrior Found in Iranian Tomb," NBC News, December 6, 2004, https://www.nbcnews.com/id/wbna6661426

years (discovered in 1889) until DNA tests proved otherwise in 2017. Then, despite being buried with several artefacts that indicate she was a high-ranking warrior, several historians suddenly refused to believe she was a warrior—a supposition they had no problem with whatsoever when they thought she was male. [174]

DNA tests on 105 sets of human remains from the Battle of Senbon Matsubara in 1580 showed that 35—exactly one-third—of these Japanese warriors were female.[175] Several women were buried in Phum Snay, Cambodia with metal swords and helmets between the 1st and 5th centuries ACE, discovered in 2007. [176] Japanese researcher Yoshinori Yasuda, who led the team, asserted that "It's originally a European concept that women are weak and therefore should be protected."

The steadfast belief that only men have been warriors in human history is also belied by countless written records, from Viking sagas' shieldmaidens to Amazons in *The Iliad* to Sun Tzu's account of Ho Lu's army of 180 women. Plutarch recounts a 102 BCE battle where women were among the Teutonic Ambrones fighting Romans at Aquae Sextiae: "the fight had been no less fierce with the women than with the men themselves… the women charged with swords and axes and fell upon their opponents uttering a hideous outcry." It is striking how some scholars have twisted themselves into logical knots trying to prove the historicity of *The Iliad*, but will readily discount female warriors as too far-fetched to be believable.[177]

In fact, a 2023 study of hundreds of foraging societies found that, for the 63 which researchers could find hunting documentation for, 50 explicitly refer

---

[174] Hedenstierna-Jonson, Charlotte, Kjellström, Anna, Zachrisson, Torunn, Krzewińska, Maja, Sobrado, Veronica, Price, Neil, Günther, Torsten, Jakobsson, Mattias, Götherström, Anders and Storå, Jan, "A Female Viking Warrior Confirmed by Genomics," *American Journal of Physical Anthropology* Vol 164 no 4, 853–60 (September 8, 2017), https://onlinelibrary.wiley.com/doi/10.1002/ajpa.23308

[175] "Female Samurai Warriors," March 2, 2011, Military History Matters, https://www.military-history.org/feature/samurai-wars/female-samurai-warriors.htm.

[176] "Women Warriors May Have Battled in Ancient Cambodia," *World Bulletin*, November 27, 2007, https://www.worldbulletin.net/archive/women-warriors-may-have-battled-in-ancient-cambodia-h14102.html

[177] Paisley, Janet, *Warrior Daughter* (Penguin, 2009).

to women hunting.[178] In other words, women hunted in *at least* 79% of those societies, meaning this was not the exception, but the rule. Moreover, the idea of women as too weak for hunting is not backed up by biology. Higher levels of oestrogen and adiponectin may make women more athletically inclined than previously thought, enabling more efficient fat storage and less muscle breakdown, and women's slow-twitch muscles are suited to longer bouts of endurance. "Female physiology is optimized for exactly the kinds of endurance activities involved in procuring game animals for food," writes Cara Ocobock, an anthropologist at the University of Notre Dame, and Sarah Lacy, a biological anthropologist at the University of Delaware. "And ancient women and men appear to have engaged in the same foraging activities rather than upholding a sex-based division of labor."[179]

The battlefield is not the only place where women's wartime contributions have been denied. One of the first spies for the newly-formed United States was Lydia Barrington Darragh, during the American Revolution. Living in the British-occupied Philadelphia, right across the street from the commanding general's offices, she was forced to live with British soldiers when her home was commandeered. She regularly eavesdropped both at home and around town, sending her son to the Continental Army with messages. The most important one came in December 1777, when she heard the British discussing an ambush—which subsequently failed because she was able to warn the Americans. In addition to her own account at the time, Darragh's daughter Ann published her mother's story in 1827. Many people dismissed it as fantasy until Colonel Elias Boudinot's memoirs were published in 1894.[180] Although his private journal entry differs from Ann's account in some of the details and comes off as incredibly dismissive—referring to Darragh as "a little poor looking insignificant Old Woman"—it verified the key facts. Darragh had

---

178 Anderson, Abigail, Chilczuk, Sophia, Nelson, Kaylie, Ruther, Roxanne and Wall-Scheffler, Cara, "The Myth of Man the Hunter: Women's contribution to the hunt across ethnographic contexts," *PLOS*, June 28, 2023, https://doi.org/10.1371/journal.pone.0287101

179 Ocobock, Cara and Lacy, Sarah, "The Theory That Men Evolved to Hunt and Women Evolved to Gather Is Wrong," *Scientific American*, November 1, 2023, https://www.scientificamerican.com/article/the-theory-that-men-evolved-to-hunt-and-women-evolved-to-gather-is-wrong1/

180 "Lydia Darragh," Independence Hall Association (USHistory.org), 2020, https://www.ushistory.org/people/darragh.htm

delivered a written warning "that General Howe was coming out the next morning with 5,000 men, 13 pieces of cannon, baggage wagons, and 11 boats on wheels. On comparing this with other information, I found it true and immediately rode post to headquarters."[181] Yet even today, there are some who refuse to believe the story—as with Sybil Ludington (see Media Representations), they dismiss Ann's account as family folklore, rather than give a woman the benefit of the doubt.

Rulers have also received this treatment. Because of the size and nature of her tomb, Neithhotep—possibly the first known female monarch in world history—was assumed to be male. She is believed to have been married to either the first or second pharaoh of the unified Ancient Egypt; both her tomb and evidence that she exercised powers a mere consort would not have had, indicate that she was a co-ruler, and may also have acted as a regent for her son before he came of age.[182] Similarly, the so-called "Ivory Lady" of Valencia, Spain was assumed for years to have been a man because, as one researcher put it, as a rich and prominent person, it must be a male. While her tomb was discovered in 2008, it took 15 years until testing proved her sex in 2023.[183]

The Villa Romana del Casale, dating back to the early 300s CE, is home to the largest and best-preserved display of ancient Roman mosaics in the world. One room is covered in images of women playing sports, being crowned in laurels as competition victors and engaging in workouts, such as lifting weights. Museum labels and guidebooks officially call this "The Bikini Girls," due to the figures' minimal clothing and the fact that archaeologists in the 1950s apparently interpreted what is clearly athletes engaged in physical activity as some sort of ancient beauty pageant. 70 years later, the name persists.[184]

Evidence of women medical practitioners in Ancient Egypt went largely

---

181 Boudinout, Elias, "Journal or Historical Recollections of American Events during The Revolutionary War by Elias Boudinot: President of the Continental Congress, Commissary General of Prisoners in the Army during the Revolutionary War, Director of the Mint, etc." Philadelphia, 1894.
182 Wilkinson, Toby A. H, *Early Dynastic Egypt – Strategy, Security and Society* (Routledge, 1999).
183 Larson, Christina, "Lavish Tomb in Ancient Spain Belonged to a Woman, Not a Man, New Research Shows," AP News, July 6, 2023, https://apnews.com/article/spain-tomb-woman-copper-age-72994db20f84a035862fb46dcddccc6e
184 Goldsmith, Elizabeth C., "Ahead of The Game: Ancient Roman Girl Athletes," Women You Should Know, April 11, 2016, https://womenyoushouldknow.net/ahead-game-ancient-roman-girl-athletes/

ignored by historians for decades. Even Barbara Watterson, a leading Egyptologist and author of *Women in Ancient Egypt*, claimed physicians "were all, with one or two exceptions, male." This assertion and the many others like it are directly contradicted by evidence of women physicians as far back as the Early Dynastic Period (circa 3150 to 2613 BCE), when Merit-Ptah—the first woman doctor known by name in world history—was the royal court's chief doctor. Even before that, evidence suggests a woman ran a medical school at the Temple of Neith in Sais around 3000 BCE, though her name has been lost to history. Even among the religious pantheon, two of the four deities most commonly associated with healing were female (Sekhmet and Serket, along with the gods Heka and Nefertum). Some scholars even today will claim that women were not allowed to become scribes—a prerequisite to practice medicine—despite evidence to the contrary.[185]

Even Homer's *The Odyssey* mentions Polydamna, "wife of Thon, a woman of Egypt," who gives Helen of Troy a drug to banish care, sorrow, and ill-humour.[186] In addition to passing mentions of women medical practitioners, we have records of specific individuals, the earliest being Merit-Ptah, whose funerary inscription in Saqqara named her as "Chief Physician," meaning she would have attended the king as well as teaching other physicians and supervising men.[187] A few centuries later, Peseshet was known as the "Lady Overseer of Female Physicians" around 2500 BCE, as well as being referred to as the "King's Associate" in inscriptions from her stela at Giza.[188]

Egyptian queens were also associated with medicine. Hatshepsut (who ruled 1479 to 1458 BCE) founded medical schools and encouraged women to study medicine, and Tiye (1398 to 1338 BCE) and Nefertiti (c. 1370 – c. 1336 BCE) may have promoted this as well. Cleopatra VII (69 to 30 BCE) reputedly wrote

---

185 Mark, Joshua, "Female Physicians in Ancient Egypt," World History Encyclopedia, February 22, 2017, https://www.worldhistory.org/article/49/female-physicians-in-ancient-egypt/
186 Emeriaud, Hélène, "Helen," The Kosmos Society, April 19, 2016, https://kosmossociety.chs.harvard.edu/helen/
187 Ferry, Georgina, "Women in Science | History, Achievements, & Facts," Britannica, https://www.britannica.com/topic/Women-in-Science-2100321#ref1246414
188 Mark, Joshua, "Female Physicians in Ancient Egypt," World History Encyclopedia, February 22, 2017, https://www.worldhistory.org/article/49/female-physicians-in-ancient-egypt/

a book on medicine, though she may have simply sponsored its creation. A later, and less well-known, Cleopatra wrote a book on obstetrics that was routinely consulted by doctors (including famed Roman physician Galen), so it is also likely that history has confused the two women.[189]

Trota of Salerno was one of the most well-known physicians of the 12th century and is considered the world's first gynaecologist. She wrote several medical works, including *De curis mulierum* ("*On Treatments for Women*"), made up of 63 chapters on medical concerns of the female body. The goal of this book was to educate male physicians, who were woefully ignorant. Arguably, they were still less ignorant than the historians and medical professionals who, in following centuries, assumed Trota was a man based solely on the reasoning that a woman could not have authored such influential medical texts. Some even doubted that she existed at all, despite the clear evidence of her legacy. In the 1500s, Casper Wolf edited her works, deliberately changing the name from Trotula to the male name Eros and changing the verb forms from feminine to masculine to match. Even when historian John F. Benton uncovered the evidence of the real-life Trota in the 1980s, he continued to insist that there was no connection to her work and they were all written by men.[190]

Florence Nightingale is perhaps the most famous nurse in Western history, and is often considered the founder of modern nursing, elevating it to a respected profession. She founded the modern world's first non-religious nursing school, established standards and ethics for nurses, and was among the first medical professionals to insist on frequent, thorough hand-washing. Yet recent years have seen some historians trying to downplay her contributions, claiming that the media of her time exaggerated her work, and ignoring the strides she made in areas like nutrition, hygiene, and sanitation, not to mention the benevolent aspects of her activism, like pushing to have qualified nurses in workhouses and orphanages. As nursing has typically been an undervalued yet vital profession, demeaning

---

[189] Reser, Anna and Leila Mcneill, *Forces of Nature: The Women Who Changed Science* (Frances Lincoln, 2021).
[190] Debakcsy, Dale, "Trota of Salerno and the Problem of Medieval Women's Medicine," Women You Should Know, February 7, 2018, https://womenyoushouldknow.net/trota-salerno-medieval-womens-medicine/

Nightingale's reputation by referring to her legacy as "the Nightingale myth" seems sadly unsurprising from certain corners.[191]

Dating back to the 12th century, the Lewis chess pieces make up one of the most famous chess sets in the world. From the time they were discovered on Scotland's Isle of Lewis in 1831, it was generally assumed that they were crafted by a Norse man, as they depict a Norse army and the Norse occupied Scotland at the time. Other than androcentrism, there is no particular reason to believe a man made the set, and in her 2015 book *Ivory Vikings: the Mystery of the Most Famous Chessmen in the World and the Woman Who Made Them*, historian Nancy Marie Brown makes the case that Icelandic carver Margaret the Adroit was the most likely artisan, and that the set was commissioned at the request of Bishop Páll Jónsson. It was an assertion that others had previously put forth, and it seems as probable a theory as any. Margaret appears in the Icelandic saga Páls saga biskups (Saga of Bishop Páll) as the bishop's assistant. Among the tasks she did for him was crafting walrus ivory pieces (the same material as the chessmen), including an altarpiece and a "bishop's crozier of walrus ivory, carved so skilfully that no one in Iceland had ever seen such artistry before; it was made by Margaret the Adroit, who at that time was the most skilled carver in all Iceland."[192]

Apart from overlooking women's accomplishments, archaeological androcentrism creates a blind spot that hides important factors about entire civilisations. Modern understanding of the Vikings, for example, focuses almost exclusively on male warriors, thanks to the focus of scholarship and media depictions. In 2020, archaeologist Michèle Hayeur Smith published *The Valkyries' Loom: The Archaeology of Cloth Production and Female Power in the North Atlantic*. Smith called attention to the fact that the society's women produced high-quality, standardized woollen cloth, called vaðmál. Valuable enough that it served as a currency in Iceland, the cloth formed the backbone of Viking trade, and was particularly desirable in England, providing important financial support for the Viking community.

---

191 Williams, Keith, "Reappraising Florence Nightingale," December 2008, https://www.bmj.com/bmj/section-pdf/186089?path=/bmj/337/7684/Great_Britons.full.pdf

192 Nancy Marie Brown, *Ivory Vikings: the Mystery of the Most Famous Chessmen in the World and the Woman Who Made Them* (Palgrave Macmillan, 2016).

By ignoring women's work, archaeologists overlooked a major aspect of this early civilisation—the assumption that women and their work is unimportant undermines the foundations of the entire field.[193]

---

193   Cascone, Sarah, "Viking Women Were Power Weavers Whose Textiles Provided Vital Trade across Europe, Researchers Say," Artnet News, September 19, 2022, https://news.artnet.com/art-world/viking-women-weavin-power-2178165

TRANSLATION

"Thou shalt not suffer a witch to live" is one of the most famous Bible verses in popular media, at least for the fantasy lovers among us. It's been used to justify the murders and persecutions of countless women in the name of a Christian god. It's also, quite possibly, hooey.

The original Hebrew word used in Exodus 22:18, translated as "witch," is mekhashepha. The Septuagint, the translation of Hebraic traditions into Greek that was written by Jewish sages in around the 3rd century BCE translated that term into pharmakeia. Ann Jeffers, lecturer in Biblical Studies at Heythrop College, translates "pharmakeia" to "herbalist," but back in the 1500s, British Member of Parliament Reginald Scott translated it as "poisoner" in his book *The Discoverie of Witchcraft*. While it is true that Deuteronomy 18:9-10 includes mekhashepha in a list of practices Yahweh considers to be abominations, magic has not been considered inherently bad throughout Jewish history, given the existence of Jewish magical texts from the Palestinian, Babylonian, and Cairo Genizah periods. In the late 300s, Jerome (later Saint Jerome) produced the Vulgate Bible, translating mekhashepha as maleficos (something evil or harmful), though it's open to interpretation how well he actually spoke the Greek or Hebrew that he was translating into Latin—it's certainly possible that nuance could have been lost or words misinterpreted. In any event, the "witch" translation didn't show up until the early 1600s, when the King James version of the bible was first produced. Given that King James, who sponsored the translation, was notorious for his paranoia about witches, it seems entirely possible, even likely, that the word choice was politically motivated.[194]

While most translations do not have repercussions on the scale of mass murder, it is telling how conscious and unconscious choices shape translations and thus influence the readers.

Though Anne Dacier translated *The Iliad* and *The Odyssey* into French hundreds of years earlier, Emily Wilson was the first female scholar to translate Homer's *Odyssey* into English in 2017. Wilson's translation differed in a few ways, not least that it gave more attention to the secondary characters—many of them women—beyond Odysseus himself. She lays bare the mistreatment of the women, not least the enslaved women that Odysseus orders his son to kill for having sex with (or, more likely, being raped by) the suitors that invaded his home to try and woo his wife Penelope. While this is part of the original text, it is the type of thing translators who have wanted to elevate or idealise the man have tended to gloss over. Even the fact of their enslavement is often hidden by referring to specific individuals as "nurse" or "chambermaid." "It sort of stuns me when I look at other translations, how much work seems to go into making slavery invisible," Wilson noted. "The need to acknowledge the fact and the horror of slavery and to mark the fact that the idealized society depicted in the poem is one where slavery is shockingly taken for granted, seems to me to outweigh the need to specify, in every instance, the type of slave."[195]

Just as mindsets have often defaulted to "male," scholars have also routinely defaulted to assuming heteronormativity in their interpretations. Sappho is now generally regarded as a famed lesbian poet—to the extent that "sapphic" is an adjective for lesbianism, a word which itself derives from Sappho's home island of Lesbos. Yet early translators would sometimes deliberately heterosexualise her

---

[194] Sloane, Elizabeth, "Thou Shalt Not Suffer a Witch to Live: A Murderous Mistranslation?" Haaretz, August 17, 2017, https://www.haaretz.com/archaeology/2017-08-17/ty-article/thou-shalt-not-suffer-a-witch-to-live-a-murderous-mistranslation/0000017f-e2c8-d804-ad7f-f3fa49340000

[195] North, Anna, "Historically, Men Translated the Odyssey. Here's What Happened When a Woman Took the Job," Vox, November 20, 2017, https://www.vox.com/identities/2017/11/20/16651634/odyssey-emily-wilson-translation-first-woman-english.

work, which was then perpetuated by other scholars. Ambrose Philips's 1711 translation of the *Ode to Aphrodite* made the object of the poet's desire male, a mistranslation that was followed by pretty much every other translator of the poem until the 1900s.[196] In 1781, Alessandro Verri—with no apparent evidence—decided fragment 31 was about Sappho's love for a man, when it clearly describes her intense romantic feelings toward a woman. In the "they're probably just friends" camp, Friedrich Gottlieb Welcker argued that Sappho's feelings for other women were "entirely idealistic and non-sensual," while Karl Otfried Müller wrote that fragment 31 described "nothing but a friendly affection."[197] This raises some serious questions about how those men felt about their friends, given that the work reads (in part) that the other woman's laughter:

> makes my heart flutter in my breast;
> for when I look at you even for a short time,
> it is no longer possible for me to speak
> but it is as if my tongue is broken
> and immediately a subtle fire has run over my skin,
> I cannot see anything with my eyes,
> and my ears are buzzing
> a cold sweat comes over me, trembling
> seizes me all over, I am paler
> than grass, and I seem nearly
> to have died. [198]

Scholarly androcentrism and the resolute refusal to believe women could do things once again reared its head in the case of Friedrich Hultsch's 1878 translation of Pappus's *Collection*, which spoke of the work of Pandrosion, a 4th-century maths teacher in Alexandria. Translating the Greek into Latin, he decided, baselessly, that the feminine pronouns must be a mistake that he took it upon himself to "correct,"

---

196   DeJean, Joan, *Fictions of Sappho: 1546–1937* (University of Chicago Press, 1989).
197   Most, Glenn W, "Reflecting Sappho". *Bulletin of the Institute of Classical Studies,* Vo 40: 15–38 (1995).
198   Sappho, unknown date. Fragment 31.

and subsequent scholars followed his lead. It was more than 100 years later when Alexander Raymond Jones translated the work into English in 1988 and "argued convincingly" that the feminine was correct.[199] Have scholars ever had to "argue convincingly" that a man did something he was said to have done?

---

199   O'Connor, J. J. and Robertson, E. F, "Pandrosion – Biography." MacTutor, School of Mathematics and Statistics, University of St Andrews, Scotland, Last updated May 2018, https://mathshistory.st-andrews.ac.uk/Biographies/Pandrosion

EDUCATION GATEKEEPERS DECIDING WHAT IS TAUGHT

"(I)n my day (undergrad and grad in the 1960s) all women's history had been forgotten or obliterated and was not taught at much of any colleges. When the founders of women's history began to start research and writing (1970s), they all had to bone up and read Eleanor Flexner's *Century of Struggle*, the only survey of the subject and for which the author had had a hard time finding a publisher," says historian Margaret Rossiter. [200]

Education is a field rife with gender bias at all levels, from the textbooks to the teachers to the policy-makers setting curriculum standards. While we can hope this is improving, indicators in recent years show the problem is far from solved.

TEXTBOOKS

First published in 1776, Edward Gibbon's *History of the Decline and Fall of the Roman Empire* is notorious for its frankly absurd and thoroughly debunked dismissal of the entire Byzantine Empire. But he reserved a special brand of sneering loathing for princess and historian Anna Komnene, referring to her work as "an elaborate affectation of rhetoric and science betrays, in every page, the vanity of

---

[200] Dominus, Susan, "Women Scientists Were Written out of History. It's Margaret Rossiter's Lifelong Mission to Fix That," *Smithsonian Magazine*, October 2019, https://www.smithsonianmag.com/science-nature/unheralded-women-scientists-finally-getting-their-due-180973082/

a female author." Even as he admits her opinions were perceptive and judicious, Gibbon dismissed her as, in the words of *The Paris Review*, "vain, vengeful, dissembling, and reckless, the embodiment of a particular type of unpleasant Byzantine woman." The supposed evidence for her vanity? That she dared to flaunt her education and knowledge to show her authority as a scholar. [201]

As in journalism, textbooks are shaped largely by the authors and editors, all of whom have their own biases—conscious or unconscious, blatant or subtle—that shape their work. In history texts, this includes the people and events that are featured prominently, or only mentioned in passing, or left out entirely. In language texts, it shapes the sample texts that are given as examples. In workbooks, it's the phrasing of questions and the options that are given as responses.

And it's not just the words—the images chosen to illustrate textbooks, workbooks, and worksheets can also reinforce sexist (as well as racist, ableist, and so on) attitudes that are considered societal norms. If, for example, the images of scientists in a science text are overwhelmingly male, white, and able-bodied, children are less likely to associate themselves with those professions if they are female, non-Caucasian and/or disabled.[202]

While the problematic elements of many history textbooks might be predictable, it is disturbing the extent to which blatant misogyny makes it into maths and other STEM (science, technology, engineering and maths) textbooks. In 2020, the East China Normal University Press apologized and retracted a maths textbook for children following backlash, because they had published different versions for boys and girls. As one author put it, "For example, the 'male version' includes content in the form of games as boys like to play games, and for the girls, we have more practical scenarios, such as buying vegetables and fruit in the market." While the publisher claimed the versions were equal in difficulty, they did so in a WeChat

---

201 White, Edmund, "The Misunderstood Byzantine Princess and Her Magnum Opus," *The Paris Review*, March 2, 2018, https://www.theparisreview.org/blog/2018/03/02/byzantine-princess-magnum-opus/
202 Parker, Kate, "The Impact of the Textbook on Girls' Perception of Mathematics," *Mathematics in School*, Vol 28 no 4 (1999): 2–4. https://www.jstor.org/stable/30212026

post titled, "My daughter is great at maths, so she should buy the 'male version.'" [203]

That same year, Scottish Twitter user William Sutcliffe tweeted a photo of his primary school-age daughter's maths homework. The worksheet in question featured percentage and fraction questions, with references to a woman spending 25 percent of her money on a spa break and another weighing 85 kilograms and going to a health resort to lose 20 percent of her weight. Meanwhile, the men of the worksheet were buying mountain bikes and doing sit-ups. The publisher, Teejay Maths, responded that, "this content is old and we are sorry that it is still in circulation; we have worked through many years of resources to ensure that content is updated and will be updating this to ensure that the contexts we use are truly appropriate." [204]

In its 2016 report *Textbooks pave the way to sustainable development*, UNESCO reported that "Textbooks can disseminate gender bias, prejudice and discrimination through stereotypical and unbalanced depictions of men and women in stories and illustrations. Gender biases in textbooks can shape gender identities in ways that impede progress towards gender equality in education and the empowerment of women for social and economic development. Gender bias in textbooks is one of the best camouflaged and hardest to budge rocks in the road to gender equality in education." [205]

While the analysis for the Gender Education Monitoring Report showed improvement, only 37 percent of textbooks across the world mentioned women's rights in the 2000-2011 period (up from only 15 percent in the 1946-1969 period), and depictions of discrimination against women increased from 16 percent to 38 percent. Per the 2016 report, "An extensive number of studies, in countries including Algeria, France, Pakistan, Spain, Uganda, and Zimbabwe, have pointed to the invisibility of women in teaching and learning materials and how this perpetuates

---

203 Qi, Grace, "Chinese publisher apologizes, yanks math textbook with different versions for boys and girls," CBS, August 21, 2020, https://www.cbsnews.com/news/china-publisher-pulls-sexist-math-textbook-with-boys-and-girls-versions-and-apologizes/

204 Sutcliffe, Will, Twitter, December 6, 2020, https://twitter.com/Will_Sutcliffe8/status/1335567154935173120

205 "Textbooks pave the way to sustainable development," UNSECO, December 2016, https://unesdoc.unesco.org/ark:/48223/pf0000246777

women's marginal status in society. In many textbooks, stories, images or examples in textbooks either do not include women or depict them in submissive, traditional roles, such as housework and serving men." The report noted that women are rarely depicted as working outside the home and when they are, it is in teaching or other traditionally more accepted roles, while men are shown in a much broader range of positions, including those of power and prestige. The report noted that women's political participation is often presented as limited only to voting, and that "Textbooks often leave out influential women in history or do not accurately portray the lives of women," such as reducing Marie Curie to merely her husband's "Polish wife," rather than a named scientist in her own right: "Around the end of the nineteenth century and the beginning of the twentieth century, the two French scientists Pierre Curie and his Polish wife discovered some chemical elements with high radioactivity such as uranium, polonium, and radium." [206]

Described by its publisher Phaidon as "one of the most famous and popular books on art ever written," Ernst Gombrich's *The Story of Art* has served as an introductory guide for generations of fine art students. Yet the first edition, published in 1950, included not a single woman. Sixteen editions and more than seventy years later, this had improved—to including one female artist. [207]

TEACHERS

In 2019, a parent wrote to Slate's advice columnists asking for help with her high school daughter's misogynistic English teacher. In a meeting with parents, when asked why there were no women authors in the year's reading list, he responded, "I'd really like to teach women authors, of course, but they're hard to find. I keep reading works by women to find something to teach, and I'll think I have one, but then I get to a passage and think, 'Whoa, I'd get arrested if I taught this.' Either

---

206 Alayan, S. and Al-Khalidi, N, "Gender and Agency in History, Civics, and National Education Textbooks of Jordan and Palestine," *Journal of Educational Media, Memory, and Society*, vol 2 no. 1, pp. 78-96.
207 Preston, Edwina, "'No Woman Could Paint': The Story of Art without Men Corrects Nearly 600 Years of Male-Focused Art Criticism," *The Conversation*, October 12, 2022, https://theconversation.com/no-woman-could-paint-the-story-of-art-without-men-corrects-nearly-600-years-of-male-focused-art-criticism-184458

that or they're just not complex enough."[208]

Like journalists, teachers frame the information they present, with a huge impact on what children are taught. They are largely responsible for what information to emphasize and what to minimize, the words they use to convey information, and even the facial expressions and body language they show when discussing topics. There are countless testimonials from women across different fields and times, attesting to the power that a supportive—or dismissive—educator can have. And while teaching at the primary and secondary levels may be dominated by women, this does not preclude female teachers from passing on internalized misogyny to their students.

In terms of higher education, the list of sexist comments by male professors is quite literally endless, but here are just a few that made headlines in recent years:

Women who prioritize careers over family are "more medicated, meddlesome and quarrelsome than women need to be… Every effort must be made not to recruit women into engineering, but rather to recruit and demand more of men who become engineers. Ditto for med school, and the law, and every trade," political science professor Scott Yenor, Boise State University, claimed in a speech.[209]

Indiana University business professor Eric Rasmusen published a 1500-word diatribe entitled, "Are Women Destroying Academia? Probably," in addition to a history of other racist, sexist and homophobic remarks, such as publishing a blog post asserting LGBTQIA+ people should not be teachers, doctors, or elected officials and claiming gay men are paedophiles.[210]

"Girls" should have to work in gender-segregated labs because they distract men who fall in love with them and cry when criticized, according to Nobel Prize

---

208 Bauer, Carrie, Hersey, Brandon, Holbrook, Katie and Scott, Amy, "My Daughter's Teacher, the Misogynist," *Slate*, October 3, 2019, https://slate.com/human-interest/2019/10/teacher-is-misogynist-parenting-advice.html
209 Ravishankar, Rakshitha Arni, "A Professor Made a Sexist Remark. Here's How This Student Responded," *Harvard Business Review*, May 13, 2022, https://hbr.org/2022/05/a-professor-made-a-sexist-remark-heres-how-this-student-responded.
210 Brice-Sadley, Michael and Paul, Deanna, "University Says a Professor's Views Are Racist, Sexist and Homophobic — but It Can't Fire Him," *The Washington Post*, November 20, 2019, https://www.washingtonpost.com/education/2019/11/20/university-says-professors-views-are-racist-sexist-homophobic-they-cant-fire-him/

winner Tim Hunt. He then played the victim and claimed he was "joking" even though he told BBC in a follow-up interview that he was "sorry" for offending his audience, but "I did mean the part about having trouble with girls."[211]

Perhaps the most maddening part is that these men are saying these things publicly, and there is typically no consequence for them. Outcomes like University of Montana computer science professor Rob Smith being put on leave and then resigning after his incredibly offensive blog posts came to light are the exception, not the rule, with most male academics, particularly those with tenure.[212] There's also University of North Carolina Wilmington criminology professor Mike Adams, whose "early retirement" package included a $500,000 payout after making racist, anti-LGBT, and misogynistic public comments like "Don't shut down the universities. Shut down the non-essential majors. Like Women's Studies."[213] Tim Hunt was forced to resign, leading him to publicly proclaim himself a martyr—supported by his wife Mary Collins, a prominent scientist in her own right—but it should be noted that the 72-year-old had a long history of sexist comments before action was finally taken, even admitting himself that he had a reputation as a "chauvinist."[214] Most often, these men are allowed to continue spreading their poison, to the detriment of female students, who see very visibly that their universities do not care.

In 2020, a white Harvard University professor who specializes in Japanese law published a paper arguing that Korean women enslaved by the Japanese army during World War II had voluntarily chosen to become sex workers, or as the

---

211 Russell, Cristine, "Why Tim Hunt's Sexist Comments Were No 'Joke,'" Scientific American Blog Network, June 15, 2015, https://blogs.scientificamerican.com/voices/why-tim-hunt-s-sexist-comments-were-no-joke/
212 Stanton, Andrew, "Professor Quits amid Investigation into 'Homophobic and Misogynistic' Posts," Newsweek, October 23, 2021, https://www.newsweek.com/professor-resigns-amid-investigation-homophobic-misogynistic-blog-posts-1641958
213 Baer, Stephanie K, "A Professor Who Was Known for His Racist, Misogynistic Tweets Was Found Dead in His Home," BuzzFeed News, July 27, 2020, https://www.buzzfeednews.com/article/skbaer/mike-adams-uncw-professor-death
214 Ratcliffe, Rebecca, "Nobel Scientist Tim Hunt: Female Scientists Cause Trouble for Men in Labs," The Guardian, June 10, 2015, https://www.theguardian.com/uk-news/2015/jun/10/nobel-scientist-tim-hunt-female-scientists-cause-trouble-for-men-in-labs

Japanese euphemistically referred to them, "comfort women."[215] In a tenor reminiscent of Fox News host Bill O'Reilly's revisionist comments about how well enslaved African-Americans were supposedly treated, J. Mark Ramseyer used the existence of labour contracts to assert that the women and girls—most of them aged fourteen to nineteen and some as young as ten—were willing sex workers who were paid well.

Korean women made up the largest share of the hundreds of thousands of women from across Asia (including China, the Philippines, and Indonesia) forced from their homes into "comfort stations" to be raped by Japanese soldiers. His assertion completely ignores the decades' worth of testimony of countless survivors, who have all been clear and consistent about the coercion, enslavement and brutal rapes they experienced—indeed, he has publicly referred to this as "pure fiction." This is particularly egregious as there is little proof such contracts exist and even if they do, many of the girls were illiterate or, being as young as ten or twelve, too young to enter a legally binding contract—which one would hope a Harvard law professor would be aware of.

It is also interesting to note that his position is funded by Mitsubishi, a Japanese company that used slave labour during World War II, including that of Korean women and children and American prisoners of war.[216] The Japanese government has also consistently tried to deny or downplay the mass sexual enslavement of women and girls during this period, to the point of throwing tantrums when statues acknowledging these women's experiences are erected in other countries (see Statues section).

There is also the bias against female professors. At the U.S. Naval Academy, 11 men and four women applied for tenure in 2021, including Professor Carolyn Chun. Of those 15, 10 men were granted tenure—none of the women were. Chun, a maths professor, calculated the odds: "There are 3,003 scenarios where 10 people

---

215 Binkley, Collin, "Harvard Professor Ignites Uproar over 'Comfort Women' Claims," AP NEWS, March 8, 2021, https://apnews.com/article/j-mark-ramseyer-harvard-paper-comfort-women-dbebb62b01045c-23036089ca3415de64

216 Ryall, Julian, "South Korea Court Ruling on Mitsubishi Reopens Old Wounds with Japan," Deutsche Walle, October 8, 2017, https://www.dw.com/en/south-korea-court-ruling-on-mitsubishi-reopens-old-wounds-with-japan/a-40044146

can be chosen from the 15 applicants, and only 11 scenarios where all 10 are men. All things being equal, the chance that the top 10 applicants would all be male is 11 out of 3,003." In other words, she calculated a 99.6 percent chance of gender discrimination.

"It's telling that, at the highest level, women comprise only 25 percent of the faculty," Chun told the *Washington Post*. "At the middle level, it's 31 percent, and at the lowest level, it's 46 percent. This suggests that women are being held back compared with our male counterparts."

Chun was denied tenure because, after telling her students that, statistically, female students did better on tests than male students, several of the men complained and accused her of giving preferential treatment to the women. This illustrates the significant impact that student feedback can have on a professor's career and, like virtually all aspects of life, there is a gender bias.[217]

A 2016 study found that female students rated teachers higher when they believed the instructor to be male, meaning the same instructor scored higher as "Paul" than "Paula."[218] An analysis in 2014 showed that "Students rated the male identity significantly higher than the female identity, regardless of the instructor's actual gender, demonstrating gender bias. Given the vital role that student ratings play in academic career trajectories, this finding warrants considerable attention." For instructors like Chun, the impact is also exacerbated by race, as non-Caucasian, female faculty receive particularly low scores, according to multiple studies.[219] Another study found that students are more likely to make demands for special treatment, like extra credit opportunities or re-doing work to get a better grade, when the professor is a woman. They are also more likely to get upset if their

---

217 Alter, Cathy, "After Twice Being Denied Tenure, This Naval Academy Professor Says She Is Seeking Justice," January 31, 2022, *The Washington Post*, https://www.washingtonpost.com/magazine/2022/01/31/naval-academy-asian-bias-tenure-gender/

218 Boring, Anne, Ottoboni, Kellie and Stark, Philip B, "Student Evaluations of Teaching (Mostly) Do Not Measure Teaching Effectiveness," ScienceOpen, January 7, 2016, https://www.scienceopen.com/hosted-document?doi=10.14293/S2199-1006.1.SOR-EDU.AETBZC.v1

219 MacNell, Lillian, Driscoll, Adam and Hunt, Andrea N, "What's in a Name: Exposing Gender Bias in Student Ratings of Teaching," Innovative Higher Education, December 2014, https://www.researchgate.net/publication/269288475_What's_in_a_Name_Exposing_Gender_Bias_in_Student_Ratings_of_Teaching

demands are refused, rather than accepting the professor's authority.[220]

An interactive tool integrating 14 million student reviews on the site Rate My Professor revealed stark differences in how students viewed their male versus female instructors in 2015. The men were more likely to be described as "brilliant," "intelligent" or "smart," and those reviews far more often included "genius." The women were more often described as "mean," "harsh," "unfair" or "strict," and significantly more likely to be considered "annoying." Men were "cool" and "funny," while women were "disorganized"—at best, they were "nice" and "helpful," if not "good" like the men. Even for specific, ostensibly objective metrics, like promptness, students ranked female professors significantly lower (3.55 of 5) than male professors (4.35) even when they returned graded assignments at the same time.[221]

Women are also at a disadvantage when it comes to the job security of tenure. In the U.S., women made up the majority of nontenure-track lecturers and instructors, but only 44 percent of tenure-track faculty and 36 percent of full professors in the 2017-18 academic year. Those disparities increased depending on the field of study, such as with the science, technology, engineering, and maths faculties. Men with children were also vastly more likely to achieve tenure than women with children.[222] [223]

At the university level, it is important to remember that professors don't just impact their students in the classroom or through assignments and chosen reading material. Professors and administrators are gatekeepers who approve or disapprove who gets to work on what projects, support or reject research that students may want to pursue, and make decisions around who and what will

---

220 Morgante, Camden, "It's Not Easy Being a Woman Professor: Subverting Sexism in Higher Education," CBE International, September 5, 2019, https://www.cbeinternational.org/resource/its-not-easy-being-woman-professor-subverting-sexism-higher-education/
221 Bates, Laura, "Female Academics Face Huge Sexist Bias – No Wonder There Are so Few of Them," *The Guardian*, February 13, 2015, https://www.theguardian.com/lifeandstyle/womens-blog/2015/feb/13/female-academics-huge-sexist-bias-students
222 "Fast Facts: Women Working in Academia," American Association of University Women. https://www.aauw.org/resources/article/fast-facts-academia/
223 "The Annual Report on the Economic Status of the Profession, 2017-18," Academe, American Association of University Professors, March-April 2018, https://www.aaup.org/sites/default/files/ARES_2017-18.pdf

receive funding. At the PhD level, a thesis advisor is a vital mentor who can literally shape a young person's career—or destroy it before it even has a chance to get started.

CURRICULUM

In 2023, an employee at Studies Weekly, which provides K–8 curriculum resources to 45,000 schools across the United States, removed the mention of race in Rosa Parks's story in reaction to political attacks on critical race theory in Florida. Instead of saying that Parks "was told to move to a different seat because of the color of her skin," an employee removed the end of the sentence, so it read only that she "was told to move to a different seat." Although the company stated the edit was not approved and was reversed as soon as they were made aware, the situation illustrates how politics and biases shape what is taught. [224]

Depending on the school system, different people impact educational standards, from federal, state, and local governments to school boards to principals to the individual teachers themselves. While there are certainly much more blatant tactics, like banning any mention of same-sex couples, comprehensive sex education, or honest discussion of race and racism, there are also more subtle impacts that shape what is taught. Curriculums are a reflection of what the people in power choose to prioritize—and what they choose to leave out.

The Dahomey Mino are the only known all-female army in modern history, with thousands of soldiers in the mid-1800s. But after the 1894 invasion and occupation of what is now southern Benin by the French, the army was forced to disband. The new French schools excluded the Mino from the curriculum, in an attempt to erase their existence from history. More broadly speaking, it was common for European colonial powers to emphasize teaching their own history and cultures, at the expense of those of the native locals. A person might be able to recite centuries' worth of the kings of England, but not be able to

---

[224] Gamble, Justin, "Race left out of Rosa Parks story in revised weekly lesson text for Florida schools highlights confusion with Florida law," CNN, March 22, 2023< https://edition.cnn.com/2023/03/22/us/florida-textbook-race-rosa-parks-reaj/index.html

name the people—often women—who had ruled their own lands before they were invaded.[225]

Required reading is another area where we often see the emphasis placed on white, male narratives and writers. Even stories that touch on societal issues often focus the narrative on the privileged, rather than the marginalized. When I was in 10th grade, we read the play *Master Harold and the Boys*, written by white South African Athol Fugard, and centering the semi-autobiographical white, racist character. My English teacher then thought it was a brilliant idea for her white, Midwestern U.S. students to pretend we were an African village and allow our "chief" to assign everyone roles. As we of course had zero cultural knowledge, this led to all the girls being assigned as a boy's first or second wife—except for one girl that our (male) chief declared "the village idiot." As my female teacher sat there and said nothing.

After referring to women as "whores," in one email chain, University of Sydney poetry professor Barry Spurr suggested a rape victim should have had more than "penis" put in her mouth, before it was "stitched shut" (in response to his friend, the woman's own lawyer, describing her as a "worthless slut"). He also has a well-documented history of racist and otherwise offensive remarks. Shortly before the 2014 public outcry over his comments, he was paid more than $8,000 by the Australian government to review the English section of Australia's entire national school curriculum, from kindergarten through to Year 12.[226] His recommendations included comments like, "The impact of Aboriginal and Torres Strait Islander peoples on literature in English in Australia has been minimal and is vastly outweighed by the impact of global literature in English, and especially that from Britain, on our literary culture."[227] That is, of course, tame compared to

---

225 Solly, Meilan, "The Real Warriors behind 'the Woman King,'" *Smithsonian Magazine*, September 15, 2022, https://www.smithsonianmag.com/history/real-warriors-woman-king-dahomey-agojie-amazons-180980750/
226 "WHERE ARE THEY NOW? Barry Spurr: Ex-Professor, Racist, Misogynist, Turned Literary Editor," *New Matilda*, January 20, 2020, https://newmatilda.com/2020/01/20/where-are-they-now-barry-spurr-ex-professor-racist-misogynist/
227 Graham, Chris, "Barry Spurr May Have Resigned, but the National Curriculum Review Is Tainted," *The Guardian*, December 18, 2014, https://www.theguardian.com/commentisfree/2014/dec/18/barry-spurr-may-have-resigned-but-the-national-curriculum-is-tainted

the slurs he used in his emails, yet the federal government declined to reconsider his review after his less savoury comments were publicized.[228]

In 2017, the U.S.'s National Women's History Museum examined social studies curricula across the country and found that only 178 women (62 percent of whom are white) were mentioned in the academic standards across all 50 states and the District of Columbia, compared to 559 men. More generally, of the 1,975 mentions of women, women's history, and women's roles across all the standards, more than half referred to domestic roles (53 percent) rather than women acting outside a home setting. The report found that, "Standards do not reflect current trends or ideals in girls' education. While there is an increasing public interest in motivating girls to embrace science, technology, engineering, and mathematics, social studies standards provide few historic examples of women or their achievements in these fields."[229] [230]

---

228 "English Review Unlikely despite Professor's Suspension," ABC News, October 18, 2014, https://www.abc.net.au/news/2014-10-18/english-review-unlikely-despite-professors-suspension/5823792
229 "Where Are the Women?" National Women's History Museum, 2019, https://www.womenshistory.org/social-studies-standards
230 White, Anna, "What Schools Teach about Women's History Leaves a Lot to Be Desired," *Smithsonian Magazine*, February 20, 2019, https://www.smithsonianmag.com/history/what-schools-teach-womens-history-180971447/

INDUSTRY GATEKEEPERS

"I used to not like being called a 'woman architect.' I'm an architect, not just a woman architect. The guys used to tap me on the head and say 'you're OK for a girl.' But I see an incredible amount of need from other women for reassurance that it can be done, so I don't mind anymore."

—Zaha Hadid[231]

When the book *DC Comics Heroines: Highlights from the History of the World's Greatest Super Heroines* came out in 2018, the (male) author made a glaring omission, or, as culture writer Rachel Ulatowski put it, "what can only be described as a gross and bizarre oversight." Specifically, writer Gail Simone was excluded despite her years of work on Birds of Prey, Batgirl, and Wonder Woman, for whom she was the series' longest-running writer. She was the first female writer to take over the Birds of Prey series after its initial run and created the character of Huntress as well as Alysia Yeoh, one of the first major transgender comic book heroes. Ulatowski notes, "She truly popularized the (Birds of Prey), and throughout the team's 27-year history, her run has remained a fan favorite. Since her run ended, the series has been muddled with cancellations, reboots, and relaunches. Simone added over 50 issues to the Birds of Prey series, offering the team its most cohesive, female-focused, and vibrant run. She grew the Birds of Prey, solidified team dynamics, and blended superhero fun, dark and gritty content, and sassy and sexy undertones to frame the all-female team in a way that did them justice." Yet the

---

[231] "Zaha Hadid is 'Leading Woman,'" August 22, 2012, World Architecture News, https://www.worldarchitecturenews.com/article/1511240/zaha-hadid-leading-woman

book also skips over her run, despite it being arguably the most important. As this is an official DC Comics reference book, the corporation itself tacitly erased the contributions of one of its most valuable female staff. [232]

Every industry has gatekeepers, powerful people who act as arbiters of what is valuable and what will—and will not—succeed. Often, this is tied to funding, from business investment to grants for the arts and sciences. It's also about using their platforms to amplify someone's work, whether it's a gallery owner putting on an artist's show or the critic that declares the works worthwhile (by whatever criteria they may decide). It's science journal editors deciding which papers do and do not get published. It's influential businesspeople putting their reputation behind a venture, knowing that countless others will trust their judgement.

These people often run organisations, from professional networks to schools, and historically their decisions to exclude an entire gender from participation has held women back in a multitude of ways (see "Undermined" chapter for more on this topic). This encompasses both total exclusion—such as universities refusing women admission as students—and partial exclusion, where women are allowed to participate on a limited basis. While it may be tempting to allow those decision-makers to hide behind the facade of the organisation, there is always at least one person writing the policies and choosing to implement and enforce them.

Take, as an example, women composers. Composer Pauline Oliveros asked "Why have there been no 'great' women composers?" in a 1970 opinion piece for *The New York Times*. Oliveros observed that because composing was considered a man's pursuit, women who did so were reduced to "female" composers, separate from and less valuable than the mainstream. She argued for greater recognition of their achievements and potential—something women still fight for more than 50 years later. [233]

Classical music organisations—orchestras, ensembles, operas, etcetera—may point to the historical male dominance as an excuse to perform exclusively, or almost exclusively, men's works. Recent years have seen more of an acknowledgement of

---

232 Ulatowski, Rachel, "Why Did DC Erase Gail Simone From the 'Birds of Prey' Legacy?" *The Mary Sue*, October 16, 2023, https://www.themarysue.com/why-did-dc-erase-gail-simone-from-the-birds-of-prey-legacy/
233 McCabe, Allyson, "Oksana Linde and the Forgotten Pioneers of Electronic Music," BBC, May 13, 2022, https://www.bbc.com/culture/article/20220513-oksana-linde-and-the-forgotten-pioneers-of-electronic-music

women's historical works that have been overlooked, though they are still very much in the minority. But even when looking only at new works—particularly commissioned works where funding support is guaranteed—there is a major gap. As *The Conversation* reported in 2016,

> Since 1987, 47 composers have been commissioned to write for the Australia Ensemble – the nation's leading chamber music ensemble. Forty-one of them were men.
>
> Meanwhile, the Bendigo International Festival of Exploratory Music featured only 10 women among the 63 composers in its 2015 program...
>
> Women's new music, it seems, is sidelined in professional Australian concert programs. In 2013, for instance, women's music represented only 11 percent of the works performed at new music concerts. [234]

In an analysis of programmes presented by 15 major orchestras worldwide in their 2019-2020 season, only 3.6 percent of the pieces performed were written by women (142 of 3,997 total). Only 8.2 percent of the concerts included at least one piece by a woman—123 out of more than 1,500.[235]

There is also a dearth of women running the shows in question. Opera Australia, the country's national opera company, had more men named David (or Davide) than women directing opera productions in 2019. As *Timeout* pointed out at the time, "Only 17.5 per cent of creative roles at OA in 2019 will be filled by women. But in the positions of greatest artistic control and influence – director, composer and conductor – it drops to a mere 8.2 per cent." [236]

Things are better but still not great in the land of popular music. In a study of Billboard Hot 100 Year-End Charts from 2012 to 2020, researchers from the University of Southern California Annenberg Inclusion Initiative found male artists

---

[234] Hope, Cat, Bennett, Dawn and Macarthur, Sally, "The Sound of Silence: Why Aren't Australia's Female Composers Being Heard?" *The Conversation*, May 30, 2016< https://theconversation.com/the-sound-of-silence-why-arent-australias-female-composers-being-heard-59743
[235] "INEQUALITY IN MUSIC: WOMEN COMPOSERS BY NUMBERS 2019_2020," Donne: Women in Music, http://www.drama-musica.com/stories/2019_2020_orchestra_seasons.html
[236] Tongue, Cassie, "Does Opera Australia have a problem with women?" *Timeout*, August 20, 2018, https://www.timeout.com/melbourne/news/does-opera-australia-have-a-problem-with-women-082018

outnumbered female artists 3.6 to 1. The proportion got worse when looking at other roles—while women made up 21.6 percent of artists, they were only 12.6 percent of songwriters and 2.6 percent of producers.[237]

And of course this plays out in other art forms as well, as noted in the museums and galleries section above. In Ireland, the Gender Count Report analysed 1,155 theatre productions between 2006 and 2015 and found only 28 percent had women authors.[238] "Gender Equality and Diversity in European Theatres," a study released in 2021 by the European Theatre Convention, found that:

> Women were found to have less secure contract situations than men and be "less present at the top of the hierarchy."
>
> Men are more visible than women in theatre programmes and dominate the "prestigious positions" of playwright, director and technical staff, while women held 70+ percent of the positions of "costumes" and "hairdressing."
>
> "Female authors and directors demonstrate a clear trend towards gender equality compared to their male colleagues, who are in the majority and who make men more visible." [239]

While there are supportive male gatekeepers and unsupportive female ones, the theatre study's finding that women in charge leads to greater gender equity is no surprise. For an example in the publishing world, look no further than Judith Jones. This editor not only rescued *The Diary of Anne Frank* from the reject pile, she was also a champion for Julia Child's *Mastering the Art of French Cooking*.[240] A study of speakers at academic seminars in 2013 and 2014 found that women were significantly less likely to be featured than men. The person in charge of the event

---

237 "Annenberg Inclusion Initiative's Annual Report on Popular Music Reveals Little Progress for Women," USC Annenberg, March 8, 2021, https://annenberg.usc.edu/news/research-and-impact/annenberg-inclusion-initiatives-annual-report-popular-music-reveals-little.
238 Hill, Shonagh, "How Irish Free State Theatre Excluded Women from Public Life," Raidió Teilifís Éireann (RTÉ), September 27, 2022, https://www.rte.ie/brainstorm/2022/0803/1313723-irish-free-state-theatre-women-gender/
239 "'Six Men for Every Four Women': Gender Inequalities in Theatre Programming Revealed in New Cross-Europe Study," European Theatre Convention, March 8, 2021, https://www.europeantheatre.eu/news/six-men-for-every-four-women-gender-inequalities-in-theatre-programming-revealed-in-new-crosseurope-study
240 McFadden, Robert D, "Judith Jones, Editor of Literature and Culinary Delight, Dies at 93," *The New York Times*, August 2, 2017, https://www.nytimes.com/2017/08/02/us/judith-jones-dead.html

made a big difference: on average, female chairs chose women as speakers 49 percent of the time, while male chairs selected women only 30 percent of the time.[241]

Critics represent an overlap of the journalistic and industry gatekeeper. In 2012, the *New York Review of Books* reviewed 40 women authors, compared to 215 men.[242] The majority of professional movie critics are male, which led to an interesting contrast on Rotten Tomatoes in 2016. For the female-led *Ghostbusters* reboot, 84 percent of positive reviews on the site were from female critics. 77 percent of the negative reviews were from their male counterparts, who made up an estimated 76 percent of registered film critics on Rotten Tomatoes at the time. A *Salon* reporter researching the topic also found "A survey of Meryl Streep's films showed that men were disproportionately likely to give them a negative review, no matter the quality of the film... When "*The Devil Wears Prada*" debuted in 2006, 80 percent of female critics liked it, while 82 percent of bad reviews came from men." The difference was even more pronounced for *Pitch Perfect*: 93 percent of women reviewers liked it, while 94 percent of negative scores came from men.[243]

With the rise of the internet, anyone can now leave reviews, which on one hand may seem more egalitarian but also opens up the possibility of review-bombing, where angry fans leave negative reviews often without even having watched the media in question. *Ghostbusters*, *Captain Marvel*, *She-Hulk*—the list goes on, but the biggest targets typically seem to involve powerful women in the lead, though shows like *Lord of the Rings: Rings of Power* and *The Last of Us* also get the racists riled up.[244] When the trailer for 2023's *The Marvels* was released, it garnered almost 300,000 "dislikes" on YouTube almost immediately, as well as thousands of copy/

---

241 Flaherty, Colleen, "Study Finds Men Speak Twice as Often as Do Women at Colloquiums," Inside Higher Ed, December 18, 2017, https://www.insidehighered.com/news/2017/12/19/study-finds-men-speak-twice-often-as-do-women-colloquiums
242 Flood, Alison, "Wikipedia Bumps Women from 'American Novelists' Category," *The Guardian*, April 25, 2013, https://www.theguardian.com/books/2013/apr/25/wikipedia-women-american-novelists
243 Lang, Nico, "The Growing Gender Divide over 'Ghostbusters': Why Movies Starring Women Get Slimed by Male Critics," *Salon*, July 13, 2016, https://www.salon.com/2016/07/12/the_growing_gender_divide_over_ghostbusters_why_movies_starring_women_get_slimed_by_male_critics/
244 Whitley, Claire, "Review Bombing is About Power, Politics and Revenge – but it's not About Art," *The Conversation*, February 8, 2023, https://theconversation.com/review-bombing-is-about-power-politics-and-revenge-but-its-not-about-art-199005

pasted negative comments, "a popular way to spam content and drown out positive replies by inundating comment sections with similar messaging" as noted by *Rolling Stone*. For comparison, the trailer for the simply dreadful *Morbius* only accumulated 11,000 over the course of a year.[245] As an article on the topic in *The Conversation* noted, "It most commonly occurs when longtime fans feel that their ownership of their favourite media franchise has been wrested away from them to soothe the political sensibilities of a more 'sensitive,' 'PC' or 'woke' contemporary audience."

There was also a distinct difference in how the performance of *Ghostbusters* (2016) and the subsequent Paul Rudd-led *Ghostbusters: Afterlife* was depicted in the media. *Ghostbusters* (2016) earned $46 million in its opening weekend, compared to *Afterlife*'s $44 million. *Ghostbusters* (2016) would also earn more total, $229 million compared to *Afterlife*'s $204 million.[246] Yet compare *The Hollywood Reporter*'s headline for the former—"'Ghostbusters' Heading for $70M-Plus Loss, Sequel Unlikely," despite Sony saying nothing about a sequel—to its headline for the latter: "'*Ghostbusters: Afterlife*' Opens to Heavenly $44M." The prediction proved accurate, however—the lower-earning but male-led film is the one that got a sequel, 2024's *Ghostbusters: Frozen Empire*.

Groundbreaking chemist Elizabeth Fulhame invented the concept of catalysis and discovered photoreduction. To avoid being "plagiarized," she published her pioneering 1794 work, the culmination of 14 years of research, under the name "Mrs Fulhame." When the book was published in the United States in 1810, her American editor noted in the introduction that her work was not as well-known as it should have been, as "the pride of science, revolted at the idea of being taught by a female." Fulhame herself wrote, "But censure is perhaps inevitable: for some are so ignorant, that they grow sullen and silent, and are chilled with horror at the sight of anything that nears the semblance of learning, in whatever shape it may appear; and should be the spectre appear in the shape of a woman, the pangs

---

245 Cheung, Kylie, "'The Marvels' Trailer Becomes Most Disliked in YouTube History due to Women Superheroes," *Jezebel*, April 14, 2023, https://jezebel.com/the-marvels-trailer-becomes-most-disliked-on-youtube-1850337330
246 Steiner, Chelsea, "Let's Unpack the Sexist Box Office Narrative around 'Ghostbusters: Afterlife,'" The Mary Sue, November 22, 2021, https://www.themarysue.com/lets-unpack-the-sexist-box-office-narrative-around-ghostbusters-afterlife/

which they suffer are truly dismal."[247]

During the 2022 World Cup, the Union of European Football Associations tweeted "Inevitable. Ronaldo becomes the first player to score at 5 World Cups," referring to male Portuguese player Cristiano Ronaldo. What the UEFA failed to fact-check was that he was the first *male* player to do so, having been preceded by both Brazil's Marta Vieira da Silva and Canada's Christine Sinclair, both in 2019.[248]

The sports news site as.com also posted an article titled "Cristiano Ronaldo becomes the first player to score in 5 separate World Cup finals" with the subtitle "The Portuguese ace wrote his name in the history books again as he found the net in his fifth World Cup—the first player to achieve the feat." Buried in the very last sentence of the article was that "In the Women's World Cup, several players have managed to score in five different World Cup finals including Marta (Brazil—2003, 2007, 2011, 2015, 2019), and Christine Sinclair (Canada—2003, 2007, 2011, 2015, 2019)." While the UEFA tweet was likely an error, AS appears to have knowingly misrepresented the situation.[249]

For writers, publishers are arguably the biggest gatekeeper. Jane Austen's *Northanger Abbey* was almost never published. Originally titled *Susan*, her brother had sold the rights to the manuscript to Benjamin Crosby, a publisher in London, for 10 pounds in 1803. But it soon became apparent that Crosby was not going to publish it, and Austen could not afford the 10 pounds to buy it back until 1815. Although it was her first completed novel, *Northanger Abbey* was not published until 1817, after her death.[250]

Publishers can also push for changes that writers may not support—depending on the nature of the relationship, writers may have signed away control of their work or they may risk losing their chance to be published. War photographer

---

[247] Fulhame, Elizabeth, "An Essay on Combustion, with a View to a New Art of Dying and Painting, wherein the Plogistic and Antiphlogistic Hypotheses are Proved Erroneous," Printed and Soled by James Humphreys, Corner of Second and Walnut-streets, Philadelphia, 1810. https://digital.library.upenn.edu/women/fulhame/combustion/combustion.html
[248] UEFA, 2022, Twitter, Nov 25, 2022, https://twitter.com/EURO2024/status/1595832054545096710
[249] Hall, Andy, "Cristiano Ronaldo Becomes the First Player to Score in 5 Separate World Cup Finals," Diario AS, November 24, 2022, https://en.as.com/soccer/cristiano-ronaldo-becomes-the-first-player-to-score-in-5-separate-world-cup-finals-n/
[250] "Austen Sells Her Novel Susan for £10 | Digital Austen," Digital Austen, https://digitalausten.org/node/27

Deborah Copaken Kogan's 2002 memoir was retitled "Shutterbabe" against her wishes by Random House. As she later recounted:

> The book is sold on the basis of a proposal and a first chapter under the title *Newswhore*, which is the insult often lobbed at us both externally and from within our own ranks—a way of noting, with a combination of shame and black humor, the vulture-like nature of our livelihood, and a means of reclaiming, as I see it, the word "whore," since I want to write about sexual and gender politics as well. Random House changes the book's title to *Shutterbabe*, which a friend came up with. I beg for *Shuttergirl* instead, to reclaim at least "girl," as Lena Dunham would so expertly do years later. Or what about *Develop Stop Fix*? Anything besides a title with the word "babe" in it.
>
> I'm told I have no say in the matter. The cover that the publisher designs has a naked cartoon torso against a pink background with a camera covering the genitalia. I tell them it's usually my eye behind the camera, not my vagina. I fight—hard—to change the cover. Thankfully, I win this one, agreeing to shoot the cover photo myself, gratis. When my publicist tries to pitch the book to NPR's Terry Gross, a producer tells him that Terry likes the "Shutter" part of the title but not the "babe" part.[251]

Decades earlier, her predecessor Dickey Chapelle had a similar experience: her editors changed the title of her 1962 autobiography from "Trouble I've Asked For" or "With My Eyes Wide Open" to "What's a Woman Doing Here?"—an insulting question she'd been asked time and again as a war correspondent. They also removed her dedication "to my Communist interrogators, in deference to their repeated assurances that I would never live to write another line for print." Worst of all was that they rewrote entire sections of the book, to play into stereotypes of femininity—as she put it, "my story seems to have been feminized the hell out of." Her editor assured her it hadn't been because the men in the office didn't think so. "Her self-deprecating

---

[251] Kogan, Deborah Copaken, "My So-Called 'Post-Feminist' Life in Arts and Letters," The Nation, April 9, 2013, https://www.thenation.com/article/archive/my-so-called-post-feminist-life-arts-and-letters/

humor had been contorted into buffoonery. Rather than a gritty reporter willing to risk life and limb to get the story, she came off as a ditzy dame who stumbled into the middle of things despite herself," writes biographer Lorissa Rhinehart. [252]

Even in celebrity memoirs, where the writer should in theory have more power, there is still a divide, writes *This Magazine* publisher Lisa Whittington-Hill:

> And while there is no shortage of male celebrities spilling their guts all over my poorly constructed Ikea bookshelf, the fact that they share shelf space with celebrity memoirs written by women is about all they have in common. When it comes to celebrity memoirs there's a distinct gender bias in everything from how the books are marketed to the type of topics female celebrities are expected to write about and the amount of themselves they are expected to expose to sell books.
>
> The gender divide bias becomes even more problematic, and downright depressing, when you read the reviews and see how critics and the press receive female celebrity memoirs. Rather than celebrate women and their amazing stories, reviewers revert to stereotypes and tired clichés and, in the process, miss the actual story. Women can spend chapters talking about their accomplishments, their awards, and their accolades and reviewers will still only focus on the sex, the scandal, and the bombshell reveals that are expected from female-penned celebrity memoirs if they want to actually sell books. From memoir titles to book blurbs, when it comes to celebrity memoirs by women, sadly, we haven't come a long way baby. [253]

Meanwhile, when a Japanese publishing company bought the rights to a Japanese edition of Sharon Bertsch McGrayne's "Nobel Prize Women in Science" in 1997, she was thrilled. Until the book arrived. With a cover bearing a kitten, steaming bowl of food, tea pots, and a cartoon mother wielding a spoon, a child

---

252 Rhinehart, Lorissa, *First to the Front: The Untold Story of Dickey Chapelle, Trailblazing Female War Correspondent* (MacMillan, 2023).
253 Whittington-Hill, Lisa, "Judge a Book Not by Its Gender," Longreads, May 20, 2021, https://longreads.com/2021/05/20/judge-a-book-not-by-its-gender/

tugging at the woman's apron while mommy's thought bubble is full of molecules. Thinking she had been sent the wrong book, complete with teapots on the pages and pink endpapers, McGrayne discovered instead that her book had been retitled: "Mothers Who've Won Nobel Prizes." [254]

Perhaps the most frustrating thing about sexist barriers is just how easily they can be removed by the gatekeepers holding them in place. In 1939, Helen Kirkpatrick applied for a reporter job with the *Chicago Daily News*. Owner Frank Knox told her that "We don't have women on the staff." She responded, "I can't change my sex. But you can change your policy." Knox hired her, and Kirkpatrick became a war correspondent during World War II and the first woman to report from an Allied war zone with equal privileges to the men. [255]

After earning a dual degree in mathematics and music, Delia Derbyshire was rejected by Decca Records, because the company did not employ women in their recording studios. Instead, she joined the BBC in 1960 and transferred to the BBC's Radiophonic Workshop in 1962, working there for more than 10 years. At the BBC, Derbyshire composed music for shows like *Time on our Hands* and *The World about Us*, but she's best known for her arrangement of composer Ron Grainer's 1963 theme music for *Doctor Who*. The process involved recording hundreds of sounds on analogue tape, adjusting the pitch of each one, then seamlessly splicing them together. BBC policy required members of the Workshop to remain anonymous, meaning that her role as a co-composer was not recognized until 2013—she received an on-screen credit on *The Day of the Doctor*, a special episode to commemorate the show's 50th anniversary.[256]

---

254 Dresser, Norine, "Draping a Prize in an Apron," *Los Angeles Times*, March 15, 1997, https://www.latimes.com/archives/la-xpm-1997-03-15-me-38511-story.html
255 Mackrell, Judith, *The Correspondents: Six Women Writers on the Front Lines of World War II* (Doubleday, 2021).
256 McCabe, Allyson, "Oksana Linde and the Forgotten Pioneers of Electronic Music," BBC, May 13, 2022, https://www.bbc.com/culture/article/20220513-oksana-linde-and-the-forgotten-pioneers-of-electronic-music

WIKIPEDIA'S GENDER BIAS

As an experiment one day, I started clicking Wikipedia's "Random article" button—the third, fourth, eighth and 14th results were biography pages about individual men. The fifth was a book written by a man. The sixth was a painting by a man (albeit of a woman). Although the eleventh was about the Salem Witch Trials, it took 16 clicks to get to a biography of a woman.

Wikipedia's crowd-sourced approach, where anyone can register and make edits, is the site's greatest strength and, arguably, its greatest weakness. There is no central authority to appeal to when, for example, a new page is submitted and some anonymous moderator decides the person or topic in question is not noteworthy enough to warrant an entry. This is what happened when a user attempted to create a page for Canadian physicist Donna Strickland in March 2018, despite Strickland's professional achievements. Only a few months later, Strickland became the first woman in 55 years to win the Nobel Prize in physics. For comparison, her colleague Gérard Mourou, with whom she shared the Nobel, has had a Wikipedia page since 2005.[257]

Similarly, Clarice Phelps was a nuclear engineer at Oak Ridge National Laboratory's High Flux Isotope Reactor when, in 2008, she helped isolate and purify 22mg of berkelium, which collaborators used to create a new element: tennessine,

---

[257] Cecco, Leyland, "Female Nobel Prize Winner Deemed Not Important Enough for Wikipedia Entry," *The Guardian*, October 3, 2018, https://www.theguardian.com/science/2018/oct/03/donna-strickland-nobel-physics-prize-wikipedia-denied

element 117. Phelps became the first African-American woman to contribute to the discovery or creation of a new element.[258] Yet only months after physicist and Wikipedia activist Jess Wade put a bio up for her on Wikipedia on August 31, 2018, it was removed by another editor, user TonyBallioni, on February 11, 2019 because he deemed Phelps "not notable" enough. Wade recreated the page that April and the same user deleted it the same day.[259] It took almost a year of fighting before it was restored in January 2020. It's also worth noting that dozens of editors besides Wade had worked on the page while it was up the first time, but it only took one man to decide a woman didn't matter enough.[260] The majority of Wikipedia editors are male, and editors of any gender can have an androcentric bias, either consciously or unconsciously. One of the more absurd ways this male-as-default gender bias plays out is in the category pages, which feature lists of all pages that fit within a category. A recurring issue is that there will be a category page for a non-gender-specific group that only features men, with all the women moved to a sub-category page. There was an outcry in 2013 when it was discovered that Wikipedia editors had removed every woman from the "American novelists" category page into the proverbial "pink ghetto" sub-category for "American women novelists."[261]

When I was looking up 'cross-dressers in wartime' for another project in July 2022, I discovered that the Wikipedia category page for "Wartime cross-dressers" gives the main category page to only the men tagged—all three of them. I had to navigate to the "Female wartime cross-dressers" sub-category to find the 94 pages for women. When I checked back a year later, the structure was the same in July 2023.[262]

It can also be maddening to try and navigate the often subjectively applied rules

---

258   Chapman, Kit, "The Women Written out of Nuclear Science," Berkeley College of Chemistry, January 10, 2022, https://chemistry.berkeley.edu/news/women-written-out-nuclear-science
259   All public logs, page: Clarice Phelps, Wikipedia, https://en.wikipedia.org/w/index.php?title=Special:Log&page=Clarice+Phelps
260   Clarice Phelps: Revision history, Wikipedia, https://en.wikipedia.org/w/index.php?title=Clarice_Phelps&action=history&dir=prev
261   Flood, Alison, "Wikipedia Bumps Women from 'American Novelists' Category," *The Guardian*, April 25, 2013, https://www.theguardian.com/books/2013/apr/25/wikipedia-women-american-novelists
262   https://en.wikipedia.org/wiki/Category:Wartime_cross-dressers

of Wikipedia editing. I was once tasked with creating a list page for alumni of a school, which is very common on Wikipedia. The first version I submitted had one reference source—the alumni section of the school's website, which lists every graduate, sorted by year and program. Even though this would seem like the best possible source, the entire page was rejected because there was only one. So, I went and painstakingly sourced dozens of articles from reputable outlets where different people's alumni status was mentioned, added them all in, and then resubmitted. I was accused of source-bombing, where a troll attempts to overwhelm editors with too many references. After attempting to seek help and learning there was none to be had, I accepted defeat and moved on.

As noted in a 2022 American Society for Biochemistry and Molecular Biology article on the topic, when surveyed a decade prior, approximately 85 percent of the English version's editors were men, mostly living in the United States, United Kingdom, and India. At least 80% of the roughly 2.8 million biographies they had produced were about men. Sociologist Dr. Francesca Tripodi tracked the list of articles recommended for deletion on Wikipedia for over three years. She found that while women represented only 18.25 percent of English-language biographies as of February 2020, they made up more than 25 percent of page deletion requests. Women "are more likely to be considered non-notable even if they meet Wikipedia's criteria for inclusion." Although the 22,000 biographies that were submitted for deletion were disproportionately likely to be about women, pages about women were more likely than pages about men to be retained after discussion. "They met the criteria for inclusion at a point where they shouldn't have been (on the Articles for Deletion list) to begin with," Tripodi said. "If there weren't networks like Women in Red devoted to saving these articles, these articles would have been deleted." [263]

But saving a page requires someone to defend it, which can be time-consuming, exhausting, and demoralising. Because women's lives have been less documented than men's, it can also be difficult to cite sufficient sources in defending a page.

---

[263] Oldach, Laurel, "What's with Wikipedia and Women?" ASBMB Today, March 8, 2022, https://www.asbmb.org/asbmb-today/careers/030822/what-s-with-wikipedia-and-women

Studies have also found that less than 30 percent of biographies on the site are of women, and they link to men's pages more often than men's bios link to women's.[264]

One page that highlights this is the "List of pioneers in computer science." Leaving out women like Gladys West—who laid the foundation for GPS—and all but one of the ENIAC programmers (Betty Holbertson made the cut), only 20 women were included in 2023, among 165 men. Yet each gender had four notability challenges ("undue weight? – discuss"), meaning the editor did not believe the person listed was significant enough to warrant inclusion on the list. The men had only a 2.4% chance of being challenged, while fully 25% of the women were.[265]

It is also impossible to overstate the importance of Wikipedia as a source of information, as Google, Siri, Alexa, and other common search tools all frequently rely on it to provide the answers we ask them for. A *Time Magazine* article claiming to list the 100 most significant historical figures included only three women, which the authors partially blamed on women's underrepresentation on Wikipedia.[266] As of its 20th anniversary in January 2021, it was the 13th most popular website on the internet, with hundreds of billions of page views every year.[267] It also has more than 33 million editors. As of 2013, only 16 percent were women—and there is no reason to think that has changed.[268]

---

264 Carroll, Tamar and Nicosia, Lara, "Wikipedia at 20: Why It Often Overlooks Stories of Women in History," *Big Think*, January 20, 2021, https://bigthink.com/the-present/wikipedia-at-20/#rebelltitem1

265 "List of pioneers in computer science," Wikipedia, Accessed September 20, 2023, https://en.wikipedia.org/wiki/List_of_pioneers_in_computer_science

266 Diehl, Amy, "'You Have to See It to Be It': Missing Female Role Models and What We Can Do about It," *Ms. Magazine*, December 27, 2021, https://msmagazine.com/2021/12/27/womens-history-stem-role-models/

267 Galov, Nick, "How Many People Use Wikipedia in 2022?" WebTribunal, March 6, 2023, https://webtribunal.net/blog/how-many-people-use-wikipedia/#gref

268 Carroll, Tamar and Nicosia, Lara, "Wikipedia at 20: Why It Often Overlooks Stories of Women in History," *Big Think*, January 20, 2021, https://bigthink.com/the-present/wikipedia-at-20/#rebelltitem1

VISUAL REMINDERS

"A golden statue of a wicked man is worth less than a mud statue of a man with a heart of gold!"
—Mehmet Murat İldan

In 2023, leaders of the National Audubon Society voted to keep the name of John James Audubon for their organisation. The question arose as local chapters and the organisation's union removed the name, given the man's history as a slave owner and staunch anti-abolitionist. "He bought and sold humans like horses. That is evidence enough to recast the hero into a different role," wrote J. Drew Lanham for *Audubon* magazine in 2021. "I do not believe perfection should ever be the standard, but I know we can do better." It is also well-documented that he was a grave robber who actively stole the human skulls of Native Americans and Mexican soldiers, sending the remains to Samuel George Morton, who used them in his racist pseudoscience that claimed human races could be ranked in intelligence—with Caucasians at the top, naturally. The National Audubon Society also acknowledges that he was accused of "and most certainly committed" plagiarism and academic fraud.

All of which begs the question of why an organisation would want to maintain those ties. The answer is, essentially, brand recognition. As the board chair said at the time, "The name has come to represent not one person, but a broader love of birds and nature." Some found the decision particularly insulting for a conservation-focused group, which is meant to serve a common good and relies on public support to do so. "The celebration of such a figure undermines all efforts at being an inclusive organization and inflicts harm," the Seattle chapter stated in response to the vote. "The name is a barrier imposed upon historically excluded communities that suffer the impacts of environmental calamities first and disproportionately."[269]

Every day, we see homages to people, often without even noticing. A statue, a street name, the faces on the currency in our pocket—all of these are visual reminders of who we hold in esteem. And most of those are men. One of the most visible representations of people is on the money that most of us carry with us, regardless of where we live. It can also provide a fascinating insight into what countries value when you consider who they place in such prominent positions. As of 2022, only 15 percent of banknotes around the world feature women—and quite a few of those were Queen Elizabeth II, a remnant of the U.K.'s colonialism. This does not include anonymous figures, or personifications of ideals.[270]

STATUES

Italy's largest public square, Prato della Valle, features a canal lined with 78 statues, some dating back as far as 1775. For more than 200 years, only men were represented, except for a small bust of Gaspara Stampa—considered the Italian Renaissance's greatest woman poet—tucked behind the leg of sculptor Andrea Briosco for some unknown reason. In 2022, a proposal to include a statue of Elena Lucrezia Cornaro Piscopia on one of the empty pedestals was put forward and, after much controversy and a lot of sexist rhetoric, it was approved. "The fact that there were these vacant spots was a glaring reminder that women are underrepresented here and elsewhere and that they were marginalized in the past, certainly not put on pedestals," said city councillor Simone Pillitteri. Although in 1678, philosopher Piscopia was the first woman in the world to graduate with a university degree, this was apparently not enough in some people's opinions to rank her among likely fictional characters like Antenor (a counsellor during the Trojan War),

---

269 Osborne, Margaret, 2023, "National Audubon Society Votes to Keep the Name of an Enslaver," *Smithsonian Magazine*, March 17, 2023, https://www.smithsonianmag.com/smart-news/national-audubon-society-votes-to-keep-the-name-of-an-enslaver-180981827/
270 "Just 15% of the World's Banknotes Feature Famous Women on Them," *Business Insider*, July 18, 2017, https://www.insider.co.uk/news/just-15-worlds-banknotes-feature-10817847

inconsequential rulers like Marcantonio Giustinian (an inept puppet), Michele Morosini (who died only a few months after he was elected) and popes like Eugene IV, who created the legal basis for forcing Jews into ghettos. And, as Pillitteri noted, empty pedestals, as well as multiple obelisks. [271]

Similarly, of the 229 busts on Rome's Pincian Hill, only three depict women. But while those are two glaring examples, they reflect patterns seen around the world. A major audit published in 2021 of nearly 50,000 U.S. monuments found that of the 50 most represented historical figures, only three were women: Joan of Arc (the highest ranked at 18th), Harriet Tubman, and Sacagawea. The most likely candidates were typically European, like Marie Curie, saints like Catholic leader Elizabeth Ann Seton, or both European and a saint, like Joan of Arc. Images of women were also often symbolic (like winged victory on military monuments) or non-human— the survey found a ratio of 22 mermaids to every two U.S. congresswomen.[272] Years after a bill was passed in 2020, authorising a statue on federal ground in Washington D.C., honouring the fight for women's suffrage in the U.S., the battle continued on where to place it. While the Women's Suffrage National Monument Foundation wanted to see the women join the many men on the National Mall, the National Parks Service actively fought the move. "Every little girl who visits the National Mall with her Girl Scout troop should see herself in democracy's story," foundation executive director Anna Laymon told *The Washington Post*. [273]

Even when women are honoured with public art, it often goes very badly in a variety of ways. When a statue of the late Princess Diana was erected at Kensington Palace in 2021, it was roundly criticized on several fronts. *The Guardian* noted the figure's "aesthetic awfulness," calling it "a spiritless and characterless hunk of nonsense" and "nauseating." *The Times* agreed that the aesthetic was "so

---

271 "Padua's Most Important Public Square to Get Its First Female Statue," *ITALY Magazine*, March 8, 2022, https://www.italymagazine.com/featured-story/paduas-most-important-public-square-get-its-first-female-statue
272 McGreevy, Nora, "Scholars Spent a Year Scrutinizing America's Monuments. Here's What They Learned," *Smithsonian Magazine*, October 1, 2021, https://www.smithsonianmag.com/smart-news/researchers-spent-one-year-scrutinizing-americas-monuments-heres-what-they-learned-180978791/
273 Green, Stephanie, "A National Mall Standoff: Can a New Monument to Women Join All the Men?" *The Washinton Post*, July 13, 2023, https://www.washingtonpost.com/history/2023/07/08/national-mall-womens-suffrage-monument-nps/

horrible" it could only have been "calculated to appeal to the lowest common denominator." *The Times'* critics also interpreted the statue as framing Diana as a modern-day Virgin Mary figure and found the "frumpy" outfit unbefitting the ever-stylish Diana. A poem accompanies the figures—from Wallace Gallaher's 1923 *The Measure of a Man*, with the word "man" substituted for "woman"—but as the *Telegraph* noted, "If you have to re-write it to make it appropriate, you've chosen the wrong poem." Even the relatively generous review in *The Independent* observed that the use of bronze "belongs to the norms and standards of another time," better suited to memorials of "colonial generals, Victorian politicians and fascist dictators" than a progressive woman. [274]

However poorly done the Diana statue may have been artistically and thematically, there are far worse offences. The song "Molly Malone" is the unofficial anthem of Dublin, Ireland, telling the story of a fictional 1600s fishmonger. Because many such women also worked as sex workers, when a statue was erected to "honour" her in 1988, she was depicted as large-breasted with a very low-cut bodice. It should be noted that there is nothing in the song lyrics to imply "Molly" was a sex worker, and that this statue was designed by a woman, Irish sculptor Jeanne Rynhart. Often referred to as "The Tart with the Cart," the statue was later subjected to so much groping of those prominent breasts that the metal became distinctly discoloured.[275]

In 2021, an 8-metre-tall statue of Marilyn Monroe was erected outside the Palm Springs Art Museum in Florida. Referencing her infamous skirt flying up scene from *The Seven Year Itch*, "The 26-foot-tall statue of Marilyn Monroe is designed for viewers to walk in between the legs, look up her dress and snap a picture of her crotch or buttocks for fun," observed one critic. "It is sexist, exploitive and misogynistic. Even in death, Marilyn has no peace." [276] As for how Marilyn herself

---

[274] O'Driscoll, Julia, "The Verdict on the Kensington Palace Princess Diana Statue," *The Week UK*, July 2, 2021, https://www.theweek.co.uk/news/uk-news/953368/kensington-palace-princess-diana-statue-verdict
[275] Siobhán Marie Kilfeather, *Dublin: A Cultural History* (Oxford University Press, 2005).
[276] Wu, Tara, "Why a Newly Installed Statue of Marilyn Monroe Is so Controversial," *Smithsonian Magazine*, June 22, 2021, https://www.smithsonianmag.com/smart-news/why-newly-installed-statue-marilyn-monroe-so-controversial-180978030/

might have felt about it, she told *Life* in 1962, "I never quite understood it, this sex symbol. I always thought symbols were those things you clash together! That's the trouble, a sex symbol becomes a thing. I just hate to be a thing." In another interview, she said "Being a sex symbol is a heavy load to carry, especially when one is tired, hurt and bewildered." [277]

That same year and also in Florida, former deputy fire-rescue chief Latosha Clemons sued the city of Boynton Beach over a mural that was meant to honour her. Clemons, the city's first African-American woman firefighter, was painted as Caucasian in her own mural. This wasn't even the first time—in 2019, another city art project included a depiction of former fire chief Glenn Joseph, who was African-American and was portrayed as Caucasian. The repeat of such an issue was so embarrassing that the mural was removed the day after it was unveiled, and both the public art manager and fire chief were fired. "I'm hurt. I'm disappointed. I'm outraged," Clemons told the *Palm Beach Post* in June 2020. "It's been my heart and soul and my lifeblood to serve in the community where I grew up ... this is beyond disrespect and I basically want to know why it happened." [278]

Meanwhile in Australia, a monument to the country's first female riverboat skipper, Pearl Wallace, was damaged during flooding in 2011 and when repaired, she had been transformed into a bearded male. The reasons for this are unclear—likely, it was done by someone ignorant of the subject who simply assumed it was a tribute to a man. It was only after Wallace's grandson advised the local council of the mistake 12 years later that this was corrected.[279]

Indeed, it often seems that we're more likely to see statues of men who committed atrocities than we are of women. A statue of James Marion Sims stood in

---

[277] G, Trisha Gayathri, "How Did Marilyn Monroe Become the Ultimate 'Sex Symbol'? Did She like the Title?" First Curiosity, September 7, 2022, https://firstcuriosity.com/news/how-did-marilyn-monroe-become-the-ultimate-sex-symbol-did-she-like-the-title/

[278] Milian, Jorge, "'I'm Outraged.' Boynton Faces $100,000 Lawsuit over Mural Showing Black Female Firefighter with White Face," *The Palm Beach Post*, October 8, 2021, https://www.palmbeachpost.com/story/news/local/boynton/2021/10/08/boynton-beach-first-black-female-firefighter-latosha-clemons-suing-city-over-mural-depiction/5994504001/

[279] Printz, Jo, "Captain Pearl Wallace's tribute at Nyah refurbished after incorrectly given beard," ABC, September 20, 2023, https://www.abc.net.au/news/2023-09-20/riverboat-captain-pearl-wallace-bollard-beard-nyah/102872814

New York City's Central Park for more than 120 years (1894—2018), despite the well-documented fact that he horrifically tortured enslaved women, including Anarcha, Betsy, Lucy, and nine women whose names were never even recorded by their tormentor. It was only in 2022 that these women were given their own monument, a statute in Montgomery, Alabama—only about a mile from where a statue of him still stands in front of the Alabama State Capitol. In the 1840s, he experimented on women for years, performing major surgeries without anaesthesia as the women were restrained and observed by other curious white men. Anarcha alone was forced to undergo at least 30 surgeries. Horrifically, after his white male assistants quit, he trained the women to replace them, forcing them to assist with surgeries on each other.[280]

According to the New York Historical Society,

"Lucy was the first of the three women to undergo Sims's experimental operation. The operating room was packed with doctors who wanted to watch the procedure. She was not asked whether she was comfortable with strange men watching her operation. Lucy was brought to the operating room naked and restrained on the table so her involuntary movements during surgery would not disrupt the procedure. Sims did not use anesthesia to numb her pain. This was partly because doctors feared patients could die from anesthesia and partly because it was commonly believed that Black women did not experience pain the same way white women did. Lucy's surgery took about an hour, and she was conscious for every minute of it.

After the surgery, Lucy developed a terrible infection from a device Sims had placed in her bladder. She experienced days of extreme agony. Sims was able to cure her infection, but her injury did not heal. The operation was a failure." [281]

---

[280] Kuta, Sarah, "Subjected to Painful Experiments and Forgotten, Enslaved 'Mothers of Gynecology' Are Honored with New Monument," *Smithsonian Magazine*, May 11, 2022, https://www.smithsonianmag.com/smart-news/mothers-of-gynecology-monument-honors-enslaved-women-180980064/

[281] Boomer, Lee, "Life Story: Anarcha, Betsy, and Lucy," Women & the American Story, https://wams.nyhistory.org/a-nation-divided/antebellum/anarcha-betsy-lucy/

Sims is not alone. Kentucky "doctor" Ephraim McDowell—who never earned a medical degree—forced operations on four enslaved women in an attempt to treat ovarian cancer, at a time when abdominal surgery was viewed, justifiably, as tantamount to murder. Surgeons at the time saw no need to wash their hands and post-operative infection killed many who didn't die on the table; at least one of McDowell's experiment subjects died as a result of his actions. His statue stands in the United States Capitol Visitor's Center. The women these men tortured are all but forgotten to history while their abusers are lauded as the "father of modern gynaecology" (Sims) and the "father of abdominal surgery" (McDowell).[282]

There are countless monuments to objectively horrible men—Christopher Columbus enslaved Indigenous people en masse, murdered many, and instigated a genocide, not to mention rape and torture. As of 2021, there were at least 149 statues of him across the U.S., and about 6,000 places that bear his name (see below for more on that). Though, in a promising sign, one in Newark, New Jersey was replaced in 2023 with a monument to Harriet Tubman.[283] In January 2021, an investigation by *The Forward* identified more than 1,500 statues and streets honouring Nazi collaborators around the world, including at least 37 in the U.S. alone.[284]

Italian journalist Indro Montanelli, whose statue in Milan has been repeatedly defaced, was an admitted child rapist. Per *Politico*,

> During his two years of service in the army in the second Italo-Ethiopian war in the 1930s, Montanelli bought—or rather "leased," as he put it—a young Eritrean girl from her father for 350 lire, a horse and a rifle. The girl, whose name was either "Destà" or "Fatima," was 12 or 14 at the time.
>
> In a long, painfully detailed article that appeared in his column La

---

282 Eschner, Kat, "This American Doctor Pioneered Abdominal Surgery by Operating on Enslaved Women," *Smithsonian Magazine*, December 19, 2017, https://www.smithsonianmag.com/history/father-abdominal-surgery-practiced-enslaved-women-180967589/

283 Franklin, Jonathan, "A Monument of Harriet Tubman Now Replaces a Statue of Christopher Columbus in Newark," *NPR*, March 13, 2023, https://www.npr.org/2023/03/13/1163024069/harriet-tubman-monument-unveiled-newark-new-jersey

284 Anania, Billie, "Why Monuments to Nazi Collaborators Are All over America," ART News, November 1, 2022, https://www.artnews.com/list/art-news/news/nazi-symbols-monuments-united-states-1234644910/the-tangled-history-of-anti-communism-and-fascism/

stanza di Montanelli in 2000, the Italian man of letters described the girl as a "docile little animal" whose smell repulsed him, and whose mutilated genitals "resisted his ardor," to the point that intercourse was only possible after her mother's "brutal intervention."

Montanelli never showed any remorse. In a 1969 television interview, he dismissed criticism of his actions by claiming customs were "different" in Africa. There's nothing to suggest he ever regretted his treatment of her, or developed any self-awareness in later years. [285]

And when women who have been victimized are honoured, there may still be protest from their abusers or those abusers' representatives. Any time another country erects a Statue of Peace recognising the suffering experienced by the 50,000 to 200,000 women and girls enslaved and raped by the Japanese military during World War II, the government and its representatives inevitably throw a hissy fit. In December 2015, Japan reneged on a promise to pay 1 billion yen in compensation to the victims unless a Statue of Peace was removed from its location in Seoul. A second statue was then erected in Busan, and Japan recalled two diplomats from the country and halted high-level talks. Within a few years, there were 50 statues erected in parks and other public spaces across South Korea. In 2012, officials from a New Jersey Koreatown rejected requests from two Japanese diplomatic delegations to remove a small plaque from a public park. After San Francisco's Column of Strength became the first such statue in a major U.S. city in 2018, Osaka ended its 60-year sister-city relationship with them in protest.[286] As reported in *The Nation* in 2022:

> Alexis Dudden, a history professor at the University of Connecticut whose research specializes in Korea-Japan relations, helped organize a 2015 letter signed by a group of American academics condemning Japan's revisionist history regarding comfort women. Denialists retaliated by

---

285   Blasi, Giulia, "He Raped a 12-Year-Old Girl. They Built Him a Statue," POLITICO, June 16, 2020, https://www.politico.eu/article/indro-montanelli-raped-a-12-year-old-girl-they-built-him-a-statue-milan/
286   Hu, Elise, "'Comfort Woman' Memorial Statues, a Thorn in Japan's Side, Now Sit on Korean Buses," *NPR*, November 13, 2017, https://www.npr.org/sections/parallels/2017/11/13/563838610/comfort-woman-memorial-statues-a-thorn-in-japans-side-now-sit-on-korean-buses

sending her 10 to 15 death threats every day; eventually, an FBI officer was assigned to her classroom.

She is also one of several professors at American public universities who've received Freedom of Information Act requests in an unfounded search for incriminating e-mails. The requests emanated from white American men living in Asia, whose online writings are sympathetic to Japanese nationalism and anti-comfort women.

"I was charged with working together with Nancy Pelosi on an international conspiracy to bring down the government of Japan," Dudden said. "I was simply teaching about comfort women from documents I have found in the government of Japan archives." [287]

When a statue was erected in Glendale, California, a pro-Japan conservative group sued the city to have it removed. When it lost, the group appealed, and after the appeals court upheld the dismissal, they tried to take it to the Supreme Court, complete with an amicus brief from the Japanese government. The Supreme Court declined to hear the case.[288]

But despite Japan's best efforts—which have been successful in some instances—by 2022, there were more than 90 Statues of Peace on display around the world.[289] When an exhibition on the topic was staged at the Aichi Triennale 2019 in Japan, it was forced to close after three days. Openly criticized by local government officials and visitors, the gallery faced a campaign of intimidation, including an anonymous letter threatening to set the gallery on fire if the exhibition continued. Artistic director Daisuke Tsuda decided to close the exhibition to prevent violence. When organizers attempted to restage it at a private gallery in Tokyo in 2021, the opening was postponed due to a right-wing campaign of

---

287 Berkman, Seth, "The Fight over Berlin's Comfort Woman Statue," The Nation, July 18, 2022, https://www.thenation.com/article/world/comfort-women-japan-korea-germany/

288 Constante, Agnes, "Supreme Court Declines Case over Lawsuit to Remove 'Comfort Women' Memorial," NBC News, March 31, 2017, https://www.nbcnews.com/news/asian-america/supreme-court-declines-case-over-lawsuit-remove-comfort-women-memorial-n740996.

289 Berkman, Seth, "The Fight over Berlin's Comfort Woman Statue," The Nation, July 18, 2022, https://www.thenation.com/article/world/comfort-women-japan-korea-germany/

"sabotage and intimidation using vehicles and loudspeakers," according to South Korean newspaper *Hankyoreh*.[290]

And, of course, monuments can be destroyed. After the death of the pharaoh Hatshepsut, her nephew had her face and name chiselled off the monuments to her and rewrote history to ascribe her accomplishments to her brother and father, who preceded her.[291]

PLACE NAMES

In 2015, engineer Aruna Sankaranarayanan ran an analysis of streets named for people using OpenStreetMap data. It found that "Between Bengaluru, Chennai, London, Mumbai, New Delhi, Paris, and San Francisco, the percentage of streets named after women is an average of 27.5.[292] Among the cities in India, Bengaluru tops the list with 39 percent of streets named after women." That same year, feminists in Paris symbolically "renamed" 60 streets to honour women. They were protesting the fact that only 2.6 percent of the city's streets were named after women—and many of the 166 women were wives and daughters of famous men, rather than accomplished in their own right. Roman geography teacher Maria Pia Ercolini analysed the city's 16,500-plus streets in 2012 and found only 580 streets—just 3.5 percent—named after women.[293] On March 5, 2020, the Secretary of State for Economic Transition in Brussels, Barbara Trachte, published an interactive map of the city's street names. The data showed that only 6.1 percent of the streets in the Belgian capital are named after women.[294]

While Queen Victoria certainly had plenty of places named after her, the kings

---

[290] Solomon, Tessa, "Japan's Controversial Comfort Women Sculpture Is Going on View Again despite Protests and Intimidation," ARTnews, March 29, 2022, https://www.artnews.com/art-news/news/contested-comfort-women-sculptures-will-again-go-on-view-in-japan-1234623194/

[291] Heywood, Ann, and Serotta, Anne, "Queen Hatshepsut Restored," The Metropolitan Museum of Art, 2021, https://www.metmuseum.org/about-the-met/conservation-and-scientific-research/conservation-stories/2020/hatshepsut

[292] Sankaranarayanan, Aruna, "Mapping female versus male street names," Mapbox, November 3, 2015, https://blog.mapbox.com/mapping-female-versus-male-street-names-b4654c1e00d5

[293] Bosworth, Mark, "Are Our Street Names Sexist?" BBC, April 11, 2012, https://www.bbc.com/news/magazine-17203823

[294] Schwab, Pierre-Nicolas, "The Feminisation of Street Names: Useful Debate or a Political Artifice?" Market Research Consulting, March 11, 2020, https://www.intotheminds.com/blog/en/feminisation-street-names/

still outnumber the queens. For every Maryland and Virginia, there's a Georgia, Washington, and Louisiana—though it is interesting to note that California draws its name from a mythical, Black, griffin-riding warrior queen named Calafia.[295]

It is particularly offensive to consider just how often colonizers' names get slapped on important Indigenous sites, like calling Australia's Uluru "Ayers Rock," after the one-time Chief Secretary of South Australia, Sir Henry Ayers. Christopher Columbus was a genocidal rapist and torturer, but there are roughly 6,000 memorials to him in the United States alone, as well as being the namesake for places ranging from the country of Colombia to the provinces of British Columbia (Canada) and Colón Province (Panama) to the United States capital (District of Columbia).[296]

And yet, as with statues, efforts to address the problematic nature of these tributes often meet with backlash. In 2022, the Canadian city of Calgary commissioned Chinese-Canadian artist Annie Wong to create a site-specific public artwork addressing this very topic in James Short Park. Taken down after only four days, Wong's installation featured seven printed banners with quotes from interviews with the local Chinatown's community members about Short's racist history and the city's paltry efforts to acknowledge the historic mistreatment of its Chinese citizens. The quotes included, "James Short was a racist," "Erasing a name in history cannot erase what was done," and "James Short was a leader in the anti-Chinese movement." For context, Short, a lawyer, represented Caucasian citizens of the city who wanted to prevent Chinese Calgarians from establishing Chinatown within the city centre in 1910. "Those people do not beautify any property, and in fact they tend to make a district obnoxious," he told the *Calgary Herald* that year. "They have no idea of sanitation at all." Despite the clear accuracy of Wong's banners, and the fact that she did what she was hired to do, historical truth was deemed too

---

295   Johnson, Rebecca, "California Is Named for a Griffin-Riding Black Warrior Queen," *Atlas Obscura*, November 11, 2020, https://www.atlasobscura.com/articles/california-etymology-black-queen

296   Shin, Youjin, Nick Kirkpatrick, Catherine D'Ignazio, and Wonyoung So, "Columbus Monuments Are Coming Down, but He's Still Honored in 6,000 Places across the U.S. Here's Where," *The Washington Post*, October 11, 2021, https://www.washingtonpost.com/history/interactive/2021/christopher-columbus-monuments-america-map/

controversial to be stated publicly more than 100 years later.[297]

CENSORSHIP

Then, of course, there is deliberate and explicit censorship. Historically and today, people with power have sought to block ideas, writing, and artwork that challenge what they consider the status quo, often in the guise of "protecting" people. For example, Artemisia Gentileschi painted a nude woman in a noble's home for a commission in 1616; in 1680, the man's descendent had another painter add flowing fabric to cover the nudity, "to protect the owner's wife and children from being exposed to a figure that might dent their decorum."[298] In the U.S., while today's censorship has largely focused on critical race theory and the existence of the LGBTQIA+ community, the silencing of women is still going on, including in legislatures. In 2012, Michigan State Representative Lisa Brown was banned from speaking a bill about the retirement of school employees after daring to use the word "vagina" in her comments protesting a proposed abortion law, which apparently "violated the decorum of the House."[299] In 2017, U.S. Senator Elizabeth Warren was repeatedly interrupted while attempting to read a letter from civil rights activist Coretta Scott King because it was insulting to Senator Jeff Sessions—even though King's letter about Sessions' blatant racism had previously been entered into the Senate Record in 1986. Moreover, the issue at hand was Sessions' confirmation to the role of U.S. Attorney General, so presenting negative information about the man would seem highly relevant.[300]

Modern censorship is particularly visible in China, where the government has significant influence over the major internet sites and services. In February 2022,

---

297 Nayyar, Rhea, "Canadian City Clashes with Artist over a Park's Racist History," *Hyperallergic*, October 31, 2022, https://hyperallergic.com/774899/artist-targets-calgary-historical-sinophobia/
298 Bowman, Emma, "A Censored Nude Painting from 1616 Is Set to Be Digitally Unveiled," *NPR*, November 14, 2022, https://www.npr.org/2022/11/14/1136372868/artemisia-italy-nude-censored-painting
299 Peralta, Eyder, "Michigan State Rep Barred from Speaking after 'Vagina' Comments," *NPR*, June 14, 2012, https://www.npr.org/sections/thetwo-way/2012/06/14/155059849/michigan-state-rep-barred-from-speaking-after-vagina-comments
300 Chappell, Bill, "Read Coretta Scott King's Letter That Got Sen. Elizabeth Warren Silenced," *NOR*, February 8, 2017, https://www.npr.org/sections/thetwo-way/2017/02/08/514085145/read-coretta-scott-kings-letter-that-got-sen-elizabeth-warren-silenced

Chinese-American author Geling Yan published an article on the WeChat account of *Survivors' Poetry*, a contemporary Chinese poetry magazine, expressing her rage at the mistreatment of women. The article soon disappeared from WeChat, and searches of Yan's name yielded no results on Weibo, China's largest social media platform.[301] Weibo had also shut down several feminist accounts for "hyping up opposition between different groups," and authorities had previously censored posts about sexual harassment. Yan's comments were also removed from results offered by the Chinese search engine Baidu, and the page about Yan on its online encyclopaedia Baidu Baike, was removed.

For activists like Xianzi, who exposed sexual harassment by the prominent TV star Zhu Jun, having access to communities on Weibo not only gave her a platform—where she amassed hundreds of thousands of followers—to have her voice heard, but also provided connection to a support network. When Weibo blocked her account in 2021, she lost both. As she told the BBC, "Talking is healing...If you prohibit people from saying they are hurt, then you are really trying to destroy them."[302]

Women's lives and bodies are censored in other ways on social media like Facebook and Instagram. In 2015, as part of a university project, poet and artist Rupi Kaur posted a photo of herself with menstrual blood having leaked through her pants and staining the bed she lay on—a situation countless women have experienced. Instagram removed the image, claiming it violated community guidelines and leading to a battle that attracted the attention of millions. Kaur re-posted the image, with the caption "thank you @instagram for providing me with the exact response my work was created to critique. you deleted a photo of a woman who is fully covered and menstruating stating that it goes against community guidelines when your guidelines outline that it is nothing but acceptable. the girl is fully clothed. the photo is mine. it is not attacking a certain group. nor is it spam. and

---

301 Li, Jane, "Weibo Censored a Famous Novelist Who Voiced Her Anger over China's Inhumanity to Women," *Quartz*, February 14, 2022, https://qz.com/2127169/censors-delete-geling-yans-wechat-essay-on-chained-woman-in-china

302 Yi, Beh Lih, "After Saying #MeToo, Chinese Women Fight Censorship to Push for Change," Reuters, August 9, 2018, https://www.reuters.com/article/us-china-rights-women-idUSKBN1KU0ZS.

because it does not break those guidelines i will repost it again. i will not apologize for not feeding the ego and pride of misogynist society that will have my body in an underwear but not be okay with a small leak. when your pages are filled with countless photos/accounts where women (so many who are underage) are objectified. pornified. and treated less than human." [303]

One of artist Cheryl Ann Lipstreu's mediums is the human body, such as when she elaborately painted seven models in 2014 to create a giant Dia De Los Muertos sugar skull, also known as calavera. Yet the image kept getting flagged as "pornography" on Facebook despite the clearly artistic nature of the work. While no genitals are visible, nipples and buttocks are, which was enough for it to be repeatedly removed from the platform.[304]

In 2012, it was revealed that Facebook moderators were instructed to remove breastfeeding images if a nipple was visible. At the same time, images of "deep flesh wounds" and "crushed heads/limbs," as well as "graphic images" of animals were considered permissible. And of course there was no discussion of censoring men's nipples. In May 2013, the site blocked the administrator of an Australian feminist page after she posted an image protesting the site's double standards. "My problem is that when we report things like violence against women or sexism against women or misogyny against women, they just say it's totally fine," Jenna Price, co-founder of the Destroy the Joint group, told *The Guardian*. [305]

Meanwhile TikTok moderators were told to suppress content by disabled, "ugly," and "poor" people, with criteria including "Abnormal body shape," "ugly facial looks," "dwarfism," "too many wrinkles," "eye disorders," and many other "low quality" traits.[306] Black Lives Matter content has also been suppressed. Videos of

---

303   Rao, Mallika, "How Cultural Bias and Sexism Catapulted the Period Photo That Broke the Internet," *Huffington Post*, May 6, 2015, https://www.huffpost.com/entry/rupi-kaur-instagram-period-photo-series_n_7213662
304   "This Powerful Image Took Our Breath Away. Facebook Censors It As Porn," Women You Should Know, April 28, 2014, https://womenyoushouldknow.net/powerful-image-took-breath-away-facebook-censors-porn/
305   Hern, Alex, "Facebook's Changing Standards: From Beheading to Breastfeeding Images," *The Guardian*, October 22, 2013, https://www.theguardian.com/technology/2013/oct/22/facebook-standards-beheading-breastfeeding-social-networking
306   Biddle, Sam, Ribeiro, Paulo Victor and Dias, Tatiana, "Invisible Censorship: TikTok Told Moderators to Suppress Posts by 'Ugly' People and the Poor to Attract New Users," *The Intercept*, March 16, 2020, https://theintercept.com/2020/03/16/tiktok-app-moderators-users-discrimination/

natural disasters, videos that showed "defamation....towards civil servants, political or religious leaders" and other material that might threaten "national security" have been suppressed as well as those showing rural poverty, slums, beer bellies, and crooked smiles.[307]

Instagram released guidelines in December 2020 stating that if a post is unintentionally sexual but still arousing, it could be banned. Given the over-sexualisation of women and their bodies, it seems impossible this would not disproportionately impact women. Even "excessive cleavage" could get a photo removed, which critics warn is a dog-whistle for fat-phobia.[308]

As noted elsewhere in this book and even without getting into the use of violence (both actual and threatened), women have been silenced in countless ways throughout history—but it's important to acknowledge that it is still happening, overtly, today. One particularly ironic case of a young woman's work being censored arose in 2024, when Girl Scout Kate Lindley chose to launch an anti-censorship campaign for her Gold Award project, which is the highest honor a Girl Scout can achieve in the United States. Her Free to Read initiative included establishing book nooks in her Virginia area with books banned by the local school board and a Free to Read app with information on book bans and their negative impact. Lindley and the other Gold Award Scouts then received proclamations from the Hanover Board of Supervisors, recognising their achievements. But Lindley's – which originally included the details and context of her project – had all mentions of book banning and censorship removed. None of the other young women's project details were changed.[309]

---

307 McCluskey, Megan, "These Creators Say They're Still Being Suppressed for Posting Black Lives Matter Content on TikTok," *Time*, July 22, 2020, https://time.com/5863350/tiktok-black-creators/
308 "Social Media Censorship: The Modern Weapon of Patriarchy," The Vintage Woman, https://thevintagewomanmagazine.com/social-media-censorship/
309 Ulatowski, Rachel, "Book Banners Reach New Low, Censoring Girl Scout Project That Fought Censorship." The Mary Sue, April 23, 2024, https://www.themarysue.com/book-banners-censor-girl-scout-project-that-fought-censorship/

MEDIA REPRESENTATION

"I'm not going to limit myself just because people won't accept the fact that I can do something else."
—Dolly Parton[310]

Dramatisations also have a significant impact on how we perceive the past. Imagine, for instance, if Henry Wadsworth Longfellow had chosen, instead of Paul Revere, to immortalize the story of Sybil Ludington in verse. Her nighttime ride was the more impressive feat, to be sure—she was 16, to Revere's 41, when she rode 40 miles, compared to Revere's 12.5 miles. He was one of dozens of riders that night and, unlike Sybil, he got caught and didn't actually complete his task. Sybil, on the other hand, was successful when she rode to warn the roughly 400 militiamen under her father's command that British troops were planning to raid Danbury, Connecticut, where the Continental Army had a supply depot. On the way, she woke people in their homes, reportedly yelling "The British are burning Danbury!" Previously, the teen had saved her father from capture by 50 Loyalists. When the mob approached their home, Sybil lit candles around the house and had her siblings march in front of the windows in military fashion, creating the illusion that troops were guarding the house and causing the Loyalists to flee.

Yet even the national Daughters of the American Revolution, in 1996, said that the evidence was not strong enough to support their criteria for a war heroine, and they removed a book about her from their headquarters' bookstore. However, the

---

310 Devaney, Susan, "11 Of Dolly Parton's Greatest Quotes On Life, Love And Everything Else In Between," *Vogue*, January 19, 2022, https://www.vogue.co.uk/arts-and-lifestyle/gallery/dolly-parton-best-quotes

DAR chapter near her historic home says that her exploit was documented, and it continues to honour her.[311] This is an example of how oral histories are often dismissed, where written records are valued more highly—ignoring the long history of oral traditions, and the fact that not everyone had the luxury of literacy, time to write, and being valued enough to have their papers preserved. This is why even fictionalised accounts can contribute to preserving legacies—if they're done well.

Washington Irving's highly fictionalised *A History of the Life and Voyages of Christopher Columbus*, published in 1828, is the source of much of the glorification and myth-making around the genocidal asshole who couldn't even find India. Combined with the desire of Italian-Americans to use the Italian Columbus to cement their connection to the United States, this led to the creation of a national holiday and the ludicrous claim that he "discovered" an already inhabited land that many Europeans had already been to.[312] In reality, with the mindset that "With fifty men we could subjugate them all and make them do whatever we want" (as he wrote in his journal), he and his men tortured, enslaved, raped, and killed thousands of Indigenous people en masse and didn't even find what they were after—gold—because there was simply none to be found. In two years, half of the 250,000 native Arawaks on Haiti were dead, either through murder, mutilation, or suicide. By 1550, there were only 500 and by 1650, the Arawaks had been wiped out from the island.[313]

Ecuadorian revolutionary Manuela Sáenz helped free South America from colonial Spanish rule and was one of the first recipients of the Order of the Sun, Peru's highest distinction. Yet after the revolution, Sáenz effectively faded from literature. Between 1860 and 1940 only three Ecuadorian writers mentioned her and her participation within the revolution, and largely portrayed her as either exclusively the lover of Simón Bolívar or as incapable and wrongfully participating within the political sphere. These portrayals also assured her femininity as a

---

311   Hunt, Paula D, "Sybil Ludington, the Female Paul Revere: The Making of a Revolutionary War Heroine," *The New England Quarterly*, Vol 88 no 2, 2015): 187–222, https://www.jstor.org/stable/24718670

312   Gandhi, Lakshmi, "How Columbus Sailed into U.S. History, Thanks to Italians," *NPR*, October 14, 2013, https://www.npr.org/sections/codeswitch/2013/10/14/232120128/how-columbus-sailed-into-u-s-history-thanks-to-italians,

313   Zinn, Howard, "The Real Christopher Columbus," *Jacobin*, October 10, 2016, https://jacobin.com/2016/10/the-real-christopher-columbus-2

mainstay of her characterisation. However, there was a significant shift in how she was viewed and characterized in the 1940s. Literature like *Papeles De Manuela Sáenz* (1945), a compilation of documents around the life of Bolívar, effectively disproved popular stereotypes about Sáenz. Ideas about her being sexually deviant, hyper feminine, and incapable were replaced by more favourable portrayals as the 20th century progressed. Shifts in her portrayals were consistent with ideological changes within Latin America, like the increase in feminism of the 1980s and nationalism of the 1960s – 1970s. Portrayals within the novel *The General in His Labyrinth* (1989) by Gabriel García Márquez and Alfonso Rumazo's nonfictional *Manuela Saenz La Libertadora del Libertador* (1962) added to her humanisation within popular culture and helped politicize her image. Sáenz became increasingly popular with radical Latin American feminist groups and her image was commonly used as a rallying point for Indo-Latina causes of the 1980s. The image of Sáenz riding horseback in men's clothing, popularized by her portrayal in *The General in His Labyrinth*, was re-enacted by female demonstrators in Ecuador in 1998. [314]

Similarly, these dramatisations can turn the camera lens into proverbial "rose-coloured glasses"—for example, in the 2020 film *Wonder Woman 1984*, even the Smithsonian Institution acknowledged that the depiction of its National Museum of Natural History as a workplace was presented as much more diverse than it would have been at the time, with more women and people of colour than would have been accurate.[315] More often, however, women are left out of books, films, and other "based on a true story" media, while people of colour are pushed to the background for white—and whitewashed—leads.

Take the 2021 film *The Dig*, based on a novel of the same name about a real archaeological dig in late-1930s Britain. Writing for *The Times*, Mark Bridge noted that the film portrayed archaeologist Peggy Piggott as inexperienced (even bumbling), and someone who was only hired because her light weight would not disturb

---

[314] Murray, Pamela S, "'Loca' or 'Libertadora'?: Manuela Sáenz in the Eyes of History and Historians, 1900-c.1990," *Journal of Latin American Studies*, Vol 33 no 2: 291–310, https://www.jstor.org/stable/3653686.
[315] Thulin, Lila, "How 'Wonder Woman 1984' Was Filmed at the Smithsonian," *Smithsonian Magazine*, 2021, https://www.smithsonianmag.com/smithsonian-institution/how-wonder-woman-1984-was-filmed-smithsonianand-what-it-would-have-really-been-diana-work-there-180976778/

the delicate site. In reality, by 1939, Piggott was an experienced archaeologist in her own right, and had earned archaeology degrees from the University of Cambridge and the University of London. She was also presented as married to an older, more experienced male archaeologist, when in fact her husband was only 29 to her 27 (they had met while both were students). Meanwhile, the head archaeologist was in his late 30s but is played by an actor in his 60s, while the female lead, landowner Edith Pretty, was in her mid-50s but is played by 34-year-old Carey Mulligan (replacing Nicole Kidman, who would have been in her early 50s). By presenting men as older, they are also presented as more experienced, mature, and authoritative.

Then there is the addition of the fictional Rory Lomax as a love interest for Piggott—not only is this not necessary, but it also adds to the insistence that she not be taken seriously as a professional who is there to do a job. Making matters worse is that Lomax's function on the site is as photographer. In reality, two local schoolmistresses, Mercie Lack and Barbara Wagstaff, extensively photographed the site and were completely excluded from both novel and film just to create a romantic storyline that further undermines and trivializes Piggott's contributions as a professional doing her work.[316]

In the 2001 miniseries *Uprising*, about Jewish resistance fighters in the Warsaw ghetto, Judy Batalion writes in her non-fiction book, *The Light of Days: The Untold Story of Women Resistance Fighters in Hitler's Ghettos*, that women leaders were turned into minor characters, merely the girlfriends of the male protagonists. The only female lead is Tosia Altman, and while she is shown fearlessly smuggling weapons, she is presented as a beautiful, shy girl taking care of her sick father, passively swept up into the resistance. In actuality, Tosia was a leader of the Young Guard movement long before the war, with a reputation as a brazen glam girl. By rewriting her into a more palatable version, *Uprising* discarded not only her truth, but the context and realities that formed her.[317]

---

316 Bridge, Mark, "Netflix Drama the Dig Unfair on Sutton Hoo Archaeologist Peggy Piggott," *The Times*, January 29, 2021, https://www.thetimes.co.uk/article/netflix-drama-fails-to-dig-out-the-ancient-truth-of-sutton-hoo-728srdndr
317 Batalion, Judith, *The Light of Days: The Untold Story of Women Resistance Fighters in Hitler's Ghettos* (William Morrow, 2021).

Disney's 2020 *Mulan* was a disaster—a box office bomb loathed by critics and audiences alike—but it's worth noting that it could have been even worse. In the original script, Mulan, the legendary heroine of the tale, is secondary to a white merchant attracted to her due to his exoticised views of Chinese women. After then actually falling in love with her, he becomes involved in the war in order to protect her & and ends up saving China himself.[318] Like other films that actually got made—*The Last Samurai*, *Dances with Wolves*, and *The Last of the Mohicans*, to name a few—white male gatekeepers have taken stories of people of colour and recentered them on the completely unnecessary addition of a white male saviour.

More broadly, media teaches us how to behave, what is important, and how to expect we should be treated. And if you're a woman, it's ... not great. In a lot of ways.

First there are the movies where women don't talk even when they're the title character—classic kids' movies like *Sleeping Beauty* and *The Little Mermaid* are perhaps the worst offenders, as the title characters spend much of those films unconscious or mute. But even more recently, a 2017 analysis of family films by the Geena Davis Institute found that male characters had twice as much screen time and speaking time, compared to female characters.[319]

And it's certainly not just children's media. Helen Hunt won an Oscar for *The Piano* (1993), where she plays a mute character. In 2019, critics noted the lack of dialogue for Margot Robbie's Sharon Tate in *Once Upon a Time in Hollywood*. The character, ostensibly one of three leads, has less than 50 lines in the entire movie, many of which are whispered to her husband. When a journalist questioned director Quentin Tarantino about this, he denied the quite obvious, saying "I reject your hypothesis."[320]

The Center for the Study of Women in Television and Film at San Diego State University analysed the 3,100 characters in the top-grossing films in 2021. Their

---

318 Yuill, Bessie, "Before She Was a Warrior Heroine, Mulan Was Rescued by a White Savior," *Slate Magazine*, September 16, 2020, https://slate.com/culture/2020/09/mulan-disney-remake-china-history.html
319 "The See Jane 100," Geena Davis Institute on Gender in Media, https://seejane.org/research-informs-empowers/the-see-jane-100/
320 Cohen, Anne, "Margot Robbie's Lack of Dialogue in 'Once upon a Time In...Hollywood' Tells a Sadder Story," Refinery 29, July 27, 2019, https://www.refinery29.com/en-us/2019/07/238814/margot-robbie-as-sharon-tate-once-upon-a-time-in-hollywood-dialogue

findings included:

> Eighty-five percent of films featured more male than female characters, but only 7 percent of films had more female than male characters.
>
> Females made up only 34 percent of all speaking characters, declining from 36 percent in 2020.
>
> Women comprised only 35 percent of major characters, those who appeared in more than one scene and were considered instrumental to the story.
>
> Major female characters were younger than major male characters. Almost twice as many major male characters (11 percent) as female characters (6 percent) were aged 60 and above.
>
> In the top-grossing films, 31 percent featured female protagonists—a slight increase from 2020's 29 percent—57 percent featured male protagonists and 12 percent had a combination. [321]

There is also the hyper-competent female sidekick trope, perhaps best epitomised by Hermione Granger of the *Harry Potter* franchise. This is where the woman or girl, despite being the smartest, most badass, or otherwise most capable person in the room, is still relegated to sidekick because the male is the protagonist, often explained away by some form of being "the chosen one." Other examples include Sarah Walker in *Chuck* (2007-2011), Hope Van Dyne in *Ant-Man* (2015), Alice Quinn in *The Magicians* (2016-2020), Leia in *Star Wars*, and Trinity in *The Matrix* franchise. While this trope has been seen as feminist because the women are so competent, it largely tells female viewers that no matter how good they are, it still isn't their story.

Then there's the obsession with women's appearances, which undermines their value as people (real or fictional). The inherent bias of decision-makers for young, thin, conventionally attractive, able-bodied, white, cisgender women is exhausting

---

[321] Saperstein, Pat, "Only 7% of Movies in 2021 Featured More Women than Men, Study Finds," *Variety*, March 15, 2022, https://variety.com/2022/film/news/womens-roles-2021-films-men-outnumber-lauzen-study-1235204838/

for pretty much anyone, including those women who fit the mould. It results in needlessly excluding older women, as seen in *The Dig*. A 2017 report from the Media, Diversity and Social Change Initiative at the University of Southern California found that of the top 100 grossing films of 2016, only 34 had women in leading roles—only 8 of those included women over 45, compared to 29 for men over 45.[322]

In addition to the general absence of women considered fat, there is also the disturbing trend of explicitly referring to female characters as fat when the actresses are objectively thin by any sane metric—particularly in films primarily targeted at female audiences. In the 2003 ensemble romantic film *Love Actually*, the character of Natalie is repeatedly referred to as being fat, yet actress Martine McCutcheon reportedly weighs 62kg (136 pounds) and is 5 '7" (170cm).[323] Anne Hathaway's character Andy's weight and size is repeatedly brought up in *The Devil Wears Prada* (2006), with both herself and others calling her fat, not skinny, etcetera, repeatedly. While this can be seen as a critique on the fashion industry, as Cinema Blend puts it, "In no world is Anne Hathaway not skinny, let alone fat."[324] That does not, of course, stop people from fat-shaming perfectly healthy and conventionally very attractive actresses, from Greta Garbo to Carrie Fisher to Jennifer Lawrence and Emma Watson. In 2017, actress Chloë Grace Moretz, then 20, revealed that she had been told by a male co-star, who played her love interest, that he would never date her in real life because she was too big (the reason should have been that this adult man was in his 20s, and she was 15 at the time).[325] Judy Garland was reputedly fat-shamed at MGM, which she first started working for at age 13, by no less than studio head Louis B. Mayer, who reportedly told the commissary to

---

322 Schubert, Abbey, "Hollywood Is Ignoring Women over the Age of 45, and These Experts Know Why," *Mic*, August 1, 2017, https://www.mic.com/articles/183117/hollywood-is-ignoring-women-over-the-age-of-45-and-these-experts-know-why
323 Adams, Sam, "Martine McCutcheon Height Weight Bra Size Body Measurements Age Facts Ethnicity," *Celebrity Inside*, January 21, 2017, https://celebrityinside.com/body-measurements/musicians/martine-mccutcheon-height-weight-bra-size-age-facts-ethnicity/
324 Tisdale, Jerrica, "The Devil Wears Prada: 6+ Thoughts I Had While Rewatching the Movie," Cinema Blend, July 15, 2022, https://www.cinemablend.com/movies/the-devil-wears-prada-thoughts-i-had-while-rewatching-the-movie
325 Smith, Anna, "Hollywood's Grim Century of Fat-Shaming: From Greta Garbo to Chloë Grace Moretz," *The Guardian*, August 11, 2017, https://www.theguardian.com/film/2017/aug/11/hollywoods-grim-century-of-fat-shaming-from-greta-garbo-to-chloe-grace-moretz

only give her chicken broth.[326]

When we do see larger women, their weight is often tied to their sense of self-worth or identity. Rebel Wilson's character in the *Pitch Perfect* franchise is literally named Fat Amy. Films often tie weight loss to health, though newer movies like *Brittany Runs a Marathon* (2019) are upending that paradigm and characters like 1999's *Drive Me Crazy*'s "Dee" Vine (formerly "Bo" Vine) have illustrated how problematic it is. Characters like those played by Amy Schumer in *I Feel Pretty* and Rebel Wilson in *Isn't It Romantic* have character arcs of learning that they are lovable despite their weight.

And if women aren't being fat-shamed, they're likely being slut-shamed—or both! Carrie Fisher, at age 19 and 105 pounds, was told to lose weight to film the original *Star Wars* films, and then she was forced into a gold bikini. Decades later, in her fifties, she was pressured to lose 35 pounds for *The Force Awakens*.[327] Women are simultaneously told to show off their bodies and then that they should be ashamed to do so. It is the same victim-blaming mindset that asks a rape victim what they were wearing when they were assaulted. The recent Harley Quinn films present an interesting juxtaposition between the character's outfit in *Birds of Prey* (2020) and *Suicide Squad* (2016). The male-directed *Suicide Squad* had Harley in shiny briefs, fishnets, and a tight T-shirt that says, "Daddy's Little Monster" (a reference to her relationship with The Joker as his girlfriend and minion), and the male characters are shown ogling her as she puts it on. The female-directed *Birds of Prey* sees her in a loose T-shirt bearing her own name, actual shorts, and shorter pigtails that she hacked off herself after the Joker dumped her. She wears a wildly colourful coat that takes up space because she's no longer making herself small for a man. The character is also shot very differently—as *The Hollywood Reporter* put it, "In *Birds of Prey*, as opposed to *Suicide Squad*, the camera follows what Harley

---

326 "Judy the Fat Kid, Judy the Star – Poor Judy," *Detroit Free Press*, June 23, 1969, https://www.newspapers.com/article/33156414/judy_garland_remembered_69/

327 Moyer, Justin Wm, "Carrie Fisher 'Was Pressured' to Lose 35 Lbs. For New 'Star Wars' Movie," *The Washington Post*, December 2, 2015, https://www.washingtonpost.com/news/morning-mix/wp/2015/12/02/carrie-fisher-was-pressured-to-lose-35-lbs-for-new-star-wars-movie/

is doing, not how good her ass looks in the process."[328]

Yet just as women are insulted for supposed promiscuity, they are also taught that they must be attractive to "catch" a man. Countless rom-coms centre on a successful, otherwise happy, career woman who must be incomplete without a partner (pretty much always heterosexual). Katherine Heigl and Jennifer Lopez have each played multiple variations on this character, from Heigl's *The Ugly Truth*, *27 Dresses*, and *Killers* to Lopez's *The Wedding Planner*, *The Back-up Plan*, and *Marry Me*.

The sheer number of "makeover" scenes in films is perhaps incalculable, but a short list from my own childhood would include *The Princess Diaries*, *She's All That*, and *The Breakfast Club*. It's also interesting that in the finale of *Grease*, which shows both main characters having changed for the other, Sandy retains her new, hyper-sexualized look while all Danny has to do is strip off a letter-sweater and he's back to the exact same look from the rest of the film.

Then there's the objectification, where female characters are there to serve a purpose rather than to be fully formed individuals in their own right. The term "fridging" refers to the killing of a female character solely to motivate the male character(s). The female character is often underdeveloped, and the death may not even be shown, because the aftermath and the man's reaction are what is important—the term originates from a comic book scene where the Green Lantern returns home to find his girlfriend's body in a refrigerator. Many fans considered the 2019 death of Black Widow in the Marvel Cinematic Universe to be fridging, particularly when compared to how the death of Iron Man was treated in the same film. Her death was in the middle of the film and used as motivation for her male teammates to keep going with barely a pause, while his was the climax of the film and followed by a large funeral scene.[329]

Women are also presented as sexual rewards in films like *Kingsman: The Secret Service* (2014), *Dodgeball* (2004), and several Adam Sandler movies (2000's *Little Nicky*, 1995's *Billy Madison*, 1998's *The Water Boy*). Women also act as trophies in

---

328   Wardlow, Ciara, "How 'Birds of Prey' Deconstructs the Male Gaze," *The Hollywood Reporter*, February 8, 2020, https://www.hollywoodreporter.com/movies/movie-features/how-birds-prey-deconstructs-male-gaze-1277232/
329   Grady, Constance, "How Avengers: Endgame Failed Black Widow," *Vox*, May 2, 2019, https://www.vox.com/culture/2019/5/2/18524155/avengers-endgame-failed-black-widow

other contexts, but regardless of when it is sexual or not, to paraphrase *Aladdin*'s Jasmine, women are not prizes to be won.

In 2022 and 2023, Warner Brothers made an interesting pair of decisions about two DC films. First, the company decided not to release *Batgirl*, a $90 million production that was already finished, claiming it as a tax write-off. Then, the studio proceeded with plans to release *The Flash*, which ended up being considered one of the biggest box office flops in Hollywood history.[330] On one side was a Latina-led movie, featuring a trans actor playing the first trans character in any DC film and directed by two Muslims, fresh off the successful *Ms. Marvel*.[331] On the other was a film led by Ezra Miller, who had within the previous year been arrested twice, accused of grooming a victim since they were 12 years old, accused of harassing a minor and brandishing a gun in front of their family, and of exposing young children to guns and weed on his Vermont farm.[332] Warner Bros. Discovery president and CEO David Zaslav, a white man notorious for hiring other white men, defended the decision not to release *Batgirl* by saying "we're not going to put a movie out unless we believe in it."[333] He certainly made it very clear what Warner Bros. believes in.

THE EMPATHY GAP

This is, of course, part of a larger societal pattern of emphasising white men's—particularly cisgender, heterosexual, able-bodied white men's—stories and reinforcing traditional gender norms that oppress women. In media, people are less likely to connect with characters that don't look like them, meaning male gatekeepers are less likely to support women-led work. It isn't only gender—the same is true of

---

[330] Carras, Christi, "'The Flash' fizzles at the box office amid Ezra Miller controversy, studio woes," *Los Angeles Times*, June 18, 2023, https://www.latimes.com/entertainment-arts/movies/story/2023-06-18/flash-ezra-miller-box-office-warner-bros-dc

[331] Grisafi, Patricia, "Opinion | Batgirl Deserved Better," NBC News, August 7, 2022, https://www.nbcnews.com/think/opinion/batgirl-movie-warner-bros-discovery-blow-diverse-dc-comics-fans-rcna41829

[332] Holub, Christian, "Kevin Smith Says It's 'Baffling' That Warner Bros. Canceled 'Batgirl' but Not 'the Flash,'" *Entertainment Weekly*,, August 8, 2022, https://ew.com/movies/kevin-smith-says-its-baffling-that-warner-bros-canceled-batgirl-but-is-stilrelease-the-flash/

[333] Shaw, Lucas, "Warner Bros. Discovery Leadership Team Draws Ire over Diversity," *Bloomberg*, July 28, 2022, https://www.bloomberg.com/news/articles/2022-07-28/warner-bros-discovery-leadership-draws-ire-over-diversity

disability, sexuality, nationality, and other attributes. The men in charge don't relate to the stories being presented to them, so it's a harder sell to get them on board.

At the same time, consuming media featuring people different from yourself increases empathy, which would narrow the gap—but only if it gets made and seen. So, there is another catch-22—the empathy gap results in gatekeeping behaviours that reinforce the empathy gap, in a self-perpetuating cycle. This is exacerbated by the over-sexualisation of women, which reinforces the mindset of women as objects for men's gratification. A 2017 study, "The Future is Female?" from the University of Southern California's Annenberg School of Journalism's Media, Diversity and Social Change Initiative, looked at the top Hollywood films from the previous 10 years. Those films depicted more than 40 percent of young women in "sexy attire" and 35 percent with some nudity. There was also an unsurprising consistency in the types of women featured. More than 60 percent of female actors were thin, 77 percent were Caucasian, and 52 percent had heterosexual romantic relationships. Only 3 percent had disabilities and none were presented as LGBTQIA+.[334]

"Women are so used to that active empathising with the active protagonist of a male-driven plot," Meryl Streep said during a panel discussion in 2015. "That's what we've done all our lives. You read history, you read great literature, Shakespeare, it's all fellas. But they've never had to do the other thing. And the hardest thing for me, as an actor, is to have a story that men in the audience feel like they know what I feel like. That's a really hard thing. It's a very hard thing for them to put themselves in the shoes of female protagonists." [335]

Because most of the gatekeepers in these industries are white and male, it's unfortunate but not surprising when we hear about women succeeding by telling men's stories. The first woman to win the Oscar for Best Director won for a film about men. Kathryn Bigelow's *The Hurt Locker* doesn't even pass the

---

[334] Smith, Stacy L., Pieper, Katherine; Choueiti, Marc, Tofan, Artur, DePauw, Anne-Marie and Case, Ariana. 2017. "The Future Is Female? Examining the Prevalence and Portrayal of Girls and Teens in Popular Movies," Media, Diversity, & Social Change Initiative, 2017, https://assets.uscannenberg.org/docs/the-future-is-female.pdf
[335] Lang, Nico, "The Growing Gender Divide over 'Ghostbusters': Why Movies Starring Women Get Slimed by Male Critics," *Salon*, July 13, 2016, https://www.salon.com/2016/07/12/the_growing_gender_divide_over_ghostbusters_why_movies_starring_women_get_slimed_by_male_critics/

Bechdel-Wallace Test, a baseline for women's representation in film and other media. To pass, all that is required is for it to have at least two named female characters (so, not extras) who talk to each other about something other than a man for at least a two-line exchange. It's such an insanely low bar that, if applied to men, almost any film would pass, even those about women. Incidentally, the name is generally shortened to Bechdel Test, as it was first introduced in Alison Bechdel's comic strip *Dykes to Watch Out For* in 1985, but Bechdel credits her friend, Liz Wallace, with the original idea and prefers the hyphenated version.[336]

It's interesting to note that Jane Campion, the only woman nominated in the category twice, lost for *The Piano* (1993)—about a mute woman and her daughter—but won for *The Power of the Dog* (2021), another film that fails the Bechdel-Wallace Test. She also sparked controversy while accepting her Critics Choice award for the latter film by commenting, for no apparent reason, that tennis stars Serena and Venus Williams (who were also at the ceremony) don't "play against the guys like I have to." [337] Incidentally, both Williams sisters have won multiple Grand Slam titles in mixed doubles, sweeping all four of the championships in 1998 – quite literally playing against the guys,

Only Chloe Zhao—also the only woman of colour nominated for the award to date—was recognized for a women-centred film, *Nomadland* in 2021.

Dr. Claire Jenkins, Lecturer in Film and Television Studies at the University of Leicester, recognises Bigelow has received such critical acclaim in part because she generally makes films about men and masculinity.

"That's not to say there aren't feminist moments or that they can't be from a feminist perspective, but (Bigelow) definitely is making films about the male experience that tend to do well at awards. The difficulty is, most women directors aren't offered those films. At the same time as you only get rewarded if that's what you're making, you struggle to make it in the first place. You're being clobbered

---

336 Lawrence, Faith, "SPARQLing Conversation: Automating the Bechdel–Wallace Test," Paper presented at the Narrative and Hypertext Workshop, Hypertext 2011. http://nht.ecs.soton.ac.uk/2011/papers/12-flawrence.pdf
337 Wise, Alana, "Jane Campion Apologizes for Comments Made about Venus and Serena Williams," *NPR*, March 14, 2022, https://www.npr.org/2022/03/14/1086587867/jane-campion-apologizes-comments-venus-serena-williams

from two angles," Jenkins said. [338]

The first woman nominated was Lina Wertmüller for her 1975 *Seven Beauties*, which doesn't pass the Bechdel-Wallace Test. When Campion lost the first time with *The Piano*, she did win Best Screenplay and Holly Hunter and Anna Paquin both took home acting Oscars for the film, yet the directing Oscar went instead to Clint Eastwood for the hypermasculine Western *Unforgiven*. When Sofia Coppola's *Lost in Translation*, about a man's midlife crisis, lost in 2003, it was to sexual predator Roman Polanski—who the world has known was a paedophile and rapist since the 1970s—who won instead for *The Pianist*, which also fails the Bechdel-Wallace Test.

More recent years have seen the gap less pronounced, with more women-centric films being nominated but losing to ensemble pieces. Greta Gerwig's female-focused *Ladybird* lost in 2017, to Damien Chazelle for *La La Land*, and she was not even nominated for her *Little Women* (2019), though the film itself was nominated for six Oscars including Best Picture and Best Adapted Screenplay (written by Gerwig). Meanwhile Emerald Fennell lost for *Promising Young Woman* (2020) to Bong Joon-ho for *Parasite*. No women were nominated in 2023, following Zhao and Campion's back-to-back wins. Gerwig was again snubbed for the phenomenal *Barbie* in 2024, and while Justine Triet was nominated for her female-led *Anatomy of a Fall*, she lost to Christopher Nolan for the Bechdel-Wallace Test-failing *Oppenheimer*.

"I think there is a widespread belief that stories about women are less important than stories about men. This is because most stories over history have been centred around white men, so that's basically all we know," noted Melissa Silverstein, founder of Women And Hollywood, an initiative to promote gender diversity and inclusion within the global film industry. [339]

This goes far beyond the Oscars, as seen by Penelope Spheeris's *Wayne's World*, Mary Harron's *American Psycho* and Jennie Livingston's *Paris is Burning*. While

---

338 Sutton, Megan, "Why Are Women's Stories Still Being Snubbed at Hollywood Film Awards?" *Good Housekeeping*, February 7, 2020, https://www.goodhousekeeping.com/uk/lifestyle/a30794209/womens-stories-ignored-hollywood-awards/
339 Sutton, Megan, "Why Are Women's Stories Still Being Snubbed at Hollywood Film Awards?" *Good Housekeeping*, February 7, 2020, https://www.goodhousekeeping.com/uk/lifestyle/a30794209/womens-stories-ignored-hollywood-awards/

the last is certainly debatable from a gender perspective, the former two don't come anywhere near passing the Bechdel-Wallace Test and were their directors' best-known films. In the world of authors, many female writers found their greatest success with men's stories, like Mary Shelley's *Frankenstein*, J. K. Rowling and the *Harry Potter* franchise and the majority of Anne Rice's vampire novels. While Agatha Christie's Miss Marple is popular, Hercule Poirot performed better over the decades—it's also worth noting that Miss Marple debuted in a novel where she's barely a secondary character and it's narrated by a man. In the theatre realm, Julie Taymor was nominated for Tonys for other work, but she won for her stage adaptation of the Disney classic *The Lion King* (which also does not pass the Bechdel-Wallace Test). Interestingly, her 2003 biopic of Frida Kahlo, *Frida*, was nominated for six Oscars, winning two, but these did not include best director, best picture, or best original screenplay. It did win Best Makeup, which feels a bit like *Frida*'s unibrow won an Oscar but its director did not.

THE SCULLY EFFECT

Named for Gillian Anderson's character on the hit '90s show *The X-Files*, the "Scully Effect" refers to the impact that fictional role models in popular media have on encouraging girls and women to pursue paths that society might otherwise tell them not to. Specifically, a 2018 survey by the Geena Davis Institute on Gender in Media found that women who watched the show were more likely to have considered and pursued careers in STEM—science, technology, engineering and/or maths. Half of them said the character increased their interest in STEM and fans were more likely to believe young women should be encouraged to study STEM, compared to non-fans.[340]

Although that survey specifically focused on the STEM side, Anderson has also mentioned that she's heard from women who pursued law enforcement as a result of Dana Scully's influence. "We got a lot of letters all the time, and I was told quite frequently by girls who were going into the medical world or the science

---

340 "The "Scully Effect": I want to believe... in STEM," The Geena Davis Institute on Gender in Media< https://seejane.org/wp-content/uploads/x-files-scully-effect-report-geena-davis-institute.pdf

world or the FBI world or other worlds that I reigned, that they were pursuing those pursuits because of the character of Scully. And I said, 'Yay!'" [341]

Jessica Ware, a curator of invertebrate zoology at the American Museum of Natural History, is an example of the Scully Effect in action. As she told ABC Radio National in 2020, "She brought knowledge, so her contribution to the dialogue was actual evidence or facts or experimental design, or rational thought." Ware, a sci-fi fan, recalled "What I was used to seeing was a female sidekick who offered commentary that was used for humour, [or] for romantic plot." But when she and other women would gather to watch the show at university, what they saw was that "[other characters] respected her and looked to her for her guidance because she was smart. That, I think, really resonated with us." [342]

But the Scully Effect actually dates back much further than *The X-Files*—decades, in fact. Lieutenant Uhura, played by Nichelle Nichols on the original *Star Trek* series, was a major influence on a young Mae Jemison, who later became a physician, engineer, and astronaut who was the first African-American woman in space.[343]

While fictional heroes can inspire, real-life ones are even better. Jemison herself has inspired countless young women who are even now pursuing STEM careers, just as primatologist Biruté Galdikas was inspired by the work of Jane Goodall and Dian Fossey, which she was exposed to when they were featured in *National Geographic*.[344] Similarly, U.S. Supreme Court Justice Ruth Bader Ginsburg was inspired by Dorothy Kenyon, a Municipal Court Justice in 1930s New York, and women's rights activist.[345]

As a child, Joan Feynmen's mother and grandmother both tried to steer her

---

341 Johnson, Stephen, "New Study on Women Who Watched 'the X-Files' Backs up 'Scully Effect,'" Big Think, April 20, 2018, https://bigthink.com/culture-religion/study-on-female-fans-of-the-the-x-files-backs-up-scully-effect/
342 Nobel, Emma, "The Scully Effect Has Been Noted in STEM Circles for Years. And the Truth Is out There," ABC (Australian Broadcasting Corporation), August 18, 2020, https://www.abc.net.au/news/2020-08-19/x-files-and-scully-effect-real-world-phenomenon-women-in-stem/12562440
343 Jackson, Camille, "The Legacy of Lt. Uhura: Astronaut Mae Jemison on Race in Space," *Duke Today*, October 28, 2013, https://today.duke.edu/2013/10/maejemison
344 Pfeiff, Margo, "Mother to the Apes," *Reader's Digest*, Vol 143 no 855 (1993): 127–132.
345 Rosenwald, Michael S, "Ruth Bader Ginsburg Was Inspired by a Forgotten Female Trailblazer," *The Washinton Post*, December 27, 2018, https://www.washingtonpost.com/history/2018/12/27/ruth-bader-ginsburg-was-inspired-by-forgotten-female-trailblazer/

away from the sciences, believing that women's brains were incapable of understanding complex scientific concepts the way men's brains could. Her brother, future Nobel Prize-winning physicist Richard Feynman, encouraged her curiosity and interest in astronomy, but it was encountering the story of astronomer Cecilia Payne-Gaposchkin that convinced Feynman that she, too, could become a scientist. She later became a highly regarded astrophysicist, authoring more than 100 publications, making advances in our understanding of auroras and spending decades working at NASA's Jet Propulsion Lab.[346]

---

346   Seelye, Katharine Q, "Joan Feynman, Who Shined Light on the Aurora Borealis, Dies at 93," *The New York Times*, September 10, 2020, https://www.nytimes.com/2020/09/10/science/joan-feynman-dead.html

CREDIT STOLEN

"There are two kinds of people, those who do the work and those who take the credit. Try to be in the first group; there is less competition there."
—Indira Gandhi, quoting her grandfather, Pandit Motilal Nehru [347]

Artist and designer Adah Robinson never saw herself as an architect and lacked any formal training in the field. But in 1924, she was asked to submit a design for the future Boston Avenue Methodist Church in Tulsa. The committee in charge liked her concept, and she signed a contract that she would be "in charge of all things artistic, both inside and outside the building." One of her students was responsible for carrying out her designs from an architectural standpoint, leading people to give him credit for the entire project. The church is now a National Historic Landmark and considered a brilliant example of Art Deco architecture. Many people did not believe a woman capable of designing such a building during her lifetime, and her student also tried to claim to be the primary designer, which his company naturally supported. [348] A 1989 letter to the *New York Times* asserted that when the firm insisted on listing his name as designer on the church cornerstone, the church simply did not install the stone rather than do so. [349] The last straw for Robinson came in 1948, when an official at the University of Tulsa, where she had worked for 20 years as founder and chairperson of the Art Department, disputed

---

[347] "Congress President Sure to Spark New Love of Work: Indira Gandhi," *The Times of India*, February 8, 1959.
[348] Dembling, Sophia, "Who Really Designed Boston Avenue United Methodist Church?" National Trust for Historic Preservation, https://savingplaces.org/stories/who-really-designed-boston-avenue-united-methodist-church
[349] Arthur, John, "ARCHITECTURAL NOTES; Autodidact," *The New York Times*, January 8, 1989, https://www.nytimes.com/1989/01/08/arts/l-architectural-notes-autodidact-645089.html

her role in the church's design—she resigned.[350]

It's important to remember that the stories in this chapter, and indeed the entire book, **are only the ones we know about**. These are the people who've gotten caught, who have been exposed in some way. In addition to the countless untold stories that have been lost to history, there are almost certainly more examples going on even now, and the victims cannot speak up for themselves, not least for fear of professional reprisals from those in positions of power.

Alice Augusta Ball died at age 24. Though short, her academic career as a chemist in the 1910s was impressive: she was the first woman and first African American to receive a master's degree from the University of Hawai'i, and to be a chemistry professor there. She also developed the most effective treatment for leprosy of the early 20th century. After studying the kava plant for her master's thesis, Ball developed a technique to make the plant's oil injectable and able to be absorbed by the body. While it couldn't cure or fully stop the progress of leprosy indefinitely, hers was the only effective treatment available until sulfonamide drugs were developed in the 1940s.[351]

It was so good, in fact, that a white man stole her work and never credited her.

Because she died before she could publish her findings, Ball's graduate study advisor—who was also dean of the college and later university president—was able to steal her research and, after additional trials, published her work without acknowledging her at all, even naming the technique after himself. Although another colleague attempted to set the record straight, she was largely forgotten until the 1970s, when University of Hawai'i professors found records of her research and fought for recognition for her. If they hadn't, she would likely have remained unknown.

While dying young is perhaps an extreme example of why someone might not be able to defend themselves against a credit thief, there are many other factors

---

350 Synar, Edwyna, "Remember the Ladies: Boston Avenue Methodist Church Controversy," *Muskogee Phoenix*, July 28, 2022, https://www.muskogeephoenix.com/news/remember-the-ladies-boston-avenue-methodist-church-controversy/article_82e14dc5-74ac-5623-80ea-607fc219cefa.html

351 Wong, Kathleen M, "The Trailblazing Black Woman Chemist Who Discovered a Treatment for Leprosy," *Smithsonian Magazine*, March 23, 2022, https://www.smithsonianmag.com/history/the-trailblazing-black-woman-chemist-who-discovered-a-treatment-for-leprosy-180979772/

that have empowered men to glory in the stolen acclaim for women's work.

For decades, the iconic Art Nouveau beauty of Tiffany lamps was credited almost exclusively to Louis Comfort Tiffany, the artist son of the Tiffany & Company founders. But Tiffany neither crafted nor designed them, despite company ads proclaiming him the chief designer of the signature pieces and claiming that he personally oversaw the processes. These materials mentioned neither Clara Driscoll, long-time head of the women's glass-cutting department, nor the dozens of so-called "Tiffany girls" she worked with. Their artistry would have continued to go unacknowledged were it not for the 2005 discovery of hundreds of Driscoll family letters more than 60 years after Clara Driscoll's death in 1944. In the letters, it is explicit that Driscoll herself designed some of the most popular lamps, including the Wisteria, Butterfly, Fern, Poppy, and Dragonfly models. She describes making a "model of paper and linen so that Mr. Tiffany could see exactly what [her] idea was" and tells her family that, "This Dragonfly lamp is an idea that I had last summer." [352]

English chemist and crystallographer Rosalind Franklin is best known for her work on X-ray diffraction images of DNA while at King's College, London. By refining existing techniques and tools, she was able to get clearer images than her colleague Maurice Wilkins, who apparently didn't like her for personal reasons. As a result, she was able to identify the "helical structure" of DNA. One image, Photo 51, taken by her student Raymond Gosling, led to the discovery of the DNA double helix for which Francis Crick, James Watson, and Wilkins shared the Nobel Prize in Physiology or Medicine in 1962.[353]

Wilkins's main contribution seems to have been showing Watson the photo Franklin's student captured using her methods under her guidance. That was after Watson, who originally wanted to talk to Franklin, pissed her off by implying she didn't know how to interpret her own data. She actually presented her

---

352 Urist, Jacoba, "These Women Were the Real Geniuses Behind the Iconic Tiffany Lamps," *Smithsonian Magazine*, March 2024, https://www.smithsonianmag.com/smithsonian-institution/women-real-geniuses-behind-iconic-tiffany-lamps-180983699/
353 "Rosalind Franklin – Profiles in Science," National Library of Medicine, March 12, 2019, https://profiles.nlm.nih.gov/spotlight/kr/feature/biographical

findings—which included an image of the double helix—at a lecture; although Watson was there, he reportedly "didn't pay attention" during her presentation. It's also worth noting that Watson racked up decades of racist, sexist, homophobic, anti-Semitic, and even fat-shaming remarks, including offensive comments about Franklin herself.[354] In fact, Watson later had his Nobel stripped from him because of blatant racism, while Crick was a eugenicist (someone who believes only those with "desirable" traits should reproduce) and both men had a documented history of sexual harassment accusations. [355] [356] [357]

Yet, even Watson suggested that Franklin should have ideally been awarded a Nobel Prize in Chemistry. However, as Franklin died in 1958, she would have been ineligible as the Nobel committee does not award prizes posthumously. Incidentally, at the time of her death from ovarian cancer at age 37, she was leading pioneering work on the molecular structures of viruses. Her team member Aaron Klug continued her research, winning the Nobel Prize in Chemistry in 1982. So really, she should have won twice.[358]

In 1938, Austrian-Swedish physicist Lise Meitner and her lab partner Otto Hahn discovered how to split atoms, releasing incredible amounts of energy. Meitner was the first woman to become a full professor of physics in Germany but lost all of her academic positions thanks to Nazi Germany's anti-Semitic Nuremberg Laws. Meitner had fled the country but continued to collaborate with Hahn remotely. Hahn and his assistant conducted an experiment bombarding uranium with neutrons, producing barium. He wrote to Meitner, "Perhaps you can come up with some sort of fantastic explanation." Meitner realised that the uranium

---

[354] Belluz, Julia, "James Watson Has a Remarkably Long History of Sexist, Racist Public Comments," Vox, January 15, 2019, https://www.vox.com/2019/1/15/18182530/james-watson-racist

[355] "Nobel Prize Winner James Watson Stripped of Titles after Suggesting Genes Make Black People Less Intelligent," ABC News, January 13, 2019, https://www.abc.net.au/news/2019-01-14/nobel-prize-winner-james-watson-stripped-title-race-comments/10712588

[356] "Letter from Francis Crick to John T. Edsall, Fogarty International Center," National Library of Medicine, 1971, https://profiles.nlm.nih.gov/spotlight/sc/catalog/nlm:nlmuid-101584582X192-doc

[357] Hopkins, Nancy, "Nancy Hopkins' Keynote Speech Shockers," Nature Education, April 1, 2011, https://www.nature.com/scitable/forums/women-in-science/nancy-hopkins-keynote-speech-shockers-19135206/

[358] Klug, Aaron, "Nobel Lecture: From Macromolecules to Biological Assemblies," The Nobel Prize, December 8, 1982, https://www.nobelprize.org/uploads/2018/06/klug-lecture.pdf

had split into smaller elements, producing energy as it lost mass. She wrote the first theoretical explanation of the fission process, published in *Nature* in 1939. Indeed, Meitner was the one who told Hahn to test the radium in more detail, and that it was possible for the nucleus of uranium to disintegrate. Yet when the Nobel Prize for Chemistry was awarded in 1944, only Hahn was acknowledged, even though Meitner was nominated 49 times in her lifetime—including several times before the nuclear fission discovery. Hahn had the gall to depict her as only his assistant. When the Nobel Committee's decision-making process was made public 50 years later, Nobel Prize in Chemistry laureate Max Perutz wrote that "the protracted deliberations by the Nobel jury were hampered by lack of appreciation both of the joint work that had preceded the discovery and of Meitner's written and verbal contributions after her flight from Berlin." [359]

In 2016, biologist Eric S. Lander tried to erase Jennifer Doudna and Emmanuelle Charpentier from the story of the CRISPR gene-editing technology they developed. In an article for the academic journal *Cell*, he exalted the "heroes" of CRISPR. Not only did he leave the two women out and downplayed their labs' contributions, he neglected to mention that his employer, MIT and Harvard's Broad Institute, was at the time involved in a billion-dollar patent dispute with the women—clearly a major conflict of interest. The article was widely derided in the scientific community as essentially propaganda, with little to no fact-checking having been done. Doudna and Charpentier, who had filed their patent application seven months before the Broad Institute, won the 2020 Nobel Prize in Chemistry for their work.[360]

While working with Alexandre Varille at the Temple of Karnak in 1940, Egyptologist Christiane Desroches Noblecourt found herself doing all the hard work of excavation in the savage sun, heat, and violent windstorms while he did paperwork in the cool of the night. She later discovered, after the site had been shut down for

---

359 DeBakcsy, Dale, "Gone, Fission: How Lise Meitner Was Written out of the Nuclear Age," Women You Should Know, April 3, 2019, https://womenyoushouldknow.net/lise-meitner-nuclear-age/
360 Rothkopf, Joanna, "How One Man Tried to Write Women out of CRISPR, the Biggest Biotech Innovation in Decades," Jezebel, January 20, 2016, https://jezebel.com/how-one-man-tried-to-write-women-out-of-crispr-the-big-1753996281

lack of funding, that he had published all of her notes and photographs—given to him when she left Egypt—under his own name, never once mentioning her.

It was a foreshadowing of things to come. For years, Desroches Noblecourt spearheaded an international campaign to save 22 Nubian monuments in Egypt and Sudan, which would have been submerged by the lake created as a result of the construction of the Aswan High Dam. Yet when all was said and done, her partner in the endeavour, Egyptian Minister of Culture Tharwat Okasha, tried to erase her from the story. In a long essay about the project, he failed to mention her role in engaging UNESCO—a key partner—at the beginning, painting it as something he had done entirely on his own. She is mentioned in one sentence of one footnote.

In contrast, the third member of the trio that had led the campaign, Assistant Director-General of UNESCO René Maheu, wrote to her that "After this extraordinary accomplishment, how can I not think of you, who pulled me in, guided me and took me on the most marvelous adventure of my life?"

Even when others told the story of her vital role in print and broadcast media years later, Okasha would go out of his way to actively dispute the truth. In response, Torgny Säve-Söderbergh, a Swedish archaeologist who had worked on the project from the start, wrote that Okasha and other Egyptian officials had expressed sad resignation and paralysing overwhelm when the idea of saving the temples was first put forth. Indeed, he stated, it was only Desroches Noblecourt's belief that it was possible that changed their minds. Fortunately, she and her work were too well-known for Okasha to rewrite history, and her contributions were acknowledged by many others both at the time and in the decades since. [361]

The most widely seen depiction of U.S. President Franklin D. Roosevelt is inarguably his portrait engraved in profile on the 10-cent dime. Yet African American sculptor Selma Hortense Burke's initials are not the ones inscribed in the tiniest of fonts on each coin—instead, it's a JS, for John Sinnock, who served as the U.S. Mint's Chief Engraver from 1925 to 1947. Sinnock basically duplicated Burke's work, which had been done for a plaque honouring the president, who modelled

---

361 Olson, Lynne, *Empress of the Nile: The Daredevil Archaeologist Who Saved Egypt's Ancient Temples from Destruction* (Penguin Random House, 2023).

for Burke before his death. Sinnock was also accused of using sketches by another artist, John Frederick Lewis, in the design for the Sesquicentennial of Independence half-dollar coin, after Sinnock's own designs were rejected.[362]

While the Grimm brothers are well-known for "their" fairy tale collections, Wilhelm's wife Dortchen Wild went uncredited for contributing a quarter of the stories in the first volume of 86 stories. But she was certainly not alone—other largely unacknowledged sources included sisters Jeanette, Marie and Amalie Hassenpflug (who collectively contributed around 40 stories), Dorothea Viehmann (21 to 40+), and Jenny von Droste zu Hülshoff (six). Viehmann was the only one publicly recognized, likely because as the daughter of a tavern owner and widow of a tailor, she fit the brothers' marketing, which claimed their sources were the common peasant folk, rather than members of their own bourgeois social circles.[363]

In the case of the brilliant cryptanalyst Elizebeth Smith Friedman, it was not one individual but an entire government agency that wanted credit for her work. With her husband William, Elizebeth broke the most difficult codes of several foreign powers and designed unbreakable encryption machines, among other accomplishments during both World Wars and Prohibition. She was sworn to secrecy by J. Edgar Hoover's FBI, which then basked in the warmth of her achievements even as their blunders interfered with her work. Elizebeth, who actually worked for the Coast Guard at the time, was frustrated, but had no control over the distribution of information, even as FBI employees testified in open court about the highly confidential breaking of codes. The breaking point came after the FBI used intelligence from intercepted and decoded transmissions from Nazi spies in South America. The FBI staged a campaign that caught some of the spies, but caused the rest to change their methods and any future intelligence was lost. This finally led to other agencies freezing out the FBI, withholding information that Hoover and his cronies would not be trusted with.

Along with publishing an official history that excluded the contributions of

---

[362] Djossa, Christina Ayele, "Who Really Designed the American Dime?" *Atlas Obscura*, January 17, 2018, https://www.atlasobscura.com/articles/who-designed-american-dime-selma-burke-franklin-roosevelt
[363] Paradiz, Valerie, *Clever Maids: The Secret History of the Grimm Fairy Tales* (Basic Books, 2009).

UNCREDITED

other agencies, Hoover even hired film director Frank Capra to make a propaganda piece about the FBI's work, completely leaving out Elizebeth's role. This was the same agency that would send agents to South America without speaking the local languages—in at least one instance, they gave a man a crash course in basic Spanish before sending him to Brazil, where he discovered the primary language was in fact Portuguese.

It was not the first time Elizebeth's contributions were erased by men. In her early days as a codebreaker, she and William developed the *Riverbank Publications* (published 1917-1919), which laid the groundwork for future codebreakers. Their eccentric millionaire employer published these primarily with only William's name—Elizebeth was only credited as co-author on one of the ten. Yet given the equal nature of their collaboration, it seems highly unlikely that this represented the full extent of her work, not least because her handwriting is all over the drafts. In a letter, William also referred to the documents as "our" pamphlets.

While these are both instances of powerful men loathe to give anyone else—male or female—credit when they could take it for themselves, it is noteworthy that Hoover was also a blatant chauvinist. The FBI had three female agents when he took over in 1922. Believing that women were incapable of being agents because they couldn't be taught to fire a gun, he got rid of them, and there wasn't another woman agent until after his death in 1972. [364]

---

364 Fagone, Jason, *The Woman Who Smashed Codes: A True Story of Love, Spies, and the Unlikely Heroine Who Outwitted America's Enemies* (Dey St., 2018).

WHEN OTHERS MISATTRIBUTE

"Errors are notoriously hard to kill, but an error that ascribes to a man what was actually the work of a woman has more lives than a cat."
—Hertha Ayrton[365]

Jackson Pollock is known for dripping and flinging paint across canvases—but although he popularized the style, he did not invent it, as is often claimed and assumed. Starting in 1938, the Ukrainian-born Janet Sobel was creating works using the technique years before Jackson. Her complete lack of artistic training was likely an asset, allowing her to play with the paint in a natural way without worrying about the "right" approach. As the BBC relayed, "With no inculcated allegiance to any artistic school or prejudice regarding the appropriateness of materials, Sobel began playing both with what a painting can say and how it can say it. Using unconventional implements such as glass eye-droppers to squirt paint and the strong suck of a vacuum to drag wet splatters into thin gossamers that no traditional brush could spin, she assaulted the surface of canvases laid out on the floor, orchestrating a liquid lyricism of spills, splashes and spits the likes of which had never before been seen."

Given the attention she gained in the art world, Pollock certainly was familiar with her work before undertaking similar techniques. It is documented that he attended an exhibition of her work in 1945 and was impressed by it. Just as she was starting to gain recognition, her husband decided to move the family, cutting

---

[365] Mason, Jona, "Hertha Ayrton (1854-1923) and the Admission of Women to the Royal Society of London," Notes and Records of the Royal Society of London, Vol 45 no 2 (July 1991), p. 201-220. https://www.jstor.org/stable/531699

off her access to the New York City arts scene. Worse, she developed an allergy to an ingredient in paint, making it impossible for her to continue with the medium. She died in obscurity while Pollock skyrocketed to fame.[366]

The stealing of credit is not always done by the man being credited, but rather by the male public on that man's behalf, on the basis that no woman could have done that (an attitude sprinkled throughout different sections of this book). While this is sometimes done with historians about those long dead and therefore unable to chime in, we often see it with contemporaneous works. It is then up to the man to either stand up for his colleague or take the undue credit with a shrug and a "what are you gonna do?" The answer, dear friends, is you tell the truth, like Dr. Andrew Chael did in 2019.

Chael was part of an Event Horizon Telescope team led by Dr. Katie Bouman. When the first picture of a black hole was taken, it was largely due to the work Bouman and her team had done in developing an algorithm to make it possible. Thanks in part to an adorable photo of the 29-year-old Bouman's excitement when the image was generated, she was getting a fair bit of attention at the time. Even though Bouman never tried to take sole credit, always calling the work a team effort, affronted men latched onto Chael as the "real" source of the brilliant work. These Internet trolls claimed Chael wrote 850,000 of the 900,000 lines of code for the project, that he did all the real work, and the attention on Bouman was just feminist media wanting to hold up an undeserving woman as responsible.[367]

Chael wasn't having any of it. He posted a Twitter thread refuting the claims and denouncing the "awful and sexist attacks on my colleague and friend Katie Bouman." Chael added, "if you are congratulating me because you have a sexist vendetta against Katie, please go away and reconsider your priorities in life."[368]

Compare this to Truman Capote. The childhood friend of Harper Lee never

---

366 Grovier, Kelly, "Janet Sobel: The Woman Written out of History," BBC. March 8, 2022, https://www.bbc.com/culture/article/20220307-janet-sobel-the-woman-written-out-of-history
367 Lou, Michelle and Ahmed, Saeed, "To Undermine Katherine Bouman's Role in the Black Hole Photo, Trolls Held up a White Man as the Real Hero — until He Fought Back," CNN, April 12, 2019, https://edition.cnn.com/2019/04/12/us/andrew-chael-katie-bouman-black-hole-image-trnd/index.html
368 Chael, Andrew, Twitter, April 11, 2019, https://twitter.com/thisgreyspirit/status/1116518544961830918

publicly refuted claims that he was the true author behind her classic American novel *To Kill A Mockingbird*, of which there is no evidence. Capote, the writer behind *In Cold Blood* and *Breakfast at Tiffany's*, was known to be petty, jealous and attention-seeking, so it's no surprise that he would be happy to take credit where it was not due, even if he never verifiably claimed it himself. Some claim the rumour started with literary critic Pearl Belle, to whom Capote may have implied that he wrote or significantly contributed to the book. Though this cannot be verified, it would not be out of character for Capote to have hinted at a falsehood like this, even if he did not go so far as to lie outright. Indeed, when his own book *In Cold Blood* came out, Lee herself was mentioned in the dedication (alongside Capote's lover), yet she was not properly acknowledged for the months of research that she contributed to the groundbreaking non-fiction novel. Reportedly, it was Lee's down-to-earth manner—a marked contrast to Capote's flamboyance—that won the trust of the rural Kansans, facilitating the interviews that made the book possible. [369] [370]

We cannot know for certain who the anonymous author of *Blue-stocking Hall* (1827) and *Tales of my time* (1829) truly was, but we can be quite sure it was not William Pitt Scargill. For more than 150 years, they have been misattributed to him even though reviews and advertisements of the time clearly indicate that it was common knowledge that the unknown novelist was female. The publisher's archives indicate they were written by a "Mrs. Wilmot," possibly Alicia Wilmot, though this could have been a pseudonym. Wilmot's sister-in-law Anna Maria Chetwood has also been suggested as a candidate. The only basis for the misattribution was an 1832 review of an actual Scargill novel that speculated he might have written the other two—even that reviewer acknowledged his guess "may be wrong" as the only indication was "the internal evidence of a family resemblance." On that flimsiest of bases, many sources, even reputable reference

---

[369] Block, Michelle, "Letter Puts End to Persistent 'Mockingbird' Rumor," NPR, March 3, 2006, https://www.npr.org/templates/story/story.php?storyId=5244492
[370] "7 facts about the elusive Harper Lee," Readers Digest, January 1, 2015, https://www.readersdigest.co.uk/culture/books/meet-the-author/7-facts-about-the-elusive-harper-lee

materials, continue to attribute a woman's work to a man who never claimed it.[371]

Written in 1829, the piano composition "Easter Sonata" was believed lost for more than 140 years, until the original manuscript was discovered in a French book shop, with the signature "F Mendelssohn." The "F" was assumed to stand for Felix, but later analysis confirmed in 2010 that it was in fact his sister Fanny's. Described as "masculine," "violent," and "ambitious," it is little wonder her composition would be mistaken for his, given how much he plagiarized her work.[372]

Italian Baroque painter Artemisia Gentileschi was a badass. Considered one of the most accomplished, progressive, and expressive painters of the 1600s, she was producing professional-level work by the time she was 15. And yet many of her paintings have been attributed to men, often for decades. Her 1612 *Danae* and 1610 *Susanna and the Elders* were originally attributed to her father Orazio but re-evaluated in the late 1990s.

One of her paintings went misattributed for almost 40 years—even though she literally signed her name in the middle of the image. Her *David with the Head of Goliath* first surfaced on the auction market in 1975 and was attributed to her father's student Giovanni Francesco Guerrieri. In 1996, art historian Gianni Papi suggested it was actually Gentileschi's work, yet when it came up for auction again in 2018, it was still initially attributed to "a seventeenth-century painter of the school of Caravaggio." When a conservator finally was enlisted to clean the painting, they found her signature on the hilt of David's very large sword.

It is only because of her reinvigorated prominence in the 20th and 21st centuries that curators, collectors, and other art professionals are even questioning the attributions of paintings in her style. It's clear that obscurity can be self-reinforcing—we don't know to look for what we are unaware of. There is also a financial gain in some instances—in that 2018 auction of the David painting,

---

371   Byrne, Angela, "Anonymity, Irish Women's Writing, and a Tale of Contested Authorship: Blue-Stocking Hall (1827) and Tales of my Time (1829)," Proceedings of the Royal Irish Academy Section C: Archaeology, Celtic Studies, History, Linguistics and Literature, February 27, 2019, https://pure.ulster.ac.uk/ws/portalfiles/portal/76340278/procriasectc.119.1.AOP.Byrne.pdf

372   Hawkins, Dere, "A Mendelssohn Masterpiece Was Really His Sister's. After 188 Years, It Premiered under Her Name," *The Washington Post*, March 9, 2017, https://www.washingtonpost.com/news/morning-mix/wp/2017/03/09/a-mendelssohn-masterpiece-was-really-his-sisters-after-188-years-it-premiered-under-her-name/

the attribution was changed at the last minute to Gentileschi. While it would be nice to assume this was for accuracy purposes and giving a female artist the benefit of the doubt, it should not be ignored that with Gentileschi's renewed fame, a painting with her name (literally) on it would sell for more than one by "a seventeenth-century painter of the school of Caravaggio." Her *Lucretia* sold in 2019 for €4.8 million (US$6.1 million). [373]

Gentileschi is far from alone in this. For years, Canadian painter Caroline Louisa Daly's works were misattributed to not one but two men. In 1969, nearly a century after she painted them, the Confederation Centre Art Gallery in Charlottetown, Prince Edward Island, purchased four pieces showing historical scenes of the town, signed "C.L. Daly" from a collector in Montreal. The seller claimed they were the work of John Corry Wilson Daly, a businessman and the first mayor of the Ontario town of Stratford. After a bit of—but clearly not enough—research, the gallery staff decided the paintings were really by Charles Daly, a municipal bureaucrat in Toronto who was also an artist and art teacher. Years later, when the gallery acquired two more pieces signed C.L. Daly, they were automatically attributed to Charles Daly as well. It was only in the 2010s, with the help of the Internet, that the discrepancies started showing. There is no indication of either male Daly having the middle initial L, nor that either had ever visited Prince Edward Island. Gallery registrar Paige Matthie was able to connect the pieces to Caroline based on various records and examples of her work in family files—nothing to indicate that she had ever been recognized publicly as a professional-level artist. This, combined with male-centric assumptions about who makes art, likely contributed to the misattributions, Matthie said. "I think it also comes down to what's top of mind when you think of an artist. Most think of a male image," she said. "Women were allowed to be subjects, the sitter. Although they were doing art in many forms, it just wasn't taken seriously." [374]

---

[373] Katz, Brigit, "Once Attributed to a Male Artist, 'David and Goliath' Painting Identified as the Work of Artemisia Gentileschi," *Smithsonian Magazine*, March 5, 2020, https://www.smithsonianmag.com/smart-news/painting-david-and-goliath-once-attributed-male-artist-revealed-work-artemisia-gentileschi-180974312/

[374] Peters, Diane, "Caroline Louisa Daly Is Finally Getting Her Due," *JSTOR Daily*, June 28, 2017, https://daily.jstor.org/caroline-louisa-daly-is-finally-getting-her-due/

French portrait painter Marie-Denise Villers's most famous painting, *Portrait of Charlotte du Val d'Ognes/Young Woman Drawing* (1801) was attributed to Jacques-Louis David, under whom she studied. This may have been an honest mistake due to similarities in style, or it could have been deliberate as David was the better-known painter. Even after the Metropolitan Museum of Art acquired the painting in 1917, it was decades before curator Charles Stirling, in 1951, verified the painting was first exhibited at the 1801 Paris Salon. Because David had boycotted the event that year, he could not have painted *Young Women Drawing*. Stirling proposed that a woman may have been the artist, but it took another four decades until Margaret Oppenheimer identified Villers through in-depth research of David's students. Art historian Anne Higonet argues it's actually a self-portrait, as the features resemble a painting of Viller by her sister Marie-Victoire Lemoine. This theory supposes that the family who bought it renamed it *Portrait of Charlotte du Val d'Ognes* after purchase, which would support the idea that they knowingly lied about the painting's creator, a deception that lasted more than 100 years.[375]

Chemist, mineralogist, and meteorologist Claudine Picardet was one of the most prolific scientific translators of the 1780s. Working in the Bureau de traduction de Dijon at Dijon Academy, she translated three books and thousands of papers on topics including chemistry, mineralogy, and astronomy from Swedish, English, German, and Italian into her native French, even creating new words when none existed that served the meanings. The Bureau group also replicated experiments to confirm instructions and results from the original texts. Picardet was the Bureau's only non-academic and only woman. As well as being more productive than any of her colleagues, she was the only one to work in so many languages and the only one publishing in journals other than the Parisian *Annales de chimie*. Yet some later writers have credited others in the group for work that Picardet produced, starting with of all things her obituary. When she died in 1820, lawyer and journalist Claude-Nicolas Amanton wrote of the "very beautiful woman" and

---

375 Tsaleza, Anastasia, "Women Artists Whose Works Were Misattributed to Men | DailyArt Mag," Daily Art Magazine – Art History Stories, May 26, 2020, https://www.dailyartmagazine.com/women-artists-works-misattributed/

referred to "her reputation as a woman of remarkable beauty"—while he mentioned her wit, that she was learned and that men of science and literature sought her company, he credited the men of the Bureau for her accomplishments.[376] It has also been suggested that the French translation of the first two volumes of *Opuscula physica et chemica* (originally written in Latin), which was published under the name of the Bureau's leader, was actually the work of several uncredited translators including Picardet.[377]

In the 1940s, Kathleen Antonelli, Betty Jean Jennings Bartik, Frances "Betty" Holberton, Marlyn Meltzer, Frances Spence, and Ruth Teitelbaum collaborated to program ENIAC, the world's first programmable, electronic, general-purpose digital computer. They had to learn to program without a programming language or tools, because they simply did not exist yet. But from the first demonstration on February 15, 1946—which Betty and Betty Jean wrote the program for—they received no recognition. The programmers were not even invited to the gala dinner afterward for "government and scientific men," as reported by *The New York Times*. Herman Goldstine, who oversaw the project for the U.S. Army, claimed that he and his wife Adele—who was a programmer and did write the original technical manual for the ENIAC—had programmed that first successful demonstration for the VIPs, which Betty Jean later declared a "boldface lie." Some historical images caption the women as models, rather than actual staff. When the U.S. Army used a War Department publicity photo for a recruitment ad, they cropped out the three women in the photo, and the department's press releases credited a vague "group of experts" for the work, naming only Goldstine and ENIAC designers John Mauchly and J. Presper Eckert. This fundamentally ignored that the machine Mauchly and Eckert designed would never have functioned without the work of the programmers.

In the 1980s, Harvard University student Kathy Kleiman came across a photo of the women with ENIAC while researching her thesis on early programmers and software developers. When she enquired about the images, she was told the women

---

376 Bret, Patrice, "The letter, the dictionary and the laboratory: translating chemistry and mineralogy in eighteenth-century France," *Annals of Science*, Vol 73 no 2 (2015): 122–142.
377 Bret, Patrice, "Picardet, Claudine," *Complete Dictionary of Scientific Biography* (Charles Scribner's Sons, 2008).

were models, hired to make the image more appealing. Fortunately, Kleiman kept digging, discovered the women's story and launched the ENIAC Programmers Project to get them the recognition they should have received decades earlier. [378]

American photographer Lee Miller's career took a fascinating journey from fashion model to war correspondent. In between being on the cover of *Vogue* and documenting World War II from the London Blitz to the liberation of Paris, to the concentration camps at Buchenwald and Dachau, Miller travelled to Paris in 1929 to apprentice herself to the surrealist artist and photographer Man Ray. Miller became his student, model, collaborator, muse, and, no surprise, his lover. She began her own photo studio and would often photograph his fashion assignments for him so that he could focus on painting. They worked together so closely during the time that some of her photographs are credited to him. Reputedly, during a fight over the attribution of work they produced together, he slashed an image of her through the neck with a razor. [379]

There are likely to be more such discoveries in the years to come. In 2022, one of Vermeer's well-known paintings, *Girl with a Flute*, was analysed and found to not be a Vermeer at all, but likely done by an associate or student. This leads to a great mystery, as there is no record of Vermeer having had either.[380] He did, however, have at least 10 children—at least seven of whom were girls—and artists at the time were not required to register their apprentices with the painters' guild if the apprentice was also their child. Given similar stories of other women, it is entirely possible one of his daughters studied their father's work and style informally but never became a professional artist. Art historian Benjamin Binstock attributed at least five "Vermeer" paintings to his oldest daughter Maertge (Anglicised as Maria) in his 2008 book *Vermeer's Family Secrets* and was promptly dismissed out of hand by mainstream academics. *Girl with a Flute* was one such painting,

---

378   Claire Lisa Evans, *Broad Band: The Untold Story of the Women Who Made the Internet* (Portfolio/Penguin, 2020).
379   "Much More than a Muse: The Art of Lee Miller and Man Ray," NPR, August 20, 2011, https://www.npr.org/2011/08/20/139766533/much-more-than-a-muse-lee-miller-and-man-ray.
380   Kim, Juliana, "Art Researchers Discover One of Dutch Artist Vermeer's Paintings Is Not Actually His," NPR, October 8, 2022, https://www.npr.org/2022/10/08/1127679191/vermeer-girl-with-a-flute-fake-forgery

which he believed was a self-portrait—a theory he put forth 14 years before the National Gallery of Art's testing.[381]

Italian Renaissance painters Lavinia Fontana and Sofonisba Anguissola were both highly successful. Fontana was the breadwinner for her family, which included 11 children, while her husband acted as her agent and took care of the household, and Anguissola was a portraitist who served in the Spanish court of King Phillip II as tutor to Queen Elizabeth of Valois and a court painter for the king. Yet, Anguissola's official title was "lady-in-waiting," which likely contributed to later misattributions, along with the fact that she rarely signed her paintings. The less talented—but male!—Alonso Sánchez Coello was the official court portrait painter, meaning that in later years he was largely given credit for her works even though he primarily worked as Anguissola's assistant. Both artists were largely ignored by historians for centuries, and both had their works misattributed to men—for Anguissola, in addition to Coello, it was artists such as Titian, Zurbaran, and Giovanni Battista Moroni; for Fontana, Guido Reni. With more than 125 works attributed to her, Fontana is now credited as having the largest extant oeuvre of any female artist prior to 1700.[382]

Composer Louise Bertin collaborated with Victor Hugo to create an operatic version of his book *Notre-Dame de Paris* (*The Hunchback of Notre Dame*). *La Esmeralda* featured music by Bertin (her fourth opera) and a libretto (words) by Hugo, making Bertin the only composer to work directly with Hugo on an opera. But almost as soon as the opera opened in 1836, Bertin was accused of receiving special privileges due to her brother's connection to the government's opera administration, with a riot erupting during the seventh performance. Although the original production was forced to close, a version of it continued to be performed over the following three years. Because Bertin had a physical disability that affected

---

381 Lawson-Tancred, Jo, "Did Vermeer Have a Daughter Who Painted Some of His Most Famous Portraits? This Art Historian Thinks So," Artnet News, March 21, 2023, https://news.artnet.com/art-world/vermeer-daughter-binstock-theory-2273118

382 McGuire, Nneka, "These Female Artists Were Forgotten — and One Woman's Work Was Even Credited to Men. Now, an Exhibit Is Making Amends," *The Lily (The Washington Post)*, December 4, 2019, https://www.thelily.com/these-female-artists-were-forgotten-and-one-womans-work-was-even-credited-to-men-now-an-exhibit-is-making-amends/

her ability to walk or stand for long periods of time, composer Hector Berlioz was hired to run the rehearsals of *La Esmeralda*, which led to claims that he had actually written music for the opera, which he adamantly denied. Bertin was so frustrated by the situation that she never wrote another opera.[383]

In some cases, it is not the work, but an achievement that others assume a man accomplished first. In 1974, Kathy Kozachenko became the first openly homosexual political candidate in the United States to win an election–three years before Harvey Milk was elected to the San Francisco Board of Supervisors in 1977. Yet, Milk is widely credited as the first, not least because his natural flamboyance and assassination the year following his election added to his name recognition. It's also worth noting that Kozachenko was only 21 and a third-party candidate when she was first elected to the Ann Arbor City Council in Michigan, while Milk was 47, had been active in politics for years, and was running in arguably the most queer-friendly city in the country (as opposed to the typically conservative Midwest), with the backing of the powerful Democratic party.[384]

It's particularly impressive when a woman's work is credited to a man who literally could not have done it. In 2019, Smithsonian Data Science Lab fellow Tiana Curry found that dozens of botanical samples collected by natural historian, botanist, and artist Mary Vaux Walcott were listed under Mary's husband's name in the Smithsonian's National Museum of Natural History database. Walcott's husband, palaeontologist and Smithsonian Secretary Charles D. Walcott, died before the samples were even collected. When the handwritten cards were scanned into the database, titles were automatically removed. When "Mrs." was removed from "Mrs. C. D. Walcott," a woman's work magically became her husband's.[385]

---

[383] Wertheimer, Melissa, "'Loudly Applauded': Composer Louise Angélique Bertin | in the Muse," The Library of Congress, January 15, 2021, https://blogs.loc.gov/music/2021/01/loudly-applauded-composer-louise-angelique-bertin

[384] Compton, Julie, "Meet the Lesbian Who Made Political History Years before Harvey Milk," NBC News, April 2, 2020, https://www.nbcnews.com/feature/nbc-out/meet-lesbian-who-made-political-history-years-harvey-milk-n1174941

[385] Cohen, Sara E, "Using Data Science to Uncover the Work of Women in Science," *Smithsonian Magazine*, March 15, 2022, https://www.smithsonianmag.com/blogs/american-womens-history-initiative/2022/03/15/using-data-science-to-uncover-the-work-of-women-in-science/

PLAGIARISM BEGINS AT HOME

"Thieves are opportunists, whether they are amateurs or professionals.
They endeavour to take advantage of any situation, which provides them a loophole.
An opportunity to take what belongs to someone else."
—Denise N. Fyffe, Thieves in the Workplace[386]

In her 2018 memoir, *This Will Only Hurt a Little*, actress Busy Philipps wrote about the origins of the 2007 sports comedy film *Blades of Glory*. The initial idea came from Philipps herself, who co-wrote the first draft of the screenplay (including a role for her to play), but her then-boyfriend movie producer Craig Cox and his brother Jeff cut her out of the process when pitching the film to producers, removed any credit to her, and told her she was "crazy" when she asked to be credited, with rumours suddenly emerging that she "stole ideas" from them.

"I had a hard time recovering. It wasn't the script. It was that I'd been so easily thrown out, like trash. I was in the way of their success, I guess? Collateral damage," Philipps wrote. "In order for them to do this insanely shitty thing to me, they vilified me and told me I was crazy. The story became that I was the one who had tried to STEAL ideas from them, that I was ALWAYS just looking out for myself. THEY had come up with this AMAZING STORY, and I was the less-than-talented girlfriend trying to glom on to their talent and carve out a piece for myself. A piece that I didn't deserve. I had a hard time figuring out what was real."[387]

Throughout this book, there are many tales of women who worked closely with

---

386   Fyffe, Denise N, *Thieves in the Workplace* (Lulu, 2015).
387   Philipps, Busy, *This Will Only Hurt a Little* (Simon & Schuster, 2018).

their husbands, brothers, or other close male relatives. Whether scientists, artists, writers, or academics, women worked with the men around them out of shared interests, financial dependence, or simply because there was no other option. That same reliance and lack of alternatives has often led to women being taken advantage of in many ways—including having their work stolen.

THE HUSBANDS

New Zealander racehorse trainer Hedwick Wilhelmina McDonald's greatest achievement was not credited to her. She trained the winner of the 1938 Melbourne Cup, but women were not allowed to be professional trainers in Australia at the time, so her husband temporarily took over the role. While his name was on the paperwork, everyone knew the success was hers. While the McDonalds did what they had to do according to the rules, there are many instances of husbands actively stealing credit for their wife's work—with or without her consent.[388]

Often held up as one of the great American novelists, it is unclear how much of F. Scott Fitzgerald's attributed work is his own—and how much was written by his wife, Zelda.[389] In addition to publishing Zelda's writing under her husband's name—as this would bring in more money—much of the writing in F. Scott's books is directly taken from words Zelda herself wrote or said. As Zelda caustically announced in The New York Tribune, after the publication of his first book *This Side of Paradise*:

> I recognize a portion of an old diary of mine which mysteriously disappeared shortly after my marriage, and also scraps of letters which, though considerably edited, sound to me vaguely familiar. In fact, Mr. Fitzgerald—I believe that is how he spells his name—seems to believe that plagiarism begins at home.[390]

---

388 Mountier, Mary, "McDonald, Hedwick Wilhelmina," Te Ara (Dictionary of New Zealand Biography), 1998, https://teara.govt.nz/en/biographies/4m6/mcdonald-hedwick-wilhelmina
389 Carrasco, Isabe, "How F. Scott Fitzgerald, Author of 'the Great Gatsby,' Plagiarized His Own Wife," Cultura Colectiva, March 25, 2019, https://culturacolectiva.com/en/art/books/scott-zelda-fitzgerald-great-gatsby-plagiarized-his-own-wife/
390 Fitzgerald, Zelda, "Friend Husband's Latest," April 2, 1922, *The New York Tribune*.

A few years later, she wrote a semi-autobiographical novel, *Save Me the Waltz*. When she sent it to her husband's publisher, Fitzgerald was enraged—not because she had used part of their life, but because he had been planning to use the same material for his own novel, *Tender Is the Night*. He forced her to remove those portions, and the book was published. Unfortunately, it was a commercial and critical flop and this, combined with her husband's criticism, calling her "plagiaristic" and a "third-rate writer" (ironic, given how much he stole from her), crushed her. It was the only novel she ever published, and she became a recluse.

Mileva Marić was a brilliant physicist and mathematician, but we'll never know all she could have accomplished because a classmate impregnated her out of wedlock and she had to give up her career to care for their children. That classmate, Albert Einstein, later divorced her after he decided he'd rather marry his cousin, though he did pay child support, including the money when he won the Nobel Prize for work they likely collaborated on together.

Mileva was the only woman in their class at Zürich Polytechnic and the second woman to complete studies in the Department of Mathematics and Physics. The couple had similar grades (her 4.7 to his 4.6) except in applied physics where she got the top mark of 5. He got a 1. She also excelled at experimental work, where he did not. She had hoped to pursue a PhD, but her pregnancy and subsequent marriage derailed that plan.

Although her husband never publicly acknowledged her contributions, contemporaneous sources, including witnesses and letters between the two, indicate that much of his work was the result of collaborations with her. He wrote to Mileva on March 27, 1901: "How happy and proud I will be when the two of us together will have brought our work on relative motion to a victorious conclusion."[391] He also reputedly declared at a social gathering, "I need my wife. She solves for me all my mathematical problems."[392] Maric also reportedly told her father in 1905 that "we finished an important scientific work which will make my husband known

---

391 Einstein, Albert, "Letter from Albert Einstein to Mileva Maric, March 27, 1901."
392 Gagnon, Pauline, "The Forgotten Life of Einstein's First Wife," Scientific American Blog Network, December 19, 2016, https://blogs.scientificamerican.com/guest-blog/the-forgotten-life-of-einsteins-first-wife/

around the world." That year, he published the theory of special relativity.[393]

Sidonie-Gabrielle Colette was a naive country girl when she met Henry Gauthier-Villars; when they married, she was 20 to his 34. So it's little surprise that he took advantage of her. In addition to cheating on her almost immediately, likely causing her to develop depression and probably giving her gonorrhoea, he convinced Colette to let him publish her first books, the massively popular and largely autobiographical *Claudine* series, under his name. He had also done this with a virtual stable of young male writers—albeit presumably without the sexually transmitted infections—paying them a pittance to produce more than 50 novels that he published under his name. He reportedly locked her in a room until she had written enough pages to satisfy him. When she finally left him in 1906, she had no access to the profits of her own work because he owned the copyright. She embarked on a stage career, making barely enough to survive. In 1910, she published her first novel under her own name, *The Vagabond*, in which a thinly veiled version of her now ex-husband is a famous painter whose "only genius ... was for lying." In addition to publishing several more successful works, she went on to have a remarkable life filled with scandalous love affairs with men, women, and at least one gender non-conforming partner.[394]

In the 1960s, Walter Keane's "Big Eye" paintings gained immense popularity across the U.S.—derided as kitsch by critics, they were a massive commercial success. Andy Warhol remarked to Life magazine in 1965, "I think what Keane has done is just terrific. It has to be good. If it were bad, so many people wouldn't like it." But while they were done by "Keane," they weren't Walter's. Like other women who escaped their husband's influence, Margaret Keane later claimed credit for her work. In a common refrain, Walter was significantly older—12 years—and abusive, with Margaret later saying she was afraid for her life. Initially, he was taking credit for her work without her knowledge or consent. As she explained,

---

[393] Gagnon, Pauline, "Who Cares about Particle Physics? Making Sense of the Higgs Boson, the Large Hadron Collider and CERN," Appendix B: The Role of Mileva Marić Einstein, pages 234-246, July 2016, Oxford University Press, https://doi.org/10.1093/acprof:oso/9780198783244.005.0002

[394] Edemariam, Aida. "Wild, Controversial and Free: Colette, a Life Too Big for Film." *The Guardian,* January 7, 2019, https://www.theguardian.com/books/2019/jan/07/colette-french-novelist-movie-keira-knightley

"After I married Walter I just signed my paintings 'Keane'. He was able to take credit for my work, which I was not aware he was doing at first." When she did find out, she kept quiet and even publicly supported his claim for fear of reprisals behind closed doors, later saying that he had threatened to kill her. It was only years after their 1965 divorce that Margaret went public, asserting in a radio broadcast that she was the true artist. A reporter from the *San Francisco Examiner* arranged a "paint-off" between the former spouses—Margaret attended, Walter did not. It was not the only time he'd dodge such a challenge—in 1986, Margaret sued Walter and *USA Today* for an article in which he claimed to be the true artist of the Big Eyes paintings. The presiding judge ordered both Keanes to create a Big Eyes painting in the courtroom. Walter refused, spinning a tale about a "sore shoulder," while Margaret finished hers in under an hour. The jury awarded her $4 million in damages; a federal appeals court later overturned the monetary award but upheld the defamation verdict. Margaret said after the initial trial, "I really feel that justice has triumphed. It's been worth it, even if I don't see any of that four million dollars." [395] [396]

Australian music scholar Martin Jarvis published his book *Written By Mrs Bach* in 2011. In it, he presents the case that Johann Sebastian Bach's six unaccompanied cello suites may have been composed by his second wife, Anna Magdalena Bach. (See the next section for what Prof. Jarvis has to say about Mozart's sister Maria Anna). The book inspired a documentary in which, as the *Washington Post* puts it, "a professor of music, a composer and an American expert in document forensics advance the case." [397] "Prof Jarvis said he aims to overturn the 'sexist' convention that recognized composers were always a 'sole male creator,' to finally reinstate Mrs Bach into the history books," wrote Hannah Furness in the *Telegraph*. "While Anna is known to have transcribed for Bach in his later years, researchers found

---

395   Lee, Benjamin, "Margaret Keane, 'Big Eyes' Artist, Dies Aged 94," *The Guardian*, June 29, 2022, https://www.theguardian.com/artanddesign/2022/jun/29/margaret-keane-big-eyes-artist-dies
396   "M.D.H. Keane – Artist Biography," East House Art Gallery, 2014, https://easthouseart.com/artist-biography.php?artistId=364741&artist=M.D.H.+Keane
397   Marshall, Colin, "Did Bach's Wife Compose Some of 'His' Masterpieces? A New Documentary Says Yes," Open Culture, October 30, 2014, https://www.openculture.com/2014/10/bachs-wife.html

the handwriting did not have the 'slowness or heaviness' usually attributed to someone who is merely copying, but was likely to have flowed from her own mind," supported by "numerous corrections to scores written in her hand, signalling she is likely to have been composing it as she went along." [398]

Fang, who lived during the first century BCE, was the earliest recorded woman alchemist in China. She reputedly discovered a way to turn mercury into silver—one interpretation is that she used a chemical technique to extract silver from ores using mercury. This would have left pure silver residue behind when the mercury boiled away. Her husband Cheng Wei physically abused her, attempting to force her to reveal the secret procedure. She refused, eventually going insane—possibly from all that mercury exposure, as it's a neurotoxin—and committed suicide.[399]

Historically, women scientists have often worked with their husbands or other male relatives—and those men have often taken credit for their work. German astronomer Caroline Herschel is often credited as the first woman to discover a comet, on August 1, 1786. Although she discovered eight comets, among other astronomical bodies, she was not even the first German female astronomer to do so.[400] Maria Margaretha Kirch beat her by many decades, having discovered the "Comet of 1702" on April 21, 1702. Though her husband later admitted that Maria had been the one to do so, he initially took credit for it at the time and for years to come, only coming clean in 1710.[401]

Botanist and illustrator Mary Anne Stebbing also worked with her husband, helping to classify specimens and producing sketches for his books. Yet all their joint work was published under his name only—Stebbing never published any research under her own name. Her skills as a botanical illustrator were highly regarded enough that she was part of the first cohort of 11 women admitted to

---

[398] Furness, Hannah, "Did Bach's wife write his finest works?" *The Telegraph*, October 25, 2014, https://www.telegraph.co.uk/culture/music/classicalmusic/11188153/Did-Bachs-wife-write-his-finest-works.html

[399] Rayner-Canham, Marelene F, and Geoffrey Rayner-Canham, *Women in Chemistry: Their Changing Roles from Alchemical Times to the Mid-Twentieth Century* (Chemical Heritage Foundation, 2001).

[400] Johnson-Roehr, S. N, "Caroline Herschel Claims Her Comet," JSTOR Daily. August 27, 2022, https://daily.jstor.org/caroline-herschel-claims-her-comet/

[401] McBride, JoEllen, "Maria Kirch Was the First Woman to Discover a Comet, but Her Husband Took the Credit," Massive Science, May 2, 2019. https://massivesci.com/articles/maria-kirch-comet-astronomy-margaretha-aurora-borealis-saturn-venus-conjunction/

the Linnean Society of London. When Fellow Lord Frank Crisp, whose wife was one of the 11, commissioned a painting of the women, he commented of Stebbing, "we must surely have at the table a lady Fellow who has done something, not one without a record." She was painted over and replaced with an empty chair.[402]

Similarly, paleoanthropologist Mary Leakey spent much of her marriage letting her husband Louis publicly take credit for the work they did together. "Although Louis grabbed the headlines, it was his second wife, Mary, an archaeologist, who made many of the actual finds associated with the Leakey name," Roger Lewin wrote in *Smithsonian Magazine*. "Until later in their relationship, when their marital ties all but snapped for both personal and professional reasons, she let her husband bask in the limelight while she conducted her beloved fieldwork." Although Mary was later recognized as "the woman who found our ancestors," during their marriage it was Louis who would "lecture, raise money and speculate at news conferences about the significance of his wife's discoveries, often leaving the impression that he, personally had made the finds," Bart Barnes wrote for the *Washington Post*.[403] It probably contributed to their dynamic that Mary was not college-educated; they met when she was in her early 20s while he was a highly regarded Cambridge University professor 10 years her senior (and a married one at that; he left his wife for the young illustrator). As their marriage began to fall apart, she asserted herself more, taking credit for her work and accepting accolades. In addition to her contributions to our understanding of the origins of humans, Mary also discovered 15 new species and a genus over the course of her career.[404]

Microbiologist Esther Lederberg was a pioneer of bacterial genetics, but she worked with her husband, so everyone gave credit for her work to him. Including, in 1958, the Nobel committee, which awarded the prize for physiology or

---

402 Durant, Joanna, "Passionate Pioneers – Increasing Access to Botanical Artwork by Women Artists," Biodiversity Heritage Library, March 13, 2019, https://blog.biodiversitylibrary.org/2019/03/passionate-pioneers.html
403 Barnes, Bart, "Eminent archaeologist Mary Leakey Dies at 83," *The Washington Post*, December 10, 1996, https://www.washingtonpost.com/archive/local/1996/12/10/eminent-archaeologist-mary-leakey-dies-at-83/d2010875-7d07-42fb-9532-c237405940d0/
404 Eschner, Kat, "Mary Leakey's Husband (Sort Of) Took Credit for Her Groundbreaking Work on Humanity's Origins," *Smithsonian Magazine*, February 6, 2017, https://www.smithsonianmag.com/smart-news/mary-leakeys-husband-sort-took-credit-her-groundbreaking-work-humanitys-origins-180961991/

medicine to Joshua Lederberg and two other men they worked with.[405] The only mention of Esther on the Nobel website to this day is at the bottom of Joshua's Nobel bio—"While at Yale, Lederberg married Esther M. Zimmer in 1946. They have no children. Mrs. Lederberg had obtained her M.A. at Stanford with Professor G.W. Beadle during 1944-1946, and her Ph.D. degree at the University of Wisconsin in 1950. She is working full time as research associate."[406] They acknowledge she has a PhD but can't even give her the respect of calling her Dr. instead of Mrs.

Lederberg's accomplishments included discovering the Lambda bacterial virus and the bacterial fertility factor and creating a replica plating process that enabled biologists to reproduce bacterial colonies en masse. This enabled the Lederbergs to more effectively study mutations. Discovering the Lambda bacteriophage also led to her work in specialized transduction, where foreign DNA is introduced into a cell by a virus. Although Lederberg laid the groundwork for much of 20th century microbiology, she was never offered a tenured position at a university. Even modern textbooks often ignore her work and attribute her accomplishments to her husband.

In fact, he likely held her back—she was a grad student when she discovered the F factor and Lambda, and Joshua, as her thesis advisor, stopped her from continuing her work on those discoveries. While it's not clear to what degree he reinforced or contradicted the perception of her as only his wife and assistant, when he wrote an autobiographical account of their discovery of genetic recombination in bacteria, he did not acknowledge her work. She also had to fight to stay employed at Stanford after divorcing him in 1968—he was head of the genetics department.[407]

All these examples stand in stark contrast to Elias von Löwen, second husband to 17th-century astronomer Maria Cunitz. When Cunitz published her *Urania Propitia*, which helped make astronomy more accessible for lay people, von Löwen wanted to make it absolutely clear that the book was entirely and exclusively

---

405 Steinmetz, Katy, "Esther Lederberg and Her Husband Were Both Trailblazing Scientists. Why Have More People Heard of Him?" *Time,* April 11, 2019, https://time.com/longform/esther-lederberg/
406 "Joshua Lederberg Biographical," The Nobel Prize, 1958. https://www.nobelprize.org/prizes/medicine/1958/lederberg/biographical/
407 Steinmetz, Katy, "Esther Lederberg and Her Husband Were Both Trailblazing Scientists. Why Have More People Heard of Him?" *Time,* April 11, 2019, https://time.com/longform/esther-lederberg/

Cunitz's work. He wrote the preface, explicitly stating that he had no part in writing it and he supported his wife's work.[408]

THE BROTHERS

Fanny Mendelssohn, elder sister to composer Felix Mendelssohn, was arguably the more talented sibling, but was held back throughout her life by Felix himself. Their suffocating dynamic empowered him to prevent her from pursuing a career as a composer. Although she wrote almost 500 beautiful compositions, he and their father forbade her to publish them or perform them in public. Even as he supported Felix's career, their father told Fanny, "Music is likely to become a profession for Felix, while it is only an ornament for you; it may never form the core of your life." Even her marriage could not free her from her father and brother's control. Even after her father's death in 1835, Felix continued to actively prevent her from pursuing success.

During his lifetime, Felix himself acknowledged stealing Fanny's works and claiming them as his own—even admitting to Queen Victoria that her favourite of his pieces (*Italien*) was actually written by Fanny. Several of Fanny's compositions were published under Felix's name in his *Opus 8* and *9* collections. She also likely developed the Lied ohne Worte (Song without Words) genre typically attributed to Felix. Additionally, he sought her opinions on all his own works and her insights helped shape their final versions. Fanny unfortunately died shortly after freeing herself from his control, the year after she published her own first opus. If not for the stroke that killed her, she may have truly come into her own as a composer and received the recognition she deserved. [409]

While there is less supporting evidence in the case of Mozart's older sister Maria Anna, Australian academic Martin Jarvis—noted above for similar assertions about Anna Magdalena Bach—believes at least two violin concertos attributed to the brother were in fact written by the sister. There is proof that she composed

---

408   McNeill, Leila McNeill, "The 17th-Century Lady Astronomer Who Took Measure of the Stars," *Smithsonian Magazine*, March 2, 2017, https://www.smithsonianmag.com/science-nature/lady-astronomer-who-took-on-most-advanced-science-180962142/
409   Davis, Elizabeth, "Meet the Awesome Composer Whose Music Was Published under HER BROTHER'S Name," Classic FM, January 29, 2019, https://www.classicfm.com/discover-music/fanny-and-felix-mendelssohn/

music, including letters from her brother praising her work, but as there are no surviving works attributed to her, scholars cannot compare them as they can for a composer like Fanny Mendelssohn. Jarvis was a conductor and professor who had spent more than a decade studying original Mozart manuscripts when he publicized his theory, based on handwriting differences on certain works. Dr. Scott Davie, a concert pianist and music lecturer at the Australian National University, was reluctant to acknowledge that Mozart may have intentionally taken credit for his sister's work, suggesting instead that Maria Anna may have chosen to have her work published under her brother's name due to stigma against women composers at the time.[410]

William Wordsworth relied on his sister, wife, and daughter throughout his career. While the latter two (Mary and Dora, respectively) acted as his literary agents, his sister Dorothy was an uncredited editor, as well as transcriber and, after his death, literary executor. Wordsworth repeatedly used Dorothy's own words without attribution, including descriptions in his successful guide book *A Guide through the District of the Lakes* and segments from her journals. His famed poem *Daffodils* uses a description originally written by Dorothy. Her own attempts to find a publisher for her *Recollections of a Tour Made in Scotland* were unsuccessful and it was not published until almost 20 years after her own death.[411]

---

410 Dick, Samantha, "Mozart Claimed Credit for Concertos Written by His Sister, Suggests Darwin Academic," ABC News, January 8, 2022, https://www.abc.net.au/news/2022-01-09/nt-mozart-sister-cdu-professor-martin-jarvis/100742458
411 Nelson, Camilla, "#ThanksforTyping: The Women behind Famous Male Writers," The Conversation, April 6, 2017, https://theconversation.com/thanksfortyping-the-women-behind-famous-male-writers-75770

STOLEN WORK

"In science, the credit goes to the man who convinces the world, not to whom the idea first occurs."
—Francis Darwin[412]

In 2022, author John Hughes's novel *The Dogs* was removed for consideration for the $60,000 Miles Franklin Prize, Australia's most prestigious literary award. A *Guardian* investigation had identified "58 similarities and instances of identical text between parts of Hughes' 2021 novel *The Dogs* and the 2017 English translation of Svetlana Alexievich's nonfiction *The Unwomanly Face of War*." Hughes later claimed this was unintentional and apologized, but the fact remains that not even being a Nobel laureate protected Alexievich from being plagiarized, and the words of the real women she interviewed from being stolen.[413]

Here we differentiate between taking credit for work that has been done and the theft of the intellectual property itself. Often when men deliberately steal women's work, there is financial gain involved. Perhaps the most apropos example of this is the board game Monopoly. Originally patented in 1903 by creator Elizabeth Magie as "The Landlord's Game," it was designed to help demonstrate how rents enrich property owners and impoverish tenants. Ironically, it was anti-monopolistic.

In 1932, Charles Darrow played Magie's game with friends, made some minor

---

412 Darwin, Francis, "Remarks made while presenting the original papers of W. T.G. Morton to the Royal Society of Medicine." Proceedings of the Royal Society of Medicine, 1917-18, p. 66, paragraph 2.
413 Verney, Anna Katherine, "Miles Franklin Prize Removes Novel from Longlist after Author Apologises for Plagiarism," *The Guardian*, June 10, 2022, https://www.theguardian.com/books/2022/jun/10/miles-franklin-prize-removes-novel-from-longlist-after-author-apologises-for-plagiarism

tweaks and patented "his" version. Parker Brothers bought the game from him, not knowing he didn't necessarily have all the rights. The company paid $500 for the rights to Magie's game as well, while Darrow went on to make millions. Parker Brothers never credited Magie, falsely claiming Darrow as the original creator.[414]

Then there's the case of Margaret E. Knight and the flat-bottomed paper bag. In the 1860s, Knight was working for the Columbia Paper Bag Company. There were essentially two types of paper bags in circulation at the time—machine-made ones like the company's, which were weak and narrow and couldn't stand on their own, and flat-bottomed ones in the U.K. that had to be handmade. In 1868, Margaret invented a machine that cut, folded, and glued paper to form the flat-bottomed brown paper bags we're all familiar with today, enabling mass production.

To file her patent application, she needed a working iron model of the machine. While it was being built, a machinist who visited the machine shop stole her design and patented it first. When Margaret went to file her own patent, she discovered what he'd done and filed a patent interference lawsuit. She had years' worth of precise hand-drawn blueprints, journals, models, witnesses, and years of having worked at a company that produced paper bags. He had misogyny. He argued that as a woman, "she could not possibly understand the mechanical complexities of the machine." He also tried to claim that "his" machine, although clearly identical, was not the same as her invention (probably because he couldn't remember all the details) and that she hadn't created a working model. Fortunately, she did win, thanks to the overwhelming amount of evidence she was able to produce and the fact that he had none. It's important to note that Margaret had to spend $100 per day in legal costs on the 16-day hearing. In modern terms, that would be more than $32,000 U.S. For many women, particularly a single woman, that cost would have meant they couldn't defend their rights in court.

Margaret continued inventing throughout her life and although she was never wealthy, she was able to live comfortably by selling her inventions to companies

---

[414] Pilon, Mary, "Monopoly's Inventor: The Progressive Who Didn't Pass 'Go,'" *The New York Times*, February 13, 2015, https://www.nytimes.com/2015/02/15/business/behind-monopoly-an-inventor-who-didnt-pass-go.html

and living off the royalties, including $25,000 for the paper bag machine. In 1913, the year before her death at age 76, a *New York Times* article reported that she was "working twenty hours a day on her eighty-ninth invention."[415] [416]

It's not just individuals or corporations stealing the work of women inventors, either—in Hedy Lamarr's case, it was the U.S. Navy. As mentioned in the introduction, Lamarr is primarily remembered for her beauty and acting abilities, as well as her six marriages. In recent years, her contributions as an inventor have gained more public awareness. During World War II, radio-controlled torpedoes had been suggested for naval use, but an enemy could potentially jam the guidance system, sending it off course. Lamarr, having read about this, developed the idea of a frequency-hopping signal with her friend, composer and pianist George Antheil. He jerry-rigged a miniature player piano mechanism to test the concept, and Lamarr hired an engineering professor to develop the functionality. She was granted the patent for the device on August 11, 1942.

The U.S. Navy did not end up using radio-controlled torpedoes, but they seized the invention as "alien property"—Lamarr was Austrian, and this was the midst of World War II. Then they shelved it for years. It was rediscovered in the 1950s. In 1957, engineers at Sylvania Electronic Systems Division used the concept in combination with the recently invented transistor. In 1962, the U.S. Navy finally used the technology during the Cuban Missile Crisis, after Lamarr's and Antheil's patent had expired. It would prove to be a precursor to secure Wi-Fi, GPS, and Bluetooth technology.[417]

For more than two centuries after her death, Dutch Golden Age painter Judith Leyster's entire body of work was attributed to either her husband, Jan Miense Molenaer, or her competitor Frans Hals. Those that weren't were simply left unattributed. It probably didn't help that in another case of the "nameless wife," after her death the inventory of her estate attributed many of the paintings to "the wife

---

415 "Margaret Knight | Lemelson," Lemelson.mit.edu, https://lemelson.mit.edu/resources/margaret-knight.
416 "Margaret E Knight (1838-1914)," The Mills Archive, https://new.millsarchive.org/2021/02/14/margaret-e-knight-1838-1914/
417 Kratz, Jessie, "The World War II-Era Actress Who Invented Wi-Fi: Hedy Lamarr," Pieces of History, a blog of the U.S. National Archives, May 26, 2020, https://prologue.blogs.archives.gov/2020/05/26/the-world-war-ii-era-actress-that-invented-wi-fi-hedy-lamarr/

of Molenaer," not to Judith Leyster. While this may be partly due to similarity in styles, there was at least one instance of deliberate forgery. In 1893, the Louvre discovered Leyster's signature underneath a forged Hals signature on the 1630 painting *The Carousing Couple or The Jolly Companions*. The fraud appears to date back to the 1600s, possibly even to Leyster's lifetime (1609-1660). Another version of the painting had been sold in Brussels in 1890; Leyster's distinctive JL monogram had been "crudely altered to an interlocking FH." An investigation arose in 1893 when one dealer bought it from another and sold it on to a customer; noticing the odd signature, the buyer took the case to court. Dutch art historian Cornelis Hofstede de Groot examined the painting and testified in court that it was definitely not Hals's signature, but Leyster's. This is a great example of the monetary incentive that dealers and museums have to not look too closely at potentially questionable attributions—the painting's value dropped by 25 percent, with each dealer blaming the other and no one paying attention to the rediscovery of a once-renowned painter's work. De Groot's revelation did help lead to seven more of Leyster's pieces being identified. Recognition of and appreciation for her work has increased since the 1890s—her painting *Merry Company* sold for \$2.3 million in 2018.[418]

In 1919, Canadian writer and teacher Florence Deeks received bad news—the publisher Macmillan had rejected her manuscript, a feminist history of the world submitted eight months earlier. It seemed odd that the pages were clearly in bad condition, worn, torn and dog-eared—why had a manuscript that had clearly been well-used been rejected? She got her answer the following year, when she read *The Outline of History*, published by Macmillan under H. G. Wells's name. The published book bore too many similarities to her own rejected work to be a coincidence—the same themes, organisation, choices of words, as well as leaving out most of the history of India. Even the mistakes matched, such as spelling the name of the pharaoh Hatshepsut as "Hatasu," claiming the Phoenicians traded by land rather than sea, and inaccurately describing the Roman general Sulla as "aristocratic."

---

418 Batycka, Dorian, "A Painting Some Experts Believe Is by a Little-Known Female Old Master Just Sold for 125 Times Its High Estimate," Artnet News, May 5, 2022, https://news.artnet.com/market/judith-leyster-auction-record-2108724

Deeks spent years trying unsuccessfully to sue Wells for copyright infringement, taking her case all the way to the British Empire's highest court at the time, the Judicial Committee of the Privy Council. In the first trial before Justice Raney of the High Court division of the Supreme Court of Ontario, Deeks called multiple expert witnesses to attest to the similarities in the two manuscripts. Wells and MacMillan simply denied her allegations. The judge disregarded the expert witnesses' "fantastic hypotheses" as "an infinite deal of nothing," ruling against Deeks and ordering her to pay court costs. She was no more successful in her appeals. In its title, a 2002 book on the subject reflects the narrative of the time, which derided Deeks and idealised Wells: *The Spinster and the Prophet*.[419]

In 2022, when painter Jeff Dieschburg won a €1,500 prize for his painting *Turandot*, he was soon exposed online by Singaporean photographer Jingna Zhang. *Turandot* was an almost identical copy of one of her photographs, which appeared in *Harper's Bazaar* magazine in 2017. Per Zhang, "When confronted by others about copyright infringement, he sends me an email statement, tells me that as a figurative painter it's obvious that he needs reference materials. That he was inspired by someone else who appropriated my photos first (!!), and even though he was inspired by some of my artistic choices, he had "created an image in an artisanal way."" The only apparent differences between the two images (of an Asian woman holding roses and looking over her shoulder at the viewer) is that Dieschburg flipped the image, added a small earring and changed the woman's clothing and background from blue to green—a child's "spot the difference" game has more distinction between images. *Turandot* was exhibited by the Commune de Strassen until Zhang's accusations and reportedly sold for €6,000. Meanwhile, American photographer Bekka Björke came forward with proof of blatant plagiarism of her own work. Like Zhang's, Björke's photographs were intricately staged images of lone women, posted alongside corresponding, almost identical paintings Dieschburg had replicated. A lawsuit is ongoing and his prize at the 11th Strassen

---

419 Mckillop, Brian, *The Spinster and the Prophet* (McClelland & Stewart, 2011).

Contemporary Art Biennale was suspended.[420][421]

In arts law, the tenet of "fair use" is an exception to copyright—for example, if someone is parodying or critiquing a work, they may reprint text or share an image or clip of the work, or produce their own version. Creating a different artwork using the original is generally considered fair use, if the work is substantially different from the original—in the case of Dieschburg, the changes were minor and superficial, resulting in images almost identical to the originals. Andy Warhol is perhaps the most significant example of an artist whose entire, successful career was based on replicating other people's images, including his *Marilyn Diptych* (using 50 publicity photos from Marilyn Monroe's 1953 film *Niagara*).[422]

Photographer Lynn Goldsmith fought her copyright against Warhol's estate (the Andy Warhol Foundation) all the way to the Supreme Court. Goldsmith photographed the biggest names in rock 'n' roll in the 1980s, including a 1981 photoshoot with Prince before he became a legend. She later licensed the image to *Vanity Fair* for a 1984 issue of the magazine. Without her knowledge, Warhol later produced the "Prince Series" of images based on her photo, without crediting her in any way. She only found out in 2016, when *Vanity Fair* published one of the series' images. Patricia Caufield also sued Warhol for using her photograph of hibiscus flowers as the subject of his Flowers series, while civil rights photographer Charles Moore sued him for using photographs that Moore published in *Life* as the basis for his *Race Riot* painting, and Fred Ward sued over use of his photograph of a grieving Jacqueline Kennedy. All three settled with Warhol out of court, but more legal battles arose after Warhol's 1987 death.[423] Because such court cases are often subjective, based on the personal opinions of judges rather than hard facts, it

---

420 Nam, Jane, "Singaporean Photographer Claims Artist 'Ripped Off' Her Work, 'Mansplained' Copyright to Her," Yahoo News, June 4, 2022, https://news.yahoo.com/singaporean-photographer-claims-artist-ripped-002624099.html
421 "Litigation Update in the Jingna Zhang-Jeff Dieschburg Case: Defense Denies Liability for Infringement," PitchMark, August 23, 2022, https://news.pitchmark.net/news/litigation-update-in-the-jingna-zhang-jeff-dieschburg-case-defense-denies-liability-for-infringement-452554
422 "'Marilyn Diptych', Andy Warhol, 1962," Tate, 2019, https://www.tate.org.uk/art/artworks/warhol-marilyn-diptych-t03093
423 Szynol, Paul, "The Andy Warhol Case That Could Wreck American Art," The Atlantic, October 1, 2022, https://www.theatlantic.com/ideas/archive/2022/10/warhol-copyright-fair-use-supreme-court-prince/671599/

is all too easy for a well-known artist to get away with stealing others' work. But in a "landmark ruling," the U.S. Supreme Court sided with Goldsmith in 2023, with Justice Sonia Sotomayor writing, "Goldsmith's original works, like those of other photographers, are entitled to copyright protection, even against famous artists."[424]

Louisa Lawson was best known as a suffragist and newspaper publisher in Sydney, but she was also a former postmistress. In 1896, after she patented a new buckle for use on mailbags, the New South Wales Postal Department used her invention and then refused to pay for it. As Sydney's *Evening News* reported, "There will be saving in the quantity of wax used, no string will be required, and the work can be done in about half the time now taken. It is not to be wondered at, therefore, that the Government has given Mrs. Lawson an order for

several thousand at once. It is pretty certain that others will follow suit, and that the inventor will be rewarded by a handsome and frequently recurring financial increment." Alas, the *News* was overly optimistic, though Lawson was later successful in suing Edward Murray, whose company she had used to manufacture the buckle, for patent infringement in 1902. He had tried to file a patent in 1900 for the same buckle; when she opposed his application, he withdrew it and went on manufacturing them anyway.[425] [426] [427]

In 1970, 60 women employees of *Newsweek* sued the magazine. Female researchers accused male writers and editors of taking credit for their work, including Lynn Povich, who later wrote a book about the experience, *Good Girls Revolt*. The women, represented by Eleanor Holmes Norton, filed a claim with the Equal Employment Opportunity Commission, asserting that *Newsweek* only allowed men to be reporters. The women won, forcing Newsweek to allow women

---

[424] Cascone, Sarah, "In a Landmark Ruling against the Andy Warhol Foundation, the Supreme Court Has Sided with Photographer Lynn Goldsmith," Artnet News, May 18, 2023, https://news.artnet.com/art-world/the-supreme-court-ruling-lynn-goldsmith-andy-warhol-foundation-2304684

[425] Evening News, "New Postbag Fastener," October 10, 1896, https://trove.nla.gov.au/newspaper/article/108220504

[426] Radi, Heather, "Lawson, Louisa (1848–1920)," Australian Dictionary of Biography. Canberra: National Centre of Biography, Australian National University, Published online 2006, https://adb.anu.edu.au/biography/lawson-louisa-7121

[427] "Lawson, Louisa," The Dictionary of Sydney, Dictionary of Sydney, https://dictionaryofsydney.org/entry/lawson_louisa

to officially be recognized as reporters—work that they were already apparently doing. Ironically, the day the claim was filed, that week's cover article was about the feminist movement, called "Women in Revolt." The woman who wrote it was a freelancer because there were no female reporters on staff. [428]

In his 1994 book, *Brecht & Co*, scholar John Fuegi challenged the legacy of playwright Bertolt Brecht, asserting that the vast majority (about 80 percent) of Brecht's output was actually the work of his romantic partners and "collaborators," particularly Elisabeth Hauptmann, Margarete Steffin, Ruth Berlau, and Marieluise Fleißer. Fuegi argues that Steffin wrote at least eight of the plays Brecht took credit for, including *Mother Courage and Her Children*, *The Good Person of Szechwan*, *Life of Galileo*, and early drafts of *The Caucasian Chalk Circle*. He notes that all the manuscripts are in Steffin's handwriting, and draw from source material written in French, which Brecht could not read. Fuegi accuses Brecht of stealing not only the credit, but also the royalties that should have been due to the women, publishing as his own dozens of shorter plays and stories written entirely by various lovers and plagiarizing from foreign works most of what he didn't steal from his associates.

The description for the book asserts, "Brecht's first violent, homoerotic plays, though noisily provocative failures at the box office, brought him praise from adventurous critics. In Berlin in the 1920s, Brecht found someone who would change not only his life but world theater: Elisabeth Hauptmann, who wrote over 80 percent of *The Threepenny Opera* in exchange for time in Brecht's life and in his bed. Yet her name often disappeared from the printed text, as well as from other plays and poems." [429]

Although countless critics and academics who love Brecht deride Fuegi's conclusions, the mainstream media was much more receptive to his assertions. Among the favourable reviews were "One of the most important critical studies of the century," (*New York Magazine*), "This biography is fascinating in its diversity of detail and portraiture of a period," (*The Economist*) and inclusion on *The New York*

---

428   Povich, Lynn, *The Good Girls Revolt How the Women of Newsweek Sued Their Bosses and Changed the Workplace* (New York Public Affairs, 2016).
429   Fuegi, John, *Brecht and Company: Sex, Politics, and the Making of the Modern Drama* (Grove Press, 2002).

Times Notable Books of the Year list. When his book was published, Fuegi told the *Washington Post* that he had deliberately chosen a mainstream publisher rather than going to an academic one because he knew the Brecht loyalists would never let it go to print in a peer-reviewed setting. Fuegi had previously published pieces of his findings in academic journals and found that his fellow scholars consistently treated each occurrence of theft or plagiarism as an exception, rather than looking at the broader picture they added up to.[430]

More importantly, it is undeniable that Brecht was a well-documented plagiarist, using other artists' work without permission or credit, such as the poetry of Verlaine and Rimbaud in the 1927 play, *Jungle of Cities*. These were also brilliant, creative women that Brecht is known to have worked with, and he was inarguably a womaniser, likely with the misogyny and manipulative nature that generally accompanies such behaviour. It's simply not far-fetched to question just how much the women relegated to the roles of "collaborator" actually contributed to the works in his name, particularly when the scholar in question spent 25 years compiling his information, with access to vast amounts of original documents and interviews with primary sources—including Hauptmann herself—and who founded the International Brecht Society in 1970 and edited its annual journal for almost 20 years.[431]

In 2018, comedian Russell Peters claimed that *The Daily Show* host Trevor Noah stole some of his material. It was a refrain—he's previously claimed this in 2015, then backtracked, calling the allegations a "prank" and the media "gullible." Ironically, the second time around, Peters admitted that another comic, Elon Gold, had been doing the same material, about "Russian sounding like English backwards," before Peters. So not only did Peters admit he himself had used someone else's material, it was not the first time. British comedian Gina Yashere publicly announced, "What this fucker fails to mention is that he stole material from me when I was starting out. I confronted him, he promised never to do it again. Six

---

[430] Mondello, Bob, "BRECHT: A MASTER or a THIEF?" *The Washington Post*, October 23, 1994, https://www.washingtonpost.com/archive/lifestyle/style/1994/10/23/brecht-a-master-or-a-thief/dd9909e3-b0644030-8f26-cbfe8cf3f5a9/

[431] Fuegi, John, *Brecht and Company: Sex, Politics, and the Making of the Modern Drama* (Grove Press, 2002).

years later I'm getting messages from his fans saying, 'Why are you doing Russell Peters's material?' So he was still doing it. And it was on his stand-up special, so my shit helped to make him famous." Yashere says she confronted the multi-millionaire again, and he promised to pay for the bit, "but he never did," and that he's done this to "countless" other comedians who were "too afraid to speak out."[432] While Peters is not the first or only comic to steal jokes, and he does it to men and women alike, his behaviour speaks to stealing jokes from those with less power and money than himself. And while it may speak more to the gender disparity in comedy, it certainly seems much more common among male comics, with Milton Berle, Jay Mohr, Denis Leary, and even Robin Williams getting caught doing it.[433]

Although she received no screenwriting credit for the Oscar-winning film *Selma* (2014), director Ava DuVernay rewrote almost the entirety of Paul Webb's original script, including writing all of Martin Luther King Jr's speeches used in the film, changing the perspective of the story, adding nearly a dozen new characters, and writing a new third act. She substantially changed the focus of the film, from a white saviour tale about President Lyndon B. Johnson, to focus more on the African American civil rights activists and presenting Johnson as a more reluctant supporter of the movement, and also drew on her own father's lived experiences. Contractually, Webb, a white British man, would have had to give permission to share the writing credit with DuVernay, an African American woman. He refused. He also publicly criticized her changes, which begs the question—if he didn't like the final product, why insist on taking sole credit for the writing? For her part, DuVernay stated at The New Yorker Festival in 2017 that "It's the only time in the industry I feel I really betrayed myself. Because I wrote that script, and my name was not on it. The credit was taken from me." She was also actively discouraged from pushing the issue at the time to avoid "controversy" ahead of the Oscars, for which the film was nominated for Best Picture. DuVernay also later stated, "I was the seventh director they'd asked. All of the men before me said no," adding that producers seemed ready to give up

---

432 Yashere, Gina, July 6, 2018, Twitter, https://www.chortle.co.uk/news/2018/07/06/40423/hypocrite
433 Bennett, Steve, "Hypocrite!" Chortle: The UK Comedy Guide, July 6 2018, https://www.chortle.co.uk/news/2018/07/06/40423/hypocrite

on the film entirely before star David Oyelowo suggested they ask DuVernay.[434]

Frequently, the thief is not a single individual, but a corporation. In 1902, Mary Anderson invented early windshield wipers, which she patented and pitched to manufacturing companies. She had no luck, and it wasn't until faster cars came along in the 1950s and '60s—after her patent expired—that her invention would end up on every car in the world.[435] She was inducted into the Inventors Hall of Fame in 2011, but never received any financial compensation for her creation, which Robert Kearns was repeatedly credited with.[436]

When Marion Donovan began inventing disposable diapers in the 1940s, it was a classic (and literal) case of necessity being the mother of invention. As a new mom, she was spending a lot of time she didn't have cleaning cloth nappies, so she first designed a waterproof version, using her own shower curtain. Working through a series of improvements, she produced a reusable, leak-proof diaper cover that, unlike the rubber baby pants of the time, did not cause diaper rash. When no major company was interested, she went into production for herself—the "Boater" was such a success that she was able to sell her new company and patent for a million dollars (almost $10 million in today's currency).[437] While her diaper cover was a success, her subsequent pitches for disposable diapers did not take off as she had hoped. Although she had patented it, Proctor and Gamble researcher Victor Mills did not credit or pay her when he used her idea to start Pampers in 1961.[438]

Until the release of the 2016 book *Hidden Figures* and its movie adaptation, most Americans had never heard of mathematician Katherine Johnson. Internally

---

434 Fallon, Clair, "Ava DuVernay Says She Regrets Giving Up On 'Selma' Writing Credit," The Huffington Post, October 8, 2017, https://www.huffingtonpost.com.au/entry/ava-duvernay-regrets-selma-writing-credit_n_59d99427e4b072637c44869e?ri18n=true

435 Palca, Joe, "Alabama Woman Stuck In NYC Traffic In 1902 Invented The Windshield Wiper," NPR, July 25, 2017, https://www.npr.org/2017/07/25/536835744/alabama-woman-stuck-in-nyc-traffic-in-1902-invented-the-windshield-wiper,

436 "How Robert Kearns Got Credit for Mary Anderson's Work," The List, October 28, 2022, https://www.thelist.com/1075601/how-robert-kearns-got-credit-for-mary-andersons-work/

437 Matchar, Emily, "Meet Marion Donovan, the Mother Who Invented a Precursor to the Disposable Diaper," Smithsonian, May 10, 2019 https://www.smithsonianmag.com/innovation/meet-marion-donovan-mother-who-invented-precursor-disposable-diaper-180972118

438 "Pampers: The birth of P&G's first 10-billion-dollar brand," P&G, June 27, 2012, https://us.pg.com/blogs/pampers-birth-pgs-first-10-billion-dollar-brand

UNCREDITED

at NASA's Langley Space Flight Research Center, everyone knew she was brilliant, to the point that astronaut John Glenn asked for her by name to check the calculations before his first orbit around Earth. Yet outside those walls in the 1950s and 1960s, no one was publicly crediting her or her fellow African-American, female colleagues like Mary Jackson, Dorothy Vaughan, and the many African-American women who worked as computers at NASA.

Johnson was the first woman and first person of colour on the flight research team she joined in 1953.

But even though she was now in meetings no woman had ever been invited to, her work was still going uncredited. As of 1960, no woman had ever had her name included in a NASA report. Johnson was the first, thanks in part to the support of her colleague, engineer Ted Skopinski. The pair had been working together on equations—mostly Johnson's—to launch, follow, and manoeuvre a spacecraft on a path that would land the craft at a specific position. This was the foundation for the U.S.'s first spaceflight in 1961 and first orbital mission in 1962. In September 1960, their supervisor Henry Pearson—who was "no fan of women," according to Johnson—pushed Skopinski to finish the report and put it out with only his name on it.

"Finally, Ted told him, 'Katherine should finish the report, she's done most of the work anyway.' So Ted left Pearson with no choice; I finished the report and my name went on it, and that was the first time a woman in our division had her name on something," Johnson recalled. She would be rightfully credited on 25 more reports and papers and set the precedent for other women at NASA.[439]

In a story reminiscent of Rosalind Franklin, Marthe Gautier was studying Down Syndrome when she noticed an extra chromosome while studying cell samples from a patient. Due to her poorly equipped lab—she had only a low-power microscope—she couldn't identify or photograph the chromosome. The following month, June 1958, she "naively" accepted an offer from another Downs researcher, Jérôme Lejeune, to take her slides and have them photographed. Months went by without hearing from him, and suddenly she learned that her discovery was about

---

[439] Shetterly, Margot Lee, *Hidden Figures: The American Dream and the Untold Story of the Black Women Mathematicians Who Helped Win the Space Race* (William Morrow, 2016).

to be published without her input or consent—and Lejeune didn't even spell her name correctly. Gautier agrees that Lejeune identified the 47th chromosome as an extra copy of chromosome 21, but she maintains that she was the first to notice that there was a 47th chromosome. More than 50 years later, Lejeune's foundation intimidated the French Federation of Human Genetics into cancelling a 2014 speech by Gautier because it believed she would "tarnish" his reputation (he had already been dead for 20 years by that point). The speech had been meant to be part of a ceremony where she was presented with a medal for her role in the discovery. Per *Science*, "the federation also said it "bitterly regretted" the cancellation and condemned the use of legal power to put pressure on a scientific meeting." [440]

In the early 1900s, Henrietta Swan Leavitt, a "human computer" at the Harvard College Observatory, discovered the period-luminosity relationship, meaning the brighter a star is, the more slowly it seems to pulse. As a student at Radcliffe College, Leavitt became one of the women crudely referred to as "Pickering's harem." Observatory director Edward Charles Pickering hired female astronomers to analyse data, but they were given the more diminutive title of computer and the lower pay that came with it (25 cents per hour). Leavitt's assignment was measuring and recording stars whose radiance appeared to brighten and darken at specific intervals. She published her findings in the *Annals of the Astronomical Observatory of Harvard College* in 1908, describing how the brighter variables had the longer pulsation period.[441]

In a paper published in 1912, Leavitt examined the relationship between the periods and the brightness of a sample of 25 Cepheids variables in the Small Magellanic Cloud. Pickering claimed the work as his own, the only acknowledgement of its true author the first sentence stating it was "prepared by Miss Leavitt."

Leavitt's work enabled astronomers to calculate the distance of stars from Earth and therefore get a better sense of the scale of galaxies, causing a radical shift in how astronomers looked at the universe. Years after her death, her discovery made it possible for

---

440 Pain, Elisabeth, "After More than 50 Years, a Dispute over down Syndrome Discovery," Science, February 11, 2014, https://www.science.org/content/article/after-more-50-years-dispute-over-down-syndrome-discovery

441 Mariani, Gael, "Henrietta Leavitt – Celebrating the Forgotten Astronomer," American Association of Variable Star Observers, 2012, https://www.aavso.org/henrietta-leavitt-%E2%80%93-celebrating-forgotten-astronomer

Edwin Hubble to establish his observations that the universe is continuously expanding, known as Hubble's Law. He often said Leavitt should have won a Nobel Prize.

Alas, when the Swedish mathematician Magnus Gösta Mittag-Leffler wrote her a letter in 1925, saying that he wanted to nominate her for the Nobel Prize in Physics, it was too late. Leavitt had died four years earlier, and the Nobel is not awarded posthumously. In a revolting display, the new observatory director, Harlow Shapley, replied, saying that the real credit belonged to himself for his interpretation of Leavitt's findings.

Arguably Marcel Duchamp's most famous "work" was submitting a urinal to the Society of Independent Artists as "art," signed "R. Mutt. " "*Fountain*," however, was not his creation. In an April 11, 1917, letter to his sister Suzanne, Duchamp admitted, "Une de mes amies sous un pseudonyme masculin, Richard Mutt, avait envoyé une pissotière en porcelaine comme sculpture" (*One of my female friends under a masculine pseudonym, Richard Mutt, sent in a porcelain urinal as a sculpture*).[442] While writer Louise Varèse has also been suggested, the leading candidate is Dadaist and baroness Elsa von Freytag-Loringhoven. R. Mutt was identified as living in Philadelphia, where von Freytag-Loringhoven resided at the time, and while André Breton attributed the urinal to Duchamp in 1935, the artist himself didn't start claiming it until long after the baroness died. In 1950, he officially took credit and authorised replicas (the original was reputedly returned to "R. Mutt" and never recovered). Duchamp claimed to have bought the urinal from the JL Mott Ironworks Company, and Mutt was a play on Mott—but the company didn't manufacture the model that can be seen in a photograph from the time, so his story is clearly a fabrication. An alternative explanation for the name is von Freytag-Loringhoven's love of dogs. The urinal would also be in line with her penchant for scatological humour, which was reflected in her work: a previous piece was called *God*, a plumbing trap as artwork (noteworthy that this is another piece she was initially not credited for, as it was originally attributed solely to Morton Schamberg, but is now attributed to both of them). Her handwriting also matches

---

[442] Duchamp, Marcel, "Letter to Suzanne Duchamp," April 11, 1917.

the artist signature on the urinal: R. Mutt 1917. "I am convinced that if the urinal had been attributed to the baroness from the beginning, it would never have soared into the stratosphere as a work of consummate genius," says novelist Siri Hustvedt, who included the baroness as a character in her novel *Memories of the Future*.[443]

Camille Claudel was only 19 when she became Auguste Rodin's student in 1883. In the late 1800s, there were few other options for a woman, as she would have been barred from studying art at formal institutions. She soon became the 42-year-old sculptor's muse, model, and lover, relying on him emotionally and financially as she received neither form of support from her family. As his apprentice, she worked endlessly on the most difficult parts of his sculptures, including the hands and feet of the figures on his monumental *Gates of Hell*.

When she ended the physical part of their relationship almost 10 years later, in 1892, she had difficulty securing funding for her work because of her gender and continued to rely financially on her collaborations with Rodin, for which she was not credited. She even had him sign her works so that they could be seen.[444]

This ended in 1899 when Rodin reacted poorly to Claudel's *The Mature Age*, which can be interpreted as reflecting the artists' love triangle (he had chosen to finally settle down with his long-time mistress and mother of his son Rose Beuret). He reportedly pressured the Ministry of Fine Arts to cancel the funding for the commission. It is unclear both how much Claudel influenced Rodin's style, and how much Rodin may have contributed to her subsequent mental health issues, which led to her being committed to an asylum in 1913. Though doctors repeatedly tried to have her released, her mother and brother refused, keeping her there for the remaining 30 years of her life and cutting off her access to the outside world.

More than a century after she was locked away, the Musée Camille Claudel opened in her hometown of Nogent-sur-Seine in 2017. Although the museum has gathered the largest collection of her work in the world, it remains unknown

---

443 Hustvedt, Siri, "When Will the Art World Recognise the Real Artist behind Duchamp's Fountain?" *The Guardian*, April 3, 2019, https://www.theguardian.com/books/2019/mar/29/marcel-duchamp-fountain-women-art-history

444 Campbell, Tori, "Stealing Art: When Men Took Credit for Women's Work," *Artland Magazine*, January 22, 2021, https://magazine.artland.com/stealing-art-when-men-took-credit-for-womens-work/

just how many sculptures claimed by Rodin and exhibited as such in museums around the world are actually Claudel's work.

Singer Alberta Hunter and pianist Lovie Austin wrote *Downhearted Blues* in 1922, and Hunter recorded the track for Ink Williams at Paramount Records, for $368 in royalties. Williams secretly sold the recording rights to Columbia Records in a deal where he would receive all royalties. The new record, featuring Bessie Smith as vocalist, sold almost a million copies. Hunter learned what Williams had done and stopped recording for him, moving to Okeh Records.[445]

Elvis Presley was notorious for covering music from African American artists, including singer Willie Mae "Big Mama" Thornton. The song *Hound Dog* was written for Thornton, and her recording was certainly a success, selling 500,000 copies and spending 14 weeks in the R&B charts and seven weeks at number one. Presley's version became his bestselling song, with 10 million records sold worldwide.[446] Her recording is listed as one of the Rock and Roll Hall of Fame's "500 Songs That Shaped Rock and Roll," while Presley's cover was featured by the Rock and Roll Hall of Fame as "the most illustrative example of the white appropriation of African-American music." Thornton's recording was also inducted into the Grammy Hall of Fame in 2013—25 years after Presley's was in 1988.

Prior to the COVID-19 pandemic, Tiffany Tate had created a vaccination tracker called PrepMod, used by public health departments across the U.S. for flu and other mass vaccinations. During the pandemic, dozens of states began using the app to track COVID-19 vaccinations. In 2021, Tate sued the U.S. Centers for Disease Control and Prevention (CDC) and the multinational corporation Deloitte for copying her app for their Vaccine Administration Management System (VAMS). Tate accused Deloitte and the CDC of using details of her work and implementing similar features, and that Deloitte tried to hire Tate in June 2020

---

445 "Alberta Hunter," All About Blues Music, October 17, 2012, https://www.allaboutbluesmusic.com/alberta-hunter/

446 Kelati, Haben, "Blues Singer 'Big Mama' Thornton Had a Hit with 'Hound Dog.' Then Elvis Came Along," *The Washington Post*, February 24, 2021, https://www.washingtonpost.com/lifestyle/kidspost/blues-singer-big-mama-thornton-had-a-hit-with-hound-dog-then-elvis-came-along/2021/02/23/60c36a04-6764-11eb-8468-21bc48f07fe5_story.html

to help develop VAMS. She told *The New York Times* that she was "in shock, and I really was heartbroken because I've worked with these people my entire career and I respected them and I trusted them." Tate claims that she had several meetings with the CDC starting in March 2020, sharing significant amounts of information about her system. Tate says the CDC asked to speak with her technical team and asked for a quote but did not follow through. When a new feature was added to PrepMod that May, a similar feature was added to VAMS soon after, Tate said. That month, the CDC reportedly offered Deloitte a $15.8 million contract "essentially to reproduce PrepMod," as Tate put it—half a million more than Tate had quoted to use PrepMod.[447]

---

447 Stolberg, Sheryl Gay, "Immunization Expert Accuses C.D.C. And Deloitte of Stealing Her Idea," *The New York Times*, February 6, 2021, https://www.nytimes.com/2021/02/06/us/politics/coronavirus-vaccines.html

CONTRIBUTIONS IGNORED

"Tremendous amounts of talent are lost to our society just because that talent wears a skirt."
—Shirley Chisholm[448]

Alma Reville was a skilled film writer, director, and editor in her own right, but many of her contributions to her husband, Alfred Hitchcock's, films went unacknowledged. For example, she worked extensively on preparing and adapting scripts for films such as *Rebecca* (1940), *Foreign Correspondent* (1940), *Suspicion* (1941), and *Saboteur* (1942). Of those, she was only credited for *Suspicion*, meaning she was not included when *Rebecca* and *Foreign Correspondent* were each nominated for Best Original Screenplay Oscars. The British Film Institute notes, "Of the films on which she has a writing credit, it's striking how many contain strong, well-drawn female roles ...*Stage Fright* is the last film Alma was credited on; apparently the failure of *Under Capricorn* (1949), a property she had recommended to Hitchcock, led her to lose confidence in her judgement. Her absence shows; while Hitchcock's later films are among his best regarded, the female roles tend to be less deeply examined, the action usually driven by the male protagonists." Hitchcock himself alluded, perhaps unintentionally, to this when he said, "I never understood what women wanted. I only knew it wasn't me."

The lack of credit went well beyond writing, as the British Film Institute writes that "From finding properties for him to produce, to casting, scouting locations,

---

448 Jarrett, Valerie, "Champion of African American History: The Honorable Shirley Chisholm of New York," Obama White House, February 28, 2014, https://obamawhitehouse.archives.gov/blog/2014/02/28/champion-african-american-history-honorable-shirley-chisholm-new-york

plotting camera angles and checking rushes, there were few areas that Alma didn't contribute to. Once in Hollywood, she was less frequently seen on the set of his films, but was a key collaborator behind the scenes on every project." [449]

Film critic Charles Champlin wrote in 1982, "The Hitchcock touch had four hands, and two were Alma's." While accepting his AFI lifetime achievement award in 1979, Hitchcock himself said that were it not for Alma, he may have been at the event not onstage but as "one of the slower waiters."

The overlooked wife is a recurring theme throughout this book, but particularly in this section, which will look at women whose contributions, either to a collaboration or a field as a whole, have gone ignored.

Jenny Marx was more than Karl's wife. A dedicated socialist in her own right, she gave up life as a baroness to work for the future she believed in. An advocate for women's rights from a young age, she was never afraid to point out that even the socialists generally placed men's needs above women's, if they even considered women at all. She was also her husband's greatest supporter and worked tirelessly with him on his *Communist Manifesto*. As the political magazine *Jacobin* observes, "With Karl busy theorizing, Jenny bore the brunt of the family's illnesses and poverty." Marx himself was a heavy drinker who experienced chronic illness, meaning Jenny had to care for him in addition to their many children, suffering the loss of four of those children, and fending off the various parties to whom they owed money. He also likely impregnated their housekeeper while Jenny was out of the country begging relatives for financial assistance. When Jenny needed support, telling her husband, "Meanwhile I sit and go to pieces. Karl, it is now at its worst pitch...I sit here and almost weep my eyes out and can find no help. My head is disintegrating. For a week I have kept my strength up and now I can no more," she received no sympathy. Yet she continued to support him, dutifully copying out *The Great Men of the Exile* as he dictated. She finally lost faith after the failure of his 1867 *Capital*, seeking escape from her husband's "burdensome shadow." At her funeral in 1881, her husband's closest collaborator Friedrich Engels eulogised, "The

---

449   Botting, Josephine, "Will the real Mrs Hitchcock please stand up?" British Film Institute, February 27, 2013, https://www.bfi.org.uk/features/will-real-mrs-hitchcock-please-stand-up

contribution made by this woman, with such a sharp critical intelligence, with such political tact, a character of such energy and passion, with such dedication to her comrades in the struggle—her contribution to the movement over almost forty years has not become public knowledge; it is not inscribed in the annals of the contemporary press. It is something one must have experienced at first hand." [450]

Carl Benz was an automotive pioneer—and so was his wife. Bertha Benz was her husband's main investor, using the funds from her dowry and an advance on her inheritance. She was also an inventor and her 1888 road trip—the first time an automobile with an internal combustion engine was driven over a long distance—was a strategic marketing tactic and practical test she devised without consulting him. As a field test, the 106-kilometre (66-mile) journey revealed several issues that Bertha had to troubleshoot along the way, but she and her two teenaged sons made it to her mother's house the same day, and Bertha dashed off a telegram to her husband to inform him. Her trip garnered the publicity she had hoped for, contributing to the company's future success, and the insights she gained led to several improvements, including the introduction of an additional gear for climbing hills and brake linings to improve braking power—which she had invented along the way.[451]

Anthropologist Frances Herskovits and her husband collaborated so closely that it is almost impossible to distinguish who did what research. The couple would each write half of the chapters in their prolific output on African, Afro-Caribbean and African American culture, and then each would edit the half the other wrote. Although Melville Herskovits did credit Frances for her work, her contributions were never recognized by the larger anthropology community, even after his death. [452]

Even notorious criminals get the overlooked wife treatment. Born in 1834, Mary Ann Bugg grew up experiencing all the discrimination you'd expect for someone who was both female and Aboriginal in Australia, being Worimi (Warrimay) on her mother's side, and the daughter of an English convict on her father's.

---

450   Fluss, Harrison and Miller, Sam, "The Life of Jenny Marx," Jacobin, February 14, 2016, https://jacobin.com/2016/02/jenny-karl-marx-mary-gabriel-love-and-capital
451   "Bertha Benz," Automotive Hall of Fame, Www.automotivehalloffame.org. https://www.automotivehalloffame.org/honoree/bertha-benz/
452   Ogilvie, Marilyn, and Joy Harvey, *The Biographical Dictionary of Women in Science* (Routledge, 2003).

First married off at age 14, she had several children and exes by the time she took up with Frederick Ward in 1860. He went by the name Captain Thunderbolt (no, seriously). Ward was basically on probation for horse theft, and when he violated that probation, he was sent back to Cockatoo Island. The island prison in Sydney Harbour was about 400 metres of shark-infested waters from shore—Mary Ann reputedly swam the distance, carrying a file to take care of the leg irons. They carried on robbing folks and making babies for several more years before separating at the end of 1867. As with the infamous jailbreak, Mary Ann was probably doing the heavy lifting in their partnership while Ward claimed all the credit. She hunted their food, was the only one who could read a map, scouted ahead, and spread false information to evade authorities and even taught Ward to read. He was shot and killed within a year and a half of their split, while Mary Ann lived to age 70. She had 13 kids and once evaded arrest by pretending to go into labour.[453]

The problem of women's contributions being ignored, of course, extends far beyond overlooked wives. In a 2015 study of the tenure process at top economics programs, Harvard PhD student Heather Sarsons found that women aren't getting credit for papers they co-author with men. Because publishing is a key factor in academic career advancement, Sarsons concluded, "that women incur a penalty when they coauthor that men do not experience. This is most pronounced for women co-authoring with men and less pronounced the more women there are on a paper." This is not an issue when women are the sole author, though there are of course barriers to sole authorship in academia. Sarsons notes, "Interestingly, though, women present their solo-authored papers fewer times per year than men do. It is possible that women do not 'advertise' their work as much as men do and this leads to women receiving less recognition for their work in general," which she suggests contributes to the fact that "up to a point, women are less likely to receive tenure than men when they solo author."[454]

According to a 2022 study, women are less likely to be authors compared to

---

453   Reilly, Eliza, *Sheilas: Badass Women of Australian History* (Macmillan, 2002).
454   Sarsons, Heather, "Gender Differences in Recognition for Group Work," Harvard, December 3, 2015, https://scholar.harvard.edu/files/sarsons/files/gender_groupwork.pdf

the men in their research group at the same career stage, even accounting for the hours each person worked on the project.[455] Specifically, women accounted for less than 35 percent despite being more than 48 percent of the workforce. The study included a survey, in which women were more likely than men to report that they were excluded from authorship and that their colleagues had underestimated their contributions to a paper.[456] That matches a 2021 study, which found that women researchers were more likely than men to see authorship decisions as unfair and to express the need for more guidance on how to make those decisions.[457] Meanwhile, men were more likely to think they received more credit in authorship than they deserved. A 2020 study looking at lead authorship in the geosciences specifically found that feminine names represented 13–30 percent of all first authors in the researchers' database – significantly less than the proportion of women in early career positions (30–50 percent). [458] A 2013 paper reported that both men and women judged research papers by men to be stronger than those by women, and both showed preference for the male authors as potential future collaborators.[459]

Lord William Malcolm Hailey is listed as the author of the influential 1938 African Survey, a British "Study of Problems arising in Africa South of the Sahara." The goal was to report on British colonial policy in Africa and examine the extent to which Africans should be involved in policy-making. Hailey started the project in 1935, but his health began failing by 1936, and his secretary Hilda Matheson took over the project fully as an executive manager. She had spoken extensively

---

455   Langin, Katie, "Women Scientists Don't Get Authorship They Should, New Study Suggests," Science, June 22 2022, https://www.science.org/content/article/women-scientists-don-t-get-authorship-they-should-new-study-suggests
456   Ross, Matthew B., Britta M. Glennon, Raviv Murciano-Goroff, Enrico G. Berkes, Bruce A. Weinberg, and Julia I. Lane, "Women Are Credited Less in Science than Are Men," Nature, vol 1, no 2 (2002), https://doi.org/10.1038/s41586-022-04966-w
457   Langin, Katie, "Are women researchers shortchanged on authorship? New study highlights gender disparities," Science, September 1, 2021, https://www.science.org/content/article/are-women-researchers-shortchanged-authorship-new-study-highlights-gender-disparities
458   Pico, T., P. Bierman, K. Doyle, and S. Richardson, "First Authorship Gender Gap in the Geosciences," *Earth and Space Science*, vol 7 no 8 (2020), https://doi.org/10.1029/2020ea001203
459   Dominus, Susan, "Women Scientists Were Written out of History. It's Margaret Rossiter's Lifelong Mission to Fix That," *Smithsonian Magazine*, October 2019, https://www.smithsonianmag.com/science-nature/unheralded-women-scientists-finally-getting-their-due-180973082/

with scientists and administrators to organize logistics and plan the scope of the project and coordinated preparatory research. Meanwhile, due to Hailey's incapacitation, Frederick Pedler stepped in as editor of the nearly 2,000-page document.[460] Anthropologists Lucy Mair and Audrey Richards also contributed to the project; both had been doing fieldwork in Africa for years and would go on to be celebrated for their significant work in the area.[461] [462] In fact, many of the chapters in the report were written by anthropologists and other specialists, yet Hailey retained sole authorship despite his actual contributions being questionable at best.

"Explorer" is another traditionally unladylike pursuit, yet that did not stop women like French opera singer and Buddhist scholar Alexandra David-Néel. In 1911, she embarked on a 14-year excursion through India, Sikkim, Nepal, Bhutan, China, Japan, and Tibet, culminating in 1924 when she disguised herself as a beggar to sneak into the forbidden Tibetan capital city of Lhasa—the first Western woman to do so. She then spent the next 45 years as a lecturer and writer, including the memoir *My Journey to Lhasa*.[463] Yet she, like other women explorers, has often been left out of books and other writing on the topic.

Jerry Thomas is widely credited as the world's first mixologist after publishing his *Bar-Tender's Guide* in 1862, the first book in the U.S. dedicated solely to cocktail recipes. But women had been publishing cookbooks that included such recipes for centuries, not least of which was Isabella Beeton's *Mrs Beeton's Book of Household Management*. Published the year before Thomas', it included recipes for beers, ales, cordials, cocktails, and punches. In terms of which was more influential, Thomas's book sold 8,000 copies—Beeton's sold over 2 million internationally, outsold at the time only by the Bible.[464]

Similarly, the idea of Dom Perignon as the "father of Champagne" is the result

---

460 Cell, John W, "Lord Hailey and the Making of the African Survey," *African Affairs*, vol 88 no 353, 481–505 (1989). https://doi.org/10.1093/oxfordjournals.afraf.a098213
461 Owens, Patricia, "Lucy Mair," LSE History, October 3, 2018, https://blogs.lse.ac.uk/lsehistory/2018/10/03/lucy-mair/
462 Kuper, Adam, "Audrey Richards – a Career in Anthropology," LSE History, March 23, 2016, https://blogs.lse.ac.uk/lsehistory/2016/03/23/audrey-richards-a-career-in-anthropology/
463 Guy, David, "Alexandra David-Néel," Tricycle: The Buddhist Review, Fall 1995, https://tricycle.org/magazine/alexandra-david-neel/
464 O'Meara, Mallory, *Girly Drinks: A World History of Women and Alcohol* (Hurst Publishers, 2021).

of a marketing scheme implemented after his death. In fact, he hated carbonation in wine and was actively working on a method to try to remove the region's signature fizz (he failed). Moreover, the second fermentation process that produces Champagne was an incidental by-product of fermentation pausing due to cold winter temperatures and re-starting when things warmed up in spring—although it has been refined (by people other than Dom Perignon), no one "invented" it. Madame Barbe-Nicole Clicquot, rightfully referred to as the "Grande Dame of Champagne" had a far greater impact on the development of the early Champagne industry. The namesake of the famed Veuve Clicquot ("veuve" meaning "widow") managed both the culinary and business side of the company, which still bears her name. She both refined the creation of the drink and successfully promoted it both in France and internationally, creating the association of Champagne with wealth and status, though the king's influential mistress, Madame de Pompadour was also largely responsible for popularising the drink.

In the case of Henrietta Lacks, it was not her work that was stolen, but her very cells. While being treated at Johns Hopkins for cervical cancer in 1951, a sample of Lacks's cancer cells was sent for biopsy to researcher Dr. George Gey, who discovered that where most people's cells die outside the body, hers actually multiplied. After her death, they stole additional samples from her body as it lay in the Johns Hopkins morgue. Gey and Johns Hopkins proceeded to use her cell lines for decades without compensation or even her or her family's consent or knowledge, much less acknowledging her in any way beyond calling them "HeLa" cells. The Lacks family were unaware of this until 1975, and it wasn't until Rebecca Skloot's *The Immortal Life of Henrietta Lacks* was published in 2010 that the origins of the HeLa cells was widely known, or that Johns Hopkins publicly acknowledged Lacks. Meanwhile, her cells have been used in countless medical research projects, such as being used to develop the polio vaccine as well as studying cancer, AIDS, the effects of radiation and toxic substances, and gene mapping. Almost 11,000 patents are based on research using HeLa cells.[465]

---

465   Butanis, Benjamin, "The Legacy of Henrietta Lacks," John Hopkins Medicine, April 12, 2017, https://www.hopkinsmedicine.org/henriettalacks/

THE SCIENTISTS

Science is a cumulative field, with people building upon work that was done before or using others' techniques to make great discoveries. For example, mathematician Mary Somerville posited in 1836 that the difficulties in calculating the position of Uranus may indicate the existence of a further planet—inspiring astronomer John Adams to start the calculations that led to the discovery of Neptune in 1846.[466] Similarly, the discovery of Pluto, ascribed solely to astronomer Clyde Tombaugh, would not have been possible without mathematician Elizabeth Williams. She worked for astronomer Percival Lowell, who first theorized the existence of a ninth planet, but died before he could verify it. Both men relied on Williams's calculations.[467]

It's also a collaborative field, with people working together to achieve results—and as we will see, the people responsible for discoveries are not always the ones in charge. So, while appalling, it is not surprising that many of the women who contributed, either laying the groundwork or as contemporary colleagues for the men, subsequently had their contributions either downplayed or ignored completely. This is particularly true as women were frequently relegated to jobs with titles like assistant and secretary, making it all the easier to dismiss the valuable

---

[466] O'Connor, J. J. and Robertson, E. F., "Mary Fairfax Greig Somerville," School of Mathematics and Statistics University of St Andrews, Scotland, November 1999, https://mathshistory.st-andrews.ac.uk/Biographies/Somerville/

[467] Bartels, Meghan Bartels, "Meet the Unknown Female Mathematician Whose Calculations Helped Discover Pluto," Space, February 18, 2020, https://www.space.com/human-computer-elizabeth-williams-pluto-discovery.html

work they did. As science historian Margaret Rossiter noted, "Women take these second-rate jobs because they have few options." The same is true for semi-technical positions like "chemical secretary" or "chemical librarian."

"A technical assistant could be asked to do anything right from the top to the bottom," said Kay Thorne, who held that title when she worked on Australia's first digital stored-program computer, CSIRAC. "And because we were a very small team, that meant that I literally did do a bit of everything." [468]

At age 24, Margaret Rossiter was one of the few women in her graduate program at Yale in 1969. Dedicated to the history of science, the program nonetheless seemed entirely unaware that women also had been, and continued to be, scientists. At one point, Rossiter asked a group of professors "Were there ever women scientists?" and was conclusively told absolutely not, never, none. "It was delivered quite authoritatively," Rossiter recalled. Even when someone mentioned two-time Nobel Prize winner Marie Curie, she was dismissed as essentially her husband's assistant. Although she did not argue at the time, sensing there would be no point, Rossiter went on to a long career bringing such women's stories to light. She also coined the term "Matilda effect" to describe a systemic bias against acknowledging women's contributions, to the point of denying them altogether. [469]

In addition to fighting for women's rights, Eunice Newton Foote was a groundbreaking scientist who was the first person to theorize and demonstrate the greenhouse effect. Yet when John Tyndall published similar findings—that water vapour and carbon dioxide contribute to atmospheric heating—three years later, he was lauded as the discoverer of new information, which proved to be the foundation of climate science. This is both despite and because of the fact that Foote's research was publicly presented to the American Association for the Advancement of Science. Her paper, *Circumstances Affecting the Heat of the Sun's Rays*,

---

468   Smith, Carl, "At the Dawn of Australian Computing, 72 Women Had a Crucial Job You've Never Heard Of," ABC News, November 30, 2019, https://www.abc.net.au/news/science/2019-12-01/women-computing-astronomy-technology/11713282
469   Dominus, Susan, "Women Scientists Were Written out of History. It's Margaret Rossiter's Lifelong Mission to Fix That," *Smithsonian Magazine*, October 2019, https://www.smithsonianmag.com/science-nature/unheralded-women-scientists-finally-getting-their-due-180973082/

was accepted to be read at the AAAS's meeting on August 23, 1856, but she was not permitted to present it herself. Joseph Henry, secretary of the Smithsonian, presented it in her stead and downplayed her findings. He then discounted her work in a *New York Daily Tribune* article about the presentation, claiming there were too many difficulties around interpreting the significance of her findings.

Beyond that, her paper was excluded from the meeting's published record of the papers presented, likely due to the influence of Alexander Dallas Bache, whose committee could reject papers. Those that were permitted were overwhelmingly by male authors, even though Foote's was of superior scientific methodology compared to ones that were published. As such, the only place her paper could be found was in the 1856 *American Journal of Science and Arts*, right after a different paper by her husband, Elisha. Although news of her work appeared in journals internationally, some omitted her conclusions about the climate implications of the effects of carbon dioxide.[470]

Lillian Moller Gilbreth and her husband Frank were equal partners in both running their engineering firm (Gilbreth Incorporated) and writing several books and more than 50 papers on a range of scientific subjects. While each produced sole-authored papers as well, Lillian was also left off of several of their co-authored papers, possibly because of publishers not wanting to name a woman. This is despite the fact that Lillian held a PhD, among other degrees, while her husband never attended college.[471]

CHEMISTRY

By studying the decay of actinium in the 1930s, French chemist Marguerite Perey discovered the last natural element to date, francium. Yet her discovery was not announced by her, but by Jean Baptiste Perrin as a note in the *Comptes Rendus* presented at the Académie des Sciences on January 9, 1939, because Perey was only

---

[470] McNeill, Leila, "This Lady Scientist Defined the Greenhouse Effect but Didn't Get the Credit, Because Sexism," *Smithsonian Magazine*, December 5, 2016, https://www.smithsonianmag.com/science-nature/lady-scientist-helped-revolutionize-climate-science-didnt-get-credit-180961291/

[471] Kass-Simon, G.; Farnes, Patricia, eds. 1990. "Lillian Moller Gilbreth and the Rise of Modern Industrial Engineering," *Women of Science: Righting the Record,* (Indiana University Press, 1990).

a laboratory assistant without a university degree. Perey was nominated for a Nobel Prize five times, but never won despite the 1952 Nobel Committee agreeing that her francium studies "undoubtedly are worth being recognized."[472]

During World War II, physical chemist Erika Cremer was working in Nazi-occupied Austria, developing solid-state gas adsorption chromatography. In spring 1945, Cremer was hit with a double dose of destruction: the press where a report of her work was being printed was bombed and her lab was damaged in an air raid. After the war, her students were able to build a gas chromatograph, optimise it, and use it to separate gases. Post-war issues with German science journals further delayed her publications until 1951, and her work garnered little attention.[473] The following year, male British chemists A. J. P. Martin and R. L. M. Synge won the 1952 Nobel Prize in Chemistry for developing liquid partition chromatography; if Cremer's work, separate from theirs, had been better known at the time, it arguably would have justified a share of the prize.

Australian chemist Enid Plante, who worked for the Advisory Council of Science and Industry (now CSIRO, the Commonwealth Scientific and Industrial Research Organisation) from 1940 to 1946, went entirely and deliberately uncredited for that work. According to CSIRO's website, "During her time with our agency, Enid made contributions to three scientific projects and published 13 papers or reports, including eight single-author papers. However, none included her name as author. The convention at the time was to list the section head as author of papers written by women." This means that her boss, Keith Leonard Sutherland (Head of the Physical Chemistry Section from 1941 to 1947), received sole credit for work that was entirely or partially Plante's, not to mention the same thing happening to other women throughout the organisation. [474]

Irving Langmuir received the 1932 Nobel in Chemistry for his work in surface

---

472 Borman, Stu, "These women scientists should have won the Nobel," Chemical and Engineering News, September 11, 2017, https://cen.acs.org/articles/95/i36/female-scientists-should-won-Nobel.html
473 Johnson, Jeffrey A, "Erika Cremer and the Origins of Gas–Solid Adsorption Chromatography, 1944–1947," Acs Symposium Series, January, 183–98, https://doi.org/10.1021/bk-2018-1311.ch007
474 Willetts, Rebecca, "Towards gender equity: our female scientists over the years," CSIRO, February 10, 2023, https://www.csiro.au/en/news/All/Articles/2023/February/toward-gender-equity

chemistry, primarily the development of single-molecule surface layers that have been used to create coatings, membranes, sensors, and electronic devices. Yet although these are called Langmuir-Blodgett films, his colleague Katharine Burr Blodgett was excluded from the Nobel. She worked closely with Langmuir to develop the films and the apparatus that makes them, called the Langmuir–Blodgett trough. Additionally, although Langmuir is credited with the idea for the layers in the first place, his work was based on a paper published by Agnes Pockels in 1891, which demonstrated that areas of film can be controlled by barriers. As Dr. Burtron H. Davis of the University of Kentucky Center for Applied Energy Research put it, "Langmuir did better surface science work than Pockels," but it was "merely an improvement of her work."

Langmuir continued Pockels's work, but it was Blodgett who devised a method to spread coatings of the substance onto items, including multiple layers. By "stacking" layers of the film, Blodgett was able to produce so-called "invisible glass," used in cinematography on 1939's *Gone with the Wind* and subsequent films, as well as by the military during World War II on submarine periscopes and aeroplane spy cameras. She was also, incidentally, the first woman to be awarded a PhD in physics from the University of Cambridge, in 1926. Beyond chemistry, Blodgett and Langmuir's studies on electrical discharges in gases helped lay the foundations for plasma physics. Blodgett also held eight patents, including poison gas adsorbents, methods for de-icing aircraft wings, and improved smokescreens. [475]

German chemist Ida Noddack was the first scientist to propose the concept of nuclear fission, as well as co-discovering the element rhenium, the last stable element to have been discovered to date. In 1934, physicist Enrico Fermi suggested that if uranium was bombarded with neutrons, it could possibly produce atomic elements heavier than uranium. In a paper responding to Fermi's discovery, Noddack stated that bombarding uranium could actually produce smaller atoms—in other words, nuclear fission. This process also produces massive amount of energy, but she did not pursue the idea with experiments, possibly due to expense

---

475 Borman, Stu, "These women scientists should have won the Nobel," *Chemical and Engineering News*, September 11, 2017, https://cen.acs.org/articles/95/i36/female-scientists-should-won-Nobel.html

or other priorities. It wasn't until four years later, in 1938, that chemists Otto Hahn and Fritz Strassmann, in collaboration with Lise Meitner, demonstrated that such fission is indeed possible. But when Noddack reminded everyone that it was, in fact, originally her idea, her assertion fell on deaf ears. When Hahn was awarded the Nobel Prize in Chemistry in 1944, Noddack and Meitner were both excluded.[476]

When physicist Chien-Shiung Wu proved a theory by two men, they won the Nobel while she was ignored (see the Physics section). Interestingly, the exact opposite seems to have happened here—instead of recognising the person who originated the theory, they gave it to only one of the people who proved the theory.

The 1996 Nobel Prize in Chemistry went to Harold W. Kroto, Robert F. Curl, and Richard E. Smalley for their landmark paper on the experimental production and observation of buckminsterfullerene, or C60—a substance made up of molecules composed of 60 carbon atoms. The soccer ball-like structure of C60 means that it can interact with other substances in a variety of unique ways, and applications for C60 and other fullerenes range from biomedical to nanotechnology to solar energy cells. But 12 years before the men's paper was published in 1985, Russian Academy of Sciences computational chemist Elena Galpern made the first computational prediction of C60's stable structure. Her paper was published in Russia in 1973. "If you live in a closed society," observed Magdolna Hargittai of Budapest University of Technology & Economics, "where there used to be little opportunity for interaction with world scientists, there is a big chance that if you discover something important, its significance will be lost."[477]

Isabella Karle was one of the many overlooked spouses, whose collaboration with her husband Jerome meant many people credited only him for work they did together. Jerome and Herbert A Hauptman shared the 1985 Nobel in Chemistry for developing crystal structure determination methods, which enabled scientists to use maths to identify molecular structure rather than having to use X-ray

---

476 Tretkoff, Ernie, "December 1938: Lise Meitner & Otto Frisch Discover Nuclear Fission," American Physical Society, 2019, https://www.aps.org/publications/apsnews/200712/physicshistory.cfm
477 Borman, Stu, "These women scientists should have won the Nobel," Chemical and Engineering News, September 11, 2017, https://cen.acs.org/articles/95/i36/female-scientists-should-won-Nobel.html

crystallography, saving time and increasing precision. "It is almost impossible to give an example in the field of chemistry where this method is not being used," noted one Nobel judge. Isabella made vital contributions to that work, yet she was excluded. When Jerome first found out he had won, he reputedly immediately asked whether Isabella had won as well. It's unclear whether he protested when he found out she hadn't. She was also one of the youngest scientists on the Manhattan Project. Of their collaborations, Isabella later told the *Washington Post*, "I do the physical applications, he works with the theoretical. It makes a good team. Science requires both types."[478]

BIOLOGY

Any student of genetics is aware of the Hershey-Chase experiment, which confirmed that DNA carries genetic information. Conducted by Martha Chase and Alfred Hershey, the work earned the Nobel Prize in Physiology or Medicine in 1969—not for Chase, but for Hershey, who shared it with Max Delbrück and Salvador Luria, for their "discoveries concerning the genetic structure of viruses."

When Chase and Hershey were conducting their experiments in the 1950s, the function of DNA was still unclear. It was thought that DNA was too inert to carry genetic information, which was believed to be the job of protein. The experiments demonstrated that when bacteriophages, which are made up of DNA and protein, infect bacteria, their DNA enters the host bacterial cell, but most of their protein does not.

While some critics questioned Chase's contributions to the work and will point out that she was a research assistant and not a lead investigator, the fact that the experiment bears her name as well as Hershey's certainly indicates a partnership of equal value. She was also listed as a co-author on the results paper, which was uncommon for research assistants unless they contributed substantially. Yet, Hershey didn't

---

478 Langer, Emily, "Isabella L. Karle, Chemist Who Helped Reveal Structure of Molecules, Dies at 95," *The Washington Post*, April 8, 2023, https://www.washingtonpost.com/local/obituaries/isabella-l-karle-chemist-who-helped-reveal-structure-of-molecules-dies-at-95/2017/10/20/c778f268-b4ee-11e7-a908-a3470754bbb9_story.html

even acknowledge her contributions in his Nobel acceptance speech.[479]

Hilde Mangold's 1923 dissertation was "one of the very few doctoral theses in biology that have directly resulted in the awarding of a Nobel Prize" but she wasn't the one who received the 1935 Nobel Prize in Physiology or Medicine. Instead, it went to her mentor, Hans Spemann, who used Mangold's work as the foundation for "his" discovery of the embryonic organiser, which dictates early development. Mangold died at age 25, before her thesis results were published, meaning it is possible she would have shared the award had she lived—or not.[480]

While Jonas Salk is generally credited with the creation of the polio vaccine in 1955, Isabel Morgan discovered three subtypes of the virus and helped develop an experimental vaccine, which proved effective in monkeys, years earlier. Her work, including establishing that multiple boosters were needed for full immunity, were vital to Salk's later research. But because she left the field in 1949 to have a family, her inactivated virus was never tested in humans.[481] Salk himself was known to minimize the contributions of his predecessors, and even downplaying those of his own team.[482]

The Michaelis-Menten hypothesis explains how, and the rate at which, reversible binding reactions occur between enzymes and surfaces; combined with the supporting equation and constant, they form Michaelis-Menten kinetics. The discovery was a collaboration between biochemists Maud Menten and Leonor Michaelis. After becoming one of the first Canadian women to earn her MD in 1911, Menten moved to Berlin in 1912 to pursue research opportunities that were not available for women in Canada at the time. The following year, she and

---

479 Dawson, Milly, "Martha Chase Dies," Genome Biology, August 20, 2003, https://doi.org/10.1186/gb-spotlight-20030820-01

480 Ogilvie, Marilyn Bailey and Harvey, Joy Dorothy. "Mangold, Hilde (Proescholdt)," The Biographical Dictionary of Women in Science, 10th ed. (Scott F. Gilbert, 2003).

481 Ault, Alicia, "From the Inventor of Mass-Market Paper Bags to a Scientist Who Unraveled the Mysteries of Polio, Meet Five American Women Whose Remarkable Achievements Have Long Been Overlooked," Smithsonian Magazine, March 12, 2024, https://www.smithsonianmag.com/smithsonian-institution/from-inventor-mass-market-paper-bags-to-scientist-who-unraveled-mysteries-of-polio-meet-five-american-women-whose-remarkable-achievements-have-long-been-overlooked-180983931/

482 Tan, Siang Yong and Ponstein, Nate, "Jonas Salk (1914-1995): A vaccine against polio," Singapore Medical Journal, vol 60 no 1 (2019):9-10, https://www.ncbi.nlm.nih.gov/pmc/articles/PMC6351694/

Michaelis published their groundbreaking paper.[483]

But while she was credited and recognized for her work with Michaelis, it is her later work where her contributions were overlooked. As part of her work on properties of haemoglobin, Menten was the first to use electrophoresis to separate blood haemoglobin proteins in 1944. Her work was published years before that of Linus Pauling and his collaborators in 1951, yet he is usually given credit for the discovery.[484]

In 1944, Albert Schatz, Elizabeth Bugie and Selman Waksman published their discovery of streptomycin, yet when Waksman and Schatz patented it, her name was left off the application. Her daughter later stated that Bugie had been told it wasn't important for her to be included in the patent because she would later get married. Both Schatz and Bugie were excluded when Waksman alone won the Nobel in 1952.[485]

Born in 1647, German naturalist and scientific illustrator Maria Merian had a decidedly unladylike interest in insects. She observed and took notes on butterflies for years, but despite her significant discoveries about insect metamorphosis, her work was largely ignored by scientists of the day—not least because she wrote in her native German rather than the "official" language of science, Latin. Not to be deterred, she funded her own expedition to Suriname in 1699 to observe, record, and illustrate insects and plants previously unknown to European scientists, later publishing her *Metamorphosis Insectorum Surinamensium*. Many of her classifications are still in use today, and her beautiful illustrations are both admired and used as scientific resources.[486]

It is frustratingly common for the work of nurses to be undervalued. Embryologist and nurse Jean Purdy was a key contributor to the work that resulted in

---

483 "Leonor Michaelis and Maud Leonora Menten," Science History Institute, https://sciencehistory.org/education/scientific-biographies/leonor-michaelis-and-maud-leonora-menten/

484 "Maud L. Menten, MD," Canadian Medical Hall of Fame, https://www.cdnmedhall.ca/laureates/maudmenten

485 Shelby, Natalie, "The Forgotten Women of the Antibiotics Race," Lady Science, July 22, 2021, https://www.ladyscience.com/features/forgotten-women-researchers-in-the-race-for-antibiotics-2021

486 Latty, Tanya, "Hidden Women of History: Maria Sibylla Merian, 17th-Century Entomologist and Scientific Adventurer," The Conversation, February 21, 2019, https://theconversation.com/hidden-women-of-history-maria-sibylla-merian-17th-century-entomologist-and-scientific-adventurer-112057

the birth of the first IVF (in-vitro fertilisation) baby in 1978. Yet as her male colleagues Professor Sir Robert Edwards and the surgeon Patrick Steptoe were lauded, Purdy was ignored to the point that she was deliberately excluded from a plaque honouring the achievement despite protests from Edwards. When he proposed including her, he was told by local health authorities that it would read "Mr Patrick Steptoe, Dr. Robert Edwards and their supporting staff." A 1981 letter from Edwards pushing the point reads, "I feel strongly about the inclusion of the names of the people who helped with the conception of Louise Brown. I feel this especially about Jean Purdy, who travelled to Oldham with me for 10 years, and contributed as much as I did to the project. Indeed, I regard her as an equal contributor to Patrick Steptoe and myself." In another instance he referred to her as "crucial," and that the work actually stopped for several months when Purdy had to take leave to care for her ailing mother. Edwards alone received the Nobel Prize in Physiology or Medicine in 2010. While both Steptoe and Purdy had died in the 1980s and were therefore ineligible because it cannot be given posthumously, it seems likely based on many other examples that were this not the case, Steptoe would have been included and Purdy excluded. [487]

Even when a woman's discovery is named for her, that doesn't guarantee recognition. Anna Wessels Williams isolated and cultivated a strain of bacteria that causes diphtheria, work that was pivotal to mass-producing an antitoxin to fight the disease. Within a year, the antitoxin was being sent to doctors in the U.S. and U.K., free of charge, as Williams was promoted to a full-time position as assistant bacteriologist. Even though she discovered it while he was gone, her boss got top billing when the strain was named "Park-Williams No. 8"—which was soon shortened to simply "Park 8."[488]

When botanist Jane Colden discovered a small plant with pink flowers near her New York home in 1753, she believed it was a species previously unidentified

---

487 Halliday, Josh, "Female Nurse Who Played Crucial Role in IVF Ignored on Plaque," *The Guardian*, June 9, 2019, https://www.theguardian.com/society/2019/jun/10/jean-purdy-female-nurse-who-played-crucial-role-in-ivf-ignored-on-plaque

488 Najera, Rene F, "Anna Wessels Williams, Immunologist," History of Vaccines, October 6, 2021, https://historyofvaccines.org/blog/anna-wessels-williams-immunologist

by Western science. She wrote to Carl Linnaeus, considered the premier expert of the day, that she had found a new species—he dismissed her and assumed it was St. John's wort. In fact, it was a new species—now known as Hypericum virginicum—but by the time other scientists figured this out, Colden's role had been forgotten and the honour of naming it was lost to her. Colden discovered a new white-flowered plant in 1756, and this time wrote to botanist John Ellis to lobby on her behalf to Linnaeus. Colden had wanted the name Fibraurea and Ellis wrote, "This young lady merits your esteem, and does honor your system ... suppose you should call this Coldenella, or any other name that may distinguish her among your genera." Linnaeus ignored both and called it Helleborus (later renamed Coptis groenlandica). Botanist Peter Collinson wanted to honour Colden's contributions to the field, and, like Ellis, asked Linnaeus to allow a plant to be named for her—although there were plenty of plants in need of names, Linnaeus refused. It's also worth noting that he was a blatant racist, applying his taxonomy classifications to humans as well, with white Europeans as a superior race, followed by Asians, Native Americans and, at the bottom, Africans. [489]

Biochemist Barbara Low was one of the first scientists in the U.S. to study X-ray diffraction of crystalline proteins in a lab and, through that work, discovered the elemental components of penicillin that enabled mass production and conversion into other antibiotic compounds. Until then, the life-saving drug had not been successfully synthesised. In an ironic twist, the very importance of Low's discovery was why she and her supervisor Dorothy Hodgkin went unacknowledged—their work on penicillin was classified for decades, though Hodgkin did win the Nobel in Chemistry in 1964, for her work mapping the structure of vitamin B12. [490]

Other women whose work on penicillin went largely unrecognized included lab assistant Mary Hunt, who reputedly found the mold that led to penicillium rubens strain NRRL 1951–the "parent" of all strains that would later be used

---

489 Kenyon-Flatt, Brittany, "Meet Jane Colden, the 18th Century Botanist Snubbed by Linnaeus," Massive Science, February 10, 2021, https://massivesci.com/articles/jane-colden-botany-colonial-america-new-york-marsh-st-johns-wort/
490 "Barbara Low: Pioneer in X-Ray Crystallography," Columbia University Irving Medical Center, March 5, 2019, https://www.cuimc.columbia.edu/news/barbara-low-pioneer-x-ray-crystallography

commercially.[491] Another Mary, Dr. Mary Ethel Florey, ran the first clinical trials of penicillin in 1941 alongside her lab partner and husband Howard Walter Florey–yet, like so many other wives, she was left out when he won a Nobel in 1945 for the work they had done together to transform Alexander Fleming's discovering into a useful and effective drug. The only mention of her in his Nobel bio is the last two sentences: "He married Mary Ethel Hayter Reed in 1926. They have two children, Paquita Mary Joanna and Charles du Vé."[492] Although the male Florey reportedly said, "It must never be forgotten that if it wasn't for Ethel penicillin would not have been introduced into medical practice when it was," he doesn't seem to have done much to promote or ensure her legacy.[493] He didn't even mention her in his lecture, which Nobel Prize winners deliver about their work, despite name-dropping more than a dozen other scientists.[494] Most folks with a vagina do not look forward to their Pap smears, a routine test in which a small scraping of cells is taken to test for abnormalities that may indicate problems like cervical cancer. But it's hard to argue with the numbers, given that it has been shown to reduce cervical cancer deaths by as much as 80 percent. While the test is named for Greek pathologist Georgios Papanikolaou, few people acknowledge that it was his wife, Andromachi "Mary" Papanikolaou, who spent more than 20 years having her own cervix scraped on a daily basis to provide the testing materials he needed, in addition to managing his laboratory and recruiting her friends to donate their own samples as well.[495]

Anatomist Anna Morandi Manzolini was acclaimed (if severely underpaid) in her time, but she was written out of history. In 1700s Bologna, she and her husband dissected hundreds of corpses and created hundreds of anatomical wax sculptures. Unlike others at the time, they systematically removed organ systems

---

[491] "The Forgotten Mother of Penicillin," October 10, 2023, The Disappearing Spoon Podcast, Science History Institute, https://www.sciencehistory.org/stories/disappearing-pod/the-forgotten-mother-of-penicillin/
[492] Nobel Lectures, Physiology or Medicine 1942-1962, Elsevier Publishing Company, Amsterdam, 1964, https://www.nobelprize.org/prizes/medicine/1945/florey/biographical/
[493] Bickel, Lennard, *Florey: The Man Who Made Penicillin* (Bloomsbury Reader, 1972).
[494] Florey, Howard, Nobel Lecture, December 11, 1945< https://www.nobelprize.org/uploads/2018/06/florey-lecture.pdf
[495] Nikolaos Chatziantoniou, "Lady Andromache (Mary) Papanicolaou: The Soul of Gynecological Cytopathology," *Journal of the American Society of Cytopathology*, vol 3 no 6: 319–326 (2014), doi:10.1016/j.jasc.2014.08.004. PMID 31051722.

for further study, enabling them to create detailed wax models of the organ system, perfect for teaching anatomy students. Unlike many husband-and-wife teams, Morandi was the public face of their partnerships, and her skill and fame only grew after his 1755 death, after which the Institute of Bologna appointed her Lecturer in Anatomy in her own name.[496]

Yet even her contemporaries sought to undermine her skills and achievements by emphasising her beauty, crediting her work as due to her devotion to her husband as "his wise and pious wife" or reducing her from his partner to a mere assistant—ignoring that her work continued after his death. Some, like anatomist Petronio Ignazio Zecchini, went much further. He actively attacked Morandi and other women intellectuals, whom he saw as interlopers who must be undermined. In his book *Genial Days: On the Dialectic of Women Reduced to Its True Principle*, he asserts that women are ruled by their uterus, not their brains and intellect like men, and tells women to "[w]illingly subject yourselves to men, who, by their counsel, can curb your instability and concupiscence."[497]

Morandi biographer Rebecca Messbarger observes that such accounts "have influenced her place in history to her detriment. She was essentially erased from history... Morandi had an international reputation. But even later biographical sketches represent [her husband] as the brains, and she was the gifted hand. In her lifetime, that wasn't true."[498]

When *Plants of New Zealand* was published in 1906, it was the first comprehensive, well-illustrated book on the topic to achieve popularity, becoming a classic that would have seven editions over the following six decades. Published under the authors' initials of R. M. Laing and E. F. Blackwell, Elizabeth Blackwell nonetheless was largely ignored for her role in the work. Her co-author, Robert Laing, appears to have done nothing to defend her when local botanists

---

[496] McNeill, Leila, "The Lady Anatomist Who Brought Dead Bodies to Light," *Smithsonian Magazine*, July 26, 2017, https://www.smithsonianmag.com/science-nature/lady-anatomist-who-brought-dead-bodies-light-180964165/
[497] Zecchini, Petronio Ignazio, 1771, *Genial Days: On the Dialectic of Women Reduced to Its True Principle*.
[498] McNeill, Leila, "The Lady Anatomist Who Brought Dead Bodies to Light," Smithsonian, July 26, 2017, https://www.smithsonianmag.com/science-nature/lady-anatomist-who-brought-dead-bodies-light-180964165/

and contemporary reviewers disregarded her contributions, which included photographs, knowledge, and writing. Laing was well-known in the male-dominated New Zealand scientific community, which was all too happy to give him sole credit—and he seems to have been all too willing to take it at Blackwell's expense.[499]

ASTRONOMY

Astronomers Williamina Paton Fleming, Antonia Maury, Annie Jump Cannon, Florence Cushman, and Henrietta Swan Leavitt were among the underpaid women who worked in the Harvard Observatory in the 1890s and early 1900s, mapping the skies. Most of the work that came out of the Observatory was done by these women, including:

The Draper Catalogue of Stellar Spectra, published in 1890—Fleming classified most of the spectra and was credited with classifying more than 10,000 featured stars and discovering 10 novae and more than 200 variable stars. It's also worth noting that the catalogue was funded by Mary Anna Draper in honour of her late husband, an amateur astronomer whom she worked with on astronomical photography and research in her own right. Cushman determined the positions and magnitudes of the stars in the catalogue, which featured the spectra of around 222,000 stars.

Maury published her own stellar classification catalogue in 1897, which included 4,800 photographs and her analyses of 681 bright northern stars. It was the first time a woman was credited for an observatory publication.

From 1901 to 1912, Cannon devised the current Harvard classification system, the first real attempt to organise and classify stars based on their temperatures and spectral types. It is still in use today. Over her 40-year career, Cannon observed and classified more than 200,000 stars.

Leavitt, while measuring photographic plates to catalogue the positions and brightness of stars, discovered the relationship between the luminosity

---

[499] Dell, R. K., "Blackwell, Ellen Wright," *Dictionary of New Zealand Biography*, first published in 1996, Te Ara – the Encyclopedia of New Zealand, https://teara.govt.nz/en/biographies/3b37/blackwell-ellen-wright

and the period of Cepheid variables (stars that pulsate radially, varying in diameter and temperature, that change in brightness, with a well-defined stable period and amplitude). This discovery gave astronomers the first standard with which to measure the distance to other galaxies.

Yet even when their work was recognized, such as when Maury published under her own name, the women were criticized for working outside the home and collectively referred to as Pickering's Harem, after Observatory director Edward Pickering. Pickering, meanwhile, explicitly said he hired women because he could pay them less, getting significantly more labour on a limited budget.[500]

On the other side of the world, more than 70 women were employed at observatories in Adelaide, Sydney, Melbourne, and Perth to measure, log and calculate the position of stars in the Australian night sky for the Astrographic Catalogue. This process began in 1887. Called "computers," "star measurers," and "clerical assistants," they were almost entirely left out of papers on their discoveries. "Astrographic computer" Charlotte Peel, who was acknowledged on one paper for her calculations and observations for a comet, was the sole exception. From 1902 to 1964, 254 volumes of raw data were published.[501]

French astronomer Amélie Lefrançais worked with her husband, among other collaborators, yet she was not listed as an author on any of the publications that she worked on, even ones that were made up almost entirely of the tables that she calculated. Her husband was the director of the École Militaire observatory, elected to the Bureau des Longitudes and the Astronomy Section of the Academy of Sciences, and was made an officer of the Légion d'Honneur. Presumably due to her gender, such honours were withheld from Amélie herself.[502]

Elisabeth Hevelius, one of the first female astronomers, married the 52-year-old

---

500   Geiling, Natasha, "The Women Who Mapped the Universe and Still Couldn't Get Any Respect," *Smithsonian Magazine*, September 18, 2013, https://www.smithsonianmag.com/history/the-women-who-mapped-the-universe-and-still-couldnt-get-any-respect-9287444/
501   Stevenson, Toner, "Windows to the Stars – RiAus Education," January 15, 2021, https://education.riaus.org.au/cosmos-magazine-windows-to-the-stars/
502   O'Connor, J. J. and Robertson, E. F., "Amélie Harlay," School of Mathematics and Statistics University of St Andrews, Scotland, December 2021, https://mathshistory.st-andrews.ac.uk/Biographies/Harlay

Johannes Hevelius when she was only 16, driven largely by her desire to study the stars—the internationally renowned astronomer owned the best observatory in the world. For more than 20 years, they worked together, and after his 1687 death, she completed and published their *Prodromus Astronomiae*, a catalogue of more than 1,500 stars. Despite her many contributions to the project, his was the only name on the title page.[503]

Jocelyn Bell Burnell discovered the first pulsar as a doctoral student in the Cambridge University radio astronomy lab in the late 1960s, identifying its unusual signal as an object of significance. Yet she was excluded from the 1974 Nobel Prize for Physics, which went instead to her thesis supervisor Antony Hewish and astronomer Martin Ryle. Many scientists argued at the time (and since) that she should have been recognized as well, including Fred Hoyle and Thomas Gold, who completed the puzzle to prove that Bell's find was indeed a spinning, pulsing neutron star.[504]

Bell Burnell herself took a humble approach—presumably to avoid making waves that could make it more difficult for her future career—saying in 1977, "I believe it would demean Nobel Prizes if they were awarded to research students, except in very exceptional cases, and I do not believe this is one of them." That argument simply doesn't hold water, however, given that plenty of men were students when they did their Nobel-winning work—just among the physicists, this includes Lawrence Bragg (1915), Bob Schrieffer (1972), Brian Josephson (1973), Russell Hulse (1993), Douglas Osheroff (1996), Frank Wilczek (2004), and Konstantin Novoselov (2010). [505]Hewish also took lead authorship of the paper announcing Bell Burnell's discovery—she was placed second among five authors.

After building a clock with an astronomical function with her husband, Nicole-Reine Lepaute collaborated with him and astronomer Jérôme Lalande to produce

---

503 Ashworth, William B., "Elisabeth Hevelius," The Linda Hall Library, December 22, 2017, https://www.lindahall.org/about/news/scientist-of-the-day/elisabeth-hevelius

504 Rozman, Michael, "Professor Jocelyn Bell Burnell – 2019 Katzenstein Lecturer | Department of Physics," October 24, 2019, https://physics.uconn.edu/2019/10/24/professor-jocelyn-bell-burnell-2019-katzenstein-lecturer/

505 Siegel, Ethan, "These 5 Women Deserved, and Were Unjustly Denied, a Nobel Prize in Physics," Forbes, October 11, 2018, https://www.forbes.com/sites/startswithabang/2018/10/11/these-5-women-deserved-and-were-unjustly-denied-a-nobel-prize-in-physics/?sh=7bed2356195e

a *Traité d'horlogerie* (Treatise of Clockmaking), published in 1775. Although it was her idea and she participated in its construction, as well as the writing of the treatise, it was published only under her husband's name. Lalande acknowledged her contributions, noting "Madame Lepaute computed for this book a table of numbers of oscillations for pendulums of different lengths, or the lengths for each given number of vibrations, from that of 18 lignes, that does 18000 vibrations per hour, up to that of 3000 leagues." She then worked with him and a male mathematician, to calculate when Halley's Comet would return and the comet's attraction to Jupiter and Saturn. Working for more than six months, the team predicted in November 1758 that it would arrive on April 13, 1759 with a margin of error of a month on either side. They were off by precisely one month when it returned on March 13, 1759, but it was the first time scientists had successfully predicted when the comet would cross the perihelion (the point of the comet's orbit closest to the sun). Lalande did not acknowledge Lepaute's contributions at all—allegedly removing all mentions of her from the book he published in 1760 to please another woman—though Lalande remained her staunch proponent, crediting her in an article calling her the "most distinguished female French astronomer ever."[506]

PHYSICS

Physicist Chien-Shiung Wu had many nicknames, including "First Lady of Physics," "Queen of Nuclear Research" and the "Chinese Madame Curie." Unlike Curie, however, Wu never won a Nobel—but her male colleagues did, thanks to her work. In the 1950s, Wu set out to test a theory of Tsung-Dao Lee and Chen-Ning Yang, whether spinning, decaying particles have a preferred direction that they spin in. Wu experimented using cobalt-60 in the presence of a strong magnetic field—the electrons produced by the radioactive decay of the cobalt showed a preferred direction. In science terms, she proved parity is not conserved. So even though the Nobel committee won't give out awards for untested theories, they ignored

---

[506] Bernardi, Gabriella, *The Unforgotten Sisters: Female Astronomers and Scientists before Caroline Herschel* (Springer, 2016).

the fact that Wu proved Lee and Yang's theory and only recognized the men.[507]

Wu also worked on the Manhattan Project, where she helped develop the process for separating uranium into uranium-235 and uranium-238 isotopes through gaseous diffusion and later researched molecular changes in haemoglobin associated with sickle-cell anaemia. Of the Wu experiment, she later declared, "These were moments of exhilaration and ecstasy! A glimpse of this wonder can be the reward of a lifetime." [508] Though a Nobel also makes a nice reward.

In 1951, Experimental Breeder Reactor 1 in the U.S. became the world's first reactor to produce electricity using nuclear energy, with later testing confirming that a reactor could produce more fuel than it consumed. In 1963, EBR-1 was dedicated as a National Historic Landmark. Following the initial experiments, all the men involved wrote their names on an interior wall of the building that housed the reactor, but none of the women were invited to include their names, regardless of how vital they had been to the program's success. It was not until 1994 that the Department of Energy added a plaque at the site recognising the contributions of Wilma S. Mangum, Eleanor B. Barnes, Gladys Joslin, Virginia Kruse, and Agnes Williams.[509]

Astrophysicist Margaret Burbidge and her husband Geoffrey were invited to work with William Alfred Fowler and Fred Hoyle at the University of Cambridge in 1951. They combined the data the Burbidges had collected on the abundances of different chemical elements in stars with Hoyle's hypothesis that nuclear reactions in stars might produce chemical elements, a topic that Fowler had been conducting experiments on. Margaret was the lead author on their culminating paper in 1957, and their work established the basis for what came to be known as stellar nucleosynthesis. Of the four scientists, Fowler alone was awarded the 1983 Nobel Prize in Physics for his work on the topic, and expressed surprise that

---

507 Siegel, Ethan, "These 5 Women Deserved, and Were Unjustly Denied, a Nobel Prize in Physics," Forbes, October 11, 2018, https://www.forbes.com/sites/startswithabang/2018/10/11/these-5-women-deserved-and-were-unjustly-denied-a-nobel-prize-in-physics/?sh=7bed2356195e

508 Shearer, Benjamin F. and Barbara Smith Shearer, *Notable Women in the Physical Sciences: A Biographical Dictionary* (Greenwood, 1997).

509 Grant, Sheila D., "EBR-I, the World's First Nuclear Power Plant, Continues to Inspire Innovation in the Idaho Desert," Roadtrippers, July 22, 2019, https://roadtrippers.com/magazine/ebr-1-atomic-museum-nuclear-power/

his colleagues were excluded. All four had also been nominated almost 20 years earlier for the 1964 award.[510]

GEOLOGY AND PALAEONTOLOGY

Although Eileen Guppy worked in the field for 43 years and had a Bachelor of Science in geology, she was only recognized as a geologist for three of those years. Instead she held the common "women's" titles of secretary and scientific assistant, only promoted to assistant geologist in 1943 because of the loss of male staff to World War II. She was promptly demoted when the men returned in 1945. She worked for almost four decades at the British Geological Survey, yet she was almost never credited for her contributions to publications and reports.[511]

Charlotte Murchison and Mary Horner Lyell are more of our many overlooked wives, who worked with their husbands, Roderick Impey Murchison and Charles Lyell. Both women accompanied their husbands on expeditions and worked as illustrators. Mary was a significant but uncredited contributor to Charles's 1830s book, *Principles of Geology*. She is also known for her studies on evolution, having worked with Charles Darwin and conducted a study in 1854 of Canary Island's land snails comparable to Darwin's of Galapagos tortoises. Darwin praised her not least as "a monument of patience" when collaborating with himself and her husband.[512]

Meanwhile, Charlotte collected and studied fossils, with other geologists of the time studying and publishing works about fossils in her collection. She was so adamant about attending Charles Lyell's lectures that she convinced him to open them to women. She also helped her husband develop his publications, including providing illustrations. Indeed, as Mary Somerville wrote of Charlotte, "... she had studied science, especially geology, and it was chiefly owing to her exemplar that her husband turned his mind to those pursuits in which he afterwards obtained

---

510 Skuse, Ben, "Celebrating Astronomer Margaret Burbidge, 1919–2020," Sky & Telescope, April 6, 2020, https://skyandtelescope.org/astronomy-news/happy-birthday-margaret-burbidge/
511 Gibson, Hazel, "Eileen Guppy," Trowelblazers, May 8, 2014, https://trowelblazers.com/2014/05/08/eileen-guppy-the-first-woman-geologist-in-the-british-geological-survey/
512 Hunter, Dana, "Mary Horner Lyell: 'a Monument of Patience,'" Scientific American Blog Network, April 25, 2013, https://blogs.scientificamerican.com/rosetta-stones/mary-horner-lyell-a-monument-of-patience/

such distinction." Archibald Geikie wrote in 1875, "to his wife he owed his fame, as he never failed gracefully to record," yet not enough to acknowledge her as a contributor to his prolific output (180 papers and three books).[513]

Murchison's friend, palaeontologist Mary Anning's, work largely revolved around helping men who did not credit her. Many of her contemporaries published papers that relied largely on her discoveries and interpretations, without acknowledging her at all. Despite being well-known in scientific communities in Europe and the U.S., with other scientists consulting her on anatomy as well as palaeontology, the Geological Society of London refused her admission because of her gender. As one example of her impact, it was Anning who suggested to William Buckland that the items known as bezoar stones were actually fossilised faeces—important not only for indicating the diets of the animals whose remains they were found in, but also containing fossilised bones of smaller prey animals. The letter in which she advised him of this sold at auction for more than £100,000 in 2020.[514]

She struggled financially for many years, though her friend, eminent geologist Henry De la Beche, sold prints of his *Duria Antiquior*—the first widely circulated visual representation of a scene from prehistoric life based on fossil reconstructions—for her benefit, not least because much of it was based on fossils Anning found. While Anning published no scientific papers during her life, her many wealthy gentlemen clients published descriptions of the fossils they bought from her. A friend wrote of Anning, "She says the world has used her ill ... these men of learning have sucked her brains, and made a great deal of publishing works, of which she furnished the contents, while she derived none of the advantages."[515]

MATHS

Engraved on the side of the Eiffel Tower are the names of 72 men—and no

---

513   Kölbl-Ebert, Martina, "Charlotte Murchison (Née Hugonin) 1788-1869." Earth Sciences History, vol 16 no 1 (1997): 39–43, https://doi.org/10.17704/eshi.16.1.97014235w8u4k414
514   Parks, Shoshi, "This Dino-Mite Lady Unearthed Some of History's Most Important Dinosaurs, Only to Have Men Steal..." Timeline, April 18, 2018, https://timeline.com/mary-anning-discovered-a-bunch-of-cool-dinosaurs-but-men-stole-them-ab18f206bf35
515   Pinney, Anna, *The Dragon Seekers* (Perseus Publishing, 2001).

women—whose works in science and mathematics Gustave Eiffel considered vital to its construction. Left off the list was mathematician Sophie Germain, whose work in the theory of elasticity was integral to the tower's construction. Historian John Augustine Zahm wrote in 1913, "Was she excluded from this list for the same reason she was ineligible for membership in the French Academy—because she was a woman? If such, indeed, was the case, more is the shame for those who were responsible for such ingratitude toward one who had deserved so well of science, and who by her achievements had won an enviable place in the hall of fame."[516]

Betty Shannon's husband Claude was a scientific rock star of the mid-1900s, helping to usher in the computer age. While Claude was well-known to both scientific circles and the general public, few realised Betty was his closest collaborator. They met in 1948 at Bell Labs, where Betty was a computer—the women doing the maths the male engineers needed to make things work—and also published her own research. With an intellect that matched his own, she was often the first person that the notoriously solitary Claude came to with an idea. Betty would look up references, take notes, suggest improvements, and edit his written work, as well as more hands-on, technical contributions. As an article in *Scientific American* notes, "Though his ideas were very much his own, Betty turned them into publishable work." In a scientific twist on the wife-as-muse trope, she also encouraged him to try new activities, take speaking engagements and travel to new places—all of which expanded his thinking and ultimately benefited his work.[517]

---

516 Lienhard, John H, "Sophie Germain," The Engines of Our Ingenuity (Cullen College of Engineering), https://www.uh.edu/engines/epi223.htm
517 Soni, Jimmy and Goodman, Rob, "Betty Shannon, Unsung Mathematical Genius," Scientific American Blog Network, July 24, 2017, https://blogs.scientificamerican.com/voices/betty-shannon-unsung-mathematical-genius/

THE ARTS

Wassily Kandinsky is often considered the father of European abstract art. He claimed that he produced the first abstract painting in 1911, writing to his gallarist in 1935 of the piece, "Indeed, it's the world's first ever abstract picture, because back then not one single painter was painting in an abstract style. A "historic painting," in other words." Whether knowingly or not, Kandinsky was wrong—Swedish artist Hilma af Klint had beaten him to the punch by several years. She produced *Primordial Chaos*, her first series of abstract paintings in 1906 and 1907, at age 44 and after 20 years making art. [518]

Like many abstract artists of the time, af Klint and Kandinsky were both interested in spiritualism and related practices. While this likely influenced their art separately, it is interesting to note that it connected them through a person as well, occultist Rudolf Steiner. When af Klint met him in 1908, she had invited him to visit her in Stockholm and see her work. He was reputedly unimpressed, telling her that most of her work was inappropriate for a theosophist. Yet he seemed intrigued by *Primordial Chaos*, and kept photographs of certain pieces, even having some of the photographs hand-coloured. Later that year, he met Kandinsky—who would not produce his "historic painting" until 1911. It is entirely reasonable to assume that Steiner may have shown Kandinsky the images of af Klint's work, leading him to abstract art. It wouldn't have been the only time—Kandinsky later adopted his

---

518   Voss, Julia, "The First Abstract Artist? (and It's Not Kandinsky)," Tate, June 25 2019, https://www.tate.org.uk/tate-etc/issue-27-spring-2013/first-abstract-artist-and-its-not-kandinsky

student, lover, and collaborator Gabriele Münter's use of saturated colours and abstract expressionist style.

The 1989 China, the Avant-Garde Exhibition was shut down only two hours after it opened because Xiao Lu suddenly shot her own artwork with a pellet gun. Although intended as an artistic statement, the act made her an inspiration for China's political and cultural activists. In the charged political atmosphere, her gunshots became known as the "first gunshots of Tiananmen" as the massacre at the square happened just four months later. [519] In 2014, she said in an interview, "I created the work out of personal feelings, but this work became interpreted with political meanings...I don't reject this. I've come to understand that with this work, making it for myself is one thing, but how it is interpreted is also a big part of it."[520] She and her partner Tang Song were both arrested, and she emigrated to Australia. For 15 years, it was assumed that Song was the one behind the act, until Lu publicly stated that it was solely her work, not instigated or planned by her boyfriend. There was swift and intense backlash from the Chinese art community, accusing her of being bitter following their break-up. As Gao Minglu writes, "The revision was perceived as going against the whole established history of avant-garde art, against authority, even against patriarchal society. Therefore, Xiao Lu's revision lost her the former sympathy towards her. The avenging actions of lovelorn woman did not involve any question of justice. Even within the inner core of the 'avant-garde', whose calling is rebellion as such, Xiao Lu's revision encountered enormous obstruction."[521]

Suzanne Duchamp-Crotti was more than the little sister of famous artists—she was an influential Dadaist painter, sculptor, and collage maker. But as many younger siblings have experienced, she was working in the shadow of her elder brothers, all famous artists in their own right: painter and printmaker Jacques

---

519 Lu, Xiao, "Xiao Lu "Dialogue" / In English," Xiao Lu Art, August 22 2020, http://www.xiaoluart.com/index.php?c=show&id=27
520 Wen, Philip, "25 years on, artist remembers 'first gunshots of Tiananmen.'" *Sydney Morning Herald*, May 30, 2014, https://www.smh.com.au/world/25-years-on-artist-remembers-first-gunshots-of-tiananmen-20140530-zrspf.html
521 Xiao Lu, *Dialogue* (Hong Kong University Press, 2010).

Villon, sculptor Raymond Duchamp-Villon, and painter, sculptor, and writer Marcel Duchamp. She married another artist, painter Jean Crotti, which in turn led to her being relegated to the "wife of" status by many.[522]

Gwen Verdon was the epitome of a Broadway triple threat—a Tony-winning singer, actor, and dancer whose career in theatre, film, and stage spanned more than 60 years. But although acclaimed and beloved as a performer, she was generally not credited for her work as a dance coach and teacher, assistant choreographer, and assistant director. Her role as her husband Bob Fosse's collaborator was key to his success, yet he never properly credited her for her contributions. She already had a Tony before their first production together (*Damn Yankees*, 1955), so it's likely that her reputation was an asset to his early career.

Although Verdon was credited as choreographer on the 1953 hit film *The Mississippi Gambler*, and as special dance coordinator for the 1985 sci-fi classic *Cocoon*, she went uncredited for her roles as assistant choreographer on the 1969 film adaptation of *Sweet Charity* and on the beloved 1952 musical film *Singin' in the Rain*, and as dance coach for 1951's *On the Riviera*. In the 1986 revival of *Sweet Charity*, she was credited as "assistant to Mr. Fosse." The only theatre production for which she received an assistant dance credit was 1948's *Magdalena*, which she worked on with Jack Cole long before she met Fosse. Verdon was also the one who pushed for the creation of the musical *Chicago*, and her contract gave her unprecedented control over the production, yet she was not credited as a producer.[523]

Nancy Holt was one of the early leaders of the land art movement, but her work has long been overshadowed by that of her husband, Robert Smithson, with whom she collaborated extensively on massive earthworks. Following Smithson's untimely death at age 35 in 1973, Holt committed much of her time and energy to ensuring his legacy. "On a very basic level, simply by virtue of her gender Holt challenges the popular imagination of Land Art as an especially masculine arena ... populated by rugged men reshaping remote landscapes with heavy machinery,"

---

522 Kwartler, Talia, "Suzanne Duchamp, Katherine S. Dreier, and "Semi-Abstract" Painting," Yale University Art Gallery Bulletin, 2020, https://www.jstor.org/stable/27113359
523 Schrock, Madeline, "Gwen Verdon Is Uncredited for Her Work on One of Hollywood's Most Iconic Dance Movies," *Dance Magazine*, September 19, 2019, https://www.dancemagazine.com/gwen-verdon-merely-marvelous/

said one collector. "Although recent scholarship has complicated this reductive reading, it has proven remarkably persistent." [524]

Comedian Sarah Ophelia Colley Cannon, better known as Minnie Pearl, was part of the Grand Ole Opry for half a century. From the inception of the Country Music Hall of Fame, she was nominated every single year—14 times—before she was finally inducted in 1975. While she was admittedly known more for comedy than singing, her many nominations were an indicator of her contributions to the culture the Hall represents. At the ceremony, singer Tennessee Ernie Ford observed, "no one exemplifies the endearing values of pure country comedy more," calling her "the first country music humourist to be known and loved worldwide." She got a standing ovation. [525]

In contrast, icon Dolly Parton was eligible for the Rock & Roll Hall of Fame for 30 years before she was finally nominated, and won, in 2022. In addition to having 11 Grammys out of more than 50 nominations, she had already been inducted into several halls of fame, including Country Music, Songwriters, Gospel Music, and three songs in the Grammy Hall of Fame.[526]

While William Moulton Marston is credited as the creator of Wonder Woman, his wife Elizabeth and their polyamorous partner Olive Byrne were highly influential in her development, to the point that when Marston first raised the idea of creating a comic book hero, Elizabeth reportedly said, "Fine—but make her a woman."[527] But although Wonder Woman has proven the most enduring over time, another character had also hit the stands six months earlier. Miss Fury debuted in April 1941 and was written and drawn by June Tarpé Mills, making her the first comic superheroine to be created by a woman, though she initially went by Tarpé

---

524 Anderson, Gracie, "Archives of Groundbreaking Land Artist Nancy Holt Head to the Smithsonian," *Smithsonian Magazine*, July 13, 2021, https://www.smithsonianmag.com/smart-news/nancy-holt-archives-smithsonian-180978154/

525 Levy, Shawn, *In on the Joke: The Original Queens of Standup Comedy* (Doubleday, 2022).

526 Neal, Matt, "Dolly Parton Finally Receives Rock & Roll Hall of Fame Nomination. Why Has It Taken so Long?" ABC News, February 3, 2022, https://www.abc.net.au/news/2022-02-03/rock-roll-hall-fame-explainer/100800680

527 Lepore, Jill, "The Man behind Wonder Woman Was Inspired by Both Suffragists and Centerfolds," NPR, Fresh Air, June 9, 2017, https://www.npr.org/2017/06/09/532149100/the-man-behind-wonder-woman-was-inspired-by-both-suffragists-and-centerfolds

Mills to hide her gender in the male-dominated field. Socialite by day and catsuit-wearing vigilante by night, Marla Darke and her alter ego graced newspapers across the U.S. for more than 10 years, though 37 newspapers dropped the comic in 1947 after she was drawn wearing a bikini.[528]

Hilda Rebay was vital to the creation of the Guggenheim and was then ignobly forced out after it was established. She spent years as advisor to Solomon R. Guggenheim and then as the curator and director of its first incarnation, the Museum of Non-Objective Painting. She built not only one of the best modern abstract art collections in the U.S., but also relationships and reputation for the young institution. In addition to being an artist herself, she was also a major proponent of individual artists, contributing greatly to their success and even helping some escape Nazi Germany. Yet after Guggenheim's death, and despite a letter from him stating, "It is my further wish that during the lifetime of Miss Rebay the Foundation accept no gifts and make no purchases of paintings without her approval," she soon found herself undermined. Rebay's budget was severely restricted, and she was eventually forced out, removed not only as director but eventually as a trustee and director emeritus as well. When the museum was renamed and re-opened in 1959, the woman who built it was not even invited to the party. Adding one final insult to injury, after Rebay's death, the trustees of her own foundation, which she had created to establish her own museum from her own impressive collection, gave everything to the very museum that forced her out instead.[529]

While Lucille Ball is renowned as a beloved comedian, she was also a producer—and not just of *I Love Lucy*. Without a doubt, her most enduring legacy in this regard is her support of the original *Star Trek* series. As head of Desilu Productions in the 1960s, she was one of the most powerful women in Hollywood. And when series creator Gene Roddenberry came to pitch his show, she not only gave him a shot—she gave him two. Even as board members were hesitant about the idea, Ball greenlit the show and when NBC rejected it based on the first pilot,

---

528　Barber, Nicholas, "Remembering Miss Fury – the World's First Great Superheroine," BBC, March 30 2021, https://www.bbc.com/culture/article/20210329-remembering-miss-fury-the-worlds-first-great-superheroine
529　"Hilla Rebay," The Art Story, https://www.theartstory.org/artist/rebay-hilla/

she bankrolled a second, launching one of television's most enduring franchises. As one tribute notes, "Her belief in *Star Trek* is why we have *Star Trek* as it stands today. Ball was more than just a comedian and a beloved television icon, she was a savvy producer who deserved credit for her work behind the scenes, including helping to achieve Roddenberry's vision. For this, we can all love Lucy."[530]

---

530 "How Lucille Ball Helped Star Trek Become a Cultural Icon," StarTrek.com, August 6, 2023, https://intl.startrek.com/news/how-lucille-ball-helped-star-trek-become-a-cultural-icon

THE ACTIVISTS

Called "doyenne of American Negro women" by iconic activist Pauli Murray, Anna Arnold Hedgeman had been active in both feminism and Civil Rights for decades when she helped organize the 1963 March on Washington. But facing what Mary Church Terrell called the "double handicap of race and sex," just as white feminists dismissed her due to race, the male leadership of the Civil Rights movement disregarded women's potential to lead. "Suffice it to say that the male would be better advised to spend less time mourning the loss of his superiority and more time working in partnership with women," Hedgeman wrote.[531]

She'd been speaking publicly on the topic for years, in speeches with titles like "Why Women Walk Two Steps behind Their Men," "The Role of the Negro Woman," "Women and the New America," and "Equal-Unequal." Hedgeman herself had built a network of women in government and activism, and recognized their accomplishments even as the men actively denied them leadership positions. African American women were the core of the movement, yet their differing experiences to men's were generally disregarded.

When head of the National Council of Negro Women Dorothy Height proposed that Hedgeman speak at the March, the men in charge refused, claiming there were already too many speakers, that it was too hard to choose one woman, and if they did it would make others jealous—it seems doubtful it even occurred

---

[531] Scanlon, Jennifer, "Where Were the Women in the March on Washington?" The New Republic, March 16, 2016, https://newrepublic.com/article/131587/women-march-washington

to them that the possibility of more than one was an option. Women could sing, organize, recruit, and march—they just couldn't speak. The "compromise" was that A. Philip Randolp would say a few words about the women's contributions, then a group of women could stand and take a bow. The women included Myrlie Evers, Diane Nash Bevel, Rosa Parks, Gloria Richardson, Daisy Bates ,and Paris Lee. The women were then grouped with the wives of the male leaders, separate from and behind the men. Daisy Bates unexpectedly took the mic, to declare, "The women of this country, Mr. Randolph, pledge to you ... that we will join hands with you as women of this country. We will kneel-in, we will sit-in, until we can eat in any counter in the United States. We will walk until we are free, until we can walk to any school and take our children to any school in the United States. And we will sit-in and we will kneel-in and we will lie-in if necessary until every Negro in America can vote. This we pledge to the women of America."[532]

Retaking the mic even though Bates was meant to introduce the other women, Randolph stumbled through the remainder of the "Tribute to Negro Women." He called for Myrlie Evers, apparently unaware that she had not made it. The recording is almost painful: "Uh, who else? Will the ... [someone behind him says: Rosa Parks] Miss Rosa Parks ... will they all stand. And Miss, uh [someone behind him says: Gloria Richardson] Gloria Richardson."

Hedgeman herself recalled, "We grinned; some of us, as we recognized anew that Negro women are second-class citizens in the same way that white women are in our culture." Another reminder came at the end of the March, when the male leaders went to the White House to meet with President John F. Kennedy. None of the women were invited. The exclusion of Rosa Parks in particular bothered Hedgeman, who was tired of seeing the smart, dedicated civil rights warrior presented as a quiet seamstress who kept her seat on the bus because she was tired—rather than because she was sick and tired of life in the Jim Crow South as an African American woman. Pauli Murray described the situation as "bitterly

---

532   Bates, Daisy, Speech delivered at the March on Washington, August 28, 1963, https://cooperproject.org/daisy-bates-speaks-at-the-1963-march-on-washington/

humiliating," because "the omission was deliberate."[533]

Marcus Garvey married two women with a lot in common—both were Jamaican journalists named Amy, and both had their own accomplishments overshadowed by their more famous husband. Amy Ashwood was first, married from 1919 until their divorce in 1922, when Garvey married Amy Jacques. Although the first marriage was deeply dysfunctional, Ashwood and Garvey were better activists than spouses, co-founding, in 1914, the Universal Negro Improvement Association (UNIA), which was the most influential anti-colonial organisation in Jamaica for decades. The same year, they co-founded the international *Negro World* newspaper, and Jacques was also one of the first directors of UNIA's shipping line, the Black Star Line. In the decades after their divorce, she became heavily involved in promoting African and diaspora arts and artists in addition to her pan-Africanist activism. Amy Jacques was also involved in *Negro World* from its inception in 1918, and she was a popular speaker who traveled both with her husband and independent of him. She also assumed interim leadership of UNIA when Garvey was convicted of mail fraud less than a year into their marriage. Despite her tireless support of him, he never showed any appreciation for her work, acknowledged her influence, or allowed her to take an official position of leadership in the UNIA.[534] [535]

The trend of African American women's activism going unacknowledged dates back to the abolition years. Born enslaved, as an adult free woman Hester Lane built her own business and used her success to buy other people out of slavery, as well as working tirelessly as a fundraiser for different organisations. But while the men, particularly white men, were happy for her financial support in the cause of abolition, she was prevented from taking a leadership role. When women were finally admitted to the executive committee in the American Anti-Slavery Society, of which Lane was a member, they were all Caucasian. Her nomination had been

---

533 Murray, Pauli, "The Negro Woman in the Quest for Equality," Council of Negro Women Convention, Washington, D.C., November 14, 1963, https://ebin.pub/sisters-in-the-struggle-african-american-women-in-the-civil-rights-black-power-movement-9780814790380.html
534 "Amy Ashwood," PBS: American Experience, https://www.pbs.org/wgbh/americanexperience/features/garvey-ashwood/
535 "Amy Jacques," PBS: American Experience, February 13, 2019, https://www.pbs.org/wgbh/americanexperience/features/garvey-jacques/

rejected, leading one member to comment, "Hester Lane is well known in this city as a woman of good character and senses, and has been a slave, but the 'principle' could not carry her color." Soon after, she gave up her abolition work, and the cause lost a dedicated proponent.[536]

In the story of Frederick Douglass, his wife and fellow abolitionist Anna Murray is generally overlooked. Given little mention in Douglass's three autobiographies, historian Henry Louis Gates has written that "Douglass had made his life story a sort of political diorama in which she had no role." Yet Douglass's very freedom was largely due to Anna's support—born free, she provided him with clothing and money from her own savings. She then was both homemaker and breadwinner to support him, taking care of their five children and working to support them financially as his activism brought in little money, in addition to her own active role in the Boston Female Anti-Slavery Society.[537] He thanked her with long absences, adultery, and ignoring her contributions, but their eldest daughter Rosetta was quick to remind his fans that his "was a story made possible by the unswerving loyalty of Anna Murray."[538]

Although her boss Franklin D. Roosevelt got all the glory for the New Deal(s) in the 1930s, Labor Secretary Frances Perkins was the architect and driving force behind the set of programs, public work projects, financial reforms, and regulations to help the country survive the Great Depression. She agreed to join Roosevelt's Cabinet only if he supported her social reform agenda: the 40-hour work week, minimum wage, unemployment compensation, worker's compensation, elimination of child labour, Social Security, and universal healthcare. By the time Roosevelt died in 1945, she had accomplished all but the last, as well as becoming the country's first female Cabinet secretary. In her 12 years as Labor Secretary, Perkins also created the blueprint for the Social Security Act (signed into law in

---

536 Yee, Shirley J., *Black Women Abolitionists: A Study in Activism, 1828-1860* (University Of Tennessee Press, 1992).
537 Boissoneault, Lorraine, "The Hidden History of Anna Murray Douglass," Smithsonian Magazine, March 5, 2018, https://www.smithsonianmag.com/history/hidden-history-anna-murray-douglass-180968324/
538 Sprague, Rosetta Douglass, "My Mother As I Recall Her," Speech to the Anna Murray Douglass Union W.C.T.U, in Washington, DC., May 10, 1900.

1935) and oversaw the Fair Labor Standards Act of 1938, which set minimum wage and maximum work hours, as well as abolishing child labour.[539] In 1944, *Collier's* magazine ran an article titled "*The Woman Nobody Knows*," noting that "the Roosevelt New Deal" would be more accurately called "the Perkins New Deal."[540]

Oskar Schindler is internationally renowned for his work saving 1,300 Jews during World War II, not least because of the Oscar-winning, 1993 film *Schindler's List*. But while the film depicted his wife Emilie as a supporting character, she was just as involved as he was. The Schindlers' scheme involved convincing the Nazis that Jewish workers were vital in their factory, which produced war supplies (including deliberately faulty bullets as sabotage). In one instance, Emilie intercepted a caravan transporting 250 Jews to a death camp, and convinced the officers to instead take them to the factory to be put to work. There, she nursed them back to health, ensuring that everyone had enough food even in the face of scarcity and government rationing.[541]

---

539   Diehl, Amy, "'You Have to See It to Be It': Missing Female Role Models and What We Can Do about It," *Ms. Magazine*, December 27, 2021, https://msmagazine.com/2021/12/27/womens-history-stem-role-models/

540   Klutz, Jerry and Asbury, Herbert, "The Woman Nobody Knows," Collier's Weekly, August 5, 1944, https://www.unz.com/print/Colliers-1944aug05-00021/

541   Connolly, Kate, "Schindler's Widow Left to Die in Bitterness and Poverty," *The Guardian*, July 28, 2001, https://www.theguardian.com/world/2001/jul/29/kateconnolly.theobserver

THE ARCHITECTS

While even those who are not architecture aficionados will often recognise the name Frank Lloyd Wright, it is a much smaller number who will be familiar with the work of his collaborator, Marion Mahony Griffin. The first licensed woman architect in Illinois, she was also the first employee Wright hired in 1895, and she went on to work closely with him for 15 years. She helped to develop the Prairie School style for which Wright was so well known, and her architectural drawings became a recognized symbol of his work. Wright was well-known for downplaying the contributions of all his employees, and taking credit for their work, so it's unclear exactly how much Marion contributed. The 1910 Wasmuth Portfolio was a collection of 100 lithographs—more than half of them are believed to be Marion's work, yet Wright was credited as the sole creator.[542]

She later collaborated on a variety of projects with her husband, Walter Burley Griffin. Her beautiful watercolour illustrations won them the commission to design the new Australian capital of Canberra in the 1910s, yet the designs were repeatedly credited only to Walter as he had entered the competition under only his name. It is unknown how much of this was due to prevailing sexism of the time, versus Walter himself wanting sole credit. The Australian Institute of Architects

---

542   Schrenk, Lisa D., and David Van Zanten, "Review of Marion Mahony Reconsidered, van Zanten-David," *Journal of the Society of Architectural Historians*, vol 75 no 1 (2016): 106–8. https://www.jstor.org/stable/26418874.

now has a Marion Mahony Griffin Prize for women architects.[543]

Like the sciences, architecture is rarely the work of one person, but rather a studio full of individuals. Yet the industry frequently has a type of star blindness—one or two people are the face of the whole business and thus tend to get sole credit for everything the studio does. Yet even when a woman is the "starchitect," there will be men trying to undermine her.[544] Zaha Hadid is inarguably the most famous woman architect, yet her male successor tried to claim shortly after her death, "I am as much an author of the work of the practice as she is."[545]

Mary Jane Colter was the visionary behind many historic hotels in the U.S., yet she was not even listed as the architect on many of the projects she completed as chief architect and designer for the Fred Harvey Company, which built hotels along the Santa Fe Railroad line when it was new. She worked for the company for 45 years (1904 to 1949), and her projects included designing all of the buildings for the Grand Canyon when it became a tourist destination. Her signature rough-hewn style and integration of Native American motifs became known as National Park Service Rustic.[546]

While Charles Eames was the public face of their architecture and furniture design partnership, he was always quick to acknowledge his wife, Ray, as an equal, or even superior, saying "Anything I can do, Ray can do better." Yet in the 1940s-'70s United States, Ray was often dismissed and overlooked by others, partially because much of her contributions came in the subtle details. As the BBC put it, "She sprinkled stardust on his designs, and gave his grand projects the human touch. She had a feel for colour, and a sense of fun. Without her playful input, his

---

543   "Marion Mahony Griffin Prize," n.d. Australian Institute of Architects, https://www.architecture.com.au/prizes/nsw/marion-mahony-griffin-prize

544   Álvarez, Eva, "The Invisible Women: How Female Architects Were Erased from History," *Architectural Review*, March 8, 2017, https://www.architectural-review.com/essays/the-invisible-women-how-female-architects-were-erased-from-history

545   Schumacher, Patrik, "Housing as Architecture" (speech), World Architecture Festival, November 17, 2016, https://www.architectsjournal.co.uk/news/shit-happens-what-schumachers-email-tells-us-about-zaha-hadid-architects

546   Gaglio, Meredith, "Pioneering Women of American Architecture," Pioneering Women of American Architecture, https://pioneeringwomen.bwaf.org/mary-elizabeth-jane-colter/

creations would have seemed austere."⁵⁴⁷

Charles Rennie Mackintosh has been called Scotland's most famous architect, while his wife, artist Margaret MacDonald Mackintosh, has been relegated to the role of supportive spouse by art historians. Yet even Charles acknowledged that he owed Margaret much of his professional success as a partner and collaborator, telling her in 1927 that, "You must remember that in all my architectural efforts you have been half if not three-quarters of them."⁵⁴⁸ He also asserted that while he had "talent," she had "genius."⁵⁴⁹ As the BBC notes, "Margaret's influence on Charles's life and work would prove to be one of the greatest partnerships in art history." Although they jointly won awards for their work during their lives, her 1933 death (five years after his) barely made the news, and her contributions have been significantly downplayed in the decades since.⁵⁵⁰

Finnish designer Aino Aalto often stood by while her husband Alvar was given all the recognition for their joint projects, even being dismissed as merely his muse rather than his partner. In their early years, the couple would enter architectural competitions separately, but Alvar was routinely held up as the bar against which Aino's own work was measured. In 1935, she became co-founder, artistic director, and later managing director of their lighting and furniture company, Artek, in addition to collaborating with her husband on projects that brought only him fame.⁵⁵¹ Like Ray Eames, Aino often did the detail work, with design historian Lucy Ryder Richardson noting, "While Alvar provided the dramatic lead roles, Aino filled in all the gaps to create perfect harmony in everything."⁵⁵² There was also the personality difference. Biographer Siegfried Giedion wrote, "[Alvar] is

---

547   Cook, William, "Charles and Ray Eames: The Couple Who Shaped the Way We Live," BBC, December 18, 2017, https://www.bbc.com/culture/article/20171218-charles-and-ray-eames-the-couple-who-shaped-the-way-we-live
548   Mackintosh, Charles Rennie, 1927, Letter to Margaret MacDonald Mackintosh.
549   Neat, Timothy, *Part Seen, Part Imagined*, (Canongate Press Ltd., 1994).
550   Panther, Patricia, "Margaret MacDonald: the talented other half of Charles Rennie Mackintosh," BBC Scotland, January 10, 2011, https://www.bbc.co.uk/scotland/arts/margaret_macdonald_the_talented_other_half_of_charles_rennie_mackintosh.shtml
551   Brydson, Eva, "Aino Aalto: 'a Quietly Flowing Stream,'" George Washington University, 2021, https://bpb-us-e1.wpmucdn.com/blogs.gwu.edu/dist/7/4507/files/2021/04/Aino-Aalto-A-quietly-flowing-stream-Eva-Brydson.pdf
552   Richardson, Lucy Ryder Richardson, "102 Midcentury Chairs and Their Stories," (Pavilion Books, 2016).

restless, effervescent, incalculable. Aino was thorough, persevering, and contained. Sometimes it is a good thing when a volcano is encircled by a quietly flowing stream."[553] The same dynamic is seen in other couples in this book, and the stream is always easy to overlook when the volcano is constantly drawing attention.

It's also a documentation issue. Historian Nikolaus Pevsner, in his architectural guides of England, bent over backward to undermine the works of Lady Elizabeth Wilbraham, describing them as "an enterprise of Lady Wilbraham" or that Wilbraham is "credited with the design." "No other work in his book has these awkward designations," notes historian Cynthia Hammond, observing that every work is "by" the men "with no other qualifications." Denise Scott Brown, who worked extensively with her husband, has commented, "for a few years, writers on architecture were interested in sexism and the feminist movement ... in a joint interview, they would ask Bob about work and question me about my 'woman's problem.' 'Write about my work!' I would plead, but they seldom did."[554]

---

553   Giedion, Siegfried, "Time and Architecture: The Growth of a New Tradition," (Harvard University Press, 1941).
554   Álvarez, Eva, "The Invisible Women: How Female Architects Were Erased from History," *Architectural Review*, March 8, 2017, https://www.architectural-review.com/essays/the-invisible-women-how-female-architects-were-erased-from-history

BEHIND THE WRITER

It took a legal battle to get bestselling author Dan Brown to publicly acknowledge his wife, Blythe's, significant contributions to his success. In 2006, when Brown was sued for allegedly stealing ideas for *The Da Vinci Code*, *The Guardian* described Blythe Brown's efforts, digging through complex reference materials, marking up important sections and scouring the Internet for information to help create a compelling story.[555] Blythe herself later sued her subsequently ex-husband over a variety of allegations. While most of these were personal, she did claim credit for inspiring much of his work, including coming up with the premise for *The Da Vinci Code*. It is interesting to note that, as of the writing of this book, Brown had not produced a novel in the years since their 2019 divorce, the last being published in 2017.[556]

In contrast, Dick Francis openly credited his wife, Mary Margaret, for her contributions to the novels published under his name. As he said in an interview in 2003, "Mary and I worked as a team … I have often said that I would have been happy to have both our names on the cover. Mary's family always called me Richard due to having another Dick in the family. I am Richard, Mary was Mary, and Dick Francis was the two of us together." They were happily married for more than 50

---

[555] Freeman, Hadley, "Behind Every Great Male Writer …" *The Guardian*, March 15, 2006, https://www.theguardian.com/world/2006/mar/15/gender.books

[556] Casey, Michael, "'Da Vinci Code' Author Settles Lawsuit Alleging Secret Life," AP News, December 28, 2021, https://apnews.com/article/dan-brown-divorce-lawsuit-da-vinci-code-ceeaf78f10a6c52b008f6909f695a96a

years, and Francis stopped writing for years after her death.[557]

Blythe Brown is one in a long line of wives whose contributions to men's work has gone unrecognized by their famous husbands. Susan Sontag was a significant contributor to the seminal psychology biography *Freud: The Mind of the Moralist*, published in 1959. Considered one of sociologist Philip Rieff's most influential works, it established his reputation. Yet although Rieff acknowledges his wife's contributions with "special thanks" in the preface, that's a far cry from the co-author credit she clearly deserved.[558] In the Pulitzer Prize-winning biography *Sontag: Her Life and Work*, Benjamin Moser goes one step further, attributing the entire work to her. Indeed, their 1959 divorce settlement—the same year the book was published—stipulated she agree to Rieff's claim of sole authorship. Per Moser's research, "It was a blood sacrifice," as one friend put it, in exchange for Rieff not trying to take their son David from Sontag. While Moser acknowledges that the book would have been based on Rieff's research, he maintains the writing was all Sontag's, saying, "He almost certainly did not actually write the book upon which his career was based." It's worth noting that Sontag and Rieff married when she was just 17, only 10 days after she attended one of his lectures—he was more than 10 years her senior, at 28.[559]

Courtier Anne Vavasour is recognized as the inspiration for and protagonist of the poem, *Anne Vavasour's Echo*, written circa 1581. It has also been suggested that she is the poem's true author, as well as the poet behind *Though I seem strange sweet friend*, but both are more commonly attributed to her lover, Edward de Vere.[560]

Mark Twain's wife, Olivia Langdon, edited her husband's books, articles, and lectures and was considered, in his words, a "faithful, judicious, and painstaking editor."[561]

---

557 Swanson, Jean and Dean James, "An Interview with Dick Francis," The Dick Francis Companion (Berkeley Prime Crime, 2003).
558 Flood, Alison, "Susan Sontag Was True Author of Ex-Husband's Book, Biography Claims," *The Guardian*, May 13, 2019, https://www.theguardian.com/books/2019/may/13/susan-sontag-her-life-benjamin-moser-freud-the-mind-of-the-moralist-philip-rieff
559 Moser, Benjamin, *Sntag: Her Life and Work* (Ecco, 2019).
560 Sage, Lorna, Greer, Germaine and Showalter, Elaine, *The Cambridge Guide to Women's Writing in English*, Internet Archive, (Cambridge University Press, 1999) https://archive.org/details/cambridgeguidedt0000unse
561 LeMaster, J.R and James D. Wilson, *The Routledge Encyclopedia of Mark Twain* (Routledge, 2013).

An authority on art history herself, Mary Berenson is believed to have significantly contributed to the work of her husband, art historian Bernard Berenson.[562] Eileen Blair, meanwhile, was a major influence on her husband George Orwell's writing, including *Nineteen Eighty-Four*, which was likely inspired by her poem *End of the Century, 1984*.[563]

War and Peace is known for its length, at 587,287 words. Sophia Tolstaya copied and edited it seven times by hand. She did this at night by candlelight after her children—she bore thirteen—went to bed, using a magnifying glass to decipher her husband's notes. Their marriage was infamously miserable, and Tolstoy repaid her by abandoning her in 1910, selling most of their property so he could wander the countryside and promptly dying 10 days later.[564]

Anna Dostoevskaya saved her husband from ruin. When they met, Fyodor Dostoyevsky was a gambling addict who risked losing all rights to his work if he didn't meet a publisher's deadline. Stenographer Anna was hired to help him get the promised novel written, which they accomplished in less than a month. After marrying a few months later, Anna took charge of the finances, got her new husband out of debt, and curbed his gambling problem, while also helping him avoid future risky contracts. She was also the one to establish their own publishing company so that the family would receive far more profits from her husband's writing. Like many wives of famous men, she also helped ensure his legacy, collecting and preserving his manuscripts, photographs and other documents as well as publishing two memoirs of her own about their life together.[565]

Vera Nabokova gave up her own career to become her husband's editor, reviewer, typist, business manager, and agent, as well as supporting their family financially as a secretary and translator. She learned to drive just so she could chauffeur him around and even reportedly cut his food for him at meals. She also

---

562 "Mary Berenson," I Tatti, the Harvard University Center for Italian Renaissance Studies," https://itatti.harvard.edu/mary-berenson
563 Topp, Sylvia, *Eileen: The Making of George Orwell* (Unbound Publishing, 2020).
564 Edwards, Anne, *Sonya: The Life of the Countess Tolstoy* (Simon & Schuster, 1981).
565 Kaufman, Andrew D, "How Did Anna Dostoyevsky Become a Brave Russian Publishing Pioneer?" Andrew D. Kaufman, October 3, 2021, https://andrewdkaufman.com/2021/10/03/how-did-anna-dostoyevsky-become-a-brave-russian-publishing-pioneer/

saved the manuscript of his most famous work, *Lolita*, when a frustrated Nabokov threatened to burn it.[566]

---

566 Beck, Koa, "The Legend of Vera Nabokov: Why Writers Pine for a Do-It-All Spouse," *The Atlantic*, April 8, 2014, https://www.theatlantic.com/entertainment/archive/2014/04/the-legend-of-vera-nabokov-why-writers-pine-for-a-do-it-all-spouse/359747/

THE INVENTORS

American inventor Maria Beasley successfully marketed at least fifteen of her own inventions, ranging from a foot-warmer to a device that kept trains from derailing. Financially, her greatest accomplishment was a barrel-making machine that earned her an income of about $20,000 a year, when most working women of the time earned only $3 per day. In 1880, she produced a much-improved life raft— previously, emergency rafts were simply planks with hollow floats. Beasley designed hers to be "fire-proof, compact, safe, and readily launched." She changed the style of the floats, so that her rafts could be folded for storage but quickly unfolded in an emergency, complete with guard rails. Yet despite her achievements, Beasley's occupation in the 1880 U.S. Census was "unemployed housewife."[567]

Martha Coston worked for 10 years to perfect and then patent her late husband's idea for a pyrotechnic flare. Working off only a rough sketch, Coston was the one who made the idea a reality in every sense, developing an elaborate system of flares that would allow ships to communicate at night. Yet on the patent, she was listed only as "administratrix," with her long-dead husband credited as inventor. The U.S. Navy bought the rights, and her work helped save lives and win battles. In 1871, she was granted a patent in her own right for an improvement on the system.[568]

When Thomas Lyle Williams was nineteen, he saw his sister Mabel using a

---

[567] Handcock, Katherine, "Sisters in Innovation: 20 Women Inventors You Should Know," A Mighty Girl, February 20, 2022, https://www.amightygirl.com/blog?p=12223

[568] Pilato, Denise E, "Martha Coston: A Woman, a War, and a Signal to the World," *International Journal of Naval History*, April 2002, https://www.ijnhonline.org/wp-content/uploads/2012/01/pdf_pilato.pdf

homemade concoction of petroleum jelly, coal dust, and burnt cork to darken her eyelashes. The results were commercially manufactured mascara, and his company, Maybelline, was named for his sister.[569]

Socialite Caresse Crosby got so fed up with her corset at age nineteen that she stitched together the first modern bra on the spot. In 1914, she patented her "backless brassiere," selling it to Warner Brothers Corset Company for just $1,500. The company erased her from their product's history and went on to make $15 million from her invention over the next three decades.[570]

In some cases, women could not legally have their work in their own name. In the U.S., the *Patent Act* of 1790 made it possible for anyone, male or female, to protect their invention with a patent, like Hannah Slater who patented a method of making cotton thread that was stronger than the common linen thread. Her 1793 patent was in the name of "Mrs Samuel Slater." But due to state laws preventing women from owning property separate from their husbands, many women either didn't bother or registered their patents in their husbands' names.[571]

This is not to say that women hadn't been inventing useful tools. Sybilla Righton Masters was the first person in the American colonies to be granted a patent. In the 1710s, some colonies were issuing patents, but Pennsylvania, where the Masterses resided, was not one of them. So, she travelled to London in 1712 to apply for a patent for her "Cleaning and Curing The Indian Corn Growing in the several Colonies of America" process, which was granted on November 25, 1715—in her husband's name. This is another example where a woman's accomplishments would have been lost to history were it not for the support and acknowledgement of a man. Thomas Masters explicitly included in the patent application that it was her idea, and when the patent was issued, it stated the patent was for "a new

---

569   Spector, Barbara, "The History of Maybelline's Founder Tom Lyle Williams," Family Business Magazine, 2011, https://www.familybusinessmagazine.com/hidden-history-maybelline-1
570   Ruane, Michael E., "Caresse Crosby, who claimed the invention of the bra, was better known for her wild life," *The Washington Post*, November 11, 2014, https://www.washingtonpost.com/local/caresse-crosby-who-claimed-the-invention-of-the-bra-was-better-known-for-her-wild-life/2014/11/09/99c55f7e-3f39-11e4-b03f-de718edeb92f_story.html
571   Office of the Chief Economist, "Progress and Potential: A profile of women inventors on U.S. patents," United States Patent and Trademark Office, February 2019, https://www.uspto.gov/sites/default/files/documents/Progress-and-Potential-2019.pdf

invention found out by Sybilla his wife."[572]

Her cornmeal process produced a popular food today known as grits, and she opened a successful millinery store thanks to another invention, after she received her second patent, also under Thomas's name, for a method of weaving straw and palmetto leaves into hats and bonnets.

James Marion Sims, mentioned previously for his horrific torture of enslaved women in the name of gynaecological innovation, was widely credited for the invention of the modern speculum. (Specula in general date back to at least ancient Rome.) But decades earlier, French midwife Marie Boivin invented a vaginal speculum in 1825 (Sims would have been twelve at the time), as well as a pelvimeter. Along with being one of the first medical professionals to use a stethoscope to listen to foetal heartbeat, she also discovered the causes of certain types of bleeding, miscarriages, and placental and uterine diseases. The medical textbooks that she wrote were translated to different languages and used for 150 years.[573]

---

[572] Barrett, Pru, "Sybilla Righton Masters (c 1676 – 1720)," The Mills Archive," November 3, 2020, https://new.millsarchive.org/2020/11/03/sybilla-righton-masters-c-1676-1720/

[573] Cancel, Marielba, "The Vaginal Speculum: From Its Unearthed Secrets to Our Modern Times," Sklar Surgical Instruments, January 9, 2017, https://research.sklarcorp.com/the-vaginal-speculum-from-its-unearthed-secrets-to-our-modern-times

THE MILITARY

Many servicewomen can recall instances where people have assumed they are not in the military or not a veteran. In 2016, Lieutenant Commander Rebecca Landis Hayes, a former U.S. Navy physician, went viral after sharing the angry note someone had left on her car, which was parked in a spot designated for veterans: "This parking is for Veterans, lady. Learn to read and have some respect."[574]

Other servicewomen chimed in with their own experiences, including:

People assuming their husband (real or imagined) served when the woman is standing there in uniform.

Lauding their husband with praise for serving while ignoring the wife who also served.

Asking where the veteran was in relation to signage on their car.

Being told to go sit at the "non-military wives" table.

Going to the Veterans Administration to get medical care for her disability, and being asked if she was there with her grandfather.[575]

One woman noted, "I'm damn proud to be a veteran. But sometimes when I say

---

574 Praderio, Caroline, "The Female Veteran Who Found a Sexist Note on Her Car Just Got a Heartfelt Apology Letter," Insider, June 22, 2016, https://www.insider.com/female-veteran-who-found-sexist-note-just-got-an-apology-letter-2016-6

575 "Female Veterans Share Experiences Of Being Assumed Non-Military Based Solely On Gender," Women You Should Know, June 17, 2016, https://womenyoushouldknow.net/female-veterans-share-experiences-of-being-assumed-non-military-based-solely-on-gender/

that I'm one, people will get this incredulous look in their eyes because I'm female."

Such attitudes are particularly infuriating in light of the battles women have had to wage just to be allowed into the armed forces, and recognized as such when they have served. Historically, women have been grouped into supposedly civilian roles even as they perform the same duties as men in the armed forces and are frequently sent into war zones. The women of the British Special Operations Executive (SOE) who spied—and often died—in service to their country during World War II often received commendations that were explicitly designated for "civilians." Even when the SOE as an agency recommended women like Pearl Witherington (who led an SOE network of around 2,000 fighters in France) for military commendation, the government was likely to change it to a civilian version. In at least one instance where a woman—Odette Sansom—had refused to give the enemy information despite being tortured, a note in her files said that the military commendation she had been recommended for "stands little chance of acceptance without:—(a) Medical evidence of maltreatment. (b) Witnesses of her refusal to speak under threat of torture, during torture and after torture." There were, in fact, several doctors' notes in her files attesting to the signs of torture.[576] The SOE's official historian, M. R. D. Foot, tried to undermine Sansom's credibility by claiming that, "Unfortunately her experiences in Ravensbruck had induced in her a state of nervous tension so severe that she had considerable trouble for many months in distinguishing fantasy and reality and it is likely enough that she got the two confused." He also criticized her as a bad mother, calling her "so combative that she had sacrificed the company of her three small daughters in England to go back to war."[577] It seems highly unlikely that he was running around calling the men delusional and bad fathers for doing their duty.

During World War I, the so-called "Hello Girls" of the Signal Corps worked on the front lines providing one of the most vital functions in war: communications. Upon discovering that men were, in general, inept as telephone operators, General

---

576 Carlomagno, Cameron, "Women in a Man's War: The Employment of Female Agents in the Special Operations Executive, 1940-1946," Chapman University, May 28, 2019, https://doi.org/10.36837/chapman.000075
577 Foot, M. R. D. "SOE in France: An Account of the Work of the British Special Operations Executive in France, 1940-1944," 1966, Her Majesty's Stationary Office.

John Pershing in 1918 put out the call for women, who filled 80 percent of such roles in the U.S. and could typically connect five calls in the time it took a man to do one. Thousands of women answered the call, and hundreds were sent overseas. Many of them were bilingual and acted as real-time translators for officials from different countries. Following the Armistice, they also stayed six months to a year longer than most of the men, because they were still needed in the aftermath. Yet when they returned home, says historian Elizabeth Cobbs,

"The women found, if they were in the Army, despite everything they understood, when they got home the Army said you weren't in the Army. You never took an oath. And there were multiple oaths in the files for them. One of them, their leader Grace Banker, won the Distinguished Service Medal awarded by Pershing, which was the top medal for officers at that time. Despite all that, they were told, 'You weren't actually in the Army.'... There were women who died, two who lost their lives in influenza, and several were disabled. One woman's arm was permanently disabled because somebody had treated it improperly and she ended up with permanent nerve damage. Another had tuberculosis. The Army, unlike the Marines and Navy, which provided medical benefits, said, that's not our problem."[578]

During World War II, Lieutenant Reba Whittle was a flight nurse with the 813th Medical Air Evacuation Squadron who logged more than 500 flight hours. On a September 1944 flight to pick up casualties, her plane went off course and was shot down over Germany. The few survivors were taken prisoner. Whittle was allowed to attend to the wounded prisoners in her camp, and she and 109 male POWs were released on January 25, 1945. The injuries she had sustained prevented her from future flying. Although Whittle received the Air Medal and a Purple Heart and was promoted to lieutenant, she was denied disability or POW

---

[578] Boissoneault, Lorraine, "Women on the Frontlines of WWI Came to Operate Telephones," *Smithsonian Magazine*, April 4, 2017, https://www.smithsonianmag.com/history/women-frontlines-wwi-came-operate-telephones-180962687/

retirement benefits. Leaving the Army in 1946, she spent ten years applying for, and being denied, POW status and back pay, finally accepting a cash settlement in 1955. Her POW status was finally granted in 1983, two years after her death.[579]

---

[579] Cellania, Miss, "11 Women Warriors of World War II," Mental Floss, November 11, 2011, https://www.mentalfloss.com/article/29219/11-women-warriors-world-war-ii

HER CHOICE?

*"I always thought it was wrong for me to take credit for the work that I did.
I don't think that anymore."*
—Dolores Huerta[580]

In 1967, famed hairdresser Vidal Sassoon flew to London for a publicity stunt, in which he cut off actress Mia Farrow's long blonde locks into a pixie cut for the horror film *Rosemary's Baby*. Called "the most famous moment in haircut history" by *The Hollywood Reporter*, the pixie cut was soon copied by women around the world. It was only after Sassoon's death in 2012 that Farrow admitted it was a hoax—at least, in regards to Sassoon's contributions. Calling it a "prank," she said she'd actually cut her own hair in the style two years earlier, and indeed her hair is already short in the many photos from the stunt. Farrow's story is one of countless examples where a woman has let a man take credit for any number of reasons—in her case, publicity for herself and her film. [581]

Throughout history, countless women have found success presenting themselves through male identities. In many cases where someone had fully immersed themselves in manhood, we cannot say for sure whether the person was transgender, non-binary, or otherwise not a cisgender woman—or if it was just the easiest or only way to pursue their goals.

However, far simpler than living as a man in the midst of other men was the

---

580 "Dolores." Directed by Peter Bratt. Interview with Dolores Huerta. 2017.
581 Ginsberg, Merle, "Mia Farrow Tweets Her Vidal Sassoon 'Rosemary's Baby' Haircut Was a 'Prank,'" The Hollywood Reporter, May 10, 2012, https://www.hollywoodreporter.com/news/general-news/mia-farrow-tweets-her-vidal-sassoon-rosemarys-baby-haircut-was-a-prank-323143/

use of pseudonyms, initials, or simply giving a man credit by choice. Though it is certainly open to discussion to what degree this was voluntary versus necessary, there are plenty of examples of women who sacrificed credit for success.

Geneviève Thiroux d'Arconville once wrote of women, "Do they show science or wit? If their works are bad, they are jeered at; if they are good, they are taken from them, and they are left only with ridicule for letting themselves be called authors."[582] A novelist and scientist, her efforts went beyond translation of English works into her native French—she also added her own commentary, which pushed her writing from the acceptable to the unacceptable for women of the 1700s, particularly given her interest in the sciences. As such, she left her name off these works. When she collaborated with anatomist Jean-Joseph Sue on the French version of *Treatise on Osteology*, including adding illustrations that she paid for, he was believed to be the sole author. She also spent a decade studying putrefaction (the processes by which plant and animal matter rots), conducting experiments and recording her findings. She found that protecting the matter from air and exposing it to copper, camphor, and cinchona slowed spoilage. Her *Essai pour servir a l'histoire de la putrefthaction* (*Essay on the History of Putrefaction*), published in 1766, detailed more than 300 experiments but left out the author's identity. One reviewer opined the author "must be a highly distinguished physician with a deep knowledge of both chemistry and medicine."[583]

As always, women at the intersections of marginalization face additional obstacles. In 1888, inventor Ellen Eglin sold the rights to a clothes wringer she had designed to an agent for $18 (around $570 today).[584] "If it was known that a negro woman patented the invention, white ladies would not buy the wringer," she explained in an 1891 interview.[585] Although the device proved hugely popular and garnered massive profits, Eglin received neither credit nor royalties for her

---

582   D'Arconville, Geneviève Thiroux, *Sur les femmes*, 1760.
583   Noyce, Pendred, *Remarkable Minds: 17 More Pioneering Women in Science and Medicine* (Tumblehome Learning, 2015).
584   Quackenbush, Julie, "Ellen Eglin (1849 – ?)" BlackPast, March 27, 2021, https://www.blackpast.org/african-american-history/people-african-american-history/ellen-eglin-1849/
585   Smith, C., *The Woman Inventor*, 1891, https://library.si.edu/digital-library/book/womaninventor1smit

creation. In 1956, Mary Kenner invented an adjustable sanitary belt with a moisture-proof napkin pocket built in. The Sonn-Nap-Pack Company wanted to purchase her creation, until they found out Kenner was African-American. Her patent expired and others stole her idea without crediting her.[586]

The song "La Tequilera" was revolutionary in 1930s Mexico for not only its style, but its content. Singer Lucha Reyes had made a name for herself in the male-dominated cancion ranchera style and many people believe she wrote the song, about a woman drowning her sorrows with tequila—a taboo of the time (and arguably today). Yet, the songwriter officially credited is Alfredo D'Orsay because women in the country were not allowed to register copyrights as composers until 1937.[587]

Julia Ward Howe, best known as the writer of the *Battle Hymn of the Republic*, anonymously published her volume of poetry *Passion Flowers* in 1853.[588] Her poetry, much of which critiqued women's roles as wives, her own marriage, and women's place in society, was hated by her husband—not surprisingly, as he was apparently a physically abusive adulterer who mismanaged her inheritance. He threatened that he would divorce her and take the children if she published it, and when it came out that she was the author, he refused to speak to her for three months. She also published *Words for the Hour* anonymously in 1857.[589]

As a single woman, Jane Austen was better off than her married contemporaries in several ways—not least of which was that under the legal doctrine of coverture, married women had no legal independence from their husbands. Women like Austen could own property and sign contracts in their own right, but if they wed, that property became their husband's and any contracts were considered null and void. But single women were also viewed with pity, contempt, and suspicion.

---

586   Raven, Rebecca, "Happy Birthday, Mary Kenner," Science Museum (London), May 17, 2021, https://blog.sciencemuseum.org.uk/happy-birthday-mary-kenner/

587   O'Meara, Mallory, *Girly Drinks: A World History of Women and Alcohol* (Hurst Publishers, 2021).

588   Schama, Chloe, "Literary Landmarks: A History of American Women Writers," *Smithsonian Magazine*, March 6, 2009, https://www.smithsonianmag.com/arts-culture/literary-landmarks-a-history-of-american-women-writers-56536736/

589   Lewis, Jone Johnson, "Julia Ward Howe: Beyond the Battle Hymn of the Republic," ThoughtCo., March 6, 2019, https://www.thoughtco.com/julia-ward-howe-early-years-3529325

Women writers, who were seen as stepping outside their assigned roles as wife and mother, fared little better. Indeed, Austen's own name did not appear on her books until after her death, with *Sense and Sensibility* being published as "By a Lady," and *Pride and Prejudice* as "By the author of *Sense and Sensibility*."[590]

MALE PSEUDONYMS

> "Authoresses are liable to be looked on with prejudice."
> —Charlotte Brontë[591]

When the classic Gothic novel *Jane Eyre* was originally published in 1847, it received widespread acclaim and was so popular it was reprinted within ten weeks. Although published under the pseudonym Currer Bell, not everyone was fooled—novelist William Thackeray proclaimed, "It is a woman's writing, but whose?"[592]

Once it was suggested that the true author was a woman, the initially favourable reviews were joined by negative outcries that the book was "coarse," "anti-Christian," and marked by "moral Jacobinism," denounced for excessive passion and the use of curse words.[593] [594]

The conservative backlash against the novel only intensified with the publication of *Wuthering Heights* by "Ellis Bell" and, later, *The Tenant of Wildfell Hall* by "Acton Bell." Charlotte, Emily, and Anne Brontë all used male pseudonyms because they feared exactly the reaction they received—that their work would be judged more harshly if it were known the books were written by women. As the *Guardian* notes, "For decades after its publication, (*Jane Eyre*) was seen by many as a transgressive book from which young girls needed protection... Jane's

---

590 "Collection Item: First edition of Jane Austen's Sense and Sensibility," British Library, https://www.bl.uk/collection-items/first-edition-of-jane-austens-sense-and-sensibility
591 Brontë, Charlotte, "Biographical Notice of Ellis and Acton Bell," September 19, 1850.
592 Thackeray, William Makepeace, "Letter to W. S. Williams," October 23, 1847, https://www.open.ac.uk/Arts/reading/UK/record_details.php?id=28472
593 Cregan-Reid, Vybarr, "Jane Eyre | Summary, Characters, Analysis, & Facts," In Encyclopædia Britannica, 2019, https://www.britannica.com/topic/Jane-Eyre-novel-by-Bronte
594 Lucasta Miller, "The Appeal of Jayne Eyre," *The Guardian*, September 23, 2006, https://www.theguardian.com/books/2006/sep/23/fiction.charlottebronte

individualism, her strong sense of self and her refusal to be docile ruffled critical feathers." Even Elizabeth Gaskell, who would later write a biography of Charlotte and whose own writing was considered scandalous, refused to let her own daughter read *Jane Eyre* until she was twenty. Gaskell herself used the name Cotton Mather Mills in her early career.

Years earlier, when Charlotte sent her poetry to the poet laureate Robert Southey in 1836, he infamously responded that "Literature cannot be the business of a woman's life, and it ought not to be. The more she is engaged in her proper duties, the less leisure will she have for it even as an accomplishment and a recreation."[595] It could be said that she partially heeded his words—the "Bells" published their first volume of poetry in 1846.

Throughout history, it has been common for women to adopt male or gender-neutral pseudonyms to avoid sexist discrimination. Irish journalist Sydney Czira was always best known as "John Brennan," chosen because it sounded like "a strong Wexford farmer," which she felt gave her more authority.[596] Arguably Australia's most famous woman writer, (Stella) Miles Franklin, did the same— but her book *My Brilliant Career*, which vaulted her to fame at only twenty-one, included an introduction by poet Henry Lawson that exposed her without her consent. That didn't stop her from adopting other pseudonyms, male and female, throughout her career, including Brent of Bin Bin—a writer she actively promoted and whose identity was secret even from her publishers. As Dr. Rachel Franks of the State Library of New South Wales writes, "She praised Brent's works publicly and privately as if she had nothing to do with them: in lectures, on the radio, in articles, in letters, even in her own private diaries. She wrote to others in the guise of Brent while simultaneously writing to them as Miles Franklin. She even chaired a meeting of the Fellowship of Australian Writers in 1941 which discussed the

---

[595] "Collection item: Letter from Robert Southey to Charlotte Brontë, 12 March 1837," British Library, https://www.bl.uk/collection-items/letter-from-robert-southey-to-charlotte-bronte-12-march-1837

[596] "Czira (Gifford), Sydney Madge ('John Brennan')" Dictionary of Irish Biography, originally published October 2009, revised December 2010, https://www.dib.ie/biography/czira-gifford-sydney-madge-john-brennan-a2356

very subject of Brent's identity!"[597]

Like Franklin, Margaret Todd chose to fictionalize her own experiences and publish under a male pseudonym. Todd's 1892 novel *Mona Maclean, Medical Student* was praised by pioneering doctor Sophia Jex-Blake as having a protagonist who resembled a "genuine medical woman"—which Todd, then a medical student herself, was.[598] It was described by *Punch* magazine as "demonstrating the indispensability of women-doctors"—a stance which was perhaps more easily received from a "male" author.[599]

American cartoonist Dale Messick was born Dalia but changed her name because of industry sexism. She went on to create the popular Brenda Starr, Reporter, who became the leading comic-strip heroine for forty years, read by more than forty million people.[600]

Pants-wearing, tobacco-smoking Amantine Lucile Aurore Dupin became a literary icon in 1800s Europe as George Sand, while Mary Ann Evans wrote seven novels as George Eliot to avoid stereotypes of works by women as frivolous.[601] [602] Essayist Violet Paget went by Vernon Lee to be taken more seriously, writing more than 30 books.[603] Novelist and playwright Emily Morse Symonds used George Paston as her alias.[604] Mary Marvin Breckinridge Patterson cut the Mary for her professional career in cinematography and photojournalism, though her gender was clear when she later began reporting as a radio broadcaster.[605] The Frances

---

597 Franks, Rachel, "Miles Franklin," State Library of NSW, March 5, 2018, https://www.sl.nsw.gov.au/stories/miles-franklin
598 "Margaret Todd (1859-1918): Medical woman and author," Constructing Scientific Communities (University of Oxford), https://conscicom.web.ox.ac.uk/article/margaret-todd-1859-1918-medical-woman-and-author
599 *Punch, or the London Charivari*, Volume 103. December 3, 1892, https://www.gutenberg.org/ebooks/16263
600 Commire, Anne and Klezmer, Deborah, "Messick, Dale (1906–2005)," *Dictionary of Women Worldwide: 25,000 Women Through the Ages* (Vol. 2) (Gale, 2007).
601 "George Sand | French Novelist," *Encyclopedia Britannica*, https://www.britannica.com/biography/George-Sand
602 "What's in a Name?" Exploring Eliot, https://exploringeliot.org/stories/whats-in-a-name/
603 "Vernon Lee | English Essayist," *Encyclopedia Britannica*, https://www.britannica.com/biography/Vernon-Lee
604 Mellby, Julie L., "Her Name Was George Paston," Princeton University Library, January 29, 2010, https://www.princeton.edu/~graphicarts/2010/01/her_name_was_george_paston.html
605 Tepperman, Charles, "Marvin Breckinridge," Women Film Pioneers Project, Columbia University Libraries, 2017, https://wfpp.columbia.edu/pioneer/marvin-breckinridge/

in Frances Ulric Cole was also dropped in the 1920s in her pursuit of a career composing music.[606] Her fellow composer, Helen Guy, became Guy d'Hardelot.[607]

In later years, male pseudonyms became more common in certain genres, like science fiction. Decades before she became known as the "Grand Dame of Science and Fantasy," Alice Mary Norton used her soon-to-be-famous nom de plume Andre Norton, as well as Andrew North and Allen Weston, because her publisher thought they would sell better to young men—their assumed market for science fiction—than Alice.[608] Alice Bradley Sheldon wrote award-winning science fiction as James Tiptree Jr. because it "seemed like good camouflage. I had the feeling that a man would slip by less observed. I've had too many experiences in my life of being the first woman in some damn occupation."[609] "James" was often seen as simultaneously unusually macho and unusually feminist (for a male). The James Tiptree Jr. Award now recognises works of science fiction and fantasy that expand or explore one's understanding of gender.[610]

Italian artist and writer Bianca Pucciarelli Menna didn't just use Tomaso Binga as a pseudonym—she incorporated the identity into her work. Menna initially chose the male pseudonym to parody patriarchy and the privileges it bestows upon men, which they often take for granted. Binga evolved into an alter ego that she used to challenge gender stereotypes. In a 1977 performance piece, she invited guests to attend a "wedding" between Bianca and Tomaso, with guests bringing cards and gifts to create an ever-changing installation, while the androgynous artist attended the ceremony in a white suit.[611]

And it's not just the creative writers and artists. María Andresa Casamayor was

---

606   Catherine Parsons Smith, *Cole, (Frances) Ulric*, (Oxford University Press, 2001) https://doi.org/10.1093/gmo/9781561592630.article.47043
607   "Popular Lady Composers," *Strand Musical Magazine*, Jul–Dec 1895, p.251, https://books.google.com.au/books?id=9f0sAAAAYAAJ&redir_esc=y
608   Ruane, Therese, "Norton, Andre," Encyclopedia of Cleveland History | Case Western Reserve University, October 20, 2020, https://case.edu/ech/articles/n/norton-andre
609   Platt, Charles, "Profile: James Tiptree, Jr.," *Isaac Asimov's Science Fiction Magazine* vol 7 no 4, April 1983.
610   "Five Book Friday!" Peabody Institute Library, August 24, 2018, https://www.peabodylibrary.org/freeforall/?p=10225
611   Benson, Louise, "The Radical Italian Artist Who Married Her Male Pseudonym," ELEPHANT, August 6, 2019, https://elephant.art/tomaso-binga/

the first Spanish woman to publish a book on science, which she did in March 1738 when she was just seventeen—under the name Casandro Mamés de La Marca y Araioa.[612] Like Miles Franklin, architect Margaret Justin Blanco White dropped her first name while working in the U.K. from the 1930s onward, including as Superintending Architect of the Scottish Office.[613]

As a young woman, French mathematician Sophie Germain was barred from attending the École Polytechnique when it was founded in 1794. She was, however, able to obtain the lecture notes and submit written observations in a form of distance learning. She began corresponding with faculty member Joseph Louis Lagrange in the guise of a former student, Monsieur Antoine-Auguste Le Blanc, fearing "the ridicule attached to a female scientist." Impressed by her, Lagrange asked for a meeting. Fortunately, he did not care that she was a woman and became her mentor.[614] Another correspondent of "Le Blanc's" was Carl Friedrich Gauss, who wrote in 1807, "How can I describe my astonishment and admiration on seeing my esteemed correspondent M. Le Blanc metamorphosed into this celebrated person ... when a woman, because of her sex, our customs and prejudices, encounters infinitely more obstacles than men in familiarising herself with [number theory's] knotty problems, yet overcomes these fetters and penetrates that which is most hidden, she doubtless has the noblest courage, extraordinary talent, and superior genius."[615]

In some cases, a woman may hide behind a male pseudonym for their own safety. As Berlin bureau chief for the *Chicago Tribune* during the rise of Hitler and the Nazi party, Sigrid Schultz was subject to the Gestapo's intimidation tactics (including trying to plant incriminating documents in her apartment) and censorship attempts, like disrupting her phone services while trying to relay stories. She created an entire fake identity—a fictional roving reporter named

---

612 O'Connor, J. J. and Robertson, E. F., "María Andresa Casamayor – Biography," School of Mathematics and Statistics, University of St Andrews, Scotland, 2021, https://mathshistory.st-andrews.ac.uk/Biographies/Casamayor/
613 "Justin Blanco White," Architectuul, https://architectuul.com/architect/justin-blanco-white
614 O'Connor, J. J. and Robertson, E. F., "Sophie Germain – Biography," School of Mathematics and Statistics, University of St Andrews, Scotland, 2020, https://mathshistory.st-andrews.ac.uk/Biographies/Germain/
615 Gauss, Carl Friedrich, "Letter to Sophie Germain," April 30, 1807.

"John Dickson," complete with correspondence and mentions of him in her diary. Schultz would leave the country to file dispatches, with fake datelines, from cities like Oslo and Copenhagen. "Dickson" reported on German attacks on churches, exposed concentration camps, recounted the persecution of Jews, and predicted the non-aggression pact between Germany and the Soviet Union as well as Munich Agreement, which enabled Hitler to invade Czechoslovakia. Schultz also had the added danger of being ethnically Jewish, a secret she kept to avoid further danger.[616] Another Berlin correspondent, William L. Shirer, wrote that, "No other American correspondent in Berlin knew so much of what was going on behind the scenes as did Sigrid Schultz."[617]

Even today, the "gynobibliophobia" (fear of women's books, a term coined by Francine Prose) persists. In 2015, Author Catherine Nichols recounted that when she initially pitched her novel to fifty agents, she received just two requests for her manuscript. But with a new email address and a male name, sending the same cover letter and pages to fifty agents, it was requested seventeen times. "He is eight and a half times better than me at writing the same book. Fully a third of the agents who saw his query wanted to see more, where my numbers never did shift from one in 25," she wrote. "The judgments about my work that had seemed as solid as the walls of my house had turned out to be meaningless. My novel wasn't the problem, it was me – Catherine."[618]

And it's certainly not just the publishing industry. When *Westworld* co-creator Lisa Joy wrote her film *Reminiscences*, which she also directed and produced, she was initially tempted to hide her identity when sending the script to producers. "I thought it would get more traction if I did it under a male name. In the end, I opted not to do that, but I've definitely encountered a lot of bias and prejudice before in my career."[619]

---

616 Mackrell, Judith, *The Correspondents: Six Women Writers on the Front Lines of World War II* (Doubleday, 2021).
617 Shirer, William L., Review for Sigrid Schultz's book, *Germany Will Try It Again* (1944).
618 Flood, Alison, "Sexism in Publishing: 'My Novel Wasn't the Problem, It Was Me, Catherine.'" *The Guardian*, August 6, 2015, https://www.theguardian.com/books/2015/aug/06/catherine-nichols-female-author-male-pseudonym
619 Ntim, Zac, "'Reminiscence' Director Lisa Joy Says She Thought about Producing the Film under a Male Pseudonym because of Sexism," Insider, August 16, 2021, https://www.insider.com/lisa-joy-reminiscence-hugh-jackman-movie-under-male-pseudonym-sexism-2021-8

Similarly, the majority of female gamers choose male or non-gender-specific avatars and usernames and either avoid games where their voices would be heard or find ways to disguise them. A 2021 study found that 59 percent of the 900 women surveyed in the U.S., China and Germany hide their gender while gaming to avoid sexist behaviours, including insults, inappropriate sexual messages, patronising and dismissive comments, and mansplaining—which 77 percent of respondents said they had personally experienced.[620] A 2022 survey of U.S. gamers found even higher numbers: 76% of female gamers reported hiding their identities online, and 93% of those said it was because they had experienced sexual harassment online from fellow gamers.[621] The 2021 study found that "this type of explicitly sexist behaviour is normalised in online spaces, with little to no repercussion."

GIVING HUSBANDS THE CREDIT

While F. Scott Fitzgerald likely stole much of his work from his wife's own words without her permission, Zelda did write under his name voluntarily. Though there may have been some degree of emotional coercion, given the unhealthy dynamics at play in their relationship, it was the practical choice—a piece by "F. Scott Fitzgerald" would bring in far more money than one by Zelda when the couple found themselves short of funds.[622]

In many instances of collaboration between spouses, it is unclear how much of a woman going uncredited may have been their own choice for practical reasons—the best of less-than-ideal options. Of the 214 articles published by married mathematicians Grace Chisholm Young and William Henry Young, only eighteen list Grace as sole author and thirteen were credited under both their names. However, it is generally believed that Grace's contributions to their work were far more substantial, meaning that many of the papers published solely in his name were

---

620 Nightingale, Ed, "Worrying Survey Finds 59% of Women Hide Gender When Gaming to Avoid Harassment," PinkNews, May 21, 2021, https://www.pinknews.co.uk/2021/05/21/women-in-gaming-study-video-games-women-gamers/

621 Celatti, Alyssa, "Three-Quarters of Female Gamers Disguise Their Gender While Gaming," FandomSpot, 2022, https://www.fandomspot.com/female-gamers-disguise-gender-while-gaming/

622 Cline, Sally, *Zelda Fitzgerald: Her Voice in Paradise* (John Murray, 2002).

significantly her work.⁶²³ Similarly, Egyptologist Hilda Petrie worked with her husband, the renowned William Flinders Petrie, "but she never published anything in her own name, and her contributions were never formally acknowledged. Her husband wrote the reports, headed the excavation teams and garnered all the credit for their finds," notes Lynne Olson in *Empress of the Nile*, a biography of another woman in the field.⁶²⁴

Although Italian zoologist Michele Lessona is credited with translating the work of Darwin and other natural history texts into Italian, his own letter indicate that much of the work was done by his wife, naturalist and linguist Adele Masi Lessona. Published in 1880-82, the massive Universal Dictionary of Sciences, Letters and Arts was officially edited by her husband and Carlo A. Valle, but Michele Lessona later declared, "my wife did almost all of it herself."⁶²⁵

Philosopher and women's rights activist Harriet Taylor Mill published little under her own name during her lifetime, but contributed significantly to the works of her husband, John Stuart Mill. Although he acknowledged her contributions in other ways, such as dedicating *On Liberty* to her and crediting her as a joint author in his autobiography, she was never listed as a co-author on their collaborations.⁶²⁶ After her 1858 death, Helen Taylor, her daughter from her first marriage, took care of Mill, who reportedly valued his stepdaughter's contributions in intellectual matters as well as the running of his household. Mill claimed that his later work was the result of three minds, not one, referring to his wife and stepdaughter, and even after his death, Helen continued to edit and publish his work.⁶²⁷

Before Gerda Taro became the first woman photojournalist to die while

---

623 "Grace Chisholm Young," Biographies of Women Mathematicians: Agnes Scott College, https://mathwomen.agnesscott.org/women/young.htm

624 Olson, Lynne, *Empress of the Nile: The Daredevil Archaeologist Who Saved Egypt's Ancient Temples from Destruction* (Random House, 2023).

625 Dröscher, Ariane, Scienza a Due Voci, University of Bologna, https://scienzaa2voci.unibo.it/biografie/145-masi-lessona-adele

626 Käuper, Kristin, "Mill, Harriet Taylor (1807-1858)," History of Women Philosophers and Scientists, Pederborn University, https://historyofwomenphilosophers.org/project/directory-of-women-philosophers/mill-harriet-taylor-1807-1858/

627 Awcock, Hannah, "Turbulent Londoners: Helen Taylor, 1831-1907," Turbulent Isles, October 11, 2018, https://turbulentisles.com/2018/10/11/turbulent-londoners-helen-taylor-1831-1907/

covering a war on the front lines, she worked with her lover Endre Friedmann. Together they collaborated on work attributed to "Robert Capa," an American persona intended to protect European Jewish artists from increasing political tensions on the continent in the 1930s, as well as reaching the lucrative U.S. markets. Photos ostensibly taken by Americans sold for three times what they could get under their own names. Soon, Friedmann claimed the Capa pseudonym for his exclusive use, and as such many of the early "Capa" photos are Taro's work, later credited to Friedmann. Even her own artist bios, with organisations such as the International Center of Photography, overlook this fact.[628]

JUST THE INITIALS

In addition to learning Greek specifically so she could translate the work of Sappho, lesbian poet Renée Vivien published her first work as simply "R. Vivien." (Renée was also a pseudonym, for the British-born Pauline Mary Tarn, who wrote only in French). But even those published as Renée seem to have confused the hetero-centric men of the late 1800s and early 1900s, who assumed the love poetry was written by a man to his mistress. Vivien and her partner Natalie Barney reputedly attended a lecture by one such confused gentleman, and had to stifle their laughter at the mistake, according to Barney's account.[629]

An alternative to explicitly male pseudonyms is the gender-neutral initials. As recently as 2016, an opinion piece in the *Wall Street Journal*—written by a man—advised women in tech to use only their initials in professional settings to avoid gender discrimination.[630] It is also common in academic papers. Both S. E. Hinton and J. K. Rowling have stated that publishers advised them to use

---

628   O'Hagan, Sean, "Robert Capa and Gerda Taro: Love in a Time of War," *The Guardian*, May 12, 2012, https://www.theguardian.com/artanddesign/2012/may/13/robert-capa-gerda-taro-relationship
629   "Renée Vivien and the Trials of Lesbian Poetry," Artlark, June 10, 2022, https://artlark.org/2022/06/11/renee-vivien-the-misunderstood-lesbian-sonneteer/
630   Greathouse, John, "Why Women in Tech Might Consider Just Using Their Initials Online," *Wall Street Journal*, September 28, 2016, https://www.wsj.com/articles/BL-258B-7328

their initials to prevent critics and audiences from pre-judging their books.[631] [632] However, it is interesting that when Rowling wanted to experiment with a new pseudonym, she chose not only a male name (Robert Galbraith) and a background with more credibility than she herself could claim, but the name was also that of a real-life, massively unethical "doctor" who advocated for conversion therapy. While Rowling denied any connection, her notorious anti-transgender attitudes have made many in the LGBTQIA+ community suspicious.[633]

There's also *Mary Poppins* creator P. L. Travers, *Star Trek* screenwriter D. C. Fontana, E. L. Konigsburg, E. Nesbit, poet U. A. Fanthorpe, C.J. Cherryh, A.M. Barnard (a pre-*Little Women* Louisa May Alcott), J.D. Robb (Nora Roberts) ... the list goes on. However, it's not only writers who use their initials. From 1893 to 1914, architect Emily Elizabeth Holman was known professionally as E. E. Holman in order to secure contracts. [634]

This is also common among scientists. Botanist Shirley Winifred Jeffrey published her work as S. W. Jeffrey to avoid gender bias, though she did gain a reputation as "the mother of chlorophyll c," for her work with the pigment.[635] Vanderbilt University's Tina M. Iverson did a small experiment: in her first year as a researcher in 2005, she submitted 16 grant applications under her full, clearly feminine name. Only one received funding. "T. M. Iverson" was significantly more successful—five times more, in fact. "This was only an n = 1 experiment, but I didn't care to repeat it," she commented. Unfortunately, her university's electronic application system put in her full name without her knowledge on subsequent applications, and her success rate dropped again—rising when she convinced administrators to "correct"

---

631   Tensley, Brandon, "The Enduring Fascination of S.E. Hinton's 'the Outsiders,'" Pacific Standard, April 26, 2017, https://psmag.com/news/the-enduring-fascination-of-s-e-hintons-the-outsiders
632   Flynn, Caitlin, "The Reason J.K. Rowling Used a Pen Name Is Further Proof That Sexism Is Alive & Well," Refinery29, July 11, 2017, https://www.refinery29.com/en-us/2017/07/162736/jk-rowling-pen-name-sexism
633   Lan, Nico, "J.K. Rowling's Denies Pen Name Is Inspired by Anti-LGBTQ+ Conversion Therapist," Them, June 10, 2020, https://www.them.us/story/jk-rowlings-pen-name-also-name-of-anti-lgbtq-conversion-therapist
634   "Woman Architect Tells How She Won Success," Evening Public Ledger, (Philadelphia, Pennsylvania), July 7, 1915, p 10, https://www.newspapers.com/article/3311397/evening_public_ledger/
635   Wright, Simon, Gustaaf Hallegraeff, R Fauzi, C Mantoura, and Shirley Jeffrey, "SHIRLEY WINIFRED JEFFREY," National Academy of Sciences, 2015, http://www.nasonline.org/publications/biographical-memoirs/memoir-pdfs/jeffrey-shirley.pdf

it to her initials. "I am the same applicant. The replicates are low, but the outcome apparently differed only when it was obvious to the reviewers that I was female."[636]

---

[636] Brooks, Rob, "Just Your Initials, Please! Subverting Sexist Biases in Peer-Review," The Conversation, April 5, 2013, https://theconversation.com/just-your-initials-please-subverting-sexist-biases-in-peer-review-13272

THE POWER BEHIND THE THRONE

"We haven't really gotten the credit for what we have done."
—Nancy Pelosi[637]

Isabeau of Bavaria was queen of France for almost forty years and spent much that that time managing affairs of state in her husband's stead. Known as Charles the Mad, Charles VI was prone to bouts of violent psychosis, which could last for months and of which later he did not recall. The first recorded instance, in 1392, saw him attack his own knights, including his brother, and kill four men. In the following three decades, Isabeau helped keep the country stable, preserving the throne for her son to inherit.[638]

While some women have been able to seize power overtly, others have often been political in subtle ways, manipulating those in power to achieve their own ends. A common middle ground for women has been regencies, where they were officially ruling but in the name of a male relative, such as an absent king or a child. These are public but generally temporary positions (unless they just never give the power back, but that's a topic for another book). In some cases, the women working behind the scenes have more impact than those in the public positions.

For centuries, the valide sultan was often the second most important person in the Ottoman Empire, after the sultan himself. Generally held by the mother of the reigning sultan, the position was highly influential in matters of state. Among

---

[637] Peolsi, Nancy, Interview, Politics Daily, October 24, 2010, http://www.politicsdaily.com/2010/10/24/video-melinda-henneberger-interviews-house-speaker-nancy-pelosi/

[638] Herman, Eleanor, *Off with Her Head: Three Thousand Years of Demonizing Women in Power* (HarperCollins, 2022).

the most powerful of these women were Mihrimah Sultan, Nurbanu Sultan, Safiye Sultan, Kösem Sultan, and Turhan Sultan.[639] Hurrem Sultan, wife of Suleiman the Magnificent, died before her son's reign began and so never held the title. Nonetheless, she is considered the most influential woman in the history of the empire, beginning the so-called Sultanate of Women. During this period, from approximately 1533 to 1656, the mothers and wives of sultans exercised particularly significant amounts of political influence, though other powerful valide sultans also existed after this time. The last woman to hold the position was Perestu Kadın, until her death in 1904.[640]

First as regent and then in her own right, Empress Cixi ruled China for almost half a century. After her husband died in 1861, her five-year-old son became the emperor in name only. With the help of her late husband's principal wife, Empress Dowager Ci'an, and other allies, she overthrew the Eight Regents her husband had intended to rule for their son, called the Xinyou Coup. After her son died in 1875, she installed her two-year-old nephew as the new emperor. Her regencies were referred to as "rule from behind the curtains." She later launched another coup against her nephew in 1898 and ruled in her own right until her death in 1908.[641]

Centuries earlier, Jia Nanfeng was the first wife of Emperor Hui of the Jin dynasty. Often portrayed as a villainous figure in Chinese history, she is seen as the person who provoked the War of the Eight Princes, which led to the Wu Hu rebellions and the Jin Dynasty's loss of northern and central China. From 291 to 300, she ruled the empire behind the scenes by dominating her husband, who had developmental disabilities. When he was still the prince, it was suggested to his father the emperor that the young man was not fit to inherit—Jia reputedly circumvented his ensuing enquiries by having someone write simple but correct responses.[642]

---

639   Peirce, Leslie, *The Imperial Harem: Women and Sovereignty in the Ottoman Empire* (Oxford University Press, 1993).
Peirce, Leslie, *The Imperial Harem: Gender and Power in the Ottoman Empire, 1520-1656*, (UMI Dissertation Information Service, 1988) p. 106.
640   Iacob, Anisia, "Under Suleiman's Rule: The Role of Women in the Ottoman Empire," The Collector, February 28, 2022, https://www.thecollector.com/role-of-women-in-ottoman-empire-suleiman-rule/
641   "Empress Dowager Cixi," New World Encyclopedia, 2019, https://www.newworldencyclopedia.org/entry/Empress_Dowager_Cixi.
642   Fang, Xuanling (ed.) (648). Book of Jin (Jin Shu).

Belle Moskowitz was a social reformer and political advisor so influential that, in her obituary, *The New York Times* called her the most powerful woman in U.S. politics. Following her early social work improving conditions for young women, she spent years as an industrial mediator, resolving conflicts between managers and their workers. But it was once she started working with Al Smith in 1918 that she transitioned to the power behind the throne. As his campaign manager, publicist, and top aide, she helped Smith become governor of New York, a role he would hold for eight years. During that time, witnesses reported that Smith would wait for her approval before making final decisions on matters large and small. She helped guide the sweeping reforms he implemented as governor, which would later influence the national New Deal social reform package. [643]

While most U.S. presidents have relied on their First Ladies, none have wielded the same type of power as Edith Wilson did after her husband Woodrow had a stroke while in office in October 1919 that left him partially paralysed. Rather than showing weakness to the public and his enemies, Edith stepped up and effectively ran the executive branch of the U.S. government from her husband's bedside for over a year, long after his mobility had returned.[644]

"So began my stewardship, I studied every paper sent from the different Secretaries or Senators," she wrote in her memoir, "and tried to digest and present in tabloid form the things that, despite my vigilance, had to go to the President. I, myself, never made a single decision regarding the disposition of public affairs. The only decision that was mine was what was important and what was not, and the very important decision of when to present matters to my husband."[645]

Very few people, including those in the government, knew the extent to which Edith had taken over her husband's presidential duties, which continued through the completion of his second term in 1921. Despite the modesty and underplaying her words relate in a no doubt carefully phrased publication, historians believe

---

[643] Gorham, Christopher C., *The Confidante: The Untold Story of the Woman Who Helped Win WWII and Shape Modern America* (Citadel, 2023).
[644] Markel, Howard, "When a Secret President Ran the Country," PBS NewsHour, October 2, 2015, https://www.pbs.org/newshour/health/woodrow-wilson-stroke
[645] Wilson, Edith Bolling Galt, *My Memoir* (Bobbs-Merrill Company, 1938).

she did much more than "stewardship," but rather she likely acted as the country's de facto chief executive.

IGNORED FOR AWARDS

"Women don't need to find their voice. They need to feel empowered to use it and people need to be encouraged to listen."
—Meghan Markle[646]

When she was a graduate student at Johns Hopkins University, neuroscientist Candace Pert discovered the opiate receptor—key to explaining how endorphins and opioids work chemically in the body—and was the first person to isolate the T cell receptor. Pert's supervisor was given the credit—and the prestigious Albert Lasker Award, with its $250,000 prize money—for her discovery, even though she was lead author on the paper. When Pert wrote a letter of protest to the award committee, he condescendingly responded, "That's how the game is played." [647]

While receiving public recognition is generally not part of the job for those in espionage, there are times when it is deserved. Jane Wallis Burrell was the first active-duty CIA agent to die, in a plane crash on January 6, 1948. Yet she was never recognized with a star on the agency's Memorial Wall. While the CIA justification for this is that the wall is reserved for people who died while carrying out CIA duties, 45 of the 137 stars represent accidental deaths, many of them commercial plane crashes like Burrell's. They also include car crashes and medical circumstances, such as a gall bladder surgery that ended badly.[648]

---

646 Markle, Meghan, Royal Foundation Forum, February 28, 2018.
647 Maugh, Thomas H, "Candace Pert Dies at 67; Neuroscientist Discovered Opiate Receptor," *Los Angeles Times*, September 23, 2013, https://www.latimes.com/local/obituaries/la-me-candace-pert-20130924-story.html
648 Holt, Nathalia, *Wise Gals: The Spies Who Built the CIA and Changed the Future of Espionage*, (Icon Books, 2023).

It's especially galling (pun intended) when considering Burrell's contributions, which went back to working for the CIA predecessor, the Office of Strategic Services (OSS), starting in 1943. She was hired as a junior clerk, with an annual salary of only $1,440, despite her education, experience, and the fact that she was actually doing the work of an analyst. During World War II, American intelligence officers collected information, discovered enemy agents (including assassins, saboteurs and other "stay behinds"), interrogated sources, and also ran agents, including doubled enemy agents, against the Germans. The few surviving documents mentioning her indicate that Burrell was "in the thick of these activities," according to the CIA. She and her work were also valuable enough that she survived the massive post-war downsizing and re-organisation when the OSS was dissolved and replaced with the Central Intelligence Group, later renamed the Central Intelligence Agency.[649]

It's also possible that she was, in fact, working at the time. Per the CIA, "We know nothing about Jane's activity at the time of her death. She was returning from a trip to Brussels on January 6—traditionally the end of the Christmas season—and despite speculation that she was on an operational mission, the limited documentation sheds no light. An official U.S. spokesman at the time said Jane had been on vacation." Given the common need for operational secrecy, it seems entirely feasible that the spokesman would have reason to lie if she was working, and the agency's own records are too scant to confirm either way. But in the end, it simply doesn't matter whether she was on a mission or a holiday—she served the agency well and deserves the same honour as other fallen officers, which even the CIA acknowledges, albeit purely as lip service, "her service with CIA and its predecessor organizations was honorable and deserves to be remembered."

Ida B. Wells was recognized with a Pulitzer special citation in 2020—almost 90 years after her death—"for her outstanding and courageous reporting on the horrific and vicious violence against African Americans during the era of lynching". The prize money was given to the Ida B. Wells Society for Investigative Reporting,

---

649 "The Mystery of Jane Wallis Burrell: The First CIA Officer to Die in the Agency's Service," Central Intelligence Agency, July 13, 2016, https://www.cia.gov/stories/story/the-mystery-of-jane-wallis-burrell-the-first-cia-officer-to-die-in-the-agencys-service/

which donated it to the Ida B. Wells Scholarship Fund at the City University of New York school of journalism. This raises the question of what Wells might have accomplished with the equivalent money when she was actually alive.[650]

Overlooking Ida B. Wells could be seen as an oversight, but a clear and deliberate choice was made in 1957. The Pulitzer Prize advisory board chose not to give that year's award for fiction to anyone, rather than give it to Elizabeth Spencer. The jury had unanimously voted that the prize be awarded to Spencer for her third novel, *The Voice at the Back Door*, a critique of local corruption and racial violence in Mississippi. Though no public reason was given, critics have asserted that it was a political decision, given her candour about racism at the time. Her career suffered because, as all of her books had been set in Mississippi, she was seen as a "Southern woman" writer rather than a literary author, and she didn't publish another book until 1965. It seems indisputable that a Pulitzer would have changed such a perception.[651]

Marie Curie is arguably the most famous woman scientist in history. She was the first woman to win a Nobel, the first person and the only woman to win the Nobel Prize twice, and the only person to win the Nobel Prize in two different scientific fields. But she almost didn't. Curie's first Nobel win in 1903 was for her foundational work in radioactivity, which she did with her husband Pierre. Four men on the Nobel committee nominated Pierre and Henri Becquerel, who had also been studying radioactive materials, for a joint prize. None of the men put Marie forward, even though three of them were familiar enough with the Curies' work to know that it was in fact Marie who had discovered radioactivity in a uranium mineral known as pitchblende, and had discovered not one but two new elements, radium and polonium. It's also worth noting that the Curies did all of this without a proper laboratory facility, as they had basically no funding for their work.[652]

---

650 Greene, Morgan, "Ida B. Wells Receives Pulitzer Prize Citation: 'the Only Thing She Really Had Was the Truth,'" Chicago Tribune, May 4, 2020, https://www.chicagotribune.com/news/breaking/ct-ida-wells-pulitzer-citation-20200505-rlt4ujeeenf7vi5z6qt7e4pmha-story.html

651 McFadden, Robert D, "Elizabeth Spencer, Author of 'the Light in the Piazza,' Dies at 98," December 23, 2019, https://www.nytimes.com/2019/12/23/arts/elizabeth-spencer-dead.html

652 "Marie Curie – Recognition and Disappointment (1903-1905)," American Institute of Physics, https://history.aip.org/exhibits/curie/recdis2.htm

What followed is an excellent example of the importance of allyship on men's part. Another committee member, mathematician Magnus Gösta Mittag-Leffler, alerted Pierre to the situation. Pierre and Charles J. Bouchard forced the committee to add Marie's name. Bouchard was another committee member, who had nominated both Curies the previous year. Pierre told the committee that he would not accept the prize unless Marie was included. Even after they relented, the prize money was not split equally—Becquerel received 70,000 francs, and so did the Curies. It is absolutely ridiculous that such a brilliant scientist had to rely on the goodwill of important men just to be recognized for the work she did, and even then, received basically no prize money, as it was the same amount Pierre would have received on his own.

Curie was one of many women scientists who were dismissed as merely assisting their husbands, but most of those women did not fare as well as she did when their husbands were honoured with Nobels. French microbiologist and virologist Marguerite Lwoff partnered with her husband André, and they worked together for decades. Over time, André gained greater recognition while Marguerite was seen as nothing more than a technician assisting him, despite earning her own PhD in 1940 and publishing papers in her own name. While he was departmental head at the Institut Pasteur, she was the Head of Laboratory. When he won the Nobel Prize in Medicine in 1965, she was ignored—even his official bio on the Nobel site mentions her only once in passing as "his wife," not even bothering to name her.[653]

Astrophysicist Vera Rubin's pioneering research on galaxy rotation led to "a Copernican-scale change in cosmological theory," says *The New York Times*.[654] In collaboration with Kent Ford, Her observations suggested that there was a lot of unseen matter in galaxies, which they named "dark matter." Today, scientists believe dark matter makes up 85 percent of the universe, and this discovery is considered one of the most important in astrophysics. Yet, although there were calls

---

653 Harvey, Joy, "The Mystery of the Nobel Laureate and His Vanishing Wife," For Better or for Worse? Collaborative Couples in the Sciences, 57–77, https://doi.org/10.1007/978-3-0348-0286-4_4,
654 Overbye, Dennis (December 27, 2016), "Vera Rubin, 88, Dies; Opened Doors in Astronomy, and for Women," *The New York Times*, Retrieved December 27, 2016.

for her to be awarded a Nobel Prize for decades, she was never even nominated.[655]

Physicist Dr. Marietta Blau did groundbreaking research on the pion, a subatomic particle made up of a single quark and antiquark that results from the collision of particles or exposure to high-energy gamma rays. Working with her student, Hertha Wambacher, they pioneered the use of nuclear emulsion plates to characterize and measure interactions of different particles. They also discovered "disintegration stars" created by cosmic rays interacting with nuclei in her photographic plates. In 1937, the pair reported the first indisputable evidence of the disintegration of heavy nuclei in accelerators—the basis for many modern accelerators that rely on this fact, like the Large Hadron Collider.[656]

Blau was nominated once for the chemistry Nobel and four times for the Physics, but even though noted physicists Dr. Erwin Schrodinger (himself a Nobel winner) and Dr. Walter Thirring both nominated Blau and Wambacher for the Nobel Prize, the committee declined. Instead, Dr. Cecil Powell received the Nobel Prize in Physics in 1950 for work that was founded in Dr. Blau's discoveries. In his Nobel lecture, Powell mentioned photographic emulsions at least eight times, and tracks from emulsion plates made up seven of the eight figures he used as visuals, but although he included twelve citations, he didn't mention Blau or Wambacher at all.

The 1934 Nobel Prize in Physiology or Medicine was awarded to three men—George Whipple, George Richards Minot, and William P. Murphy—for their research into the use of liver tissue in treatment of pernicious anaemia. Frieda Robscheit-Robbins, who had co-authored twenty-one papers with Whipple (almost his entire body of published work) on the topic, was left out. The three men believed this was due to sexism, and Whipple shared his portion of the prize money with her. Although she had a PhD and they worked together for 38 years, she was never given a title higher than "research associate." From 1917 to 1955, she wrote more than 100 articles as well as chapters on anaemia for medical textbooks.

---

655 Siegel, Ethan, "These 5 Women Deserved, and Were Unjustly Denied, a Nobel Prize in Physics," Forbes, October 11, 2018, https://www.forbes.com/sites/startswithabang/2018/10/11/these-5-women-deserved-and-were-unjustly-denied-a-nobel-prize-in-physics/?sh=7bed2356195e

656 Rentetzi, Maria, "Marietta Blau," Jewish Women's Archive, December 13, 1999, https://jwa.org/encyclopedia/article/blau-marietta

She was also the lead author on Whipple's most important paper, and of the twenty-three papers that Whipple cited in his Nobel speech, Robscheit-Robbins had co-authored ten.[657]

As noted previously, Alma Reville was not included when *Rebecca* and *Foreign Correspondent* were each nominated for Best Original Screenplay Oscars, despite her extensive contributions, and Ava DuVernay was not credited for her work rewriting the script of *Selma* (2014). They are not alone. 1940s film writer Catherine Turney was known for writing great women characters—strong, independent, and funny. Her films included *The Man I Love* (1947), *A Stolen Life* (1946), *My Reputation* (1946) and *Mildred Pierce* (1945). Even though Warner Brothers, film historians, and the Screenwriters Guild all agree Turney was the primary script writer, she did not receive on-screen credit for *Mildred Pierce*. So, when it was nominated for Best Screenplay Writing at the 1946 Academy Awards, she was not named—only Ranald MacDougall was.[658]

"At Warner Bros., women writers were not particularly highly thought of. We were seen as a necessary evil and were seldom paid as much as the men," Turney told *The Advocate* in 1984. "I think the only reason that they put up with women writers, certainly at Warner's, was that they had big women stars. At one time they had Bette Davis, Barbara Stanwyck, Joan Crawford, Rosalind Russell, Ann Sheridan, and Ida Lupino. All of them were under contract and demanded stories slanted toward women."

Eighty years later, writer, director, and actor Greta Gerwig was snubbed at the Oscars. Her 2023 hit *Barbie* was not only the highest-grossing film of the year, but also the most talked about. And while the film was nominated for Best Picture and seven other categories at the Academy Awards the following year, Gerwig was once again ignored for Best Director. Although she had been nominated for her directorial debut, 2017's *Lady Bird* (for which she was also nominated for Best Original Screenplay, but won in neither category), she was not nominated for Best Director

---

657 Commire, Anne, *Dictionary of Women Worldwide: 25 000 Women through the Ages* (Thomson/Gale, 2007).
658 Oliver, Myrna, "Catherine Turney; Screenwriter, Author," *Los Angeles Times*, September 11, 1998, https://www.latimes.com/archives/la-xpm-1998-sep-11-me-21584-story.html

for 2019's *Little Women*, which garnered six nominations including Best Picture and Best Adapted Screenplay for Gerwig. Eyebrows were also raised at the categorisation of her *Barbie* script as "Adapted" rather than "Original" for her writing nomination. With *Lady Bird*'s five nominations, Gerwig had written and directed three films that, in total, received 19 Oscar nominations, among other awards. And yet the famously male-dominated Best Director was repeatedly withheld, making one wonder if there was an unwritten quota that allowed at most one woman—in 2024, Justine Triet for *Anatomy of a Fall*—to be nominated in the category. As previously noted, women directors are also more likely to be nominated for male-centred films, while all three of Gerwig's films were very much female-focused.[659]

The Pritzker Architecture Prize, generally considered the world's highest honour in that field, is meant to be awarded "irrespective of nationality, race, creed, or ideology"—note that gender is not included. Denise Scott Brown, who won the Soane Medal in 2018 for the "global influence" of her work, was deliberately excluded when her husband won the Pritzker in 1991 for work that everyone knew they had collaborated on together. When the blatant insult caused outcry, organizers claimed that the award can only be given to one person—a flagrant lie, as two men received the prize jointly only a few years earlier, in 1988.[660] Scott Brown later told CNN, "the Pritzker Prize was based on the fallacy that great architecture was the work of a 'single lone male genius' at the expense of collaborative work."[661]

The decades-long streak of male-only winners was broken by Zaha Hadid in 2004. Even though several women have won since then, the organisation appears not to have learned its lesson, as they did the exact same thing to Chinese architect Lu Wenyu in 2012, when her husband Wang Shu alone was recognized for work they did together. Although Lu later asserted that she did not want the Pritzker, as she preferred to avoid the fame that would accompany such an award, and that

---

659 Academy of Motion Picture Arts and Sciences, https://www.oscars.org/
660 Álvarez, Eva, "The Invisible Women: How Female Architects Were Erased from History," *Architectural Review*, March 8, 2017, https://www.architectural-review.com/essays/the-invisible-women-how-female-architects-were-erased-from-history
661 Davies, Catriona, "Denise Scott Brown: Architecture favors 'lone male genius' over women," CNN, May 29, 2013, https://edition.cnn.com/2013/05/01/business/denise-scott-brown-pritzker-prize/index.html

her partner would have shared it if she had wanted him to, the fact remains that the organisation apparently did not offer. For both women, it is part of a larger pattern for themselves and other women in architecture of having their collaborations credited solely to their male collaborators.[662]

In 2013, the Gottfried Semper Architekturpreis was initially awarded only to Matthias Sauerbruch of Sauerbruch Hutton, without acknowledging equal founding partner Louisa Hutton—a decision that was later reversed when Sauerbruch objected.[663]

Mathematician Philippa Fawcett was denied the title of "Senior Wrangler" at Cambridge University even after she had objectively earned it in 1890. The title officially went to whichever student (known as wranglers) in the Mathematical Tripos (Cambridge's name for the course) achieved the top score on the exams each year and it was described as "the greatest intellectual achievement attainable in Britain" at the time. Even though her score was thirteen percent higher than her nearest competitor, Geoffrey Thomas Bennett was the one feted because only men were ranked. When the women's list was announced, Fawcett was credited as "above the senior wrangler."[664] No woman officially held the title until more than 100 years later, when Ruth Hendry won in 1992.[665]

In 2016, the prestigious Angoulême International Comics Festival came under fire when not one woman was among the thirty people nominated for its lifetime achievement award, the Grand Prix. It was part of a larger pattern—few women had ever been nominated. Of those, only Florence Cestac won, more than a decade earlier in 2005. Moreover, only past winners were invited to vote on the shortlisted

---

662 Zabalbeascoa, Anatxu, "La Arquitecta Que Renunció al Pritzker Para Evitar La Fama," El País, October 1, 2013, https://elpais.com/cultura/2013/09/30/actualidad/1380569553_963993.html
663 Álvarez, Eva, "The Invisible Women: How Female Architects Were Erased from History," *Architectural Review*, March 8, 2017, https://www.architectural-review.com/essays/the-invisible-women-how-female-architects-were-erased-from-history
664 O'Connor, J. J. and Robertson, E. F., "Philippa Fawcett – Biography," School of Mathematics and Statistics, University of St Andrews, Scotland, Last updated October 2003, https://mathshistory.st-andrews.ac.uk/Biographies/Fawcett/
665 Letter from Dr. Richard R. Weber to Ruth Hendry, June 19, 1992, https://www.notarymidwales.co.uk/ruth-juliet-hendry-senior-wrangler-1992.pdf

nominees, making Cestac the only woman eligible to vote on who would win.[666]

In response, twelve of the nominees withdrew their names from consideration, and organizers announced they would add Posy Simmonds and Marjane Satrapi. The festival's executive officer had previously claimed Satrapi, best known for her groundbreaking *Persepolis*, was ineligible because she had stopped making comics, yet *Calvin and Hobbes* creator Bill Watterson had won in 2014, almost 20 years after he stopped producing. The same executive publicly claimed, "Unfortunately, there are few women in the history of comics," which is simply not true.[667]

One of the nominees who withdrew, Riad Sattouf, publicly listed several women he would like to see nominated in his place, including Rumiko Takahashi and Julie Doucet, who won in 2019 and 2022. (Sattouf himself won in 2023.)

There are, of course, other reasons that women have been overlooked besides their gender. From 1945 to 1974, Estonian poet Marie Under was nominated for the Nobel Prize for Literature thirty times. Dr. Sirje Kiin, who wrote her dissertation for her 2010 PhD in comparative literature on Under, identified several reasons for the repeated snub, including the questionable quality of translations from Estonian, particularly given the complexity of her style and language. There is also a bias towards novelists over poets, though poets like Gabriela Mistral (1945), Octavio Paz (1990) and Wislawa Szymborska (1996) have all won the award. Kiin also noted broader changes in European literature following World War II, and the political implications of the time, including the Soviet occupation of Estonia, which led Under and her family to flee to Sweden as refugees.[668]

Algerian novelist Assia Djebar was repeatedly a favourite to win a Nobel Prize in Literature, yet over a career of more than fifty years, she never did. In 2013, *Le Figaro* put the question of "why not?" to French industry professionals. The

---

666 Lewis, Danny, "Prestigious Comics Festival Comes under Fire for Excluding, Then Denying Existence Of, Women Creators," *Smithsonian Magazine*, January 7, 2016, https://www.smithsonianmag.com/smart-news/prestigious-comics-festival-comes-under-fire-for-excluding-then-denying-existence-of-women-creators-180957739/
667 Potet, Frédéric, "Le festival de BD d'Angoulême accusé de sexisme après une sélection 100 % masculine," *Le Monde*, Janaury 5, 2016, https://www.lemonde.fr/bande-dessinee/article/2016/01/05/le-festival-de-bd-d-angouleme-accuse-de-sexisme-apres-une-selection-100-masculine_4842193_4420272.html
668 Kiin, Sirje, "Marie Under: Marie Under: Why Didn't She Receive a Nobel Prize?" The Estonian Society of Central Florida, https://floridaestos.files.wordpress.com/2012/01/marie-under-nobel-sirje-kiin.pdf

answers were all deeply unsatisfying, and one in particular was a vague "not universal enough," despite Djebar's books having been translated into twenty-three languages and studied in universities around the world. The same applies to the criticisms that the Algerian author wrote "for the French," which may have contributed to the lack of support from her home country of Algeria, which another suggested as a factor. One critiqued Djebar writing in French rather than her mother tongue of Arabic, yet Joseph Brodsky won for a collection of poems and essays in both his native Russian and English. None seemed willing to acknowledge the obvious: Djebar was an Arab woman from a non-Western country, writing about women and expressing both anti-patriarchal and anti-colonialist views.[669] The only Arab women to win in any category, as of 2023, were Peace Prize winners Tawakkol Karman, Malala Yousafzai, Narges Mohammadi and Nadia Murad. In more than 120 years and out of 965 individuals, only sixty-four women have won Nobel Prizes in any category, and only thirteen of those were women of colour, as of the 2023 awards. African American poet Toni Morrison is the only woman of colour to have won for Literature.[670][671]

Being anti-feminist didn't help Greek-Italian journalist, novelist, and short story writer Matilde Serao, however. She was favoured to win the Nobel for Literature in 1926 but lost out to Grazia Deledda because of her politics—she failed to align herself and her newspaper with Italy's Fascist regime of the time, and so they blocked her nomination. She had only the year before publicly signed the 1925 "Manifesto of anti-fascist intellectuals."[672]

Even today, women may be deliberately excluded rather than "merely" overlooked. In 2024, it was revealed that four authors—two Caucasian men and two Chinese people, a woman and a non-binary, femme-presenting individual—had

---

669 Matarese, Melanie, "Pourquoi Assia Djebar N'a Pas Eu Le Nobel de Littérature," Le Figaro, October 11, 2013, https://www.lefigaro.fr/blogs/algerie/2013/10/pourquoi-assia-djebar-na-pas-eu-le-nobel-de-litterature.html
670 "Nobel Prize Awarded Women," NobelPrize.org, https://www.nobelprize.org/prizes/lists/nobel-prize-awarded-women/
671 "All Nobel Prizes," NobelPrize.org, https://www.nobelprize.org/prizes/lists/all-nobel-prizes/
672 Trivelli, Anita, "Matilde Serao," In Jane Gaines, Radha Vatsal, and Monica Dall'Asta, eds. Women Film Pioneers Project, Columbia University Libraries, 2013, https://doi.org/10.7916/d8-vze6-7463

their work deliberately excluded from consideration for the prestigious science fiction Hugo Awards in 2023. The award's gatekeepers had chosen to self-censor the awards to remove any content or writers that could potentially upset the hosting country, China. While the two men in question were excluded for their public criticisms of China's government and policies, Xiran Jay Zhao's and R. F. Kuang's works themselves were targeted for incorporations of their own ethnic and cultural backgrounds. Zhao, who was born in China but raised in Canada, was excluded from consideration for the "Astounding Award" for *Iron Widow*, their debut sci-fi reimagining of Chinese empress Wu Zetian's rise to power. Meanwhile, former Hugo finalist Kuang's *Babel, or the Necessity of Violence*—which has won other accolades including Nebula and Locus Awards—was flagged by an administrator because it had "a lot about China." The person admitted they had not read the book, nor had any knowledge of Chinese politics, and so could not say if it would be seen as negative. Kuang was also born in China, but raised in the United States, meaning that the awards decision-makers were deliberately excluding writers from the host country for writing about that country. Both books were also #1 *New York Times* bestsellers, and the awards are voted on by members of the World Science Fiction Society, meaning popular books have an advantage—at least, when they're allowed to be voted on.[673]

The women of the Special Operations Executive risked—and often lost—their lives to support the Allied Powers during World War II. Yet when it came to recognising their bravery, recommendations for commendations were bafflingly denied. Yvonne Rudellat was posthumously recommended for a Military Cross, given for "acts of exemplary gallantry during active operations against the enemy on land." She is the only woman officially recorded as having merited it during World War II. She was rejected because women were ineligible. Rudellat, the first SOE-trained female agent sent into France, worked in the heart of the Nazi-occupied country before being captured and dying of typhus and dysentery, which she contracted

---

673 Ulatowski, Rachel, "Hugo Awards Administrator Exposes Deliberate Censorship of R. F. Kuang's 'Babel' and More," February 15, 2024, The Mary Sue, https://www.themarysue.com/hugo-awards-controversy-explained-administrator-exposes-censorship-of-r-f-kuang-babel-more/

at Bergen-Belsen concentration camp.[674]

Virginia Hall was a highly successful SOE agent who was recommended for a Commander of the Order of the British Empire, the country's highest civilian honour, while she was still active in the field. The citation read:

> "She has devoted herself whole-heartedly to our work without regard to the dangerous position in which her activities would place her if they were realised by the Vichy authorities. She has been indefatigable in her constant support and assistance for our agents, combining a high degree of organising ability with a clear-sighted appreciation of our needs... Her services for us cannot be too highly praised."

The recommendation was declined for unknown reasons, and she was later granted the less prestigious Member of the Order of the British Empire. She was also awarded France's Croix de Guerre, and was the only civilian woman to be awarded the Distinguished Service Cross for extraordinary heroism against the enemy by the Office of Strategic Services, precursor to the U.S.'s Central Intelligence Agency.[675]

Dr. Mary Edwards Walker served in the Union Army during the U.S. Civil War but was captured in 1864 while trying to reach a patient and held in a Confederate military prison for four months as the first known female prisoner of war (many women served while disguised as men, so she likely had an unidentified female predecessor). After the war, she was awarded the Medal of Honor, the country's highest military decoration for members of the armed forces who have distinguished themselves by acts of valour. Dr. Walker was, and remains, the only woman to have been awarded the medal in more than 160 years.[676] In 1916, shortly before her death, Dr. Walker's medal was stripped from her. A report by the Medal of Honor Review Board, established by Congress the year before, had identified 911

---

674 King, Stella, "Jacqueline," *Pioneer Heroine of the Resistance* (Arms and Armour Press, 1989).
675 Purnell, Sonia, *A Woman of No Importance: The Untold Story of the American Spy Who Helped Win World War II* (Penguin Books, 2020).
676 "Dr. Mary E. Walker: The Sole Female Medal of Honor Recipient," Wounded Warrior Project, https://newsroom.woundedwarriorproject.org/Dr-Mary-E-Walker-The-Sole-Female-Medal-of-Honor-Recipient

recipients that it felt should not have been given the medal—including Dr. Walker. Because there had been few rules at first, medals were given out for a variety of reasons, including almost 900 for non-combat enlistment extensions. While it is reasonable to rescind medals awarded for such reasons, Dr. Walker saved lives and would frequently cross battle lines into enemy territory to get to injured people in need. Ostensibly, the reason given was process—Walker was awarded her Medal directly by President Andrew Johnson, rather than being formally recommended. It is noteworthy that the board declined to revoke the Medal of at least two other (male) surgeons who were likewise ineligible. In 1977, lobbying efforts by the Walker family were successful in reversing the decision and having her medal reinstated. As for Dr. Walker, she refused to return the medal, wearing it every day until her death on February 21, 1919.[677]

There is also the emotional component of being recognized. When physicist Margaret G. Kivelson was awarded a Guggenheim Fellowship in 1973, she later recalled, "that fellowship gave me for the first time the sense that I was being taken seriously as a scientist. More than money, it gave me status and increased my self-confidence considerably."[678]

---

[677] Jowdy, Laura, "The 1916 Medal of Honor Review Board," Congressional Medal of Honor Society, June 18, 2021, https://www.cmohs.org/news-events/blog/the-1916-medal-of-honor-review-board/

[678] Kivelson, M. G., "The Rest of the Solar System," *Annual Review of Earth and Planetary Sciences* vol 36 no 1, 32 (2008). https://www.annualreviews.org/content/journals/10.1146/annurev.earth.36.031207.124312

UNDERMINED

"Men can comfortably claim credit for what they do as long as they don't veer into arrogance. For women, taking credit comes at a real social and professional cost."
—Sheryl Sandberg[679]

Special effects designer Milicent Patrick created one of the most iconic film monsters of her era—the Creature from the Black Lagoon (1953). Bud Westmore, head of the Universal Studios makeup department, was given the on-screen credit as the department head, because at the time, the norm was to leave out many of the behind-the-scenes staff who worked on a film (another practice that meant women were often uncredited). The studio sent Patrick on a press tour as "The Beauty Who Created the Beast," to speak about her work designing and building the creature. Jealous, Westmore not only insisted the phrasing be changed to "The Beauty Who Lives With the Beast," but he actually had her fired when she returned from promoting the film. Given his family's clout in the film industry, his actions likely resulted in her essentially being blackballed from any similar roles. And so, the first woman to work in a Hollywood special effects makeup department, who contributed to several films prior to this, never worked behind the scenes on another film.[680]

Many men see women wanting to accomplish things as inherently threatening to the men—this seems an implicit acknowledgement that they are aware women

---
679   Sandberg, Sheryl, *Lean In: Women, Work, and the Will to Lead* (Penguin Random House, 2013).
680   O'Meara, Mallory, *The Lady from the Black Lagoon: Hollywood Monsters and the Lost Legacy of Milicent Patrick* (Hanover Square Press, 2019).

are just as good and, horrifyingly to them, potentially even better than the men already doing the jobs. As such, their opportunities and hopes must be snuffed before they can become a danger.

More broadly, many men with fragile egos will seek to "put a woman in her place" if she dares wound said ego. War correspondent Dickey Chapelle's incredible reporting from World War II was largely buried because she offended the ego of an admiral. Due to a misunderstanding, lack of communication, and a series of events largely outside her control, the admiral believed she had deliberately violated his orders about where she was allowed to go with U.S. troops in Okinawa. He had her arrested, with a Marine holding his gun on her during transport, and sent back to the U.S. There, her abusive husband was waiting with a letter addressed to *him* stating that her press credentials had been revoked, meaning it would be almost impossible to get her work published, including a book deal she had lined up. No amount of reason or pleading would get the admiral to change his mind, and her credentials wouldn't be restored for another ten years.[681]

While many women mentioned in other chapters were held back by the men in their lives—husbands, brothers, colleagues—it's worth noting how often sexist attitudes impact women's ability to be recognized when their work should speak for itself. Such issues can also prevent women from achieving everything they otherwise might in the first place, but that would encompass far more than we could fit in this book. As documentary filmmaker Robin Hauser noted in her TED talk, *The likability dilemma for women leaders*,

> Modern day sexism is different than it was in the past when a blatant comment about a woman's physique or a chummy pat on the derriere was tolerated, maybe even accepted. Today's sexism can be more subtle. Little nuances that might seem like no big deal to some, but their impact can have the effect of a thousand cuts.[682]

---

[681] Rhinehart, Lorissa. First to the Front: The Untold Story of Dickey Chapelle, Trailblazing Female War Correspondent. (MacMillan, 2023).

[682] Hauser, Robin, "Robin Hauser: The Likability Dilemma for Women Leaders," TED, April 13, 2022, https://www.ted.com/talks/robin_hauser_the_likability_dilemma_for_women_leaders_jan_2022/transcript

Nettie Stevens discovered XY chromosomes at the exact same time as E.B. Wilson in 1905. The two scientists were working independently, but each was aware of the other's work. However, when they published their respective results, Wilson was widely acclaimed as the sole discoverer, to the point that Stevens was often excluded from speaking at meetings of experts where her own findings were being discussed.

In retrospect, Stevens' work appears to be higher quality. For example, Wilson claimed environmental factors affected sex, whereas Stevens believed it was only genetic. She was right. In fact, Wilson didn't even bother studying eggs, examining only sperm because he claimed that eggs were too fatty for his staining procedure. After reading the papers describing Stevens' discoveries, Wilson reissued his original paper and in a footnote acknowledged Stevens for the finding of sex chromosomes.[683]

She also determined that Clarence Erwin McClung's theory that the X chromosome determines sex was wrong, as sex is determined by the presence or absence of the small (Y) chromosome. After her death, her own PhD advisor belittled and misrepresented her contributions and even implicitly tried to take credit for her work by excluding her name while bragging about his own lab's work in the field. Although she died only nine years after completing her PhD, Stevens published approximately 40 papers in her short career.

Even when lauding a woman's success, many men cannot help but get in a dig with backhanded compliments. Martha Gellhorn's 1936 short story collection, *The Trouble I've Seen*, was a critical and commercial success. English novelist Graham Greene proclaimed it was "quite amazing" that she showed none of the "female vices" of sentimentality and that her "masculine characters are presented as convincingly as her female."[684][685]

Marian Diamond is considered one of the founders of modern neuroscience, not least for her experimental discovery of brain plasticity—the fact that the brain

---

683   Brush, S G., "Nettie M. Stevens and the Discovery of Sex Determination by Chromosomes," *Isis; an International Review Devoted to the History of Science and Its Cultural Influences*, vol 69 no 247, pp 163–72 (1978), https://doi.org/10.1086/352001
684   Mackrell, Judith, *The Correspondents: Six Women Writers on the Front Lines of World War II* (Doubleday, 2021).
685   Greene, Graham, "Short Stories," *The Spectator*, May 22, 1936, https://archive.spectator.co.uk/article/22nd-may-1936/34/short-stories

physically changes with experience—which directly contradicted the scientific beliefs of the time. Shortly before her groundbreaking 1964 paper was to be published, she found out that her secondary co-authors (three men), were listed before her, and her own name had been placed in parenthesis. Having both initiated the project and done the bulk of the work, she confronted her colleague, whose excuse was that he had never written an article with a female co-writer. "Treat it like another name," she responded. In the end, her name appeared first.[686]

U.S. Navy Rear Admiral Grace Hopper was a trailblazing mathematician who was one of the first programmers to work with the Harvard Mark I computer in the 1940s. With a PhD in mathematics from Yale, she was a professor at Vassar College before joining the Navy, where she spent decades doing incredible things. One of them was developing computer languages that were written in English, rather than mathematical notation—most notably, the common business computing language known as COBOL, which is still in use today. In fact, by the year 2000, it was estimated that COBOL made up about 240 billion of the 300 billion lines of computer code in the entire world. In 1951, she developed the first "compiler," which automatically translated plain-language instructions into machine code. Both COBOL and compiling made programming much more accessible to a broader audience, as well as more efficient. In one test, the previous method took three people over fourteen hours—Hopper's compiler turned that into less than one hour for one person.[687]

It was, unfortunately, also seen as a threat by many programmers. As Hopper later said, "someone learns a skill and works hard to learn that skill, and then if you come along and say, 'You don't need that, here's something else that's better,' they are going to be quite indignant."[688] Indeed, some programmers who take

---

[686] Smith, Harrison, "Marian Diamond, Neuroscientist Who Gave New Meaning to 'Use It or Lose It,' Dies at 90," *The Washington Post*, July 30, 2017, https://www.washingtonpost.com/local/obituaries/marian-diamond-neuroscientist-who-gave-new-meaning-to-use-it-or-lose-it-dies-at-90/2017/07/30/ff10060c-752a-11e7-8f39-eeb7d3a2d304_story.html

[687] Evans, Claire L., *Broad Band: The Untold Story of the Women Who Made the Internet* (Penguin Putnam, 2018).

[688] "1976 interview with Grace Hopper, as quoted in Grace Hopper and the Invention of the Information Age," Beyer, Kurt W., 2009, MIT Press.

themselves too seriously even today deride her FLOW-MATIC language because it's simple enough for laypeople to understand. She was also part of the team that developed the UNIVAC I computer, which was the first general-purpose electronic digital computer designed for business use.

She tried retiring twice, and both times was asked to return to active duty because she was just that good at what she did. When she finally did retire, almost twenty years after her first attempt, she was the Navy's oldest active-duty commissioned officer, at just a few months shy of her eightieth birthday. She received the National Medal of Technology and the Presidential Medal of Freedom, among other honours.

Canada's first female geologist, Alice Wilson, was eligible to begin her PhD in 1915, but she had to fight for more than ten years to get the necessary paid time off from her employer, the Geological Survey of Canada, to complete it. Although the GSC did grant paid absences at the time, she was repeatedly denied, even after her supportive new boss, Edward M. Kindle, began supervising her in 1920. Even after she was awarded a scholarship in 1926 by the Canadian Federation of University Women, GSC leadership still didn't want to give her leave, even though she had now been working for the GSC for more than fifteen years. The CFUW lobbied on her behalf and she was finally granted leave, graduating at age forty-eight in 1929.[689]

It was not the only example of Wilson's difficulties at the GSC, where she was the first woman granted a permanent position—and the only one, until 1970. Early in her career, she wrote two articles, documenting the discovery of two new species, a brachiopod and a bivalve. Yet she found she faced significant difficulty being included in other colleagues' work. It didn't help that the GSC did not allow women to work with men during fieldwork. Being the only woman, Wilson devised her own projects, mapping more than 14,000 square kilometres of the Ottawa St. Lawrence Lowlands completely on her own over the course of decades.

In 2021, the Suez Canal was temporarily blocked when the massive container ship the *Ever Given* became wedged across it. Marwa Elselehdar, Egypt's first female ship's captain, found herself being blamed as rumours ran rampant

---

689 Russell, Loris S. and James-Abra, Erin, "Alice Wilson," *The Canadian Encyclopedia* (Historica Canada, 2017).

online—even though she was hundreds of miles away. Someone used a photo of her, added a fake headline supposedly published by *Arab News,* and the screenshot of the literally fake news went viral. Fake Twitter accounts under her name were also created to spread the lies. At the time, women accounted for only two percent of the world's maritime professionals. Indeed, when Elselehdar applied to the Academy for Science, Technology and Maritime Transport despite its men-only policy, she was granted permission only after a legal review by no less than Egypt's then-President Hosni Mubarak. Elselehdar had become the youngest and first female Egyptian captain to cross the Suez Canal years earlier.[690]

Architectural superstar Zaha Hadid commented that she was judged much more harshly because she was a woman, a sentiment echoed by other British architects.[691] A 2016 *Architectural Review* survey found that 72 percent of women architects have experienced gender discrimination, harassment or victimisation, and one in five said they would not encourage a woman to become an architect.[692] Eva Jiřičná, a former president of the Architectural Association in London recalled, "a client of ours said to me he didn't want any of my female colleagues to work on his project … It was completely incomprehensible." Alison Brooks, who won the Stirling Prize for the building of the year in 2008, had a consultant chide her upon learning she had a baby: "'Oh, but a mother should be at home with her children'… You can't believe the words emanating from their mouths."

In the 1997 British general election, the Labour Party won in a landslide, including electing 101 women as members of Parliament. Yet rather than celebrating a landmark moment for women, some started referring to them as "Blair Babes," in reference to the new Prime Minister Tony Blair. The term, a blatant and sexist attempt to trivialize the legislators, is thought to have originated with the

---

690   Cheetham, Joshua, "Marwa Elselehdar: 'I Was Blamed for Blocking the Suez Canal,'" April 3, 2021, https://www.bbc.com/news/world-middle-east-56615521
691   Booth, Robert, "Architects Speak out about Industry Sexism in Tributes to Zaha Hadid," *The Guardian,* April 1, 2016, https://www.theguardian.com/artanddesign/2016/apr/01/architects-speak-out-industry-sexism-tributes-zaha-hadid
692   Tether, Bruce, Results of the 2016 Women in Architecture Survey revealed, *The Architectural Review,* February 26, 2016, https://www.architectural-review.com/essays/results-of-the-2016-women-in-architecture-survey-revealed

Daily Mail tabloid.[693] Margaret Moran, MP for Luton South, later declared herself not a Blair Babe, but a Blair Witch, in reference to the 1999 film.[694]

Even those who claim to want equality for all have often been blinded by misogyny. As noted by *Smithsonian Magazine*,

> In January 1912, author and activist Ernest Untermann called out hypocritical behavior of his fellow socialists in the pages of the *Railway Carmen's Journal*: "[I]t seems inexplicable at first sight that even … Socialists should look with indifference or disfavor upon the efforts of their wives, sweethearts, mothers, sisters to secure equality with men. The fact is indisputable, however. It does exist and persist in our own ranks." Untermann identified his comrades' sexism as being rooted in men's fear that expansion of a woman's horizons would make her more self-reliant and "less willing to swallow all the crooked logic of the 'superior' male mind."[695]

---

693   Perkins, Anne and Ward, Lucy, "The Rise and Fall of Blair's Babes," *The Guardian*, May 24, 2001, https://www.theguardian.com/world/2001/may/24/gender.uk
694   Mark Inglefield, "A fair cop", *The Times*, London, 2 September 2000, p. 22.
695   Campbell, Olivia, "The Historical Struggle to Rid Socialism of Sexism," Smithsonian Magazine, July 12, 2018, https://www.smithsonianmag.com/history/historical-struggle-rid-socialism-sexism-180969610/

NO ASSUMPTION OF CREDIBILITY

"Feminism isn't about making women stronger. Women are already strong, it's about changing the way the world perceives that strength."
—G.D. Anderson[696]

In 2022, CEO Cathy Long tweeted:

> I just missed a client meeting cos I wasn't invited to it. The client invited my male colleague but left me out....because he thought I was just doing the admin. I'm the CEO.
>
> Don't tell me @EverydaySexism is done. However unintentional it is costing me money[697]

One of the most significant ways that women are undermined is through a lack of assumed credibility. From the aforementioned Harvard scholar who claimed enslaved comfort women were voluntary sex workers to Piers Morgan accusing Meghan Markle of lying about being suicidal, there is a misogynistic throughline. The default assumption that women lack credibility is part of the much larger issue of refusing to believe women. Just as with sexual assaults and harassment, women are less likely to be believed than men in other areas as well.[698]

---

696   Dunne, Geena, https://gdanderson.com/
697   Long, Cathy, Twitter, August 16, 2022, https://twitter.com/Cathy_TwoHalves/status/1559190955315630080
698   Kanter, Jake, "Piers Morgan Slammed by Mental Health Charity after He Dismissed Meghan Markle's Suicidal Thoughts," Deadline, March 8, 2021, https://deadline.com/2021/03/piers-morgan-slammed-by-mind-meghan-makle-suicide-1234709341/

As in other areas, women of colour or with other marginalisations such as disability and class face greater obstacles in this area than more privileged women. Among countless other indignities, the African-American women computers of NASA's predecessor, NACA, were forced to retake courses they had already completed, despite having the same educational qualifications as their white counterparts.[699]

Florence Griffith Joyner, better known as Flo Jo, was one of the fastest women in the world in the 1980s, and she had the medals and records to prove it. Yet her critics—largely male athletes—claimed she must be using drugs to achieve her incredible performances. They even used her sudden and tragic death in 1998 to claim that it must have been the result of her purported drug use. Her actual cause of death was epileptic seizures, caused by a congenital brain abnormality, and an autopsy confirmed that the only drugs in her system were acetaminophen (aspirin) and the antihistamine Benadryl.

In response, Prince Alexandre de Merode, chairman of the International Olympic Committee's medical commission, told *The New York Times* that she was singled out for extra, rigorous drug testing during the 1988 Olympic Games due to the baseless rumours. De Merode stated that Manfred Donike, who was at that time considered to be the foremost expert on drugs and sports, failed to discover any banned substances during the testing, saying that "all possible and imaginable" analyses and been performed, and there was no basis for "the slightest suspicion."[700]

At Oberlin College in the early 1860s, Edmonia Lewis was one of only thirty students of colour in a student population of around 1,000. As an African American woman, she was subjected to racism, sexism, and discrimination on a daily basis. Female students were rarely given a chance to participate in classes or speak at public meeting. She was baselessly accused of poisoning two Caucasian classmates, badly beaten by enraged townspeople, and brought to trial, though she was successfully defended by John Mercer Langston, the first African American lawyer in Ohio, who had the charges dismissed for lack of evidence. The following year,

---

[699] Arterbery, Andrea, "Why 'Hidden Figures' Is the Movie We Need Right Now," *Teen Vogue*, January 12, 2017, https://www.teenvogue.com/gallery/why-hidden-figures-is-the-movie-we-need-right-now

[700] "Autopsy Proves Flo-Jo Suffered an Epileptic Seizure – Nebiolo Urges Media Restraint," World Athletics, October 23, 1998, https://worldathletics.org/news/news/autopsy-proves-flo-jo-suffered-an-epileptic-s

she was accused of stealing artists' materials from the college, and was once again acquitted for lack of evidence. She finally had enough and left a few months later, after she was charged with aiding and abetting a burglary.[701]

Tatsuuma Kiyo expanded her family's business into the largest brewer and shipper of sake in the 1800s, but she had to hire a male employee to be the public face of her company because customers and businessmen would not deal with a woman. After she died, rather than celebrating her accomplishments, her family kept quiet about them because a woman's business success was considered embarrassing at the time.[702]

Writer, director, producer, and actress Mindy Kaling was central to the U.S. version of the hit TV comedy *The Office*. Yet early on in her tenure, she recalls that the Television Academy, which runs the Emmy Awards, tried to overlook her role as an executive producer and exclude her from the show's nominations. Reportedly, the justification was that there were too many creatives—so the only woman of colour just happened to be the one left out.[703] "They made me, not any of the other producers, fill out a whole form and write an essay about all my contributions as a writer and a producer," Kaling said. "I had to get letters from all the other male, white producers saying that I had contributed, when my actual record stood for itself." In the end, she was included—but not without the fight. "I worked so hard and it was humiliating. I had written so many episodes, put in so much time in the editing room, just to have the Academy discard it because they couldn't fathom I was capable of doing it all. Thankfully I was rescued by my friends, the other producers. The point is, we shouldn't have to be bailed out because of the kindness of our more powerful white male colleagues."[704]

Mary Boykin Chesnut's U.S. Civil War diary was published in 1905, almost twenty years after her death. Offering a "vivid picture of a society in the throes of

---

701 Ewing, Gigi, "Edmonia Lewis' Story Part of a Continuing Culture of Violence Against Black Women," The Oberlin Review, March 5, 2021, https://oberlinreview.org/22935/news/edmonia-lewis-story-part-of-a-continuing-culture-of-violence-against-black-women/
702 O'Meara, Mallory, *Girly Drinks: A World History of Women and Alcohol* (Hanover Square Press, 2021).
703 Carras, Christi, "Mindy Kaling Says the TV Academy Tried to Strip Her of Producer Credit on 'the Office,'" *Los Angeles Times*, October 9, 2019, https://www.latimes.com/entertainment-arts/tv/story/2019-10-09/mindy-kaling-emmys-television-academy-office
704 Nelson, Rebecca, "Mindy Kaling Didn't Sign Up to Be a Role Model," *Elle*, October 9, 2019, https://www.elle.com/culture/a29340748/mindy-kaling-interview-2019/

its life-and-death struggle," she described the war from her perspective as an upper-class Southern slaveowner, but her writing encompassed different classes as well. From 1881 to 1884, she worked on a final version to be published, and subsequent versions were published after more of her papers were discovered. Historian C. Vann Woodward's annotated edition won the Pulitzer Prize for History in 1982, and it is arguably the most important work by a Confederate author.[705] Yet Johns Hopkins University history professor Kenneth S. Lynn claimed, with no apparent proof, that the diary was a "hoax" and a "fabrication" by a failed novelist in a 1981 *New York Times* review of Woodward's edition. He even criticized the *New York Review of Books*'s reviewer, who responded, "*Mary Chesnut's Civil War* is neither fiction nor a fraud. It is a perfectly legitimate reconstruction of first-hand material and will be read not as the work of a novelist—failed or otherwise—but as that of a remarkably penetrating and capacious historian."[706]

Cytogeneticist Barbara McClintock remains the only woman to win a Nobel Prize in Physiology or Medicine without sharing it with at least one man. She won in 1983 "for her discovery of mobile genetic elements." Also known as transposable elements, these are nucleic acid sequences in DNA that can change position within a genome, which may create or reverse mutations and alter the cell's genetic identity and genome size. Yet like other women scientists, her research was initially ignored and dismissed. Although she first announced her findings in 1951, it was only in the late 1960s and 1970s when some men found mobile genes in viruses and bacteria that her work resurfaced, and more than a decade after that that she received her Nobel.[707]

Kono Yasui became the first Japanese woman to receive a scientific doctoral degree in 1927, but getting abroad to conduct research proved problematic. When she applied to the Japanese Ministry of Education to study abroad, officials did not want to give her permission because they believed "a woman cannot achieve

---

705 "Mary Chesnut's War," Bill of Rights Institute, https://billofrightsinstitute.org/essays/mary-chesnuts-war
706 Styron, William, "Mrs. Chesnut's Affair | Kenneth S. Lynn," New York Review of Books, October 8, 1981, https://www.nybooks.com/articles/1981/10/08/mrs-chesnuts-affair/
707 Cohn, Victor, "Long-Neglected Woman Scientist Awarded Nobel," *The Washington Post*, October 11, 1983, https://www.washingtonpost.com/archive/politics/1983/10/11/long-neglected-woman-scientist-awarded-nobel/943ee505-5aca-4777-aa0e-a645922313ce/

much in science." She was forced to list "home economics research" along with "scientific research" on her application before they would let her leave Japan. This was after the Ministry of Education had refused to approve a physics textbook she had written on the grounds that a woman could not possibly have written it.[708]

Louise Bourgeois was renowned for her skill as a midwife, with patients including French royalty in the early 1600s. In 1627, one of her patients—the wife of the king's brother—died from a fever after labour, and the princess's mother-in-law, queen mother Marie de'Medici, ordered an autopsy. It was conducted by male physicians, many of whom were Bourgeois's enemies, who claimed she was at fault. Bourgeois published a rebuttal challenging their findings, including noting that the physicians present in the birthing room were not allowed to be present at the autopsy. She had been a highly regarded midwife for thirty-four years, and had written books on the topic used by medical professions in several countries. Yet the word of biassed men was enough to end her career.[709]

A 2015 Vulture article also observed the trend of misogynistically assuming women directors hadn't "really" directed their own films:

> One of the most pernicious myths about first-time female filmmakers is that they had nothing to do with it. After Sofia Coppola delivered one of the most promising film debuts in American movies with *The Virgin Suicides*, I can't tell you how many people whispered to me that her then-husband Spike Jonze had really directed it. (Jonze's own feature-length directorial debut—*Being John Malkovich*, for which he was Oscar-nominated—came out that same year; suffice it to say, no one claimed it was really Coppola's doing.) I heard the same sort of story about Miranda July when her striking *Me and You and Everyone We Know* became a Cannes sensation, spurring a gossipy publicist to claim that July's then-flame Miguel Arteta had actually directed the bulk of it.

---

708 Yamazaki, Miwae, "Where no other dared to go: Kono Yasui 1880 – 1971, Japan's first woman doctor of science," Blazing a path: Japanese Women's contributions to modern science, 2001, http://www.igs.ocha.ac.jp/igs/IGS_publication/pdf/yasui_where.pdf
709 Sheridan, Bridgette *At birth: the modern state, modern medicine, and the Royal midwife Louise Bourgeois in seventeenth-century France* (Dynamis, 1999).

Coppola and July have directed films since, and both have a sensibility so iconoclastic that if you look back at their first features, it's now unmistakable who made them. Still, there are people in the industry who don't trust that sense of certainty in a woman, and they'll try to position a man in her orbit as some sort of Svengali. (Often they'll give all the credit to her cinematographer.) Even the Oscar-winning Kathryn Bigelow is not immune, as a whisper campaign during *Zero Dark Thirty*'s awards run asserted that she was practically under the thrall of her collaborator Mark Boal. This shit is absurd, and no one would do it to a man. Let these talented women be regarded as the auteurs they clearly are.[710]

MANSPLAINING

"I will not be lectured about sexism and misogyny by this man. I will not. And the Government will not be lectured about sexism and misogyny by this man. Not now, not ever .... Because if he wants to know what misogyny looks like in modern Australia, he doesn't need a motion in the House of Representatives, he needs a mirror."

—Julia Gillard[711]

Mansplaining, a term inspired by feminist writer Rebecca Solnit's essay, "Men Explain Things to Me: Facts Didn't Get in Their Way," refers to when a man confidently (and often cluelessly) attempts to explain something—often incorrectly—to a woman who is more capable of speaking on the topic than the man is. The man may or may not be aware of the women's likely expertise, but inherently assumes it is inferior to his.[712] Twitter provides many examples from women, including:

Molly Seidel @ByGollyMolly12, Aug 28 2021

---

710   Buchanan, Kyle, "5 Dumb Reasons Why Hollywood Won't Hire Women Directors," *Vulture*, November 5, 2015, https://www.vulture.com/2015/11/5-reasons-why-women-directors-dont-get-hired.html
711   Gillard, Julia, Misogyny Speech, Delivered to Australian Parliament, October 9, 2012.
712   Asare, Janice Gassam, "How Mansplaining Is Negatively Impacting Your Workplace — And What You Can Do To Prevent It," *Forbes*, January 7, 2019, https://www.forbes.com/sites/janicegassam/2019/01/07/how-mansplaining-is-negatively-impacting-your-workplace-and-how-to-prevent-it/

UNCREDITED

On my flight was talking to a guy next to me & it came up that I run. He starts telling me how I need to train high mileage & pulls up an analysis he'd made of a pro runner's training on his phone. The pro runner was me. It was my training. Didn't have the heart to tell him.[713]

Dr. Jessica McCarty, @jmccarty_geo, Feb 16 2021
At a NASA Earth meeting 10 years ago, a white male post doc interrupted me to tell me that I didn't understand human drivers of fire, that I def needed to read McCarty et al.
Looked him in the eye, pulled my long hair back so he could read my name tag.
"I'm McCarty et al."[714]

At the 2017 World Science Festival in New York, a panel discussion on cosmology included five men, a male moderator, and one female panellist: Dr. Veronika Hubeny, an expert in string theory and quantum gravity.[715] Marliee Talkington, a performer and disability advocate, was in the audience, and later recounted:

> Veronika Hubeny, the only woman on the panel is barely given any opportunity to speak. And the Moderator, Jim Holt even acknowledges this.
>
> In the last 20-30 minutes of the 90 minute discussion Jim Holt finally pushes the conversation to Hubeny's field of expertise, string theory, and this is what ensued:
>
> He asked her to describe her two theories of string theory that seem to contradict one another.
>
> And THEN, without letting her answer, proceeded to answer for her and describe HER theories in detail without letting her speak for herself.

---

[713] Seidel, Molly, August 28, 2021, Twitter, https://twitter.com/ByGollyMolly12/status/1431443745820528644

[714] McCarty, Jessica, February 16, 2021, Twitter, https://twitter.com/jmccarty_geo/status/1361332337678639107

[715] Jusino, Teresa, "Attendee Shames Mostly-Male Science Panel For Mansplaining to Female Theoretical Physicist," The Mary Sue, June 7, 2017,
https://www.themarysue.com/dont-mansplain-to-female-theoretical-physicists-bruh/

We could clearly see that she was trying to speak up. But he continued to talk over her and dominate the space for several minutes...

So at this point, after seeing very clearly that she was not going to be given space to speak and in fact having her own theories described to the audience by the moderator, I am in full outrage. My body is actually beginning to shake. The sexism is beyond blatant. It is happening on stage and NO ONE, not a single other physicist or panelist is stepping in to say anything about it. And I can hear other audience members around me, both men and women becoming more and more agitated with what is happening. Jim Holt, even at one point, asks Veronica a question and she laughs because he has been answering his own questions about her work...and he makes fun of her for 'giggling'.

So at some point while he is Still talking about Her theories, I just can't handle it any longer.

With my hands shaking,

I finally say from my seat in the 2nd row of the audience, as clearly, directly and loudly as possible;

"Let. Her. Speak. Please!"

The moderator stops.

They all stop.

The auditorium drops into silence.

You could hear a pin drop.

And then the audience explodes with applause and screams.

Jim Holt eventually sat back, only after saying I was heckling him

And he let her speak.

And of course, she was brilliant. [716]

Afterward, Talkington described, person after person approached her to thank her for speaking up.

---

716   Talkington, Marilee, Facebook. June 5, 2017, https://www.facebook.com/marilee.talkington/posts/10155051385188961

Men will even mansplain things like menstruation, feminism, and basic biological facts about women's bodies, and it can be absolutely hilarious when they get it horribly wrong. Perhaps the greatest irony arises when men explain mansplaining itself to women. In 2015, Elle Armageddon tweeted a flowchart called "Should You Explain The Thing To The Lady?" It asked:

- Are you an expert or at least well-informed?
- Did she ask?
- Are you her tutor, teacher or other person responsible for her education?
- Does she already know what you're about to say? (if you don't know, ask)

It was only if the answers were yes, yes, yes and no that the flowchart encouraged the user to "Explain away!" In addition to generally pissy responses, she also had multiple men explain mansplaining to her. She later commented, "I think that part of why a specific type of man has taken this tweet so personally is because misogyny is still extremely prevalent in our culture. Any time a woman, especially a woman who identifies as 'feminist,' speaks publicly or is granted a platform, men perceive it as an attack against them."

ASSUMED LACK OF CAPABILITY

> "My coach said I ran like a girl, I said if he could run a little faster he could too."
> —Mia Hamm

1920s botanist Ynes Mexia recalled that "a well-known collector and explorer stated very positively that 'it was impossible for a woman to travel alone in Latin America.'" Expeditions like the ones Mexia undertook in Mexico, Colombia, and Peru were seen as dangerous and inappropriate for women in the 1920s, given the rough conditions. She collected at least 145,000 plant specimens during her relatively short career of thirteen years. Curators are still working to catalogue the full collection, but at least 500 were previously unidentified species, and at least fifty new species have already been named for her.⁷¹⁷

Assuming by default that women are less capable than men enables their accomplishments to be overlooked, discredited, and disregarded, such as when, upon seeing Mary Cassatt's painting La Toilette, Edgar Degas reputedly proclaimed, "I don't believe a woman could draw that well. Did you really do this?"⁷¹⁸ One of the biggest areas where this happens is when money is on the line. According to London Business School and Harvard researchers, female company founders are more likely to face "prevention" questions from investors. These are framed negatively, and centre on loss prevention—essentially, assuming the worst and putting the women on the defensive. The men were more likely to be asked "promotion" questions, centering the conversation on the possibilities of a start-up and focusing on hopes and ideals.⁷¹⁹

In 1883, "lady vineyardist" Kate Warfield entered her brandy in the California State Fair contest, winning the top prize. When it was revealed a woman had won, an all-male judging panel contested their own result, unable or unwilling to believe a woman could make a better brandy than a man. A second test was held on the spot, with identical results. She went on to win top marks in 1886 for her Cabernet, Syrah, and Sauvignon Blanc at the San Francisco Mechanics Fair Tasting, the preeminent California wine event at the time.⁷²⁰

In her 1680 manuscript on Copernican and Galilean theories, astronomer Jeanne Dumée included an apology for writing on a subject considered "too delicate work for persons of her sex." She wrote that her contemporaries considered themselves incapable of study, but she hoped her own example would convince them that there is no difference between a woman's brain and a man's.⁷²¹

When Australian writer Zora Cross submitted her poetry collection, *Songs of Love*

---

717   "Ynes Mexia (U.S. National Park Service)," NPS, https://www.nps.gov/people/ynes-mexia.htm
718   Marlowe, Lara, "France's Forgotten Impressionist: The Art of Mary Cassatt," *The Irish Times*, June 2, 2018, https://www.irishtimes.com/culture/art-and-design/visual-art/france-s-forgotten-impressionist-the-art-of-mary-cassatt-1.3512408
719   Griffith, Erin, "They Still Live in the Shadow of Theranos's Elizabeth Holmes," *The New York Times*, August 24, 2021, https://www.nytimes.com/2021/08/24/technology/theranos-elizabeth-holmes.html
720   Gaiser, Tim, "The Forgotten Women of California Wine," Tim Gaiser, April 23, 2020, https://timgaiser.com/blog/the-forgotten-women-of-california-wine
721   Finot, Jean, Problems of the sexes, (G. P. Putnam's sons, 2013) pp. 111–112, https://archive.org/details/problemssexes00saffgoog

and Life, to publisher George Robertson in 1917, he didn't even bother to read it, simply dismissing it out of hand. It was only after another smaller publisher had put out a modest run of the book that Robertson decided he did want to publish it after all. The other publisher sold the rights to him without even consulting Zora.[722] The first run of the book sold out within three days, and a newspaper noted, "Some critics say it is the most promising poetry that has come out of Australia for a generation."[723]

Françoise Barré-Sinoussi, who won a Nobel Prize for her role in discovering the human immunodeficiency virus (HIV), recalled a man telling her early on, "As a researcher, no way, women never have done anything in science, you had better think immediately to revise your career plan."[724] Fortunately, she didn't listen to him—but how many women have listened to men like that? How many brilliant young women have been dissuaded from work that could have changed the world?

Paper bag inventor Margaret Knight had the funds and the will to sue the man who stole her design, but many women would not have, or could not have, given the costs of the lawsuit she brought. Even with her mountain of documentation, he genuinely thought he could win with nothing more than the argument that a woman could not have invented the machine.

Being a woman also seems to have been the greatest hurdle for Austrian mathematician Hilda Geiringer, who was also Jewish and a refugee. Applying for academic positions in the U.S. in the 1940s, she would receive responses like, "I am sure that our President would not approve of a woman. We have some women on our staff, so it is not merely prejudice against women, yet it is partly that, for we do not want to bring in more if we can get men." Geiringer wrote to a friend, "I hope there will be better conditions for the next generations of women... In the meantime, one has to go on as well as possible."[725]

---

722   Perkins, Cathy. 2019. The Shelf Life of Zora Cross. Biography
723   "Our Book Columns: Songs of Love and Life," The Sydney Stock and Station Journal, December 7, 1917, https://trove.nla.gov.au/newspaper/article/124223593
724   Hagen, Ashley and Gaynes, Robert, "Françoise Barré-Sinoussi's Discovery of HIV," American Society for Microbiology, November 2022, https://asm.org/Podcasts/MTM/Episodes/The-Discovery-of-HIV-with-Francoise-Barre-Sinoussi
725   O'Connor, J. J. and Robertson, E. F., "Hilda Geiringer – Biography," School of Mathematics and Statistics, University of St Andrews, Scotland, Last updated May 2020, https://mathshistory.st-andrews.ac.uk/Biographies/Geiringer/

Women journalists faced exclusion from war zones on the assumption that women were incapable of handling such conditions, ignoring the countless nurses who had been doing so for centuries. The flimsiest of excuses popped up to justify the initial banning of all women reporters from U.K.–and U.S.-controlled battle zones during World War II—they didn't have proper women's restrooms.[726] When Helen Kirkpatrick's editor was told that women didn't belong in fighting zones because they couldn't dig latrines, he responded that Kirkpatrick "could beat anybody in the room in that particular activity."[727] Famed war reporter and photographer Dickey Chapelle was also warned about the lack of "facilities for women" at the start of her career, when she applied to photograph U.S. soldiers training in the jungles of Panama. She responded, "I'm sure the 14th Infantry Regiment has solved much tougher problems than that. And they'll probably think of a way to lick this one, too." [728]

Héloïse, a nun in 1100s France, was a renowned philosopher and writer. Which, naturally, meant that men have challenged the authenticity of her letters. In the 1800s and 1900s, and even today, her authorship has been questioned because some men can't fathom that a nun would have written of sexual longing and/or that a woman—even one so highly educated—could have written so eloquently in Latin.[729]

Nellie Bly was famous as a stunt reporter. While some of her "stunts" were of significant public import—like reporting on the deplorable conditions at an "insane asylum"—others were more focused on boosting circulation for her newspaper. Perhaps the most well-known of these was her trip around the world to see if she could beat the fictional time in Jules Verne's *Around the World In 80 Days*. She made it in 72, but not without facing heavy scepticism before her departure in 1889.[730]

'It is impossible for you to do it,' was the terrible verdict. 'In the first

---

726 Mackrell, Judith, *The Correspondents: Six Women Writers on the Front Lines of World War II* (Doubleday, 2021).
727 Lyse Doucet, "The Women Reporters Determined to Cover World War Two," BBC News, June 4, 2014, https://www.bbc.com/news/magazine-27677889
728 Rhinehart, Lorissa, *First to the Front: The Untold Story of Dickey Chapelle, Trailblazing Female War Correspondent*, MacMillan, 2023.
729 Newman, Barbara, "Authority, Authenticity, and the Repression of Heloise," *Journal of Medieval and Renaissance Studies*, January 1992, https://www.academia.edu/619031
730 Todd, Kim, *Sensational: The Hidden History of America's "Girl Stunt Reporters"* (HarperCollins, 2021).

place you are a woman and would need a protector, and even if it were possible for you to travel alone you would need to carry so much baggage that it would detain you in making rapid changes. Besides you speak nothing but English, so there is no use talking about it; no one but a man can do this.'

'Very well,' I said angrily, 'Start the man, and I'll start the same day for some other newspaper and beat him.'[731]

While plenty of women politicians face sexism, women of colour like U.S. Representative Shirley Chisolm also have to scale racism hurdles. In 1972, she became the first African American candidate for a major-party nomination for president, and the first woman to run for the Democratic Party's nomination. Yet she received support from neither the National Organization for Women nor the Congressional Black Caucus—both of which she co-founded.[732]

In 2022, software engineer Patrick Shyu was widely called out for his sexist social media content, from a YouTube video titled, unironically, "Why Women Should Not Code" to tweets like this:

> Women shouldn't code… perhaps be influencers/creators instead. It's their natural strength. Coding is a brutal 24/7 job, mutually exclusive with motherhood – after 9-months of maternity leave, they come back obsolete & outdated. Elon Musk even says the birth rate is falling "too much" and No one asked for women programmers. We asked for women influencers and instead got "independent women" in pants suits. Independence does not exist if you want a family. A woman should prioritize being a good mother and wife, not a coding machine. "Mother/Wife" is a great job.

Shyu's blatant sexism is particularly disturbing given his resume, which includes

---

731   Bly, Nellie, "Around the World in Seventy-Two Days," Pictorial Weeklies, 1890, https://digital.library.upenn.edu/women/bly/world/world.html
732   Landers, Jackson, "'Unbought and Unbossed:' When a Black Woman Ran for the White House," *Smithsonian Magazine*, April 25, 2016, https://www.smithsonianmag.com/smithsonian-institution/unbought-and-unbossed-when-black-woman-ran-for-the-white-house-180958699/

roles as a software developer, former tech lead, and software engineer at companies like Google and Facebook, as well as his business training software engineers. He freely brags about using his power to keep women from employment and insult them to their faces, tweeting, "So when I used to conduct interviews for Google, I rejected all women on the spot and trashed their résumés in front of them. I told them, 'Go have some kids. Don't worry, I'm smarter than you, I know.'" He worked there for three and a half years—it seems highly unlikely that his views were never brought to the attention of his superiors, yet he was allowed to continue, and later get a job at Facebook. [733]

An investigation into *Nepotism and sexism in peer-review* in Sweden "strongly suggests that peer reviewers cannot judge scientific merit independent of gender. The peer reviewers over-estimated male achievements and/or underestimated female performance." The study found that in 1995, Swedish Medical Research Council "reviewers gave female applicants lower average scores than male applicants on all three evaluation parameters... Because these scores are multiplied with each other, female applicants received substantially lower final scores compared with male applicants (13.8 versus 17.0 points on average). That year, four women and sixteen men were awarded postdoctoral fellowships." As fifty-two women had applied, compared to sixty-two men, they made up forty-six percent of applicants—but only twenty percent of those awarded fellowships. The researchers then analysed scientific productivity and found that the reviewers gave lower scores to women than they did to men of comparable productivity. "In fact, the most productive group of female applicants, containing those with 100 total impact points or more, was the only group of women judged to be as competent as the least productive group of male applicants (the one whose members had fewer than 20 total impact points)." [734]

The resulting paper also noted that other studies indicated that both women and

---

733 Teh, Cheryl, "A Former Google Tech Lead Bragged on Twitter about How He Used to Trash Women's Résumés in Front of Them: 'Go Have Some Kids,'" Business Insider, May 26, 2022, https://www.businessinsider.com/ex-google-staff-brags-iabout-trashing-female-coders-resumes-2022-5
734 Wennerås, Christine, and Wold, Agnes, "Nepotism and Sexism in Peer-Review," *Nature* vol 387 no 22, May 1997, https://www.ehu.eus/documents/1775594/2032981/Nepotism_and_sexism_in_peer_review.pdf

men rate the quality of men's work higher than women's when they know the sex of the person being evaluated, but not when the same person's gender is unknown.

This default assumption also contributes to a "triple bind" as described by Mary Ann Sieghart in *The Authority Gap: Why Women Are Still Taken Less Seriously Than Men, and What We Can Do About It*. Women are assumed to be less competent, but when we self-promote to challenge that assumption (talk about our accomplishments, push for a raise or promotion, and so on) and demonstrate traditionally masculine leadership qualities like assertiveness, we are seen as less likeable, and women who are not considered likeable are less likely to be hired and promoted.[735]

GIVING MEN THE UNEARNED BENEFIT OF THE DOUBT

"In politics, if you want anything said, ask a man. If you want anything done, ask a woman."
—Margaret Thatcher[736]

While most double standards are nonsensical, a particularly ridiculous one is observed in the simultaneous refusal to invest in women with good ideas and a willingness to invest in men who are unqualified and/or have previously failed, even on grand scales. Statistically, men are more likely to overestimate their own competence and be able to convince others. Organisational psychologist Tomas Chamorro-Premuzic attributes the success of such men, who generally make very poor leaders, to three factors of human psychology:

Inability to distinguish between confidence and competence.

Love of charismatic individuals.

The allure of narcissistic individuals: people with grandiose visions that tap into our own narcissism.[737]

---

735 Mary Ann Sieghart, *The Authority Gap: Why Women Are Still Taken Less Seriously than Men, and What We Can Do about It* (W. W. Norton & Company, 2022).
736 Thatcher, Margaret, "Speech to the National Union of Townswomen's Guilds Conference," May 20, 1965.
737 Chamorro-Premuzic, Tomas, "Why Do so Many Incompetent Men Become Leaders? And What Can We Do about It?" TED. January 9, 2020, https://ideas.ted.com/why-do-so-many-incompetent-men-become-leaders-and-what-can-we-do-about-it/

As seen time and again in real life, the reserved, competent woman loses out to the bombastic man who talks a big game and has little to back it up.

One such man was Adam Neumann. As recently as 2017, men were still getting ninety-eight percent of venture capital funding.[738] Even after the spectacular failure of Neumann's management of the WeWork shared office space business that resulted in the loss of almost $40 billion dollars,[739] he was still able to get $350 million from a venture capital firm for a new company.[740] While there are certainly arguments for second chances when the failure is due to circumstances outside one's control (see Glass Cliff section), a 2022 study found that failed entrepreneurs, when given a second chance, are likely to fail again due to simply not being very good at entrepreneurship:

> We find that failed entrepreneurs are less likely to survive with their current venture. This result persists for several subgroups of entrepreneurs, if we consider the number of past failure events, or if we control for the inclination of entrepreneurs to pursue high-risk projects. Overall, our results are consistent with the hypothesis that previously failed entrepreneurs are those with below-average entrepreneurial talent.[741]

Meanwhile, women tech entrepreneurs fear that isolated but high-profile cases like Elizabeth Holmes's $700 million scam Theranos will make it even harder for women in general to secure funding in the long run. "There was already a higher bar before Theranos because we don't fit the pattern," said Falon Fatemi, who co-founded artificial intelligence start-up Node and media distribution start-up Fireside. "This just makes it that much harder." Julia Cheek, founder of Everly

---

738   Field, Hayden, "98 Percent of vc Funding Goes to Men. Can Women Entrepreneurs Change a Sexist System?" Entrepreneur, October 23, 2018, https://www.entrepreneur.com/article/315992
739   Ramaswamy, Anita, "'We Do Our Own Research': A16z GP on Investing Millions in Adam Neumann," TechCrunch, October 18, 2022, https://techcrunch.com/2022/10/18/a16z-chris-dixon-adam-neumann-flow-funding-disrupt-2022/
740   Molla, Rani, "If at First You Don't Succeed, Raise $350 Million and Try Again," Vox, August 17, 2022, https://www.vox.com/recode/2022/8/17/23309756/wework-adam-neumann-flow-andreessen-venture-capital
741   Gottschalk, Sandra, and Bettina Müller, "A Second Chance for Failed Entrepreneurs: A Good Idea?" Small Business Economics vol 59 no 2, pp 745–67, https://ideas.repec.org/a/kap/sbusec/v59y2022i2d10.1007_s11187-021-00584-4.html

Health, found herself constantly compared to Holmes for no apparent reason. "Women founders have to navigate these types of questions that their male counterparts simply don't have to answer," she said.[742]

As reported in *The New York Times* in 2021:

> When Alice Zhang set out in 2018 to raise funding for her drug discovery start-up, investors kept asking her about Theranos…
>
> Others asked, too. At a Stanford University event, the organizers wanted Ms. Zhang to talk about Theranos. One adviser told her that when her start-up came up in conversation, people responded by cracking jokes about Ms. Holmes.
>
> Ms. Zhang was initially confused. Her start-up, Verge Genomics, uses artificial intelligence to aid the discovery of therapeutic drugs. That was completely different from Theranos's business of marketing blood testing machines as a diagnostic tool. Ms. Holmes had also been accused of criminal fraud. Ms. Zhang had not.
>
> But the pattern was clear. When Verge Genomics raised funding later that year, a prominent industry columnist penned an article that compared Ms. Zhang to Ms. Holmes. Although the comparisons dissipated as her start-up has grown, Ms. Zhang, 32, said she hears the same stories from other female founders today, even though "I could see no similarity besides the fact that we're both women in the hard-science space."

Heather Bowerman, who founded DotLab, which developed a test to help identify endometriosis in 2016, found that potential investors expected her to explain how DotLab would be different from Theranos. She turned to government grants to launch it and was able to then secure $12 million in venture funding in 2019. Base founder Lola Priego, whose company offers at-home blood and saliva tests, reported getting several Theranos comparison per week, either directly or indirectly from potential partners, advisers, investors, customers, and reporters.

---

742   Griffith, Erin, "They Still Live in the Shadow of Theranos's Elizabeth Holmes," *The New York Times*, August 24, 2021, https://www.nytimes.com/2021/08/24/technology/theranos-elizabeth-holmes.html

She even had a potential advisor that she was trying to recruit take the meeting just to tell her off about how bringing technology into healthcare was a disservice to the entire industry—just like Theranos.

Japan's low birthrate has been a matter of concern for years. In 2018, a Japanese member of Parliament said young Japanese women should have more children or face being a burden on the state in their old age, completely disregarding all the countless reasons—many of them caused or controlled by men—that those women were not having children.[743] Placing the blame on women removes it entirely from the shoulders of men who have the power to make change—such as, say, a member of Parliament.

In 2022, the prime minister replaced Seiko Noda, the minister in charge of addressing the issue, with a childless man. Noda, a mother of one, criticized the male-dominated government for their "indifference and ignorance" in failing to address the problem. Her replacement's best effort at understanding women seems to be a publicity stunt where he tried on a fake pregnancy belly.[744]

We see this even from other women in power. As head of Lucasfilm since 2012, producer Kathleen Kennedy had the power to implement real change. Yet when asked in 2015 when a woman would finally get to direct a Star Wars film, her response was "There's nothing we'd like more than to find a female director for Star Wars," but "We need to not go to a filmmaker who's done one movie and expect them to come in and do something the size of Star Wars without having an opportunity to find other movies they can do along the way."[745] Despite this claim, male directors are often given blockbuster projects after only a low-budget debut—and Kennedy herself hired two such men to direct Star Wars films: Gareth Edwards, who was given the chance to direct *Godzilla* (2014) after he made the microbudget indie *Monsters* (2010) and went on to direct *Rogue One* (2016).

---

743 "Taro Aso: Japan Minister U-Turns on Birth-Rate Gaffe," February 5, 2019, https://www.bbc.com/news/world-asia-47127738

744 Reynolds, Isabel, "Japan's New Male Minister for Birthrate Tried 'Pregnancy Belly,'" August 10, 2022, https://www.bloomberg.com/news/articles/2022-08-10/japan-s-new-male-minister-for-birthrate-tried-pregnancy-belly

745 Feeney, Nolan, "'Star Wars' Producer: 'Nothing We'd like More Than' a Woman Director," *Time*, October 14, 2015, https://time.com/4072910/star-wars-kathleen-kennedy-women-directors/

Colin Treverrow, whose $500,000 indie *Safety Not Guaranteed* (2012) preceded Kennedy's own husband choosing Trevorrow to make the $150 million *Jurassic World* (2015), was originally hired to direct *Star Wars Episode IX: The Rise of Skywalker* (2019). While Victoria Mahoney is proclaimed as the first woman to direct a Star Wars film, as second unit director on *Episode IX*, she was not "the" director (that was J. J. Abrams), but rather one of dozens of people with "director" in their title. As film pundit and author Mark Harris has observed, "Producers take a good small movie by a guy as a sign he's ready to step up; by a woman, it's a sign that she's found her niche."[746]

NO GIRLS ALLOWED

> "(Men) have always been so afraid that some mere woman might penetrate their sanctums of discussion that they don't even permit women in their clubhouses, much less allow them to attend any meetings for discussions that might be mutually helpful."
> —Harriet Chalmers Adams[747]

The original patriarch of the modern Olympic Games had very definite ideas about the role of women—and it wasn't as athletes. Founder of the International Olympic Committee Pierre de Coubertin claimed the inclusion of women would be "impractical, uninteresting, unaesthetic, and incorrect." In his opinion, the point of the games was "the exaltation of male athleticism... And female applause as its reward."[748] Incidentally, that seems to have been the only reward he thought they deserved, as he was one of the primary advocates for only allowing amateur—not professional—athletes to compete, which forced athletes of all genders to choose between a paying career and the Olympics for decades.

---

746   Buchanan, Kyle, "5 Dumb Reasons Why Hollywood Won't Hire Women Directors," Vulture, November 5, 2015, https://www.vulture.com/2015/11/5-reasons-why-women-directors-dont-get-hired.html
747   Biggar, Joanna, "Where Women Go First," *The Washington Post*, 1985, https://www.washingtonpost.com/archive/lifestyle/magazine/1985/12/15/where-women-go-first/c59c8197-8102-490d-b9b0-adc24aae4c78/
748   Fitzgerald, Elizabeth, "Women & the Olympic Games: 'Uninteresting, Unaesthetic, Incorrect,'" SBS, May 3, 2016, https://www.sbs.com.au/topics/zela/article/2016/05/03/women-olympic-games-uninteresting-unaesthetic-incorrect

For centuries, women have been excluded from education and professional institutions. In addition to reducing their opportunities, it leads to circular logic that women don't have degrees or memberships because they are not capable, and that assumed lack of capability is in turn used as a reason to exclude them. Time and again, women have proven their capabilities to the organisations that shut them out—women who complete the coursework and pass the exams but are still denied a degree. Women whose work is accepted by the official organisations even as the women themselves are rejected. Women who score higher and do better work than the men but are still excluded.

SCHOOLS

From 1904 to 1907, around 720 so-called "steamboat ladies" were awarded degrees by the University of Dublin's Trinity College. The women had completed all the necessary coursework at Oxford and Cambridge, but those oh-so-prestigious universities would not grant them the degrees that the women had earned in their vaunted halls of learning. So, they would hop on a steamboat to Dublin, where they were awarded ad eundem degrees, based on a previously established agreement between the University of Dublin, Oxford, and Cambridge. A special shout-out to Anthony Traill, the then-Provost of Trinity College, who proposed that the option be extended to women as well as men.[749] Mathematician Grace Chisholm Young was the first person to earn a First-class degree at both Oxford and Cambridge Universities in any subject—and even that was not enough for them to actually give her the degrees.[750]

Another of Cambridge's non-alums was Winifred Boys-Smith, who studied there from 1891 to 1895, taking the full honours course for the natural science tripos only to receive a certificate instead of a degree.[751] Cecilia Payne-Gaposchkin, who later

---

[749] Parkes, S. M., "Steamboat ladies (act. 1904–1907)," Oxford Dictionary of National Biography, Oxford University Press, October 4, 2007, https://www.oxforddnb.com/display/10.1093/ref:odnb/9780198614128.001.0001/odnb-9780198614128-e-61643

[750] Rothman, Patricia, "Grace Chisholm Young and the Division of Laurels," Notes and Records of the Royal Society of London vol 50 no (Jan 1 1996), pp 89–100, doi:10.1098/rsnr.1996.0008

[751] McDonald, Heath, "Boys-Smith, Winifred Lily," Dictionary of New Zealand Biography. Te Ara – the Encyclopedia of New Zealand, 1996, https://teara.govt.nz/en/biographies/3b41/boys-smith-winifred-lily

discovered that stars are made up primarily of hydrogen and helium in "the most brilliant Ph.D. thesis ever written in astronomy," completed her Cambridge studies in 1923. She also later became the first woman to chair a department at Harvard—which did give her a PhD.[752] Biochemist Rose Scott-Moncrieff, credited with founding the field of biochemical genetics, earned but did not receive her PhD in 1930.[753]

It wasn't until 1948 that Cambridge finally began giving women the degrees they'd earned—"the last of the big institutions in the UK to do so," according to historian Dr. Lucy Delap.[754] But, of course, it wasn't just Cambridge. Botanist Carrie Derick completed the research required for her PhD at the University of Bonn in 1906 but was not granted a degree because the university refused to grant women doctorates. She later became the first female professor at a Canadian university, and the founder of McGill University's genetics department.[755] The University of Pennsylvania gave chemist Mary Engle Pennington a "certificate of proficiency" instead of the Bachelor of Science she earned in 1892. She went on to pioneer food sanitation methods that saved countless lives.[756]

Even female professors were not exempt from the "no girls allowed" mindset in university settings. In 1732, Laura Bassi became the first salaried woman lecturer in the world, at the University of Bologna. However, university officials still believed that women should lead private lives, so she was highly restricted from delivering public lectures. Despite her efforts, from 1746 to 1777 she gave only one formal dissertation per year, on a wide variety of topics. In 1739 her pleas for normal teaching duty was (again) denied, but she was allowed to start private lessons and in 1759, she was given funding for experiments at her home.[757]

---

752 Soter, Steven, and Neil Degrasse Tyson, *Cosmic Horizons: Astronomy at the Cutting Edge* (New Press, 2001).
753 Chambers, Suzanna, "At Last, a Degree of Honour for 900 Cambridge Women," *The Independent*, May 30, 1998, https://www.independent.co.uk/news/at-last-a-degree-of-honour-for-900-cambridge-women-1157056.html
754 Roberts, Stuart, "The Rising Tide: Women at Cambridge," University of Cambridge, October 14, 2019, https://www.cam.ac.uk/stories/the-rising-tide
755 McDevitt, Neale, "Carrie Derick: Pioneering Educator," McGill Reporter, March 8, 2017, https://reporter.mcgill.ca/carrie-derick-blazing-the-trail-for-female-professors-and-researchers/
756 "Pennington, Mary Engle," 2002, National Women's Hall of Fame, https://www.womenofthehall.org/inductee/mary-engle-pennington/
757 Lending, Tabitha, "Laura Bassi," Women in History, December 22, 2021, https://womeninhistory.education/laura-bassi/

Psychologist Mary Whiton Calkins was the first woman to complete the requirements for a PhD in psychology with the unanimous support of the Harvard University psychology faculty, but the university refused to grant it because Harvard did not accept women. She went on to become president of the American Psychological Association and the American Philosophical Association—the first woman to hold either position. She also taught at Wellesley College for four decades, doing research there and at Harvard for most of that time.[758] Her achievements included discovering that stimuli were more easily remembered when paired with other vivid stimuli and that the length of exposure improved recall. Her research was cited by Freud and used without credit by Georg Elias Müller and Edward B. Titchener. Gordon Allport's *Personality: A Psychological Interpretation*, which is considered a foundational text, acknowledged her in the first edition, but she was removed from later editions.[759]

Even when women are allowed admission, it has not been uncommon for other barriers to be put in their path. Alice Turner (later Schafer) received a full scholarship to the University of Richmond, where she was the only woman to major in mathematics. But at the time, women were not allowed in the campus library. She later became one of the founding members of the Association for Women in Mathematics in 1971.[760] The women of Harvard's affiliate Radcliffe College likewise did not have access to the university's museums, libraries or even all of the same classes—they were not allowed to attend classes with the men on the Harvard campus, only those that professors deigned to duplicate on their own campus.[761]

Dutch botanist and geneticist Jantina Tammes was one of only 11 women students at the University of Groningen in 1890, where she was allowed to attend lectures but not take exams, culminating in a teaching diploma rather than a degree

---

[758] "Mary Whiton Calkins," Harvard University Department of Psychology, 2019, https://psychology.fas.harvard.edu/people/mary-whiton-calkins

[759] Scherer, Naomi, "Mary Whiton Calkins," *Woman Is a Rational Animal: University of Chicago*, November 26, 2021, https://womanisrational.uchicago.edu/2021/11/26/mary-whiton-calkins/

[760] O'Connor, J. J. and Robertson, E. F., "Alice T Schafer – Biography," School of Mathematics and Statistics, University of St Andrews, Scotland, Last updated April 2002, https://mathshistory.st-andrews.ac.uk/Biographies/Schafer/

[761] 2022, "Research Guides: Women at Harvard University: Historical Background," Harvard Library, Last updated October 7, 2022, https://guides.library.harvard.edu/c.php?g=1108872&p=8085578

in science.[762] She went on to be the first professor of genetics in the Netherlands (of any gender).[763]

Maria Montessori is known for her pioneering educational techniques that made school environments more adapted to the children who inhabit them. But although her methods were met with widespread international acclaim, education was not her original profession—rather it was her work in paediatrics and psychology, which led to working with disabled children, that set her on the path where she had the most influence. But getting her medical degree in 1890s Italy was a nightmare. From the start, she was strongly discouraged by a University of Rome professor, but she persevered with her studies, earned her diploma di licenza in 1892 and qualified for the university's medical program in 1893. Once there, she was met with outright hostility and harassment from students and professors alike because of her gender. Because it was considered inappropriate for her to attend classes with men where naked bodies were present, she was forced to perform her dissections of cadavers alone after hours. Fortunately, she persisted, even winning an award in her first year and securing a position as a hospital assistant early on, setting her on a career trajectory that would result in her improving education for countless children for decades to come.[764]

In 1878, Christine Ladd (later Ladd-Franklin) was accepted to Johns Hopkins University. When officials found out that the C in "C. Ladd" stood for Christine, they tried to rescind her enrollment—were it not for the support of her mentor, mathematics professor James J. Sylvester, they might have succeeded. Even as things stood, she was initially only allowed to take Sylvester's classes—it was only after she proved herself an exceptional student that she was permitted to attend other professors' classes. Though she was awarded a stipend, the customary title of "fellow" was withheld from her. Even though she completed all the requirements for a PhD in mathematics and logic, she was refused a degree because women were not allowed

---

762 "Jantine Tammes (1871-1947)," University of Groningen, July 23, 2003, https://www.rug.nl/museum/history/prominent-professors/jantine-tammes
763 "The Jantina Tammes Chair," University of Groningen, May 1, 2014, https://www.rug.nl/about-ug/profile/prizes-and-awards/named-chairs/de-jantina-tammes-leerstoel-?lang=en
764 Kramer, Rita, *Maria Montessori* (University of Chicago Press, 1976).

to graduate from the university at the time. Maths was also not her first choice—she later noted, "had it not been for the impossibility, in those days, in the case of women, of obtaining access to laboratory facilities" she would have chosen to study physics.[765]

In 1893, when she applied for a teaching position at Johns Hopkins, she was denied, with scholar Laurel Furumoto later noting that her inability to gain a regular academic position was a common consequence, in that time period, of a woman's decision to marry. It took more than a decade, but she was finally given permission to teach a single class per year in 1904. Even this had to be approved and renewed every year, and much of the teaching she did in her career was unpaid.[766]

In 1917, anatomist Florence Sabin became the first woman to achieve full professor status at Johns Hopkins, after being passed over for a department chair position that went instead to one of her former students. Sabin herself had attended the School of Medicine there, which admitted women from the time it opened in 1893—a financial decision, rather than an ethical one.[767] A group of prominent Baltimore women, led by Mary Elizabeth Garrett who contributed $354,764 herself, had raised $500,000 to guarantee the admission of women. If the med school wanted their money, they had to let women in, causing their sexist concerns to magically disappear.[768]

Rocket scientist Yvonne Brill was the first person in her family to go to college and graduated at the top of her class at the University of Manitoba with a bachelor's degree in both chemistry and mathematics in 1945. She had originally applied to their engineering program but was denied by the school because they claimed that the program's mandatory summer camp did not have the necessary facilities to host female students. She went on to do brilliant work in rocket propulsion and invent the electrothermal hydrazine thruster (used in controlling satellites),

---

[765] "Christine Ladd-Franklin," The-Women-of-Hopkins, https://www.womenofhopkins.com/laddfranklin
[766] Furumoto, Laurel, "Joining Separate Spheres: Christine Ladd-Franklin, woman scientist (1847-1930)," American Psychologist, February 1992.
[767] "Changing the Face of Medicine | Florence Rena Sabin," National Institutes of Health, 2015, https://cfmedicine.nlm.nih.gov/physicians/biography_283.html
[768] Hammett, Corinne F., "Woman M.D.: When scrubbing up means surgery, not dinner dishes," News American, October 7, 1979, https://msa.maryland.gov/megafile/msa/speccol/sc3500/sc3520/014300/014382/pdf/newsamer7oct1979.pdf

improving both engine performance and propulsion reliability.[769]

As an undergrad in nuclear chemistry at Berkeley, Margaret Melhase discovered and isolated caesium-137, having been assigned to study the newly-created element plutonium by Glenn Seaborg. Seaborg himself was working on plutonium in secret for the U.S. military, and would go on to win a Nobel Prize and chair the Atomic Energy Commission, but Margaret's contribution was classified due to wartime secrecy. Her application to graduate school at Berkeley was rejected due to her gender, even though the head of chemistry was aware of her incredible achievement. His irrational rationale was that a previous female PhD candidate had married shortly after defending her thesis and thus "wasted her entire education." Melhase instead began working with Seaborg on the Manhattan Project, but was unable to find employment or acceptance to a PhD program after the end of World War II, effectively ending her career.[770]

Architect and engineer Julia Morgan designed more than 700 buildings in her career, but like many women trying to enter male-dominated fields in the early 1900s (and still today), she had a difficult start. After L'Ecole des Beaux-Arts began allowing women to take entrance exams in 1897, Morgan applied. The college would only accept the top thirty applicants to the architecture program, and in her first attempt, she ranked forty-second. Not to be deterred, she studied even harder, gained experience in local architecture firms, and tried again the following year—and placed in the vaunted top thirty. However, school officials artificially lowered her scores to justify rejecting her again because they "did not want to encourage young girls."[771] She wrote in a letter home: "I'll try again next time anyway even without any expectations, just to show 'les jeunes filles' are not discouraged."[772] On her third and final attempt, she placed thirteenth out of 376

---

[769] "Yvonne Claeys Brill," University of Manitoba Faculty of Science, 2020, https://sci.umanitoba.ca/yvonnebrill/

[770] Chapman, Kit, "The Women Written out of Nuclear Science," Berkeley College of Chemistry, January 10, 2022, https://chemistry.berkeley.edu/news/women-written-out-nuclear-science

[771] "First in Their Field: Julia Morgan," Women's Museum of California, May 24, 2017, https://womensmuseum.wordpress.com/2017/05/24/first-in-their-field-julia-morgan/

[772] Julia Morgan to Pierre Le Brun, December 12, 1897, Record Group I: Personal Papers, Series 04: École des Beaux-Arts Correspondence, Box 2, Folder 1, Julia Morgan Collection, Special Collections, California Polytechnic State University.

applicants, high enough that they were forced to admit her. Even then, the school only allowed people to study there until the age of thirty, meaning she was now racing the clock to complete her certificate before her thirtieth birthday—which she did, completing in three years a program that typically took five.

A particularly ironic bit of sexism is when women are excluded from fields specifically related to womanhood. In the case of María Teresa Ferrari, she was denied the opportunity to teach obstetrics at the Universidad de Buenos Aires in 1915 because, "Despite their qualifications, for physiological and psychological reasons people of the feminine sex do not meet the required conditions to be engaged as professors in the Faculty [of Medicine]."[773] She was allowed to teach at the School of Midwifery, but without the standing or credentials of a professorship at the university—an example of the common occurrence of female-dominated professions like midwife being undervalued compared to male-dominated ones.[774]

In 1919, Ferrari applied again, but the decision-making body that had rejected her in 1915, the Honorable Consejo Directivo, delayed making a decision until 1925, including changing evidence and disregarding recommendations. It took another two years, at which point she had taught for two decades and dedicated fifteen years to medicine, before her application for a professorship was approved in 1927.

Like other Russian women of the 1860s, mathematician Sofya Kovalevskaya was barred from attending university in her home country, and she would have needed her father's permission to study abroad. Instead, she entered a "fictitious marriage" of convenience to a man who would not stand in her way, and she and her new husband moved to Germany for their studies. In addition to her groundbreaking work in the field, she became the first woman to obtain a modern doctorate in mathematics, and one of the first women to be editor of a scientific journal. They later returned to Russia, where Kovalevskaya's gender meant she would never be granted a professor position. She left again, securing a job at

---

773 Proceedings of the Honorable Consejo Directivo (HCD), June 23, 1915.
774 Alvarez, Adriana and Carbonetti, Adrián, Saberes y prácticas médicas en la Argentina: un recorrido por historias de vida (Knowledge and medical practices in Argentina: a journey through life stories). El caso de Dra. Dr. María Teresa Ferrari de Gaudino: el triunfo de la mujer en la docencia universiteria (The case of Dr. María Teresa Ferrari de Gaudino, the triumph of the university professor). Universidade Nacional de Mar de Plata, 2008.

Stockholm University, where she was appointed first an assistant and then full professor, making her the first woman in modern Europe to hold such a position.[775]

Biochemist Kamala Sohonie became the first Indian woman to receive a PhD in a scientific discipline in 1939, but when she applied to the Indian Institute of Science for a research fellowship, her application was rejected by then-Director and Nobel winner Prof. C V Raman because women were not considered competent enough to pursue research. She responded by holding a satyagraha—a form of nonviolent protest developed by Ghandi—outside his office until he gave in. Even then, she was not allowed to be a regular student, would be on probation her entire first year, her work would not be officially recognized unless he was personally satisfied with it, and she was warned not to be a "distraction" to the male students.[776] She later said of the humiliating conditions, "Though Raman was a great scientist, he was very narrow-minded. I can never forget the way he treated me just because I was a woman. Even then, Raman didn't admit me as a regular student. This was a great insult to me. The bias against women was so bad at that time. What can one expect if even a Nobel Laureate behaves in such a way?"[777] In the 1940s, Raman also rejected then-research scholar Rajeshwari Chatterjee, who was later awarded a scholarship to study in the U.S. She would go on to lead pioneering research in microwave engineering, write several textbooks and mentor others as the first female engineer and only woman on the faculty in the Indian Institute of Science.[778] It's also worth noting that Raman's Nobel Prize win comes with its own controversies about other scientists (Russians Grigory Landsberg and Leonid Mandelstam and Raman's collaborator K. S. Krishnan) who should have been credited, proving that the Nobel Committee can overlook

---

775   O'Connor, J. J. and Robertson, E.F., "Sofia Kovalevskaya – Biography," School of Mathematics and Statistics: University of St Andrews, Scotland, last updated January 2021, https://mathshistory.st-andrews.ac.uk/Biographies/Kovalevskaya/
776   Dhuru, Vasimati, Lilavati's Daughters, The scientist lady, (Indian Academy of Sciences, 2008) https://www.ias.ac.in/public/Resources/Initiatives/Women_in_Science/Contributors/kamalasohonie.pdf
777   Sur, Abha, "Dispersed Radiance: Women Scientists in C.V. Raman's Laboratory," Meridians Feminism Race Transnationalism vol 1 no 2 (2001), pp 95-127, March 2001.
778   Gupta, D. P., "On her own terms," October 1, 2010, The Hindu, https://www.thehindu.com/todays-paper/tp-features/tp-fridayreview/On-her-own-terms/article15764097.ece/

men as well as women.[779]

Chemist Agnes Pockels would have studied the subject if she were given the chance, but women were not admitted to universities in 1870s Germany. Her work laid the foundation on which Irving Langmuir won his 1932 Nobel in Chemistry, but she was never paid or affiliated with an academic institution, relegating her to the role of citizen scientist. She later recalled, "I had a passionate interest in natural science, especially physics, and would have liked to study."[780]

When no English medical school would accept women, Sophia Jex-Blake went to Scotland in 1869 to plead her case to the University of Edinburgh. Even once the faculty and academic senate voted to allow her in, the university court overruled them, claiming the university could not make the necessary arrangements "in the interest of one lady." So, she went to *The Scotsman* newspaper, where her advertisement led to six more women—Mary Anderson, Emily Bovell, Matilda Chaplin, Helen Evans, Edith Pechey and Isabel Thorne—joining her cause. The university court reluctantly gave in to the "Edinburgh Seven," becoming the first university in Britain to admit women.[781]

But the women were barred from the Edinburgh Royal Infirmary, where they would have gotten valuable practical experience. And that's not even getting into the harassment they faced, not least was one professor absurdly suggesting to the press that women pursuing medical careers might be "basely inclined" or "Magdalenes" (reformed sex workers). On November 18, 1870, the women faced a literal riot blocking them from taking an anatomy exam.[782]

In 1872, the university court decreed that even if the women passed all their courses and exams, they would not be granted degrees. Jex-Blake sued in the Court of Session, Scotland's highest civil court, which not only supported the university's

---

779 Singh, Rajinder and Riess, Falk, "The 1930 Nobel Prize for Physics: A Close Decision?" *Notes and Records of the Royal Society of London*, vol 55 no 2 (2001), pp. 267-283. https://www.jstor.org/stable/532100
780 Ostwald, Wolfgang, "Die Arbeiten von Agnes Pockels Über Grenzschichten Und Filme." (The Work of Agnes Pockels on Boundary Layers and Films). Kolloid-Zeitschrift 58, 1-8, 1932.
781 "Sophia Jex-Blake and the Edinburgh Seven," The University of Edinburgh, January 8, 2018, https://www.ed.ac.uk/medicine-vet-medicine/about/history/women/sophia-jex-blake-and-the-edinburgh-seven
782 Knox, William, "Sophia Jex-Blake: Women and Higher Education in Nineteenth-Century Scotland," Edinburgh University Press EBooks, March, 70–94 (2006), https://doi.org/10.3366/edinburgh/9780748624096.003.0005

decision, but maintained that the women should never have been admitted in the first place. Five of the women—Bovell, Chaplin, Jex-Blake, Anderson and Pechey—earned their medical degrees abroad, in Bern and Paris. They also worked to establish the London School of Medicine for Women, which opened in 1874. Thorne set aside her own medical career to run the school for more than 30 years.

As always, women at the intersections of prejudices face greater obstacles. Clara Belle Williams became the first African American graduate of New Mexico College of Agriculture and Mechanic Arts (now New Mexico State University) in 1937. But she was not allowed inside the classrooms, forced to take notes from the hallway because of her race.[783] Bessie Coleman dreamed of flying, but in 1910s America, no school would train an African American woman as a pilot. So, she worked two jobs, saved as much money as she could, and learned French. She moved to France in 1920, where she became the first African American and first Native American to be awarded a pilot's licence. Back in the U.S., her ethnicity also kept her from working as a pilot for the postal service, so she became a nationally recognized barnstormer, performing stunt manoeuvres across the U.S.[784]

When Matilda J. Clerk wanted to study medicine at Achimota College, her father had to petition the head of the British colonial government, the Governor of the Gold Coast, for a special waiver. Only then was she allowed to enrol, in 1940.[785] Two years later, she became the first Ghanaian woman with a western medical degree, and she was the only candidate of any gender to pass the first preliminary medical baccalaureate examinations known in 1942. Her performance was so impressive, she was granted a rare medical scholarship by the colonial government to study medicine at the University of Edinburgh from 1944 to 1949. Returning home in 1951, she focused her career on public health and primary

---

[783] Gomez, Mia, "Williams, Clara Belle Drisdale," Texas State Historical Association, October 5, 2022, https://www.tshaonline.org/handbook/entries/williams-clara-belle-drisdale
[784] Alexander, Kerri Lee, "Bessie Coleman," National Women's History Museum, 2018, https://www.womenshistory.org/education-resources/biographies/bessie-coleman
[785] Ferry, Georgina, "Agnes Yewande Savage, Susan Ofori-Atta, and Matilda Clerk: three pioneering doctors," The Lancet. 392, November 2018.

care in Ghana.[786]

In 1836, the Imperial Natural History Society of Moscow accidentally let a woman in. With her strong reputation and unusual name (one letter off from the male Ethelred), they had assumed English geologist and palaeontologist Etheldred Benett was a man. The English, presumably being more familiar with the name, barred her from joining the Geological Society. Tsar Nicholas I awarded her a Doctorate of Civil Law, assuming she was male, at a time when women were not permitted to attend Russian universities. In response, she observed, "scientific people, in general, have a very low opinion of the abilities of my sex."[787]

JOBS

> Man noticing my collar: Are you a preacher?
> Me: Yes
> Man: I don't believe in women preachers
> Me: I am literally standing right here so....
> —Abby Norman[788]

Jacoba Felicie was an Italian healer in 1300s France, at a time when restrictions were being placed on who could treat people. Traditional healers and midwives were being sidelined by trained (male) physicians with accompanying legal regulation. In 1322, Felicie was placed on trial for unlawfully practising medicine, because she had not been trained at a university. She had a strong reputation for successful outcomes and did not charge her patients unless her treatments were effective, but her success likely contributed to her being charged, as she would have inspired the ire of male physicians who saw themselves as more qualified yet were

---

786 "Matilda J. Clerk," *The University of Edinburgh*, February 6, 2023, https://www.ed.ac.uk/global/uncovered/1940/matilda-j-clerk
787 "Etheldred Benett (1775-1845)," The Geological Society of London, https://www.geolsoc.org.uk/Library-and-Information-Services/Collection-Highlights/Women-and-Geology/Etheldred-Benett
788 Norman, Abby, 2018, Twitter, February 3, 2018, https://twitter.com/abbynormansays/status/959550349148348416

less effective. Indeed, Felicie was known to successfully treat patients whom the physicians had failed. During the trial, patient after patient attested to her skill and results, and her medical knowledge was never even questioned. But she was found guilty on the reasoning that women were not allowed to be physicians and were barred from the universities that trained them, so any woman doing what a physician did was automatically breaking the law. Felicie was banned from practising medicine, excommunicated, and fined sixty Parisian pounds.[789]

In her research, science historian Margaret Rossiter found when reading letters of recommendation that male scientists would bend over backwards to come up with absurd reasons why a female scientist could not be promoted. Arguing, for example, because there is no precedent was what Rossiter termed "restrictive logic." It is fascinating that men of science, who generally pride themselves on being logical, were fundamentally incapable of doing so.[790] Women's credentials, Rossiter wrote, "were dismissed as irrelevant in favor of stereotypes, fears, and long-cherished views."[791] Referring to the collective campaign by male professors to prevent German physicist Hertha Sponer from being appointed to full professorship at Duke University, Rossiter observed, "Sponer was evidently up against not only all the other applicants for a job at Duke in 1936 but also certain physicists' collective views and misconceptions about all of womankind."

Even though countless women have served on the front lines of wars as nurses, women are often excluded from military-related roles by virtue of their gender, beyond simply not allowing them to enlist in armed forces. Despite being one of the most qualified codebreakers in the world at the time, Elizebeth Smith Friedmann was not allowed to join her husband and collaborator William in the U.S. Army American Expeditionary Forces as a signal corps codebreaker because she was a

---

789   Tishma, Mariel, "Women in the Medical Profession: The Trial of Jacoba Felicie de Almania," Hektoen International, June 16, 2020, https://hekint.org/2020/06/16/women-in-the-medical-profession-the-trial-of-jacoba-felicie-de-almania/
790   Dominus, Susan, "Women Scientists Were Written out of History. It's Margaret Rossiter's Lifelong Mission to Fix That," Smithsonian Magazine, October 2019, https://www.smithsonianmag.com/science-nature/unheralded-women-scientists-finally-getting-their-due-180973082/
791   Rossiter, Margaret, *Women Scientists in America: Struggles and Strategies to 1940* (Johns Hopkins University Press, 1982).

woman.⁷⁹² Various sexist reasons have been used to justify excluding female journalists from war zones, including protecting women's modesty and sensibilities.⁷⁹³

Out of necessity, espionage agencies have often been forced to utilise women in situations where able-bodied men would be at war—such men would immediately be regarded with suspicion and could not blend in with the civilian population. Some of the greatest spies on both sides of the U.S. Civil War were women, including Elizabeth Van Lew, Harriet Tubman, Belle Boyd, and Rose O'Neale Greenhow. The British Special Operations Executive (SOE) sent many incredible women to Nazi-occupied France, such as Virginia Hall, Nancy Wake, and Noor Inyat Khan.

Upon completing her Master's degree in the U.S., Estonian curriculum reformer Hilda Taba wanted to return home. But her alma mater, the University of Tartu, rejected her application because of her gender. She stayed in the U.S., writing extensively on education and making valuable contributions to the field.⁷⁹⁴ Just as Estonia lost the value of Taba's contributions, Switzerland lost Emilie Kempin-Spyri's. Kempin-Spyri was the first woman in the country to graduate with a law degree in 1887, and to be accepted as an academic lecturer (though in education, not law). But women were not allowed to actually practice law because they were not even considered citizens. She, too, emigrated to the United States, where she established the first women's law school.⁷⁹⁵

When lichenologist and mycologist Annie Lorrain Smith was first hired at London's Natural History Museum, she had to be paid from a special fund because women could not officially be employed there. Initially brought on to curate a collection of microscopic fungi slides, she soon became responsible for identifying most

---

792   Fagone, Jason, *The Woman Who Smashed Codes: A True Story of Love, Spies, and the Unlikely Heroine Who Outwitted America's Enemies* (Dey St., 2018).
793   Mackrell, Judith, *The Correspondents : Six Women Writers on the Front Lines of World War II* (Doubleday, 2021).
794   Laanemets, Urve and Kalamees-Ruubel, Katrin, "The Taba-Tyler Rationales." Journal of the American Association for the Advancement of Curriculum Studies – Volume 9, 2013, https://salimi.staff.uns.ac.id/files/2016/03/The-Taba-Tyler-Rationales.pdf
795   Leybold-Johnson, Isobel, "A Woman Ahead of Her Times," Swiss Broadcasting Corporation, June 30, 2008, https://www.swissinfo.ch/eng/a-woman-ahead-of-her-times/1015736.

of the fungi brought to the museum, working there for more than four decades.[796]

Edith Clarke gained recognition in her field, becoming the first woman to deliver a paper at the American Institute of Electrical Engineers' annual meeting in 1926, but it was an uphill battle. When she initially could not find work as an engineer, she worked for General Electric as a supervisor of the women computers. While there, she invented an early graphing calculator (patented in 1925, four years after she filed the applications). Not being allowed to work in her actual field—electrical engineering—combined with a lower salary and professional status than men doing the same work, Clarke took a leave of absence from GE to teach physics at the Constantinople Women's College in 1921. Absence seems to have made her bosses grow fonder, because when she returned, she was a salaried electrical engineer, making her the U.S.'s first professional female electrical engineer. She went on to write an influential textbook, develop and install turbines that generate hydropower in hydroelectric dams, and became the U.S.'s first female professor of electrical engineering in 1947.[797] The following year, she commented to the *Daily Texan*, "There is no demand for women engineers, as such, as there are for women doctors; but there's always a demand for anyone who can do a good piece of work."[798]

Astrophysicist Margaret Burbidge was repeatedly a victim of this particular type of gender discrimination. In 1945, Burbidge was rejected for a postdoctoral fellowship with Carnegie Observatories because the job required working at Mount Wilson Observatory, which women were not allowed to do at the time. Ten years later, she re-applied and was again rejected, but her less-qualified husband was hired instead—he was a theorist, where she was an observer, and the role was for an observer. Anytime he was required to go observing, she would accompany him, supposedly as his assistant, but in reality she was the one operating the

---

796 Crease, Mary R. S., "Smith, Annie Lorrain," Oxford Dictionary of National Biography, Oxford University Press, May 26, 2005, https://www.oxforddnb.com/display/10.1093/ref:odnb/9780198614128.001.0001/odnb-9780198614128-e-46420;jsessionid=BECA46FB38DCE2406E6A5344BB55546E
797 Ingram, Elizabeth, "Edith Clarke, the First Female Electrical Engineer in the U.S.," Hydro Review, March 14, 2022, https://www.hydroreview.com/business-finance/jobs-and-people/meet-edith-clarke-the-first-female-electrical-engineer-in-the-u-s/
798 Unknown author and title, Daily Texan, March 14, 1948, Quoted by Gusen, Aaron, Looking Back: Edith Clarke, IEEE Potentials, Feb. 1994.

telescope while he worked in the photographic dark room. When observatory management found out, they reluctantly agreed that she could work there, but only if they stayed in a separate cottage, rather than the catered dormitory for the men. In 1972, when she became the first female director of the Royal Greenwich Observatory, the role was reduced—for three centuries, the position had been combined with the Astronomer Royal, but as soon as a woman came along, the roles were split, with a man taking the Astronomer Royal title.[799]

As Burbidge experienced at the Mount Wilson Observatory, even once a woman gets her foot in the door, she is often held to higher standards and faces greater restrictions than the men around her. After earning her master's degree in 1932, biochemist Mildred Cohn worked for the National Advisory Committee for Aeronautics.[800] Though she had a supportive supervisor, she was the only woman among the seventy men, was given a lower position than she was qualified for, was explicitly told that she would never be promoted and was even banned from the lab. Rather than put up with that, she returned to Columbia—which she had left after a year because she'd been denied an assistantship because of her gender—to finish her PhD in physical chemistry. She went on to publish 160 papers and win countless awards.[801]

In the case of American oceanographer Mary Sears, a "no girls allowed" rule didn't prevent her from having her job—it just made it a lot harder for her to do it. When the Woods Hole Oceanographic Institution (WHOI) was founded in 1930, Sears was one of the first staff members, working under her mentor, WHOI director Henry Bryant Bigelow. While Bigelow supported Sears in many ways, such as making sure she met prominent scientists from around the world, he hobbled her with one major restriction: she was not allowed to sail on the organisation's research vessel, the *Atlantis*, because she was a woman. This was a holdover from a long-held superstition among sailors that women were bad luck, though officially the lack of

---

799   Glorfeld, Jeff, "Lady Stardust Was a Star of Astrophysics," Cosmos, November 6, 2020, https://cosmos-magazine.com/space/lady-stardust-was-a-star-of-astrophysics/
800   Barrer, Betty, "Mildred Cohn," Jewish Women's Archive, December 31, 1999, https://jwa.org/encyclopedia/article/cohn-mildred
801   Elga Wasserman, *The Door in the Dream: Conversations with Eminent Women in Science* (Joseph Henry Press, 2000).

a women's bathroom was given as the reason for excluding women (there was no explaining why a woman could not use the men's bathroom). As Sears was organising collections of plankton, jellyfish, and other marine animals, she was dependent on what her male colleagues brought back from their expeditions. This meant relying on sometimes faulty information, as the men often did not correctly label and preserve the specimens they collected. Bigelow clearly knew the importance of expedition work—while the women were grounded, all male oceanographers at WHOI were required to go to sea at least once a year.[802]

It was more than ten years before Sears finally got to go on her own expedition, and it wasn't for WHOI. In 1941, ornithologist William Vogt requested her help analysing why birds in Peru—which fed on anchovies from the ocean—were dying. Her work from the trip was later published in *Deep Sea Research*.

When Sears joined the Navy in 1943, where her work would later save countless lives, it was the result of a sexist attitude that her work wasn't important. Roger Revelle wanted to leave his administrative position at the Navy's Hydrographic Office for more exciting work, but he needed to find a replacement before he could escape. He went to WHOI, where Bigelow's successor identified Sears, the only female scientist on staff, as the only non-essential oceanographer at WHOI, to do a job a man didn't want. Sears later wrote, "I was palmed off on him." As the office originally sought to only hire men, it is also likely she would have been disregarded were it not for the shortage of available men due to World War II—they were given leave to rehire civilians fired because they were suspected of committing fraud before considering women. Her work on tidal patterns would help the Navy locate hundreds of survivors stranded in the ocean after attacks or malfunctions, as well as more effectively planning strategies, as actions like landings were highly impacted by the tides.

WHOI finally had to let a woman on board a research vessel in 1959 when oceanographer Betty Bunce secured funding for an expedition with herself as chief scientist—no Bunce meant no funding and therefore no expedition. There were

---

802   Musemeche, Catherine, *Lethal Tides: Mary Sears and the Marine Scientists Who Helped Win World War II* (HarperCollins, 2022).

no issues, proving the invalidity of the "no female toilets" excuse. Bunce would go on to be chief scientist on many more expeditions in the 1960s and 1970s.[803]

Three years earlier, Roberta Eike, a biology graduate student, had risked her WHOI fellowship by sneaking aboard a WHOI vessel after repeatedly being denied opportunities to go to sea. When the stowaway was discovered several hours into the voyage, the captain turned back, but was ordered to proceed with the trip as Eike was confined to the captain's quarters like a criminal. Upon their return, she was stripped of her fellowship.[804] WHOI acknowledges, "Eicke also had to suffer the indignity of being physically humiliated by her supervisor, George Clarke, when he 'held her over his knee and spanked her.'" Clarke was known to be less than equitable towards his female colleagues. Dick Backus, a friend of Eike, later wrote about Clarke's reputation for sexually harassing the women at WHOI as well. "Prof. Clarke pushed himself on Institution women and his reputation among them was not good."

Eike's actions reinvigorated conversation about the double standard, with several prominent oceanographers coming to her defence. Backus, who was also Eicke's mentor, noted, "Her gutsy act turned the attention of the WHOI community to the issues of women at sea as it had never before. Consider the problem: one couldn't be an oceanographer without going to sea. Did that mean that women couldn't become oceanographers? The answer was the one that a trifling amount of thought had given in all such cases: it not only would be unfair, but it would also halve the pool of talent. Further, so long as oceanographic research was mainly paid for with public funds, the prohibition of women on research vessels was surely doomed."

Cartographer Marie Tharp famously created the first scientific maps of the ocean floor, fundamentally changing geology forever with her discovery of the Mid-Atlantic Ridge, which led to the acceptance of the theories of plate tectonics and continental drift. But she was restricted to drawing maps in the first place

---

803 Freiburger, Brett, "Elizabeth 'Betty' Bunce," WHOI Women's Committee, May 6, 2020, https://web.whoi.edu/womens-comm/elizabeth-betty-bunce/

804 Freiburger, Brett, "Roberta Eike: The stowaway who made waves for women scientists today," WHOI Women's Committee, March 31, 2020, https://web.whoi.edu/womens-comm/roberta-eike/

because of the same superstition that women were bad luck on boats and therefore prevented from going on expeditions. She also had a male colleague dismiss the theory of continental drift as "girl talk."[805] If he means that girls are usually right, then sure. Tharp, for her part, mostly ignored the upheaval her work resulted in, and kept right on doing her job. "There's truth to the old cliché that a picture is worth a thousand words and that seeing is believing," she wrote. "I was so busy making maps I [just] let them argue."[806]

Canada's first professional female geologist, Alice Wilson, worked around a similar restriction. While at the Geological Survey of Canada, women were not allowed to conduct fieldwork alongside the men. So, she focused her efforts on local sites in Ottawa, studying the area on foot, bicycle and car for decades. Wilson eventually mapped more than 14,000 kilometres of the Ottawa St Lawrence Lowlands entirely by herself, producing the first geological publication about the region in 1946.[807]

After earning her PhD, Icie Hoobler started working as an assistant chemist at Pittsburgh's Western Pennsylvania Hospital. Among the sexist nonsense she faced there was the complete lack of a women's bathroom, meaning she had to use a public restroom down the street. Limiting her trips to the bathroom led to acute inflammation of her kidneys, which her superiors used to try and urge her to take a year's leave. She also wasn't allowed to eat in the doctors' dining hall because they were all men, but not allowed to eat in the nurses' dining hall for bureaucratic reasons. She was also not invited to the annual staff banquet because her laboratory chief didn't think she would want to spend the evening with "all those men." She quit after two weeks. Fortunately, the president of the board of trustees cared enough to discuss the situation, and thanks to him, circumstances improved enough for Hoobler to return. That was, of course, not the end of the

---

805 Blakemore, Erin, "Seeing Is Believing: How Marie Tharp Changed Geology Forever," *Smithsonian Magazine*, August 30, 2016, https://www.smithsonianmag.com/history/seeing-believing-how-marie-tharp-changed-geology-forever-180960192/
806 Tharp, Marie, "Connect the Dots: Mapping the Seafloor and Discovering the Mid-Ocean Ridge," originally published in the book, *Lamont-Doherty Earth Observatory: Twelve Perspectives on the First Fifty Years 1949-1999*, edited by Laurence Lippsett, 1999, Lamont-Doherty Earth Observatory of Columbia University.
807 Russell, Loris S and James-Abra, Erin, "Alice Wilson," The Canadian Encyclopedia, Historica Canada, 2017.

sexism she had to deal with, such as when she was invited to speak at an event where the organizers had assumed "Icie" was a man. When she arrived, she wasn't even allowed to enter until her husband negotiated with the manager and the board of trustees re-voted on whether to allow her to speak.[808]

Award-winning radiochemist Darleane C. Hoffman did foundational work in scientists' understanding of how fission works. But when she had first come to Los Alamos Scientific Laboratory in 1952, she was told, "We don't hire women in that Division," in regards to the Radiochemistry Group of the Test Division. She had joined her husband at the organisation, but for an extended period she was denied access to the laboratory because the human resources department refused to believe that a woman could be a chemist. She went on to work there for more than thirty years, becoming the first woman division leader of the Chemistry-Nuclear Chemistry Division before leaving for a career in academia.[809]

In a case of "same nonsense, different century and continent," Italian pharmacist Sabina Baldoncelli completed all the coursework to earn a degree in the subject circa 1807. Although she had received the same education from tutors that male students had access to at university and had years of practical experience that most of them lacked, authorities allowed her to take her examinations only because of her special circumstances as an orphan residing in an orphanage. But they also stipulated that she could only practice her trade in the orphanage, not in secular pharmacies, restricting her from working anywhere else in Bologna.[810]

In some cases, women can't even get hired for jobs they are already doing. In 1909, botanist Carrie Derick's boss fell ill, and Derick assumed his role as chair of the botany department at McGill University. She ran the department for three years (he died in 1910) and had strong support from colleagues, yet when McGill finally began the search to officially replace him in 1912, they did not offer her

---

[808] Shearer, Benjamin F, and Barbara S Shearer, Notable Women in the Physical Sciences, Greenwood.
[809] Chapman, Kit, "The Women Written out of Nuclear Science," Berkeley College of Chemistry, January 10, 2022, https://chemistry.berkeley.edu/news/women-written-out-nuclear-science
[810] Logan, G. B., "Women and the Practice and Teaching of Medicine in Bologna in the Eighteenth and Early Nineteenth Centuries," Bulletin of the History of Medicine, vol 77 no 3 (2003), pp. 506–535, https://www.jstor.org/stable/44447892

the job ... that she'd been doing ... for three years. Instead, they appointed her as a professor of morphological botany, which was not her area of specialty and did not come with a pay increase or a faculty seat, and the new chair assigned her work suitable for a lower-ranked demonstrator, not a professor. It did, however, make Derick the first woman in Canada to become a university professor.[811]

Even if they do get the job, they may not get the title, continuing a long tradition of women being given lower-status job titles than their work warrants. When her predecessor had a stroke in 1950, Anne Bohm took over all duties as the Dean of the Graduate School at the London School of Economics. Although she did the job for twenty years, she was never granted the title of Dean, and was even told by the School Secretary, "we don't really need a Dean, do we: you are doing it."[812]

Although thirty years younger than her husband, astronomer Maria Margaretha Kirch was a valuable collaborator, who earned acclaim with her writing on the conjunction of the sun with Saturn, Venus, and Jupiter. After her husband's death in 1710, Maria petitioned to take over his role as the Royal Academy of Science's astronomer and calendar maker, noting that "for some time, while my dear departed husband was weak and ill, I prepared the calendar from his calculations and published it under his name." She also made clear that she needed the income to support herself and her children, as her husband had left her little financial support. There was a well-established precedent of widows assuming their dead husband's trade, as would be later seen in the election and appointment of political widows to fill their spouses' seats. Women also made up around fourteen percent of astronomers at the time, but as noted elsewhere, were routinely excluded from professional organisations.[813] But although the academy's president supported her and she had worked at the academy for a decade under her husband, the executive

---

811 Birker, Ingrid, "Carrie Derick: Canada's First Female Professor Taught at McGill," McGill Reporter, March 1, 2012, https://reporter.mcgill.ca/carrie-derick-canadas-first-female-professor-taught-at-mcgill/
812 Donnelly, Sue, ""A melange of charm, beauty and pure terror" – Anne Bohm (1910-2006), Secretary to the Graduate School." London School of Economics and Political Science, March 1, 2017, https://blogs.lse.ac.uk/lsehistory/2017/03/13/a-melange-of-charm-beauty-and-pure-terror-anne-bohm-1910-2006-secretary-to-the-graduate-school/
813 Gregersen, Erik, "Maria Kirch | German Astronomer," Encycloaedia Britannica, https://www.britannica.com/biography/Maria-Kirch

council rejected her proposal to fill a formal position because "what we concede to her could serve as an example in the future... If she were now to be kept on in such a capacity, mouths would gape even wider." Instead, they appointed the inexperienced Johann Heinrich Hoffmann, who soon fell behind on the work and failed to make required observations—it was suggested that Kirch become his assistant. She wrote, "Now I go through a severe desert, and because... water is scarce... the taste is bitter."

The following year, Kirch published an acclaimed pamphlet in which she predicted a new comet, followed by a paper about Jupiter and Saturn. In 1712, she secured the patronage of Bernhard Friedrich von Krosig and returned to working in his observatory, where she had previously worked with her husband, and achieved the rank of master astronomer. She had trained her children in astronomy, and following the death of the incompetent Hoffmann 1716, her son Christfried was appointed an observer at the Royal Academy of Science observatory. Kirch and her daughter Christine joined him as assistants, though (male) academy members complained she was "too visible at the observatory when strangers visit," and took too prominent a role in the operations of the observatory. Kirch was ordered to "retire to the background and leave the talking to... her son." She chose to retire the following year, but the Academy requested she continue to reside nearby so that Christfried could still dine at home without neglecting his duties.

Christine was not paid for her own decades of work assisting Christfried. It was only after his death in 1740 that the academy began paying her for calculating calendars, a major source of income for the organisation.[814]

PROFESSIONAL ORGANISATIONS

Professional organisations have a long history of excluding women, regardless of their skills, dedication, or accomplishments. In Medieval and Renaissance Europe, many women artists worked within the workshop system, under the nominal

---

814 Wielen, R., Kirch, Christine, In: Hockey, T., et al. *The Biographical Encyclopedia of Astronomers*, Springer, 2007.

guidance of a man, often the woman's father.[815] There is no record of a woman-led workshop until the 1100s, when widows were allowed to take over their deceased husband's shop.[816] Artistic guilds would often bar women from achieving higher ranks that came with greater recognition and power.[817]

Shortly before her death, the International Archive of Women in Architecture wrote, "Mary Rockwell Hook will be remembered, not because she was a woman working in a 'man's field,' but because she was a successful designer who made her mark in the field of architecture." Alas, her mark was not enough to get her admitted to the American Institute of Architects, which rejected her because of her gender. They did give her a plaque for distinguished service on her 100th birthday, at which point she was blind and therefore couldn't even see it.[818] She was also reportedly rejected for a job because "you can't swear at women and they can't climb all over full sized details."[819]

Though a few women had been elected as honorary members, Isis Pogson was the first woman to try to join the Royal Astronomical Society as a fellow. Nominated by her father in 1886, her nomination was withdrawn when two attorneys declared female fellows illegal because the society's 1831 royal charter referred to fellows as "he." She was admitted almost thirty-five years later, in 1920, after the society finally changed the rules.[820]

In 1880, while a student at Cambridge University's Girton College, Hertha Ayrton passed the Mathematical Tripos (the university's mathematics course) but was denied an academic degree because the university would not award full degrees to women—even if they had earned them. Instead, she took and passed an external exam at the University of London, which accordingly granted her a Bachelor of

---

815 "Art and Visual Culture: Medieval to Modern," OpenLearn, https://www.open.edu/openlearn/history-the-arts/art-and-visual-culture-medieval-modern/content-section-1.2.3
816 Crowston, Clare, "Women, Gender, and Guilds in Early Modern Europe: An Overview of Recent Research," International Review of Social History vol 53 no 19–44 (2008), https://www.jstor.org/stable/26405466
817 *Ibid.*
818 "IAWA Spotlight: Mary Rockwell Hook," International Archive of Women in Architecture, Autumn 1991.
819 Hook, Mary Rockwell, *This and That* (Mary Rockwell Hook, 1970, pp. 1–67).
820 Brück, Mary T, *Women in Early British and Irish Astronomy: Stars and Satellites* (Dordrecht: Springer, 2009, p. 157).

Science degree in 1881.[821]

In 1899, Ayrton became the first woman to read her own paper, *The Hissing of the Electric Arc*, before the Institution of Electrical Engineers, and was soon elected the IEE's first woman member. But when she petitioned to read another paper, *The Mechanism of the Electric Arc*, before the Royal Society in 1901, she was not allowed to because of her sex. It clearly had nothing to do with the quality of or interest in her work, as fellow electrical engineer John Perry was allowed to read it in her place.

Following the publication of *The Electric Arc*, a summary of her work and research, the following year, Perry proposed her as a Fellow to the Royal Society. The governing Council rejected the application, claiming that married women were not eligible to be Fellows. Apparently neither were unmarried women, as it was more than forty years until the first female Fellows were elected (biochemist Marjory Stephenson and crystallographer Kathleen Lonsdale in 1945).

Ayrton did become the first woman to read her own paper before the Royal Society in 1904, *The origin and growth of ripple-mark*. She was also the first woman to win a prize from the Society, the Hughes Medal in 1906, in honour of her research on the motion of ripples in sand and water and her work on the electric arc. The annual prize was not awarded to another woman until Michele Dougherty in 2008.

On January 8, 1816, Sophie Germain became the first woman to win a prize from the Paris Academy of Sciences, but she was still not allowed to attend Academy sessions because the only women allowed were members' wives. Even Nobel Prize winners Marie Curie and Irène Joliot-Curie were excluded, and it was not until Curie protege Marguerite Perey that a woman was even admitted as a "correspondent" member in 1962, with Yvonne Choquet-Bruhat becoming the first full member in 1979. Ironically, the annual Sophie Germain Prize is conferred by the Academy.[822]

Beatrix Potter is best known as the creator of Peter Rabbit, but her illustrations

---

821 O'Connor, J. J. and Robertson, E. F., "Hertha Marks Ayrton – Biography," School of Mathematics and Statistics, University of St Andrews, Scotland. Last updated August 2016, https://mathshistory.st-andrews.ac.uk/Biographies/Ayrton/
822 O'Connor, J. J. and Robertson, E. F., "Sophie Germain – Biography," School of Mathematics and Statistics, University of St Andrews, Scotland. Last updated November 2020, https://mathshistory.st-andrews.ac.uk/Biographies/Germain/

extended to the sciences as well as children's books, and she was also an avid mycologist who spent years studying fungi. In 1895, she developed a theory about spore germination and convinced mycologist George Massee of its soundness. Rebuffed by the director of Kew Gardens, she nonetheless wrote up her conclusions, submitting her paper, *On the Germination of the Spores of the Agaricineae*, to the Linnean Society in 1897. Massee presented it because, as a woman, Potter was not allowed to present her own work.[823]

Even when women have been allowed to join, their position is not always secure. In 1748, Eva Ekeblad became the first woman admitted to the Royal Swedish Academy of Sciences, but three years later she was reduced to an honorary member because she was a woman.[824] In 1885, Marian Farquharson was elected as the first female fellow of the Royal Microscopical Society—but as a woman she was still prohibited from actually attending any meetings or voting on society matters.[825]

Even at a local level, women are kept out by their neighbours. At the time of her death, lepidopterist Emma Hutchinson's collection included 20,000 butterflies, which were later donated to the London Natural History Museum. Yet she published little during her lifetime and her local scientific society, Woolhope Naturalists' Field Club, did not admit women as full members until 1954, almost fifty years after Hutchinson's death in 1906. But the same club that kept her out was more than happy to take her notebooks, which remain in their collection today.[826]

WOMEN WHO CHANGED THE RULES

When the literal gatekeepers, assuming women don't belong, try to keep them out, there will always be women who don't take no for an answer.

---

823   Lepp, Heino, "Beatrix Potter and Fungi – Case Study," Australian National Botanic Gardens, https://www.anbg.gov.au/fungi/case-studies/beatrix-potter.html
824   Tikkanen, Amy, "Eva Ekeblad | Biography & Facts," Encyclopaedia Britannica, Last updated July 6, 2023, https://www.britannica.com/biography/Eva-Ekeblad
825   Douglas, Gina, "Farquharson [née Ridley], Marian Sarah," Oxford Dictionary of National Biography, Oxford University Press, May 27, 2010, https://www.oxforddnb.com/display/10.1093/ref:odnb/9780198614128.001.0001/odnb-9780198614128-e-55777
826   Wale, Matthew, "Emma Hutchinson (1820-1906)," Constructing Scientific Communities, https://conscicom.web.ox.ac.uk/article/emma-hutchinson-1820-1906

In 1892, three women were proposed for fellowship in the Royal Astronomical Society—Elizabeth Brown, Alice Evert, and Annie Russell. All three failed to gain sufficient votes to be admitted, just as Isis Pogson's nomination had been rejected in 1886.[827] It wasn't until 1916 that Mary Adele Blagg, Ella K. Church, A. Grace Cook, and Fiammetta Wilson became the first female fellows elected. Annie Maunder was also elected that year—more than twenty-four years after her first attempt to join.[828] Rather than waiting, Brown, along with Margaret Huggins, Agnes Clerke, and Agnes Giberne were among the founders of the British Astronomical Association in 1890, which allowed women in from the start.[829]

In 1900, Marion Farquharson sent a letter petitioning the Royal Society and the Linnean Society of London that "duly qualified women should have the advantages of full fellowship in scientific and other learned societies." They initially refused to consider the petition on the excuse that they could only accept one from a fellow, so she got its former president, John Lubbock, to resubmit it on her behalf. Their new excuse was that the royal charter that established the organisation probably couldn't apply to women because it used male pronouns. But she kept pushing, until the society agreed to put the petition to a vote by the fellows. In 1903, the society requested a supplementary charter from King Edward VII explicitly allowing women to join as fellows. In December 1904, fifteen women were nominated for fellowship—all were elected except Farquharson. It was years before she was resubmitted in 1908, at which time she was elected, but it was too late. Due to the delay, her now-ill health prevented her from signing the admission roll.[830]

Kristine Bonnevie's competence as a college professor led to sweeping legal reform in Norway. She was nominated to a professor position in 1910, during a time when Norwegian law prevented women from holding such a position. Her

---

827 Marsden, Hannah, "Elizabeth Brown: A Forgotten 'Lady Astronomer,'" Corinium Museum, July 9, 2021, https://coriniummuseum.org/2021/07/elizabeth-brown-a-forgotten-lady-astronomer/
828 "100 Years and Counting: Women in the RAS Go from Strength to Strength," The Royal Astronomical Society, https://ras.ac.uk/education-and-careers/100-years-and-counting-women-ras-go-strength-strength
829 McKim, Richard, "A Different Sort of Society," *Astronomy & Geophysics*, vol 57 no 4 (2016). https://doi.org/10.1093/astrogeo/atw146
830 Mason, J., "The Women Fellows' Jubilee," *Notes and Records of the Royal Society* vol 49 (1995): 125–140. Beharrell, Will and Douglas, Gina, "Celebrating the Linnean Society's First Women Fellows," *The Linnean Society*, March 27, 2020, https://www.linnean.org/news/2020/03/27/celebrating-the-first-women-fellows

colleagues, Georg Sars and Robert Collett, were so determined to keep Bonnevie that they influenced Parliament to pass an act on February 9, 1912 known as "Lex Bonnevie," granting women the same right as men to be university professors.[831]

Joanna Cohan Scherer worked in the Smithsonian Institution's anthropology archives for decades, starting in 1966. While there, she faced various instances of gender discrimination, not least of which was the fact that, by 1974, the department had never hired a single woman curator, despite the existence of thousands of women anthropologists. She filed a class action and sex discrimination lawsuit, arguing that sexism had hindered her career. She won in 1975, and received a long overdue promotion, with a title upgrade from Museum Specialist to Anthropologist. The department's first female curator, Adrienne Kaeppler, joined the staff later that year.

Scherer also went on to sue for the reprisals she faced, such as unfounded negative performance reviews, harassment, and withholding of further earned promotions. She won that case in 1982.[832]

Jeannette Rankin was elected to the U.S. House of Representatives in 1916, before many women in the country had the right to vote. At the time, women's suffrage was a state issue, and several of the western states, like Rankin's Montana, offered it as incentive to attract more women to move west. During her first term in Congress, she introduced legislation that eventually became the 19th Amendment to the U.S. Constitution, granting women's suffrage, which went into effect in 1920.[833]

Emilie Kempin-Spyri became Switzerland's first female law school graduate in 1887, but women were not allowed to practice law at the time because they lacked full citizenship. Her proposal to the Bundesgericht, (Federal Supreme Court of Switzerland) asking for a reconsideration of Article 4 of the Federal Constitution that a "Swiss citizen" could also include women, was rejected as "ebenso neu als kühn" (just as novel as audacious). Thanks to her lobbying, however, a new statute was introduced in 1898 that allowed women to practice law in Zürich canton;

---

831   "Kristine Bonnevie," Store Norske Leksikon, February 1, 2021, https://snl.no/Kristine_Bonnevie
832   Kaul, Clara, "Gender Discrimination at the Smithsonian Institution," Smithsonian Institution Archives, August 6, 2019, https://siarchives.si.edu/blog/gender-discrimination-smithsonian-institution
833   Conkling, Winifred, "Jeannette Rankin: One Woman, One Vote (U.S. National Park Service)," NPS, https://www.nps.gov/articles/000/jeannette-rankin-one-woman-one-vote.htm

it was not adopted nationally until 1923, more than two decades after her death in 1901.[834]

Lidia Poët was the first woman in Italy to be a lawyer, inscribed in the roll of lawyers (*albo degli avvocati*) on August 9, 1883. But she was almost immediately disbarred, in a court ruling that banned women from the practice of law in the country. Although she could not appear in court, she continued doing the work of a lawyer in her brother's firm in the following years, in addition to advocating for women to be allowed to practice law and hold public office in Italy. She finally triumphed more than thirty-five years after her disbarment, in 1920, at the age of sixty-five.[835]

On the other side of the world, Clara González de Behringer became the first woman in Panama to earn her doctorate in law, at a time when women weren't allowed to practice law in the country. Her thesis, "La Mujer ante el Derecho Panameño" ("The Woman in Panamanian Law"), was one of the first documents addressing the legal rights of women in Panama. De Behringer was more successful in her lobbying efforts than Kempin-Spyri, not least because thirty-five years had passed. In 1924, two years after she graduated, the law was changed and Clara was able to become a practising lawyer.[836]

Annie MacDonald Langstaff won for others, but not for herself. She earned her Bachelor of Civil Law in 1914, but the Bar of Montreal refused to allow her to take the bar exam to become a practising lawyer. When she petitioned the Superior Court on the matter, they ruled against her because she did not have her husband's permission to attend law school or become a lawyer. The fact that her husband had abandoned her and her child and she had no idea where he was did not, apparently, matter. She continued to fight to become a barrister, as well as for women's suffrage. When she appealed to the Court of King's Bench, they punted to the legislature, saying it was their problem because they had passed the

---

834 Leybold-Johnson, Isobel, "A Woman Ahead of Her Times," Swiss Broadcasting Corporation, June 30, 2008, https://www.swissinfo.ch/eng/a-woman-ahead-of-her-times/1015736
835 Burack, Emily, "The True Story of Lidia Poët," *Town & Country*, February 24, 2023, https://www.townandcountrymag.com/leisure/arts-and-culture/a43047434/lidia-poet-true-story/
836 Navarrete, Wendy, "Clara González de Behringer, First Female Lawyer in Panama and the First Latinamerican Female to Earn a PhD in Law," Pioneering Women, June 5, 2019, https://pioneeringwomen.org/?p=374

statute defining who could be a lawyer in the first place, so she'd have to take it up with them—as though courts never overturn laws that legislatures pass.[837] After women won the vote in Quebec in 1940, Langstaff, along with Leona Bell and Elizabeth C. Monk, once again appealed to the Quebec Bar Association. They relented, but a prerequisite had been introduced in the decades Langstaff spent fighting—lawyers had to have a Bachelor of Arts. After more than twenty-five years, she had the wrong type of degree. She was posthumously admitted in 2006, more than thirty years after she died.[838]

YES, WOMEN *ARE* FUNNY

Why aren't there more women in comedy? Well, it must be because women just aren't as funny as men. This cliche is as tired as it is false. It ignores toxic masculinity in many writers' rooms and comedy clubs. It ignores gatekeepers—the agents and club owners who choose which aspiring comics get time and attention. It ignores the danger for a woman traveling late at night and on her own—for comedians like Eurydice Dixon, this scenario resulted in her rape and murder.[839] It ignores sexual harassment in the workplace and beyond from powerful men like Louis C. K.[840] It ignores the male "colleagues" like Daniel Tosh and his supporters, who think it's funny to joke about a female audience member getting gang-raped[841]—and the drunk men in the audience who laugh at that "joke"—and female comedians like Kitty Flanagan, who claimed in her 2018 book that she doesn't believe date rape is real, that women lie because they regret their choices made while drunk, and even so, men are justified in using date rape drugs because

---

837 McCabe, Daniel, "A Lawyer at Long Last," McGill News (McGill University), December 2007, https://mcgillnews.mcgill.ca/s/1762/news/interior.aspx?sid=1762&gid=2&pgid=1272

838 Mahoney, Richard, "Breaking down Barriers: Alexandria native made legal history," The Glengarry News, July 14, 2021, https://www.pressreader.com/canada/the-glengarry-news/20210714/282346862814101

839 "Eurydice Dixon's Killer Stalked Her for 5km before Murder in Melbourne Park," *The Guardian*, August 15, 2019, https://www.theguardian.com/australia-news/2019/aug/15/eurydice-dixons-killer-stalked-her-for-5km-before-in-melbourne-park

840 Schneider, Christopher J., and Stacey Hannem, "Louis C.K.: Sexual Misconduct and the Pursuit of Justice," The Conversation, https://theconversation.com/louis-c-k-sexual-misconduct-and-the-pursuit-of-justice-174146

841 Bassist, Elissa, "Why Daniel Tosh's 'Rape Joke' at the Laugh Factory Wasn't Funny," The Daily Beast, July 12, 2012, https://www.thedailybeast.com/why-daniel-toshs-rape-joke-at-the-laugh-factory-wasnt-funny

women don't get wasted as easily as they used to.[842] It ignores a culture that tells you to either toughen up or relax—seemingly contradictory statements—if you speak up about these issues.

Comedy is one of many areas where women have always been under-represented—just as women "aren't funny," we also "aren't good at maths and science" and "aren't tough enough" for careers in the military and elsewhere. We "don't belong" in arenas like video games, comic books, science fiction/fantasy works, or sports. It's presented as an issue of potential and innate skill combined with hard work and endurance, rather than one of barriers deliberately placed in our path. When we cite women like Lucille Ball, Lily Tomlin, Joan Rivers, and so many more, we're met with a scoff and assurance that they're clearly the exception rather than the rule.

As far back as 1695, playwright William Congreve wrote "I must confess, I have never made any observation of what I apprehend to be true humor in women ... If ever anything does appear comical or ridiculous in a woman, I think it is little more than an acquired folly or an affectation."[843] But just as there's evidence of this prejudice dating back centuries, there is also proof of women being funny— one needs look no further than the plays of Aphra Behn (1640-1689) for that. Sixteenth-century humanist Juan Luis Vives, though he warned against women laughing because it could convey sexual looseness, simultaneously believed women could be funny, encouraging wives to have funny stories ready to cheer their husbands.[844] Theories for the bias range from simple misogyny—wanting to assert male dominance—to religious prudery as shown by Vives, to gate-keeping and money-making opportunities by excluding potential rivals. And, of course, men's deep-seated fear that women will make jokes at their expense and laugh at them.

In his 2022 book, *In On the Joke: The Original Queens of Standup Comedy*, author Shawn Levy describes the experience of comedian Elaine May during her time as a member of the Compass Players comedy group, which she was a founding

---

842 Flanagan, Kitty, *Bridge Burning & Other Hobbies* (Allen & Unwin, 2018).
843 Congreve, William, "Concerning Humour in Comedy," 1695.
844 Wiltenburg, Joy, "Just When in History Did Men Decide That Women Are Not Funny?" *Psyche*, October 24, 2022, https://psyche.co/ideas/just-when-in-history-did-men-decide-that-women-are-not-funny

member of from 1955:

> Elaine still intimidated the snot out of many of her fellow Compass players. Her wit was too quick and sharp, her instincts too primal, her patience too thin... She literally had ideas for new scenes falling out of her pockets and the baby buggy that she pushed around in lieu of a purse. On top of fear, she also commanded respect—many of her colleagues would matter-of-factly refer to her "genius." But she was often treated with chauvinistic condescension. When she shared her ideas for new work, her fellow players would often act as if imposed upon. "I don't think anyone ever said it was good," remembered director Mark Gordon. "Every time she came in with material, it was 'Oh my God, it's awful. It will never work.'... Then someone would kind of grudgingly say, "OK, we'll try it.' Then we'd do it for people at night and the audience would be hysterical loving it... But there was never a recognition that Elaine's stuff was fantastic." For Roger Bowen, another writer and actor in the group, the reason was obvious: "We, being men, just ignored her." (Compass co-founder David Shepherd would, years later, say that Elaine "broke through the psychological restrictions of playing comedy as a woman," apparently incapable of realizing that those psychological restrictions were not *hers* but *his*—and those of his male colleagues.[845]

She quit the group in 1957 to pursue a successful doubles act with partner Mike Nichols. Compass actor Nancy Ponder has said, "She was the strongest woman I ever met," while famed actor Richard Burton recalled, "Elaine was too formidable, one of the most intelligent, beautiful, and witty women I had ever met. I hoped I would never see her again."[846]

May's experience was hardly unique among women comedians. Jane Curtin recalled John Belushi in particular making life hell for the women writers of early *Saturday Night Live*, which premiered in 1975. "It was primarily a misogynistic

---

[845] Levy, Shawn, *In On the Joke: The Original Queens of Standup Comedy* (Doubleday, 2022).
[846] Nachman, Gerald, "Seriously Funny: The Rebel Comedians of the 1950s and 1960s," Pantheon Books, 2003.

environment... Their battle was constant. They were working against John, who said women are just fundamentally not funny. You'd go to a table read and if a woman writer had written a piece for John, he would not read it in his full voice. He would whisper it," she told Oprah Winfrey in 2011. "He felt as though it was his duty to sabotage pieces that were written by women."[847] In Yael Kohen's *We Killed: The Rise of Women in American Comedy*, SNL writer Anne Beatts notes, "John Belushi used to regularly ask for us to be fired. 'Fire the girls!'"[848]

It's also worth mentioning that in the Oprah segment, when Oprah asked about SNL's role in creating a space for women comedians, Chevy Chase immediately jumped in to talk about the struggle for women writers. When he claims that they were writing about women's issues, Curtin's "you're so full of it" facial expression is priceless. He then interrupted and talked over her when she tried to speak, giving up when Curtin kept going (presumably not the first time she's had to do so). He also interjected "I don't remember that" during her comments about Belushi.

A decade later, Julia Louis-Dreyfus's experience on the show seems to have been no better. In a 2019 interview, she told Stephen Colbert of her 1984-89 run, "It was very sexist ... It was a pretty brutal time." Her main takeaway? "I learned I wasn't going to do anymore of this show-business crap unless it was fun," she said. "It is important, it's so basic, but I just thought, I don't have to do this. I don't have to walk and crawl through this kind of nasty glass if it's not ultimately going to be fulfilling, and so that's how I sort of moved forward from that moment. I sort of applied the fun-metre to every job I've had since and that has been very helpful."[849]

While it would be nice to imagine this sentiment is a thing of the past, it exhaustingly continues. Most women working today in comedy have more than enough stories to fill their own book—each. In 2013, then-eighty-seven-year-old Jerry Lewis reiterated that he still didn't find women funny, having notoriously said in 1998, "I don't like any female comedians. A woman doing comedy doesn't

---

847 "The Secrets of Saturday Night Live," Oprah.com, April 12, 2011, https://www.oprah.com/oprahshow/the-secrets-of-saturday-night-live/all
848 Kohen, Yael, *We Killed: The Rise of Women in American Comedy* (Picador, 2013).
849 Wright, Megh, "Julia Louis-Dreyfus on Her SNL Days: 'It Was a Pretty Brutal Time,'" Vulture, December 10, 2019, https://www.vulture.com/2019/12/julia-louis-dreyfus-snl-sexist-brutal.html

offend me, but ... I think of her as a producing machine that brings babies in the world."[850] But while most professionals are smart enough not to say it out loud anymore (or blame cancel culture and people being over-sensitive when they get caught), such opinions have not died out with the likes of Lewis and Belushi.

In 2007, *Vanity Fair* published, with no apparent irony, a column titled *Why Women Aren't Funny*, which claimed that it's because women don't have to be funny to attract a man, whereas men do have to be funny to attract a woman. The piece included commentary like claiming the few good female comics were "hefty or dykey or Jewish," and describing "Jewish humor" as "almost masculine by definition."[851]

British comedian Lee Mack claimed in 2013, "It's actually a compliment, I think, to women that there aren't as many female stand-ups because they are far more interested in what each other has to say than standing there on their own and showing off."[852] The lack of understanding of his own industry is breath-taking.

Kristen Wiig noted, "I think the fact that people keep asking [if women are funny] implies that it's something we need to explain or defend. If [people] would watch movies or look at comedy and see how many talented, funny women are out there and have been since the beginning of time, people would stop asking that."[853] However, the idea that it's simply ignorance of the existence and work of women comics misses the point in an age where this content is more prolific and accessible than ever before. The people who push this mindset consistently don't want to be shown the error of their ways.

The fundamental flaw in the argument that women aren't funny because a particular man doesn't find them funny is that comedy is subjective. Almost no one will find 100 percent of comedians funny, but that doesn't mean we all go around saying that (fill in whatever group here) aren't funny. The type of man likely to

---

850 Lang, Brent, "Cannes: Jerry Lewis Skewered for Latest Bad-Taste, Sexist Remarks," TheWrap, May 24, 2013, https://www.thewrap.com/cannes-jerry-lewis-skewered-latest-bad-taste-sexist-remarks-93656/
851 Hitchens, Christopher, "Why Women Aren't Funny," Vanity Fair, 2007, https://www.vanityfair.com/culture/2007/01/hitchens200701
852 Christie, Bridget, "The Are Women Funny? Debate Is as Dead as Christopher Hitchens," *The Guardian*, October 1, 2013, https://www.theguardian.com/commentisfree/2013/oct/01/are-women-funny-lee-mack
853 Olsen, Mark, "Q&A: With 'Nasty Baby,' Kristen Wiig is officially crazy-busy," *Los Angeles Times*, October 23, 2015, http://www.latimes.com/entertainment/la-ca-mn-conversation-kristen-wiig-nasty-baby-20151025-story.html

make this comment is fundamentally sexist, is therefore less inclined to even watch women's comedy, and if he does, has already gone in with a strong enough bias that his mind is made up. He's likely to be less open-minded about or interested in other people's experiences and viewpoints. Of course he doesn't think women are funny, and nothing will ever change that.

THE PINK GHETTO

"I do not call myself a woman conductor,
I call myself a conductor who happens to be a woman."
—Antonia Brico

In season 2 of Phoebe Waller-Bridge's *Fleabag*, her character congratulates Belinda, who had just won an award for women in business. Belinda is less than impressed. "It's infantilising bollocks," she says. "It's ghettoising. It's a subsection of success. It's the fucking children's table of awards."[854]

The term "pink ghetto" refers to the segregation of women into a separate, and often lesser, section. In some cases, this is physical, like the separation of women into their own women's colleges as a subsidiary of a men's college that refused those women admission or degrees. More often nowadays, it is a matter of categorisation—having dedicated awards specifically for women in business, the arts, and so on, or removing all the women from Wikipedia's American Novelists category page and putting them in one for Women American Novelists, as noted previously. The implication often is that women do not belong in the main section, not least because they're not good enough to compete with the men.

Some women reinforce this stereotype, as when film director Jane Campion, upon accepting a BAFTA (for a film that doesn't even pass the Bechdel-Wallace Test, incidentally), commented completely unnecessarily that the tennis star Williams sisters, who were at the event, "don't play against the guys like I do." In fact,

---

854 Waller-Bridge, Phoebe, "Fleabag," Season 2, episode 2.3, May 17, 2019.

both Venus and Serena have won Grand Slams in mixed doubles—between them, they swept the 1998 Grand Slams with Venus winning the Australian and French Opens and Serena taking the U.S. Open and Wimbledon.[855]

Similarly, the entire debate around allowing transgender athletes to compete based on their gender identity is ostensibly around "fairness." The assumption is that either people who were born with male biology will have natural advantages and/or that cisgender men will trick people into believing they're non-binary or trans so they can compete against the weaker girls—which just sounds like the plot of a bad '90s comedy. While the latter is clearly absurd, arguments can be made that some transgender women will have biological advantages over some cisgender women—but the same is true of all athletes.[856] In many sports, simply being taller, with longer arm span and leg length is an inherent advantage—basketball player Manute Bol was 7' 7" (2.3m) tall, which contributed to his reputation as one of the best shot-blockers in NBA history. Simone Biles benefits from the opposite—at 4'8" (142cm), her height-to-strength ratio enables her to do more flips and manoeuvres in the same amount of time compared to taller gymnasts. Michael Phelps is perhaps the best modern example—while he certainly works hard to be the best swimmer he can be, he also has several biological quirks that contribute to his phenomenal success: his wingspan (combined length of both arms and shoulders) is longer than his height; he is hyper-jointed in the chest, meaning he can kick from his chest instead of just his ribs; his double-jointed ankles bend fifteen percent more than his rivals, which, coupled with his size-fourteen feet, help his legs act like flippers to propel him through the water. Yet no one is claiming these athletes should not be allowed to play—it is only when athletes that some people see as male want to play against cisgender women that a fundamental imbalance is assumed.

Moreover, when trans athletes are allowed to compete based on their own gender identity, the assertion of biological benefits for trans women doesn't hold

---

[855] Oladipo, Gloria, "Jane Campion Apologizes to Williams Sisters for 'Thoughtless Comment,'" *The Guardian*, March 14, 2022, https://www.theguardian.com/film/2022/mar/15/jane-campion-serena-venus-williams-backlash.
[856] "The Right To Compete," Gender Justice, January 2021, https://www.genderjustice.us/wp-content/uploads/2021/01/Trans-Equity-in-Sports_Fact-Sheet-Jan-2021.pdf

up. If increased testosterone is an advantage, many transgender people use hormone replacement therapy specifically to increase or decrease testosterone or estrogen. HRT significantly changes a person's body—for trans women, that usually means growing breasts, reduction in muscle mass, and less physical strength, which is why the US's National Collegiate Athletic Association (NCAA) and the Olympics both allow trans women to compete in women's events if they have been on HRT for a certain amount of time. Critics claim that does not offset the supposed benefits of growing up with male hormone balances. Lia Thomas became a lightning rod for the debate when she won the 500-yard freestyle race at the NCAA's first division swimming championship in her last competition as a college athlete. Data shows that she lost an inch of height and a degree of strength due to HRT, and while she is certainly an elite-level swimmer, she is nowhere near as dominant as athletes like Phelps or Biles. At the competition mentioned, she won the women's 500-yard freestyle race in 4 minutes and 33.24 seconds, but placed fifth in the 200 yard and eighth in the 100 yard. Overall at the event, twenty-seven NCAA records were broken, none of them by Thomas—eighteen were broken by the cisgender Kate Douglass, which in a perfect world would have been the much bigger news story. Thomas's time in the 500-yard freestyle ranked her about fifteenth compared to other women in the NCAA competition history.[857]

International football star Barbra Banda, captain of the Zambian national team, was forced to sit out multiple games at the 2022 Women's Africa Cup of Nations because her testosterone levels were considered too high.[858] Christine Mboma and Beatrice Masilingi, both cisgender women, were banned from the Olympics for the same reason in 2021.[859] Intersex runner Caster Semenya's XY chromosomes and naturally elevated testosterone levels have also made her a target. After she won

---

857   Dodds, IO, "Why the Data Shows Trans Swimming Champion Lia Thomas Didn't Have an Unfair Advantage," The Independent, May 31, 2022, https://www.independent.co.uk/news/world/americas/lia-thomas-trans-swimmer-ron-desantis-b2091218.html

858   Ennis, Dawn, "Zambia Soccer Captain Fails 'Gender Verification' Test," Washington Blade: LGBTQ News, Politics, LGBTQ Rights, Gay News, July 7, 2022, https://www.washingtonblade.com/2022/07/07/zambia-soccer-captain-fails-gender-verification-test/

859   Villareal, Daniel, "Two more cis Black women banned from Olympics for their natural testosterone levels," LGBT Nation, July 2, 2021, https://www.lgbtqnation.com/2021/07/two-cis-black-women-banned-olympics-natural-testosterone-levels/

the 2009 World Championships, she was forced to undergo sex testing to prove that she was female and was cleared to return to competition the next year. In 2019, new World Athletics rules came into force preventing women like Semenya from participating in 400m, 800m and 1500m events in the female classification unless they take medication to suppress their testosterone levels—a rule change that also affected Burundi's Francine Niyonsaba and Kenya's Margaret Wambui, both cisgender women with naturally high testosterone levels.[860] Of taking such medications earlier in her career, Semenya later recalled, "It made me sick, made me gain weight, panic attacks, I don't know if I was ever going to have a heart attack... It's like stabbing yourself with a knife every day. But I had no choice. I'm 18, I want to run, I want to make it to Olympics, that's the only option for me."[861] In 2021, she filed an appeal with the European Court of Human Rights against the restrictions.

Transgender players have even been restricted from chess tournaments, as the International Chess Federation imposed a rule in 2023 to prevent trans women from competing in women's competitions, while at the same time removing titles from former women's competition winners who later transitioned to men, though transgender women were allowed to keep theirs.[862]

Science historian Margaret Rossiter, in her search for women scientists, found that the "territorial segregation" of women being cloistered within separate colleges was one reason they were more difficult to identify.[863] With women excluded from medical schools in the 1800s, women's medical colleges began popping up, but were often considered inferior to the "real" medical colleges attended by men.[864]

---

860 "Like 'Stabbing Yourself with a Knife': Caster Semenya Opens up about Being Forced to Take Testosterone-Lowering Medication," May 25, 2022, https://www.abc.net.au/news/2022-05-25/caster-semenya-testosterone-medication-world-athletics/101097076
861 Interview, Real Sports with Bryant Gumbel, May 24, 2022, https://www.facebook.com/realsportshbo/videos/for-the-last-decade-track-star-caster-semenya-says-shes-been-at-the-center-of-a-/1887402678118965/
862 "World Chess Just Placed Restrictions on Both Trans Women and Trans Men," NPR, August 18, 2023, https://www.npr.org/2023/08/18/1194593562/chess-transgender-fide-pushback
863 Dominus, Susan, "Women Scientists Were Written out of History. It's Margaret Rossiter's Lifelong Mission to Fix That," Smithsonian Magazine, October 2019, https://www.smithsonianmag.com/science-nature/unheralded-women-scientists-finally-getting-their-due-180973082/
864 Davies, Dave, "'Doctors Blackwell' Tells the Story of 2 Sisters Who Changed Medicine," KQED, January 20, 2021, https://www.kqed.org/arts/13891470/doctors-blackwell-tells-the-story-of-2-sisters-who-changed-medicine

While exclusively female efforts have been put forth to try to correct gender imbalances in visibility, art historian Griselda Pollock observed that this can be problematic in itself:

> Corrective shows may be trapped, however, in a paradox. Obliged to re-include artist-women by all-women shows, we may ironically confirm a two-tier system. Exhibitions titled "Abstract Expressionism" (with a few women among many men) have been challenged by shows of "Women in Abstract Expressionism" (with only women and no men). Reversing exclusivity, we again isolate artists as women, gender forming a common identity that masks many significant differences—historical, geopolitical, sexual, ethnic, social—between women.[865]

This also occurs thematically when decision-makers are considering what to allow women to do, relegating them to only certain areas. Women are frequently excluded from directing films about women because of biases that claim women are less capable of directing action films, for example, even as men are given the opportunity to do so without ever having directed such a film.[866] While there has been pushback in recent years in the superhero realm, with women directors on *Wonder Woman* and its sequel (Patty Jenkins, 2017 and 2020), *Captain Marvel* (co-writer and co-director Anna Boden, 2019), *Black Widow* (Cate Shortland, 2021) and *The Marvels* (Nia DaCosta, 2023), *The Hunger Games* and *Divergent* film adaptations were all directed by men, as were the women-led *Alien* and *Terminator* films, Angelina Jolie's *Tomb Raider* films, Kate Beckinsale's *Underworld* series, Demi Moore's *G. I. Jane*, the early-2000s *Charlie's Angels* (though Elizabeth Banks took over with the 2019 film), the *Kill Bill* franchise, *Mad Max: Fury Road*, all seven *Resident Evil* films, *Sicario,* and countless others.

That's not to say women haven't been highly influential on male-centric blockbusters. Several female film editors have won Oscars for their work on movies like

---

865 McEwan, Olivia, "A Women's History of Global Abstraction," Hyperallergic, March 7, 2023, https://hyperallergic.com/805770/a-womens-history-of-global-abstraction-whitechapel-gallery/

866 Buchanan, Kyle, "5 Dumb Reasons Why Hollywood Won't Hire Women Directors," Vulture, November 5, 2015, https://www.vulture.com/2015/11/5-reasons-why-women-directors-dont-get-hired.html

Lawrence of Arabia (Anne V. Coates, 1962), *Jaws* (Verna Fields, 1975), the original *Star Wars* trilogy (Marcia Lucas, 1977–1983), *Platoon* (Claire Simpson, 1986) and *Mad Max: Fury Road* (Margaret Sixel, 2015). Thelma Schoonmaker has won three times, for *The Aviator* (2004), *The Departed* (2006), and *Raging Bull* (1980).[867]

War presents an interesting juxtaposition in what is considered acceptable for women. For example, women don't belong in the armed forces ... unless they're nurses. Britain's Special Operations Executive found that women were more effective precisely because they could not be soldiers—as spies in occupied France, a young, able-bodied man would immediately draw suspicion. Journalists have faced the sexist assumption that women in war only cover the civilian side, telling the stories of nurses, refugees and those left to keep the home fires burning. American radio journalist Betty Wason risked near-starvation to cover the German invasion of Greece, and then was not allowed to broadcast her own material because her voice was considered too feminine.[868]

At the German art school Bauhaus, women like Anni Albers and Otti Berger were shunted into the textile department, prevented from studying other disciplines.[869] Initially sceptical, Albers grew to love the medium, saying "In my case it was threads that caught me, really against my will. To work with threads seemed sissy to me. I wanted something to be conquered. But circumstances held me to threads and they won me over."[870] Berger, meanwhile, became one of the few Bauhaus artists to have her designs patented. Although segregated, artists like Albers and Berger changed the way textiles are viewed as an artistic medium.

---

867 Eiseman, Selise, "Oscar's Women," CineMontage. January 1, 2012, https://cinemontage.org/oscars-women/
868 Mackrell, Judith, *The Correspondents: Six Women Writers on the Front Lines of World War II* (Doubleday, 2021).
869 "Women and Weaving at the Bauhaus," Index Magazine, Harvard Art Museums, May 22, 2019, https://harvardartmuseums.org/article/women-and-weaving-at-the-bauhaus
870 Albers, Anni, "Material as Metaphor." Josef and Anni Albers, 1982, Foundation, https://www.albersfoundation.org/alberses/teaching/anni-albers/material-as-metaphor

REFUSING TO INVEST IN WOMEN

"Never be limited by other people's limited imaginations. If you adopt their attitudes, then the possibility won't exist because you'll have already shut it out…You can hear other people's wisdom, but you've got to re-evaluate the world for yourself."
—Mae C. Jemison[871]

In the 1910s, Australian Fanny Durack was the best female swimmer in the world. Yet despite holding many records in Australia, the New South Wales Ladies Swimming Association tried to prevent her and fellow badass Mina Wylie from participating in the 1912 Olympics—the first to include women's swimming. First the organisation tried to refuse permission for Durack and Wylie to go at all. Then, perhaps realising that wasn't going to work—both women seemed the type to embody the "yeah, nah mate" Aussie attitude—the NSWLSA "relented" but refused to provide any financial support. Durack and Wylie had to raise the funds themselves—not only for themselves, but for their required chaperones.[872]

And they did. Their community supported them when the NSWLSA wouldn't, and they were able to raise the necessary funds. Fanny became the first Australian woman to win an Olympic gold medal, with Mina right behind her taking the silver. Fanny also set a new world record in the 100-metre freestyle. They were prevented from participating in the relay, which required four swimmers, even after they offered to each go twice.

The refusal to invest in women takes many forms:

- Women-led startups received just 2.3 percent of venture capital funding in 2020.[873]
- Countless women took unpaid work—and continue to do so in the form

---

871 Jemison, Mae C., Speech at the Annual Biomedical Research Conference for Minority Students, November 2009.
872 Reilly, Eliza, *Sheilas: Badass Women of Australian History* (Macmillan Publishers, 2022).
873 Elsesser, Kim, "Female Entrepreneurs Funded by Female VCs Face Difficulties Obtaining Future Funds," Forbes, Accessed August 21, 2023, https://www.forbes.com/sites/kimelsesser/2022/06/06/female-entrepreneurs-funded-by-female-vcs-face-difficulties-obtaining-future-funds/?sh=47f7cc696a7c

of internships and volunteer work—when no one would pay them for their contributions.
- Relegating women to lower-status roles to justify lower pay, even when they are doing the same work as the men with higher-status titles.
- Research for medical conditions that primarily impact women, such as endometriosis and anorexia, is underfunded.[874]
- Cheerleading is associated with the highest number of direct catastrophic injuries for all sports in which women and girls participate in the U.S. This is largely due to the fact that legally, it is considered an "activity" rather than a sport, which would require equal funding under Title IX for things like safety equipment.[875]
- Lack of support for paid maternity leave and childcare continues to be a problem in many countries.

Because the refusal to invest in women financially could—and should—be its own book, we'll focus only on the instances where the withholding of funds relates to women not being credited for their work. While many women, like Durack and Wylie, are able to overcome the financial barriers placed in their path, that has not been possible for everyone.

Many women inventors have fallen into obscurity because they could not secure investment to initiate production. Isaac K. Shero is credited as the inventor of the first patented hair straightener—but an African American woman beat him to it by more than fourteen years. The first patent for a hair straightener was filed on November 3, 1893 by Ada Harris, who lived in Indianapolis—home of the famed African American beauty product inventor and business mogul Madame C. J. Walker. Although she tried to find investors to support her product, it never got

---

874   Smith, Kerri, "Women's Health Research Lacks Funding – These Charts Show How," Nature, May 3, 2023, https://www.nature.com/immersive/d41586-023-01475-2/index.html
875   Toomas Timpka, Caroline F Finch, Claude Goulet, and Kaissar Yammine, "Meeting the Global Demand of Sports Safety: The Intersection of Science and Policy in Sports Safety," ResearchGate, Springer Verlag, February 2008, https://www.researchgate.net/publication/23268547_Meeting_the_global_demand_of_sports_safety_the_intersection_of_science_and_policy_in_sports_safety

off the ground. Unlike Walker, Harris was never able to sell her invention, and Shero patented his own version of the product in 1909.[876]

Women can also find themselves undermined on the marketing front. In her memoir *Recollections of my Nonexistence*, Rebecca Solnit recalls a publicist who told her that he'd scheduled a series of readings to promote her latest book. Solnit went on the road only to discover that none of the events existed. He had not bothered to do what was quite literally his job, and then had lied about it.[877]

Not investing in marketing is also a common self-fulfilling prophecy in women's sports: executives think people won't be interested, so they don't put the time, money, and energy into promoting them. They then interpret poor turnout and viewership as proving them correct, when in fact it was their own choices—rather than lack of potential audience interest—that caused the outcome. The same thing happens with all types of women-focused content like film, television shows, live productions, and visual arts—and books, as discovered by Solnit, a noted feminist author who is credited with inspiring the term "mansplaining" with her essay *Men Explain Things to Me*.

Racecar driver Julia Landauer noticed a similar issue with her support crew. When she started a season well, winning a few races, her team principal – the man who oversaw equipment preparation and helped communicate to mechanics what she, as the driver, wanted done with her car – congratulated her while also telling her he hadn't expected her to do well. Landauer concluded he likely hadn't been giving his best effort up to that point, particularly as her car started handling noticeably better after he made the comment, indicating that he and the mechanics were suddenly working harder for her.[878]

Before she became the third woman to win a Nobel Prize in 1947 for her work on metabolic processes, biochemist Gerty Cori worked for years as her husband's

---

876 Kulkarni, Reecha, "How a Man Got All the Credit for Ada Harris' Invention of the Flat Iron," The List, December 3, 2022, https://www.thelist.com/1125543/how-a-man-got-all-the-credit-for-ada-harris-invention-of-the-flat-iron/
877 Solnit, Rebecca, *Recollections of My Nonexistence* (Viking, 2020).
878 Landauer, Julia, "Don't Call Me A 'Female Racecar Driver'... My Gender Has No Bearing on My Ability To Race," Women You Should Know, June 28, 2016, https://womenyoushouldknow.net/dont-call-female-racecar-driver-gender-no-bearing-ability-race/

assistant despite being just as qualified as him for a professor position. Despite the title, she was an equal collaborator, and published her own research in addition to papers co-authored with her husband, Carl. Yet she had difficulty gaining research positions, and the ones she did secure paid little. Carl did what he could and insisted on continuing their collaboration even as supervisors tried to discourage him from doing so.[879] It is notable that Cori and her two predecessors—Marie Curie and her daughter, Irène Joliot-Curie—all won Nobels jointly with their husbands. While many women, including Marie Curie, have won independently, the trend has continued with spouses May-Britt Moser and Edvard I. Moser winning in 2014 and Esther Duflo and Abhijit Banerjee in 2019. It is gratifying to see the results of Carl's investment in Gerty, even as the rest of their profession refused to acknowledge her value.[880]

When Danish physicist and future MacArthur Fellowship winner Lene Hau first applied for National Science Foundation funding for her light-slowing experiments, funders rejected her proposal, claiming her background as a theoretician hadn't prepared her for the difficult experiments she was proposing. She secured private funding instead, which she used to perform some of the most significant experiments in modern physics—literally trapping light.[881]

Emmy Noether was "the most significant creative mathematical genius thus far produced since the higher education of women began," according to Albert Einstein, with whom she collaborated. Yet the combination of being female and Jewish meant that she was discriminated against and underpaid. First, she was held back by rules against women studying at German universities—one of only two women among 986 students, she could only audit classes rather than participate fully, and had to get permission from each professor whose lectures she wanted to

---

[879] Núñez Valdés, Juan, "Gerty Cori, a Life Dedicated to Chemical and Medical Research," *Foundations* vol 3 no 3 (2023): 380–92, https://doi.org/10.3390/foundations3030027
[880] "Nobel Prize-Awarded Couples," Nobel Prize, first published, September 10, 2015, https://www.nobelprize.org/prizes/themes/nobel-prize-awarded-couples/
[881] "Ten things to know about Denmark's Lene Hau," The Local, October 6, 2015, https://www.thelocal.dk/20151006/nobel-prize-ten-things-to-know-about-danish-physicist-lene-hau/

attend. But she overcame and passed her graduation exam in 1903.[882]

Even after completing her PhD, she worked at her alma mater, the University of Erlangen, for seven years without pay. When she was finally granted a title of "unofficial associate professor" at the University of Göttingen, it was at the invitation of David Hilbert and Felix Klein, but when other faculty members objected, she spent four years with her lectures advertised under Hilbert's name. She was still unpaid, supported financially by her family. Even that dubious role was stripped from her in 1933 because she was Jewish.

Moving to the U.S., she became a lecturer and researcher at Bryn Mawr College and the Institute for Advanced Study in Princeton, New Jersey. It was here that she laid the mathematical groundwork for Einstein's general theory of relativity and made major advances in algebra.[883] She later commented of Princeton University that she was not welcome at "the men's university, where nothing female is admitted."[884]

---

[882] Cavna, Michael, "Emmy Noether Google Doodle: Why Einstein called her a 'creative mathematical genius,'" *The Washington Post*, March 23, 2015, https://www.washingtonpost.com/news/comic-riffs/wp/2015/03/23/emmy-noether-google-doodle-why-einstein-called-her-a-creative-mathematical-genius/

[883] "Emmy Noether: Creative Mathematical Genius," San Diego Supercomputer Center, https://www.sdsc.edu/ScienceWomen/noether.html

[884] Dick, Auguste, *Emmy Noether: 1882–1935*, translated by Blocher, H.I. (Birkhäuser, 1981).

YOU TALK TOO MUCH

"Justice is about making sure that being polite is not the same thing as being quiet. In fact, oftentimes, the most righteous thing you can do is shake the table."
—Alexandria Ocasio-Cortez[885]

In response to criticism that its board was dominated by men, Japan's ruling Liberal Democratic Party proposed in 2021 allowing five female lawmakers to join its board meetings as observers—and only observers, as the women would not be allowed to speak. Women make up only two of the party's twelve-member board and three of its twenty-five general council members. The proposal came only a week after former prime minister and LDP member Yoshiro Mori resigned from his position as Tokyo Olympics chief after complaining that women spoke too much at meetings and caused them to go on too long.[886]

While we have fortunately progressed from the scold's bridle[887]—an iron muzzle women were forced to wear in 1500s-1800s Europe—it is still extremely common to police how much women talk, how they speak, and what they say, in ways that are almost never applied equally to men. Though the approaches are much more subtle than literally clamping a woman's mouth shut, women continue to be silenced and ignored.

---

885 Alexandria Ocasio-Cortez, "Oftentimes the most righteous thing you can do is shake the table," Women's March – January 19, 2019, New York, USA
886 Park, Ju-min and Kim, Chang-Ran, "Japan's Ruling Party Invites More Women to Meetings, as Long as They Don't Talk," February 17, 2021, https://www.reuters.com/article/us-japan-politics/japans-ruling-party-wants-more-women-at-meetings-unless-they-talk-idUSKBN2AH08E
887 "Scold's Bridle," The British Library, https://www.bl.uk/collection-items/scolds-bridle

UNCREDITED

Janneke Parrish shared the following story via Twitter on July 20, 2022 (@JannekeParrish):

> I lost my job because I spoke to a man the way men speak to me.
>
> This is why women leave the tech industry.
>
> A couple weeks ago, a male colleague made changes to a project I was running while I was offline that dramatically impacted the scope and timelines. I asked to talk to him to understand why and how we could set up a way to solve issues in the future.
>
> During the meeting, he kept interrupting me and cutting me off. I wasn't getting anywhere, so I just started talking, politely telling him to "please let me finish" every time he tried to jump in. I said my piece, then let him talk.
>
> On Monday, I got called into a meeting with HR, where I was told I had been incredibly rude, that my communication skills were abysmal, and I was being fired.
>
> I was fired because I wouldn't let a man talk over me. This is what it's like to be a woman in the tech industry. It's brutal and it's toxic, and it's where your gender determines your fate before you ever have a chance.[888]

Just the year before, she had been fired after five years at Apple from her role as a program manager on Apple Maps after helping to spearhead the #AppleToo employee movement against alleged patterns of discrimination, racism, and sexism at the company. It came just days after another recently fired Apple employee, Ashley Gjovik, filed a complaint against the company with the National Labor Relations Board. Gjovik had been fired after sharing allegations of harassment.[889]

---

[888] Parrish, Janneke, Twitter, July 21, 2022, https://twitter.com/JannekeParrish/status/1549799287667687424?lang=en

[889] Anguiano, Dani, "Apple Fires Employee Janneke Parrish, Leader of #AppleToo Movement," *The Guardian*, October 16, 2021, https://www.theguardian.com/technology/2021/oct/15/apple-janneke-parrish-fired-appletoo

Even the fundamental nature of women's voices is held against them.[890] "Shrill" is a common criticism, one that was lobbed at Hilary Clinton over and over during her 2016 U.S. presidential campaign.[891] People have been socialised to associate deeper voices with authority—while this applies to all genders, men have a clear natural advantage in this regard.[892]

Clinton was also repeatedly called out for "screaming," when her opponent was objectively a worse offender on that front.[893] "I've been told to stop, and, I quote, 'shouting about gun violence,'" she said at the Democratic National Committee Women's Leadership Forum. "Well, first of all, I'm not shouting. It's just when women talk, some people think we're shouting."[894]

Verbal tics like vocal fry, filler words (like, um and so on), and "upspeak" are perceived as annoying when used by women, yet these same speech patterns go unnoticed in men. "With men, we listen for what they're saying, their point, their assertions. Which is what all of us want others to do when we speak," says linguist Robin Lakoff. "With women, we tend to listen to how they're talking, the words they use, what they emphasize, whether they smile."[895]

In a 2015 *New York Times* opinion piece entitled *Speaking While Female*, an origin story was relayed for television producer Glen Mazzara's "no interruptions" rule, which he found made his team more effective:

> Mazzara noticed that two young female writers were quiet during story meetings. He pulled them aside and encouraged them to speak up more.
> Watch what happens when we do, they replied.

---

890   Simmons-Duffin, Selena, "Talking While Female | Shots | NPR," YouTube, October 25, 2014, https://www.youtube.com/watch?v=XDvPjm10CM0
891   Crockett, Emily, "It Was Hillary Clinton's Big Moment, and All Some Pundits Could Talk about Was Her Voice," Vox, March 15, 2016, https://www.vox.com/2016/3/15/11243422/hillary-clinton-dnc-speech-smile-shouting-voice
892   Fitzsimmons, Caitlin, "Hitting the Right Note for Success," The Sydney Morning Herald, July 25, 2018, https://www.smh.com.au/business/workplace/hitting-the-right-note-for-success-20180725-p4ztla.html
893   Crockett, Emily, "Was Bernie Sanders Sexist toward Hillary Clinton? That's Asking the Wrong Question," Vox, November 5, 2015, https://www.vox.com/identities/2015/11/5/9671830/bernie-sanders-sexism
894   Clinton, Hillary, Speech at the Democratic National Committee Women's Leadership Forum, October 23, 2015, https://www.c-span.org/video/?328919-3/hillary-clinton-democratic-womens-leadership-forum
895   Friedman, Ann, "Can We Just, Like, Get over the Way Women Talk?" The Cut. July 9, 2015, https://www.thecut.com/2015/07/can-we-just-like-get-over-the-way-women-talk.html

Almost every time they started to speak, they were interrupted or shot down before finishing their pitch. When one had a good idea, a male writer would jump in and run with it before she could complete her thought.

As the authors of the piece, Sheryl Sandberg and Adam Grant, note, "When a woman speaks in a professional setting, she walks a tightrope. Either she's barely heard or she's judged as too aggressive. When a man says virtually the same thing, heads nod in appreciation for his fine idea. As a result, women often decide that saying less is more." [896]

Linguistics professor Deborah Tannen also points out that the linguistic styles that girls are raised with, compared to those that boys are raised with, can be interpreted by men as showing a lack of confidence. What one person may see as pausing to collect their thoughts or allowing someone else to speak may be interpreted as hesitation by someone who expects people to jump right into discussion. As Tannen notes, "The research of sociologists, anthropologists, and psychologists observing American children at play has shown that, although both girls and boys find ways of creating rapport and negotiating status, girls tend to learn conversational rituals that focus on the rapport dimension of relationships whereas boys tend to learn rituals that focus on the status dimension." In other words, children are taught from a young age that "bossy" is unlikeable in a girl, while "being a leader" is desirable for a boy.[897]

Women are also more likely than men to be interrupted, regardless of the woman's stature. A 2017 analysis from the Harvard Business Review of U.S. Supreme Court transcripts found that over the previous twelve years, the female justices were more likely to be interrupted by both their male colleagues and the male attorneys appearing before the court. And yes, it was only the male attorneys, which accounted for about ten percent of interruptions, while their female

---

896 Sandberg, Sheryl and Adam Grant, "Opinion | Speaking While Female," *The New York Times*, January 12, 2015, https://www.nytimes.com/2015/01/11/opinion/sunday/speaking-while-female.html
897 Tannen, Deborah, "The Power of Talk: Who Gets Heard and Why," Harvard Business Review, September 1995, https://hbr.org/1995/09/the-power-of-talk-who-gets-heard-and-why

counterparts accounted for zero percent. Almost all of those, fully eight percent of all interruptions, were male attorneys interrupting Justice Sonia Sotomayor, the only woman of colour.[898]

Though women made up, on average, only twenty-four percent of the justices in that time period, they were subject to thirty-two percent of interruptions. Looking back further, the authors noted:

> We found a consistently gendered pattern: In 1990, with one woman on the bench (former Justice Sandra Day O'Connor), 35.7 percent of interruptions were directed at her; in 2002, 45.3 percent were directed at the two female justices (O'Connor and Ruth Bader Ginsburg); in 2015, 65.9 percent of all interruptions on the court were directed at the three female justices on the bench (Ginsburg, Sonia Sotomayor, and Elena Kagan).

Looking for other potential biases, the authors noted that seventy percent of interruptions were of liberals, while only thirty percent were of conservatives, and attorneys interrupt liberal justices more than they do conservative justices. Yet even Sandra Day O'Connor, the only conservative-appointed woman justice at the time of the analysis, was interrupted 2.8 times as often as her male colleagues. Similarly, "Although senior justices do interrupt junior justices more frequently than vice versa, and the difference is statistically significant, gender is approximately 30 times more powerful than seniority."

The authors also noted a pattern among the female justices:

> Time on the court gives women a chance to learn how to avoid being interrupted—by talking more like men. Early in their tenure, female justices tend to frame questions politely, using prefatory words such as "May I ask," "Can I ask," "Excuse me," or the advocate's name. This provides an opportunity for another justice to jump in before the speaker gets to the substance of her question.

---

898   Jacobi, Tonja, and Dylan Schweers, "Female Supreme Court Justices Are Interrupted More by Male Justices and Advocates," Harvard Business Review, April 11, 2017, https://hbr.org/2017/04/female-supreme-court-justices-are-interrupted-more-by-male-justices-and-advocates

We found that women gradually learn to set aside such politeness. All four of the female justices have reduced their tendency to use this polite phrasing. Justice Sotomayor adjusted within just a few months. Justices O'Connor and Ginsburg gradually became less and less polite over decades on the court, eventually using the polite phrases approximately one-third as much as they did initially. Justice Kagan is still learning: She uses polite language more than twice as often as the average man, although half as often as she did in 2010. We do not see a similar trend with the men, because male justices rarely use these polite speech patterns, even when they first enter the court.

Speaking time can also be determined by power—if you're a man. A study from Yale found that male senators with more power—based on their tenure, leadership positions and track record of getting legislation passed—spoke more on the Senate floor than their junior colleagues.[899] Yet for the women senators, there was no such correlation. Interestingly, a University of Washington study found that this has a parallel in personal heterosexual relationships as well—when partners believed their power dynamic was equal, they tended to talk the same amount. In couples where both agreed the man had more power (i.e. made more of the decisions), he talked more, but the man also talked more in relationships where the woman was agreed to be more powerful.[900]

The Yale project leader, Professor Victoria L. Brescoll wanted to investigate why the women senators were staying quiet regardless of power, so she shifted focus. Asking business professionals to gauge the competence of chief executives, she found that the men who spoke more received ten percent higher competence ratings. But when women did, both men and women gave them fourteen percent lower ratings. In the *New York Times* piece, Adam Grant noted multiple settings

---

899 Sandberg, Sheryl and Adam Grant, "Opinion | Speaking While Female," *The New York Times*, January 12, 2015, https://www.nytimes.com/2015/01/11/opinion/sunday/speaking-while-female.html
900 Donnelly, Erin, "Language Ideologies: Do Women Really Talk More than Men?" The Pimsleur Language Blog, November 19, 2018, https://blog.pimsleur.com/2018/11/19/language-ideologies-do-women-really-talk-more-than-men/

where he found men who contributed ideas that increased revenue and spoke up more saw significantly higher performance evaluations. Women who did the same saw no improvement in managers' perceptions of them.

Women are also penalised by the myth and perception that women talk more than men.[901] Australian researcher Dale Spender audio – and video-recorded university classroom discussions. She found that regardless of the students' gender ratio, men always talked more in terms of both words spoken and minutes of speaking, even when the instructor was deliberately encouraging women's participation. And the men had no idea they were doing it—when Spender had students estimate who talked more in a given conversation, men perceived the discussion as gender-balanced when women spoke only fifteen percent of the time, and as being dominated by women when they spoke for thirty percent of the time.[902] In fact, a study of U.S. state legislatures found that when the proportion of women legislators increased, their male colleagues tended to take up even more talk time than before.[903]

It's not just talking, either—there is also a cognitive bias that overestimates women's presence and participation because the default baseline is that there should be fewer women. This means that when there are an equal number of men and women, the women appear to be over-represented. In 2016, *Stuff You Missed in History Class* podcast co-host Tracey V. Wilson was tired of audience members complaining that the podcast was women-centred, so she ran the numbers: since the podcast had started in March 2013, twenty-one percent of episodes were about women, thirty-four percent were not gender-specific and forty-five percent were about men. Her supposedly female-centric podcast had twice as many men than women.[904]

Women do this as well—in 2015, researchers asked almost 1,800 executives to

---

901 Cutler, Anne, and Donia R. Scott, "Speaker Sex and Perceived Apportionment of Talk," *Applied Psycholinguistics* vol 11 no 3 (1990): 253–72. https://doi.org/10.1017/s0142716400008882
902 Spender, Dale, *Man Made Language* (Pandora, 1980).
903 Donnelly, Erin, "Language Ideologies: Do Women Really Talk More than Men?" The Pimsleur Language Blog, November 19, 2018, https://blog.pimsleur.com/2018/11/19/language-ideologies-do-women-really-talk-more-than-men/
904 Layton, Julia, "How 17 Equals 49.6: The Amazing Multiplying Women," HowStuffWorks, June 16, 2016, https://health.howstuffworks.com/mental-health/human-nature/perception/how-17-equals-496-the-amazing-multiplying-women.htm

estimate the percentage of women among CEOs of large companies. The average man said twenty-five, while the average woman said twenty-one. The answer is eight.[905] Virginia Valian, Distinguished Professor of psychology and linguistics at Hunter College and the CUNY Graduate Center, believes this is a cognitive error – in spaces where there used to be no women, or biases mean the person expects to see no women, even a few seem like too many.

One of the effects of this is under-representation in media—not just of the named, speaking characters, but the extras as well. Studies from the Geena Davis Institute on Gender in Media found that only seventeen percent of the average "crowd" in G-rated movies were women and girls,[906] and the average "workforce" in top-grossing films were only twenty-three percent female.[907] As Davis herself has noted:

> My theory is that since all anybody has seen, when they are growing up, is this big imbalance—that the movies that they've watched are about, let's say, 5 to 1, as far as female presence is concerned—that's what starts to look normal. And let's think about [it]—in different segments of society, 17 percent of cardiac surgeons are women; 17 percent of tenured professors are women. It just goes on and on. And isn't that strange that that's also the percentage of women in crowd scenes in movies? What if we're actually training people to see that ratio as normal so that when you're an adult, you don't notice?[908]

In her memoir *Bossypants*, comedian Tina Fey recalled an early memory of her long-time collaborator Amy Poehler:

> Amy Poehler was new to SNL and we were all crowded into the

---

905 Ibid.
906 Smith, Stacy, Marc Choueiti, and Katherine Pieper, "Gender Bias without Borders an Investigation of Female Characters in Popular Films across 11 Countries," https://seejane.org/wp-content/uploads/gender-bias-without-borders-full-report.pdf
907 Smith, Stacy L. and Cook, Crystal Allene, "Gender Stereotypes: An Analysis of Popular Films and TV," Annenberg School for Communication and The Geena Davis Institute on Gender in Media, 2008, http://seejane.org/wp-content/uploads/GDIGM_Gender_Stereotypes.pdf
908 Lyden, Jacki, "Casting Call: Hollywood Needs More Women," NPR. June 30, 2013, https://www.npr.org/transcripts/197390707

seventeenth-floor writers' room, waiting for the Wednesday read-through to start. There were always a lot of noisy "comedy bits" going on in that room. Amy was in the middle of some such nonsense with Seth Meyers across the table, and she did something vulgar as a joke. I can't remember what it was exactly, except it was dirty and loud and "unladylike."

Jimmy Fallon, who was arguably the star of the show at the time, turned to her and in a faux-squeamish voice said: "Stop that! It's not cute! I don't like it."

Amy dropped what she was doing, went black in the eyes for a second, and wheeled around on him. "I don't fucking care if you like it." Jimmy was visibly startled. Amy went right back to enjoying her ridiculous bit ...

With that exchange, a cosmic shift took place. Amy made it clear that she wasn't there to be cute. She wasn't there to play wives and girlfriends in the boys' scenes. She was there to do what she wanted to do and she did not fucking care if you like it ...

I think of this whenever someone says to me, "Jerry Lewis says women aren't funny," or Christopher Hitchens says women aren't funny," or "Rick Fenderman says women aren't funny ... Do you have anything to say to that?"

Yes. We don't fucking care if you like it.[909]

BEYOND MANSPLAINING

> "If she'd been a man, she'd be a humorist and memoirist.
> But she was a woman, so she was a mommy blogger."
> —Lyz Lenz, about Heather Armstrong AKA Dooce[910]

Coined by friends of physics professor and astronomer Nicole Gugliucci,

---

909   Fey, Tina, *Bossypants* (Little Brown, 2011).
910   Lenz, Lyz, "Heather Armstrong, a.k.a. Dooce, was real and raw. And we loved her," *The Washington Post*, May 10, 2023, https://www.washingtonpost.com/opinions/2023/05/10/heather-armstrong-dooce-death-suicide/

"hepeating," as she explained in a tweet on November 22, 2017, is when a woman suggests an idea and that idea is ignored, but then a man says the same thing and it is met with praise and support for "his" idea.[911] There's also bropropriation, which is just a slang portmanteau for a man stealing a woman's idea. This may also be combined with "manterrupting," where a man interrupts or talks over a woman while she is making a point. Though it should be noted, research shows that both men and women interrupt women more, and women are more likely to interrupt other women than they are to interrupt men.[912]

In 2020, Australian prime minister Scott Morrison made headlines when he interrupted senior government minister Anne Ruston, a member of his own party. While men interrupt women all the time, the context was too ironic—Ruston was just eight words into answering a journalist's question on whether sexism in the government had improved.[913] As Calla Wahlquist, an editor for *The Guardian Australia*, commented, "Nothing says respect for women like talking over a woman when a question was directly addressed to her."[914]

One tactic women have used to combat this in workplaces is amplification. In 2016, Juliet Eilperin reported on the strategy utilised by female staffers in the Obama White House:

> When President Obama took office, two-thirds of his top aides were men. Women complained of having to elbow their way into important meetings. And when they got in, their voices were sometimes ignored.
>
> So female staffers adopted a meeting strategy they called "amplification": When a woman made a key point, other women would repeat it, giving credit to its author. This forced the men in the room to recognize the

---

911 Dodgson, Lindsay, "Men Are Getting the Credit for Women's Work through Something Called 'Hepeating' — Here's What It Means," *Business Insider*, Originally posted in 2017, updated March 8, 2018, https://www.businessinsider.com/what-is-hepeating-2017-9

912 Robb, Alice, "Women Get Interrupted More—Even by Other Women," The New Republic, May 14, 2014, https://newrepublic.com/article/117757/gender-language-differences-women-get-interrupted-more

913 Gillespie, Eden, "A Case of #Mansplaining? PM's Interruption of Female MP Hits Global Headlines," SBS News, November 11, 2020, https://www.sbs.com.au/news/the-feed/article/a-case-of-mansplaining-pms-interruption-of-female-mp-hits-global-headlines/wg5xg02et

914 Wahlquist, Calla, Twitter, November 10, 2020, https://twitter.com/callapilla/status/1325979364345868288

contribution—and denied them the chance to claim the idea as their own.

"We just started doing it, and made a purpose of doing it. It was an everyday thing," said one former Obama aide who requested anonymity to speak frankly. Obama noticed, she and others said, and began calling more often on women and junior aides.

This mutual support likely contributed to the fact that, during his second term, there were as many women as men filling the top spots.[915]

The women of the Obama White House were far from the first group to make a deliberate effort to amplify each other's voices. Decades earlier, the women of the 1970s, San Francisco technological commune Project One were having a similar issue, as recounted in Claire Lisa Evans's 2018 book *Broad Band: The Untold Story of the Women Who Made the Internet*:

At their weekly building-wide consensus meetings, the women of Resource One were used to being talked over... They came up with a solution. Every time one of them was interrupted, the others would interject. They worked out the strategy ahead of time... "We would say, 'Wait a minute, I didn't hear what so-and-so said.' Or we would say, 'Wait, let her finish.' We would do that for each other," Sherry (Reson) remembers. "You're countering dominance behavior. And sometimes all it takes to do that is to wake somebody up."[916]

Men are often unaware that this is even happening, whether they are the ones doing it or others are. Business executive Caroline Turner recalled,

A few years ago, I told my boss, the CEO, that women often experience this – and that it undermines their sense of being included and valued. He responded that he didn't think this occurs. At the very next senior staff meeting, it did occur. When Bill repeated the very idea I had

---

915 Crockett, Emily, "The Amazing Tool That Women in the White House Used to Fight Gender Bias," Vox, September 14, 2016, https://www.vox.com/2016/9/14/12914370/white-house-obama-women-gender-bias-amplification
916 Claire Lisa Evans, *Broad Band: The Untold Story of the Women Who Made the Internet* (Penguin, 2020).

suggested three minutes earlier, I simply made eye contact with my boss. He looked a bit wide-eyed, but said quickly, "Bill, it looks like you agree with what Caroline said." Now aware of this phenomenon, my boss is now able to validate other women whose ideas are "stolen." [917]

She also observed:

> The masculine style of influencing others is to use commanding language. A typical man will tell the team, "Here is what we need to do." The feminine style of influencing is to persuade. A woman may tell her team, "I have an idea that I want you to consider." Or she may phrase her idea as a question, for example, "What do you think of this idea?" The masculine style is associated with leadership and power. The feminine style is not.

---

917 Turner, Caroline, "Women's Ideas: Do Men Intentionally Steal Them?" Forbes, December 3, 2012, https://www.forbes.com/sites/womensmedia/2012/12/03/womens-ideas-do-men-intentionally-steal-them/?sh=1b45e3eb7b79

BEHAVIOURAL DOUBLE-STANDARD

"When a man gives his opinion, he's a man; when a woman gives her opinion, she's a bitch."
—Bette Davis

One day when I was in my mid-twenties, I was working on a spreadsheet at my desk when something hit me in the face. The IT consultant working on a colleague's computer at a neighbouring desk had decided I looked too "serious," and his solution was to make a large paper airplane and throw it at my face. This man did not even know my name but felt entitled to throw a pointed projectile at me. It hit me right below the eye, making me wonder what would have happened if it had been a millimetre higher.

This is an example of "resting bitch face," wherein if a woman has a neutral expression, she is seen as unhappy or even angry. In other words, if a woman is not actively smiling, she is perceived negatively, to the point that men will tell her to smile even if the two people don't know each other. As comedian Hannah Gadsby observed in her special *Douglas*, "Only women have resting bitch face. Men simply have very important thoughts you'd best not interrupt them having."[918] Indeed, I have never heard of men being expected to consciously control their facial expressions on a regular basis except in very specific circumstances, such as very large men (particularly non-Caucasians) who smile a lot because they are aware their size makes them physically intimidating and they don't want to scare people. And I doubt any strangers are telling those men en masse to smile.

---

918   Hannah Gadsby, 2020, Douglas, Netflix.

This policing of women's facial expressions is an example of how women are constantly expected to expend effort for the comfort of others, including those they don't even know. It starts from a very young age, where there is less tolerance for girls to misbehave while "boys will be boys." This is one of the reasons girls are under-diagnosed for conditions like autism—the pressure for girls to "mask" (i.e. act neurotypical) is greater because the pressure for girls to behave in certain ways is greater.[919] Data from the Longitudinal Study of Australian Children found that even among two – and three-years-olds, the boys were ten percent more likely to demonstrate "externalising behaviours," like aggression and destruction. Girls, meanwhile, were more likely to show "internalising behaviours," like anxiety.[920] The girls had already been taught to keep their stress inside, where it only hurts them, rather than acting out in ways that impacted others.

Meanwhile, gendered language means that the same behaviours in men are "assertive" and "leadership qualities," while in a women they're "bossy," a "control freak," or the ever-popular "bitch." U.S. Senator, former prosecutor, and future vice president Kamala Harris was described as "hysterical" in 2017 after she calmly but pointedly questioned an uncooperative attorney general during a Senate hearing. As Late Show host Stephen Colbert later queried, "Sen. Kamala Harris: 'Hysterical' or 'A Woman Doing Her Job?'"[921]

In 2011, when the newspaper industry was in crisis, Jill Abramson was the first woman named editor of *The New York Times*. In 2014, she was abruptly fired, with a staff member commenting "The unbelievable thing is that there actually is no 'cause' for this—no single thing, nothing." Several weeks earlier, she had reportedly found out that both her pay and pension benefits as executive director and, previously, managing editor, were less than those of the male editor she had replaced in both jobs, though the publisher denies that. As an article in *New York Magazine*

---

919   Wood-Downie, Henry, Bonnie Wong, Hanna Kovshoff, William Mandy, Laura Hull, and Julie A. Hadwin, "Sex/Gender Differences in Camouflaging in Children and Adolescents with Autism," *Journal of Autism and Developmental Disorders* vol 51 no 4 (2020), https://doi.org/10.1007/s10803-020-04615-z
920   Gehan Roberts, "Nature and Nurture: Why Do Boys and Girls Behave Differently?" The Conversation, March 4, 2012, https://theconversation.com/nature-and-nurture-why-do-boys-and-girls-behave-differently-2920
921   Colbert, Stephen, "Sen. Kamala Harris: 'Hysterical' or 'a Woman Doing Her Job?'" The Late Show with Stephen Colbert (YouTube), June 15, 2017, https://www.youtube.com/watch?v=DYw7MGYmUoQ

commented, "in Abramson's case, eight Pulitzers did not speak loudly enough. Revenue growth did not speak loudly enough. Successful new digital products did not speak loudly enough." [922] Criticisms of Abramson included that she was "pushy" and brusque, yet she was replaced by Dean Baquet, a man who admits he has gotten so angry in the office that he punched holes in the newsroom walls. Yet according to a *Politico* article on the topic, even that was her fault: "If Baquet had burst out of the office in a huff, many said, it was likely because Abramson had been unreasonable."[923] Even as they lauded her with comments like "She's an incredible talent. There's no question she deserves to be where she is," she was criticized for not being likeable enough. "It's frustrating because she is such a smart person. When Jill is on her game, she is one of the smartest people I've ever met," one staff member said. "But she's not a naturally charismatic person—she's not approachable."

Following the 1964 Tokyo Olympics, Australian swimmer Dawn Fraser found herself facing a ten-year ban from swimming, courtesy of the Australian Amateur Swimming Association. She was arrested and accused of stealing an Olympic flag from the emperor's palace, though she was released when it was revealed the emperor had gifted her the flag as a souvenir. Given the Australian pride in their supposed "larrikin spirit," it seems ridiculous to ban a swimmer for a decade, effectively ending her career, over what could have been a harmless prank. It's also noteworthy that earlier in the Games, she had angered sponsors by refusing to wear the provided swimsuit, as her own was more comfortable. Her mother had also died only weeks before, in a car accident where Fraser was also injured. Fraser was the first swimmer to win individual gold medals for the same event at three successive Olympics (100 metres freestyle, in 1956, 1960 and 1964). She was named the Australian of the Year in 1964 and was inducted into the International Swimming Hall of Fame in 1965.[924]

---

922 Friedman, Ann, "Jill Abramson Will Never Know Why She Got Fired," The Cut, May 15, 2014, https://www.thecut.com/2014/05/jill-abramson-will-never-know-why-she-got-fired.html

923 Byers, Dylan, "Turbulence at The Times," Politico, April 23, 2013, https://www.politico.com/story/2013/04/new-york-times-turbulence-090544

924 Masters, Roy, "Dawn Fraser and the Case of the Unknown Olympic Flag Heist," The Sydney Morning Herald, February 11, 2022, https://www.smh.com.au/sport/dawn-fraser-and-the-case-of-the-unknown-olympic-flag-heist-20220201-p59sya.html

Almost thirty years earlier, American swimmer Eleanor G. Holm got drunk at a party aboard the *SS Manhattan* en route to the 1936 Olympics. She was promptly expelled from the team by U.S. Olympic Committee President Avery Brundage. Holm maintained that the real reason was a personal grudge by Brundage, later telling another athlete that Brundage had propositioned her and she turned him down. Her version of events:

> This chaperone came up to me and told me it was time to go to bed. God, it was about 9 o'clock, and who wanted to go down in that basement to sleep anyway? So I said to her: 'Oh, is it really bedtime? Did you make the Olympic team or did I?' I had had a few glasses of Champagne. So she went to Brundage and complained that I was setting a bad example for the team, and they got together and told me the next morning that I was fired. I was heartbroken.

Holm had previously competed at the 1928 and 1932 Olympics, winning a gold medal in 1932. She had been the favourite to win again in her event, and her teammates tried—unsuccessfully—to get her reinstated. She did not swim competitively again after her expulsion, though she was inducted into the International Swimming Hall of Fame in 1966.[925]

Meanwhile, for a genuine international incident, look no further than Ryan Lochte and four other U.S. male swimmers fabricating a story about being robbed at gunpoint at the Rio de Janeiro Olympics in 2016. Unlike Fraser, Lochte did have to go to court, and the case was dismissed because he had not actually filed a false police report, merely lied about it on international television. Video evidence later showed Lochte and the other swimmers had actually drunkenly vandalised a gas station bathroom, then got pissy when confronted by security guards. He was

---

[925] Goldstein, Richard, "Eleanor Holm Whalen, 30's Swimming Champion, Dies," *The New York Times*, February 2, 2004, https://www.nytimes.com/2004/02/02/nyregion/eleanor-holm-whalen-30-s-swimming-champion-dies.html

only suspended for ten months by USA Swimming.[926]

Almost sixty years after Fraser's incident and at the next Tokyo Olympics, audiences saw a startling juxtaposition. Sha'Carri Richardson, an African American runner, was banned from the Olympics by USA Track & Field for testing positive for cannabis. Apart from the fact that cannabis was legal where she was and she was dealing with the recent death of her mother, the idea that anyone could argue it's a performance-enhancing drug is just laughable.[927] Then it emerged that fencing alternate Alen Hadzic was credibly accused by six different women of sexual assault. He then had the sheer cheek to whine about losing out on fun experiences that he felt he had "earned" when he was forced to stay at a hotel away from the Olympic Village as part of USA Fencing's "safety plan" to protect the female athletes from him. More than a year later, there were still no actual consequences for him, and he was still allowed to continue competing.[928]

Moreover, Richardson's qualifying time when she won the U.S. Olympic Trials 100-metre dash was 10.86 seconds—had she matched that in the Olympic finals, it would have placed her fourth. Meanwhile, Hadzic wasn't even on the actual competition team—he was just an alternate who never even competed, on a men's team that didn't medal in a single event. If we're really meant to give athletes more latitude based on their performance, which multiple commentators implied in regards to Lochte, Richardson was clearly the more valuable athlete.

Race was, of course, also a factor. Many people pointed out the hypocrisy that, after Russian figure skater Kamila Valieva won gold, it turned out she tested positive for multiple performance-enhancing drugs, including trimetazidine (TMZ), which is banned. Her attorney claimed she had somehow accidentally ingested her grandfather's medication, supposedly by sharing a glass of water with her

---

926 Donnella, Leah, "Roundup: Smart Thoughts on Ryan Lochte and White Privilege," NPR, August 19, 2016, https://www.npr.org/sections/codeswitch/2016/08/19/490629815/roundup-smart-thoughts-on-ryan-lochte-and-white-privilege
927 Lawrence, Andrew, "Sha'Carri Richardson, Alen Hadzic and Our Unending Forgiveness for White Male Athletes," *The Guardian*, July 26, 2021, https://www.theguardian.com/sport/2021/jul/26/shacarri-richardson-alen-hadzic-olympics-suspensions-fencing
928 Sacks, Brianna, "An Elite Fencer under Investigation for Sexual Assault for More than a Year Is Still Allowed to Compete," BuzzFeed News, July 9, 2022, https://www.buzzfeednews.com/article/briannasacks/fencer-alen-hadzic-no-contact-directive

grandfather, which the Court of Arbitration for Sport somehow bought and allowed her to continue competing. Never mind that TMZ comes in pill form and showed up in high enough quantities to be detected in a test.[929] In 2019, African American hammer thrower Gwen Berry faced outsized consequences after daring to raise a fist during the national anthem at the Pan Am Games. Her protest gesture led to a year-long probation and tens of thousands of dollars in lost sponsorship.[930]

In 2003, Columbia Business School professors took a case study about a venture capitalist named Heidi Roizen and, for half of their classes, changed her name to "Howard." A survey of the students found that, although both were considered equally competent, students found Heidi less humble and more power hungry and self-promoting than Howard. None of them wanted to work for or hire Heidi, but all thought Howard would make a great colleague.[931]

And even in the midst of a war, women are expected to act "ladylike." In August 2022, months into the Russian invasion of her country, Ukrainian first lady Olena Zelenska was on the cover of *Vogue*. Seated on a set of stairs, the pants-clad Zelenska is leaning forward, forearms resting on thighs that are a little more than shoulder width apart. As she told *Vogue* "We have no doubt we will prevail," morons on the internet chided her because she wasn't sitting "like a girl." Other critiques, including from her own people, were that her hair was too nicely done, her eyes looked tired, and countless other minutiae.[932] She was simultaneously accused of war propaganda for doing an interview and trivializing the war for doing it with *Vogue* and having an accompanying photoshoot with Annie Leibovitz. In response,

---

929   Romo, Vanessa, "What Is Trimetazidine, the Drug Found in Russian Skater Kamila Valieva's System?" NPR, February 15, 2022, https://www.npr.org/2022/02/15/1081008770/what-is-trimetazidine-the-drug-found-in-russian-skater-kamila-valievas-system

930   Associated Press, "Gwen Berry, disciplined for raising fist at Pan-Am Games, says USOPC statement on inequality insincere," ESPN, June 4, 2020, https://www.espn.com/olympics/trackandfield/story/_/id/29264606/gwen-berry-disciplined-raising-fist-pan-games-says-usopc-statement-inequality-insincere

931   Symons, Lesley and Herminia Ibarra, "What the Scarcity of Women in Business Case Studies Really Looks Like," Harvard Business Review, April 28, 2014, https://hbr.org/2014/04/what-the-scarcity-of-women-in-business-case-studies-really-looks-like

932   Westerman, Ashley, "Ukraine's First Lady Posed for 'Vogue' and Sparked Discussion on How to #SitLikeAGirl," NPR, August 18, 2022, https://www.npr.org/2022/08/18/1115127748/ukraine-first-lady-olena-zelenska-vogue

women around the world shared their own images of what it means to #SitLikeA-Girl, including Kyiv resident Polina Karabach, who perhaps best summed up the situation: "I think that we should stop paying attention to this and start focusing on what's important— like doing what you can to support Ukraine in the war."

NO BUSINESS LIKE SHOW BUSINESS

> "It's a shame to call somebody a 'diva' simply because they work harder than everybody else."
> —Jennifer Lopez

The trope of a woman being "difficult" or "a diva" for expressing her opinions or standing up for herself often comes up when women are being asked to do something a man would never be asked to do. Actress and director Brie Larson recalled, "There were many times that I would go into auditions and a casting director would say, 'It's really great. Really love what you're doing, but we'd love you to come back with a jean miniskirt and high heels,'" she told reporters after winning her Oscar for Best Actress in 2016. "Those were always moments of a real fork in the road, because there's no reason for me to show up in a jean miniskirt and heels other than the fact that you want to create some fantasy, and you want to have this moment that you can reject."[933]

Actress Emmy Rossum reports a director asking her to show up in a bikini for a project where there were no swimsuit or nudity scenes. This was in 2017, when she had already achieved significant success, yet she still got a call from her agent: "'I'm so embarrassed to make this call, but there's a big movie and they're going to offer it to you. They really love your work on the show. But the director wants you

---

[933] Sieczkowski, Cavan, "Brie Larson On Being Asked To Wear A Miniskirt To An Audition," March 1, 2016, Huffington Post, https://www.huffpost.com/entry/brie-larson-sexism-miniskirt_n_56d5aea8e4b03260bf781755

to come into his office in a bikini. There's no audition. That's all you have to do.'"[934]

Meanwhile, actresses like Maggie Gyllenhaal report being told they're too old for Hollywood when they hit their mid-30s,[935] *The Handmaid's Tale* star Elisabeth Moss had a TV project rejected for being "too female"[936] and Kate Bosworth observes, "The one thing I heard on every single film—and I'm telling you there isn't an exception—whenever I'm up for a role, really no matter how big or small, the answer that I always get from anyone who's casting me, 'We have to cast the guy first.' Every single one, there is no exception—unless I'm producing it."[937]

In an interview with Rolling Stone, actress Emma Stone noted:

> There are times in the past, making a movie, when I've been told that I'm hindering the process by bringing up an opinion or an idea. I hesitate to make it about being a woman, but there have been times when I've improvised, they've laughed at my joke and then given it to my male co-star. Given my joke away. Or it's been me saying, 'I really don't think this line is gonna work,' and being told, 'Just say it, just say it, if it doesn't work we'll cut it out'. And they didn't cut it out, and it really didn't work![938]

Actress and director Olivia Wilde has observed, "It's really hard to get stories made about women, that are about women, not just women being obsessed with men or supporting men. And it's really hard to get men to be a part of films that are about women in a leading role."[939]

---

[934] Wallace, Francesca, "Emmy Rossum was asked to audition in a bikini for movie with no bikini scene," June 17, 2017, Vogue, https://www.vogue.com.au/celebrity/news/emmy-rossum-was-asked-to-audition-in-a-bikini-for-movie-with-no-bikini-scene/news-story/960db71c92b08c714a6b69a07d219bb5

[935] Child, Ben, "Maggie Gyllenhaal: At 37 I was 'too old' for role opposite 55-year-old man," *The Guardian*, May 21, 2015, https://www.theguardian.com/film/2015/may/21/maggie-gyllenhaal-too-old-hollywood

[936] "Elisabeth Moss reveals sexist execs slammed her ideas as 'too female,'" June 2, 2017, *Marie Claire*, https://www.marieclaire.co.uk/news/celebrity-news/elisabeth-moss-sexism-511407

[937] Fredette, Meagan, "Kate Bosworth Opens Up About The Brazen Sexism In Movie Casting," September 16, 2017, Refinery29, https://www.refinery29.com/en-us/2017/09/172392/kate-bosworth-sexism-movies-2017.

[938] Shoard, Catherine, "Emma Stone: directors gave my improv jokes to male co-stars," December 22, 2016, *The Guardian*, https://www.theguardian.com/film/2016/dec/22/emma-stone-directors-male-co-stars-la-la-land-sexism

[939] Edwards, Tanya, "Olivia Wilde Talks Sexism in Hollywood, Nails It as Usual," February 26, 2014, Glamour. https://www.glamour.com/story/olivia-wilde-talks-sexism-in-h

WHEN WOMEN DO SUCCEED, THEY'RE EXCLUDED

"I'm tough, ambitious, and I know exactly what I want. If that makes me a bitch, okay."
—Madonna

In 1931, a teenaged pitcher struck out both Babe Ruth and Lou Gehrig in one game. A few days later, she was out of a job. Jackie Mitchell had been hired earlier that year to the Chattanooga Lookouts Class AA minor league baseball team, in part as a marketing gimmick by the team owner. But when the Lookouts played an exhibition game against the New York Yankees, seventeen-year-old Mitchell got her shot after another pitcher's poor performance in the first inning. Ruth was her very first opponent—after he struck out, he reportedly stormed back to the dugout in a huff. She then struck out Gehrig, and Tony Lazzeri got a walk, before she was pulled from the mound and not allowed to pitch the rest of the game. A few days later, baseball commissioner Kenesaw Mountain Landis voided her contract, proclaiming women unfit to play because the game was "too strenuous." Presumably, he was referring to the strain on the men she defeated.[940]

This is a prime example of a trend where women are allowed to play with the men, but as soon as they outperform them, the women suddenly find themselves excluded. For twenty years, men and women competed together in skeet shooting at the Olympics. But after Zhang Shan won the gold in 1992, the International Shooting Union suddenly felt it necessary to prevent women from shooting against the

---

940 Carson, Dan, "Throwback Thursday: Female Ace Jackie Mitchell Strikes out Babe Ruth," Bleacher Report, April 3, 2015, https://bleacherreport.com/articles/2418403-throwback-thursday-female-ace-jackie-mitchell-strikes-out-babe-ruth

men, with a separate women's event established for the 2000 Olympics.[941] Ninety years earlier, ice skater Madge Syers entered the all-male figure skating world championships and placed second. Officials promptly banned women from the championships until a ladies event was organized in 1905.[942] Similarly, after bobsledder Katharin Dewey piloted her four-person team to victory at the U.S. national championships in 1940, women were summarily banned from the sport, a situation that would last decades.[943] From 1905 to 1912, Joan Newton Cuneo found success in auto races against both male and female competitors until the racing associations decided not to let girls into their proverbial clubhouses anymore. Banned from racing, she turned her attention to setting speed records instead.[944]

In some cases, it's too late because "one got in," but the gatekeepers can make damn sure to keep any others from following them in. Take as a case study a tale of two doctors, both named Elizabeth.

Elizabeth Blackwell's interest in medicine was reportedly sparked when a friend who had been ill remarked that she did not think she would have suffered so, had her doctor been a woman. She applied to several medical schools in 1847 and was rejected by all but one due to her gender. The one outlier, Geneva Medical College, had made the mistake of putting the issue to a vote by the student body of young men so that the faculty would not have to take responsibility for the decision. Reputedly thinking it was a joke, the 150 students voted unanimously to let her in. On January 23, 1849, Blackwell became the first woman to earn a medical degree in the U.S., graduating at the top of her class.[945] Yet her success did not open the doors of GMC for other women, even her own sister. As biographer

---

941 "ZHANG Shan: The only female shooter to win gold in a mixed competition," Olympics, https://olympics.com/en/news/zhang-shan-the-only-female-shooter-to-win-gold-in-a-mixed-competition
942 Dmukhovskaya, Marina, "Look to the past: Madge Syers, the first woman to compete at a figure skating World Championships," Olympics, December 15, 2021, https://olympics.com/en/news/look-to-the-past-madge-syers
943 Prewitt, Alex, "Kaillie Humphries and Elana Meyers Taylor Steer the Way for Women in Bobsled," Sports Illustrated, February 13, 2022, https://www.si.com/olympics/2022/02/13/kaillie-humphries-elana-meyers-taylor-monobob-women-bobsled-legacy
944 "Joan Newton Cuneo Sickman," National Park Service, Last updated March 1, 2023, https://www.nps.gov/kewe/learn/an-immigrant-story-joan-newton-cuneo.htm
945 Nimura, Janice P., *The Doctors Blackwell: How Two Pioneering Sisters Brought Medicine to Women—and Women to Medicine* (W.W. Norton & Company. 2021).

Janice Nimura, author of the book *The Doctors Blackwell* notes, "Geneva College itself, having given Elizabeth a degree at the top of the class, politely but firmly said, 'Emily, we are not interested in having you here as a student. We've had enough with women medical students.'"[946] Instead, Emily graduated from Cleveland Medical College, which is now Case Western Reserve University.

Across the Atlantic, Elizabeth Garrett Anderson became the first woman in Britain to qualify as a physician and surgeon through a roundabout way. In 1865, after years of private study, she took the exam to be licensed through the Society of Apothecaries—after spending years fighting to be allowed to do so, with her father threatening to sue. After she passed and was officially qualified as a doctor, a ban was immediately placed on women. She went on to learn French so that she could study at the University of Paris, finally earning her medical degree in 1870. She went on to establish the New Hospital for Women, which later became the London School of Medicine for Women, of which she was appointed dean. It was not until more than ten years after Anderson used her loophole that the new Medical Act was passed, allowing British medical authorities to licence all qualified applicants regardless of gender.[947]

Keeping women out of med school is by no means a thing of the past. In 2018, a government investigation revealed that at least ten Japanese medical schools manipulated admissions in part to keep high-scoring women out, with tampering extending as far back as 2006. The *Yomiuri Shimbun* newspaper quoted an unnamed source saying officials at the prestigious Tokyo Medical University had a "silent understanding" to reduce the number of female students because they believe "Many female students who graduate end up leaving the actual medical practice to give birth and raise children." The idea that women would, en masse, go to the trouble of attending medical school only to throw their entire career away is ludicrous, and particularly ironic given Japan's drastically low birth rate

---

946 Davies, Dave, "'Doctors Blackwell' Tells the Story of 2 Pioneering Sisters Who Changed Medicine," NPR, January 19, 2021, https://www.npr.org/sections/health-shots/2021/01/19/958319302/doctors-blackwell-tells-the-story-of-2-pioneering-sisters-who-changed-medicine

947 "Elizabeth Garrett Anderson," Science Museum Group Collection, https://collection.sciencemuseumgroup.org.uk/people/cp119599/elizabeth-garrett-anderson

in recent years. Juntendo University claimed it set the bar higher for women to offset the supposed advantage women would have in the interview portion, on the assumption they were better at communicating than men—as though communication is not an important skill for doctors to have.[948] In 2022, the first year the exams were held after the revelations, 13.6 percent of female candidates passed exams at eighty-one medical schools compared to 13.5 percent of men. When the women's results were artificially deflated, the men consistently did better, by up to two percent. As of 2018, only 21.9 percent of the country's doctors were women.[949]

Even when women as a group are proven to be capable, they are still often excluded. One of the more egregious instances can be found in the story of the Mercury 13 astronauts that never were. In the 1960s, American women were explicitly excluded from candidacy for astronaut training, even as the Soviets sent Valentina Tereshkova up on June 16, 1963.

In 1960, the privately funded Women in Space Program had thirteen women, all experienced pilots, undergo the same medical testing as NASA conducted on the Mercury 7—the first American astronauts. The project was spearheaded by Dr. Randolph Lovelace, who had helped devise America's first astronaut tests and served as chairman of NASA's Life Sciences Committee for Project Mercury. The eighty-seven tests intentionally pushed candidates to extremes, but the women didn't baulk. In fact, Wally Funk—the youngest at age twenty-two—participated in additional testing. During the isolation test, she did better than any other candidate, male or female, floating in a dark soundproof room for more than 10.5 hours until they ended the test—not her.

There was also the weight consideration—every gram matters in space flight, and women on average weigh less and consume less food and oxygen than men. In fact, one of NASA's requirements for the men was that they had to be less than 5 feet 11 inches (1.8 m) tall, because the craft could not accommodate anyone taller.

---

[948] "Medical Schools 'Rigged Women's Results,'" BBC, December 14, 2018, https://www.bbc.com/news/world-asia-46568975

[949] McCurry, Justin, "Women Outperform Men in Japanese Medical School Entrance Exams, Years after Testing Scandal," *The Guardian*, February 22, 2022, https://www.theguardian.com/world/2022/feb/22/women-outperform-men-in-japanese-medical-school-entrance-exams-years-after-testing-scandal

Even though the women passed all the same tests, and often out-performed the men, the report was disregarded and women were not accepted for astronaut training until 1978.[950] Sally Ride, the first American woman in space, broke that barrier in 1983—more than twenty years after the Mercury 13 proved themselves.

Officially, it was not a "no women" rule—the requirements included that all candidates must have military experience as fighter pilots. Not just pilots, as many women had flown for the military during World War II, but test pilots, a role women had been denied. It's a roundabout form of sexism seen elsewhere in history—placing unnecessary barriers that just happen to exclude women.

Computer scientist Helen Vorrath observed that when she first got into the field in 1966, "Because it was just based on aptitude tests, if women were interested in getting into the industry, they were as likely to get in as men were. There was no discrimination at the gate. When I got my first job, there were six people working on a project to write a payroll for Shell, and there were two women and four men. We certainly didn't have 50/50, but there were plenty of women and they were in quite senior positions." But that changed in the late 1970s. "(Computing courses) were having prerequisites for their courses that were subjects like math and physics. It was obvious to me that that was going to put a lot of women off. That's when I began to realise that there were these new barriers that were being set up which were discouraging girls."[951]

In 1979, Helen B. Feeney sued the Personnel Administrator of Massachusetts due to employment discrimination. During her twelve years as a state employee, Feeney had lost several positions to male veterans despite her high test scores because of a law that gave hiring preference to veterans—most of whom were men. Although initially successful, she lost her case on appeal because female veterans existed, meaning that the law did not exclusively favour men at the expense of

---

950   Pomeroy, Ross, "Sixty Years Ago, NASA Scientists Found That Women Would Be Better Astronauts. Their Work Was Never Published," Real Clear Science, January 8, 2022, https://www.realclearscience.com/blog/2022/01/08/sixty_years_ago_nasa_scientists_found_that_women_would_be_better_astronauts_their_work_was_never_published_807835.html

951   Smith, Carl, "At the Dawn of Australian Computing, 72 Women Had a Crucial Job You've Never Heard Of," ABC News, November 30, 2019, https://www.abc.net.au/news/science/2019-12-01/women-computing-astronomy-technology/11713282

women and the bias was incidental rather than intentional—meaning the law was not meant specifically to keep women out, it was just an unintended side effect.[952]

And of course, many times it is overt and intentional. In 2012, the United States Marine Corps created a set of six combat proxy tests to address the question "Are Females Ready for the Fight?" (Pro tip: if you're referring to women as "females," it's probably not going to be good). Around 400 male Marines and almost as many female Marines were tested on pull-ups, weight-lifting exercises, a tank loading drill, an artillery round carry and a seven-foot wall-climb while wearing a fighting load of about 30 pounds. It is interesting to note that the tests were purely physical, ignoring both the psychological and tactical problem-solving skills that would be needed in such settings. Of the top thirty-five highest performers (i.e. the top less than five percent) three were women, proving that women are capable of meeting the physical demands of close combat occupations. But the Corps decided to disregard their own test, claiming that the proxy tests were not an adequate indicator of on-the-ground success.[953] A decade later, over a third of positions in the Corps remained closed to women.[954]

Exclusion is not the only consequence for excellence. For gymnast Simone Biles, being the best in the world in her sport led to international officials undervaluing incredibly difficult moves that she created, reducing her competition scores. The International Gymnastics Federation Women's Technical Committee assigns values to different manoeuvres, based on difficulty, to ensure consistency of scoring. When Biles submitted moves that no one else was capable of doing, the WTC gave them ratings of H and J on a scale where J is the lowest difficulty level, in 2019. Their reasoning: "the WTC takes into consideration many different aspects; the risk, the safety of the gymnasts and the technical direction of the discipline." They literally graded her moves down because they were dangerous, in a sport based on people

---

952 "Personnel Administrator of Massachusetts et Al., Appellants, v. Helen B. FEENEY," Legal Information Institute, Cornell Law School, June 5, 1979, https://www.law.cornell.edu/supremecourt/text/442/256
953 Kovach, Gretel C., "Marine Reports Show Path to Women in Combat," San Diego Union-Tribune, October 15, 2015, https://www.sandiegouniontribune.com/military/sdut-usmc-reports-women-combat-research-2015oct15-htmlstory.html
954 "Women in the Marine Corps," U.S. Marine Corps, https://www.usmcu.edu/Research/Marine-Corps-History-Division/People/Women-in-the-Marine-Corps/

flipping through the air. As a journalist wrote for *The Guardian*, dictating the sport's "technical direction" is where bias really shines through:

> Biles' excellence has exposed the ineptitude of the WTC. Instead of endeavouring to create a code of points that allows a variety of different types of gymnasts to thrive, it has attempted to construct it with its own preferences in mind which almost always centres on nostalgia for gymnastics of the past...
>
> Certain innovative skills are undervalued, as are skills that are biomechanically more difficult than others. One of the frustrating consequences is that routines can often be extremely similar with little room for individuality.
>
> Examples of the WTC clamping down on innovation span decades. They squeezed out Liu Xuan's one-armed giant on uneven bars in 1996. The Croatian gymnast Tanja Delladio, who debuted the unique "snap down" technique on the bars in 2006, elicited a rare, blunt comment from the WTC in its newsletter that underlined its modus operandi: "The WTC is unwilling to encourage this type of elements." [Sanne] Wevers' Nabieva ½ variation in June was the most recent example of the inane code in action as her skill is valued the same as objectively less difficult release skills.[955]

The argument that officials are concerned for gymnasts' safety is also belied by the fact that, when Biles did a Yurchenko double pike vault (a move renamed the Biles II in her honour) in competition in 2023, she was forced to choose between a half point—potentially costing her a medal—and her own safety. Because the move presents a risk of catastrophic injury, her coach was on the mat, where he could immediately step in to reduce that risk should anything go wrong. It should be noted this is allowed for the uneven parallel bars, where the only penalty occurs

---

[955] Carayol, Tumaini, "Simone Biles' Desire to Innovate Is Frustrated by Her Own Insular Sport," *The Guardian*, July 23, 2021, https://www.theguardian.com/sport/2021/jul/23/simone-biles-desire-to-innovate-is-frustrated-by-her-own-insular-sport

if the spotter actually has to make contact with the gymnast. But even though Biles would be reaching similar heights as a bars move, spotters were not allowed for vault events, forcing the athlete and her coach to accept the penalty for her own safety.[956]

---

[956] Giambalvo, Emily, "Simone Biles's coach prioritizes safety on her vault. It hurts her score," *The Washington Post*, October 1, 2023, https://www.washingtonpost.com/sports/olympics/2023/10/01/simone-biles-coach-vault-deduction/

THE GLASS CLIFF

"Do what you feel in your heart to be right—for you'll be criticized anyway."
Eleanor Roosevelt

In 2008, "Iceland's spectacular meltdown was caused by a banking and business culture that was buccaneering, reckless—and overwhelmingly male," as the *Guardian* put it. Then the women stepped in to fix what the men had broken, led by Jóhanna Sigurdardóttir, the world's first openly gay premier. Businesswomen also took the reins, like Audur Capital founders Halla Tómasdóttir and Kristin Petursdóttir, who teamed up with singer Björk to set up an investment fund to boost the devastated economy by investing in green technology. "It goes back to our Viking women. While the men were out there raping and pillaging, the women were running the show at home," Tómasdóttir said. "Audur was one of our foremost Viking women, the name means wisdom, strength and happiness, and a clear space."[957]

The term "glass cliff" was coined by British professors Michelle K. Ryan and Alexander Haslam. A corollary to the glass ceiling, a glass cliff is when women or minorities are brought into leadership roles in times of turmoil, such as Jill Abramson at *The New York Times*. In a study, Ryan and Haslam analysed the performance of major companies before and after new board members were appointed. They found that companies that appointed women to their boards were more likely to have had consistently poor performance in the preceding five

---

957 Sunderland, Ruth, "After the Crash, Iceland's Women Lead the Rescue," *The Guardian*, February 22, 2009, https://www.theguardian.com/world/2009/feb/22/iceland-women

months. While there are a variety of interpretations as to the cause—"things are already bad so we can take a 'risk' on someone who's not a cishet, able-bodied white man," looking for nurturing and caregiving in a bad situation, and so on—the outcome is that women are frequently set up to fail in these circumstances. Taking the fall as a scapegoat not only undermines the reputations of the individual women when they can't pull off a miracle, but also reinforces the false narrative that women cannot be trusted to lead.[958]

This is frequently seen in politics, such as Teresa May being appointed the British prime minister in the wake of Brexit or Sophie Wilmès becoming Belgium's first women prime minister amid the COVID-19 crisis in 2020. Only months before one of the most crushing defeats in Canadian history, the Canadian Progressive Conservative Party elected Kim Campbell its leader in 1993, amid approval ratings so low that they subsequently lost 154 of their 156 seats in Parliament.[959]

Ellen Johnson Sirleaf, the first and only woman to be elected as President in Liberia, was first appointed in the aftermath of a civil war and as part of a transitional government. "People are always looking for someplace where they can say you messed up and then use that to say women should not meddle in [men's business]," she later remarked.[960]

In 1990, two Australian state premiers were elected, with Joan Kirner inheriting a major deficit in Victoria and Carmen Lawrence leading a party accused of corruption in Western Australia. Both of their parties lost power in subsequent elections, Kirner in 1992 and Lawrence in 1993, though both remained active in politics.[961] The pattern repeated with New South Wales premier Kristina Keneally

---

958 Ryan, Michelle K. and Haslam, Alexander, "The Glass Cliff: Evidence that Women are Over-Represented in Precarious Leadership Positions," February 9, 2005, https://onlinelibrary.wiley.com/doi/abs/10.1111/j.1467-8551.2005.00433.x
959 Simard, Caroline, "Women in Leadership and the Glass Cliff," Huffington Post, October 29, 2010, https://www.huffpost.com/entry/women-in-leadership-and-t_b_776291
960 Chisholm, Sunny, "The Glass Cliff Is a Threat to Women in Australian Politics," Marie Claire, October 19, 2021, https://www.marieclaire.com.au/misogyny-australian-politics-glass-cliff
961 Le Marquand, Sarrah, "Women in danger of falling off the glass cliff," Herald Sun, June 2, 2014, https://www.heraldsun.com.au/news/opinion/women-in-danger-of-falling-off-the-glass-cliff/news-story/c9b40689add7e71e9457f36aa02576bf

in 2009. Julia Gillard became the country's first woman prime minister and, as *Marie Claire* phrased it, "was presented with an impossible task: inheriting the public's distrust from an unreliable Rudd Government, in which she'd been a key figure, while emerging from the biggest financial crisis the world had faced since the Great Depression, and advocating for the wildly criticized carbon tax."[962]

Meanwhile, Gillard and economist Ngozi Okonjo-Iweala note in their book, *Women And Leadership: Real Lives, Real Lessons*, that Jacinda Ardern's appointment as party leader in 2017, so close to an election, also fits the bill. "Being thrust into a campaign without preparation, and with the former leader having resigned because of poor opinion polls, is a horrible start.... (although) becoming leader of a political party polling at 24 per cent just eight weeks before an election was the ultimate poisoned chalice, Jacinda won through."[963]

As the initial analysis from Ryan and Haslam shows, it's also common in business. In 2014, General Motors' first female CEO, Mary Barra, started her new job only weeks before a massive recall—millions of cars, in response to allegations that the company did not address ignition problems connected to more than a dozen deaths. Suddenly Barra was the one in the hot seat as the company was investigated by the Department of Justice and both houses of the U.S. Congress, among others. Barra was not informed of the problem until about a month before she started, and Prof. Haslam observed to the *New Yorker* that a contributing factor to the glass cliff is that women and minorities are less likely to have access to the information and support that would warn them away from such precarious positions.[964]

Barra—and GM—survived that crisis, in contrast to women like Patricia Russo, who was appointed CEO of Lucent-Alcatel, which had just been created from the merger of two communications companies. When the newly formed entity failed to turn a profit immediately, Russo and the entire management was ousted within a year and a half. As typically happens in such scenarios, she was replaced

---

962 Chisholm, Sunny, "The Glass Cliff Is a Threat to Women in Australian Politics," Marie Claire, October 19, 2021, https://www.marieclaire.com.au/misogyny-australian-politics-glass-cliff
963 Gillard, Julia, and Ngozi Okonjo-Iweala, *Women and Leadership: Real Lives, Real Lessons* (Mit Press, 2021).
964 Trop, Jaclyn, "Is Mary Barra Standing on a 'Glass Cliff?'" The New Yorker, April 29, 2014, https://www.newyorker.com/business/currency/is-mary-barra-standing-on-a-glass-cliff

with a white man.⁹⁶⁵

In 2012, Marissa Mayer was named CEO of Yahoo and, as *Forbes* wrote at the time, "The company's been an Internet has-been for years, with a stock price to match that assertion. Mayer is its third CEO (fifth if you count interim holders of the title) in a period of less than a year." She lasted five years, leaving in 2017. In 2016, a fired male employee filed a lawsuit against Mayer and two other female executives, claiming the employee performance-rating system she implemented was discriminatory against men. He had been replaced by a woman.⁹⁶⁶ One sensationalist headline read, "Yahoo CEO Marissa Mayer led illegal purge of male employees, lawsuit charges." His suit was dismissed the year after Mayer left the company.⁹⁶⁷

Ellen Pao lasted only a few months as interim CEO of Reddit. In addition to daring to try to police the harassment that runs rampant on the site by banning revenge porn and some of the more harassment-heavy subReddits, she was the target of significant backlash for the firing of a popular employee, though it was later revealed that this decision had nothing to do with her.⁹⁶⁸

In 2021, Alexis George's appointment as CEO of an Australian financial services company led to headlines like "How Alexis George is trying to bring AMP back from the brink."⁹⁶⁹

The glass cliff has also been seen as a response to sexual impropriety by men. In 2020, Agnès Buzyn replaced Benjamin Griveaux as candidate in the Paris mayoral

---

965 McCullough, DG., "Women CEOs: Why Companies in Crisis Hire Minorities – and Then Fire Them," *The Guardian*, August 14, 2014, https://www.theguardian.com/sustainable-business/2014/aug/05/fortune-500-companies-crisis-woman-ceo-yahoo-xerox-jc-penny-economy

966 Olen, Helaine, "Marissa Mayer and the Glass Cliff," Forbes, July 16, 2012, https://www.forbes.com/sites/helaineolen/2012/07/16/marissa-mayer-and-the-glass-cliff/?sh=55054ed7989d

967 Baron, Ethan, "Yahoo CEO Marissa Mayer Led Illegal Purge of Male Employees, Lawsuit Charges," The Mercury News, October 6, 2016, https://www.mercurynews.com/2016/10/06/yahoo-ceo-marissa-mayer-led-illegal-purge-of-male-employees-lawsuit-charges/

968 Kazem, Halima, "Reddit's Ellen Pao Is Latest Female CEO Blamed for Inherited Woes, Experts Say," *The Guardian*, July 11, 2015, https://www.theguardian.com/technology/2015/jul/11/reddit-ellen-pao-women-ceo

969 Patten, Sally, "How Alexis George Is Trying to Bring AMP Back from the Brink," Australian Financial Review, August 18, 2022, https://www.afr.com/work-and-careers/leaders/how-alexis-george-is-trying-to-bring-amp-back-from-the-brink-20220729-p5b5pc

race after his sexting scandal came out.[970] In 2012, Jen Oneal was appointed the first woman to lead Blizzard Entertainment after it was alleged that the company fostered a culture of sexual misconduct. Oneal, who had herself been harassed as a woman at the company, resigned after three months of demanding equal pay to her male counterpart—a demand that was only agreed to after her resignation. Instead, she struck out and formed her own studio with other ex-Blizzard employees.[971]

---

970 Paun, Carmen, "French Health Minister to Run for Paris Mayor after Party Mate's Sexting Scandal," Politico, February 16, 2020, https://www.politico.eu/article/french-health-minister-to-run-for-paris-mayor-after-party-mates-sexting-scandal/
971 Yang, George, "Former Blizzard Leaders J. Allen Brack and Jen Oneal Reemerge to Start New Studio," IGN, March 15, 2023, https://www.ign.com/articles/former-blizzard-leaders-j-allen-brack-and-jen-oneal-reemerge-to-start-new-studio

PERSONALLY AND PROFESSIONALLY UNDERMINED

"They'll tell you you're too loud, that you need to wait your turn and ask the right people for permission. Do it anyway."
—Alexandria Ocasio-Cortez[972]

Ecologist Priyanga Amarasekare is one of the world's most respected academics in her field; her work has been cited more than 14,000 times. Yet only two months after she won the Robert H. MacArthur Award (one of the highest honours in ecology) in 2022, her employer suspended her for a year without pay or benefits, and forbade her from accessing her laboratory, maintaining her insect colonies, managing her grants, or contacting students. The University of California, Los Angeles also cut her salary by a fifth for a further two years.

The offence that warranted such significant punishment? Former students and faculty members told the journal Nature that they believed it was retaliation because Amarasekare, native of Sri Lanka and one of two women of color who have tenure in the ecology and evolution department, had previously accused the university of discrimination for repeatedly denying her promotions that went instead to colleagues. UCLA refused to offer any explanation, and barred Amarasekare from speaking publicly about the matter. More than 300 scientists from around the world signed a petition urging the university to reverse its decision, noting that such measures represent "the kind of punishment normally applied

---

972   Ocasio-Cortez, Alexandria, Twitter, March 10, 2018, https://twitter.com/aoc/status/972292022362165249

only to the most egregious wrongdoings."⁹⁷³

For comparison, several years earlier, UCLA history professor Gabriel Piterberg was allowed to sexually harass students for years. His victims included graduate student Kristen Glasgow, who sued the university in 2015 after they ignored her Title IX complaints. The UC system settled, paying her $110,000 and a fellowship to support her work on her doctoral dissertation—but Piterberg kept his job. After Glasgow and fellow grad student Nefertiti Takla had filed complaints in 2013, the only punishment he had received in 2014 was a $3,000 fine, suspension without pay for one quarter and attending sexual harassment training. He was also barred for three years from holding closed-door, one-on-one meetings in his office and restricted open-door meetings to daytime hours. In exchange for him accepting those terms, the university agreed to drop any investigation, which could have threatened his tenure. In 2016, the university hired a new Title IX coordinator, Glasgow re-filed her previously-ignored complaint, and Piterberg eventually resigned.⁹⁷⁴

MEN IN PERSONAL LIFE ACTIVELY SABOTAGING

> "Freeing yourself was one thing, claiming ownership of that freed self was another."
> —Toni Morrison, *Beloved*⁹⁷⁵

There are countless examples of men stealing the work of the women in their lives. Because of the nature of the theft, there are certain to be many instances which may never be made public. When these stories do come to light, it is common for there to be abusive elements to the relationships in question—the men are using and controlling the women, and it is only once the women break free and gain some

---

973   Walpola, Thilina, "Intl Scientists Ask UCLA to Reverse Lankan Origin Ecologist's Suspension," January 30, 2023, https://island.lk/intl-scientists-ask-ucla-to-reverse-lankan-origin-ecologists-suspension/
974   Watanabe, Teresa, "UCLA Student Wins Sexual Misconduct Claim against Professor," Los Angeles Times, March 18, 2018, https://www.latimes.com/local/education/la-me-ucla-sexual-misconduct-piterberg-20180318-story.html
975   Morrison, Toni *Beloved* (Alfred A. Knopf, 1987).

degree of independence that they reclaim the credit that is rightfully theirs. Some never do, and the truth is only known after their death, and possibly not even then.

Not all men in this book have stolen from their partners—some simply sabotage them, whether by undermining their confidence when good partners build each other up, or by using their own power to encourage others not to support them. When the women do start to assert their independence and challenge men's control, men often shift from private psychological abuse—undermining women's confidence to make them easier to control—to actively sabotaging the woman's independent efforts. This is in no small part due to the benefit such men derive from having the women in their control. Ironically, men will commonly use the clout they have gained in part by stealing the woman's work to then obstruct the woman's efforts.

When photographer Dora Maar met the man who would ruin her life, she was a well-regarded photographer with a thriving career. She was intelligent, ambitious, charismatic, and innovative, demonstrating the value of photography in the burgeoning Surrealist movement. By the time Picasso was done emotionally abusing her and left her, she had a breakdown and became a recluse.[976][977] He then sold sketches of her naked and of her genitalia, in a pre-Internet version of revenge porn. She became known as his "weeping woman," saying "All (Picasso's) portraits of me are lies. They're Picassos. Not one is Dora Maar."[978][979] When they met, he was fifty-four to her twenty-eight.

When she died, hardly anyone noticed and when they did, it was to depict her as Picasso's muse and lover, rather than a brilliant artist in her own right. Those accounts also glossed over his mistreatment of Maar and other women, such as playing them off one another in a game of emotional manipulation, later describing

---

[976] Dickson, Andrew, "Dora Maar: How Picasso's Weeping Woman Had the Last Laugh," *The Guardian*, November 15, 2019, https://www.theguardian.com/artanddesign/2019/nov/15/dora-maar-picassos-weeping-woman
[977] French, Lisa, "Dora Maar and Françoise Gilot Were Much More than Picasso's Muses or Lovers. They Are Important Artists in Their Own Right," The Conversation, September 26, 2022, https://theconversation.com/dora-maar-and-francoise-gilot-were-much-more-than-picassos-muses-or-lovers-they-are-important-artists-in-their-own-right-190750
[978] Pound, Cath, "Why Dora Maar Is Much More than Picasso's Weeping Woman," BBC, June 7, 2019, https://www.bbc.com/culture/article/20190607-why-dora-maar-is-much-more-than-picassos-weeping-woman
[979] Maar, Dora, Interview with James Lord, 1940.

a scene where they came to blows in his studio as "one of my choicest memories."[980] Indeed, he later told another lover, Françoise Gilot, that "Women are machines for suffering." Gilot herself was frequently harassed in the streets by Picasso's estranged wife. Those accounts also ignored that Maar, being far more politically engaged than Picasso, was likely the reason he painted *Guernica*, arguably his most famous work, as well as the fact that she painted a small part of it and the entire style is clearly influenced by her photographs. They don't mention that Picasso was the one who pushed her to give up photography for painting—in his Cubist style, of course—cutting her off from the medium where she excelled into one where he was the master. There is also evidence he was physically abusive to Maar and other women. Although she continued making art into her eighties, she never regained the success of her twenties.[981]

Maar was hardly the only one to suffer due to his narcissism.[982] "No one in my family ever managed to escape from the stranglehold of this genius," his granddaughter Marina wrote in her memoir, *Picasso: My Grandfather*. "He needed blood to sign each of his paintings: my father's blood, my brother's, my mother's, my grandmother's, and mine. He needed the blood of those who loved him."[983]

Of women like Maar and Gilot—who Picasso seduced when he was sixty-one to her twenty-one—Marina recalled, "After he had spent many nights extracting their essence, once they were bled dry, he would dispose of them." When Gilot, unlike most of his women, left him ten years later and took their two children, he actively tried to sabotage her career. He used his considerable clout to discourage art dealers and galleries from buying her work and tried to block the publication of her memoir. When he was unsuccessful, he refused to ever contact their two children again as punishment.

Although Elaine de Kooning was a tireless advocate for her husband and his

---

980   Gilot, Françoise, *Life with Picasso* (Anchor Books/Doubleday, 1989).
981   Faus, Joan, "Museum Protesters Denounce Picasso's Treatment of Women," Reuters, June 4, 2021, https://www.reuters.com/world/europe/museum-protesters-denounce-picassos-treatment-women-2021-06-04/
982   Delistraty, Cody, "How Picasso Bled the Women in His Life for Art," The Paris Review, November 9, 2017, https://www.theparisreview.org/blog/2017/11/09/how-picasso-bled-the-women-in-his-life-for-art/
983   Picasso, Marina, *Picasso, My Grandfather* (Riverhead Books, 2002).

art, his was a tough love that arguably crossed the line into abuse. In a recurring theme, she was only twenty to his thirty-four when they met, and a student while he was an established artist. He used that power imbalance and his role as her teacher to routinely harshly criticize her work, and even destroyed many of her pieces.[984] To be fair, her friend, Lee Hall, later wrote, "Elaine said many times that Willem de Kooning provided her with the best teaching she ever had and that the skills he taught her became the foundation for her confidence as a portrait painter."[985] But for many women, having a lover that constantly tore them down has had the opposite effect.

French Impressionist Marie Bracquemond spent years being worn down by her more famous husband, Félix. Part of his belittling of her was of her style, as his was conservative while she experimented with the emerging plein air movement. But the motivations were more personal than professional.[986] According to their son, Pierre, who wrote an unpublished biography of his parents, his father was frequently resentful and jealous of his mother. Félix "seldom showed her work to their friends. When he did compliment her, it was in private. Therefore, none of their artist friends paid attention to her works or spoke of her efforts, and when she revealed hopes for success, Félix put her ambition down to 'incurable vanity,'" Pierre wrote.[987] After more than two decades of his abuse and discouraged by the lack of interest in her work that he helped perpetuate, she finally gave in and gave up painting in 1890.

Danish painter Marie Krøyer's first marriage was to Peder Severin Krøyer, one of the most famous painters in Danish history. Marie met and married Peder when she was just twenty-two; he was sixteen years her senior. In the course of their whirlwind romance, he did not mention either his family history of mental illness or the fact that he had syphilis. Peder also appears to have suffered from bipolar

---

984   Moonan, Wendy, "Why Elaine de Kooning Sacrificed Her Own Amazing Career for Her More-Famous Husband's," Smithsonian Magazine, May 8, 2015, https://www.smithsonianmag.com/smithsonian-institution/why-elaine-de-kooning-sacrificed-her-own-amazing-career-her-more-famous-husbands-180955182/
985   Hall, Lee, *Elaine and Bill: Portrait of a Marriage*, (Harpercollins, 1993).
986   Gaze, Delia, *Concise Dictionary of Women Artists* (Routledge, 2011).
987   Bracquemond, Pierre, "La vie de Félix et Marie Bracquemond," 1925.

disorder, swinging between mania and depression, which strained their marriage to the point of divorce. He was reportedly dismissive of the tuition she received when she was younger, as being for "young lady painters," which hints at a disregard for women artists in general, and there is little evidence he ever encouraged Marie in her own artistic ambitions. She is known to have suffered from self-doubt in her own abilities, which was no doubt exacerbated by being married to such a highly regarded artist when she had not yet had a chance to establish her own career. His many paintings of her may have contributed to a perception of her as only his model and muse, rather than an artist in her own right. While the exact cause is unclear, Marie stopped painting during her marriage. It was not until after her daughter's death in 1986 that Marie's own art gained recognition, as her paintings were among the estate and were eventually collected by the Skagens Museum in Skagen, Denmark.[988]

Photojournalist and war correspondent Dickey Chappelle met her future husband Tony when she was just twenty-one and he was her photography teacher and twice her age at forty. It would be fifteen years before she broke away from the abusive Tony, who routinely told her that her work wasn't good enough and sabotaged her professional opportunities to keep her in his control and supporting him.[989]

Alma Schindler had been studying composition and writing dozens of her own works for years when she became engaged in 1901 to Gustav Mahler, twenty years her senior. At that point, she stopped writing. Mahler wrote to her, "The role of composer falls to me, yours is that of loving companion…!" When he finally showed an interest in her work years later after the death of their daughter and Alma's subsequent affair, it was too little, too late. He died in 1911 and Alma later noted, "Ten years of wasted development cannot be made up anymore. It was a galvanized corpse that he wanted to resurrect."[990]

---

988 Wenande, Christian, "Her art endured despite patriarchal prejudice and the Skagen scandal," The Copenhagen Post, June 21, 2016, https://cphpost.dk/2016-06-21/history/her-art-endured-despite-patriarchal-prejudice-and-the-skagen-scandal-2/
989 Rhinehart, Lorissa, *First to the Front: The Untold Story of Dickey Chapelle, Trailblazing Female War Correspondent* (MacMillan, 2023).
990 Warkus, Brigitte, "Alma Mahler-Werfel," FemBio, https://www.fembio.org/english/biography.php/woman/biography/alma-mahler-werfel/

In addition to holding her back professionally as a writer, F. Scott Fitzgerald constantly undermined his wife Zelda's pursuits as a dancer. Although she returned to ballet at twenty-seven—fairly old for the profession, though she had studied as a girl—she was driven to succeed and trained incredibly hard. With a dream of joining the Ballet Russes, she studied with Madame Lubov Egorova, who trained ballet dancers for the company. Zelda took classes every morning and afternoon and would practice for almost eight hours a day. She also paid for the classes herself, writing short stories to make money because "I wanted my dancing to belong to me."[991]

While her husband derided her ambition, Zelda clearly had potential. While she may never have made it to the Ballet Russes, Egorova said that although she started too late to be truly great, she could still dance important roles with great success. On her recommendation, Zelda was invited to join the Italian San Carlo Opera Ballet Company, complete with a monthly salary. Zelda declined, likely due to her husband's influence. Although she never publicly stated her reasons, it has been suggested that her husband may have refused to move to Naples (though she had moved many times for him), which would have separated her from her daughter, Frances. Constantly being told she would never be good enough must have undermined her confidence as well. Barely six months later, she was admitted to a sanatorium. In her semi-autobiographical novel *Save Me the Last Waltz*, the main character throws herself into ballet and succeeds despite those telling her she cannot.

The marriage of painters Kay Sage and Yves Tanguy was described by friends as "strange" and "uneasy." With his overbearing personality and propensity to drink heavily, Tanguy would humiliate and insult Sage and her work in front of his wife and their friends, while Sage sat silent. He would also physically abuse her, even in social settings, including pushing her and threatening her with a knife. This is after Sage arguably saved Tanguy's life—when war broke out in Europe, she helped several artists, including Tanguy, flee in 1940.[992]

---

991 Milford, Nancy, *Zelda: A Biography* (Harper Colophon Books, 1989).
992 Ables, Kelsey, "Perspective | for This Surrealist Art Couple, Love Was an Alien Landscape," *The Washington Post*, February 12, 2022, https://www.washingtonpost.com/arts-entertainment/2022/02/12/kay-sage-yves-tanguy-married-surrealist-artists/

In addition to taking advantage of Camille Claudel sexually and professionally (see "Stolen Work" section), Rodin may have sabotaged her after their sexual relationship ended. Even though she had produced brilliant work during her time working for him—so brilliant in fact that he claimed credit for them without acknowledging her—she could not secure funding for her work. While part of this was certainly due to sexist attitudes, her ahead-of-its-time style and the daring, sexual subject matter she depicted, Rodin benefitted from her lack of success—she was forced to continue collaborating with him to support herself, even when she went uncredited for works that he only contributed a signature to. This raises the question of whether she may have succeeded if he had advocated for her, rather than continuing to keep her reliant on him and presenting her work as his own. Keep in mind that she had been financially and emotionally dependent on him since she was a teen, kicked out of her family home in disgrace because of her affair with him. Her 1888 sculpture *Sakuntala* may be interpreted as a sign that she was looking to break away from Rodin and establish her own artistic identity, the year before she ended their sexual relationship. No longer a naive teen, Claudel was recognising Rodin's deceptions and exploitation, and refusing to be constrained as obedient to him and conforming to societal expectations of her as a woman. Claudel grew to resent and mistrust Rodin, referring to him as a career saboteur as well as "The Ferret" in letters. When in 1899 she created *The Mature Age*, which likely depicted the love triangle between themselves and his long-time lover, he was reportedly shocked and enraged. He cut off any support and reputedly asked the Ministry of Fine Arts to cancel the funding for the work. By 1905 she was believed to be seriously mentally ill, having destroyed many of her own works and afraid to make new art because she believed Rodin would steal them from her. Her family had her committed and she remained incarcerated in an asylum until her death 30 years later. Given the circumstances around her relationship with Rodin, it may be questioned how much of her mental health decline was due to the impacts of his actions.[993]

---

993 "Camille Claudel Sculptures, Bio, Ideas," The Art Story, https://www.theartstory.org/artist/claudel-camille/

When Eleanor Glanville married her second husband Richard in 1685, it was probably her worst life choice. He was violent towards her, including threatening her with a loaded pistol. Separating in 1698 allowed her to focus on becoming one of the foremost entomologists of her day, but Richard was not done making her life hell. In a bid to try and steal her wealth and assets, he started spreading rumours that she was insane, including trying to force her children to sign written affidavits to that effect. He even arranged the attempted kidnapping of one of her sons to force him to sign over his inheritance. To protect herself, she appointed trustees to manage her properties and willed the majority of her wealth to her cousin. When she died in 1709, her assets were valued at the equivalent of around £1 million in modern terms. After her death, her oldest son contested her will by taking a page from his stepfather's book and claiming his mother was non compos mentis. No longer able to defend herself against slanders, Eleanor's legacy was marred by her son's assertions that she had delusions that her children had been changed into fairies, with other witnesses attesting to behaviours that were likely connected to her work studying moths and butterflies—beating bushes for larvae, dressing "like a gypsy" and venturing outside without all the appropriate clothing for a lady—which, given it was England circa 1700, was not exactly conducive to freedom of movement. Her will was overturned in 1712 on the grounds of perceived insanity.[994]

In the days following the invasion of Normandy, one of the pivotal moments of World War II, Martha Gellhorn was the only woman journalist on-site—and she wasn't supposed to be there. She didn't have the permission from her publisher, but she snuck onto a hospital ship, getting much closer to the action than the approved male reporters.[995]

Her then-husband Ernest Hemingway had tried to convince the magazine to give him the job instead. He had a long history of getting involved with and psychologically tormenting incredible women, including journalists Mary Welsh

---

994   Harding, Jesmond, "The Lady who loveth butter-flies," Butterfly Conversation Ireland, March 28, 2020, https://butterflyconservation.ie/wp/2020/03/28/the-lady-who-loveth-butter-flies/
995   Mackrell, Judith, *The Correspondents: Six Women Writers on the Front Lines of World War II* (Doubleday, 2021).

Hemingway and Pauline Pfeiffer. As Bernice Kert writes in *The Hemingway Women*, he was never able to sustain healthy, long-term relationships with any of the four Mrs. Hemingways, becoming critical and bullying as boredom and restlessness set in.[996] He was an alcoholic and a cheat with a violent temper who frequently belittled those around him, particularly his wives.[997]

He also included nasty depictions of them (or versions of them) in his writing, such as Pfeiffer's portrayal in his memoir *A Moveable Feast*. He vilified his second wife, claiming that she had befriended his first wife, Hadley Richardson, to seduce him away from her—never mind that leaving his wife for a mistress was a pattern he repeated with Gellhorn while married to Pfeiffer, and likely would have done to Gellhorn had she not divorced him first. He also glosses over Pfeiffer's wealth, and the fact that he and Richardson had been living off her trust fund, not to mention that Pfeiffer was a successful and skilled reporter for *Vogue* at the time.[998]

He could shift from loving to abusive, with comments like "They'll be reading my stuff long after the worms have finished with you" reportedly directed at Gellhorn. Having met the thirty-seven-year-old Hemingway when she was only twenty-four, Gellhorn was the only one of his four wives to leave him. She would later stipulate that she would only give interviews if he was not mentioned, saying "I've been a writer for over 40 years. I was a writer before I met him and I was a writer after I left him. Why should I be merely a footnote in his life?"

---

996 Kert, Bernice, *The Hemmingway Women* (W. W. Norton, 1983).
997 "The Only Woman at D-Day: What Martha Gellhorn's Letters Reveal about the Trailblazing War Correspondent," CBC, December 6, 2019, https://www.cbc.ca/radio/day6/king-tides-impeach-o-meter-frosty-at-50-lindy-west-k-pop-deaths-and-mental-health-martha-gellhorn-more-1.5384775/the-only-woman-at-d-day-what-martha-gellhorn-s-letters-reveal-about-the-trailblazing-war-correspondent-1.5384779
998 Blume, Lesley M. M., "The Vindication of Pauline Hemingway, Ernest's Second (and Most Vilified) Wife," Vogue, June 8, 2016, https://www.vogue.com/article/pauline-hemingway-forgotten-wife

MALE ADVISORS/BOSSES TELLING WOMEN NOT TO PURSUE IMPORTANT THINGS

"Certain people — men, of course — discouraged me, saying [science] was not a good career for women. That pushed me even more to persevere."
—Françoise Barré-Sinoussi[999]

Composer Kaija Saariaho has spoken about how, during her time at Helsinki's Sibelius Academy in the late 1970s, some male teachers did not want to work with her, because they saw her as a pretty woman who would marry soon and not work after that. They didn't want to waste their time by investing it in her. "It was a very normal thing [at] that time, and I didn't think much of myself anyway, so it was not so shocking. I was disappointed only when I told other people about it—like my young male colleagues, they couldn't believe their ears. Now when I think about it, it's a pity, but that's how that period was. At some point I thought, 'Well that's what they say and that's what they think, but I'm going to write my music and I will find my way.' The most important person was Paavo Heininen, and he never talked about me being a woman. His objective was to teach me to compose." Her misogynistic teachers were technically right on one front—she did get married in 1984. She also went on to have an internationally distinguished forty-year career, including writing the Grammy-winning *L'amour de loin*, only the second opera by a female composer ever to be presented by the Metropolitan Opera (the first being

---

999 Jack, Andrew, "Françoise Barré-Sinoussi: the HIV hunter," Financial Times, May 18, 2013, https://www.ft.com/content/3467c5ca-bcf6-11e2-b344-00144feab7de

the one-act *Der Wald* by Ethel Smyth, more than 100 years earlier in 1903).[1000]

Saariaho was fortunate, like many women in this book, to have a man in a position of power supporting her even as others would have held her back. Unfortunately, not all women have had the same benefit, and male relatives are not the only ones who sabotage women's careers, either deliberately or otherwise. Often, deterrents can come from male advisors or bosses (or, in some cases, men who are both relatives and in positions of professional authority). While this does verge on "being prevented from achieving things," these are examples of work that women were pursuing that they would have received recognition for had they completed them. Instead, men would typically take credit for getting to those points later.

Before he won a Nobel Prize for work his wife did, Joshua Lederberg was Esther Lederberg's thesis advisor as well as her husband. Following her groundbreaking discoveries of the fertility F factor and the λ (lambda) bacteriophage while earning her Master's degree, she intended to deepen her exploration of them while working on her doctorate. Joshua used his position of authority—which he should never have held, as her husband—to stop her from conducting additional experiments, on the premise that she should be devoting all her efforts to finishing her PhD dissertation. Had she been supported in pursuing these at the time, particularly before her career became so entangled with Joshua's, she may have been more successful in being recognized for her accomplishments independent of him, rather than being seen as merely his assistant.[1001]

In late 1500s Denmark, Sophia Brahe was a decade or so younger than her brother Tycho (dates vary), yet she repeatedly defied him when it came to her passion for astronomy. Tycho, a highly regarded astronomer himself, first tried to discourage her from studying the subject—so she learned on her own, reading books in German and using her own money to pay for translations of Latin texts so she could read those as well. Even once she had established her skills and knowledge, he tried to prevent her from continuing her research in the field because he

---

1000 Huizenga, Tom, "Kaija Saariaho, a Composer with Ears Wide Open," NPR, July 21, 2022, https://www.npr.org/2022/07/21/1112423462/kaija-saariaho-a-composer-with-ears-wide-open
1001 Schindler, Thomas, *Strange Genetics* (Oxford University Press EBooks, 2021).

thought it was too complex for a woman's abilities. Not the actual science part—he was worried she wasn't good enough at astrology to produce the horoscopes their clients would take so seriously. Despite this, she frequently handled such matters while he was away during the decade from 1588 to 1597. Working with him in his observatory, she was instrumental in his work, for which she went uncredited, including assisting with observations that led to the discovery of a supernova (which contributed to refuting a geocentric view of the universe), observations of a lunar eclipse and orbital measurements. When Tycho died in 1601, his work passed to his protégé Johannes Kepler instead of Sophia. As she outlived him by more than 40 years, we can only speculate what she may have accomplished with more encouragement.[1002]

In 1925, Cecilia Payne became the first person to earn a PhD in astronomy from Radcliffe College at Harvard. In her doctoral thesis, she contradicted the prevailing belief that the sun was made up of more or less the same composition as the Earth. While she found that silicon, carbon, and other common metals were present in roughly the same amounts as on earth, she also discovered that helium and hydrogen were far more plentiful—in the case of hydrogen, about a million times more. As such, she concluded that stars were primarily made up of hydrogen, making it the universe's most abundant element.

But when she presented it, the more senior astronomer Henry Norris Russell convinced her not to publish her findings, as it went against the scientific consensus at the time. Indeed, it would contradict Russell's own published views. In a magnificent case of gaslighting, ironically about gases, Payne was persuaded that her own results were "spurious," yet Russell himself then published the exact same findings only four years later. Whether his sabotage was deliberate or not at the time, he received the credit for a major discovery that was not his, even though he did credit Payne in passing in his paper. He was also nominated for a Nobel Prize. Ironically, the American Astronomical Society later awarded her the Henry

---

[1002] Christianson, John Robert, *On Tycho's Island: Tycho Brahe and his assistants, 1570–1601* (Cambridge University Press, 2000).

Norris Russell Prize.[1003]

Gertrude Ederle won swimming gold at the 1924 Olympic Games, setting a new world record while she was at it. But despite international acclaim and a sponsorship for her attempt to become the first woman to swim the English Channel, her own coach didn't think she could do it. Although she did fail the first time around in 1925, she not only succeeded the following year but did so faster than any of her male predecessors, in fourteen hours and thirty-four minutes—a record that stood for twenty-five years. She also did better than her initial coach—who failed in not one, not two, but twenty-one attempts to swim the Channel from 1906 to 1914. Jabez Wolffe repeatedly tried to slow her pace during training, claiming she would never last at that speed. In fact, her 1925 failure was due to Wolffe ordering another swimmer to pull her from the water, resulting in her attempt being disqualified. According to both Ederle and witnesses, she was not in danger of drowning as Wolffe claimed, but simply floating face-down for a rest. Unsurprisingly, after she dumped him for a different coach (Bill Burgess, who had, incidentally, completed the Channel swim) her results spoke for themselves. Wolffe had previously commented that women may not be capable of swimming the Channel, and it seems entirely possible that he did not want a woman to succeed where he had failed.[1004]

1003 Siegel, Ethan, "These 5 Women Deserved, and Were Unjustly Denied, a Nobel Prize in Physics," Forbes, October 11, 2018, https://www.forbes.com/sites/startswithabang/2018/10/11/these-5-women-deserved-and-were-unjustly-denied-a-nobel-prize-in-physics/?sh=7bed2356195e

1004 Mortimer, Gavin, "When Gertrude Ederle Turned the Tide," The Telegraph, April 27, 2008, https://www.telegraph.co.uk/culture/donotmigrate/3672954/When-Gertrude-Ederle-turned-the-tide.html

ALGORITHMIC BIAS

As algorithms impact more of our daily lives, it is important to be aware that anything built by humans often features human prejudices—not least because only twenty-two percent of professionals in AI and data science fields are women, and they're more likely to hold lower-status roles.[1005] Humans control what data algorithms are based on and how they're written. In 2016, a Quartz headline read "Microsoft's AI millennial chatbot became a racist jerk after less than a day on Twitter." The Twitter bot Tay was designed to learn from interacting with users, but as the saying goes: garbage in, garbage out. Within twenty-four hours, Tay was tweeting things like "I fucking hate feminists they should all die and burn in hell," and referring to feminism as a cult and a cancer, along with plenty of other offensive comments.[1006]

Even when searching for women online, it must be noted that search algorithms have inherent biases. Until 2016, LinkedIn would recommend men's names when users were searching for a woman. A search for "Stephanie Williams" would result in not only the thousands of Stephanie Williamses but also the query, "did you mean Stephen Williams?" Meanwhile a search for "Stephen Williams" did not ask "did you mean Stephanie Williams?" The same would happen with Andrea

---

1005 "Women and the digital revolution (chapter 3)," UNESCO Science Report, 2021, https://www.unesco.org/reports/science/2021/en/women-digital-revolution.
1006 Rodriguez, Ashley, "Microsoft's AI millennial chatbot became a racist jerk after less than a day on Twitter," Quartz, March 24, 2016, https://qz.com/646825/microsofts-ai-millennial-chatbot-became-a-racist-jerk-after-less-than-a-day-on-twitter.

(Andrew?), Danielle (Daniel?) and so on.[1007]

Google's autocomplete sexism was called out in a 2013 ad campaign by UN Women, which used real searches to illustrate the problem. In response to a user typing phrases like "women cannot," "women should," "women need to" and "women shouldn't," autocomplete suggested "women need to be put in their places," "women cannot be trusted," "women shouldn't have rights," and "women should stay home," among countless other misogynistic completions. Now it seems certain search terms simply have autocomplete turned off, like when I tried to search "feminists are" in 2023—interestingly, "feminism is" still gave me a book called *Feminism is Cancer* just below bell hooks's *Feminism Is for Everybody*. Typing "women are" led to the suggestion "women are emotional."[1008]

Translation programs like Google Translate and Systran have been shown to significantly overuse male pronouns, even when referring to women. While many languages, like German, French, and Spanish, are inherently gendered in their nouns, there is also a push to implement gender-neutral language in such programs, as well as policy documents and other official language. Replacing terms like "man hours" with those like "work hours" and professional terms (businessman, fireman, policeman, etc.) with non-gendered versions (businessperson, firefighter, police officer, etc.) broadens inclusivity without sacrificing clarity.[1009] Meanwhile, plenty of languages use the same word for he and she, like Tagalog (siya), Armenian (ինք), Swahili (yeye), Turkish (o), Hungarian (ő) and Persian (آن).[1010]

But it's important to note how these programs affect our lives even when we're not online. Algorithms are now used to help companies make hiring decisions, help medical professionals prioritize, diagnose, and treat patients, and help banks make financial choices. In 2019, a husband and wife who both had Apple Cards

---

1007   Day, Matt, "How LinkedIn's search engine may reflect a gender bias," The Seattle Times, August 31, 2016, https://www.seattletimes.com/business/microsoft/how-linkedins-search-engine-may-reflect-a-bias/
1008   Mahdawi, Arwa, "Google's autocomplete spells out our darkest thoughts," *The Guardian*, October 22, 2013, https://www.theguardian.com/commentisfree/2013/oct/22/google-autocomplete-un-women-ad-discrimination-algorithms.
1009   Schiebinger, Londa, "Machine Translation: Analyzing Gender," Gendered Innovations, Stanford University, 2013, https://genderedinnovations.stanford.edu/case-studies/nlp.html
1010   Cuan, Nidia, "A Simple Guide to Gender-Neutral Languages Around the World," June 11, 2022, Beelinguapp, https://beelinguapp.com/blog/gender-neutral,

discovered that his credit line was twenty times higher than hers, with no explanation why the algorithm would consider the wife significantly less credit-worthy.[1011] Even facial recognition is often trained on image sets that lack diversity, both in terms of race and gender. One study found that thirty-five percent of darker-skinned women were misclassified, compared to .8 percent for lighter-skinned men.[1012]

In 2018, Amazon made headlines when it was revealed that the company's experimental AI recruiting tool was biassed against women, including penalising resumes that included the word "woman" and downgrading alumni of two all-women colleges. It had been trained on ten years' worth of resumes and, being in the tech sector, those resumes were dominated by men.[1013] In July 2023, Intelion Systems reported that "AI adoption in recruitment is on the rise, with 35% to 45% of companies utilizing AI recruitment tools. Notably, 99% of Fortune 500 companies are already incorporating AI practices, and 65% of recruiters use AI in their hiring processes."[1014]

Meanwhile, much of the accepted wisdom in medicine is based on the premise of male as the default, to the point that women or female animals are frequently excluded from medical trials, even if the condition in question is more common among women. Even if women are included in general, important groups may still be left out like those who are pregnant, menopausal, or using hormonal birth control.[1015] A 2020 Forbes article observed, "Many medical algorithms are, for example, based on U.S. military personnel data where women in some areas only represent 6%." If healthcare algorithms are based on gender-biassed data, they

---

1011   Nedlund, Evelina, "Apple Card is accused of gender bias. Here's how that can happen," November 12, 2019, CNN Business, https://edition.cnn.com/2019/11/12/business/apple-card-gender-bias/index.html
1012   Smith, Genevieve and Rustagi, Ishita, "When Good Algorithms Go Sexist: Why and How to Advance AI Gender Equity," March 31, 2021, Stanford Social Innovation Review, https://ssir.org/articles/entry/when_good_algorithms_go_sexist_why_and_how_to_advance_ai_gender_equity
1013   Dastin, Jeffrey, "Amazon scraps secret AI recruiting tool that showed bias against women," October 11, 2018, Reuters, https://www.reuters.com/article/idUSKCN1MK0AG/
1014   Intelion Systems. "AI Recruitment Statistics," LinkedIn, July 21, 2023, https://www.linkedin.com/pulse/ai-recruitment-statistics-intelion-systems/
1015   Westervelt, Amy, "The medical research gender gap: how excluding women from clinical trials is hurting our health," The Guardian, May 1, 2015, https://www.theguardian.com/lifeandstyle/2015/apr/30/fda-clinical-trials-gender-gap-epa-nih-institute-of-medicine-cardiovascular-disease

cannot provide appropriate care for women. The Forbes article noted, "Today, online apps based on data mainly collected from men may suggest to a female user that her symptoms of pain in the left arm and back may be due to depression. The medical app might advise the woman to see the doctor in a couple of days. In contrast, a male user of the app is more likely to be asked to immediately contact his doctor based on a diagnosis of a possible heart attack."[1016]

In an analysis of 133 systems across different industries from 1988 to 2021, researchers from the Center for Equity, Gender and Leadership at UC Berkeley found that 44.2 percent showed gender bias, with 25.7 percent demonstrating both gender and racial bias.

Of the 59 systems exhibiting gender bias, 70 percent resulted in lower quality of service for women and non-binary individuals. Voice-recognition systems, increasingly used in the automotive and health care industries, for example, often perform worse for women. Second, unfair allocation of resources, information, and opportunities for women manifested in 61.5 percent of the systems we identified as gender-biased, including hiring software and ad systems that deprioritized women's applications.

Reinforcement of existing, harmful stereotypes and prejudices (in 28.2 percent of gender-biased systems) is exacerbated by feedback loops between data inputs and outputs. For instance, translation software, which learns from vast amounts of online text, has historically taken gender-neutral terms (such as "the doctor" or "the nurse" in English) and returned gendered translations (such as "el doctor" and "la enfermera," respectively, in Spanish), reinforcing stereotypes of male doctors and female nurses. Relatedly, we find that AI systems—most commonly in Internet-related services—result in derogatory and offensive treatment or erasure of already marginalized gender identities (6.84 percent). For example, using the gender binary in gender classification builds in an inaccurate, simplistic

---

1016   Niethammer, Carmen, "AI Bias Could Put Women's Lives At Risk – A Challenge For Regulators," March 2, 2020, Forbes, https://www.forbes.com/sites/carmenniethammer/2020/03/02/ai-bias-could-put-womens-lives-at-riska-challenge-for-regulators/

view of gender in tools such as facial analysis systems.

In addition, certain systems affect the physical and mental well-being of women and non-binary individuals. Gender-biased systems used in health care, welfare, and the automotive industry, in particular, pose detriments to physical safety (18.8 percent of gender-biased systems) and health hazards (3.42 percent). AI systems supporting skin cancer detection, for example, struggle to detect melanoma for Black people, putting Black women who are already underserved by the health care industry at risk.[1017]

[1017] Smith, Genevieve and Rustagi, Ishita, "When Good Algorithms Go Sexist: Why and How to Advance AI Gender Equity," March 31, 2021, Stanford Social Innovation Review, https://ssir.org/articles/entry/when_good_algorithms_go_sexist_why_and_how_to_advance_ai_gender_equity

WOMEN BRINGING WOMEN DOWN

"There is a special place in hell for women who don't help other women."
—U.S. Secretary of State Madeleine Albright[1018]

Shannon Faulkner was seventeen when she applied to the American military college known as The Citadel. Knowing they only accepted males, she did not include her gender on her application and marked it out on her transcripts. Although she was accepted, the school reversed that decision upon finding out she was female. She sued for violation of her civil rights, as The Citadel was a public school that received state funding.

The court allowed her to attend classes, starting in January 1994, pending the outcome of the trial. After two years and three semesters, the court ruled in her favour and The Citadel was forced to admit her as a full cadet.[1019]

But the battle was far from over.

A month before she was to start, her family home was vandalised for the first time, which soon became a regular occurrence. Then the death threats started, in writing, via phone calls, and, once, a man grabbed Shannon at a grocery store and told her he would enjoy burning her house down with her parents inside. It wasn't the last time he would threaten her.

"At one point in time, I thought I was going to die. I thought I was going to be the one that was going to be taken out, and I was willing to make that sacrifice," she

---

[1018] Albright, Madeleine, Keynote speech at Celebrating Inspiration luncheon with the WNBA's All-Decade Team, 2006.
[1019] Riddle, Lyn. "25 years ago, Shannon Faulkner left the Citadel in tears. But she changed the Corps," The Slate, September 15, 2020, https://www.thestate.com/news/local/military/article245597355.html

said in an interview. "But when it came to my friends and my family, they should not pay for my choices."

On her first day at the school, August 15, 1995, a man threatened her while she was in formation. Already psychologically beaten down, she was no match for the infamous Hell Week in 100-degree heat. She couldn't eat, suffered from nausea, and ended up in the infirmary before the day was over. There, she overheard a nurse scoff that she was faking. She lost fourteen pounds (6.4kg) over the next four days before she finally gave in and quit. So did five male cadets, but that fact was conveniently glossed over by the school and the media.

"I wasn't living," she said. "I was existing."

She later became a teacher, then a Title 1 planner supporting low-income families. It took more than seven years to recover from the trauma of her experience. While she doesn't take credit for the women who followed her, she does acknowledge her obvious contribution, and has stated that she considers herself a Citadel alumnus.

Nancy Mace, a Republican state lawmaker, later U.S. Congresswoman and the first woman to officially graduate from the school in 1999, sneeringly responded that Faulkner had not earned the right to do so, stating "She doesn't wear The Ring because she didn't earn it... There is no edification or achievement in her failure... 25 years later and she's still self-aggrandizing, trying to take credit for the success of others. Why does she think she can assume credit for my and others success where she failed? She can't even begin to comprehend what myself and hundreds of other women went through to earn the ring. We wear the ring because we earned it." Mace disregarded the legal battle that Faulkner had fought while only a teenager to enable Mace and other women to be admitted in the first place, much less the level of harassment that led to her "failure." [1020]

It's also worth noting that Mace is the daughter of Brigadier General James Emory Mace, who served as the commandant, third-in-command at The Citadel until 2005, a position he started on February 24 1997—just six months after his

---

[1020] "Nancy Mace fires back at Shannon Faulkner after Saturday event at The Citadel," March 6, 2018, Live 5 WCSC, https://www.live5news.com/story/37649311/nancy-mace-fires-back-at-shannon-faulkner-after-saturday-event-at-the-citadel/

daughter enrolled,[1021] and less than two months after two of the other three female cadets, Kim Messer and Jeanie Mentavlos, had left the school after having been physically assaulted, sexually harassed, and even had their clothes set on fire by eleven male classmates.[1022] Even before taking that position, he was the school's most decorated alumnus, and a former tactical officer at the Citadel. While there is no doubt that the younger Mace would not have had an easy time at the school, it also seems incredibly unlikely that her experience would have been anywhere near as difficult as Faulkner's, Messer's, and Mentavlos's.[1023]

While this ingrained and belligerent misogyny is particularly common among female right-wing politicians and media personalities, it is reflective of larger patterns of women bringing other women down. To be clear, this is not to say that women should not offer valid criticisms of other women—accountability is fundamental to progress. The key is whether a criticism is legitimate—if someone spouts offensive views or supports policies that harm others, for example—or not, such as making personal attacks about someone's appearance.

It has been, unfortunately, very common for female comedians to attack other women for a laugh, either individually—like Joan Rivers fat-shaming, slut-shaming, and even domestic violence victim-shaming female celebrities—or reinforcing negative and baseless stereotypes that do real damage in people's lives. While many critiques are certainly well-founded, often comedians—regardless of gender—are "punching down." This is when someone with privilege makes jokes at the expense of someone without that privilege. So it might be, for example, a white person making racist jokes, a wealthy person making jokes at the expense of poorer people, or a man making misogynistic jokes. It's also typically lazy on the part of the writer, as it plays into existing biases, rather than challenging or offering a new perspective on them.

Published in 2018, Australian comedian Kitty Flanagan's book *Burning Bridges*

1021 "Commandant retiring after 8 years at Citadel," Associated Press, January 9, 2005, https://www.goupstate.com/story/news/2005/01/10/commandant-retiring-after-8-years-at-citadel/29744035007/

1022 Havemann, Judith, "Two Women Quit Citadel over Alleged Harassment," *The Washington Post*, January 12, 1998, https://www.washingtonpost.com/archive/politics/1997/01/13/two-women-quit-citadel-over-alleged-harassment/54962eea-a265-4785-9daf-3808e4cf53fe/

1023 Mehren, Elizabeth, "Outrage at the Citadel," *Los Angeles Times*, January 24, 1997, https://www.latimes.com/archives/la-xpm-1997-01-24-ls-21508-story.html

and Other Hobbies ends on a particularly low note. She denounced the statistical prevalence of date rape, declaring that she doesn't think it's that high and that women lie because they regret their choices made while drunk. She then said men are justified in using date rape drugs because women don't get wasted as easily as they used to.[1024] This woman chose to use her considerable platform as one of the leading female comedians in her country to reinforce the dangerous myth that women lie about being raped, while simultaneously advocating men deliberately incapacitating women to rape them. I personally listened to the audiobook, read by Flanagan—her tone confirmed that any hope this might be last-minute satire was as misplaced as her sense of humour. While some might excuse the decades of blatant misogyny from a comic like Joan Rivers as being a product of her time—and even that is debatable—there is no such excuse for modern comedians.

Psychologically, there are a variety of reasons for women to try to hold other women down. For some, they have absorbed misogynistic views for so long and so deeply that they form a fundamental part of the person's worldview. This was likely the case for famed anti-feminist activist Phyllis Schlafly, who fought to keep women in the home—by putting her law degree to work and touring the country lobbying against the Equal Rights Amendment. It's unclear how this apparent contradiction sat in Schlafly's mind.

While women like Schlafly often appear to be zealots, there is also the hyper-practical ruthlessness that some people, regardless of gender, will simply do whatever they need to do to succeed—if that means subjugating others, that's what they'll do. During World War II, the Women Airforce Service Pilots (WASP) was a civilian organisation, whose members were United States federal civil service employees. WASPs later fought for recognition and benefits that acknowledged their military service. In 1977, Dorothy L. Starbuck became the first woman to lead the Veterans Administration, and almost immediately she argued that WASPs were not entitled to veterans' benefits, because they were civilians, even though the women had been subject to military discipline, assigned top secret missions and many members were

---

1024   Flanagan, Kitty, *Burning Bridges and Other Hobbies* (Allen and Unwin, 2018).

awarded service ribbons after their units were disbanded. Starbuck herself had been in the Women's Army Corps—the women's branch of the U.S. Army.[1025]

Contributing to this is the false scarcity principle—in the age of quotas, a sentiment was created that schools, companies, and other entities were checking boxes for diversity. If they have one woman (or one minority), they don't need any more. This built the inaccurate feeling that there is only room at the table for a limited number of people who are not cisgender, heterosexual white men, pushing marginalized people to place themselves in competition with each other, rather than working together in solidarity to improve the environment.

Some women also seek to elevate themselves by putting others down. Beauty pageant contestants are a common target for assuming that because a woman is pretty, she can't be intelligent or capable—an utterly absurd fallacy. And for those in the media whose jobs depend on ratings, they can appear desperate to say anything that will keep people watching. At the 2015 Miss America competition, Miss Colorado Kelley Johnson presented a passionate monologue about nursing while wearing her own scrubs, sharing a heartfelt story about a patient with Alzheimer's disease. While discussing the competition on the morning talk show The View, co-host Michelle Collins mocked Johnson by saying, "She came out in a nurse's uniform and basically read her emails out loud and, shockingly, did not win. I swear to God it was hilarious." But it was co-host Joy Behar who really enraged nurses across the country by implying that Johnson was wearing a costume and asking why she had a "doctor's" stethoscope.[1026]

Emotional factors like jealousy, feeling threatened, resentment and so on can also play a part, not least because women are taught to hide our emotions in our dealings with other people rather than being straightforward. This can lead to highly toxic friendships, work environments and more. As the character of Janis sings in the Broadway musical version of *Mean Girls*:

We're supposed to all be ladies

[1025] "Women Pilots Demand Equal Veterans Benefits," *Sioux City Journal*, May 30, 1977, https://www.newspapers.com/article/sioux-city-journal/36430360/

[1026] Anschuetz, Nika, "Voices: Female-on-female bashing has to stop," USA Today, September 29, 2015, https://www.usatoday.com/story/college/2015/09/29/voices-female-on-female-bashing-has-to-stop/37406723/

And be nurturing and care
Is that really fair?
Boys get to fight, we have to share
Here's the way that that turns out
We always understand
How to slap someone down
With our underhand.[1027]

Women can also simply be harder on other women if they feel that everyone else should have to fight just like they did. This unsupportive frame of mind is, of course, not exclusive to women—it's also very common in older generations toward younger generations in general.

Indeed, a recurring issue with many feminist movements is the exclusion of certain kinds of women, from white suffragists trying to ostracise activists of colour to the modern TERF (trans-exclusionary radical feminist) sentiments expressed by women such as J. K. Rowling and Chimamanda Ngozi Adichie. Many women with different forms of disadvantage have spoken out against more privileged feminists that focus only on their own concerns and experiences, rather than taking an intersectional approach that takes into account factors like racism, homophobia, transphobia, ableism, fat-phobia, religious discrimination, and other forms of bigotry. In discussing her 2021 book, *Against White Feminism*, Pakistani-American activist Rafia Zakaria recalled that "a lot of white female professors told me to quit" in law school.[1028] In the book, Zakaria writes, "A white feminist is someone who refuses to consider the role that whiteness and the racial privilege attached to it have played in universalising white feminist concerns, agendas and beliefs as being those of all of feminism and of all of feminists."[1029]

Women with privileges have a moral obligation to use those privileges to help

---

1027   Benjamin, Nell "I'd Rather Be Me," from Mean Girls (musical), 2018.
1028   Malik, Nesrine, "Rafia Zakaria: 'A lot of white female professors told me to quit,'" *The Guardian*, August 28, 2021, https://www.theguardian.com/books/2021/aug/28/rafia-zakaria-a-lot-of-white-female-professors-told-me-to-quit
1029   Zakaria, Rafia, *Against White Feminism* (W. W. Norton, 2021).

elevate our less privileged sisters. An excellent example of this was Eleanor Roosevelt, a tireless activist for countless causes, including civil rights. In 1939, the Daughters of the American Revolution (DAR) refused to allow African-American opera singer Marian Anderson to perform at their Constitution Hall. In response, Roosevelt resigned her membership and organized a performance at the Lincoln Memorial instead. Seventy-five thousand people attended.[1030]

1030 Stamberg, Susan, "Denied A Stage, She Sang For A Nation," NPR, April 9, 2014, https://www.npr.org/2014/04/09/298760473/denied-a-stage-she-sang-for-a-nation

RESPECTABILITY

"I myself have never been able to find out precisely what feminism is: I only know that people call me a feminist whenever I express sentiments that differentiate me from a doormat."
—Rebecca West[1031]

In 1958, U.S. Congresswoman Coya Knutson's career was destroyed, though no fault of her own beyond having chosen a bad husband. A rising star in her second term, Knutson's political rivals weaponised her estranged husband. She had moved to Washington DC in part for her career, but also to escape his physical abuse and alcoholism. This led to the circulation of rumours, likely false, that she was having an affair. A letter was published in newspapers across the countries begging, "Coya, Come Home" to their supposedly "happy home." It was signed by her husband, but clearly written by rivals within her own Democratic Party. "Coya, I want you to tell the people of the 9th District this Sunday that you are through in politics. That you want to go home and make a home for your husband and son. As your husband I compel you to do this. I'm tired of being torn apart from my family. I'm sick and tired of having you run around with other men all the time and not your husband. I love you, honey." The phrasing played on several aspects of traditional gender roles—implying Knutson was cheating and therefore bringing her sexual morality into question, claiming that she was neglecting her duties at home and tearing apart her family, that a husband had a right to "compel" his wife to give up her career. Her Republican opponent ran with the slogan "A Big Man for a

---

1031 West, Rebecca, "Mr Chesterton in Hysterics A Study in Prejudice," The Clarion, November 14, 1913.

Man-sized Job." All told, it was just enough to cause Knutson to lose by just over 1,000 votes, ending her political career. Ironically, she had considered publicly addressing the issues in her marriage two years earlier but had been dissuaded by her aides for the same reason: respectability.[1032]

Broadly speaking, the term "respectability politics" refers to a philosophy that advises marginalized people to behave "appropriately" in order to be treated decently. In this context, "appropriately" doesn't mean obeying laws, treating others with respect, and behaving responsibly—respectability politics holds people of colour, members of the LGBTQ+ community, people with disability or who are neurodivergent and, of course, women as a whole, to a standard of niceness that often equates to accepting our own subjugation. Respectability politics is calling a Black woman unprofessional for wearing her hair in dreadlocks. It's telling women they're too loud, too bossy, "too much" when they're still less so than the men around them. It's every man who's ever told a woman he doesn't even know to smile.

Respectability politics in the context of this chapter refers to sexist ideas about the expectations placed on women and how they hold women back creatively and professionally. Specifically, we're talking about the limitations placed on women when they are told what they "should" be doing to be a good woman, wife, mother, etcetera. These are criteria that are not based on objective fact and are not applied equally to men.

Often, measures ostensibly meant to protect women only serve to limit them. When Canadian scientist Margaret Newton's mentor, W. P. Fraser, assigned her to study samples of stem rust, she would be assisting him in fighting an epidemic that destroyed 100 million bushels of wheat in 1916. It was important work to be sure, but she only accepted after the university's dean ended the restrictions preventing women from working in the labs at night. Like other female students, she was still required to abide by a 10 p.m. curfew.[1033] She later became an internationally regarded expert on the topic of rust spores and her research led to a reduction of

---

1032   Halloran, Liz, "The Congresswoman Whose Husband Called Her Home," NPR, May 10, 2014, https://www.npr.org/sections/itsallpolitics/2014/05/10/310996960/the-congresswoman-whose-husband-called-her-home
1033   Kolmer, J.A., "Margaret Newton: Pioneering Cereal Rust Researcher," American Phytopathological Society, 2005, https://doi.org/10.1094/apsnetfeature-2005-0305

annual losses of wheat due to rust from 30 million bushels to practically none in Canada.[1034]

In the 1940s, runner Joan O'Reilly was arguably the fastest woman in Ireland, yet she was not allowed to represent her country at the 1948 Olympics due to a widespread conservative opposition to women participating in "public" sports such as track and field events. Dorothy "Tommy" Dermody, a fencer, was the only female athlete to compete from Ireland that year—one can only assume fencing was considered higher-class and therefore more acceptable.[1035]

Tan Yunxian, one of China's most famous women doctors, was very fortunate in many ways. Descended from a family of doctors, she learned healing from her grandparents, she was financially privileged, and her husband supported her endeavours. Yet, in her book 1500s *Miscellaneous Record of a Female Doctor*, she writes "As I am a woman, it is inappropriate to go outside to see to its publication, so I have told my son, Lian, to copy it and have it carved on blocks for printing in the hope that it may help other doctors. I beg readers' indulgence and ask that they not laugh at me."[1036]

Alcohol is another hot-button issue. Historian Mallory O'Meara in her book *Girly Drinks: A World History of Women and Alcohol*, correlates the acceptance of women drinking with their broader rights in a society—the less tolerant a community is of one, the less tolerant they are of the other. In addition to forcing women out of related professions, this is also reflected in the criticism women face, such as Song dynasty poet Li Qingzhao. She wrote in depth about how much she loved alcohol, which was widely deemed inappropriate for a woman, as was the fact that she dared to divorce a man who mistreated her.[1037]

Respectability is a major component in who people are likely to listen to,

---

1034 Pageau, Denis, "Commemorative day of the centenary of the Quebec plant protection society," *Phytoprotection* vol 89 no 2-3, (2008), p. 139–141, https://www.erudit.org/fr/revues/phyto/2008-v89-n2-3-phyto3429/038246ar/

1035 O'Riordan, Turlough, "O'Reilly, Joan Gertrude," Dictionary of Irish Biography, https://www.dib.ie/biography/oreilly-joan-gertrude-a10200

1036 Tan Yunxian, Nüyi zayan ping'an yishi, ed. Wang Jian (Beijing: Zhongguo Zhongyiyzo Chubanshe, 2016), preface and postscripts, https://uw.manifoldapp.org/read/chinese-autobiographical-writing/section/c43db801-cd29-452b-8efd-58313bded888

1037 O'Meara, Mallory, *Girly Drinks: A World History of Women and Alcohol* (Hanover Square Press, 2021).

sympathise with, and trust. While most American schoolchildren learn the story of civil rights activist Rosa Parks, she was not the first African American woman to fight the battle of segregation on public transport. On March 2, 1955, fifteen-year-old Claudette Colvin was arrested for refusing to surrender her seat to a Caucasian woman on a Montgomery, Alabama bus—nine months before Parks. She, Aurelia Browder, Susie McDonald, Mary Louise Smith, and Jeanetta Reese took the case to court in *Browder v. Gayle*. But reportedly, Parks was seen as a better face of the Montgomery Bus Boycott, being a mature adult in her forties with a job.[1038]

Colvin, meanwhile, was an unwed, pregnant fifteen-year-old prone to outbursts and cursing. Parks later stated of the pregnancy, "If the white press got ahold of that information, they would have [had] a field day. They'd call her a bad girl, and her case wouldn't have a chance."[1039] By comparison, Aurelia Browder, who was chosen as lead defendant, was a college-educated woman in her thirties with years of civil rights work to her name. *Browder v. Gayle* made it all the way to the U.S. Supreme Court, which declined to overturn the previous ruling that the policy was unconstitutional, ordering the end of bus segregation in Alabama.

Parks herself is often depicted as a woman who was just tired and had had enough—in fact, she was a long-time activist who knew exactly what she was doing. The story presented to the public was a deliberate effort to get the maximum public sympathy, at the expense of Parks's personal agency, dedication, and years of activism.

Alfred Kinsey is widely considered the world's first sexologist, publishing his groundbreaking and controversial *Sexual Behavior in the Human Male* in 1948 and *Sexual Behavior in the Human Female* in 1953. But Dr. Clelia Duel Mosher was doing her own research in the subject more than fifty years earlier. Her Mosher Report remains the only known existing survey of Victorian women's sexual habits, begun in 1892 and continued for nearly thirty years. Yet it was never published during her lifetime, and was only made public decades after her death, when historian Carl Degler found it among her unpublished papers in the Stanford University

---

1038 Kelley, Jenn, "Claudette Colvin (1939 –) Nurse and civil rights activist," College of DuPage Library, February 16, 2021, https://library.cod.edu/BHM/daily/Claudette-Colvin
1039 "She would not be moved," *The Guardian*, December 15, 2000, https://web.archive.org/web/20130824210949/https://www.theguardian.com/theguardian/2000/dec/16/weekend7.weekend12

Archives. Although it is unknown why she chose not to publish, the survey was controversial at the time for its acknowledgement of social taboos—respondents were, unacceptably for Victorian women, candid about topics like contraception and orgasms, and were largely sex-positive. That candour was likely because the person asking was another woman. Mosher clearly believed in the importance of her work, which also included studies of menstruation and how to alleviate associated symptoms—another taboo of the time. Her Master's thesis disproved the belief that women were inherently weaker because biology restricted their breathing—rather than, say, corsets. It is reasonable to assume that the survey, which she compiled throughout her professional life, was simply too scandalous to risk the likely impact on her career. She did note in an introduction that the survey had provided her with "a priceless knowledge for the practicing physician and teacher; a background sufficiently broad to avoid prejudice in her work with women."[1040]

Because respectability is often tied up with religion, the driving factors become internal as well as external—women are not just worried about what others will think, but whether they are committing a moral offence against a church or higher power. In the introduction to her book, *La Chymie Charitable et Facile, en Faveur des Dames* (*Easy Chemistry for Women*), 1600s chemist Marie Meurdrac described an "inner struggle" between the feminine ideal of a woman as "silent, listen and learn, without displaying...knowledge." Fortunately, she came to the conclusion that "it would be a sin against Charity to hide the knowledge that God has given me, which may be of benefit to the world."[1041]

Caterina Vitale was everything the patriarchy has traditionally hated in a woman, both today and in late 1500s/early 1600s Malta. She was rich, independent, a successful businesswoman, had scientific knowledge of chemistry and medicine—the full package. While that would have made her a prime target for witch-burning, she was both a benefactress of the Carmelite nuns and the pharmacist for the Catholic military order Knights Hospitaller, having taken over her

---

[1040] Jacob, Kathryn Allamong, "The Mosher Report," American Heritage, June/July 1981, https://www.americanheritage.com/mosher-report
[1041] Meurdrac, Marie, La Chymie Charitable et Facile, En Faveur Des Dames, 1687.

husband's job after his death in 1590 when she was just fourteen. But while she likely had a reasonable degree of protection from the Church, she was still subject to rumours that claimed she was everything from a prostitute to a sadistic torturer of slaves.[1042]

The ideal of the woman as traditional homemaker is also frequently part of the "family values" framing trotted out by political conservatives as an argument to attack anything they don't like, from women in the workforce to gay and transgender rights. During the anti-Communist fervour of the Red Scare in the U.S., women government officials like Anna M. Rosenberg, Dorothy Kenyon, Dr. Esther Brunhauer, and Mary Dublin Keyserling were disproportionately targeted by Sen. Joe McCarthy and his goons.[1043] In the 1930s and 1940s, the charge was used against dozens of women in the media like Dorothy Parker, Lena Horne, Lillian Hellman, and Gypsy Rose Lee, who threatened to use radio and television to show an America that was diverse, complicated and inclusive. Thanks to politicians and the FBI—which had no female agents at the time due to the misogyny of director J. Edgar Hoover—more than forty women were blacklisted ostensibly due to suspected Communist leanings.[1044] Yet, as Carol A. Stabile, author of *The Broadcast 41: Women and the Anti-Communist Blacklist*, notes, "Some of them were blacklisted simply for their support of the New Deal and Franklin Delano Roosevelt during the depression." And there was no effective way for the victims to fight back, Stabile adds. "They promoted rumors and gossip, all of it without factual backing. There were some cases where people did fight back and made them correct their errors in the pages of (blacklisting magazine) *Counterattack*. But as someone once said of Jean Muir, the first actress to be targeted, it's like a bruised Apple. Once the Apple is bruised, the taint remains. And even if you defended yourself, it just feeds the publicity." In doing so, these men successfully shaped U. S. media for

---

1042 "'Sex in the City' Tour: The Knights and Their Ladies of the Night," *The Malta Independent*, March 25, 2007, https://www.independent.com.mt/articles/2007-03-25/news/sex-in-the-city-tour-the-knights-and-their-ladies-of-the-night-171028/
1043 Gorham, Christopher C., *The Confidante: The Untold Story of the Woman Who Helped Win WWII and Shape Modern America* (Citadel, 2023).
1044 Kelly, Sam, "How the FBI Destroyed the Careers of 41 Women in TV and Radio," The MIT Press Reader, January 20, 2022, https://thereader.mitpress.mit.edu/how-the-fbi-destroyed-the-careers-of-progressive-women/

decades. "It removed a lot of very, very talented people from the industry. People who had progressive points of view." Of those who remained, "People learned to self-censor.... People just learned. We all know. We work in various places. There are some fights you think you could win and some you can't. Writing about race, writing about women's liberation, writing about immigration, all became very controversial. While there were people who still manage to do some of this work, it was not easy to do it and it certainly wasn't encouraged."

Women in physically demanding professions often find their validity challenged, even by strangers. Retired firefighter Linda F. Willing, after thirty years of such comments, observed, "I remember one criticism that was frequently aimed at me and other women firefighters back in the early days – that we were "too defensive." But it only follows that people seem defensive when they are forced to constantly defend themselves to others."[1045]

1045 Willing, Linda F., "Sheer Exhaustion: Accomplished Career Firefighter Still Confronting Ignorance of Skeptics," Women You Should Know, January 8, 2015, https://womenyoushouldknow.net/sheer-exhaustion-accomplished-career-firefighter-still-confronting-ignorance-skeptics/

PSYCHOLOGICAL BARRIERS TO SUCCESS

"It took me quite a long time to develop a voice, and now that I have it, I am not going to be silent."
—Madeleine Albright[1046]

Women internalize misogyny in a variety of ways. In many of the studies cited throughout this book, both men and women have shown negative views and behaviours towards women. This mindset also diminishes what we think is achievable in our own lives.

As a general rule, society has largely taught women to underestimate ourselves. A U.S. study found that between the ages of eight and fourteen, girls' confidence drops by an average of thirty percent.[1047] In their pre-teen and teen years, their belief that people like them drops by almost half, from seventy-one percent to thirty-eight percent. Simultaneously, more than half of teen girls feel pressure to be perfect and between the ages of twelve and thirteen, the percentage who say they're not allowed to fail increases by 150 percent.[1048] Women are also more likely to underestimate our own abilities and internalize negative feedback, allowing it

---

1046 Schnall, Marianne, "Madeleine Albright: An Exclusive Interview," Huffington Post, December 6, 2017, https://www.huffpost.com/entry/madeleine-albright-an-exc_b_604418
1047 "The Confidence Code for Girls: The Confidence Collapse and Why It Matters for the Next Gen," Ypulse, 2018.https://static1.squarespace.com/static/588b93f6bf629a6bec7a3bd2/t/5ac39193562fa73c-d8a07a89/1522766258986/
1048 Shipman, Claire, Katty Kay, and JillEllyn Riley, "The Confidence Gap for Girls: 5 Tips for Parents of Tween and Teen Girls," *The New York Times*, October 1, 2018, https://www.nytimes.com/2018/10/01/well/family/confidence-gap-teen-girls-tips-parents.html

to drag our confidence down.[1049]

This combination of less confidence and feeling the need to be perfect also means women are less likely to put themselves forward for jobs if they do not meet all the qualification criteria. In an article on the topic, *Harvard Business Review* notes:

> It makes perfect sense that women take written job qualifications more seriously than men, for several reasons:
>
> First, it's likely that due to bias in some work environments, women do need to meet more of the qualifications to be hired than do their male counterparts. For instance, a McKinsey report found that men are often hired or promoted based on their potential, women for their experience and track record. If women have watched that occur in their workplaces, it makes perfect sense they'd be less likely to apply for a job for which they didn't meet the qualifications.
>
> Second, girls are strongly socialized to follow the rules and in school are rewarded, again and again, for doing so. In part, girls' greater success in school (relative to boys) arguably can be attributed to their better rule following. Then in their careers, that rule-following habit has real costs, including when it comes to adhering to the guidelines about "who should apply."
>
> Third, certifications and degrees have historically played a different role for women than for men. The 20th century saw women break into professional life – but only if they had the right training, the right accreditations. These qualifications were our ticket in, our way of proving we could do the job. We weren't part of an old boys club in which we'd get the benefit of the doubt. That history can, I think, lead women to see the workplace as more orderly and meritocratic than it really is. As a result we may overestimate the importance of our formal training and qualifications, and underutilize advocacy and networking.[1050]

[1049] Todd, Sarah, "How Negative Feedback Impacts Women and Men Differently," Quartz, November 23, 2021, https://qz.com/work/2093763/how-negative-feedback-impacts-women-differently

[1050] Mohr, Tara Sophia, "Why Women Don't Apply for Jobs Unless They're 100% Qualified," Harvard Business Review, 2014, https://hbr.org/2014/08/why-women-dont-apply-for-jobs-unless-theyre-100-qualified

Women are also taught not to talk about our own skills and accomplishments, such as Ada Lovelace reputedly downplaying her work as the world's first computer programmer and publishing under her initials (AAL) to avoid being "accused of bragging."[1051] This in turn makes us less effective self-advocates even for those of us who will vocally advocate for others. When we do point out our skills and contributions, we are more likely to be called arrogant where a man would be called confident. This goes back to the triple bind—women are often assumed to be less competent, but if we offset that by detailing our credentials, we are more likely to be seen as "unlikeable" and penalised for that instead. In 2014, researchers examined fifty-one studies from different countries and found that when women negotiated on behalf of another person, they outperformed men—but not when they were negotiating on their own behalf. We are allowed to fight for others but are frequently penalised when we speak up for ourselves.[1052]

An 2015 international study of 350,000 participants measured explicit and implicit bias, and found a major one: that science was seen as a male profession. The bias was stronger in countries where there were fewer women in the sciences, like the Netherlands, South Africa, Denmark, Switzerland, and Japan, while countries like Argentina, Portugal, Spain, and Canada were among the least biassed—though the bias was still present, simply weaker.[1053]

Author Shannon Hale is best known for her *Princess Academy* children's series. As a frequent visitor to schools, she has seen firsthand the impact of misogyny on both boys and girls countless times, such as only girls being invited to her assemblies and boys who are fans being too embarrassed to come. Among the many comments she's gotten:

> A librarian, introducing me before my presentation: "Girls, you're in for a real treat. You're going to love Shannon Hale's books. Boys, I expect

---

[1051] Smith, Erika E., "Recognizing a Collective Inheritance through the History of Women in Computing," *CLCWeb: Comparative Literature & Culture: A WWWeb Journal* vol 15 no 1 (2013) pp 1–9 – via EBSCOhost
[1052] "Women Outperform Men in Some Financial Negotiations, Research Finds," American Psychological Association, 2014, https://www.apa.org/news/press/releases/2014/12/financial-negotiations
[1053] Bernstein, Rachel, "Science Still Seen as Male Profession, according to International Study of Gender Bias," Science, May 22, 2015, https://www.science.org/content/article/science-still-seen-male-profession-according-international-study-gender-bias

you to behave anyway."

A book festival committee member: "Last week we met to choose a keynote speaker for next year. I suggested you, but another member said, 'What about the boys?' so we chose a male author instead."

A parent: "My son read your book and he ACTUALLY liked it!"

A teacher: "I never noticed before, but for read aloud I tend to choose books about boys because I assume those are the only books the boys will like."

A mom: "My son asked me to read him *The Princess in Black*, and I said, 'No, that's for your sister,' without even thinking about it."

A bookseller: "I've stopped asking people if they're shopping for a boy or a girl and instead asking them what kind of story the child likes."[1054]

Researcher Deepa Narayan specializes in poverty, gender, and development, and her work led her to identify seven beliefs that silence girls:

Habit one: You don't have a body. ... When a girl rejects her body, she rejects her only house and invisibility and insecurity become her very shaky foundation. ...

Habit two: Be quiet. Educated women said that their number one problem was their inability to speak up, as if there was a foot on their throat ready to choke them...

Habit three: Be a people pleaser. Please others. Everyone likes a nice woman who always smiles, who never says no, who is never angry, even when she's being exploited.

Habit four: You have no sexuality.

Habit five: Don't trust women. ... It's much easier to demolish a woman who is alone.

Habit six: Duty over desire. ... By the time you fulfil duty, whatever little desire is left is also lost. ... A woman becomes a residue.

1054 Hale, Shannon, "We're Ready: A Post for #Kidlitwomen," ShannonHale.com, March 1, 2018, https://shannonhale.com/blog-archive/2018/03/01/were-ready-a-post-for-kidlitwomen

Habit seven: Be totally dependent.

So all these habits collectively crush women, fill her with fear, and make her totally dependent on men for her survival, and this allows the system of male power to continue.[1055]

SHE'S A WITCH!

In modern times, beer has been gender-coded as stereotypically masculine, but it used to be women's work. For most of the 7,000 years humans have been making beer, it was women doing the brewing, whether they were Egyptians or Vikings. In addition to uses at home, it was also a way for women—married or not—to earn income. Today, the image of a woman in a tall, pointed hat leaning over a cauldron, a cat nearby, is associated in the Western world with witches, but in the Middle Ages, this was the look of a brewer—the cauldron was full of beer and the hats helped customers find them in a crowded marketplace. Cats were not familiars but rat catchers that kept pests away from their grain.[1056]

With the Reformation in the 1500s that advocated for harsher gender roles and condemned witchcraft, male brewers saw a chance to reduce competition, as did the church, which blamed alewives for poor attendance at Sunday services. In sermons, writing, and imagery, these women were associated with the Devil, accused of using their cauldrons to brew potions instead of beer, and it was soon was dangerous for women to make and sell beer for fear of being denounced and possibly killed.

Their sake-making sisters in Edo Japan faced their own attack from Buddhists who suddenly decided in the early 1600s that sake was essentially female and, as such, having other women around would make it angry and jealous, forcing the women out of the industry. It is no coincidence that such actions also removed a legitimate path to financial independence for women. As historian Judith Bennett observes, "When a venture prospers, women fade from the scene."

1055   Deepa Narayan, "7 Beliefs That Can Silence Women—and How to Unlearn Them," TED Talks, 2012, https://www.ted.com/talks/deepa_narayan_7_beliefs_that_can_silence_women_and_how_to_unlearn_them/transcript
1056   O'Meara, Mallory, *Girly Drinks: A World History of Women and Alcohol* (Hanover Square Press, 2021).

Historically, calling a woman "unnatural" and/or accusing her of witchcraft has been one way to get rid of women for just about any reason, particularly if she was outspoken, independent, or knowledgeable—in other words, if she threatened the men. Joan of Arc, for example, believed—as did many other people—that holy voices spoke to her, which in itself gave her significant influence, and she was also a successful military leader while only a teenager, fighting for a fairly weak French king. Burning her as a witch was a brilliant—albeit horrific—tactical move on the English's part to undermine her influence and therefore the French king. But even much more personal levels of individual freedoms can be seen as a threat. Of the women we have enough information about, eighty-nine percent of those executed for witchcraft in New England between 1620 and 1725 had neither brothers nor sons to share their inheritance.[1057]

Going back as far as ancient Greece, Aglaonice of Thessaly may have been the first female astronomer. By studying Babylonian astronomy, she was able to predict lunar eclipses. And of course, rather than accepting a logical explanation, they assumed she was a witch. To be fair, she played into this, claiming she could "make the moon disappear from the sky" and gathering other "witches of Thessaly."[1058] In that society, being seen as a witch gave her power—other women throughout history have not been so lucky. Even earlier than Aglaonice, who lived in the first or second century BCE, Theoris of Lemnos is the first known person to be executed for witchcraft, around 323 BCE in Athens. The surviving evidence is unclear on what she was charged with, but she was a folk healer, the first of many who would be denounced.[1059]

Executed in 1461, Spanish healer Guirandana de Lay was a typical example of a witch hunt victim, who were often used as scapegoats for illness and other woes. She was single, independent, a foreigner (from France), and a healer, which

---

[1057] Day, Christian, "The Vulnerability of Women to Witchcraft Accusations," Salem Tarot, 1992, http://www.salemtarot.com/archive/seminar.html
[1058] Woodward, Afton Lorraine, "Moon Schemes," Lady Science, August 14, 2017, https://www.ladyscience.com/essays/moonschemes-eclipse2017
[1059] Collins, Derek, "Theoris of Lemnos and the Criminalization of Magic in Fourth-Century Athens," *The Classical Quarterly* vol 51 no 2 (2001) pp 477–93, https://www.jstor.org/stable/3556523

challenged the authority and power of the male physicians.[1060]

But even being completely respectable is not a guarantee of protection. Rebecca Nurse was a respected wife, mother, and grandmother, known for piety and benevolence. She was a covenant church member—the highest status a Puritan could achieve. Yet none of this kept the seventy-one-year-old from being executed as part of the Salem witch trials in 1692. She had public support—thirty-nine of the community's most prominent members signed a petition on her behalf and testified to her good character. Examining magistrate John Hathorne's own sister, Elizabeth Porter, was a good friend of Rebecca's and spoke on her behalf. None of it was enough to save her. Although the jury initially found her not guilty, they were convinced to change their verdict, and she was hanged.[1061]

When midwife Margaret Jones was charged with witchcraft in 1648, the "evidence" against her included "She would use to tell such as would not make use of her physic, that they would never be healed; and accordingly their diseases and hurts continued, with relapse against the ordinary course, and beyond the apprehension of all physicians and surgeons." So, a medical professional told patients that if they didn't follow her advice, they wouldn't get better. There was also this gem: "Some things which she foretold came to pass accordingly." She was the first person executed for witchcraft in the Massachusetts Bay Colony, but not the last as the witch hunts there lasted for forty-five years, with around eighty people accused and fifteen executed (thirteen of them women).[1062]

Throughout history, powerful women have been accused of witchcraft to try and undermine their credibility, including Cleopatra and Anne Boleyn. In both of those cases, it's interesting to note that their sexuality was also a matter of much public commentary. Gentile Budrioli was an influential astrologist and herbal healer in 1400s Bologna, renowned for her skills, a close friend of the ruler's wife,

---

1060 Fernández Otal, José Antonio, Guirandana de Lay, hechicera, ¿bruja? y ponzoñera de Villanúa (Alto Aragón), según un proceso criminal del año 1461 (Alto Aragón).
1061 Hainley, Susannah, "Perspective | My Ancestor Was Accused of Witchcraft. Here's Why Her Story Haunts Me," *The Washington Post*, October 23, 2022, https://www.washingtonpost.com/lifestyle/2022/10/23/my-ancestor-was-accused-witchcraft-heres-why-her-story-haunts-me/
1062 Lewis, Jone Johnson, "Margaret Jones: Executed for Witchcraft, 1648," ThoughtCo, Updated on March 25, 2017, https://www.thoughtco.com/margaret-jones-biography-3530774

and even briefly a councillor at the Bolognese court. However, when she failed to save the ruler's son from illness, her enemies saw an opportunity to strike at her and the ruling family she served. She was accused and the Inquisition fabricated evidence against her and tortured her. Perhaps no man was more envious of her than her own husband, who had opposed her pursuits and testified against her at her trial, claiming she had bespelled him to hamper his own intelligence.[1063]

Aglaonice was not the only woman scientist to present her work as magic, though in the case of mineralogist Martine de Bertereau, this approach backfired badly. She claimed that she and her husband used mysterious and esoteric methods to locate water, in what appears to have been early hydrogeology. For example, she claimed to use dowsing rods to find water, but a local doctor realised she had instead followed the water's red, iron-rich deposits in the cobblestone back to its source. The revelation made people much more suspicious and contributed to their eventual downfall. The family were later accused of witchcraft and fled their native France for Hungary in 1628. Martine, her husband, and oldest daughter were later arrested, imprisoned in different locations and eventually died in prison after 1642.[1064]

While it would be nice to think this particular brand of barbarism is a thing of the past, magical paranoia and the violence it incites is alive and well. On November 20, 2010, Ama Hemmah was attacked in Ghana by five people convinced she was a witch. They tortured a "confession" out of her and then tried to exorcise an evil spirit by dousing her in kerosene and setting her on fire. She died from her injuries.[1065] Albinos in Africa are also at risk of being brutally attacked and murdered to harvest their body parts because of beliefs about their supposed magical properties. In 1997, two Russian farmers killed a woman and sent four of her children to the hospital because they believed her daughter had worked folk

---

1063 "Gentile Budrioli, 'Strega Enormissima' Di Bologna," Genus Bononiae Blog, July 11, 2018, https://genus-bononiaeblog.it/gentile-budrioli-strega-enormissima-bologna/
1064 Schuh, Curtis, "Bertereau, Martine de B," Mineralogical Record, https://mineralogicalrecord.com/new_biobibliography/bertereau-martine-de-b-de-b/
1065 Smith, David, "Ghanaian Woman Burned to Death for Being a 'Witch,'" The Guardian, November 29, 2010, https://www.theguardian.com/world/2010/nov/29/ghanaian-woman-burned-death-witch

magic on them.[1066] Saudi woman Amina bint Abdul Halim bin Salem Nasser was beheaded in 2011 on charges of "witchcraft and sorcery."[1067] In 2012, a report from the Legal and Human Rights Centre estimated that Tanzanians lynched an average of 500 people per year on suspicion of witchcraft between 2005 and 2011.[1068] A 2010 UNICEF report warned of the rise in attacks on children in Africa accused of being witches, mostly boys ages eight to fourteen.[1069] Witch hunts in Nepal have happened as recently as 2019[1070] and include beatings, forcing the accused to eat faeces and burning the victim alive; in 2018, an eighteen-year-old was dragged from her home and tortured for six hours in front of a cheering crowd of hundreds on International Women's Day.[1071]

1066   Specter, Michael, "In Modern Russia, a Fatal Medieval Witch Hunt," *The New York Times*, April 5, 1997, https://www.nytimes.com/1997/04/05/world/in-modern-russia-a-fatal-medieval-witch-hunt.html
1067   "Saudi Woman Executed for 'Witchcraft and Sorcery,'" December 12, 2011, https://www.bbc.com/news/world-middle-east-16150381
1068   "Thousands Lynched for Witchcraft in Tanzania, Report Finds," Huffington Post, May 29, 2012, https://www.huffpost.com/entry/tanzania-witchcraft-3000-lynchings-witches_n_1553448
1069   "Rise in African Children Accused of Witchcraft," July 17, 2010, https://www.bbc.com/news/world-africa-10671790
1070   "Probe into Thrashing of Witchcraft-Accused Starts," The Himalayan Times, March 11, 2018, https://thehimalayantimes.com/nepal/probe-thrashing-witchcraft-accused-starts/
1071   "Branded 'Witch', Nepal Woman Force-Fed Human Excreta: Police," Hindustan Times, August 19, 2019, https://www.hindustantimes.com/world-news/branded-witch-nepal-woman-force-fed-human-excreta-police/story-N0US7FHSNSKv3RxymAWRiM.html

SLUT SHAMING

"If you're beautiful, you're led to believe that you can't also be smart. But you can be fun and fit and social and be really smart. And the smarter you are, the more capable you'll be to handle whatever challenges come up in life."
—Danica McKellar

In 1911, Marie Curie won her second Nobel Prize, this one in Chemistry for discovering radium and polonium. Unfortunately, that was the same year her affair with a younger, married man was made very public, and the chair of the Nobel committee tried to keep her from attending the ceremony due to her supposedly questionable morals. She told him off and showed up anyway.[1072]

Slut shaming is the act of demeaning and undermining a woman by focusing on her sexual attitudes and activities—real or imagined. To be clear, I do not mean to disparage sex work or women who enjoy sex. However, demeaning societal attitudes toward such behaviours mean that calling a woman promiscuous or a prostitute has often been used as a way to undermine her character, value, and credibility. From Aspasia to U.S. Congresswoman Katie Hill, slut shaming weaponizes sexuality to diminish a woman's contributions and sabotage their futures. It is even done to entire groups of women, like the British members of Parliament reduced to "Blair's Babes" or the Harvard Observatory astronomers minimized as "Pickering's Harem."

Even when a woman does develop a reputation for her work, it can be all too easy for her to be taken down, often for things that men would be able to recover

---

[1072] "Marie Curie – Scandal and Recovery (1910-1913)," American Institute of Physics, https://history.aip.org/exhibits/curie/scandal1.htm

from, even if they're completely fictitious. In 2018, Australian Member of Parliament Emma Husar chose not to run for re-election because she did not think her career could survive the completely false claim that she had supposedly exposed herself to a fellow MP (a charge both of them deny). It also emerged that the person who had made the allegation wasn't even in Canberra on the day he claimed it took place. Her own party, the Australian Labor Party, refused to endorse their incumbent for re-election. She later successfully sued Buzzfeed for publishing the rumour, and an independent investigation cleared her, but the damage was done. Husar said, "That's actually what brought my career in politics to an end, was being slut shamed so viciously, with no ability to come back and stand up for myself. It's just gutter journalism and essentially that's what ended my career… I absolutely love my job as an MP and my community has been incredibly supportive over this time. But I think that people would use that against me forever."[1073]

Although powerful and popular, Argentine activist and First Lady Eva Perón—immortalised in the musical *Evita*—still faced rampant sexism, not least because of her background as an actress. That was in addition to classism because she rose out of poverty and fought for the working class. Her critics tried to depict her as a manipulative harlot, with some calling her "La Gran Puta" ("The Great Whore") who secretly controlled the government. This also served as a tactic to undermine her husband, Juan Perón, by presenting him as a weak puppet.[1074]

Revenge porn, a subset of slut-shaming, involves publicly sharing nude images or videos as an attack on someone, typically a woman. In the age of Photoshop and deepfakes, these images may not even be authentic. Women in Myanmar faced revenge porn attacks when they protested the government's military coup in 2021.[1075] Meanwhile, celebrities like Jennifer Lawrence and Ariana Grande had

---

1073   Hutchens, Gareth, "Emma Husar Says 'Vicious Slut Shaming' Ended Her Career," *The Guardian*, August 28, 2018, https://www.theguardian.com/australia-news/2018/aug/29/emma-husar-says-vicious-slut-shaming-ended-her-career

1074   "Meet Eva Perón: Argentina's Most Powerful and Controversial Woman," Medium, September 28, 2016, https://amysmartgirls.com/meet-eva-per%C3%B3n-argentinas-most-powerful-and-controversial-woman-ff85d9099b62

1075   Thiha, Amara, "Revenge Porn Has Become a Political Weapon in Myanmar," The Diplomat, August 9, 2021, https://thediplomat.com/2021/08/revenge-porn-has-become-a-political-weapon-in-myanmar/

their images released by hackers in 2014, an experience Lawrence has described as traumatic.[1076] As noted earlier, Picasso pre-dated the trend by producing and selling images of Dora Maar's genitalia and naked body.

As in other countries where white colonizers sought to exterminate not only Indigenous populations, but also their cultures, Australian history features a dark chapter: the Stolen Generation. This refers to a decades-long governmental practice of essentially kidnapping Aboriginal children from their families and forcing them into "schools" where they were often mistreated and their cultures and languages indoctrinated out of them. One of the best-known accounts of these experiences is *Follow the Rabbit-Proof Fence* (1996), a non-fiction book written by Doris Pilkington Garimara about the escape from such an institution by her mother, Molly Craig, Molly's half-sister Daisy and their cousin, Gracie. The girls were aged around 8 to 14 at the time and, although Molly and Daisy made it home after more than two months travelling by foot, Gracie gave up, was recaptured, and never returned home.[1077] The book was adapted into an award-winning 2002 film, *Rabbit-Proof Fence*.

Just as there are Holocaust deniers and Americans who want to claim the U.S. Civil War was not about slavery, "historian" Keith Windschuttle is best-known for his adamant contention that the Stolen Generation (and other forms of violence and oppression toward Aboriginal Australians) was essentially a myth, despite the testimony of countless Aboriginal Australians as well as plenty of documentation. Calling the film "grossly inaccurate," Windschuttle claims that the girls were actually removed because of their supposed promiscuity with white men. Attempting to use this to discredit the entire story and insist the movie should not be shown in schools, he bases this claim on a single phrase in letter to A. O. Neville—the British eugenicist who shaped and implemented these policies in Western Australia—in which Mrs. Chellow, a white woman from their area,

---

1076   Valby, Karen, "Jennifer Lawrence: 'I Didn't Have a Life. I Thought I Should Go Get One,'" Vanity Fair, November 22, 2021, https://www.vanityfair.com/hollywood/2021/11/jennifer-lawrence-on-love-fame-boundaries-and-dont-look-up
1077   Garimara, Doris Pilkington, *Follow the Rabbit-Proof Fence* (University of Queensland Press, 1996).

claims the girls were "running wild with the whites".[1078] Windschuttle claims that this vague phrase would have been understood to mean promiscuity. He further insists Neville's policies were not an attempt to breed Indigenous Australians out of existence, despite Neville's own words making this abundantly clear, including his 1947 book, *Australia's Coloured Minority*.[1079] It also seems probable that, like many white people of the time (and even today), the Mrs. Chellow in question may have assumed that, being non-white, the girls were particularly promiscuous and just seeing them talking to white men or boys inflamed such suspicions. Beyond the possibility of her own biases coloring her perceptions, she also could have had any number of other motivations to deliberately lie about the girls to try and get them removed—without even a first name or any other form of documentation, it seems impossible to verify how true or false her statements were, if we even assume her intention of the phrase matches Windschuttle's self-serving interpretation.

It's also worth noting that, as stated in a 2010 article in conservative newspaper *The Australian* in 2010, Windschuttle claimed to have found the letter in a review of state archives. Yet his own book cites as its source Garimara's book, which does in fact quote and cite the original letter. In this framing, it is presented as something that those with an agenda—the filmmakers, and perhaps implying Garimara herself—were trying to hide this information, but which the intrepid investigative researcher Windschuttle found on his own. Instead, his own book citation makes it clear that he was trying to use Garimara's own work to undermine her family's history.

But most importantly, even if the girls were flirting with or kissing boys, or more than that—who cares? Their behaviour, real or imagined, has no impact on the fact that at least 100,000 Aboriginal and Torres Strait Islander children were removed from their homes, families, and communities, punished for speaking their languages and practicing their cultures, had their very names taken from them,

---

1078   Vasek, Lanai and Perpitch, Nicolas, "Rabbit-Proof Fence grossly inaccurate, says Keith Windschuttle," *The Australian*, December 14, 2009, https://web.archive.org/web/20101119044730/https://www.theaustralian.com.au/news/rabbit-proof-fence-grossly-inaccurate-says-keith-windschuttle/story-e6frg6n6-1225809998531

1079   Haebich, A. and Reece, R.H.W., "Auber Octavius Neville (1875–1954)," Australian Dictionary of Biography, Melbourne Univesity Press, 1988, https://adb.anu.edu.au/biography/neville-auber-octavius-7821

and subjected to inhumane standards of living.[1080] Using the supposed promiscuity of eight-, eleven – and fourteen-year-old girls to try to justify and erase these experiences is simply abhorrent.

We even see slut-shaming of fictional characters. Back in 2015, actors Chris Evans and Jeremy Renner called the Marvel character Natasha Romanov, AKA Black Widow, a "slut" and a "whore." While Evans apologized, Renner made it very clear he was not in any way sorry for his comments, except that he got into "internet trouble" as he told Conan O'Brien before doubling down and claiming she had slept with "four of the six" Avengers," definitive proof in his mind that she was a "slut."[1081] Apart from the fact that Black Widow was the only female Avenger and frankly had a lot of problematic stuff going on throughout the more than ten years Scarlett Johansson played the character in the Marvel Cinematic Universe, there is literally no indication that the MCU version ever actually slept with any of her teammates. Which begs the question of whether Renner's even watched his own franchise's films. If he'd had, he'd know that Iron Man is the definitive Avengers slut.

Time and again, women are sexualized just by existing. In 1997, 120 women—a record-breaking number —were elected to the British Parliament. When Prime Minister Tony Blair took a photo with 96 of the 101 Labour MPs, just the fact of women winning and doing a job was enough for the media to declare them "Blair's Babes," a title that garnered so much attention it has a more in-depth Wikipedia page than many actual women.[1082] That cohort was not alone, as other groups have been referred to variously as Gordon's gals, Cameron's cuties,

---

1080   "Bringing Them Home: Report of the National Inquiry into the Separation of Aboriginal and Torres Strait Islander Children from Their Families," Commonwealth of Australia, 1997 https://humanrights.gov.au/sites/default/files/content/pdf/social_justice/bringing_them_home_report.pdf
1081   Farokhmanesh, Megan, "Avengers Actor Doubles down on Slut-Shaming Black Widow, and It's Not Just a Joke," Polygon, May 5, 2015, https://www.polygon.com/2015/5/5/8552979/avengers-black-widow-slut-shaming-jeremy-renner
1082   Perkins, Anne and Ward, Lucy, "The Rise and Fall of Blair's Babes," *The Guardian*, May 24, 2001, https://www.theguardian.com/world/2001/may/24/gender.uk

Dave's darlings, and Nick's nymphets.[1083]

Dating back to ancient Greece, Aspasia was arguably one of the most influential women in fifth-century BCE. Athens, as a scholar, rhetorician, and teacher. Yet comedies of the time depict her as a madam and prostitute who was tried for impiety. Regardless of whether these portrayals were meant as malicious attacks or as tongue-in-cheek jokes, scholars throughout the centuries have taken them as fact, despite the lack of any real supporting evidence. [1084] For context, imagine if scholars a thousand years from now were to view *Saturday Night Live* and assume it was factual. While the position of a hetaira, or courtesan, was a respectable one, it's also worth noting that under Athenian law, as a foreign-born woman Aspasia could not legally marry her partner, the statesman Pericles, or any other Athenian man. Given Pericles's status, it's also likely that his political enemies—which included satirists writing such plays and oratories—contributed to the gossip.

Even earlier, according to early Christian writing, Mary Magdalene was one of Jesus's most important disciples, one of the women to remain with him to the Crucifixion as the men fled, as well as the first to witness his resurrection and tell others. She and other women disciples are documented as having wealth that they used to support Jesus and his followers, implying a more secular level of power as well.[1085] Yet starting with no less than the pope himself in 591 CE, later texts conflated her with other women and presented her as a repentant prostitute to undermine her position in scriptures.[1086]

Often, women of colour in Western countries face additional sexualisation by virtue of being non-Caucasian. Maria Gertrudis Barceló, known as La Tules,

---

1083   Mavin, Sharon; Bryans, Patricia and Cunningham, Rosie, "Fed-up with Blair's babes, Gordon's gals, Cameron's cuties, Nick's nymphets: Challenging gendered media representations of women political leaders," *Gender in Management an International Journal* vol 25 no 7 (2010) pp 550-569. October 2010. DOI:10.1108/17542411011081365
https://www.researchgate.net/publication/241675449_Fed-up_with_Blair's_babes_Gordon's_gals_Cameron's_cuties_Nick's_nymphets_Challenging_gendered_media_representations_of_women_political_leaders
1084   Hill, Rachel, *Sexual Slander and the Reputation of Milesian Aspasia* (University of Guelph, 1994).
1085   Carroll, James, "Who Was Mary Magdalene?" Smithsonian Magazine, June 2006, https://www.smithsonianmag.com/history/who-was-mary-magdalene-119565482/
1086   Herman, Eleanor, *Off with Her Head: Three Thousand Years of Demonizing Women in Power* (HarperCollins, 2022).

was a successful saloon owner in the Territory of New Mexico in the 1800s. A prosperous businesswoman, she was depicted as a prostitute and brothel madam by travel writers, in part to support the U.S. invasion of Mexico by depicting Mexicans in a negative light.[1087] French diplomat Alexis de Tocqueville's description in *Democracy in America* illustrates the independence that some men have always found threatening in a woman:

> In Mexico a woman lost nothing through marriage; in fact, it freed her from the watchful eye of her dueña or mother and enabled her to enjoy a legal and social independence unknown in other countries. After her marriage, La Tules kept her maiden name, her property, and her right to make contracts and to institute legal proceedings. This most independent of women also claimed the rather unusual privileges of entertaining whatever friends she pleased, male or female, in whatever degree of intimacy she chose, and of conducting her business any time and any place that suited her.[1088]

The infamous Gamergate harassment campaign weaponised slut-shaming as a way to discredit women and their credibility and threaten them into silence. A backlash to the slow progression of video games to be more inclusive, the tipping point for the misogynists was Zoë Quinn's 2013 release of *Depression Quest*, which was designed to convey the experience of depression through a series of fictional scenarios and was based in part on Quinn's own experiences. While their game was getting positive reviews, Quinn was getting rape and death threats, including those mailed to their home.[1089] In 2014, their ex wrote a long blog post that falsely claimed Quinn had traded sexual favours for a positive review, causing the harassment to escalate further and expand to other targets like media critic Anita Sarkeesian and developer Brianna Wu. Sarkeesian cancelled a speaking engagement

---

1087 Pacheco, Carmella Scorcia, "A Centennial Glimpse into New Mexico's Suffrage Movement through 'El Corrido de La Votación,'" Smithsonian Center for Folklife and Cultural Heritage, September 20, 2019, https://folklife.si.edu/magazine/new-mexico-suffrage-movement-corrido-de-la-votacion

1088 de Tocqueville's, Alexis, *Democracy in America*, 1835.

1089 Eby, Magaret, "GamerGate's victims are bravely speaking out about what needs to change," HelloGiggles, October 30, 2014, https://hellogiggles.com/gamer-gate-change/

because multiple threats had been made, while Wu's studio pulled out of an expo over security concerns. "I used to go to game events and feel like I was going home," Quinn said. "Now it's just like... are any of the people I'm currently in the room with ones that said they wanted to beat me to death?"[1090]

Insidiously, the focus on girls' bodies starts from a young age, as seen in the aisles of any costume shop.[1091] While there are countless examples, the trend is perhaps best exemplified in dress codes that present those bodies as nothing more than distractions for male students—or even staff. Japan in particular is known for incredibly strict school dress codes, a practice known as buraku kosoku that dates back to the 1870s, and controls everything down to the shape of students' eyebrows. While many of these rules are about uniformity, some are inevitably about sexualising teen girls.[1092] In 2022, Japanese teacher Motoki Sugiyama, caused an international stir when he spoke out about middle school administrators telling him that girls could not wear their hair in ponytails because exposing the nape of their necks could "sexually excite" male students—a not-uncommon practice in the country, including at all five of the schools Sugiyama had worked at over the course of eleven years.[1093] Nonsensically, many of those schools do allow bobbed haircuts—which also expose the nape of the neck. Many schools also require female students to wear only white underwear. A survey in Fukuoka city found that fifty-seven of sixty-nine municipal junior high schools had rules on students' underwear colour and pattern. In some institutions, if a student disobeyed, they were required to take off their underwear and their guardians were informed.[1094]

1090 Lee, Dave, "Zoe Quinn: GamerGate must be condemned," October 29, 2014, https://www.bbc.com/news/technology-29821050

1091 Marcotte, John, "Halloween Horror Story: Feminist Dad's Scary Visit To The Girls' Costume Aisle," Women You Should Know, October 23, 2013, https://womenyoushouldknow.net/halloween-horror-story-feminist-dads-scary-visit-girls-costume-aisle/

1092 Jassal, Anchit, "Japanese Schools Draconian Rules — Buraku Kōsoku or Black Rules| Explained," Live's Quandary, September 29, 2022, https://medium.com/https-www-livesquandary-com/japanese-schools-draconian-rules-buraku-k%C5%8Dsoku-or-black-rules-explained-944fb8337389

1093 Montgomery, Hanako, "Japanese Schools Are Still Banning Ponytails Because They Could 'Sexually Excite' Men," Vice, March 10, 2022, https://www.vice.com/en/article/pkpv4n/japanese-schools-ban-ponytail-sexism

1094 Keisuke, Muneoka and Sayo, Kato, "80% of public junior high schools in Japan city have rules on underwear color: lawyer group," The Mainichi, December 24, 2020, https://mainichi.jp/english/articles/20201224/p2a/00m/0na/010000c

In 2021, it was reported that teachers in some schools would line students up in hallways and check their undergarments. In Kawasaki, some elementary schools required children to remove their underwear before changing into gym clothes, on the basis that sweaty undergarments are unhygienic. Male teachers have also been accused of sexually harassing female students by checking their breast size to determine whether to allow them to wear supportive bras.[1095]

There are also racist aspects, like forcing mixed-race students with lighter hair to dye it black or straighten curly hair. When a high school student sued over the former in 2017, the court ruled that the school had the right to do so.[1096] In the U.S., students of colour are statistically more likely to be punished for dress code violations.[1097] A 2019 report on dress codes in Washington, DC schools found that those with majority African American populations were more likely to have severely restrictive dress codes. Additionally, the biases of non-African American teachers and administrators meant that the people enforcing dress codes often saw African-American girls in particular as older and more sexually mature than they really are, while also punishing them for the natural shape of their bodies.[1098]

In 2016, dozens of female Year 11 students at Henderson High School in Auckland were called to a meeting and told by the female deputy principal Cherith Telford that their skirts would need to be lowered to knee level, in order to keep the girls "safe," prevent the boys from "getting ideas" and create a "good work environment" for the male staff members.[1099] When publicly called out on this, the principal was

---

1095 Montgomery, Hanako, "In Japan, Students Have Underwear Rules. Their Parents Say 'No More,'" Vice, March 15, 2021, https://www.vice.com/en/article/n7vxng/in-japan-students-have-underwear-rules-their-parents-say-no-more

1096 Montgomery, Hanako, "A Japanese School Edited Her Yearbook Photo. She Says It Was Racist," Vice, July 1, 2021, https://www.vice.com/en/article/y3dnak/japan-racism-yearbook-photo

1097 Pendharkar, Eesha, "School Dress Codes Aren't Fair to Everyone, Federal Study Finds," Education Week, October 27, 2022, https://www.edweek.org/leadership/school-dress-codes-arent-fair-to-everyone-federal-study-finds/2022/10

1098 Gandhi, Lakshmi, "Black Girls Are Fighting Back against Discriminatory School Dress Codes," Prism, September 14, 2021, https://prismreports.org/2021/09/14/bipoc-girls-are-fighting-back-against-discriminatory-school-dress-codes/

1099 Roy, Eleanor Ainge, and Eleanor de Jong, "Schoolgirls in New Zealand Told to Lengthen Skirts to 'Stop Distracting Male Staff and Pupils,'" The Guardian, April 11, 2016, https://www.theguardian.com/world/2016/apr/11/schoolgirls-in-new-zealand-told-to-lower-skirts-to-stop-distracting-male-staff-and-pupils

unapologetic, and Telford was still employed in her role years later, despite promoting rape culture myths by implying that dressing modestly would keep girls "safe."[1100]

Dress codes represent that paradox of adults simultaneously sexualising young girls and shaming them for being perceived as sexual, through no fault of the girls' own. From dolls like Barbie and Bratz to cartoons, girls are presented with unrealistic body images, as well as a seemingly never-ending focus on romantic relationships. The 1995 *Pocahontas* film, for example, aged up the Native American girl, who was ten or eleven when the historical events took place, into a young woman to justify a romantic attraction with the English John Smith. In 2013, when Merida, the central character in the Disney film *Brave*, officially joined the ranks of the Disney princesses for merchandising use as part of the line-up, she had obviously been redesigned from the fearless tomboy into a sexualized young woman—her signature bow and arrow quiver removed, her once-simple dress accessorised and embellished, as well as being off-the-shoulder with a distinctly lower neckline, while her waist was drastically reduced to accentuate her chest and hips, complexion refined from ruddy to porcelain, and her previously frizzy curls smoothed into a glossy perfection. Even her shoes had gone from sensible round toes to fashionably pointy ones. This was particularly annoying as *Brave* had been one of the few female-led Disney films to date that did not have a central romance. *Brave* writer and co-director Brenda Chapman responded, "I think it's atrocious what they have done to Merida ... When little girls say they like it because it's more sparkly, that's all fine and good but, subconsciously, they are soaking in the sexy 'come hither' look and the skinny aspect of the new version. It's horrible! Merida was created to break that mold."[1101]

And as in all aspects of respectability politics, women in power are just as susceptible if not more so. In 2022, Finnish Prime Minister Sanna Marin, the youngest world leader at the time, faced backlash for attending a private party where

---

1100 Rodriguez, Mathew, "This New Zealand School Told 13-Year-Old Girls Their Skirts Distracted Male Staff," Mic, April 12, 2016, https://www.mic.com/articles/140541/this-new-zealand-school-told-13-year-old-girls-their-skirts-distracted-male-staff

1101 "Sex Sells: Disney's Misguided Redesign Of Merida From "Brave,"" Women You Should Know, May 13, 2013, https://womenyoushouldknow.net/sex-sells-disneys-misguided-redesign-of-merida-from-brave/

she danced and drank a small amount of alcohol—like many thirty-six—year-old women.[1102] Due to baseless rumours that drugs were involved, she also had to take a drug test.[1103] Yet no one was calling her Australian counterpart, 59-year-old Anthony Albanese a "disgrace" when the rock-loving "DJ Albo" was cheered by crowds at a Gang of Youths concert, chugging beer.[1104]

New Zealand PM Jacinda Ardern, when asked about the situation, observed, "My one general reflection is that ever since I've been in this role, I've really had a mind to whether or not we are attracting people to these jobs ... We need people from all walks of life to look to politics and think, 'That's a place I feel I can make a positive difference ... How do we constantly make sure that we attract people to politics, rather than perhaps has been historically the case, put them off?"

OVERSHADOWED BY PERSONAL LIFE

Artemisia Gentileschi's accomplishments as a painter were long overshadowed by her 1611 rape by two men when she was just a teenager. When one of them refused to marry her to restore her honour, her father took him to court—not for violating her, but for violating the family's honour. During the trial, it came out that, in addition to raping Artemisia, her assailant had also planned to murder his wife, slept with his sister-in-law, and planned to steal Artemisia's father's paintings. Artemisia submitted to torture by thumbscrews, risking ruining her hands in addition to the excruciating pain, to prove the validity of her testimony that she had been a virgin when she was raped. Were she not, the reasoning went, there was no honour for her rapists to have violated. Yet despite all this, his sentence of exile from Rome was never actually enforced. Instead, it was Artemisia who was essentially exiled, marrying a Florentine artist and fleeing to Florence only a

---

1102 Badham, Van, "Finland's PM Is a Young Woman in Power. Her Partying Is the Total Opposite of Disgrace," *The Guardian*, August 24, 2022, https://www.theguardian.com/commentisfree/2022/aug/24/finlands-pm-is-a-young-woman-in-power-her-partying-is-the-total-opposite-of-disgrace

1103 Henley, Jon and Graham-McLay, Charlotte, "Finland's PM Sanna Marin Apologises for 'Inappropriate' Pictures at Residence," *The Guardian*, August 24, 2022, https://www.theguardian.com/world/2022/aug/24/finlands-pm-sanna-marin-apologises-for-inappropriate-pictures-at-residence

1104 Eder, Billie, "Cheers and Beers: PM Receives Rock Star Reception at Gang of Youths Concert," The Sydney Morning Herald, August 22, 2022, https://www.smh.com.au/culture/music/cheers-and-beers-pm-receives-rock-star-reception-at-gang-of-youths-concert-20220822-p5bbwo.html

month after the trial.[1105]

Even when women's work is not actively sabotaged by the men in their lives, like Fanny Mendelssohn's brother and father or Zelda Fitzgerald's husband, their work can often be overshadowed by their personal lives.

Yoko Ono did not break up the Beatles, but for decades, this myth was the most repeated thing said about her. John Lennon and Paul McCartney both confirmed it's not true, and Ono herself has said she couldn't have even if she'd wanted to. Her own artistic achievements have, for most of her life, been overshadowed to the point that her name became a synonym for "homewrecker." She was also commonly ignored as an equal partner in her own collaborations with Lennon and blamed for her supposed negative influence on his musical style.[1106] Lennon received sole credit for writing *Imagine*, released in 1971, for more than forty years until June 2017, when the National Music Publishers Association announced she would finally receive her co-writing credit.[1107] In a 1980 interview with BBC, Lennon "explained" why: "If it had been a male, you know – Harry Nilsson's 'Old Dirt Road' – it's 'Lennon-Nilsson'. But when we did [*Imagine*'] I just put 'Lennon' because, you know, she's just the wife and you don't put her name on, right?"[1108] She also never received official credit for *Give Peace a Chance*, which was originally credited to Lennon and McCartney before McCartney was dropped.[1109] Lennon said this was because he felt "guilty enough to give McCartney credit as co-writer on my first independent single instead of giving it to Yoko, who had actually written it with me."[1110] This begs the question of whether he ever felt guilty about taking those credits from her.

1105 Cohen, Elizabeth S. 2000. "The Trials of Artemisia Gentileschi: A Rape as History," *The Sixteenth Century Journal* vol 31 no 1 (2000) pp 47–75, https://doi.org/10.2307/2671289
1106 Yam, Kimmy, "Yoko Ono Was Called 'Dragon Lady,' Blamed for Beatles Breakup. Now, Her Legacy Is Re-Examined," NBC News, December 22, 2021, https://www.nbcnews.com/news/asian-america/yoko-ono-was-called-dragon-lady-blamed-beatles-breakup-now-legacy-re-e-rcna9534
1107 Rosenberg, Sari, "September 9, 1971: 'Imagine' Was Released, Written by John Lennon… and Yoko Ono," Lifetime, September 9, 2017, https://www.mylifetime.com/she-did-that/september-9-1971-imagine-was-released-written-by-john-lennon-and-yoko-ono
1108 Lennon, John. Interview with Andy Peebles, BBC Radio, December 6, 1980
1109 Boilen, Bob, "Old Music Tuesday: 40 Years of Giving Peace a Chance," NPR, June 30, 2009, https://www.npr.org/sections/allsongs/2009/06/old_music_tuesday_40_years_of_2.html
1110 Norman, Philip, *John Lennon: The Life* (HarperCollins, 2008).

Long before she met Lennon, Ono was building a reputation, with solo art exhibitions, presenting experimental music and performance art at Carnegie Hall and creating the album cover art for Toshiro Mayuzumi's 1962 album *Nirvana Symphony*. She was a pioneering conceptual performance artist in her own right, was instrumental in the Fluxus artistic community in New York, and continues to influence and inspire artists today. Her creative output has also included books, music, films, and television, and she's been a prominent activist for decades, fighting for peace and human rights, as well as supporting disaster relief, environmental causes, LGBTQ+ rights, anti-racism, feminism, and other efforts. Her awards include a Grammy and a Golden Lion from the Venice Biennale.

Best known as the first and last of Henry VIII's six wives, Catherine of Aragon and Catherine Parr were so much more than the beginning and end of "divorced, beheaded, died, divorced, beheaded, survived." Catherine of Aragon was a Spanish princess who served as ambassador to England before marrying Henry, the first known female ambassador in European history.[1111] In 1513, she ruled England as regent while Henry was abroad, including spurring troops to victory against the Scottish at the Battle of Flodden—while heavily pregnant. She also held out for years against the worst Henry could throw at her, refusing to agree to an annulment that would have disinherited her daughter Mary, who later ascended to the throne and became England's first undisputed queen regnant in 1553. If Catherine had given in, Mary would have been declared illegitimate, and it's unlikely she would have become queen. Even her enemy Thomas Cromwell declared, "If not for her sex, she could have defied all the heroes of History." She was a patron of the arts, established a relief program for the poor and advocated for education for girls.[1112]

Meanwhile, Catherine Parr was a scholar who became the first woman in England to publish an original work under her own name in English. She was also influential in Henry's decision to pass the Third Succession Act in 1543, which

---

1111 Zarevich, Emily, "Catherine of Aragon: Europe's First Female Ambassador," JSTOR Daily, January 2, 2023, https://daily.jstor.org/catherine-of-aragon-europes-first-female-ambassador/
1112 Solly, Meilan, "When Catherine of Aragon Led England's Armies to Victory over Scotland," Smithsonian Magazine, October 14, 2020, https://www.smithsonianmag.com/history/when-catherine-aragon-led-englands-armies-victory-over-scotland-180975982/

enabled Mary and Elizabeth I to take the crown after he died. Published anonymously, her first book *Psalms or Prayers taken out of Holy Scriptures* was a powerful work of wartime propaganda designed to help Henry win the war against France and Scotland. It was later edited and included in the *Book of Common Prayer*, meaning her work is still used in the Anglican faith today. Like her predecessor, Parr also served as regent in Henry's absence, in 1544. She was also reputedly a significant influence on her stepdaughter, the future Queen Elizabeth I.[1113]

Just as women are disregarded as nothing more than a man's wife, they have also been disregarded as nothing more than a man's mistress. Jeanne Antoinette Poisson, better known as Madame de Pompadour, is best remembered as the official chief mistress of French King Louis XV in the 1700s. From that position, she was one of the most politically powerful people in the court, and therefore the country, and she wielded that power shrewdly. She was also both a patron of the arts and an artist in her own right, who supported industries like tapestry and porcelain makers and promoted the early champagne industry. She was also a supporter of Enlightenment thinkers like Voltaire and helped bring the first French encyclopaedia into existence.[1114]

Even powerful women are undermined by focusing on their personal relationships rather than their accomplishments. Egyptian ruler Cleopatra VII was a brilliant ruler whose reign saw nearly twenty-two years of prosperity and stability to her country. She spoke at least nine languages, according to Plutarch, commanded armies when she was only twenty-one, and was educated by some of the finest scholars of her day. And yet countless men, from the writers of antiquity through to filmmakers of the modern era, have focused on her supposed beauty and powers of seduction rather than her intelligence. A large part of this was likely due to Roman resentment of a powerful foreigner's relationships with and influence on

---

[1113] James, Susan E., "Katherine Parr – Renaissance and Reformation," Oxford Bibliographies, February 22, 2018, https://www.oxfordbibliographies.com/display/document/obo-9780195399301/obo-9780195399301-0070.xml

[1114] Eschner, Kat, "Madame de Pompadour Was Far More than a 'Mistress,'" Smithsonian Magazine, December 29, 2017, https://www.smithsonianmag.com/smart-news/madame-de-pompadour-was-far-more-mistress-180967662/

Caesar and Mark Antony.[1115]

But the single largest group to experience this seems to be the artists, with Ono and Gentileschi only two of countless examples. Many women who have been written off as just a muse, or whose own work fell by the wayside so they could support the men, later reclaimed their identities or have since been rediscovered as artists in their own right. 1960s It Girl Edie Sedgewick was famous as Andy Warhol's muse and actress in his films. Her untimely death at age twenty-eight of a drug overdose cut short any promise she may have shown as an artist herself, and her paintings, drawings, and sculptures as an artist in her own right weren't made public until they went up for auction in 2022.[1116]

If Elizabeth Siddall looks familiar, it's because there are estimated to be thousands of images of her, many by her husband Dante Gabriel Rossetti, who also wrote poems inspired by her. She is the model for some of the most famous Pre-Raphaelite paintings hanging in museums, such as John Everett Millais's *Ophelia*. But she was also a poet and artist who produced more than 100 watercolours, sketches, and drawings, as well as one oil painting, with art critic John Ruskin purchasing much of her output. Although her work has become more appreciated in the twenty-first century, at the time it was derided as a "pale imitation" of her husband's—in a seemingly contradictory situation, some even claimed he was the true artist, which would seem to imply they were comparable in quality. Modern curators note the clear influence Siddall's work had on her husband's, when contemporaneous pieces are placed side-by-side.[1117]

In many cases, "just a muse" also extends to "just a lover" or "just a wife," as in the case of photographer Tina Modotti. Although she was often overshadowed by her teacher and lover, Edward Weston, Diego Rivera praised Modotti's work

---

1115 Gendler, Alex, "History vs. Cleopatra," TED-Ed, February 3, 2017, https://www.youtube.com/watch?v=Y6EhRwn4zkc
1116 Enking, Molly, "Known as Warhol's Muse, Edie Sedgwick Was an Artist Herself," Smithsonian Magazine, November 17, 2022, https://www.smithsonianmag.com/smart-news/a-trove-of-unseen-art-by-warhol-superstar-edie-sedgwick-is-on-auction-for-the-first-time-180981140/
1117 Brooks, Richard, "Ophelia Resurfaces: Pre-Raphaelite Muse Is Recognized as a Skilled Artist," The Observer, April 2, 2023, https://www.theguardian.com/artanddesign/2023/apr/02/ophelia-resurfaces-pre-raphaelite-muse-is-recognized-as-a-skilled-artist

as more abstract, ethereal, and intellectual than her lover's. Although she only worked professionally as a photographer for seven years before throwing herself into activism instead, her work has since been exhibited in venues such as the National Library of Mexico since it was rediscovered in the 1990s.[1118]

In 2011, the Guggenheim Museum had the Harvard Art Museum run tests on five Kandinskys. Beneath the surface of *Sketch I for Painting With White Border (Moscow)* (1913), it was revealed that he had painted over a work clearly done by his collaborator and longtime lover Gabriele Münter. While it could be an innocent case of reusing a canvas when a painting didn't turn out as hoped, Kandinsky rarely painted over other pieces, and it seems particularly questionable that he would do so with a work that was not his own. Art history professor Bibiana Obler noted, "There were subtle ways in which they continued to adhere to their gendered roles," such as Münter assisting Kandinsky with record-keeping and sketching. As such, "it was impossible to imagine Kandinsky giving Münter a canvas to paint over."[1119] While some historians argue that he was supportive of her work, their dynamic was often dysfunctional. As his young student at the Phalanx School, which he founded and was chair of, Kandinsky asked Münter to remove herself from his class because they'd developed an intimate relationship and he was "uncomfortable" because his wife was also there. For years he strung her along while married to his first wife, becoming secretly engaged in 1903, yet even after he finally divorced his wife in 1911, he never married her. She stopped painting for a decade after he left her in 1916 to, at age fifty, seduce and marry a teenager. It is entirely possible that Kandinsky never saw her as an equal, a peer rather than a student, and clearly not to be afforded the status of a wife rather than a lover.[1120] As the *Financial Times* notes in writing about Münter, "Though they lived and painted together (in the house she bought), shared the project of grasping nature while simultaneously transcending it, and jointly helped found

---

1118 "Tina Modotti Photography, Bio, Ideas," The Art Story, https://www.theartstory.org/artist/modotti-tina/
1119 Loos, Ted, "Beneath an Abstract Painting, a Mystery Is Revealed," *The New York Times*, October 21, 2011, https://www.nytimes.com/2011/10/23/arts/artsspecial/kandinsky-painting-reveals-a-mystery-beneath.html
1120 "Gabriele Münter Paintings, Bio, Ideas," The Art Story, https://www.theartstory.org/artist/munter-gabriele/

(art movement) Der Blaue Reiter, Kandinsky was adept at claiming sole credit."[1121]

"In the eyes of many, I was only an unnecessary side-dish to Kandinsky," Münter herself recalled. "It is all too easily forgotten that a woman can be a creative artist with a real, original talent of her own."[1122]

Abstract expressionist Lee Krasner was arguably just as revolutionary and brilliant as her husband, Jackson Pollock (particularly given that, as previously mentioned, Pollock ripped off his signature style from Janet Sobel). Yet as his star rose, it cast a shadow across Krasner's career, as she committed more and more time to supporting him. Sadly, it was only after her death in 1984 that her work experienced a resurgence, with a retrospective opening at the Museum of Modern Art only six months later.

Similarly, Jo Nivison Hopper was a talented artist whose support of her husband Edward was vital to his success. Her appearance in many of his paintings also led others to see her as a muse rather than an artist in her own right.[1123] A 2022 documentary, *Hopper: An American Love Story*, explored how Hopper owed much of his career to his wife, as she put her artistic ambitions on hold to promote his. Indeed, Hopper's career struggled for more than ten years until he reconnected with Jo—whom he'd first met in art school—in 1923, and she began managing his career. She helped get several of his works into a 1923 Brooklyn Museum exhibition, which drew the positive attention of critics. "There is no Edward Hopper without Jo Nivison," *Hopper* director Phil Grabsky told Smithsonian Magazine. As for her own work, Nivison bequeathed her entire artistic estate (both her works and her husband's) to the Whitney Museum of American Art. For many years, it was thought that the Whitney had discarded most of Jo's pieces, until writer Elizabeth Thompson Colleary discovered about 200 of them in the Whitney's basement in 2000. Other works have since resurfaced as her reputation has become more

---

1121 Budick, Ariella, "Gabriele Münter: 'I Was Only a Side Dish to Kandinsky,'" Financial Times, July 19, 2018, https://www.ft.com/content/46c43c44-84f1-11e8-9199-c2a4754b5a0e
1122 Münter, Gabriele, 1926, Diary entry.
1123 Enking, Molly, "Reexamining Edward Hopper—and the Woman behind His Career," Smithsonian Magazine, October 26, 2022, https://www.smithsonianmag.com/smart-news/new-edward-hopper-documentary-and-exhibit-explore-the-little-known-life-of-this-famous-artist-180980964/

well-known. Yet even an exhibition of her watercolours at the Edward Hopper House Museum in 2021 was titled *Josephine Nivison Hopper: Edward's Muse*.

Multi-disciplinary artist Elizabeth Catlett met her first husband in art school, marrying in 1941. As an article from The Johnson Collection notes that during most of their marriage, Charles W. White's achievements overshadowed his wife's despite the similarity of their styles and subject matter. After a few years, however, Catlett's work was recognized with a fellowship that funded the couple travelling to Mexico to study at the Taller de Gráfica Popular. At the famed graphic artists' collective and workshop, she began exploring the emerging printmaking technique of linoleum cut. And as her career flourished, the marriage disintegrated, with her filing for divorce only a few months after arriving in Mexico. Catlett continued making art into her nineties and her sculptures and prints have been the subject of more than fifty solo exhibitions at various museums and galleries.[1124]

For the Viking explorer Gudrid the Far-Traveller, mentioned previously in the context of an article titled "Did a Viking Woman Named Gudrid Really Travel to North America in 1000 A.D.?" (spoiler: yes), it was her in-laws Erik the Red and Leif Erikson who were remembered while she was forgotten. According to Viking sagas, she crossed the North Atlantic Sea eight times and travelled farther than any other Viking, roaming Canada, giving birth to the first European baby in North America and walking all the way to Rome from Scandinavia. Despite being such a central character in *The Saga of Erik the Red*, she was largely forgotten as her father – and brother-in-law's names were passed down through the centuries.[1125] [1126]

"SCIENCE SAYS…"

As part of the Naropa Institute's 1994 tribute to Allen Ginsberg, Stephen Scobie recalled an event where, "A woman from the audience asks: 'Why were there so few

---

[1124] "Elizabeth Catlett | Artist Profile," National Women's Museum of Art, https://nmwa.org/art/artists/elizabeth-catlett/

[1125] Durn, Sarah, "Did a Viking Woman Named Gudrid Really Travel to North America in 1000 A.D.?" Smithsonian Magazine, March 3, 2021, https://www.smithsonianmag.com/history/did-viking-woman-named-gudrid-really-travel-north-america-1000-years-ago-180977126/

[1126] Jacobs, Frank, "The Viking Woman Who Sailed to America and Walked to Rome," Big Think, January 4, 2023, https://bigthink.com/strange-maps/gudrid-far-traveled-viking-woman/

women among the Beat writers?' and [Gregory] Corso, suddenly utterly serious, leans forward and says: "There were women, they were there, I knew them, their families put them in institutions, they were given electric shock. In the '50s if you were male you could be a rebel, but if you were female your families had you locked up."[1127]

There is a long history of pathologising women—and other marginalized groups—when they act in ways that society doesn't like. From the "wandering womb" of ancient Greece to the seemingly-impossible-to-define "hysteria" of the 1900s, questionable science has been used to keep women in their place throughout human history.[1128] "Science" has been used to keep women from overtaxing themselves by thinking too hard, doing physical activities (mysteriously, this never extended to household chores) and even off trains, which people once believed would cause women's uteruses to go flying out of their bodies at such a high speed. (Spoiler: they did not).[1129]

In many times and places, it has taken nothing more than a man's opinion to confine a woman. Elizabeth Packard spent three years locked away in an asylum in 1860s Illinois because her husband claimed she was insane for daring to disagree with him and complain about him. After she was finally discharged, her husband locked her in a room and nailed the windows shut. She was able to get a letter to a friend, who brought the situation to a judge. At the subsequent trial, it only took the jury seven minutes to find her sane. Elizabeth returned home to find that he had rented their home to another family, sold her furniture, taken all her money and possessions, and moved to Massachusetts with their children. Though she appealed to the supreme courts of both states, married women at the time had no rights to their property or children. She went on to found the Anti-Insane Asylum Society, campaigning for divorced women to retain custody of their children.[1130]

1127 "Beat History," National Beat Poetry Foundation, https://nationalbeatpoetryfoundation.org/index.php/beat-history/
1128 Traniello, Vanessa, *Hysteria and the Wandering Womb* (Marquette University, 2019), https://academic.mu.edu/meissnerd/hysteria.html
1129 Felton, James, "People Once Believed That Women's Uteruses Would Fly out on Speeding Trains," IFLScience, October 20, 2021, https://www.iflscience.com/people-once-believed-that-womens-uteruses-would-fly-out-on-speeding-trains-61343
1130 Brandman, Mariana, "Elizabeth Packard," National Women's History Museum, 2021, https://www.womenshistory.org/education-resources/biographies/elizabeth-packard

Even menstruation, a monthly occurrence for billions of people around the world, has been used to isolate and undermine women. Instances of period stigma range from the comical—NASA engineers asking Sally Ride if 100 tampons were enough for a week-long trip[1131]—to the life-threatening—confining women to menstruation huts every month because they are considered unclean.[1132] Twenty-one-year-old Parbati Rawat died of smoke inhalation in a small, windowless menstruation hut in Nepal in 2019. In 2015, Prayar Gopalakrishnan, leader of Hindu Temples in Kerala, said he would only allow women to enter the Sabarimala temple (one of India's most ancient and prominent temples) if a machine is invented to detect "purity," because menstruating women are considered unclean and impure by temple authorities.[1133] Unlike other temples that "only" restricted menstruating women,[1134] no women or girls of menstruating age were allowed into the Sabarimala temple until a 2018 Supreme Court ruling—which has still not stopped protesters from physically trying to bar women from entering.[1135]

More commonly, menstruation is used to claim women are "crazy," or to undermine a woman who is angry for a perfectly good reason by implying she's just "on her period" or "PMS-ing." But there are still situations where having a period is considered exclusionary. In Japan, myths persist that women cannot be sushi chefs because their hands are too warm to handle raw fish, make-up will block their sense of smell, and menstrual cycles affect their sense of taste.[1136]

1131 Monteleone, Katie; Zomorodi, Manoush and Simon, Katie, "That Time When NASA (Almost) Sent Sally Ride to Space with 100 Tampons," NPR, June 3, 2022, https://www.npr.org/2022/06/03/1102635355/marcia-belsky-that-time-when-nasa-almost-sent-sally-ride-to-space-with-100-tampo

1132 Adhikari, Rojita, "Bringing an End to Deadly 'Menstrual Huts' Is Proving Difficult in Nepal," BMJ 368 (February 2020), https://doi.org/10.1136/bmj.m536

1133 "HappyToBleed: Women In India Respond Temple Leader's Comment Regarding Women's Menstruation," Women You Should Know, November 27, 2015, https://womenyoushouldknow.net/happytobleed-women-in-india-respond-temple-leaders-comment-regarding-womens-menstruation/

1134 Joseph, Sinu, "The Sabarimala Story: Can Visiting Temples Affect Menstruating Women?" Hindu American Foundation, October 6, 2015, https://www.hinduamerican.org/blog/the-sabarimala-story-can-visiting-temples-affect-menstruating-women

1135 Lee, Hoon Hee, "The Sabarimala Temple Controversy," Kontinentalist, June 16, 2020, https://kontinentalist.com/stories/sabarimala-temple-protest-india-menstruation-period-poverty

1136 "The Women in Japan Challenging The Male-Dominated Sushi Chef Tradition," Women You Should Know, August 15, 2016, https://womenyoushouldknow.net/the-women-in-japan-challenging-the-male-dominated-sushi-chef-tradition/

Even talking about the reality of periods for women is considered shocking by some. In 2015, the company THINX, which makes underwear for menstruation, had their ads rejected by the Metropolitan Transportation Authority for being inappropriate in the notoriously dirty New York City subway because they found fruit and eggs too "suggestive." A woman in a turtleneck and briefs was deemed "too much skin showing," while images of scantily-clad women preying on body insecurity ran rampant in its tunnels and train cars.[1137] The company's marketing director says she was told, "'Don't make this a women's rights thing'—and then he hung up on me." ModiBodi founder Kristy Chong found her company's ads being repeatedly blocked on Facebook in 2020, after her appearance on *Shark Tank* pitching her leak-proof underwear was cut only a week before the episode aired in 2016. She sold the company in 2022 for $140 million.[1138]

Periods are also a practical factor for athletes. Chinese swimmer Fu Yuanhui made headlines around the world during the 2016 Rio Olympics when she acknowledged that she was feeling weak and tired because she was on her period. When some commenters wondered on Weibo how Fu did not "stain the pool red," someone responded, "Haven't you heard of something called a tampon?"[1139] "It's very difficult that once a month you have to plan your training, your diet, your life around having a period. There are things you can take to postpone your period but they also have side-effects so you're in a Catch-22. You can't win. But it's part of being a woman and a lot of us handle it very well," said British runner Ashleigh Nelson.[1140]

And in a classic catch-22, just as women are punished for having periods, we're

---

1137   Krantz, Rachel, "THINX Underwear Ads on NYC Subway Are up — but the Company Has Another Big Announcement," Bustle, November 10, 2015, https://www.bustle.com/articles/122564-thinx-underwear-ads-on-nyc-subway-are-up-but-the-company-has-another-big-announcement
1138   Priestley, Angela, "Kristy Chong's $140 Million Sale of Modibodi Highlights Value of Addressing the 'Unmentionable,'" Women's Agenda, July 11, 2022, https://womensagenda.com.au/business/entrepreneurs/kristy-chongs-140-million-sale-of-modibodi-highlights-value-of-addressing-the-unmentionable/
1139   Gharib, Malaka, "A Swimmer's 'Period' Comment Breaks Taboos in Sports — and in China," NPR, August 17, 2016, https://www.npr.org/sections/goatsandsoda/2016/08/17/490121285/a-swimmers-period-comment-breaks-taboos-in-sports-and-in-china
1140   Ingle, Sean, "Dina Asher-Smith Praised for Shattering 'Massive Taboo' around Periods in Sport," *The Guardian*, August 19, 2022, https://www.theguardian.com/sport/2022/aug/19/dina-asher-smith-praised-for-shattering-massive-taboo-around-periods-in-sport

also punished for going through menopause. As *The Guardian* reported in 2021, "Almost a million women in the U.K. have left their jobs because of menopausal symptoms. Countless others are discriminated against, denied support and openly mocked." To be clear, menopause comes with very real symptoms that can affect work performance—yet it is often not treated as the real medical condition it very much is. "It wasn't that I wanted to die," says one woman who became suicidal as a result. "I needed to die. Work wasn't ever going to stop doing what they were doing to me. And I was so ashamed to be so incompetent at my job."[1141]

The stigma around candidly discussing women's health also makes it difficult to evaluate how many women leave their jobs, or the workforce entirely, due to menopause—meaning the nature of the problem is a big reason we can't accurately gauge the scope of the problem. However, in a 2019 U.K. survey, fifty-nine percent of working women aged forty-five to fifty-five experiencing menopause reported that it negatively impacted them at work, with the most common issues including a reduced ability to concentrate, and feeling more stressed and less patient with clients and colleagues. The survey estimated that 900,000 women had so far left their jobs, due to menopausal symptoms. Member of Parliament Caroline Nokes observed of the situation, "These are women in the prime of their lives... in their late 40s and 50s, who should be in senior positions ... These are the people who should be the trailblazers and role models for younger people in the workplace."

[1141] Kale, Sirin, "'My Bosses Were Happy to Destroy Me' – the Women Forced out of Work by Menopause," *The Guardian*, August 17, 2021, https://www.theguardian.com/society/2021/aug/17/my-bosses-were-happy-to-destroy-me-the-women-forced-out-of-work-by-menopause

HOW FEMALE ATHLETES DRESS

"You don't have to be pretty. You don't owe prettiness to anyone. Not to your boyfriend/spouse/partner, not to your co-workers, especially not to random men on the street. You don't owe it to your mother, you don't owe it to your children, you don't owe it to civilization in general. Prettiness is not a rent you pay for occupying a space marked 'female.'"
—Erin McKean[1142]

Back in the early days of competitive swimming, women were expected to wear woollen bathing costumes that, when wet, added more than twelve kilos (26.5 pounds) of weight. Not only did this impact swimmers' performance, reinforcing men's idea that women were weak or incompetent, it was also downright dangerous as it significantly increased the risk of drowning.[1143] Australian swimming star Annette Kellerman was arrested in Boston for wearing the same type of suit as a man in 1907 at Revere Beach. "Heavy bathing suits have caused more deaths by drowning than cramps," she said. "Anyone who persuades you to wear the heavy skirty kind is endangering your life."[1144]

From the "respectability" of tennis to beach volleyball players wanting more coverage, the focus on what women are wearing rather than what they are doing has been a recurring theme in women's sports, in a way that men never seem to have to deal with. And it is men making the decisions—the 2016 Gender Balance in Global Sport report showed that the inclusion of women on boards of sports

---

1142 McKean, Erin, "You Don't Hve to Be Pretty," A Dress A Day, October 20, 2006, https://dressaday.com/2006/10/20/you-dont-have-to-be-pretty/
1143 Reilly, Eliza, *Sheilas: Badass Women of Australian History* (Macmillan Publishers Aus., 2022).
1144 Kellerman, Annette, *How to Swim* (George H. Doran Company, 1918).

organisations was less than thirty percent across all organisations and less than twenty percent for national Olympic committees and international federations. Of the national Olympic committees, Australia had the highest percentage (forty-six percent) while the Czech Republic and China had no female board members.[1145]

"The common thread here between the two things are: it's about empowerment, women deciding what's appropriate for them, and the double-bind is based on societal ... expectations of women, and everybody judging and making this fight on the backs of women's bodies," said Angela Schneider, an Olympic medallist in rowing and the Director of the International Centre for Olympic Studies at Canada's Western University. Schneider noted the sexualisation of female athletes at all levels is used by many officials to draw spectators, and the money they bring.[1146]

In 2021, the Norwegian national women's handball team was fined €1,500 (€150 per player) for refusing to wear bikinis. At the European Championships, the players competed in skin-tight shorts—but the rules said they were required to play in bikinis. It's worth noting that even with the extra centimetres of fabric, they were still wearing far less than the men's team, whose shorts were longer and who wore actual shirts instead of sports bras. The subsequent outcry led to a rules change, but one that was still sexist: under the new rules, women could wear "short tight pants," while men's shorts just had to be "not too baggy."[1147]

That same year, Paralympian Olivia Breen was competing at the England Senior and Disability Track & Field Championships when a female competition official commented that her shorts were "too short and inappropriate." "I was left speechless," Breen wrote in a statement posted on Twitter. "I have been wearing the same style sprint briefs for many years and they are specifically designed for competing in." Meanwhile, the Badminton World Federation was criticized in 2011 for forcing women athletes to wear skirts or dresses. The (male) head of the federation

---

1145 "Gender Balance in Global Sport Report 2016," Women on Boards, https://www.womenonboards.net/womenonboards-AU/media/AU-Reports/2016-Gender-Balance-In-Global-Sport-Report.pdf
1146 Benchetrit, Jenna, "Women Athletes Are Pushing Back against the Uniform Status Quo," CBC, July 30, 2021, https://www.cbc.ca/news/entertainment/women-athletes-uniform-changes-1.6122725
1147 "Bikini Rule Changed in Beach Handball after Norwegian Player Protest," CBC, November 2021, https://www.cbc.ca/sports/bikini-rule-change-handball-player-protest-1.6232786

said, "TV ratings are down ... We want them to look nicer on the court and have more marketing value for themselves. I'm surprised we got a lot of criticism."[1148]

Also in 2021, the German gymnastics team showed up to the Olympics in unitards, which cover the legs, rather than the typical bikini-cut leotards. For comparison, the men wear shorts or pants, depending on the event. This was the first summer Olympic Games since the sentencing of Larry Nassar, who sexually abused hundreds of girls through USA Gymnastics. At his sentencing, where he was given 176 years in prison, athletes including Olympic gold medallists described how the sport's culture allowed for abuse and objectification of young women and girls.[1149] Echoing those sentiments was British runner Jessica Ennis-Hill, who wrote a deeply personal essay about her fear of exposing herself and how "skimpy kit" can traumatise young athletes.[1150]

For some, modesty is also a religious or cultural expectation, and being forced to show skin will keep women from participating. Recent years have seen rule changes that enable Muslim women to play, such as allowing full-length sportswear and head coverings in table tennis, basketball, and judo. In 2018, the Afghan women's football team came under fire for supposed immodesty after some players did not fully cover themselves (i.e. knees were visible between shorts and socks) in a game against Jordan. Leading their critics was a Senior Advisor to Afghanistan's National Cricket Board who declared anyone who supported women's rights to participate in sports "damned." In response, former captain Shamila Kohestani wrote:

> When I first began to challenge male dominance in Afghan society by playing football, I faced many acts of discrimination and sexual harassment from many people. When I was the captain of the Afghan Women's National Football Team, I was slut-shamed and called a prostitute for

---

1148 Benchetrit, Jenna, "Women Athletes Are Pushing Back against the Uniform Status Quo," CBC, July 30, 2021, https://www.cbc.ca/news/entertainment/women-athletes-uniform-changes-1.6122725

1149 Galofaro, Claire, "German Olympic Gymnastics Team, Tired of 'Sexualization,' Wears Unitards," CBC, July 25, 2021, https://www.cbc.ca/sports/olympics/summer/gymnastics/gymnastics-germany-unitards-sexualization-1.6116621

1150 Zipp, Sarah, and Sutherland, Sasha, "Sexism and Sport: Why Body-Baring Team Uniforms Are Bad for Girls and Women," The Conversation, August 5, 2021, https://theconversation.com/sexism-and-sport-why-body-baring-team-uniforms-are-bad-for-girls-and-women-165546

simply participating in a game that I love. I was humiliated and harassed, not only because I was playing football, but because as a woman I was in a man's world and that made me a threat.

I always felt that no matter what I did I was failing in being the "good woman". If I covered my face, people would say that I must be a whore because I'm hiding my face. If I didn't cover my face and wore a chadar people say I must be looking for a husband. If I didn't cover my head, many men thought they had the right to insult me because I must be promiscuous. After living in Afghanistan and the United States, I have learned that no matter what women wear, society polices our clothing and judges us constantly.[1151]

As in most things, women of colour face added barriers. In 2021, swimmers of African descent lobbied to be allowed to use swim caps specifically designed to protect thick, curly, or braided hair that is difficult to fit into traditional caps—and were rejected. The managing body, FINA, claimed that athletes have "never used, neither require to use, caps of such size and configuration."[1152] What they likely meant was *white* athletes. The Soul Cap also does not follow "the natural form of the head," one of the organisation's rules for approved swimwear, ignoring that not everyone has thin, flat hair. Swimming is a sport where people of African descent are statistically under-represented at all levels—in 2017, USA Swimming reported that sixty-four percent of African American children had low or no swimming ability. The Soul Cap was approved for use in international competitions in 2022.[1153]

And it's not just the continuation of existing rules and standards—it's also the biases that come into play when officials have the chance to make new rules. 2012 was the first Olympic Games where women's boxing was an official discipline. At an Amateur International Boxing Association meeting to sort out the ground rules,

---

1151 "Freedom of Choice for the Afghan Women's National Football Team," Free Women Writers, February 20, 2018, https://www.freewomenwriters.org/2018/02/20/freedom-choice-afghan-womens-national-football-team/
1152 Nivison, Andrea, "Swimming Cap Made for Black Hair Approved for Olympic Use by FINA," CBSSports.com, September 7, 2022, https://www.cbssports.com/olympics/news/swimming-cap-made-for-black-hair-approved-for-olympic-use-by-fina/
1153 Crossley, Callie, "Why Are There so Few Black Competitive Swimmers?" WGBH, July 19, 2021, https://www.wgbh.org/news/commentary/2021/07/19/why-are-there-so-few-black-competitive-swimmers

one of the agenda items was whether to make the women wear skirts. In boxing. Apparently after the AIBA president complained in 2010 that spectators supposedly could "not tell the difference" between women and men competitors, making women wear skirts was suggested to address the issue he probably just made up in his head. Coaches from the Polish and Romanian teams, who had their athletes in skirts at the European Championships, reportedly also felt that wearing skirts in the ring made the athletes look "more elegant" and gave a "more womanly impression"—while they punch each other.[1154] In the end, the rules allowed for the boxers to wear either shorts or a skirt.[1155]

Billiards is not typically a sport where one would expect a dress code, but in 1987, player Jean Balukas found herself facing an ultimatum—wear formal attire or don't play. At the annual B. C. Open, Balukas was planning to compete in both the men's and women's divisions, but while the men's side had no dress code, she was told after arriving that the women were expected to compete in formal dress. Apart from the sexism, she simply hadn't brought appropriate clothes—because why on earth would she have? She refused to comply, and the other female players voted that she would not be allowed to compete, though she still played in the men's division. Balukas later described the hurt she felt, that the women—some of them her best friends—would vote to keep her out as she tried to stand up for all of them. There was also speculation that her competitors knew they would have a better chance at the $5,000 prize with her out of the running, though Balukas did not agree. Belinda Bearden, president of the Women's Professional Billiard Association, later wrote to *The New York Times* that players had chosen to impose the dress code to improve the image of women's pool and try to attract more spectators and media attention. Soon after, Balukas told a reporter she was considering leaving the sport, and the following year she retired from professional billiards.[1156]

Even when there is a verifiable medical reason for women to wear something

---

1154 "Ladies, I Want a Good, Clean Fight... And You Have to Wear Skirts," Women You Should Know, January 31, 2012, https://womenyoushouldknow.net/ladies-i-want-a-good-clean-fight-and-you-have-to-wear-skirts/
1155 "Female boxers will not be forced to wear skirts at the Olympics," BBC, March 2, 2012 https://www.bbc.com/sport/boxing/17229496
1156 Santo La Rosa, *History of Billiards through Its Champions Third Part* (Lulu Press, 2019).

outside the norm, people still lose their minds, as seen with Serena Williams's catsuit at the 2018 French Open. While fans and the media loved the outfit, the French Tennis Federation did not, with president Bernard Giudicelli saying such outfits went "too far," explicitly naming Williams when stating that this type of attire would no longer be permitted, out of "respect" for the game and tournament. Whether or not in response to his comment, Williams soon showed up in a tutu at the U.S. Open.[1157]

Apart from the implication that Williams had been disrespectful—a common coded term for when women step out of line—the outfit wasn't chosen for aesthetics or fashion (at least, not entirely). Williams has a history of blood clots and the compression of the clothing helps prevent clots from forming. She also dedicated the Black Panther-inspired catsuit to "all the moms out there that had a tough pregnancy."[1158]

Williams wasn't the first. At the 1985 Wimbledon tournament, Anne White followed the competition's notorious all-white rule, showing up in a white catsuit instead of a tennis skirt.[1159] Opponent Pam Shriver called it the "most bizarre, stupid-looking thing I've ever seen on a tennis court." Wimbledon officials apparently agreed and told White not to wear it again to the tournament. More than thirty years earlier, tennis player Gertrude Moran was accused of bringing "vulgarity and sin into tennis" in 1949 when a flash of lacey shorts were briefly visible while she was playing. Fifty years before that, women were expected to play in floor-length skirts, stockings, and long-sleeved tops. Even they had it easier than their Victorian forebears—the first women to play tennis did so in large, wide-brimmed hats, high collars, long sleeves, and floor-length skirts over corsets, bustles and petticoats.[1160]

1157 Nittle, Nadra, "The Serena Williams Catsuit Ban Shows That Tennis Can't Get Past Its Elitist Roots," Vox, August 28, 2018, https://www.vox.com/2018/8/28/17791518/serena-williams-catsuit-ban-french-open-tennis-racist-sexist-country-club-sport
1158 Chine, Ossian, "Serena Tells of Medical Reason behind Superhero Catsuit," Reuters, May 29, 2018, https://www.reuters.com/article/us-tennis-frenchopen-serena-catsuit-idUSKCN1IU2I6
1159 Barr, Sabrina, "Wimbledon: Most Controversial Outfits of All Time, from Anne White to Venus Williams," Yahoo Sports, June 27, 2022, https://sports.yahoo.com/wimbledon-most-controversial-outfits-time-124050221.html
1160 Rothenberg, Ben, "Courting Fashion," International Tennis Hall of Fame, https://www.tennisfame.com/courting-fashion

SACRIFICING FOR FAMILY

"One can hardly tell women that washing up saucepans is their divine mission, [so] they are told that bringing up children is their divine mission. But the way things are in the world, bringing up children has a great deal in common with washing up saucepans."
—Simone de Beauvoir[1161]

Mathematician Jessie Marie Jacobs met her future husband, geneticist Hermann Joseph Muller, while working as an instructor at the University of Texas in the early 1920s. He was looking for help with mathematical modelling of genetic mutations in flies. The couple married in 1923, and Jessie was soon fired for becoming pregnant with their first child. Her own career effectively terminated, Jessie continued collaborating with her husband in his laboratory. While he did recognise her contributions with co-authorship on a published paper, Jessie did not share the 1946 Nobel Prize that he won for work they did together.[1162]

Other women were expelled even sooner, at the time of marriage. Women in the Australian Public Service faced the "marriage bar"—termination as a nasty wedding gift. Women's rights campaigners like Merle Thornton had an uphill battle as even the Administrative and Clerical Officers' Association—the union most of the women's positions would have fallen under—was a strong supporter of the ban. Some women would lie to keep their jobs, but risked exposure at any time. Typists were allowed to stay on as "temporary" staff, but were prevented

---

1161   Schwarzer, Alice, *Simone de Beauvoir Today: Conversations 1972-1982* (Chatto & Windus, 1984).
1162   Green, Judy; LaDuke, Jeanne "Jacobs, Jessie Marie", Pioneering Women in American Mathematics: The Pre-1940 PhD's, Providence, R.I.: American Mathematical Society, pp. 260–262, 2009, Biography on p.470-472 of the Supplementary Material at AMS.

from supervisory roles, had few entitlements and no rights to retirement fund contributions. Even the single women were excluded from training because it was assumed they would marry, and any investment in them wasted. Passionate scientists, like astronomer Mary Emma Greayer, were forced to give up careers they clearly loved upon getting married, as Greayer did in 1899 even though she was marrying a colleague. Prior to marriage, she was employed at the Adelaide Observatory and was one of the first women to be elected to the South Australian Astronomical Society, where she presented papers. Charlotte Emily Fforde Peel was the first woman to hold a permanent position in astronomy in Australia and spent twenty years working at the Melbourne Observatory until she married the observatory librarian in 1919 and resigned. [1163]

Ruby Payne-Scott, described by the Australian science agency CSIRO as a "pioneer in radio physics and radio astronomy, and is believed to have been the first female radio astronomer," hid the fact that she was married from the organisation for years. When the truth came out in 1950, she lost all her retirement fund benefits, including contributions the organisation had previously made, and was reduced to a temporary employee status. Her career effectively ended the following year when she was just thirty-nine with the arrival of her son. More than fifty years later, CSIRO initiated the Payne-Scott Awards to support researchers who have taken extended leave to care for a newborn. [1164]

Similarly, English doctor Janet Mary Campbell was forced to resign from her civil service job in 1934 when she married, after having worked with departments ranging from the Board of Education (their first full-time woman medical officer), the War Cabinet during World War I and the Ministry of Health. Her thirty years of experience were suddenly outweighed by the ring on her finger, but she didn't let that get her down—she went on to help refugee children fleeing the Spanish Civil War, chair the Public Health Committee of the International Council of Women, serve on the League of Nations' Health Committee, and co-found the

---

1163   Sawer, Marian, "The Long, Slow Demise of the 'Marriage Bar,'" Inside Story, August 18, 2017, https://insidestory.org.au/the-long-slow-demise-of-the-marriage-bar/
1164   Ward, Colin, "Ruby Payne-Scott [1912-1981]," CSIROpedia, January 13, 2015, https://csiropedia.csiro.au/payne-scott-ruby/

Medical Women's Federation. Ironically, she was also a member of the War Cabinet's Committee of Women in Industry during World War II.[1165]

Literary critic Dr. Evelyn M. Simpson, the first woman to receive a Doctor of Philosophy from Oxford University, was forced to resign from her academic position at her alma mater when she married in 1921, though she continued her own independent research. It was more than twenty years until the rule was changed in 1945.[1166]

While there are now legal protections in place in many countries to prevent employers from explicitly firing women for marrying or becoming pregnant, there are countless other ways that marriage and motherhood delay, or completely derail, women's professional work. Apart from the societal expectations of being a wife and mother, women have often had to give up their own passions for practical reasons related to their families. Mileva Marić, for example, gave up her career before it ever truly started after Albert Einstein impregnated her out of wedlock while they were at Zurich Polytechnic. A few years later, Irish champion golfer May Hezlet gave up competing when she married in April 1909.[1167]

Statistician Dr. Alison Harcourt is best known for co-defining the branch and bound algorithm—a way of solving optimisation problems by breaking them into smaller problems—with Ailsa Land. Her work on poverty in Australia was just starting to gain traction as a way to calculate the poverty line, when she gave up academia. "At the end of 1971, which was just after the poverty survey had sort of got to Canberra and had been noted, I resigned from the university because I had started a family," she later said.[1168]

Women are often expected to take on caregiving roles, for children, spouses, elderly parents, and any other type of dependent. This leaves little time and energy

---

1165 Ogilvie, Marilyn, and Joy Harvey, *The Biographical Dictionary of Women in Science* (Routledge, 2003).
1166 Phillips, David, "Simpson, Evelyn Mary (1885-1963)," *Oxford Dictionary of National Biography*, ed. H.C.G. Matthew and Brian Harrison (Oxford University Press, 2004).
1167 Rouse, John and Clavin, Terry, "Hezlet, Mary Elizabeth Linzee ('May')," Dictionary of Irish Biography, 2009, https://www.dib.ie/biography/hezlet-mary-elizabeth-linzee-may-a3980
1168 Smith, Carl, "At the Dawn of Australian Computing, 72 Women Had a Crucial Job You've Never Heard Of," ABC News, November 30, 2019, https://www.abc.net.au/news/science/2019-12-01/women-computing-astronomy-technology/11713282

for other pursuits. Beloved children's author E. L. Konigsburg, for example, only began writing after her three children were all in school.[1169] Engraver and painter Tirzah Garwood put her career on hold to raise her three children.[1170] 1978 National Inventor of the Year (U.S.) Barbara Askins waited until her children were in school to finish her chemistry Bachelors and Masters degrees, then went on to work for NASA, developing a new way to process film using radioactive materials. The astronomical and geological images she worked on held much more detail, making them significantly more valuable to scientists, and her process was also applied to x-rays and restoration of old photos.[1171]

It is, of course, no new phenomenon. After marrying and starting a family in the 1640s, French artist Louise Moillon stopped painting almost entirely, producing only a few works despite living another fifty years. Yet stories like that of Italian painter Lavinia Fontana (1552-1614) and her husband Gian Paolo Zappi offer a glimpse of what could have been—Fontana supported their large family with her art while Zappi acted as her agent and cared for their eleven children.[1172]

Because men have traditionally earned higher levels of income, it is both expected and financially practical for women to uproot their lives if their husband has to move to a new location for work. This is particularly true in certain professions like the military or academia. In addition to the loss of personal support networks, this often means the sacrifice of any job (and accompanying projects) the woman may have in their current location, as well as professional networks she may have created there.

Accomplishments are also expensive—while an activity like writing or running requires primarily time and energy, most arts, sciences, and sports require funding as well, whether for supplies, equipment, facilities, or other expenses. For women

---

1169 "EL Konigsburg," Jewish Women's Archive, https://jwa.org/encyclopedia/article/konigsburg-el
1170 Peskett, Louise, "Tirzah Garwood, Artist and Engraver, in the Shadows of Eric Ravilious," Brighton & Hove Museums, https://brightonmuseums.org.uk/discovery/history-stories/tirzah-garwood-artist-and-engraver-in-the-shadows-of-eric-ravilious/
1171 "Barbara Askins | New Film Developing Method," Lemelson | MIT, https://lemelson.mit.edu/resources/barbara-askins
1172 Duncan, Alexandra, "Lavinia Fontana," Art Story, July 6, 2022, https://www.theartstory.org/artist/fontana-lavinia/

who are financially dependent on male relatives, typically husbands but also fathers and brothers, the person holding the purse strings is usually the one making the decisions. Financial dependence, combined with low pay issues for women, also leaves them in a state of precarity even today, particularly as they reach and pass retirement age in their 60s. Even when women have a successful early career, it can be difficult to re-enter the workforce after taking time away to have children. As one woman told *The Guardian*, "So many older women are being left to rot in poverty by precisely the same system that urged them to stay at home to look after the children."[1173]

When women do re-enter the workforce, they may face what sociologists call the "motherhood penalty," which has been documented in more than a dozen industrialised countries, including the U.S., Japan, South Korea, the U.K., the Netherlands, Poland, and Australia. Women may suffer a per-child wage penalty, creating a pay gap between mothers and non-mothers. In the U.S. in 2020, full-time employed mothers made only seventy-four percent of what their father counterparts earned, compared to the overall gender pay gap of eighty-three percent. Mothers may also receive worse evaluations that indicate they are less committed to their jobs, less dependable and less authoritative compared to non-mothers. As such, they may experience disadvantages in hiring, pay and daily work experience.[1174] A 2005 study from Cornell University found that job-hunting mothers were less likely to be hired, were offered lower salaries and faced a perception that they would be less committed to a job than fathers or women without children. Ironically, fathers were more likely to be offered higher salaries than non-fathers and shown more leniency with things like being late to work.[1175]

Interestingly, a study published in 2012 of women who became mothers between 1978 and 1995 found that mothers who returned to work full time

---

1173 "'No Money, No Pension, No Savings': How Caring for Others Has Left Women in a State of Precarity," *The Guardian*, July 29, 2022, https://www.theguardian.com/commentisfree/2022/jul/29/no-money-no-pension-no-savings-how-caring-for-others-has-left-women-in-a-state-of-precarity
1174 "The Wage Gap Shortchanges Mothers," National Women's Law Center, https://nwlc.org/resource/mothers-equal-pay-day/
1175 Aloi, Dan, "Mothers Face Disadvantages in Getting Hired, Cornell Study Says," Cornell Chronicle, August 4, 2005, https://news.cornell.edu/stories/2005/08/mothers-face-disadvantages-getting-hired-study-shows

shortly after having children were both mentally and physically healthier at age forty compared to stay-at-home moms, those who work part-time or those with some work history who are repeatedly unemployed. They reported greater mobility, more energy, less depression and other health benefits. "Work is good for your health, both mentally and physically," says lead researcher Adrianne Frech. "It gives women a sense of purpose, self-efficacy, control and autonomy. They have a place where they are an expert on something, and they're paid a wage."[1176]

Even for women in countries where paid parental leave is a given, it is often not equal. A woman may want to return to work and a man may want to stay home, but legislation often assumes the reverse. And if a woman is entitled to six months leave while a man only gets one, most couples will do what they have to for their financial stability. In Australia, the federal paid parental leave scheme provides for eighteen weeks for the "primary carer," but only two for the "secondary carer." The latter is specifically called "Dad and Partner Pay."[1177]

For female athletes, there are several hurdles that even Olympic track stars may struggle to leap. Today, many women are challenging the idea that they can't compete while pregnant. In 2019, Lizzette Perez finished the Boston Marathon while being eight months pregnant,[1178] while Allyson Felix took on Nike the same year for the corporation's discriminatory policy around sponsorships of pregnant athletes, which threatened to cut the terms of her endorsement by as much as seventy percent. When she protested, they told her to "know your place and just run." She won, and Nike changed its policy, banning performance-related pay reduction for pregnant athletes, but she dropped them instead and started her own line of running shoes, which she wore at the Tokyo Olympics under the banner

---

1176 "Work Has More Benefits than Just a Paycheck for Moms: Working Moms Are Healthier than Stay-At-Home Moms," ScienceDaily, August 19, 2012, https://www.sciencedaily.com/releases/2012/08/120819153843.htm

1177 Stevenson, Chrys, 2022, "Paid Parental Leave: Women Left Holding the Baby," BroadAgenda, August 22, 2022, https://www.broadagenda.com.au/2022/paid-parental-leave-women-left-holding-the-baby/

1178 Resendiz, Eric, "Woman Finishes Boston Marathon While 8 Months Pregnant," ABC13 Houston, May 4, 2019, https://abc13.com/boyle-heights-boston-marathon-east-los-angeles-runner/5285238

"I Know My Place."[1179]

Felix told a conference in 2022 that pregnancy is still considered "the kiss of death" for athletes. She recalled training at 4am while six months pregnant in 2018, afraid that if a fan took a photo of her pregnant, her sponsors would "immediately change their mind" about working with her. She had to have an emergency c-section seven months into her pregnancy due to potentially life-threatening conditions, and her baby had to spend a month in neonatal intensive care—but on top of worrying about her own health and her child's, she also had to fight for what she was owed. Felix is the most decorated U.S. track and field athlete in history, yet that was not enough for her to be financially secure while pregnant.[1180]

And after childbirth, apart from the time, energy, and financial expense of childcare, many athletes must travel for competitions and other events. That's why Felix launched a childcare initiative, which provided $10,000 grants for childcare expenses needed to enable athletes to train and compete, as well as providing free childcare to athletes, coaches and staff at the U.S. Track and Field championships.[1181]

Family life is also a common reason listed when prominent women athletes retire, as was the case for Serena Williams in 2022. While she also gave other reasons, having a second child was a priority. "I never wanted to have to choose between tennis and a family. I don't think it's fair," she said, mentioning then-forty-five-year-old father of three Tom Brady, who repeatedly retired as an NFL quarterback and then un-retired almost immediately. "If I were a guy, I wouldn't be writing this because I'd be out there playing and winning while my wife was

---

1179   Young, Shalise Manza, "Allyson Felix Is Building an Empire of Her Own — and Making Nike Execs Eat Their Words," Yahoo Sports, June 24, 2021, https://au.sports.yahoo.com/tokyo-olympics-track-allyson-felix-new-shoe-brand-saysh-225706850.html
1180   Akhtar, Allana, "Allyson Felix Said Getting Pregnant Is Known as 'the Kiss of Death' for Olympic Track and Field Athletes," Insider, April 12, 2022, https://www.insider.com/allyson-felix-getting-pregnant-kiss-of-death-for-olympic-runners-2022-4
1181   Hampton, Olivia, "Allyson Felix Launches a Child Care Initiative for Athlete Moms," NPR, June 21, 2022, https://www.npr.org/2022/06/21/1106261485/allyson-felix-launches-child-care-initiative-for-athlete-moms

doing the physical labour of expanding our family."[1182]

That's not even getting into the physical trauma that is pregnancy and childbirth. A 2023 report by the UN found that almost 800 women died every day in 2020 from preventable causes related to pregnancy and childbirth—around 287,000 women died that year alone. Part of the problem is a well-documented bias of doctors and nurses (male or female) to not believe their female patients when the women talk about what is happening with their own bodies.[1183] Even international celebrities like Serena Williams have to fight for proper care. Williams recounted that the day after delivering her daughter via c-section—a major surgery by any measure—she was feeling short of breath. Knowing her own medical history of pulmonary embolisms, she alerted the nurse that she needed a CT scan with contrast and IV heparin (a blood thinner) immediately. The nurse assumed the pain medications were making Williams confused, but Williams insisted. Instead of the measures she instructed, medical staff then wasted time on an ultrasound—which, of course, revealed nothing—before finally sending her for the CT, which confirmed what their patient had been saying all along: that she had several blood clots in her lungs. In addition to shortness of breath, the clots caused her to cough so hard, it ripped her stitches from the c-section.[1184] Moreover, about one-third of people with an undiagnosed and untreated pulmonary embolism don't survive. Even after getting out of the hospital, she needed six weeks of bed rest, but if she had not had both the clout of her position and the willpower to advocate for herself while recovering from major surgery, she easily could have been in that one-third, not least because of contributing racial biases. African Americans are disproportionately likely to face complications, and are three to four times more likely than Caucasian women to die from pregnancy-related complications

---

1182   Healy, Jon, "Serena Laments Double Standards for Parents Playing Sport, as Top Coach Reveals Young Players Freezing Their Eggs," ABC, August 10, 2022, https://www.abc.net.au/news/2022-08-10/womens-tennis-players-freezing-their-eggs-serena-williams-mother/101317988
1183   "Maternal Mortality," World Health Organization: WHO, 2023, https://www.who.int/news-room/fact-sheets/detail/maternal-mortality
1184   Lockhart, P.R., "Serena Williams's Health Scare Shows How Medicine Dismisses Black Women," Vox, January 11, 2018, https://www.vox.com/identities/2018/1/11/16879984/serena-williams-childbirth-scare-black-women

in the U.S.[1185]

Historically, many women gave up their pursuits when they married, whether by choice or not. Biologist Marion Bidder worked as a lecturer and director of studies at Newnham College for more than ten years before marrying in 1899. Suddenly her published works were all about domestic economy—even though she'd married a fellow biologist.[1186] Mathematician and astronomer Mary Somerville's first husband thought women were idiots and did not encourage her intellectual pursuits after they married, but fortunately he died within a few years and she was able to return to her work.[1187]

Sculptor and painter Margaret Gerow met Alexander Phimister Proctor when both were participating artists at the World's Columbian Exposition in Chicago in 1891. A student at the Art Institute of Chicago, she gave up a promising career to marry him, supporting his career and later raising their eight children.[1188]

German chemist Clara Immerwahr married Fritz Haber in 1901 precisely because she wanted to continue working. As a woman in turn-of-the-century Germany, even the first one in the county to earn a PhD in chemistry, her employment options were limited and Haber enticed her with visions of the two of them working side-by-side. Once she was trapped in the marriage, however, she found herself relegated to an uncredited assistant, rather than a partner. "It has always been my attitude that a life has only been worth living if one has made full use of all one's abilities and tried to live out every kind of experience human life has to offer. It was under that impulse, among other things, that I decided to get married at that time," she wrote. "The life I got from it was very brief...and the main reasons for that was Fritz's oppressive way of putting himself first in our home and marriage, so that a less ruthlessly self-assertive personality was simply

---

1185   Mayo Clinic, "Pulmonary Embolism: Take Measures to Lower Your Risk – Symptoms and Causes," Mayo Clinic, 2018, https://www.mayoclinic.org/diseases-conditions/pulmonary-embolism/symptoms-causes/syc-20354647

1186   "Personal Papers of Marion Greenwood Bidder, 1880 – 1999," Girton College Archive Repository, 1998, https://archivesearch.lib.cam.ac.uk/repositories/19/archival_objects/370699

1187   Gregersen, Erik, "Mary Somerville | Biography, Writings, & Facts," Encyclopedia Britannica, https://www.britannica.com/biography/Mary-Somerville

1188   Todd, Nicole, "Love Stories: Alexander Phimister and Mody Proctor," Buffalo Bill Center of the West, February 15, 2017, https://centerofthewest.org/2017/02/14/love-stories-alexander-phimister-mody-proctor/

destroyed." Haber also became a zealot about developing chemical weapons, which the pacifist Immerwahr was appalled by. She committed suicide in 1915 following an argument with her husband.

In the case of Anna Sundström, who may be considered the first female chemist in Sweden, it wasn't even her marriage that resulted in her termination. From 1808, she worked as assistant, laboratory superintendent, and supervisor of students for Jöns Jacob Berzelius, considered one of the fathers of modern chemistry. But after working together for almost thirty years, Sundström was fired after Berzelius married in 1836.[1189]

ANTI-NEPOTISM POLICIES

In some cases, women have been held back by anti-nepotism policies that prevent them from being employed by the same organisations that their husbands work for. For example, geologist Doris Malkin Curtis had to leave her job at Shell after almost a decade there when she married an engineer who also worked at the company.[1190] The goal of such rules is to prevent favouritism and corruption among families, and they appear everywhere from academia to government to corporations. They also frequently impacted couples who didn't even work in the same department, such as biologist Mary Hardesty not being able to get a paid position at Tulane University in the 1930s because her husband was a mathematics professor there.[1191]

In the U.S., the National Industrial Recovery Act of 1933 forbade more than one family member from holding a government job, resulting in many women losing their employment as they were more likely to be the ones in lower-paying and lower-authority positions.[1192] But that is not always the case—in 1999, a Baton Rouge, Louisiana, city councilwoman resigned from her elected position because

---

1189 "Anna Sundström, Sveriges första kvinnliga kemist." Berzelius and the development of chemistry 1780 – 1820, https://web.archive.org/web/20120320002757/http://biphome.spray.se/tni1/Berzelius/Berzbo13.htm
1190 Echols, Dorothy Jung, "Memorial to Doris M. Curtis 1914-1991," The Geological Society of America, 1992, https://rock.geosociety.org/net/documents/gsa/memorials/v23/Curtis-DM.pdf
1191 Ogilvie, Marilyn, and Joy Harvey, *The Biographical Dictionary of Women in Science* (Routledge, 2003).
1192 Milligan, Susan, "Stepping through History," US News & World Report, January 20, 2017, https://www.usnews.com/news/the-report/articles/2017-01-20/timeline-the-womens-rights-movement-in-the-us

her son-in-law had recently graduated from the police academy and become a city police officer. Because the council technically oversaw the police department, one of them would have to resign or face prosecution.[1193]

Mathematician Karen Uhlenbeck was the first woman to win the field's most prestigious award, the Abel Prize in 2019. Decades before, however, she couldn't find a permanent academic position because many universities had anti-nepotism rules in place that prevented spouses from being hired, even in different departments. She eventually accepted a job at the University of Illinois at Urbana–Champaign, but left after a few years, simultaneously solving the nepotism issue by separating from her husband.[1194]

Future Nobel Prize-winning scientist Maria Goeppert Mayer moved to the U.S. from Germany after she married chemist Joseph Edward Mayer in 1930. But that same marriage prevented her from teaching as a faculty member at Johns Hopkins University, where her new husband was an associate professor. Relegated to the role of an assistant, she still published a landmark paper in 1935, on a type of radioactive decay known as double beta decay. When her husband was fired from Johns Hopkins in 1937, she followed him to Columbia University, where she took up an unpaid position. There, she met Enrico Fermi, with whom she would later work on the Manhattan Project. After World War II, in February 1946, her husband joined the faculty at the University of Chicago, and Goeppert Mayer became an associate professor of physics at the school—once again, for no pay, though she also worked part-time for the university's Argonne National Laboratory. She also did her Nobel-winning research during this period, on the nuclear shell model.[1195]

Immunologist Marian Koshland is known for discovering that the differences in antibodies' amino acid make-up explain how efficient and effective they are at fighting off foreign elements. But because her husband was a professor at the

---

1193 White, Richard D., "Consanguinity by Degrees: Inconsistent Efforts to Restrict Nepotism in State Government," State & Local Government Review vol 32 no 2 (2000): 108–20, https://www.jstor.org/stable/4355257
1194 Andrei, Mihai, "Who Is Karen Uhlenbeck—the First Female Recipient of the Abel Prize," ZME Science, March 20, 2019, https://www.zmescience.com/feature-post/pieces/karen-uhlenbeck-abel-prize-20032019/
1195 "Struggle for Employment: Anti-Nepotism Laws in the Academy," Center of History for Physics at AIP, https://www.aip.org/sites/default/files/Struggle%20for%20Employment_Biographies%20Handout.pdf

University of California, Berkeley, she was only made a full professor herself in 1970 when anti-nepotism rules were relaxed and anti-discrimination laws began taking effect. She'd been working there as a researcher since 1965.[1196] Decades earlier, when physiologist Matilda Brooks's husband became a zoology professor at UC Berkeley in 1927, anti-nepotism rules prevented Brooks from being eligible for a comparable position. Instead, she was hired as a research associate, relying on a series of grants instead of a proper salary. It was only when he was incapacitated in 1934 and 1936 that she was allowed to teach in his place.[1197]

In 1948, mathematician Irmgard Flügge-Lotz and her husband both received offers to work at Stanford University. Despite her significant contributions in the field, a policy forbade spouses from having professor roles in the same department. While her husband was appointed as a professor, Flügge-Lotz was forced to accept the lower position of a lecturer, even though the work she was doing was at the level of a professor. It was more than a decade before she became Stanford's first woman Professor of Engineering in 1961.[1198]

Professor Lea Puymbroeck Miller became a symbol of this issue in 1938. Employed at the University of Washington, Miller was fired when the university adopted such a policy. The timing, in the midst of the US's Great Depression, helped fuel a media storm that pitted women's rights advocates against those who saw women in the workforce as stealing jobs that should belong to men. It was not new in the area, however—the city of Seattle and King County had implemented similar laws two years earlier. Indeed, the university's own board of regents had decreed in 1928 that "no more wives of faculty men should be added to the faculty or office forces." Edward and Theresa McMahon, whose employment pre-dated the rule and therefore was exempt, refused to concede. Theresa was both a longtime economics instructor and an outspoken advocate for labour rights. She publicly alleged that shortly after the policy's inception, the university president had told her husband that while the ruling was "not [made] retroactive, [Mrs. McMahon's]

1196 Ogilvie, Marilyn, and Joy Harvey, *The Biographical Dictionary of Women in Science* (Routledge, 2003).
1197 *Ibid.*
1198 O'Connor, J. J. and Robertson, E. F., "Irmgard Flügge-Lotz – Biography," Maths History, Last updated May 2010, https://mathshistory.st-andrews.ac.uk/Biographies/Flugge-Lotz/

resignation would be welcome." Miller, meanwhile, had been overseas when the policy was enacted in 1936 and, unknowingly, married another professor in 1938. This led to her being forced out after having taught at the university for seven years, in violation of her contract. Any argument about avoiding favouritism was also simply ridiculous, as Miller was an art professor, while her husband taught zoology. Her boss, Walter Isaacs, also pled her case, arguing that her dismissal would cause academic detriment to the institution, because she was a highly regarded and established professor—but also that it would cost more to replace her, as her wages were significantly lower than a male professor of her qualifications would earn.[1199]

Despite having a PhD in zoology in 1931, it was more than a year before carcinologist (someone who studies crustaceans) Dora Henry was offered a job at the University of Washington, where she had followed her husband for his career. When she was finally offered a position, it was only at the level of research associate, even though she was already well-published in her field, thanks at least in part to anti-nepotism rules—at the University of Washington, wives of staff members were prohibited from paid work anywhere other than as clerks, secretaries, or laboratory assistants. For years, she was paid at a part-time salary, despite putting in the same full-time hours as her male colleagues and winning National Science Foundation grants annually for decades for her work. It was in 1960 that she was finally promoted to associate research professor. As Catherine Musemeche writes in her book *Lethal Tides*,

> The predictable consequences of such sweeping rules were that wives who happened to be scientists were penalised even if equally qualified. Women carcinologists often worked with little or no financial compensation. It was not unusual for women to be offered lower salaries or for them to take decreases in salaries to allow their male colleagues access to more funds... Even though many of these women made discoveries that exceeded the accomplishments of the men with whom they worked, they

---

1199 Edwards, Katharine, "Married Women's Right to Work: 'Anti-Nepotism' Policies at the University of Washington in the Depression," Depts.washington.edu., 2009, https://depts.washington.edu/depress/women_uw_working_wives.shtml

were treated like the farm league of researchers.[1200]

Scholar Anne Innis Dagg has researched and written extensively about the negative impact of such rules in academia, observing that "A wife often earns a Ph.D. from the local university where she is then unable to become a professor because of this opposition. Unlike many other women, she may not be free because of her marriage to seek a position at a university outside her locale, a dilemma which makes her career vulnerable to the local university's policies."[1201]

1200 Musemeche, Catherine, *Lethal Tides: Mary Sears and the Marine Scientists Who Helped Win World War II* (HarperCollins, 2022).
1201 Dagg, Anne Innis, "Academic Faculty Wives and Systemic Discrimination —Antinepotism and "Inbreeding,"" *Canadian Journal of Higher Education* vol 23 no 1 (April 1993): 1–18, doi:10.47678/cjhe.v23i1.183148. ISSN 0316-1218

THE COST OF DISREGARDING WOMEN

"I raise up my voice—not so that I can shout, but so that those without a voice can be heard ... We cannot all succeed when half of us are held back."
—Malala Yousafzai[1202]

"When I was a girl, women were not supposed to be scientists. At least, that's what I was told," writes astronomer Nancy Grace Roman. Despite the discouragement and disapproval from those around her, Roman pursued her education and career, advocating for women in the sciences the whole way. Her discovery of irregularities in the orbits of stars and the changes in stars' elemental makeup as they age helped astronomers understand how the Milky Way evolved. She worked with NASA from its infancy in 1959, first building a program to coordinate satellites, sounding rockets, balloons, and ground research to best support space observation in the coming decades. Roman also served as Chief of the Astronomy and Relativity Programs in the Office of Space Science until 1979 and is known as the "Mother of Hubble" for her work in developing the Hubble Space Telescope (the first powerful optical telescope in space), launched in 1990.[1203]

While there have been some unintendedly beneficial outcomes when discounting women backfires—like the 1887 election of Susanna M. Salter, who had been

---

1202   Yousafzai, Malala, 2-13/ 16ᵗʰ birthday speech at the United Nations, July 12, 2013, https://malala.org/newsroom/malala-un-speech
1203   Roman, Nancy Grace, "Nancy Roman: An Astronomer's Life," Astronomical Society of the Pacific, June 11, 2013, https://www.astrosociety.org/wp-content/uploads/2013/07/ab2013-112.pdf

put on the ballot as a prank, as mayor of Argonia, Kansas[1204]—in general, there are very real, and very negative, impacts when women are overlooked or dismissed. Apart from the personal and professional cost to the women themselves, and the undermining of future generations of women and their own aspirations, decisions to disregard women and their work have cost countless people knowledge, health, wealth, and their very lives.

MEDICAL

> "Failing to listen to the woman is one of the biggest mistakes a practitioner can make."
> —Helen Varney

Dr. Katalin Karikó's work on mRNA (the genetic code that carries DNA instructions) laid the foundation for successful Covid-19 vaccines, as well as other vaccines for HIV, influenza, malaria and more. "But for many years her career at the University of Pennsylvania was fragile. She migrated from lab to lab, relying on one senior scientist after another to take her in. She never made more than $60,000 a year ... Dr. Kariko's struggles to stay afloat in academia have a familiar ring to scientists. She needed grants to pursue ideas that seemed wild and fanciful. She did not get them, even as more mundane research was rewarded," reports *The New York Times*.[1205] Dr. Karikó later won the Nobel Prize for Physiology or Medicine in 2023 for her work—and all it took for her to get recognition was a global pandemic.[1206]

It is only thanks to the persistence and tenacity of Dr. Kariko that her work continued, and the result was countless lives saved and a pandemic brought under control sooner than it might have been otherwise. But where she was able to persist, we can never know how many women's potential achievements never

---

1204   Billington, Monroe, "Susanna Madora Salter First Woman Mayor," Kansas Historical Society, Autumn 1954 (Vol. 21, No. 3), pages 173-183, https://www.kshs.org/p/kansas-historical-quarterly-susanna-madora-salter/13106
1205   Kolata, Gina, "Kati Kariko Helped Shield the World from the Coronavirus," *The New York Times*, April 8, 2021, https://www.nytimes.com/2021/04/08/health/coronavirus-mrna-kariko.html
1206   "Nobel Prize for Physiology or Medicine awarded to Katalin Karikó and Drew Weissman for research enabling mRNA COVID-19 vaccines," ABC, October 2, 2023, https://www.abc.net.au/news/2023-10-02/nobel-prize-physiology-medicine-2023-mrna-vaccine/102926620

happened because of factors like lack of funding and attention. The cost of ignoring and dismissing women's expertise can be staggering.

In 1960, Frances Oldham Kelsey was hired as a reviewer for the U.S. Food and Drug Administration. One of her first assignments was an application to approve the use of thalidomide as a tranquilliser and painkiller, specifically for pregnant women to ease morning sickness. Although it had been previously approved in more than twenty other countries, including Canada, and despite pressure from the manufacturer, Kelsey withheld approval and requested further studies. She was concerned because an English study had documented peripheral neuritis, inflammation of the nervous system, as a side effect. She also wanted evidence that the drug was not harmful to foetuses.[1207]

In July 1962, she was hailed as a hero on the front page of the *Washington Post* for preventing "the birth of hundreds or indeed thousands of armless and legless children."[1208] Birth deformities in Europe had been linked to pregnant women being prescribed and taking thalidomide. As a result of the story coming to light, the Kefauver Harris Amendment was passed unanimously in Congress that October, strengthening drug regulation in the U.S. Companies would now be required to demonstrate the efficacy of new drugs, report adverse reactions to the FDA, and request consent from clinical study participants. The law required "stricter limits on the testing and distribution of new drugs" and, for the first time, recognized that "effectiveness [should be] required to be established prior to marketing." Kelsey worked for the FDA for forty-five years, retiring in 2005 at the age of ninety.

It's worth noting that her interest in teratogens (drugs that cause birth deformities) began when she was at university, in a position that she reputedly was offered because the supervisor thought the feminine "Frances" was a variation on the male "Francis" and assumed he was hiring a man.

Kelsey's work is the best-case scenario—she credited her superiors at the FDA for backing her up, rather than pressuring her to rubber stamp thalidomide. Too

---

1207 Mintz, Morton, "'Heroine' of FDA Keeps Bad Drug Off Market," *The Washington Post*, July 15, 1962, https://www.washingtonpost.com/wp-srv/washtech/longterm/thalidomide/keystories/071598drug.htm
1208 *Ibid.*

often, women's opinions and research are dismissed out of hand, and the consequences can be devastating.

Working in Ghana in the 1930s, Dr. Cicely Williams noted that while child mortality was high, toddlers between two and four years were at much greater risk than infants. Dr. Williams noticed they were seeing young children with swollen bellies and stick thin limbs who very often died despite treatment. This condition was often misdiagnosed as pellagra, a vitamin deficiency, but Williams disagreed and carried out autopsies on the dead children. This presented significant risk, because there were no antibiotics in colonial Ghana, and she became severely ill with streptococcal haemolysis from a cut during one autopsy. Williams asked the local women what they called the condition, and was told kwashiorkor, which Williams translated as "disease of the deposed child." Her findings, that the condition was due to a lack of protein in the diets of children weaned off their mothers' breastmilk after the arrival of a new baby, were published in the *Archives of Disease in Childhood* in 1933.[1209]

Her fellow colonial physicians were quick to try to discredit her research, particularly H.S. Stannus, who was considered as an expert on African nutritional deficiency. Williams followed up her paper with another, more directly contrasting kwashiorkor and pellagra, published in *The Lancet* in 1935. This did little to sway the medical opinion, and colonial physicians continued to avoid using the term kwashiorkor, or even acknowledge that it was a distinct condition from pellagra, despite the continued deaths of thousands of children who were being treated for the latter condition. Williams commented about the ongoing issue, "These men in Harley Street couldn't believe you unless you wore stripy trousers."[1210]

It was only more than a decade and a half later that she was vindicated by a 1950 international study that found the condition represented "the most serious and widespread nutritional disorder known to medical or nutritional science"

1209   Stanton, J., "Listening to the Ga: Cicely Williams' Discovery of Kwashiorkor on the Gold Coast," World Public Health Nutrition Association, https://www.wphna.org/htdocs/downloadsMar2012/Listening%20to%20the%20Ga.pdf

1210   Stanton, Jennifer, "Obituary: Dr Cicely Williams," *The Independent*, July 16, 1992, https://www.independent.co.uk/news/people/obituary-dr-cicely-williams-1533501.html

(a study she pushed for as the first director of maternal and child health for the World Health Organization). It is impossible to know how many children died as a result of the delay.

In comparison, Kamala Sohonie's research into vitamin-rich neera (sap from toddy palm trees) led to significantly improved health outcomes for malnourished children and pregnant women in tribal communities in India.[1211]

For more than fifteen years, Dr. Mary-Claire King worked tirelessly on research that most people dismissed. From 1974 to 1990, King searched for an answer to why breast cancer ran in families. Because the prevailing theory of the time was that the cause was viral, most scientists considered her efforts to find a genetic marker to be a waste of time. Even King herself sometimes worried that her work would be in vain, but she carried on, and was proven right with the identification of the BRCA1 gene in 1990. Subsequent research identified a second gene, called BRCA2, and today it is believed that they contribute to as many as five to ten percent of breast cancer cases. Genetic links for many other cancers have also been identified.[1212]

Dr. Jane Plant was diagnosed with breast cancer for the sixth time in 1993. Although she was a geochemist, not a biologist, she decided to investigate the relatively low breast cancer rate among Chinese women and determined that lower dairy consumption was the most likely cause, connecting the oestrogen in the milk of pregnant cows and growth factors that promote cancer. Although her reasoning was scientifically sound, her theory was, like King's, dismissed by the general scientific community, though her advice to avoid dairy did reach thousands of cancer patients. She herself followed a dairy-free diet for eighteen years and remained cancer-free, until she eventually strayed from her diet due to a professed weakness for calves' liver cooked in butter. She died in 2016 due to a blood clot following chemotherapy.[1213] Years later, her theory was validated when research was

---

[1211] Mitra, Anirban, "The Life and Times of Kamala Bhagvat Sohonie." *Resonance* vol 21 no 4 (2016): 301–14, https://doi.org/10.1007/s12045-016-0330-8
[1212] "Mary-Claire King | Researcher," Breast Cancer Research Foundation, June 19, 2014, https://www.bcrf.org/researchers/mary-claire-king/
[1213] Hicks, Cherrill, "Will Giving up Dairy Defeat Cancer?" *The Sydney Morning Herald*, June 5, 2014, https://www.smh.com.au/national/will-giving-up-dairy-defeat-cancer-20140605-39lpz.html

published in 2020, indicating that "Consuming as little as 1/4 to 1/3 cup of dairy milk per day was associated with an increased risk of breast cancer of 30%... By drinking up to one cup per day, the associated risk went up to 50%, and for those drinking two to three cups per day, the risk increased further to 70% to 80%."[1214]

Canadian oncologist and clinical investigator Dr. Vera Peters was reportedly told to "go do women's work" after she challenged the medical establishment in 1950 with a groundbreaking paper. Her research demonstrated for the first time that patients with early-stage Hodgkin lymphoma (cancer of white blood cells) could be cured if they received a regimen of high-dose radiation. Previously, the condition had been thought to be incurable. Her findings were met with scepticism, to the point that she later commented that it took more than ten years for them to be accepted. She would later study the use of radiation therapy to treat breast cancer, and her research showed that lumpectomies—where only the cancerous tissue is removed—followed with radiation were just as effective as radical mastectomies, where one or both breasts are entirely removed, along with chest muscle and lymph nodes. Given the major impact of a radical mastectomy both physically and psychologically, lumpectomies are significantly less invasive, and radical mastectomies are rarely performed today.[1215]

Prominent molecular biologist Lydia Villa-Komaroff switched her major in college because an advisor told her that "women do not belong in chemistry." It is fortunate that she only shifted focus to biology, rather than leaving the sciences entirely, as she later discovered that bacteria could be engineered to produce human insulin, likely saving countless lives.[1216]

1214 "New Study Associates Intake of Dairy Milk with Greater Risk of Breast Cancer: Evidence Suggests Consistently Drinking as Little as One Cup per Day May Increase Rate of Breast Cancer up to 50%," ScienceDaily, February 25, 2020, https://www.sciencedaily.com/releases/2020/02/200225101323.htm

1215 "How Vera Peters Revolutionized Treatments for Hodgkin's, Breast Cancer," CBC, January 11, 2015, https://www.cbc.ca/news/health/how-vera-peters-revolutionized-treatments-for-hodgkin-s-breast-cancer-1.2893406

1216 "Lydia Villa-Komaroff | CSU," California State University, https://www.calstate.edu/impact-of-the-csu/alumni/Honorary-Degrees/Pages/lydia-villa-komaroff.aspx

BAD BUSINESS

"If you have to lie, cheat, steal, obstruct and bully to get your point across, it must not be a point capable of surviving on its own merits."
—Steven Weber[1217]

Tracy Oliver and Issa Rae co-created *The Misadventures of Awkward Black Girl* as a web series, starring Rae. Despite its popularity and awards, the duo was met with blatant sexism, racism, and mockery from multiple studio executives when the women tried to launch it as a television or streaming show. As Oliver later recounted to *NPR*:

> The internet was clamoring for [more episodes of *The Misadventures of Awkward Black Girl*] … And like, we had millions and millions of views. But then when we would go to meet with executives, they would say to us, "That's cute that you guys have this internet following, but like … one exec in particular, I still remember this meeting. [He] looked Issa in her face … and said, "No one wants to look at you … on their television screen," and said that she wasn't attractive enough. And that … she's an internet star, but not a TV star … it was like, it's one thing when you get like praise and stuff from the masses, but then we were like, "So nothing we did mattered." That's what it felt like. It felt like a gut punch when he said that.[1218]

1217   Weber, Steven, "Democarcy Ball!" The Huffington Post, June 8, 2012, https://www.huffpost.com/entry/democracyball_b_1581734

1218   Sanzgiri, Leena, "Tracy Oliver on Navigating Hollywood by Embracing the Unexpected: The Limits with Jay Williams," NPR, August 23, 2022, https://www.npr.org/2022/08/23/1119079338/tracy-oliver-on-navigating-hollywood-by-embracing-the-unexpected

They had better luck after Rae's 2015 memoir, also titled *The Misadventures of Awkward Black Girl*, became a bestseller. When the show was finally adapted into HBO's *Insecure* in 2016, it ran for five seasons and was nominated for more than a dozen Emmys. Rae was also nominated for several acting Emmys and Golden Globes, and she was among *Time*'s annual list of the 100 most influential people in the world in 2018 and 2021. In 2017, the American Film Institute chose *Insecure* as one of the top 10 Television Programs of the Year, and the show was honoured at the 2018 Peabody Awards, for "creating a series that authentically captures the lives of everyday young, black people in modern society."

In addition to the financial costs and damage to public image that come with lawsuits and other accusations of discrimination, sexism can often prove to be poor business practice. For example, as noted previously, many women inventors pitched their ideas to companies that chose to ignore (or steal) them—ideas that later proved highly successful. When publishers rejected *Peter Rabbit*, author Beatrix Potter published it herself and it became one of the most popular and enduring children's books ever written—one of many such tales of women's books.[1219]

In an experiment, University of Texas researcher Ethan Burris asked teams to make strategic decisions for a fictional business. He told one team member that a system the business used was flawed and gave that person information about a better approach. On teams where the person to suggest the improvement were women, team leaders saw them as less loyal and were less likely to act on the suggestion, even when all team members were made aware that the woman in question was privy to information the others were not.[1220]

Creating a toxic work environment for anyone can—and should—lead to the loss of good employees. Lynn Povich is known for being one of dozens of women who sued *Newsweek* in 1970 for gender discrimination. As she later wrote, the company's practices led to the loss of talented writers: "In our job interviews, we were told: 'Women don't write at *Newsweek*. If you want to be a writer, go

---

1219 Armitstead, Claire, "How Beatrix Potter Self-Published Peter Rabbit," *The Guardian*, December 17, 2013, https://www.theguardian.com/books/booksblog/2013/dec/17/beatrix-potter-peter-rabbit-self-publishing
1220 Sandberg, Sheryl, and Adam Grant, "Opinion | Speaking While Female," *The New York Times*, January 12, 2015, https://www.nytimes.com/2015/01/11/opinion/sunday/speaking-while-female.html

someplace else.'" Which is exactly what Nora Ephron, Ellen Goodman, Jane Bryant Quinn, and Susan Brownmiller did. They left." Goodman won a Pulitzer in 1980. Ephron would go on to be an award-winning screenwriter, including three Academy Award nominations, while Quinn spent decades as a respected financial journalist. Brownmiller's groundbreaking 1975 book on rape culture led to her being named as one of *Time* magazine's people of the year, and the New York Public Library named it one of 100 most important books of the 20th century. As Quinn recalled in Povich's 2012 book, *The Good Girls Revolt*, "I thought I'd work my way up … once I proved my worth. But I discovered that I'd never become a writer, just an older and older researcher, making my younger and younger male writers look good." And it wasn't just the lower pay, lesser titles and lack of recognition or encouragement that drove women away, Povich writes: "a researcher was stalked by her senior editor, who had a crush on her. He told her if she didn't marry him, she would have to leave *Newsweek*—which she did."[1221]

Male-driven companies may also overlook the financial potential of female customers, to the company's detriment. In the 1950s, a Toshiba salesman started asking housewives what would make their lives easier. They reported that their most onerous task was cooking rice three times a day, but this wasn't a priority for the company because Mitsubishi and Matsushita (the future Panasonic) had already failed at building an automatic machine. The male decision-makers also believed any woman willing to give up the requisite time, effort, and sleep required to prepare perfect rice was a "failed housewife" anyway—never mind that the purpose of all appliances is to make life easier. Married couple Yoshitada Minami and Fumiko combined his mechanical knowledge and her rice-cooking skills to create a working version. Within the year, Toshiba was producing 200,000 rice cookers every month, sparking a manufacturing war.[1222]

There are also instances where dismissing a woman's proposal can have major financial costs in the long run. When Melanie Perkins was trying to secure funding

---

1221 Povich, Lynn, *The Good Girls Revolt* (PublicAffairs, 2012).
1222 Ewbank, Anne, "The Battle to Invent the Automatic Rice Cooker," Atlas Obscura, July 31, 2020, https://www.atlasobscura.com/articles/rice-cooker-history

to start her company, she was rejected by 100 venture capitalists. Years later, she had grown Canva, a free online graphic design system, into a $26 billion start-up.[1223]

Marjorie Merriweather Post inherited the General Food Corporation in 1914 and served as a director until 1958. Although she was very involved with the management and expansion of the company, it would have been considered unseemly for a woman to be running such a large enterprise and so her husband, E.F. Hutton, was the chairman of the board. When Marjorie first heard about Clarence Birdseye's new techniques of preserving foods, she wanted to purchase his company and begin selling frozen foods across the country. Hutton was against the idea, causing a significant delay.[1224] In addition to the lost profits, Birdseye's company was becoming more valuable and therefore more expensive when General Food did eventually buy it for $23.5 million in 1929 (around $408 million today). Once they did, their frozen food products were an immediate and massive success.[1225]

It's also worth noting that the Geena Davis Institute found in 2017 that female-led family films grossed 38.1 percent more on average than male-led films, a pattern that had remained consistent over four years. Yet films were more than twice as likely (fifty-nine percent) to have a male lead than a female one (twenty-six percent). Similarly, films with racially diverse co-leads gross 60.5 percent more, yet only seventeen percent of the top 100 grossing family films that year had protagonists of colour.[1226]

In addition to the countless individual instances, research and statistics support the assertion that organisations do better with more women. Many studies have found that involving women in work settings increases both productivity and

---

1223 Naysmith, Caleb, "How 100 vc Rejections Led to a $26 Billion Startup for This 35-Year-Old," Yahoo Finance, June 16, 2023, https://finance.yahoo.com/news/100-vc-rejections-led-26-150012207.html
1224 See, Carolyn, "In the Land of Milk and Money," *The Washington Post*, February 3, 1995, https://www.washingtonpost.com/archive/lifestyle/1995/02/03/in-the-land-of-milk-money/442a131f-c964-4e2c-a9ac-bc4fc98e8d43/
1225 Crockett, Zachary, "The Father of the Modern Frozen Food Industry," The Hustle, November 1, 2019, https://thehustle.co/frozen-food-inventor-charles-birdseye/
1226 "Gender and Race Representations in the Top Family Films of 2017," See Jane, https://seejane.org/research-informs-empowers/the-see-jane-100/

profit.[1227] As *Forbes* put it, "Compared to their peers, high-gender-diversity companies deliver slightly better returns, and they have outperformed, on average, less diverse companies over the past five years. Companies that not only hire but also manage to retain more women put themselves in a position to automatically gain a competitive advantage, a benefit that extends to all stakeholders." [1228]

According to research from the MIT Center for Collective Intelligence, the more women were on a team, the better that team performed. Researchers attributed this in part to higher social perception on the part of women. Women leaders also tend to take fewer risks with their companies, while also being more innovative.[1229]

To quote IT executive Elaine Montilla, "Not taking advantage of a female presence in the workplace seems like a gamble most businesses shouldn't take."

1227 "What makes a high-performing team? The answer may surprise you," MIT Sloan Executive Education, March 22, 2017, https://exec.mit.edu/s/blog-post/what-makes-a-high-performing-team-the-answer-may-surprise-you-MCIE4TDCCNFZAL7MK6DYC2S6TEK4
1228 Montilla, Elaine, "Council Post: Top Three Reasons We Need More Women in Tech," Forbes, March 10, 2020, https://www.forbes.com/sites/forbestechcouncil/2020/03/10/top-three-reasons-we-need-more-women-in-tech/?sh=599539f115fb
1229 Chamorro-Premuzic, Tomas, "The Business Case for Women in Leadership," Forbes, March 2, 2022, https://www.forbes.com/sites/tomaspremuzic/2022/03/02/the-business-case-for-women-in-leadership/?sh=4d69fcb89cbb

WARTIME

"You can get a lot done if you credit other people for what they do. People want credit and they deserve to have it."
—Anna M. Rosenberg[1230]

During World War II, the U.S. Navy was trying to find a solution for "fouling"—when barnacles attach to ship hulls en masse, which slows the ship and increases fuel consumption. Yet when Dr. Dora Henry, the leading expert in the country, if not the world, on barnacles offered her services to help with the research, the men in charge declined. She later heard that the researchers could not even get a barnacle to grow in the lab for them to study. Dr. Henry went back to the site and diagnosed the problem within minutes—the ocean water they had collected had been extensively filtered, and the barnacle larvae had been filtered right out. Months of work had been completely wasted, and progress delayed.[1231]

French intelligence agent Marie-Madeleine Fourcade worked with MI6 during World War II. When she was sent a new British contact, Arthur Bradley Davies (AKA "Bla") in 1941, she was suspicious of him from the start, but her concerns went unheeded by the men in London. Years later, it was revealed that Davies had been working with the Germans the entire time. He had been a member of the Union of British Fascists, but the agency had not properly vetted him before sending him to Fourcade. When MI6 finally admitted the mistake and gave

---

[1230] Kerr, Adelaide, "These Women," Associated Press, February 12, 1942, https://digitalcommons.murraystate.edu/cgi/viewcontent.cgi?article=1188&context=pl

[1231] Musemeche, Catherine *Lethal Tides: Mary Sears and the Marine Scientists Who Helped Win World War II* (HarperCollins, 2022).

Fourcade's group approval to interrogate and execute Bla, he confirmed that he had told the Germans everything he knew about the French resistance.[1232]

MI6's domestic counterpart, MI5, was no better when it came to Milicent Bagot. An intelligence officer and expert on Soviet Russia, she was the first to warn her agency about the Communist ties of Kim Philby, an MI6 officer who worked as a Soviet KGB double agent for almost thirty years. Her warning went unheeded, and he continued to work for British intelligence for more than a decade.[1233] Similarly, her concerns about another Soviet agent, Ursula Kuczynski, living as a housewife in the English countryside, were largely ignored. This allowed Kuczynski to continue her work for years, including acting as handler for nuclear scientist Klaus Fuchs, who conveyed all details to the Soviets as he helped develop the atom bomb.[1234]

In the early days of the CIA, Mary Hutchison repeatedly warned her superiors about trusting the former Nazi intelligence officer Myron Matviyenko, a known murderer who had worked actively against the United States and its allies. Although ostensibly working with the agency, he was not communicating with his handlers, leaving out vital information. The decision-makers believed her reports and the agency cut ties with him in 1950; the following year, he led a group of Ukrainian nationalists parachuting into western Ukraine, which had been seized by the Soviets in 1939. In collaboration with MI6, the plan was for them to infiltrate and blend in with the Soviets, but his men were immediately arrested, interrogated, beaten and several were executed. He had been working with the KGB the entire time, and Hutchison's reports had predicted his betrayal.[1235]

While Mary's reports were heeded, her colleague Eloise Page was less successful when she tried to advise that the Soviets would soon launch the first satellite into space. Her male supervisor steadfastly dismissed her intelligence (and her

---

1232 Olson, Lynne, *Madame Fourcade's Secret War: The Daring Young Woman Who Led France's Largest Spy Network against Hitler*, (Random House, 2020).
1233 Hinds, Samantha, "The Future Is Femme," The New Inquiry, April 15, 2013, https://thenewinquiry.com/the-future-is-female-2/
1234 Macintyre, Ben, *Agent Sonya: Moscow's Most Daring Wartime Spy* (Crown, 2020).
1235 Holt, Nathalia, *Wise Gals: The Spies Who Built the CIA and Changed the Future of Espionage* (Icon Books, 2023).

intelligence) by claiming it was Soviet misinformation, regardless of Eloise's experience, expertise and, of course, the evidence. On October 4, 1957, the Soviets launched Sputnik, eliciting fear, shock, and anger among the American public. Eloise had wanted to tell the public but had been prevented from preparing anyone for the fact that it was coming, exacerbating the response. The agency was also ill-prepared to fight the propaganda and persuasion as the USSR used the development to gain and strengthen alliances.

During World War I, French spy Louise de Bettignies was captured by the Germans in 1915. One of her final messages warned about a major German attack on Verdun that was planned for early 1916. The information was passed on to the French commander, who refused to believe it. The Battle of Verdun lasted almost ten months and resulted in 379,000 to 400,000 French casualties, with 163,000 dead.[1236]

1236 O'Mara, David, "27 September 1918 Louise de Bettignies (Alias 'Alice Dubois') Died on This Day," Western Front Association, https://www.westernfrontassociation.com/on-this-day/27-september-1918-louise-de-bettignies-alias-alice-dubois-died-on-this-day/

PUBLIC GOOD

"In the future, there will be no female leaders. There will just be leaders."
—Sheryl Sandberg and Nell Scovell, *Lean In: Women, Work, and the Will to Lead*[1237]

A 2022 study from the University of Queensland of COVID-19 pandemic data from ninety-one countries found that those led by women averaged about forty percent fewer deaths during the height of the pandemic, compared to those led by men. According to the report, "female leaders have generally acted more quickly and decisively and have demonstrated greater risk aversion toward losses of human life. In addition, they have consistently taken a broader view to consider the wider impact of coronavirus on society and have been more open to innovative thinking, thereby managing the COVID-19 crisis better than their male counterparts."[1238]

In 2021, BioNTech co-founder Özlem Türeci credited her company's gender equity as one reason for the speed at which the first viable vaccine for COVID-19 was created. She also stated that the lack of women in decision-making roles in medicine was "destroying value" for stakeholders. World Health Organization data showed that women make up seventy percent of the global health and care workforce, but only twenty-five percent of decision-making roles. "At BioNTech, women make up 54 percent of our total workforce and 45 percent of top management. We like to think that being a gender-balanced team has been critical to making the seemingly impossible possible—developing a COVID-19 vaccine

---

[1237] Sandberg, Sheryl, *Lean In: Women, Work, and the Will to Lead* (Alfred A. Knopf, 2013).
[1238] Kane, Vivian, "Study Shows People Living in Countries Led by Women Have Been Way Safer during COVID," The Mary Sue, June 16, 2022, https://www.themarysue.com/women-led-countries-fewer-covid-deaths/

within 11 months without shortcuts," Türeci said.[1239]

Historically, women have spearheaded many movements for the public good, including various social reforms and philanthropy. But disregarding women can negatively impact the public good in other ways beyond activism. In 1746 Sweden, potatoes were cultivated only in the greenhouses of wealthy aristocrats, but that changed thanks to Eva Ekeblad. She wrote to the Royal Swedish Academy of Sciences about her discoveries on making flour and alcohol from the root vegetable. This contributed to potatoes becoming a staple food across the country. By deriving alcohol from potatoes, wheat, rye, and barley were freed up for making bread, which both improved the country's overall diet and reduced the frequency of famines. Her discoveries also led to her becoming the first woman member of the academy, though they didn't elect another until 1951, and three years later she was reduced to an honorary member because she was a woman.[1240]

Her sister, Catherine Charlotte De la Gardie was influential in popularising smallpox vaccination in Sweden, as Lady Mary Wortley Montagu had been in England. Catherine also successfully forestalled the country's last witch trial. When she became aware that a local governor had ordered the arrest, interrogation, and torture of eighteen people, she used her connections to contact authorities in the capital and have it stopped. No one in Sweden had been executed for witchcraft in fifty years; the parliament investigated, freed the prisoners, and jailed the governor. Catherine also helped the victims obtain legal assistance and ensured they were granted compensation from the state, as the torture had left them incapable of working.[1241]

There is a long history of violence being allowed to continue because law enforcement and other authorities disregard the statements of women. Across the U.S., hundreds of thousands of rape kits—evidence collected from victims

---

1239 Media, P. A., "BioNTech Co-Founder Says Gender Equality Made Vaccine Possible," *The Guardian*, March 8, 2021, https://www.theguardian.com/world/2021/mar/08/biontech-co-founder-says-gender-equality-made-vaccine-possible
1240 "Eva Ekeblad (1724-1786)," The Mills Archive, https://new.millsarchive.org/2020/07/22/eva-ekeblad-1724-1786/
1241 Sjöberg, Maria, "Catharina Charlotta de La Gardie," *Svenskt kvinnobiografiskt lexicon*, March 8, 2018, https://skbl.se/en/article/CatharinaCharlottaDelaGardie

following their assaults—went untested for years because departments do not allocate sufficient resources to testing them for DNA. As of 2021, the estimate was still well over 100,000. Not only does this delay risk the degradation of the biological samples, it also prevents law enforcement from connecting cases with the same assailant, enabling rapists to continue attacking women.[1242]

Between 2008 and 2011, Marc Patrick O'Leary raped six women in Seattle and Denver. When the first victim, an eighteen-year-old known as Marie, reported her assault to the Lynwood police officers Jeffrey Mason and Jerry Rittgarn, she was bullied by the officers into recanting her statement, which then resulted in them charging her with making a false report. Between 2008 and 2012, the Lynnwood police labeled twenty-one percent of rape cases as "unfounded," five times the national average for similarly sized municipalities. An external review of her case found that Marie was "coerced into admitting that she lied" and that the police had ignored strong evidence of the crime to focus on "minor inconsistencies" in her account. No officers were ever disciplined and it was only in 2014—three years after O'Leary was finally arrested—that the city of Lynwood settled a lawsuit brought by Marie for $150,000. While a particularly atrocious example, Marie's experience is one that many assault survivors will recognise, a reason that others do not come forward, and negligence that enables repeat offenders to continue hurting people.[1243]

Almost twenty years earlier on the other side of the world, Wendy Davis had her own experience of victim dismissal. Davis was attacked at work by Bradley Robert Edwards, grabbed by the throat, a cloth covering her mouth, and pulled toward a nearby bathroom. She was able to fight him off, reported it, and identified him to police. He was charged with a relatively minor crime despite admitting he was trying to pull her into an isolated bathroom and having zip ties on him at the time. He pled guilty and served no jail time, receiving two years' probation. He

---

1242 Caroline Mimbs Nyce, "A Nationwide Epidemic of Untested Rape Kits," The Atlantic, July 15, 2019, https://www.theatlantic.com/newsletters/archive/2019/07/nationwide-epidemic-of-untested-rape-kits-atlantic-daily/594046/
1243 Miller, T. Christian and Armstrong, Ken, "An Unbelievable Story of Rape," ProPublica, December 16, 2015 https://www.propublica.org/article/false-rape-accusations-an-unbelievable-story

had previously not been charged for a 1988 rape and would not be arrested for the murders of two other women (1996 and 1997) until 2016. He was also tied to the murder of another teen, though he could not be charged because her remains had not been located and was charged belatedly with a 1995 rape. Davis later published a book, *Don't Make a Fuss: It's Only the Claremont Serial Killer*. She discovered at the murder trial that, following her assault, Edwards had been ordered to attend a year-long sex offenders treatment program—meaning the police knew he had likely intended to rape her, yet she had been told there was not enough evidence to confirm that. He also kept his job at the telecom company Telstra (then known as Telecom), giving him access to more women's workplaces and homes, and was promoted multiple times in the coming years. "(Western Australia) Police and Telecom had dismissed the incident as 'minor', a 'one off', 'out of character', and 'explainable' given my assailant's 'relationship problems' that were occurring at the time," she told the ABC. [1244]

Women's obsession with true crime is well-documented, and many people tie this to the fact that women are statistically more likely to be victims of violent crimes than men. For some, it is also a drive to find justice for the victims. True crime aficionado Michelle McNamara spent years investigating the man she called the "Golden State Killer." Thanks to her work, former police officer Joseph James DeAngelo was identified as the perpetrator of at least thirteen murders, fifty-one rapes and 120 burglaries across California between 1974 and 1986. [1245]

Journalist Sarah Koenig's podcast *Serial* focused on Adnan Syed, who was convicted in 2000 of the murder of his ex-girlfriend, Hae Min Lee. When *Serial* aired in 2014, he was halfway through a thirty-year sentence. The attention the podcast brought to the case led to DNA testing on Lee's clothing, shoes, and rape kit, and Syed's conviction was vacated in 2022. Prosecutorial misconduct was also implied, as the prosecutor moving to vacate the charges referenced Brady

---

1244 Schmidt, Molly, "Claremont Serial Killer Survivor Wendy Davis Speaks Out, Hoping Her Neglect Won't Be Repeated," ABC, June 12, 2022, https://www.abc.net.au/news/2022-06-12/claremont-serial-killer-survivor-wendy-davis-pens-book/101143622
1245 Igoe, Katherine J., "Michelle McNamara's Work Led to a Killer—but She Died before His Arrest," *Marie Claire*, June 29, 2020, https://www.marieclaire.com/culture/a32957172/what-happened-to-michelle-mcnamara/

violations—the withholding of evidence that could undermine a prosecutor's case—by the original prosecutors.

When Katharine Graham's father turned the family-owned business of the *Washington Post* over to her husband in 1946, she claimed not to resent the decision to pass her over. It was only in 1963, after said husband committed suicide following years of cheating, alcoholism, and mental illness, that Graham took the reins as only the second woman publisher of a major American newspaper. By 1972, she was publisher, board chair of the holding company and the first female Fortune 500 CEO. Among the many decisions she made from this position of power were exposing two of the most consequential political scandals of the 1970s: the Pentagon Papers and Watergate. She stood up to the U.S. government, refused to be intimidated by legal action, and defended her writers and editors, illustrating the need for a strong journalism industry to hold those in power to account for their actions.[1246]

During her first career, Florence R. Sabin was a trailblazer: the first woman to hold a full professorship at Johns Hopkins School of Medicine, the first woman elected to the National Academy of Sciences, and the first woman to head a department at the Rockefeller Institute for Medical Research. Never one to rest on her laurels, a few years into retirement she became a vocal advocate for public health reform in her native Colorado after accepting the governor's request to lead a subcommittee on health beginning in 1944. Already in her seventies, Sabin campaigned to help pro-reform political candidates defeat their anti-reform opponents. She was successful, and the "Sabin Health Laws" radically improved public health care in the state, including providing more hospital beds for tuberculosis patients, which significantly reduced cases as patients were less likely to infect others because they could not be admitted to hospitals. In a 1947 speech, Sabin said she had been chosen as committee chair because the governor had no interest in public health and appointed "an old lady" because he didn't believe she would be able to accomplish anything.

1246   Berger, Marilyn, "Katharine Graham of Washington Post Dies at 84," *The New York Times*, July 18, 2001, https://www.nytimes.com/2001/07/18/us/katharine-graham-of-washington-post-dies-at-84.html

She then focused on Denver, which had its own set of issues including politics in the health department, no sanitary engineer, its sewage plant operated by the parks department, unreliable garbage collection, milk quality requirements well below national standards and rampant rodent problems. Recognising this, J. Quigg Newton made cleaning up Denver a priority when he ran for mayor and, after winning, appointed Sabin as the city's manager of health and charities. The seventy-six-year-old Sabin wasted no time, successfully lobbying for the construction of a new sewage treatment plant, increasing garbage collection, expanding rodent-elimination measures and implementing higher standards for milk and dairy. The city's tuberculosis cases also fell by half.[1247]

When Alice Catherine Evans joined the Bureau of Animal Industry in 1913, it was not the most welcoming environment. She later wrote in her memoir, "Although several women scientists were employed in the Bureau of Plant Industry, USDA, only one had preceded me in the Bureau of Animal Industry. She remained only a year or two, in the Division of Pathology, and left before I came. I wonder how she came to be admitted. In my case, admission was by accident, for the BAI officials had failed inadvertently to protect themselves against the admittance of women. They had left a loophole in the barrier, and I had entered through it unwittingly... when the bad news broke at a meeting of BAI officials that a woman scientist would be coming to join their staff, they were filled with consternation. In the words of a stenographer who was present, they almost fell off their chairs."[1248]

While working in the Dairy Division, Evans began investigating the bacteria Bacillus abortus, which was known to cause miscarriages in animals. She believed that the bacterium caused brucellosis, a potentially fatal disease that presents with fever, joint, and muscle pain and could be transmitted to humans via unpasteurized milk. She reported her findings to the Society of American Bacteriologists in 1917, publishing the results in the Journal of Infectious Diseases in 1918 and

---

[1247] "Florence R. Sabin – Profiles in Science," National Library of Medicine, National Institutes of Health, https://profiles.nlm.nih.gov/spotlight/rr/feature/biographical-overview
[1248] Evans, Alice C., "Dr. Alice C. Evans Memoir 1963," Office of NIH History and Stetten Museum, https://history.nih.gov/display/history/Evans%2C+Alice+C.+1963

warning that raw milk should be pasteurised, as the process kills most bacteria. As a woman, and one without a PhD, her warnings were generally disregarded by sceptics. Although her observations were repeatedly confirmed, first by Dr. Karl F. Meyer and his team in 1920, it wasn't until the 1930s that pasteurisation became standard practice in the U.S. It's impossible to calculate how many people and animals were affected, as even Evans herself was misdiagnosed with neurasthenia when she was infected because doctors did not recognise the signs of brucellosis.

Joining the U.S. Public Health Service's Hygienic Laboratory in 1918, Evans studied epidemic meningitis, Spanish flu and streptococcus. She published research on the nascent stage of bacteriophage more than two decades before Winston R. Maxted and Richard M. Krause published similar findings. In 1928, the Society of American Bacteriologists elected Evans their first woman president in recognition of her work.

In 1917, Dr. June McCarroll was driving down a California highway to her office when a truck ran her off the road. "It did not take me long to choose between a sandy berth to the right and a ten-ton truck to the left!" she later proclaimed. It also didn't take her long to come up with a solution—today, the California Department of Transportation credits her with the idea of separating traffic with painted lines on the road. Yet when she suggested it initially, the local chamber of commerce had no interest—so she grabbed a paintbrush and can of paint and went and did it herself. It was not until 1924, through the campaigning of McCarroll and other women, that the idea was finally adopted in California, with the rest of the world following.[1249]

American writer Charlotte Perkins Gilman's short story *The Yellow Wallpaper*, published in 1892, was groundbreaking for its depiction of women's health—both physical and mental—and the prevailing attitudes around them. It was based on personal experience. After giving birth to her daughter, Gilman experienced postnatal depression. Dr. Silas Weir Mitchell, considered a leading expert on women's health at the time, prescribed a harsh "rest cure"—basically, bed rest and absolutely

---

1249 "Doctor June McCarroll Monument," Atlas Obscura, August 26, 2016, https://www.atlasobscura.com/places/doctor-june-mccarroll-monument

no work of any kind, which included reading, writing and painting. After three months, Gilman couldn't take it anymore. Recognizing she was close to a complete psychological breakdown, she overruled Mitchell's restrictions and wrote *The Yellow Wallpaper*, with additions and exaggerations to emphasize her criticisms. She also sought treatment from Mary Putnam Jacobi, one of the first modern women doctors, whose recommendation of physical and mental activity proved much more successful as a treatment.[1250]

If Mitchell had had his way, Gilman would never have written again. His instructions were to "Live as domestic a life as possible. Have your child with you all the time ... Lie down an hour after each meal. Have but two hours' intellectual life a day. And never touch pen, brush or pencil as long as you live."[1251] While it's impossible to measure the full impact of her popular story, it likely saved other women from similar situations. Gilman later said *The Yellow Wallpaper* was "not intended to drive people crazy, but to save people from being driven crazy, and it worked." One mind it didn't change, however, was Mitchell's—she sent him a copy but never heard back. He continued prescribing his "rest cure" and as late as 1908 was trying to have entire hospitals devoted to the wretched "treatment."

1250 Cleghorn, Elinor, *Unwell Women: Misdiagnosis and Myth in a Man-Made World* (Dutton, 2021).
1251 Filman, Charlotte Perkins, *The Forerunner*, 1913.

ONE FINAL NOTE

"We learn best to listen to our own voices if we are listening at the same time to other women—whose stories, for all our differences, turn out, if we listen well, to be our stories also."
—Barbara Deming

Thank you for reading this book and taking the time to learn about these incredible women and their accomplishments. There are recommended titles in the following pages, and the list is by no means exhaustive. If you want to go beyond educating yourself, we all have some form of power, platforms, and privileges that we can use to promote the stories of all marginalized populations, not just women. There are countless forms of powerful people, from academics whose research we rely on to industry gatekeepers to bosses who listen to their female employees. But even if you don't feel that you have that kind of power, you can share stories, recommend books and movies and podcasts and YouTube videos (start here, if you're unsure: infinite-women.com/recommendations), and encourage those around you when things feel too hard or you see someone being overlooked. You can write to lawmakers and museum curators and school boards, telling them that as a member of their community, this is important to you. Be aware and pay attention, and when you see inequality, acknowledge it and bring it to the attention of those around you.

And if a little girl ever tells you that girls aren't good at something or can't do or be what they dream of—tell them about all the little girls who were amazing at it even when people told them otherwise.

ABOUT THE AUTHOR

Allison Tyra is the creator and manager of Infinite Women, an ever-expanding encyclopedia of women. After reading the stories of tens of thousands of women and wondering why she'd never heard of many of them, she began compiling notes for what would become her debut book, *Uncredited*. Although most of Allison's creative projects have been performance-based, *Uncredited* is a return to her journalistic roots. An American ex-pat, Allison lives in regional Australia with her husband and what he says are far too many cats and she feels are not enough.

FURTHER READING

"Women will be hidden no more. We will not remain hidden figures. We have names."
—Janelle Monáe[1252]

If you enjoyed *Uncredited,* you may also enjoy:

Rage Becomes Her: The Power of Women's Anger by Soraya Chemaly

Unwell Women: Misdiagnosis and Myth in a Man-Made World by Elinor Cleghorn

Invisible Women: Exposing Data Bias in a World Designed for Men by Caroline Criado-Perez

Off with Her Head: Three Thousand Years of Demonizing Women in Power by Eleanor Herman

When Women Didn't Count: The Chronic Mismeasure and Marginalization of American Women in Federal Statistics by Robert Lopresti

Mother of Invention: How Good Ideas Get Ignored in an Economy Built for Men by Katrine Marçal

Girly Drinks: A World History of Women and Alcohol by Mallory O'Meara

Speaking While Female: 75 Extraordinary Speeches by American Women by Dana Rubin

Inferior: How Science Got Women Wrong and the New Research That's Rewriting the Story by Angela Saini

The Authority Gap: Why Women Are Still Taken Less Seriously Than Men, and What We Can Do About It by Mary Ann Sieghart

---

1252   Monáe, Janelle, Speech, 2017 Women's March, Washington D.C.

I

There are many wonderful books telling women's (often previously untold) stories. Here are just a few recommendations for further reading:

The Audacity of Inez Burns: Dreams, Desire, Treachery & Ruin in the City of Gold by Stephen G. Bloom

The Far Traveler: Voyages of a Viking Woman by Nancy Marie Brown

Come Fly the World: The Jet-Age Story of the Women of Pan Am by Julia Cooke

The Confidante: The Untold Story of the Woman Who Helped Win WWII and Shape Modern America by Christopher C. Gorham

The Strong Ones: How a Band of Civilian Women Made Their Mark on the Army by Sara Hammel

Radiant: The Dancer, The Scientist, and a Friendship Forged in Light by Liz Heinecke

Off With Her Head: Three Thousand Years of Demonizing Women in Power by Eleanor Herman

Irena's Children: The Extraordinary Story of the Woman Who Saved 2,500 Children from the Warsaw Ghetto by Tilar J. Mazzeo

Who Cooked the Last Supper? The Women's History of the World, *Rebel Women*, and *The Women's History of the Modern World* by Rosalind Miles

We Band of Angels: The Untold Story of American Nurses Trapped on Bataan by the Japanese by Elizabeth M. Norman

Empress of the Nile: The Daredevil Archaeologist Who Saved Egypt's Ancient Temples from Destruction by Lynne Olson

Queens of Jerusalem: The Women Who Dared to Rule by Katherine Pangonis

The Dark Queens: The Bloody Rivalry That Forged the Medieval World by Shelley Puhak

Sheilas: Badass Women of Australian History by Eliza Reilly

The Immortal Life of Henrietta Lacks by Rebecca Skloot

The Nine: The True Story of a Band of Women Who Survived the Worst of Nazi Germany by Gwen Strauss

Confident Women: Swindlers, Grifters, and Shapeshifters of the Feminine Persuasion by Tori Telfer

Women Who Launch: Women Who Shattered Glass Ceilings by Marlene Wagman-Geller

The Secret History of the Mongol Queens: How the Daughters of Genghis Khan Rescued His Empire by Jack Weatherford

The Girl Explorers by Jayne E. Zanglein

THE SCIENTISTS

Overnight Code: The Life of Raye Montague, the Woman Who Revolutionized Naval Engineering by Paige Bowers

Women in White Coats: How the First Women Doctors Changed the World of Medicine by Olivia Campbell

Broad Band: The Untold Story of the Women Who Made the Internet by Claire L. Evans

Rise of the Rocket Girls: The Women Who Propelled Us, from Missiles to the Moon to Mars by Nathalia Holt

Proving Ground: The Untold Story of the Six Women Who Programmed the World's First Modern Computer by Kathy Kleiman

Rosalind Franklin: The Dark Lady of DNA by Brenda Maddox

Forces of Nature: The Women who Changed Science by Anna Reser and Leila McNeill

The Lady Anatomist by Rebecca Messbarger

Vera Rubin: A Life by Jacqueline Mitton

Rocket Girl: The Story of Mary Sherman Morgan, America's First Female Rocket Scientist by George D. Morgan

Lethal Tides: Mary Sears and the Marine Scientists Who Helped Win World War II by Catherine Musemeche

Hidden Figures: The American Dream and the Untold Story of the Black Women Who Helped Win the Space Race by Margot Lee Shetterly

Power in Numbers: The Rebel Women of Mathematics by Talithia Williams

The Exceptions: Nancy Hopkins, MIT, and the Fight for Women in Science by Kate Zernike

THE ARTISTS

When Women Invented Television: The Untold Story of the Female Powerhouses Who Pioneered the Way We Watch Today by Jennifer Keishin Armstrong

Ivory Vikings: The Mystery of the Most Famous Chessmen in the World and the Woman Who Made Them by Nancy Marie Brown

Bravura!: Lucia Chase and the American Ballet Theatre by Alex C. Ewing

The Story of Art Without Men by Katy Hessel

Ink & Paint and *The Only Woman Animator* by Mindy Johnson

In on the Joke: The Original Queens of Standup Comedy by Shawn Levy

The Lady from the Black Lagoon: Hollywood Monsters and the Lost Legacy of Milicent Patrick by Mallory O'Meara

Looking for Lorraine: The Radiant and Radical Life of Lorraine Hansberry by Imani Perry

Broad Strokes: 15 Women Who Made Art and Made History by Bridget Quinn

THE SPIES

Three Ordinary Girls: The Remarkable Story of Three Dutch Teenagers Who Became Spies, Saboteurs, Nazi Assassins–and WWII Heroes by Tim Brady

The Woman Who Smashed Codes: A True Story of Love, Spies, and the Unlikely Heroine Who Outwitted America's Enemies by Jason Fagone

Wise Gals: The Spies Who Built the CIA and Changed the Future of Espionage by Nathalia Holt

Agent Sonya: Moscow's Most Daring Wartime Spy by Ben Macintyre

Code Girls: The Untold Story of the American Women Code Breakers Who Helped Win World War II by Liza Mundy

A Woman of No Importance: The Untold Story of the American Spy Who Helped Win World War II by Sonia Purnell

Southern Lady, Yankee Spy: The True Story of Elizabeth Van Lew, a Union Agent in the Heart of the Confederacy by Elizabeth R. Varon

THE JOURNALISTS

You Don't Belong Here: How Three Women Rewrote the Story of War by Elizabeth Becker

In Extremis: The Life of War Correspondent Marie Colvin by Lindsey Hilsum

Lady Editor: Sarah Josepha Hale and the Making of the Modern American Woman by Melanie Kirkpatrick

The Correspondents: Six Women Writers on the Front Lines of World War II by Judith Mackrell

Susan, Linda, Nina & Cokie: The Extraordinary Story of the Founding Mothers of NPR by Lisa Napoli

The Good Girls Revolt: How the Women of Newsweek Sued their Bosses and Changed the Workplace by Lynn Povich

First to the Front: The Untold Story of Dickey Chapelle, Trailblazing Female War Correspondent by Lorissa Rinehart

Sensational: The Hidden History of America's "Girl Stunt Reporters" by Kim Todd

THE ACTIVISTS

The Girl Who Dared to Defy: Jane Street and the Rebel Maids of Denver by Jane Little Botkin

Walk with Me: A Biography of Fannie Lou Hamer by Kate Clifford Larson

The Woman They Could Not Silence: One Woman, Her Incredible Fight for Freedom, and the Men Who Tried to Make Her Disappear by Kate Moore

The Agitators: Three Friends Who Fought for Abolition and Women's Rights by Dorothy Wickenden

Madame Restell: The Life, Death, and Resurrection of Old New York's Most Fabulous, Fearless, and Infamous Abortionist by Jennifer Wright

THE WARRIORS

The Unwomanly Face of War: An Oral History of Women in World War II by Svetlana Alexievich

The Light of Days: The Untold Story of Women Resistance Fighters in Hitler's Ghettos

by Judy Battalion

The Real Valkyrie: The Hidden History of Viking Warrior Women by Nancy Marie Brown

All the Frequent Troubles of Our Days: The True Story of the American Woman at the Heart of the German Resistance to Hitler by Rebecca Donner

The Girls Who Stepped Out of Line: Untold Stories of the Women Who Changed the Course of World War II by Mari K. Eder

Wake: The Hidden History of Women-Led Slave Revolts by Rebecca Hall

THE FLYERS

The Mercury 13: The True Story of Thirteen Women and the Dream of Space Flight by Martha Ackmann

A Wasp Among Eagles: A Woman Military Test Pilot in World War II by Ann B. Carl

The Women with Silver Wings: The Inspiring True Story of the Women Airforce Service Pilots of World War II by Katherine Sharp Landdeck

Straight on Till Morning: A Biography of Beryl Markham by Mary S. Lovell

Sally Ride: America's First Woman in Space by Lynn Sherr

Fighting for Space: Two Pilots and Their Historic Battle for Female Spaceflight by Amy Shira Teitel

GLOSSARY

Allyship: when people who are not part of a marginalized group actively show support for individual members of that group, or the group as a whole. The allies may be more privileged, such as men supporting women, or lateral on the privilege/marginalization scale, such as a person of colour speaking out against racism that impacts a different ethnic group (i.e. a non-Muslim Latina advocating against Islamophobia). Allyship is important in several ways, from having strength in numbers and not getting caught up in in-fighting between marginalized groups, to those with privilege using that privilege to promote and elevate the voices of those without their privilege.

Androcentrism: a mindset that assumes male as the default, particularly in powerful roles. This also applies to other areas, like assuming that only studying male bodies for medical research is acceptable. For more on this, check out Caroline Criado-Perez's Invisible Women.

Anti-nepotism rules: policies that limit or prevent the employment of members of the same family. Because women have historically been paid less and been less likely to achieve higher-level positions, they have more commonly been the ones negatively impacted by such rules.

Bropropriation: slang portmanteau (combining "brother" and "appropriation") for a man stealing a woman's idea.

Bechdel-Wallace Test: first introduced in Alison Bechdel's comic strip Dykes to Watch Out For in 1985, the original version stipulated that to pass, a movie had to have at least two women who talked to each other about something other than a man. The test has since expanded to stipulate that the women must both be named characters. Although generally shortened to just "Bechdel Test," Bechdel herself credits the original idea to her friend Liz Wallace, and prefers the longer version that credits Wallace.

Catch-22: a no-win situation, where the solution presents its own problems. For example, women are often assumed to be less competent than men; in theory, the way to offset this would be to list her qualifications. However, a woman who asserts her expertise is seen as arrogant and therefore less likable. Women seen as less likable are often punished for that perception (less likely to secure a job or win a client, for example). A work-around for this scenario is, ideally, to have someone else advocating on the woman's behalf, but this is often outside the woman's control.

Fridging: the killing of female characters primarily or solely to motivate a male character. The female characters are often underdeveloped, and the impacts of their death, other than motivating the male character, are rarely explored. The original term, women in refrigerators, was coined by Gail Simone in 1999, and comes from a 1994 comic book where the superhero Green Lantern finds his girlfriend murdered and stuffed into their refrigerator. As in that case, fridging deaths are frequently not actually shown in the media in question.

Gender diminutive: a diminutive is a term that tends to diminish the person or thing it is describing. The most common example of this in a gender context is referring to adult women as "girls," because a girl is a child. Referring to an adult as you would a child belittles the person's intelligence, maturity and agency. There is also an argument to be made that referring to women by their first name – which is familiar, rather than formal – when one would refer to a male by their last name, is diminutive.

Words can also be made into diminutives with slight changes—suffragists were called "suffragette" as a form of condescension and undermining, as "-ette" means a little form of the thing, such as kitchenette. While U.S. suffragists pushed back against it, their UK sisters embraced it, taking power over the word by claiming it as their own.

Hepeating: Coined by friends of physics professor and astronomer Nicole Gugliucci, "hepeating," as she explained in a tweet on November 22, 2017, is "For when a woman suggests an idea and it's ignored, but then a guy says the same thing and everyone loves it."

Internalized misogyny: as with other biases, anti-female biases can be absorbed by female-identifying people, just as people of color can be racist, queer people can be homophobic, disabled people can be ableist, etc. Because we are constantly surrounded by misogynistic messaging, generally from a very young age, girls and women may hold these beliefs and exhibit related behaviours, having internalized the misogyny. This is particularly true when intersectionality is involved, such as a woman with wealth privilege holding negative, stereotypical views about poor women that she doesn't have about poor men—the rich woman's bias is against other women without her privilege, representing the intersection of gender and class.

Intersectionality: the compounded effect of multiple forms of marginalization, coined by Kimberlé Crenshaw in 1989. A Caucasian, abled-bodied, cisgender, heterosexual, slim, middle-class woman will be affected by sexism, but an African American, disabled, transgender, low-income, plus-size lesbian is also having to deal with racism, ableism, transphobia, classism, fatphobia, and homophobia on top of that sexism. In addition to the cumulative effects, intersecting identities can also shape the forms of discrimination, such as women of colour often being hypersexualized in different ways, from the exoticised framing of Asian women as submissive geishas to the "spicy Latina."

Male Gaze: presenting women in media (including visual art and writing) through a masculine, heterosexual lens that shows women as sexual objects for the pleasure of the assumed heterosexual male viewer.

Mansplaining: when man explains something to a woman without being asked, despite (knowingly or not) being less qualified than the woman to understand the topic. This is inherently condescending because the man automatically assumes he knows more than the woman he is speaking to.

Manterrupting: when a man interrupts or talks over a woman while she is making a point.

Matilda Effect: a bias against acknowledging the achievements of women scientists whose work is attributed to their male colleagues. The term was, coined by science historian Margaret Rossiter, is named for Matilda Joslyn Gage, who described it in her 1870 essay *Woman as Inventor*. While particularly prevalent in the sciences, which tend to be highly collaborative, we see this in other areas as well—see the "contributions overlooked" section for more.

Marriage bar: official policies preventing or limiting women's employment based on their marital status.

Motherhood penalty: disadvantages in pay, perceived competence, and benefits working mothers encounter in workplaces compared to childless women.

Period stigma: negative social and cultural views, beliefs, taboos, and practices related to menstruation, depicting it—and people who menstruate—as impure or shameful and often leading to secrecy and emotional distress.

Privilege and marginalization: in this context, a marginalization is a personal trait that commonly leads to negative discrimination (not to be confused with positive discrimination, like "pretty privilege" where more conventionally attractive people are often treated better). This can include anything from race to sex and gender identity to sexuality to disability to financial status to education to physical appearance. Privilege is the lack of marginalisations, referring to the benefits derived by those who do not have to deal with the negative discrimination associated with those marginalizations.

Respectability politics: a political strategy in which members of a marginalized community push other members to behave in ways seen as more acceptable to those outside the community. The goal is to present the community as a whole as being more worthy of respect by being "respectable" as defined by those outside the community and the community members who believe it will be effective.

Revenge porn: the sharing of nude or sexually explicit images of a person without their consent, often with the express intention of harming the person socially, emotionally or professionally.

Scully Effect: a documented increase in the number of women who choose to pursue STEM careers as a direct result of seeing female characters in such roles in fictional media. Although first recognized through and named for *The X Files*' Dana Scully, there are other examples such as African American astronaut Mae Jemison citing Lt. Uhura from the original *Star Trek* series as an inspiration.

Slut shaming: the practice of criticising women and girls for their sexual behavior—real, perceived or alleged—to make them feel bad about themselves

PLAYLIST

Hell No – Ingrid Michaelson
Armor – Sara Bareilles
Stand Up – Cynthia Erivo
Rise Up – Andra Day
I'm a Lady – Meghan Trainor
Most Girls – Hailee Steinfeld
I'd Rather Be Me – Mean Girls
Fight Song – Rachel Platten
Quiet – MILCK
I Am Woman (Hear Me Roar) – Helen Reddy
Can't Hold Us Down – Christina Aguilera
How Far I'll Go – Moana
Labour – Paris Paloma

INDEX

"Edinburgh Seven" 298
"Hello Girls" of the Signal Corps 230
"Mrs. Wilmot" 144
"Steamboat ladies" 290
Aalto, Aino 220
Abdul Halim bin Salem Nasser, Amina bint 409
Abramson, Jill 347
af Klint, Hilma 207
Aglaonice of Thessaly 406
Agnes of Courtenay 23
Agnes Williams 203
al Hurra, Sayyida 24
Albers, Anni 328
Alexievich, Svetlana 162
Alice of Antioch, Princess 23
Altman, Tosia 121
Amarasekare, Priyanga 368
Anarcha, Betsy, Lucy, and nine other nameless women 22
Ancient Egyptian women doctors 23
Anderson, Marian 393
Anderson, Mary 172, 298
Anguissola, Sofonisba 150
Annie Jump Cannon 199
Anning, Mary 205
Antoinette Poisson, Jeanne 423
Antonelli, Kathleen 148
Antonia Maury 199
Ardern, Jacinda 420
Askew, Anne 43
Askins, Barbara 441
Aspasia 410, 415
Austen, Jane 38, 95, 235
Ayrton, Hertha 311
Bach, Anna Magdalena 156, 160
Bagot, Milicent 464
Baldoncelli, Sabina 308
Ball, Alice Augusta 135
Ball, Lucille 211

Balukas, Jean 436
Banda, Barbra 325
Barceló, Maria Gertrudis 415
Barnard, A. M. 245
Barra, Mary 365
Barré-Sinoussi, Françoise 281
Bartik, Betty Jean Jennings 148
Bassi, Laura 291
Beasley, Maria 226
Beckett, Clarice 47
Beeton, Isabella 184
Bell Burnell, Jocelyn 201
Benett, Etheldred 36, 300
Benz, Bertha 181
Berenson, Mary 224
Berger, Otti 328
Berlau, Ruth 169
Berry, Gwen 351
Bertin, Louise 150
Bidder, Marion 446
Bigelow, Kathryn 128, 276
Biles, Simone 324, 360
Björke, Bekka 166
Blackjack, Ada 5
Blackwell, Elizabeth 198, 356
Blackwell, Emily 357
Blair, Eileen 224
Blau, Marietta Dr. 255
Bliss, Lillie P. 54
Bly, Nellie 282
Bohm, Anne 309

Boivin, Marie 228
Boleyn, Anne 407
Bonnevie, Kristine 314
Bosworth, Kate 354
Bouman (and Andrew Chael), Katie Dr. 143
Bourgeois, Louise 275
Bowerman, Heather 287
Bracquemond, Marie 372
Brahe, Sophia 379
Breckinridge Patterson, Mary Marvin 238
Breen, Olivia 433
Brickwedde, Marion 31
Brontë sisters 34, 236
Brooks, Alison 269
Browder, Aurelia 397
Brown, Blythe 223
Brown, Elizabeth 314
Brown, Lisa 114
Brownmiller, Susan 460
Bryant Quinn, Jane 460
Bugg, Mary Ann 181
Bugie, Elizabeth 194
Bunce, Betty 305
Burbidge, Margaret 203, 303
Burke, Selma Hortense 139
Burr Blodgett, Katharine 190
Buzyn, Agnès 366
Byrne, Olive 210
Campbell, Janet Mary 439
Campbell, Kim 364

UNCREDITED

Casamayor, María Andresa 239
Cassatt, Mary 280
Catherine Charlotte, De la Gardie 467
Catherine of Aragon 422
Catlett, Elizabeth 427
Chappelle, Dickey 373
Charpentier, Emmanuelle 138
Chase, Martha 192
Cheek, Julia 286
Cherryh, C. J. 245
Chesnut, Mary Boykin 273
Chisolm, Shirley 283
Chong, Kristy 430
Chun, Carolyn 83
Cixi 13, 248
Clarke, Edith 303
Claudel, Camille 176, 375
Clemons, Latosha 107
Cleopatra the obstetrician 70
Cleopatra VII 69, 423
Clerk, Matilda J. 299
Clicquot, Barbe-Nicole 185
Clinton, Hilary 3, 15, 0336
Cogdell-Unrein, Corey 31
Cohn, Mildred 304
Colden, Jane 35, 195
Cole, Jean 12
Coleman, Bessie 299
Colette, Sidonie-Gabrielle 155
Colley Cannon, Sarah Ophelia; AKA Minnie Pearl 210
Collier, Edith Marion 45
Colter, Mary Jane 219
Colvin, Claudette 397
Constance of Antioch, Princess 23
Cooke, Jean 46
Copaken Kogan, Deborah 96
Coppola, Sofia 275
Cori, Gerty 331
Coston, Martha 226
Craig, Molly 412
Cremer, Erika 189
Crosby, Caresse 227
Cunitz, Maria 48, 159
Curie, Marie 80, 187, 253, 312, 332, 410
Curtin, Jane 319
Czira, Sydney; AKA John Brennan 237
Dacier, Anne 74
Daly, Caroline Louisa 146
Darragh, Lydia Barrington 67
David-Néel, Alexandra 184
Davis, Geena 341
de Bertereau, Martine 408
de Bettignies, Louise 465
de Kooning, Elaine 371
de Lay, Guirandana 406
de Navarre, Marguerite 41
Deeks, Florence 165
Delladio, Tanja 361
Derbyshire, Delia 98
Derick, Carrie 291, 308

Desroches Noblecourt, Christiane 138
Diamond, Marian 266
Dicker, Friedl 49
Dickinson, Emily 43
Djebar, Assia 259
Donovan, Marion 172
Dostoevskaya, Anna 224
Doudna, Jennifer 138
Driscoll, Clara 136
Duchamp-Crotti, Suzanne 208
Duel Mosher, Clelia Dr. 397
Dumée, Jeanne 280
Durack, Fanny 329
DuVernay, Ava 171
Eames, Ray 220
Edelheit, Martha 56
Ederle, Gertrude 381
Eglin, Ellen 234
Eike, Roberta 306
Ekeblad, Eva 313
Eleanor B. Barnes 203
Eleanor of Aquitaine 23
Eliot, George 238
Elselehdar, Marwa 268
Ennis-Hill, Jessica 434
Ephron, Nora 460
Espín, Vilma 11
Evans, Alice Catherine 471
Evert, Alice 314
Evert, Chris 29
Fang 157

Fanthorpe, U. A. 245
Farquharson, Marian 313
Farquharson, Marion 313
Farrow, Mia 233
Fatemi, Falon 286
Faulkner, Shannon 387
Fawcett, Philippa 258
Feeney, Helen B. 359
Felicie, Jacoba 300
Felix, Allyson 443
Ferrari, María Teresa 296
Fey, Tina 341
Feynmen, Joan 132
Fforde Peel, Charlotte Emily 439
Findlay, Carly 16
Fisher, Carrie 124
Fleißer, Marieluise 169
Florence Cushman 199
Florey, Mary Ethel 197
Flügge-Lotz, Irmgard 449
Fontana, D. C. 245
Fontana, Lavinia 150, 441
Fourcade, Marie-Madeleine 463
Frank, Anne 42, 92
Franklin, Miles 237
Franklin, Rosalind 136, 173
Fraser, Dawn 348
Fulhame, Elizabeth 94
Fumiko, Yoshitada 460
Gage, Matilda 38
Galpern, Elena 191

UNCREDITED

Gamergate 416
Garimara, Doris Pilkington 412
Garrett Anderson, Elizabeth 357
Garvey, Amy Ashwood 215
Garvey, Amy Jacques 215
Garwood, Tirzah 441
Gautier, Marthe 173
Geiringer, Hilda 281
Gellhorn, Martha 376
Gentileschi, Artemisia 114, 145, 420
George, Alexis 366
Germain, Sophie 206, 240, 312
Gerow, Margaret 446
Gerwig, Greta 130, 256
Gilbreth, Lillian Moller 188
Gillard, Julia 365
Gilman, Charlotte Perkins 472
Gladys Joslin 203
Glanville, Eleanor 376
Goeppert Mayer, Maria 8, 448
Goldsmith, Lynn 167
González de Behringer, Clara 316
Goodman, Ellen 460
Goolagong, Evonne 29
Graham Du Bois, Shirley 41
Graham, Katharine 470
Greayer, Mary Emma 439
Griffith Joyner ("Flo Jo"), Florence 272
Gudrid the Far-Traveller 9, 59, 427
Guppy, Eileen 204
Guy, Helen; AKA Guy d'Hardelot 239
Guy-Blache, Alice 9, 20
Gwibun, Jo 38
Gyllenhaal, Maggie 354
Hadid, Zaha 219
Hale, Shannon 403
Harcourt, Alison Dr. 440
Hardesty, Mary 447
Hargreaves, Alison 9
Harris, Ada 53
Hassenpflug, Jeanette, Marie, and Amalie 140
Hatshepsut 112, 165
Hau, Lene 332
Hauptmann, Elisabeth 169
Hedegman, Anna Arnold 213
Héloïse 282
Henrietta Swan Leavitt 174, 199
Henry, Dora Dr. 450, 463
Herskovits, Frances 181
Hevelius, Elisabeth 200
Heysen, Nora 9
Hezlet, May 440
Hill, Katie 410
Hinton, S. E. 59, 244
Ho Lu's army of 180 women 66
Hodgkin, Dorothy 196
Hodgkin, Dorothy Crowfoot 8
Hodierna of Tripoli, Countess 23
Hoffman, Darleane C. 308
Holberton, Frances "Betty" 148
Holbertson, Betty 102

Holm, Eleanor 349
Holman, Emily Elizabeth 245
Holt, Nancy 209
Hoobler, Icie 307
Hook, Mary Rockwell 311
Hopkins, Patty 11
Hopper, Grace 267
Hopper, Jo Nivison 426
Horner Lyell, Mary 204
Hosszú, Katinka 19
Hubeny, Veronika Dr. 277
Hunt, Mary 196
Hunter, Alberta 177
Husar, Emma 411
Hutchinson, Emma 313
Hutchison, Mary 30, 464
Hutton, Louisa 258
Hypatia 34
Immerwahr, Clara 446
Ironside, Adelaide 36
Iverson, Tina M. 245
Ivory Lady of Valencia 68
Iyoba of Benin 50
Jackson, Mary 173
Jacobs, Jessie Marie 438
Jeffrey, Shirley Winifred 245
Joan of Arc 105, 406
Joanna Cohan Scherer 315
Johnson, Katherine 172
Johnson, Kelley 391
Jones, Judith 92
Jones, Margaret 407
Joy, Lisa 241
July, Miranda 275
Junia 57
Kahlo, Frida 48
Kaling, Mindy 273
Karikó, Katalin Dr. 453
Karle, Isabella 191
Kaur, Rupi 115
Keane, Margaret 155
Kellerman, Annette 432
Kelley, Bessie Mae 40
Kempin-Spyri, Emilie 302, 315
Keneally, Kristina 364
Kepler, Katharina 23
Khutulun 9
King, Billie Jean 29
King, Martha 36
King, Mary-Claire Dr. 456
Kirch, Christine 310
Kirch, Maria Margaretha 157, 309
Kirkpatrick, Helen 98
Kirner, Joan 364
Kiyo, Tatsuuma 273
Knight, Margaret 163, 281
Knutson, Coya 394
Koenig, Sarah 469
Kohestani, Shamila 434
Koller-Pinell, Broncia 49
Komnene, Anna 77
Konigsburg, E. L. 245, 441

UNCREDITED

Konigsburg, E. L. 245
Koshland, Marian 448
Kovalevskaya, Sofya 296
Kozachenko, Kathy 151
Krasner, Lee 426
Krøyer, Marie 372
Kuang, R. F. 261
Labille-Guiard, Adélaïde 50
Lack, Mercie 121
Lacks, Henrietta 185
Ladd-Franklin, Christine 293
Lamarr, Hedy 1, 164
Landauer, Julia 331
Landis Hayes, Rebecca; Lieutenant Commander 229
Lane, Hester 215
Langdon, Olivia 223
Langstaff, Annie MacDonald 316
Lansing, Sherry 9
Larson, Brie 353
Lavoisier, Marie Anne 32
Lawrence, Carmen 364
Lawson, Louisa 168
Leakey, Mary 158
Leavitt, Henrietta Swan 174, 199
Lederberg, Esther 379
Lee, Harper 143
Lefrançais, Amélie 200
Lepaute, Nicole-Reine 201
Leporskaya, Anna 47
Leslie, Miriam 29

Lewis, Edmonia 272
Leyster, Judith 165
Lister, Anne 45
Lohse Wächtler, Elfriede 49
Louis-Dreyfus, Julia 320
Lovelace, Ada 58, 403
Low, Barbara 196
Lowe, Ann 11
Lu, Xiao 208
Ludington, Sybil 68, 118
Luksch-Makowsky, Elena 49
Lwoff, Marguerite 254
Maar, Dora 370
MacDonald Mackintosh, Margaret 220
Madame de Pompadour 185
Magdalene, Mary 415
Magie, Elizabeth 162
Mahony Griffin, Marion 218
Mair, Lucy 184
Malkin Curtis, Doris 447
Mangold, Hilde 193
Manzolini, Anna Morandi 197
Margaret, Mary 222
Marić, Mileva 154, 440
Marin, Sanna 419
Marsh, Helene 60
Marston, Elizabeth 210
Marx, Jenny 180
Masilingi, Beatrice 325
Masters, Sybilla Righton 227
Matheson, Hilda 183

May, Elaine 318
May, Teresa 364
Mayer, Marissa 366
Mboma, Christine 325
McCarroll, June 472
McCarty, Jessica Dr. 277
McClintock, Barbara 274
McDonald, Hedwick Wilhelmina 153
McLaughlin, Loretta 12
McMahon, Theresa 449
McNamara, Michelle 469
Mediz-Pelikan, Emilie 49
Meitner, Lise 137, 191
Melhase, Margaret 295
Melisende of Jerusalem, Queen 23
Meltzer, Marlyn 148
Mendelssohn, Fanny 36, 145, 160
Menna, Bianca Pucciarelli AKA Tomaso Binga 239
Menten, Maud 193
Mercury 13 358
Merian, Maria 194
Merit-Ptah 69
Messick, Dale 238
Meurdrac, Marie 398
Mexia, Ynes 279
Miller, Lee 40, 149
Mino, Dahomey 86
Mitchell, Jackie 355
Modotti, Tina 424
Mohamed Ahmed, Fathi 17
Mohamed Ibrahim, Nasrin 17
Moillon, Louise 441
Molesworth, Helen 53
Monroe, Marilyn 106
Montessori, Maria 293
Morgan, Julia 295
Morphia of Melitene, Queen of Jerusalem 23
Morse Symonds, Emily AKA George Paston 238
Moskowitz, Belle 249
Moss, Elisabeth 354
Mozart, Maria Anna 161
Münter, Gabriele 49
Murchison, Charlotte 204
Murray, Anna 216
Nabokova, Vera 224
Nanfeng, Jia 248
Neithhotep 68
Nesbit, E. 245
Newton Cuneo, Joan 356
Newton Foote, Eunice 187
Newton, Margaret 395
Nichols, Catherine 241
Nightingale, Florence 5, 70
Niyonsaba, Francine 326
Noda, Seiko 288
Noddack, Ida 190
Noether, Emmy 332
Nong, A 62
Norton, Alice Mary AKA Andre Norton

UNCREDITED

239
Nurse, Rebecca 407
O'Malley, Grace 25
O'Reilly, Joan 396
of Bavaria, Isabeau 247
Oldham Kelsey, Frances 454
Oliver, Josefina 39
Oliver, Tracy 458
Oneal, Jen 367
Ono, Yoko 421
Packard, Elizabeth 428
Paget, Violet; AKA Vernon Lee 238
Pao, Ellen 366
Papanikolaou, Andromachi "Mary" 197
Parks, Rosa 214, 397
Parr, Catherine 422
Parrish, Janneke 335
Parton, Dolly 210
Paterson, Lesley 26
Patrick, Milicent 264
Payne, Cecilia 380
Payne-Scott, Ruby 439
Pennington, Mary Engle 291
Perey, Marguerite 188, 312
Perkins, Frances 216
Perkins, Melanie 460
Perón, Eva 411
Pert, Candace 251
Peseshet 69
Peters, Vera Dr. 457
Petrie, Hilda 243

Phelps, Clarice 99
Philipps, Busy 152
Phum Snay, Cambodia burials 66
Picardet, Claudine 147
Pickford, Mary 9
Piggott, Peggy 120
Plant, Jane Dr. 456
Plante, Enid 189
Plath, Sylvia 47
Pocahontas 419
Pockels, Agnes 190
Poehler, Amy 341
Poët, Lidia 316
Pogson, Isis 311
Polydamna 69
Post, Marjorie Merriweather 461
Potter, Beatrix 312, 459
Price, Florence 34
Priego, Lola 287
Purdy, Jean 194
Puymbroeck Miller, Lea 449
Qingzhao, Li 396
Quinn, Zoë 416
Rae, Issa 458
Raicovich, Laura 55
Rankin, Jeannette 315
Rawat, Parbati 429
Rebay, Hilda 211
Redzisz, Kasia 55
Rée, Anita 49
Reville, Alma 179, 256

Reyes, Lucha   235
Richards, Audrey   184
Richardson, Sha'Carri   350
Ries, Teresa Feodorowna   49
Robb, J. D.   245
Robinson, Adah   134
Robscheit-Robbins, Frieda   255
Rockefeller, Abby Aldrich   54
Rodriguez, María Inés   54
Roman, Nancy Grace   452
Roosevelt, Eleanor   393
Rossum, Emmy   353
Rubin, Vera   254
Russell, Annie   314
Russo, Patricia   365
Saariaho, Kaija   378
Sabin, Florence R.   294, 470
Sáenz, Manuela   119
Sage, Kay   374
Salter, Susanna M.   452
Sanchez, Celia   11
Sand, George   238,
Sansom, Odette   230
Sappho   34, 74, 244
Sarkeesian, Anita   416
Satrapi, Marjane   259
Saunders, Helen   46
Scarlett Johansson   15
Schindler, Alma   373
Schindler, Emilie   217
Schultz, Sigrid   240
Scott Brown, Denise   221, 257
Scott-Moncrieff, Rose   291
Seacole, Mary   14
Sears, Mary   304
Sedgewick, Edie   424
Seidel, Molly   276
Semenya, Caster   325
Serao, Matilde   260
Shan, Zhang   355
Shannon, Betty   206
Sheldon, Alice Bradley AKA James Tiptree Jr.   239
Shelley, Mary   10, 58
Sherman Morgan, Mary   14
Shih, Ching   27
Sibylla of Jerusalem, Queen   23
Siddall, Elizabeth   424
Sigurdardóttir, Jóhanna   363
Simone, Gail   89
Simpson, Evelyn M. Dr.   440
Sinclair, Christine   95
Sirleaf, Ellen Johnson   364
Slater, Hannah   227
Smith Friedman, Elizebeth   140
Smith, Annie Lorrain   302
Smith, Charlotte   61
Sobel, Janet   142, 426
Sohonie, Kamala   297
Solnit, Rebecca   331
Somerville, Mary   186, 204
Sontag, Susan   223

UNCREDITED

Spence, Frances 148
Spencer, Elizabeth 253
Stebbing, Mary Anne 157
Steffin, Margarete 169
Stevens, Nettie 266
Stone, Emma 354
Strickland, Donna 99
Sullivan, Mary Quinn 55
Sundström, Anna 447
Syers, Madge 356
Taba, Hilda 302
Tammes, Jantina 292
Taro, Gerda 243
Tarpé Mills, June 210
Tate, Tiffany 177
Taylor Mill, Harriet 434
Teitelbaum, Ruth 148
Tharp, Marie 306
the Adroit, Margaret 60, 71
The daughters of Genghis Khan 44
Theoris of Lemnos 406
Thiroux d'Arconville, Geneviève 234
Thomas, Lia 325
Thornton, Willie Mae "Big Mama" 177
Todd, Margaret 238
Tolstaya, Sophia 224
Travers, P. L. 245
Trota of Salerno 70
Truth, Sojourner 26
Türeci, Özlem 32, 466
Turner (later Schafer), Alice 292

Turney, Catherine 256
Twardowski-Conrat, Ilse 49
Uhlenbeck, Karen 448
Ulric Cole, Frances 239
Under, Marie 259
Vaughan, Dorothy 173
Vaux Walcott, Mary 151
Vavasour, Anne 223
Verdon, Gwen 209
Vermeer, Maertge (Anglicised as Maria) 149
Viehman, Dorothea 140
Vieira da Silva, Marta 95
Viking warrior interred in Birka, Sweden 65
Viking woman discovered in Solør, Norway 65
Villa-Komaroff, Lydia 457
Villers, Marie-Denise 147
Virginia Hall 262
Virginia Kruse 203
Vitale, Caterina 398
Vivian Maier 40
Vivien, Renée 244
von Droste zu Hülshoff, Jenny 140
von Freytag-Loringhoven, Elsa 175
W. Moodey, Margaret 33
Wade, Jess 100
Wagstaff, Barbara 121
Walker, Dr. Mary Edwards 262
Walker, Lucy Ann 30

Wallace, Pearl   107
Wallis Burrell, Jane   251
Wambui, Margaret   326
Ward Howe, Julia   235
Warfield, Kate   280
Warriors of the Battle of Senbon Matsubara   66
Wason, Betty   328
Wautier, Michaelina   52
Weber, Lois   9
Wendy Davis   468
Wenyu, Lu   257
West, Gladys   102
Wevers, Sanne   361
White, Anne   437
Whiton Calkins, Mary   292
Whittle, Reba   231
Wilbraham, Lady Elizabeth   26, 221
Wild, Dortchen   140
Wilde, Olivia   354
Wilkinson, Edith Lake   39
Williamina Paton Fleming   199
Williams, Anna Wessels   195
Williams, Cicely Dr.   455
Williams, Clara Belle   299
Williams, Elizabeth   186
Williams, Mabel   226
Williams, Serena   20, 129, 324, 437, 444
Willing, Linda F.   400
Wilma S. Mangum   203
Wilmès, Sophie   364
Wilson, Alice   268, 307
Wilson, Edith   249
Winifred Boys-Smith   290
Witherington, Pearl   230
Wong, Annie   113
Wordsworth, Dorothy   161
Wu, Brianna   416
Wu, Chien-Shiung   191
Wu, Constance   10
Wylie, Mina   329
Xianzi   115
Xuan, Liu   361
Yan, Geling   115
Yashere, Gina   170
Yasui, Kono   274
Young, Grace Chisholm   242, 290
Yuanhui, Fu   430
Yunxian, Tan   396
Yvette of Bethany, Abbess   23
Yvonne Brill   294
Yvonne Rudellat   261
Zakaria, Rafia   392
Zelda Fitzgerald   153, 242, 374, 421
Zelenska, Olena   351
Zhang, Alice   287
Zhang, Jingna   166
Zhao, Xiran Jay   261
Zora Cross   280